CHALLENGES
of LIVING

In memory of Bill Reid, our model of lifelong learning.
To our students, whose questions and insights facilitate
our reflective practice as educators.

A Multidimensional Working Model for Social Workers

CHALLENGES of LIVING

Elizabeth D. Hutchison
Virginia Commonwealth University

Holly C. Matto
Virginia Commonwealth University

Marcia P. Harrigan
Virginia Commonwealth University

Leanne W. Charlesworth
Nazareth College of Rochester

Pamela A. Viggiani
Nazareth College of Rochester

SAGE Publications
Los Angeles • London • New Delhi • Singapore

For information:

Sage Publications, Inc.
2455 Teller Road
Thousand Oaks, California 91320
E-mail: order@sagepub.com

Sage Publications India Pvt Ltd.
B 1/I 1 Mohan Cooperative Industrial Area
Mathura Road, New Delhi 110 044
India

Sage Publications Ltd.
1 Oliver's Yard
55 City Road
London EC1Y 1SP
United Kingdom

Sage Publications Asia-Pacific Pte Ltd.
33 Pekin Street #02-01
Far East Square
Singapore 048763

Printed in the United States of America

Library of Congress Cataloging-in-Publication Data

Challenges of living: A multidimensional working model for social workers / Elizabeth D. Hutchison . . . [et al.].
    p. cm.
Includes bibliographical references and index.
ISBN-13: 978-1-4129-0899-3 (pbk. : alk. paper)
    1. Social service. 2. Social problems. I. Hutchison, Elizabeth D.

HV40.C42356 2007
361.3'2—dc22

                                            2006031961

Printed on acid-free paper.

07 08 09 10 11 10 9 8 7 6 5 4 3 2 1

Acquiring Editor:	Kassie Graves
Editorial Assistant:	Veronica Novak
Production Editor:	Sarah K. Quesenberry
Copy Editor:	Barbara Coster
Typesetter:	C&M Digitals (P) Ltd.
Proofreader:	Jennifer Ang
Indexer:	Sheila Bodell
Cover Designer:	Janet Foulger
Marketing Manager:	Carmel Withers

Contents _____

Acknowledgments _____

L ike any writing project, the ideas in this book have been incubating for a number of years. Over those years, we have been informed by each others' work on various other projects and by our conversations with each other. Our ideas have also been shaped by the work and contributions of many others who are far too numerous to begin to call out. For the senior author, the seeds of this book were planted during collaborative curriculum planning with colleagues at Virginia Commonwealth University and enriched, particularly, by her several years of cherished collaboration with Stephen Gilson, who is now on the faculty at the University of Maine. We are grateful to Stephen for his contributions to our understanding of biological contributions to human behavior and his keen sense of social justice. Marcia Harrigan expresses her gratitude to Drs. Kia Bentley, Janice Berry-Edwards, Rosemary Farmer, and Joe Walsh for the gracious sharing of their own scholarship and for their suggestions that helped to shape her ideas.

We are grateful to Dean Frank Baskind at Virginia Commonwealth University and Professor Virginia David, Chair of the Department of Social Work at Nazareth College, for supporting us in all of our endeavors. The senior author is grateful to Dean Baskind and her colleagues at Virginia Commonwealth University for the opportunity to be on research leave in the final weeks of completing the book. We all owe a debt of gratitude to the library staffs at Virginia Commonwealth University and Nazareth College, recognizing that their advancements in making materials electronically accessible lightened our load and gave us more snippets of time to connect with our families.

We are lucky to be working again with the folks at Sage. Art Pomponio was a cheerleader in the early stages of bringing our incubating ideas into written form, and Kassie Graves has been a very competent, focused, yet gentle shepherd through the last stages of turning a once unwieldy manuscript into a book. At a key point, Jerry Westby greased the wheels. Veronica Novak was a constant throughout the long months and diligently did her part to keep the project moving. When the drafting and redrafting finally came to an end, Sarah Quesenberry worked the magic of turning words into a book. We were pleased to have Barbara Coster's competent copyediting assistance once again. There are many others at Sage who work behind the scenes doing crucial tasks that are invisible to authors. We sense your presence and appreciate all that you do.

We are also grateful for the support and encouragement of students, family, and colleagues. They enrich our lives and provide us with protective webs of connectedness. Chuck, thank you for waiting patiently weekend after weekend for Marcia to be (really) finished with her chapters. Chuck and Hutch, thank you for your good humor while assisting us with the various computer glitches.

Finally, we are grateful to the following reviewers who read an earlier draft of the book and provided helpful feedback:

Parris Baker, Gannon University
Sandra Chesborough, St. Cloud State University
Ann Dannerbeck, University of Missouri
Dorie J. Gilbert, University of Texas at Austin
Richard A. Longoria, University of Texas at Austin
Samuel MacMaster, University of Tennessee
Kimberly A. Mann, Chicago State University

Elizabeth D. Hutchison

Holly C. Matto

Marcia P. Harrigan

Leanne W. Charlesworth

Pamela A. Vigianni

1

A Working Model

Elizabeth D. Hutchison,
Virginia Commonwealth University

E very day, social workers meet up with complex challenges faced by individuals, families, communities, and organizations. In this book, we are presenting and demonstrating a working model to help social workers understand the many and varied challenges they will encounter in their work.

_____ Why a Challenges of Living Approach?

Social work scholars have long attempted to find frameworks for organizing social and behavioral science knowledge about human behavior in a way that is useful for the varied roles that social workers play. Two popular approaches are a social systems approach and a life course approach. Each of those approaches makes important contributions to the understanding of the complexities of human behavior encountered by social workers (see Hutchison, 2003a, 2003b). Each has been evaluated, however, to be more helpful for the social work assessment process than for guiding intervention. In this book, we are proposing another organizational framework that we think will assist social workers to move from scientific understanding to intervention. We call this approach a *challenges of living approach,* because it is organized around specific challenges of living that social workers confront and it proposes a way of thinking about the wide range of challenges of living that move social workers to action. Because this approach is quite specific about how it draws on general knowledge from the social and behavioral sciences, it can serve as a working model for searching for and integrating the best possible evidence about any challenge of living social workers encounter in their work.

The idea of challenges of living as an organizing framework is not a new idea. From the early days of the social work profession, social work scholars have focused on knowledge of client problems as the basis for intervention (e.g., Meyer, 1993; Perlman, 1957; Richmond, 1917). Although we write in this same tradition in this book, we have chosen to use the language of "challenge" rather than "problem." By dictionary definition, *problem* means a situation that presents perplexity or difficulty, and *challenge* means a call to engage in a contest or struggle (Mish, 1998). We are using challenge here to mean a difficult situation that calls for engagement and action.

We think a challenges of living approach makes sense for organizing knowledge for social workers because all social work methodologies are used to address troubling situations that are to be prevented, altered, improved, or managed. Social work intervention begins with assessment of "what the trouble seems to be" (Kirk & Reid, 2002, p. 54) as a basis for a plan of action. A challenges of living approach also makes sense because social and behavioral scientists often engage in systematic study of specific problematic conditions. Consequently, social workers can and should efficiently draw on existing empirical research about general classes of people and/or situations. Stuart Kirk and William Reid suggest that social work practitioners and social and behavioral scientists share an interest in difficult situations, although the nature of their interests is somewhat different. Social workers want to know how to help clients cope with challenging situations, and social researchers want to understand the causes of human problems.

Social workers encounter many challenges of living in their work. Indeed, any client situation may involve multiple challenges. The knowledge base for social work is very broad because of the extensive range of problems addressed by social workers and the diverse roles in the professional social work repertoire. Writing of this breadth of focus, Carol Meyer (1993) suggested that "theoretically, there is almost no end to what a social worker might have to know" (p. 15). It is not the purpose of this book to present a comprehensive encyclopedia of knowledge about the full range of challenges of living that become the focus of social work intervention. Rather, we want to present a working model that can be used to develop understanding of any challenge of living encountered and provide examples of application of the model. The working model gives a structure to facilitate the transfer of general knowledge about human behavior to discrete practice challenges (i.e., problems, populations, and settings). It includes a set of questions that guides the social worker in acquiring a base of knowledge that goes beyond, and serves as a screen for, data about the unique situation faced by the social worker.

The social and behavioral science knowledge base is ever growing and always changing. What we know about a specific challenge of living can be outdated quickly. However, if we have an organizational framework for thinking about relevant sources of knowledge, the work of developing understanding of the challenges faced by client situations will be far less daunting. We will be able to update our knowledge when necessary, and perhaps more important, we will be able to mine the available scientific knowledge about novel challenges that we encounter. In this way, we can modify existing intervention methods and/or develop new methods to align the plan of action with what "the trouble seems to be."

In this chapter, we describe the working model, and in Chapters 3–10, we demonstrate the use of the model to develop understanding of eight challenges of living: financial impoverishment, community violence, child maltreatment, traumatic stress disorders, substance abuse, obesity, HIV/AIDS, and major depression. We have not followed any classification system to select the exemplar challenges of living, nor are we suggesting one. We have attempted to choose exemplars that are considered to be major contemporary social work as well as public health problems that present across the life course, that are faced by communities as well as individuals and families, that represent a range of challenges to physical and mental health, and that cut across race, culture, ethnicity, social class, gender, and sexual orientation. The final chapter, Chapter 11, overviews the themes of Chapters 3–10, noting both commonalities and differences across the challenges of living.

The Working Model

Kirk and Reid (2002) suggest that frameworks for organizing knowledge for social work practice must present "a multidimensional matrix framed by client problems, intervention targets, and client characteristics" (p. 72). The working model presented in this book focuses primarily on client problems (challenges of living), but it also provides tools for thinking about intervention targets and client characteristics. The intent is to present a model of knowledge acquisition that assists social workers to "notice" the complexity of the multidimensional situations they encounter. Several social work scholars have written about the tendency of social workers to shrink from the complexity of the situations they encounter, to simplify and narrow the focus in the face of challenging situations (see, e.g., Begun, 1993; Gambrill, 2003a; Gibbs & Gambrill, 1999; Meyer, 1993). Our working model raises seven questions that, taken together, help social workers attend to the complexity of the challenges they face in their work:

1. Who is affected (pattern of occurrence)?

2. What are the current theories of causation, or association, related to the challenge of living?

3. What are the multidimensional (biological, psychological, social, and spiritual) developmental risk and protective factors?

4. What are the consequences of the challenge of living? Are different people affected in different ways?

5. How have people attempted to cope with the challenge of living?

6. What social justice issues are involved?

7. What do the answers to the above questions suggest about action strategies (practice implications)?

Patterns of Occurrence

One way of understanding a challenge of living is to ask "who is affected," what are the patterns of occurrence? The answer to this question has particular relevance for the development of preventive interventions. Social workers can draw on the field of public health, where epidemiological research has addressed this question. **Epidemiology** is the study of the distribution of disease and health in a population (Kaplan & Sadock, 2002). Epidemiological research can identify causal factors of diseases, social problems, and troubling situations as well as the different patterns of occurrence across age, gender, socioeconomic status, cultural groups, geographic regions, and so on (Nash & Randolph, 2004). For example, epidemiological research tells us that, in the United States, women are 2 times more likely than men to be diagnosed with major depression during their lifetime (Gorman, 2006) and that males are 3 times as likely as females to be both victims and perpetrators of homicide (Krug, Dahlberg, Mercy, Zwi, & Lozano, 2002). Epidemiological research has also been used for international comparisons, for example, in 2000, for one definition of relative poverty (40% of median income), 14.1% of children in the United States, 1.3% of children in Finland, and 17.1% of children in Mexico lived in poverty (Luxembourg Income Study, 2004). With this attention to patterns of distribution, an epidemiological approach is crucial for social work's attention to human diversity and social justice.

We want to interject a word here about terminology and human diversity. As we attempted to uncover what is known about human diversity in relation to specific challenges of living, we struggled with terminology to define identity groups. We searched for consistent language to describe different groups, and we were dedicated to using language that identity groups would use to describe themselves. However, we ran into challenges endemic to our time related to the language of diversity. First, it is not the case that all members of a given identity group at any given time embrace the same terminology for their group. Second, as we reviewed literature from different historical moments, we recognized the shifting nature of terminology. In addition, even within a given historical era, we found that different researchers used different terms and had different decision rules about who comprises the membership of identity groups. So, in the end, you will find that we have not settled on fixed terminology that is used consistently to describe identity groups. Rather, we use the language of individual researchers when reporting their work, because we want to avoid distorting their work. We hope you will not find this too distracting. We also hope that you will recognize that the ever-changing language of diversity has both constructive potential to find creative ways to affirm diversity and destructive potential to dichotomize diversity into *the norm* and *the other*.

To interpret epidemiological research, it is important to understand two types of statistics used in that research, prevalence and incidence. **Prevalence** is a rate of the number of existing cases (of a troubling situation) at a particular point in time divided by the total population studied. For example, in 2003, 929,985 people in the United States were estimated to be HIV infected, for a prevalence rate of 0.0033. **Incidence** is the rate of new occurrences of a troubling situation within a given time period. For example, in 2003, the estimated number of new diagnoses of HIV in the United States was 43,171, for an incidence rate of 0.00015 (Centers for Disease Control and Prevention [CDC], 2004b). Oftentimes, prevalence rates are reported in terms of the number per 100,000 of the population.

Theories of Causation

Much of what we "know" about challenges of living is organized into **theories**, or "systems of concepts and hypotheses designed to explain and predict phenomena" (Kirk & Reid, 2002, p. 18). Theories help us bring order to the vast, and exploding, information about human behavior, calling attention to patterns and relationships. As Anne Fortune and William Reid (1999) suggest, the theories that social work practitioners find most useful are those that produce explanatory or causal hypotheses, those that provide the "whys" of challenges of living. However, unlike medicine, where researchers seek "cause" by isolating specific biological mechanisms of causation, social scientists must live with the reality that, for the social world, "it may never be possible to identify causes and their effects fully" (Fraser, 2004, p. 6). Social science theorists rely on research that indicates that one variable is likely to influence another, and they attempt to build theory that explains these associations.

In the process of building knowledge about a specific challenge of living, we think it is important to begin by surveying the range of current explanatory theories. Because human behavior is subject to many influences, no one theory is likely to account for the complexity of a particular challenge of living. Attending to the range of explanatory theories brings more variables into view and prepares us to recognize the multiple factors influencing difficult situations. As Berlin and Marsh (1993) assert, this theoretical pluralism obligates social workers to engage in critical analysis of the strengths and limitations of a variety of theoretical frameworks. In the final chapter of the book, we analyze the **empirical research** evidence, the information produced by careful, purposeful, and systematic observation, for the various theoretical perspectives discussed throughout the book.

Multidimensional Risk and Protection

For the past several decades, researchers across several disciplines have been studying challenges of living through the lens of multidimensional developmental risk and protection. They have attempted, with much success, to identify **antecedent factors** of troubling situations, those factors that came before the troublesome situation, in several personal and environmental dimensions. A number of large-scale longitudinal studies have been a real boon to this line of inquiry (see, e.g., Masten & Garmezy, 1985; Rutter,

2000; Werner & Smith, 2001). The researchers have identified **risk factors**, or factors that increase the probability of developing and maintaining problem conditions. Some researchers call these *vulnerability factors*. More recently, researchers have also been interested in individuals who have adapted successfully in the face of risk factors (see, e.g., Luthar, 2003). They have identified **protective factors**, or factors (resources) that decrease the probability of developing and maintaining problem conditions. They have begun to recognize the power of humans to use protective factors to assist in a self-righting process over the life course, to be resilient in the face of adversity, a process known as **resilience** (Vaillant, 2002; Werner & Smith, 2001). Sometimes protective factors are just the other end of a continuum from risk factors; intelligence is a factor for which this is the case. This is not always the case, however. For example, having a teenage mother is a risk factor, but having a mother at the upper end of child-bearing age has not been found to be a protective factor (Rutter, 2003).

Scholars in the fields of developmental psychology, clinical psychology, psychiatry, and behavior genetics have used a multidimensional developmental risk and protective approach to understand developmental psychopathology, as well as psychological resilience. The field of community epidemiology has used a similar approach to understand the prevalence of disease across communities, as well as the experiences that can break the chain of risk; they use the language of prevention rather than protection (e.g., Brunner, 1997; Kellam & Van Horn, 1997; Kuh & Ben-Shlomo, 1997). Immunization against disease is one of the clearest and best-known public health prevention interventions. Both groups of researchers have observed that risk factors often co-occur with, are bundled with, other risk factors, resulting in a pileup of stress. They describe this as *cumulative risk* and find that higher numbers of risk factors result in more problems.

To date, research on risk, protection, and resilience has been guided by ecological theories and supports the idea that both risk and protective factors occur along multiple dimensions of person and environment. There is growing consensus about a common set of risk factors and a common set of protective factors, usually categorized as individual attributes, family qualities, and aspects of systems outside the family. However, some researchers have suggested that, in future studies, there is a need to extend the types of risk and protective factors investigated; they note that there is a tendency to continue to study the same factors over and over because of findings from previous studies (Luthar & Zelazo, 2003). Unfortunately, risk and protective factors cannot be identified unless they are included in the research design. After a review of the research on resilience, Suniya Luthar and Laurel Zelazo suggest several directions for future research:

- More attention to biological and genetic factors
- More attention to protective factors during adulthood that can modify the impact of early risk
- More recognition of the mutual, two-way influence of factors across biological, psychological, social, and spiritual dimensions

- More attention to understanding the mechanisms or processes by which risk factors cause vulnerability and protective factors reduce vulnerability
- More attention to ethnicity and social class

In the working model proposed here, we suggest use of a biopsychosocial-spiritual framework to examine multidimensional risk and protection. We suggest that challenges of living be analyzed by focusing attention on one aspect of this framework at a time: biological risk and protection, psychological risk and protection, social risk and protection, and spiritual risk and protection (see Exhibit 1.1 for a description of each). This is a somewhat artificial way to go about examining the knowledge base because of the linked and overlapping nature of these dimensions. However, we encourage this approach because we want to avoid the tendency in the literature to limit the focus to psychosocial factors and neglect attention to biological and spiritual dimensions. It is also the case that different disciplines have attended to different dimensions, and the literatures on the different dimensions are scattered across several disciplines. We recommend, however, that once the dimensions have been analyzed separately, an attempt should be made to weave them back together into an integrated story of risk and protection.

Biological Risk and Protection	Genetic influences The body's biochemical, cell, organ, and physiological systems
Psychological Risk and Protection	Cognitions Emotions
Social Risk and Protection	Family Peer group Community Formal organizations Social institutions
Spiritual Risk and Protection	Search for meaning and purpose Religion

Exhibit 1.1   Biopsychosocial-Spiritual Risk and Protection

Biological Risk and Protection

Genes can be the source of both risk and protection for major physical and mental diseases/disorders. Prenatal and perinatal complications and premature birth are also risk factors for a number of challenges of living (Werner & Smith, 2001). In addition, social and psychological experiences can affect brain development, produce changes in neuronal connections, and facilitate or moderate gene expression (Luthar & Zelazo,

2003). In the chapters to come, you will read, particularly, about how early deprivation and trauma alter neurobiological mechanisms that regulate cognitions, emotions, and behaviors and link to a number of physical and mental health challenges.

Psychological Risk and Protection

Looking across several major longitudinal studies, a number of psychological factors show up on common lists of both risk and protective factors, with one extreme of the continuum producing risk and the other extreme producing protection. At one end of the continuum, cognitive abilities, self-perceptions, temperament, self-regulation skills, and outlook on life produce risk. At the other end of the continuum, each of these factors has been found to be protective (see Masten & Powell, 2003).

Social Risk and Protection

When we speak of the social dimension, we are covering quite a large territory, from the parent-child relationship to the global geopolitical context. The social world is itself quite multidimensional. Researchers typically divide the social world into the **proximal environment** of the family and the **distal environment** beyond the family. Existing research emphasizes the supremely important role of the proximal environment of the family, finding evidence for the importance of factors such as parenting quality, family cohesion, family structure, family social class, and family disruption. Certainly, families are the most regular and intensive contact for most individuals, but when researchers fail to put these family qualities into wider cultural, economic, and political contexts, there is a risk of "blaming the victim." Researchers have begun to find risk and protection in systems outside the family, in terms of peer groups, school quality, neighborhood quality and cohesion, the built physical environment, health and social service resources, war and community violence, and discrimination.

Spiritual Risk and Protection

When we speak of the spiritual dimensions, we are referring to both spirituality and religion, terms that are sometimes confused. **Spirituality** is a personal search for meaning, purpose, connection, and morality. **Religion** is a systematic set of beliefs, practices, and traditions observed within a particular social institution over time. Until recently, behavioral science researchers have paid very little attention to spiritual risk and protection. Consequently, our discussions throughout this book are somewhat thin in terms of spiritual risk and protection. There is growing evidence in the empirical literature to support the idea that spiritual resources can serve as an important protective factor in adulthood to mitigate early risk (see, e.g., Kendler et al., 2003; Vaillant, 2002; Werner & Smith, 2001). James Garbarino (1999) reports that communities devoid of spiritual anchors serve as a risk factor for male violence and other high-risk behaviors in adolescence.

Some researchers have found that some types of religious beliefs and affiliations serve as protection while other types serve as risk (Pargament, 1997).

Biopsychosocial-Spiritual Integration

After teasing these dimensions (biological, psychological, social, and spiritual) apart, each chapter pulls them back together to present an integrated story of risk and protection for specific challenges of living. This will give a more holistic view of the overlapping factors and reciprocal relationships among the dimensions that create risk and protection. Comparison across challenges of living, presented in Chapter 11, will illuminate co-occurrence, bundling, overlaps, and cumulative risk and protection.

Consequences

The risk and protection approach is based on the idea that risk and protective factors precede troubling situations and have influence on them. It is also the case that troubling situations have consequences for future human behavior and for the health of individuals, families, communities, and societies, and they sometimes serve as risk for other challenges of living. When social workers are involved in improving rather than preventing troubling situations, it is important to understand the consequences as well as the antecedents of these situations.

Before we proceed, however, it is important to note that the human life course is not such a simple linear process. Quite often many conditions co-occur, and sometimes it is difficult to discern from the literature whether a particular condition preceded another condition, was a consequence of that condition, or simply occurs simultaneously with it. The chapters of this book demonstrate the circular and reinforcing nature of challenges of living, for example, family poverty serves as a risk for community violence, and community violence contributes to the ongoing impoverishment of a neighborhood.

With these caveats in mind, it is still the case that researchers have identified some likely consequences of specific challenges of living, consequences that are widely experienced as an outgrowth of the challenging situation, and we will be reporting those. But just as there are different patterns of occurrence of specific challenges of living among various demographic groups, research is beginning to identify some group-based differences in the impact that challenges of living have on people. For example, Glen Elder's (1974) longitudinal research on children and the Great Depression found that family economic hardship has more long-term detrimental effects if it is experienced in early childhood than if it is experienced in middle childhood or adolescence. In another piece of longitudinal research following a cohort born on the island of Kauai in 1955, Emmy Werner and Ruth Smith (2001) found that males are more negatively affected by child neglect and economic hardships in early childhood than females. On the other hand, females are more negatively affected by family disruption than males during adolescence.

Attempts to study differential consequences are relatively new and somewhat spotty in the literature, and we do not have a lot of such evidence to report. Where such research exists, we think it is important for social workers to be aware of the stories told about human diversity, and we report on that evidence.

Ways of Coping

When faced with difficult situations, individuals, families, communities, and organizations usually make efforts to contend with the stress and minimize the damage. In other words, they tend to take up the challenge of the difficult situation. These efforts have come to be called **coping**, and the strategies used are called *coping strategies*. Social workers should be curious about the coping strategies that client systems have already tried and should make every effort to give clients credit for their coping efforts. We also can benefit from familiarity with the research about how people attempt to cope with specific challenges of living and which coping strategies produce the most successful results.

Researchers have found that people adapt their choice of coping strategies to the situation at hand, but coping also is influenced by personal biology and psychology (Aldwin, 2000). In addition, cultural norms set the parameters for acceptable ways of coping with particular challenges of living. Resources for coping also vary across the life course. Not surprisingly, some coping strategies produce better outcomes than others. Some coping strategies will help to eliminate or minimize the difficult situation, and other coping strategies will serve to maintain or even exacerbate the situation. The choice of coping strategy can also have other consequences down the developmental line. The method of coping can serve as risk for other difficult situations later in life; this is the case when the method of coping involves escaping into alcohol or other drugs. The method of coping can also serve as protection down the line if it includes goal-directed behavior and use of positive spiritual and religious resources.

Social Justice Issues

The National Association of Social Workers (NASW) Code of Ethics identifies social justice as one of six core values of social work. The stated ethical principle for this value is "social workers challenge social injustice" (National Association of Social Workers [NASW], 1999). To challenge injustice, we must first recognize it and understand the ways that it is embedded in a number of societal institutions (Hutchison, 2003c). There are at least two reasons that this is not always a simple matter. First, institutional arrangements assign privilege, or unearned advantage, to some groups and disadvantage to other groups, but when we inhabit privileged positions, we tend to take our advantages for granted, to see them as "normal and universal" (Bell, 1997, p. 12). Therefore, we may have trouble "seeing" the injustices in the situations we encounter. Second, available theory and research about specific challenges of living do not always attend to patterns of injustice related to challenging situations. For example, if researchers focus only on individual and family attributes and fail to examine the societal contexts of these attributes, individual and family pathology will be identified, but harmful social and economic arrangements will not be. Sometimes we will need to search the literature carefully to develop understanding of social justice issues.

Recent scholarship in the social sciences has emphasized the ways in which three types of social identity—gender, race, and class—are used to develop hierarchical social structures "within which people form identities and through which they realize their life chances" (Stoller & Gibson, 2000, p. 4). These social categories are associated with systems of privilege and disadvantage, and, consequently, often convey either risk or protection. Race of color and low economic position show up on the list of common risk factors, cutting across challenging situations, and female gender is a risk factor for some troubling situations. Persons with disabilities and sexual minorities are other groups that face institutional discrimination, disadvantage, and risk.

At this point in history, it is important to note that the United States surpasses other similarly developed nations in income inequality, and the rate of inequality has been growing since the early 1970s (Hutchison & Waldbillig, 2003). This is particularly troubling given the persistent finding, as you will see in subsequent chapters, that financial impoverishment is a risk factor for a host of social ills and challenges of living. A growing international research literature suggests that high levels of inequality are bad, not only for individuals at the bottom of the hierarchy, but also for the social health of a nation, showing up in such social health indicators as childhood mortality, secondary school enrollment, violence, and life expectancy (Auerbach & Krimgold, 2001). Clearly, this issue cannot be addressed just at the micro level of individuals and families but requires that social workers provide leadership for political action and advocacy work.

Practice Implications

Because we are writing for social workers, each chapter will include discussion of the implications of the available theory and research for social work practice, focusing on modifiable factors that may alleviate difficult situations. From this perspective, the risk factor and protective factor approach is inherently a model of intervention. It suggests that efforts can focus on eliminating or reducing multidimensional risk factors and/or on increasing multidimensional protective factors. This will require that social workers intervene with social institutions, organizations, communities, and small groups, as well with families and individuals.

The Organization of the Book

We want to emphasize that we see the multidimensional working model presented in this book as an essential but partial component of your preparation for competent practice focused on specific challenges of living. It is only useful when combined with consideration of the unique features of the individual case, critical self-reflection, and analysis of relevant ethical issues. Chapter 2 presents these four interrelated elements in the process of knowing and doing in social work: knowledge about the case, knowledge about the self, values and ethics, and general knowledge from the social and behavioral sciences. Because we think it will help you to understand the working model and its applications if you have real-life stories about the challenges of living we are using to illustrate the working model, we begin Chapter 2 with four life stories that are used throughout the chapters of the book. Chapters 3–10 demonstrate how the working model presented in this chapter can be used to build knowledge of existing theory and research about selected challenges of living, including financial impoverishment, community violence, child maltreatment, traumatic stress, substance abuse, obesity, HIV/AIDS, and major depression. Finally, Chapter 11 synthesizes the elements of the working model across these eight exemplar challenges of living.

Learning Activities

1. Working in small groups, choose a challenge of living, other than the ones presented in this book, of interest to you (e.g., homelessness, adolescent pregnancy, cancer). Use the databases in your university library to research the pattern of occurrence of this challenge of living in the United States. What is the prevalence of the challenge of living? How is it distributed across different groups, such as those distinguished by gender, socioeconomic class, race, ethnicity, and so forth? How has the prevalence been changing over time?

2. Working in the same small groups with the same challenge of living, search the library databases for risk factors and protective factors for this challenge of living. Make an exhibit that summarizes your preliminary findings of the risk factors and protective factors for this challenge of living.

2

Elements of Knowing and Doing in Social Work

Elizabeth D. Hutchison,
Virginia Commonwealth University

Leanne W. Charlesworth,
Nazareth College of Rochester

Holly C. Matto,
Virginia Commonwealth University

Marcia P. Harrigan,
Virginia Commonwealth University

Pamela A. Viggiani,
Nazareth College of Rochester

Four Life Stories

Life Story #1: David Loefeler

David Loefeler was born in 1967 in rural upstate New York. He is the eldest of six siblings, all born within 9 years of one another into a German American family. David begins to tell you about himself by describing his childhood. He explains that he grew up on a dairy farm, where his family's energies were almost exclusively focused on the daily maintenance of the farm. David remembers, even as a very young child, having the responsibility of completing a seemingly endless list of chores. He often says, with nervous laughter, that his father ruled the house with a "heavy hand" and expected hard work from everyone, especially his boys. When they disappointed him, he sometimes resorted to physical violence. David was the most frequent target of his violent outbreaks.

David's father died after a short battle with lung cancer a few years ago. David says that he feels responsible for his father's death because he was not able to help his father hold onto and revive the now defunct family farm. He explains that his father was forced to sell the farm and declare bankruptcy when David was in his early 20s. David thinks that giving the farm up—and then watching it fall apart under new ownership—was the true cause of his father's death. He mentions that he often thinks about what might have been if he'd only pulled his act together in time to help his father save the farm.

With more nervous laughter, David comments that this isn't the only thing he did wrong in his life; he has always been a "screw-up." He says that he started drinking and smoking at a very young age, with easy access to his father's cigarettes and alcohol. He stopped going to school as a teenager, and although his mother seemed upset about this, her opinion never held much weight in the family, and his father was happy to have the extra help.

When David was 17, his long-time girlfriend became pregnant, and with their parents' approval, they married before the child was born. At 23 years of age, David, his wife, and their three daughters lived with David's parents. David's father initially helped support David and his family financially in return for David's more than full-time work on the farm, but as the farm began to face serious financial difficulties, both families found themselves financially destitute.

David mentions that this is probably when his substance abuse problem truly began. He says that he actually cannot remember many details from this time period, other than a great deal of fighting in the house. His wife threatened to leave many times and eventually moved back to her parents' home with their three daughters. David held a variety of odd jobs during this period, but the pay was dismal and he was fired repeatedly for showing up under the influence. When David's father told him he was no longer welcome at his parents' home, David encountered a turning point in his life. A cousin allowed David to sleep on his couch for a few weeks. This cousin eventually convinced David to get help from a substance abuse treatment program and encouraged him to seek assistance in order to complete his education and find a new vocation.

Today, David is living with his wife and their youngest daughter in a suburban area 30 miles away from where they grew up. David recently completed his associates degree at a community college. However, David's struggles are not over. He has been unable to hold down a steady job, primarily because he struggles with depression and anxiety issues. He mentions to you that he has been diagnosed with various learning disabilities and several different "mental illnesses" and that he struggles with the side effects of the many different psychotropic medications he has tried. He also shares that just last week his wife told him that their youngest daughter is four months pregnant and uncertain about the father's identity.

Life Story #2: Sondra Jackson

Sondra is a middle-aged, attractive African American woman. She and her younger sister, Estella, were born in Chicago. Born less than 2 years apart, they were always extremely close. Sondra's mother and father were childhood sweethearts, and shortly after they married, they moved from a small town full of extended family in rural Alabama to Chicago. Sondra and Estella have never lived anywhere else. Sondra's mother, Freda, and father, James, always had high expectations for the girls. However, Freda often could not supervise the girls in the way that she would have liked. Both girls were watched by a neighbor while Freda worked as a beautician and James worked for a local steel company.

During their early years, Sondra and Estella both did well in school, and Sondra was especially used to receiving praise from her teachers and peers. When Sondra and Estella were in junior high school, the family suffered a major, unexpected loss. James died suddenly from a heart attack. Freda was devastated. Luckily, the family's church community offered a great deal of support, and after several months, Freda slowly began to recover. The church took on even more importance in her life, and Sondra noticed it was the only place her mother seemed her old self.

Unfortunately, in the years that followed James's death, Freda did not have the energy to closely monitor her daughters as they navigated adolescence. While Sondra excelled in school and was considered a student leader, Estella began skipping school frequently and eventually dropped out completely. Sondra tried to convince Estella that her behavior was not good for their mother, but Estella seemed unable to think about anything other than having a good time. Sondra was especially worried about Estella's experimentation with cigarettes and alcohol. As Sondra graduated from high school at the top of her class, it became apparent that Estella needed help, but even Sondra couldn't reach her anymore.

After high school, Sondra went on to attend a local secretarial training program. Her teachers thought that staying close to home was the best choice for her, since she seemed to always be worried about keeping track of her sister and taking care of her mother. After graduating from the training program, Sondra was hired by a large, local company. Within a year of taking this secretarial job, Sondra met a successful businessman named Michael, with whom she fell in love. Six months into the relationship, Sondra found herself pregnant. When she told Michael about the pregnancy, he seemed indifferent and told her he would need some time to think about the situation. Sondra tried to give Michael time, but before long she realized that he had no intention of continuing the relationship with her. In fact, she discovered he had started a relationship with another woman. She vowed to never again be such a fool, but she had already grown to love the child growing inside of her.

By the time Sondra's son, Isaiah, was born, Estella rarely visited or called Sondra anymore, and Sondra suspected that Estella was prostituting herself in order to support an addiction to heroin. Freda's life revolved around church and now Isaiah. Freda often told

Sondra to have faith that the Lord would take care of Estella and bring her home eventually. Freda happily agreed to watch Isaiah so that Sondra could continue working. In fact, Sondra missed only 1 month of work when Isaiah was born, and she was known at work as an excellent secretary.

When Isaiah entered middle school, Sondra began to realize that the neighborhood she had grown up in was not what it used to be. Many of the long-time neighborhood residents had moved to the suburbs or elsewhere during the last several years. Isaiah's middle school was no longer well respected, and most of Isaiah's new friends worried Sondra. Sondra noticed that Isaiah's appearance and interests were changing, and she found herself worrying about his safety. She talked to Isaiah about transferring to a suburban school district and began to look at homes in the neighboring suburbs.

When Sondra tells you about the last few years of her life, her eyes grow moist with tears. Sondra explains that while she was busy working and meeting with her realtor, Isaiah was becoming quickly swept up in the danger within their community. No matter how often Sondra asked Freda to make sure Isaiah came directly home after school and did not go outside again, both Sondra and Freda seemed unable to make Isaiah obey their orders.

One day after his 17th birthday, Isaiah was murdered in his neighborhood. The police told Sondra the shooting was drug related and seemed to spend little time on the case. Sondra goes on to explain that only a month after Isaiah's death, her mother suffered a serious stroke. Sondra spent all of her free time at the hospital, attempting to keep track of her mother's care. One evening, as Sondra sat in her mother's hospital room, Freda suffered her most serious and ultimately fatal stroke.

In the past few months, Estella has returned to Sondra's life. Estella has told Sondra she is HIV positive. She is now living with Sondra and attending an outpatient substance abuse treatment program. Sondra says she needs Estella, but she often feels like she does not even know her. She also does not know where Estella will fit into her new family, because Sondra has recently learned that she is the grandmother of a newborn child. A child protective services (CPS) worker recently came to Sondra's home and told her that she was identified as the paternal grandmother of a baby boy born exposed to cocaine at a local hospital. The CPS worker asked Sondra if she would consider becoming a kinship care provider for this child, once he is ready to leave the hospital.

Life Story #3: Elias and Claudia Salvatierra

Elias and Claudia had been teenage sweethearts in the Dominican Republic (DR). Their families had known each other for many years. Both families came from a rural area outside the capital, Santo Domingo, where they made a modest living tending the sugarcane fields for the government. They experienced very few problems and had much autonomy in the fields, except when, because they were darker-skinned Dominicans, they were sometimes mistaken for illegal Haitians, who often crossed into the DR to escape poverty and violence in their own country. Elias remembers one story his grandfather told about being detained by the Dominican government for several days until he could prove his citizenship. In recent years, as the service sector's economic opportunities began to eclipse agricultural opportunities, families such as theirs were left with few options. Jobs became scarce in the sugarcane fields, but neither Elias's nor Claudia's family wanted to move into the city, because they had heard crime was rising steadily there, with the military even being brought in at times to try to maintain order.

So when Elias completed school, he and Claudia married at ages 18 and 16 and Elias searched desperately for a job. He had heard of friends who had left the DR on boats to Puerto Rico to escape the increasing unemployment rate in the DR—some never making it to their destination. And he had heard that the Colombian drug traffickers, who had been increasing their operations in the DR, would offer lucrative but risky financial opportunities. Claudia was adamant, however, that Elias should hold out for a more "conventional" service sector job as long as he could. After piecing together some money from various short-term jobs he found with friends and relatives, Elias finally got a job working as a mechanic in a local car repair shop. The two lived with Claudia's parents and her two younger siblings in her parents' one-story family home. Claudia became pregnant within 6 months of marriage and gave birth to a healthy baby boy whom they named Elias, after his father. He was called Junito (Little Junior) to avoid confusion.

The minimal income that Elias made as a mechanic and the small supplement that Claudia brought in as a child care provider was not enough, and Elias grew frustrated with his dependence on Claudia's parents. Elias had an uncle, Victor Manuel, in the United States who had moved to a large East Coast city 8 years prior to make a "better life" for himself. Victor Manuel had a good, stable job as a mechanic and was able to send money home regularly to help the family left behind. His uncle told him that there were jobs in the United States for those who wanted to work and that his family would be willing to support them until they could get on their feet. Elias decided that he would immigrate first and send for Junito and Claudia to join him later.

Two and a half years passed, and Claudia decided that although Elias said he was still not ready to take care of her in the United States, she would join him. Junito, who was 6, would stay with his grandparents, Sergia and Tomas, until arrangements could be made for his safe passage. In the United States, Claudia and Elias resided with Victor Manuel and his family in their small three-bedroom apartment. Elias seemed quite comfortable in this new world, with many friends and much support from his coworkers, but Claudia cried often and missed Junito terribly. With limited education and English skills and lack of a formal work history or job training experience, it took Claudia 6 months to find a job, but she finally found employment as a housekeeper in a hotel, where she worked long hours for minimum wage.

Claudia and Elias grew increasingly bitter toward one another, with verbal altercations often escalating into physical violence. Elias often left Claudia alone, spending nights and weekends out with friends and blaming her for their hardships. Soon Claudia discovered that she was pregnant. They still could not send for Junito, and Victor Manuel's wife,

Alejandra, was upset with what she had begun to describe as the "invasion" of her home. She had supported her husband in helping his family, but after 3 years and now the news of a baby, she began to pressure her husband to "get rid" of Elias and Claudia. Victor Manuel approached Elias and told him that he would give him enough money to pay for a deposit and first month's rent on an apartment. And so, when Claudia was 6 months pregnant, they moved into a modest two-bedroom apartment.

Claudia experienced much joy with the birth of her twin daughters, one of whom she named Sergia, after her mother, and called Yayi, and the other she named Isabel. But she missed her son and consistently talked to him by phone and wrote him letters. Elias rarely spoke to Junito, complaining about all the money he has sent home. Claudia tried to find peace with this, convincing herself that the anger came from the drinking and was not a lack of love, as Elias showed much ability to care for his daughters when he was away from the bottle. As Elias continued to drink, their relationship continued to deteriorate. When he had been drinking, Elias often made derogatory comments about Claudia's weight. Claudia had started a progressive weight gain after Junito was born. Her weight had leveled off for a few years but had been progressively increasing after coming to the States. Since the birth of the twins, she has been 60 pounds overweight. Claudia considered leaving Elias but was terrified of being alone, knowing she had to provide for three children. In the time she had been in the United States, she had learned little English, and Elias was her voice to the outside world.

Junito at 11 years old was a happy child who excelled academically with the support of his family. Sergia spoke frequently and kindly of Junito's parents, telling him stories about his mother and sharing the photos Claudia sent. Sergia feared that Junito would forget his parents, but Junito consoled his grandmother by telling her that he remembered them clearly. Actually, he had no recollection of his father and could only remember his mother because of the pictures. Sadly, when Junito turned 13, his grandmother was diagnosed with advanced-stage colon cancer and was given 6 months to live, and they began to make the arrangements for Junito to come to the United States. Sergia died at home with her family at her side. Junito was torn with grief and did not want to move to the United States.

Two months before Junito's 14th birthday, he arrived in the United States. When he arrived, his mother burst into tears, because her little boy now towered over her. Junito had mixed emotions. He greeted his father passively, because he was like a stranger to him. Yayi and Isabel hugged their brother. As the months passed, Elias continued to be mostly absent from the home, and when he was there, Elias and Junito were unable to communicate effectively. Claudia worked many long hours, and Junito was often responsible for caring for his younger sisters. School became the hardest adjustment, even though he had always excelled in school and enjoyed the work back in the DR. Although he had studied English for 3 years in school, he was unprepared for the school culture of the United States, and he quickly fell behind.

Junito began staying out late at night. His parents received calls from the school about his excessive absences and academic failures. Junito began spending time with other kids of whom Claudia and Elias did not approve, and he was found drinking Elias's alcohol on several occasions. In a fit of anger, Elias signed him out of school and brought him to work at the mechanic shop. Elias felt that this behavior would easily be changed if Junito could learn the meaning of "hard work." Junito worked hard at the shop, but soon his 15-year-old girlfriend, Analiz, became pregnant. Claudia offered to care for Analiz and the new baby and allowed them to live in their apartment. Analiz moved in with Junito's family and bore a son, Nicolas. Junito was overwhelmed by the responsibility of caring for a family, and the money he made at the shop never seemed to be enough.

Junito began selling marijuana and occasionally cocaine on the side to try and supplement his income. He began spending more and more time with his friends. His family heard that he was affiliating himself with gang members, and sometimes he disappeared for days. Claudia and Analiz were distraught. One night, when Junito resurfaced after a week's disappearance, Elias, in a drunken rage, kicked him out of the house and told him to never come back. It was evident that Junito was not only selling drugs but had begun using them himself as well.

Case contributed by Gabrielle Robles, MSW, Albany, New York

Life Story #4: Tran Thi Kim (Kim Tran)

Kim Tran lives in Orange County, California, in a neighborhood that is predominantly Vietnamese. She is 17 years old, the third child born to parents who are Vietnamese refugees whose families escaped to the United States in the late 1970s and early 1980s. Both of Kim's parents were in their early teen years when their families escaped from Vietnam by boat; each family spent 2–3 years in refugee camps before making their way to Southern California.

Kim has only spotty knowledge about her parents' lives in Vietnam and about their escape to the United States and has learned not to ask questions that make her parents and extended family members sad. She has often thought, however, that there is a deep sadness that runs through her family. She knows that both of her grandfathers were in the South Vietnamese military and were imprisoned by the Viet Cong for several years. She has heard that both grandfathers escaped from prison and moved their families around until they were able to escape from Vietnam by boat. She has occasionally overheard conversations about some of the hardships the families faced during and after the war years. She is aware that both her mother's and father's families were separated either during the escape from Vietnam or by pirate attacks on the boats. Her paternal grandfather and some of her mother's siblings have never been heard from since. She knows that both of her parents entered school when they reached California, but neither completed high school. They had had little opportunity for schooling during the war years and the turmoil that followed the war in Vietnam, language was a major barrier, and their income was needed at home. As the oldest son, Kim's father was responsible for his mother and younger siblings. Kim also knows that her grandparents held on to their Buddhist faith through all their trials, but since her paternal grandmother's death, her parents have failed to keep up these religious traditions.

Kim remembers her early years with some fondness. Her paternal grandmother lived with her, her parents, and siblings, and her maternal grandparents and uncles and aunts lived nearby. They were embedded in a large Vietnamese community that provided much support and cultural connection. When she was a small child, she loved to spend time with her maternal grandmother visiting the shops in Little Saigon, especially the herb shops. She found pleasure in hearing the old men sitting around speaking animatedly in Vietnamese. She has fond memories of Chinese New Year, the colorful dresses her mother, aunts, and grandmothers wore, and the little red *lai-see* envelopes of good luck money that were given to the children. There were tensions at home, however. Kim's paternal grandmother was sad and withdrawn and refused to leave the apartment, even to socialize in the tight Vietnamese neighborhood. The grandparents were critical of the ways that Kim and her siblings were acculturating, and this often led to family arguments. As she grew older, Kim became the special focus of these arguments, because she was more determined than her siblings to break with "the old traditions." Soon even her siblings were critical of her lack of respect for the family elders. In spite of these conflicts at home, Kim was a strong student, more so than her older brother and sister, and she had good friends in the neighborhood.

When Kim was 10, her paternal grandmother and maternal grandfather died within a few months of each other. About this time, she became aware of a lot of conflict between her mother and father. Her father worked two jobs, by day as a dishwasher in a restaurant and by night cleaning office buildings in Little Saigon. Her mother worked an evening shift as a waitress. She was good at what she did and was soon working in the best restaurant in Little Saigon. Tension with her husband increased as she grew in confidence and became more independent and assertive at home. This ran counter to his expectations for his wife, and many loud arguments ensued at home. Kim's father began to come home less and less, and when he was home, he had little interaction with the family. When Kim's brother and sister graduated from high school, they juggled full-time work with part-time study at the community college. They were not home very much either.

By the time Kim was in her second year of high school, she was the only one at home in the late afternoons, evenings, and weekends. She was lonely and began to feel abandoned. She started to hang out more with other youth in the neighborhood. She had been aware that there was a growing Vietnamese youth gang presence in the neighborhood, and one day when she was visiting with one of her friends after school, the friend told her that a youth gang had taken up residence down the street. A few days later, Kim and her friend met up with some members of this gang when they were all hanging out at a coffee shop. Over a month's time, Kim became friendly with several of these gang members, including the gang leader, and began to hang out with them. They began to invite her into their house. At first, she refused, but after a few invitations she agreed to come for a visit, and soon she was hanging out at the house on a regular basis. She began to feel a sense of family in this gang house that she had been missing.

Kim's parents and siblings became aware of her relationship with the gang members and ordered her to break all ties with the group. When she refused, they were outraged at her lack of respect and ostracized her. Kim moved into the gang house. She continued to attend school and perform well there, but now she had a place to go to be with other people after school. She was expected to cook and to clean the gang house and to provide sex for the gang leader, of whom she had become very fond. After a few weeks, when the funds were running low in the house, Kim was informed that the gang was planning a "home invasion" of a wealthy Vietnamese family. She was given the job of carrying the guns of the gang leader. Kim was frightened, but her friends assured her that there was nothing to worry about, that the family would not report the crime, because they had no trust in the police, having lived through a time in Vietnam when the police were enemy rather than protector. Kim realized that she was on a hazardous path, but she was also excited and stimulated by the danger of living *giang ho* (a Vietnamese street expression for the gang lifestyle).

Knowing and Doing

You have just read four life stories that could be encountered in social work practice. You probably noted that all four of these situations are complex and multidimensional. You might be wondering what needs to be done in each of these situations, what can be done, and how you would go about it. Social workers, like all professional practitioners, must find a way to move from knowing to doing, must translate "knowing about" and "knowing that" into "knowing how" (Ryle, 1949). Each generation of social work students learns that the process of translation is not as straightforward as they had hoped. Like architects, engineers, physicians, and teachers, social workers are confronted with complex problems and case situations that are unique and uncertain (Argyris & Schön, 1974). In such complex situations, several elements are involved in the process of moving from knowing to doing. We identify four interrelated elements that we think are the most important ingredients in the process of "knowing how" to do social work: knowledge about the case, knowledge about the self, values and ethics, and general knowledge from the social and behavioral sciences. A brief description of these four elements is presented in Exhibit 2.1.

Although all four elements are essential in social work practice, the focus of this book is on the fourth element, general knowledge from the social and behavioral sciences. In Chapter 1, we outlined a working model for organizing social and behavioral science knowledge to enhance multidimensional understanding for social work practice. In this chapter, we want to explain the importance of each of the four elements noted above and convey our belief that all four elements are intertwined in the process of doing social work. We also want to emphasize that each of these elements presents its own complexities

Knowledge About the Case	Understanding of the situation that has become problematic: • Who is involved? • How are they involved? • What are the relationships between the players? • What are the societal, cultural, and community contexts of the situation? • What are the contextual constraints and resources? • What factors are maintaining the problematic situation? • How are players functioning? • How have the players attempted to cope? • How would the players like to go about resolving the problematic situation? • What resources does the agency have?
Knowledge About the Self	• Understanding of one's own thinking processes (metacognition) • Understanding of one's own emotions (emotional intelligence) • Understanding of one's own social location
Values and Ethics	• Service • Social justice • Dignity and worth of the person • Importance of human relationships • Integrity (trustworthiness) • Competence
General Knowledge From the Social and Behavioral Sciences	• Theory about human behavior • Intervention theory • Research about human behavior • Intervention research • Theory and research for specific oppressed populations

Exhibit 2.1   Four Interrelated Elements in the Process of Moving From Knowing to Doing

and ambiguities, and each requires critical appraisal and reflection as well as thoughtful integration. We are telling you this now because we want to prepare you for the inevitability that social work education, social work practice, and this book will stretch your capacity to tolerate ambiguity and uncertainty. That is important because, as Carol Meyer (1993) has suggested, "There are no easy or simple [social work] cases, only simplistic perceptions" (p. 63). There is evidence that beginning social workers have a tendency to terminate the learning process too early, to quest for answers, as opposed to appreciating the complexity of the process that may lead to multiple possible solutions (Gambrill, 1990). Our goal in writing this book is to provide a framework for considering the complexities of situations encountered in the practice of social work, situations such as those experienced by the families and communities of David Loefeler, Sondra Jackson, Elias and Claudia Salvatierra, and Kim Tran.

Knowledge About the Case

We are using *case* here to mean *situation,* a situation that has become problematic for some person or collectivity, resulting in social work intervention. Our first task as social workers in action is to develop as good an understanding of the situation as possible. Who is involved in the situation and how are they involved? What is the nature of the relationships of the different players? What are the societal, cultural, and community contexts of the situation? What are the contextual constraints as well as the contextual resources for bringing change to the situation? What elements of the case are maintaining the problematic situation? How has the client system functioned in the situation, and what attempts have been made to cope with it? What preferences does the client system have about the types of intervention to use? What is the culture, and what are the resources of the social agency to whose attention the case is brought? You might begin to think about how you would answer some of these questions in relation to the situations of David Loefeler, Sondra Jackson, Elias and Claudia Salvatierra, Kim Tran, their families, and their communities.

Every situation is unique, and the nature of the situation influences the type of information needed to understand it. For example, medical information is an important aspect of the knowledge about the case for some situations but not for others. Information about psychotropic medications is an important aspect of knowledge about David Loefeler's current situation. Developmental history is more important for some situations than for others. For example, the developmental trajectory of Junito's attachment relationships is an important aspect of his unfolding story. In general, however, social workers should think of the situation in broad terms, incorporating a biopsychosocial-spiritual perspective and recognizing the interconnectedness of factors (see Hutchison, 2003a). Social workers should be competent at doing community assessments as well as individual and family assessments (Fraser & Galinsky, 2004). For example, it will be important for a social worker working with youth in Kim Tran's community to understand the history and the culture of the community as well as the nature of the gang presence in the community.

While social work intervention will not focus on all aspects of a case, the intervention should be connected to the "whole story" (Kirk & Reid, 2002; Meyer, 1993). It is important for the social worker to "notice" the impact of biological and social structural variables that are relatively intractable in order to view people in their circumstances, even while working with individuals and focusing on the most "fixable" aspects of the situation. To illustrate this point, Carol Meyer (1993) gives the example of direct social work practice with homeless persons. She notes that "the lack of housing is beyond the reach of professional clinical skills. Yet, to assess the psychosocial situation of a homeless person without reference to the harsh reality of lack of housing in the community would be a distortion of the case, perhaps leading the practitioner to view the client as deliberately rootless" (p. 60).

In addition, agency context will influence what a social worker attends to. For example, a social worker working at a homeless outreach center, whose agency mission is to provide services to a homeless population in targeted areas of the city, might emphasize case knowledge about client housing history, available resources, the community's experience with the presence of homelessness, and so on. On the other hand, a social worker working in a substance abuse treatment program who learns of a client's homeless status during an intake interview might focus predominantly on the client's health/mental health information, current family situation, and the way that homelessness and substance abuse are intertwined in the story while giving less attention to the community's attitude toward the presence of homeless adults or the relationship between the program and its surrounding community resources related to housing stability. These examples offer some understanding of the differential impact the agency context might have on knowledge acquisition and utilization with two clients who present as "homeless."

"Starting where the client is" is a long-standing adage in social work. This adage holds whether we are talking about individuals, families, groups, communities, or organizations. In practical terms, this means that social workers must understand how the client system sees the situation. What story(ies) do they tell themselves about the situation? What beliefs do they hold about it? What do they want to see happen? What do they value, and what preferences do they hold for the change process? Although the client's/clients' views hold supreme importance and prevail in intervention planning, it is important to acknowledge that every story is a partial story and the client's/clients' story, like all human stories, is vulnerable to gaps, bias, and contradiction. The social work literature has long suggested that for every difficult situation presented to social workers, there is both an "objective" and a "subjective" signification, the way the situation appears to external observers and the meaning it has for the client (see, e.g., Meyer, 1993; Perlman, 1957). For example, as social workers, we may see Kim Tran's situation primarily in terms of her growing enmeshment in a youth gang, but she might see her story to be primarily one about building a sense of family and connection in the midst of a disruption in her biological family that runs counter to the high value of family in her culture.

We hope you are beginning to see that developing knowledge about the case is not a simple matter of taking in data. The case must be "built" (Meyer, 1993) or "constructed" (Franklin & Jordan, 2003). We must select and order the information at hand and decide if further information is needed from the client system or other possible informants. And we must acknowledge that in selecting information, we "select out" other pieces, ultimately stringing together a series of microdecisions and practice judgments that reflect our construction of what is relevant and important. We must search for recurring themes as well as contradictions in the data. We must apply rules of evidence and logic to move from case study to case construction, particularly where contradictions exist (Alter & Egan, 1997; Chapel, 2004; Gambrill, 1990). Exhibit 2.2 presents an overview of the process and skills involved in using evidence and logic for case construction. We should continuously ask, "What other explanations are there for the situation?"

The process of case construction also calls for putting what we know about the case against social and behavioral science knowledge. The social work assessment process has been described as "a form of logical analysis, where a practitioner comes to know his or her case through acknowledgement of the client's own story, interpreted through the screen of

Process	Skills
Select relevant evidence (general knowledge)	Knowledge acquisition and organization Analytic
Apply evidence to practice challenge (case-specific knowledge)	Inferential
Interpret evidence (both case-specific and general knowledge)	Evaluative
Identify action alternatives	Generative Analytic
Weigh the risks/benefits of action alternatives with clients	Analytic Reflective
Select action alternative and implement in contract with client system	Creative Reflective Evaluative

Analytic—to deconstruct and closely inspect the different pieces of evidence
Inferential—to make new connections and hypotheses based on the available evidence
Evaluative—to come to some conclusions, interpretations, and/or recommendations
Generative—to expand upon existing evidence with alternative possibilities and new ideas
Reflective—to examine different angles and to move back and forth between these differences
Creative—to go beyond the evidence and explore novel possibilities

Exhibit 2.2   Evidence and Logic

an available knowledge base" (Meyer, 1993, p. 17). In the process, we ask ourselves, How is this case similar to what is reported in the literature, and how is it different? What is the local environmental context for this case?

Before moving to a discussion of the second element, knowledge about the self, it is important to note that knowledge about the case is influenced by the quality of the relationship between the social worker and client(s). Social workers need what Howard Gardner (1993, 1999) calls "**interpersonal intelligence**," intelligence about relationships (Matto, Berry-Edwards, Hutchison, Bryant, & Waldbillig, 2006). Interpersonal intelligence includes the capacity to understand the moods, temperaments, motivations, and intentions of other people; the capacity to recognize the symbol systems of other cultures; and the capacity to work effectively with others. There is good evidence that people are likely to reveal more aspects of their situation if they are approached with commitment, an open mind, warmth, empathic attunement, authentic responsiveness, and mutuality (see Berry-Edwards & Richards, 2002). The integrity of the knowledge about the case is related to the quality of the relationship, and the capacity for relationship is related to what Gardner calls intrapersonal intelligence and we refer to as knowledge about the self.

Knowledge About the Self

In his book *The Spiritual Life of Children,* Robert Coles (1990) wrote about the struggle of a 10-year-old Hopi girl to have her Anglo teacher understand Hopi spirituality. Coles suggested to the girl that, perhaps, she could try to explain her tribal nation's spiritual beliefs to the teacher. The girl answered, "But they don't listen to hear *us;* they listen to hear themselves" (p. 25). This young girl has captured, in a profound way, a major challenge to our everyday personal and professional communications, the tendency to approach the world with preconceived notions that we seek to validate by attending to some information while ignoring other information. To guard against this tendency, social workers need **intrapersonal intelligence**, the capacity to understand oneself, including one's desires, fears, and abilities, and the capacity to use information about the self to regulate interactions with others. Three types of self-knowledge are particularly important to social workers: understanding of one's own thinking processes, understanding of one's own emotions, and understanding of one's own social location.

It is essential that social workers engage in **metacognition**, which means thinking about our own thinking (Franklin & Jordan, 2003). We must be aware of our beliefs and perceptions and how they may lead us to overlook, discount, or misinterpret information. We need to work to keep an open mind that is receptive to surprise and uncertainty. Jack Mezirow's (1998) transformative learning theory emphasizes the importance of developing a mind-set that avoids unexamined acceptance of one's own subjective experiences. This calls for "deep and continuous self-criticism" (Wallace & Brody, 1994, p. 4), perhaps the most challenging commitment we make when we decide to become professional social workers. This type of self-reflection can be aided by journaling, dialoguing with others, and "seeing" ourselves and others through the representations from the humanities (art, literature, music, etc.; Brockbank, McGill, & Beech, 2002; Smith, 2002; Viggiani, Charlesworth, Hutchison, & Faria, 2005). Paula Nurius (1995) also reminds us that we need to develop a generative dimension to our critical thinking, "the ability to create and move beyond what is to see and contribute to what could be" (p. 114). In other words, we need to be self-critical in our understanding of what we see, and we must also be creative in seeing the possibilities in a situation (Seymour, Kinn, & Sutherland, 2003).

Social workers also need what Daniel Goleman (1995) calls **emotional intelligence**, which includes recognition of one's own emotional states, self-control, self-motivation, zeal, and persistence. We need to understand what emotions get aroused in us when we hear client stories and when we contemplate the uncertainties of the case, and we need to be able to use our own emotions in ways that are helpful and avoid using them in ways that are harmful. Although writing about physicians, Gunnar Biorck (1977) summarized well the importance for social workers to possess Goleman's traits of self-control, social motivation, zeal, and persistence when he commented that practitioners make "a tremendous number of judgments each day, based on inadequate, often ambiguous data, and under pressure of time, and carrying out this task with the outward appearance of calmness, dedication and interpersonal warmth" (p. 146).

It is also essential for social workers to identify and reflect on their own **social location**, where they fit in a system of social identities, such as race, ethnicity, gender, social class, sexual orientation, religion, ability/disability, and age. The literature on culturally sensitive social work practice proposes that a strong personal identity in relation to important societal categories, and an understanding of the impact of those identities on other people, is essential for successful social work intervention across cultural lines (see Lum, 2003a). In recent years, with renewed professional commitment to the promotion of social justice and "oppression-sensitive" practice (Ho, Rasheed, & Rasheed, 2004, p. 6), more attention has been paid to the need for social workers to understand where they fit in a system of societal privilege and disadvantage and to understand how that location might affect their social work relationships (e.g., Kondrat, 1999). We must make a conscious attempt to see our professional selves as clients see us (Hall McEntee et al., 2003).

Values and Ethics

The process of developing knowledge about the case is a dialogue between the social worker and client system, and social workers have a well-defined value base to guide the dialogue. Six core values of the profession have been set out in a preamble to the Code of Ethics established by the National Association of Social Workers (NASW) in 1996 and revised in 1999 (NASW, 1999). These values are service, social justice, dignity and worth of the person, importance of human relationships, integrity, and competence. Each of these values has implications for the process of building knowledge about the case and for moving from knowing to doing. As suggested in Chapter 1, we see social justice as such an important value for social workers that it is given an important place in the working model of the book. Here we discuss three other core values: dignity and worth of the person, integrity, and competence. Before turning to that discussion, we want to note that the NASW Code of Ethics makes no attempts to prioritize the six core values and, therefore, provides little guidance in situations where competing values come into conflict. Indeed, social workers often confront ethical dilemmas in our work, when we must resolve the competing values represented in practice situations. Resolving such conflicts requires critical appraisal on the part of the social worker.

As demonstrated in Exhibit 2.3, the Code of Ethics articulates an ethical principle for each of the core values. The ethical principle for the value *Dignity and Worth of the Person* is "Social workers respect the inherent dignity and worth of the person" (NASW, 1999). An important aspect of that principle is the idea that clients have the paramount role in constructing the case from the beginning (Dybicz, 2004; Gambrill, 2004). Defining the problem and planning the intervention is a joint effort of social workers and the client systems they serve. Recent developments in evidence-based medical care suggest that scientific evidence about best practices for specific health problems must be harmonized with patient preferences (Gambrill, 2003a). This idea is consistent with social work's long-standing valuing of socially responsible self-determination. Respect for the dignity and worth of the person does not mean, however, that we will accept the client system's view of what is best without examination. For example, with involuntary clients, such as those in the child welfare or criminal justice system, client self-determination must be balanced against duty to serve and duty to protect.

---

1. **Value:** Service

    Ethical Principle: Social workers' primary goal is to help people in need and to address social problems.

2. **Value:** Social Justice

    Ethical Principle: Social workers challenge social injustice.

3. **Value:** Dignity and Worth of the Person

    Ethical Principle: Social workers respect the inherent dignity and worth of the person.

4. **Value:** Importance of Human Relationships

    Ethical Principle: Social workers recognize the central importance of human relationships.

5. **Value:** Integrity

    Ethical Principle: Social workers behave in a trustworthy manner.

6. **Value:** Competence

    Ethical Principle: Social workers practice within their areas of competence and develop and enhance their professional expertise.

Exhibit 2.3   Core Values and Ethical Principles in NASW Code of Ethics

SOURCE: Copyright © 1999, National Association of Social Workers, Inc., NASW Code of Ethics. Reprinted with permission.

The ethical principle for the value *Integrity* is "Social workers behave in a trustworthy manner." Trustworthiness means being transparent about what is being done and the reasons for it. It also means being honest about both the certainties and the uncertainties of the case and of the social and behavioral knowledge base used as a screen for the case (Dybicz, 2004; Gambrill, 2003a). It means informing clients about the known risks and benefits related to their current status based on the best science about risk and protection (Gambrill, 2004). It means recognizing what we don't know, but it also means having the desire to know and a commitment to search for the best possible evidence about the client situation and ways to resolve the difficulties in it.

The ethical principle for the value *Competence* is "Social workers practice within their areas of competence and develop and enhance their professional expertise." In an interview with Eileen Gambrill (2003b), Robyn Dawes articulated the essence of this ethical principle simply and clearly in this way: "Ethical practice is one which recognizes what science there is" (p. 29). Competence requires understanding the limitations of the available science for considering the situation at hand, but it also requires using the strongest available evidence to make practice decisions. As suggested by Peterson (1995), "Wherever pertinent research has been done and well-tested theories are available, we need to take the high ground, we need to seize it, hold it, and work from it in the public benefit" (p. 980). This is where general knowledge from the social and behavioral sciences comes into the picture. As you read the following section, please bear in mind that social work practitioners are not expected to hold all useful theories and research evidence in their heads. We must, however, know how to access this information, analyze it systematically, and integrate it holistically.

General Knowledge From the Social and Behavioral Sciences

As suggested above, ethical social workers are always searching/recalling what is known about the situations they encounter, turning to theory and empirical research from the social and behavioral sciences for this information. This general knowledge serves as a screen against which the knowledge about the case is considered. Because of the breadth and complexity of social work practice, usable knowledge must be culled from diverse sources and a number of scientific disciplines; contradictory ideas must be held simultaneously and, where possible, coordinated to develop an integrated picture of the situation (Miller, 2002). This is, as you might guess, not a simple project. It involves selecting and weighing available evidence and analyzing its relevance to the situation at hand (Gambrill, 2004). The purpose of the working model presented in this book is to provide structure for this searching/recalling, selecting, and weighing process. Such a structure can facilitate critical thinking processes by encouraging a comprehensive exam-ination of alternative hypotheses.

You may already know that social and behavioral science theory and research has been growing at a fast pace in modern times, and you will often feel, as McAvoy (1999) aptly put it, that you are "drowning in a swamp of information" (p. 19), both case information and sci-entific information. Phillip Dybicz (2004) considers it a strength of the profession that social workers have been more willing than other social and behavioral scientists and pro-fessionals to wade into the swamp. Ironically, at the same time that you are drowning in a swamp of information, you will also be discovering that the available scientific information is incomplete. Of particular importance to the model presented in this book is the fact that one way scientific information is often incomplete is the failure of existing research to use samples that can be generalized to many populations served by social workers. Because of their smaller numbers, members of minority groups may not be included, or included in sufficient numbers, to allow generalization to the group. In addition, language and literacy difficulties may arise with both written surveys and interviews (Goodson-Lawes, 1994). As we weigh the bountiful, but incomplete, evidence, we must maintain a "critical, as opposed to a reverential, attitude" toward both theory and research (Greenwood, 1976, p. 305). To accomplish this attitude, standards are needed for critical appraisal of both theory and research. Exhibit 2.4 provides criteria for evaluating both theory and research.

Criteria for Evaluating Theory

Coherence and conceptual clarity. Are the concepts clearly defined and consistently used? Is the theory free of logical inconsistencies? Is it stated in the simplest possible way, without oversimplifying?

Testability and evidence of empirical support. Can the concepts and propositions be expressed in language that makes them observable and accessible to corroboration or refutation by persons other than the theoretician? Is there evidence of empirical support for the theory?

Comprehensiveness. Does the theory include the multiple dimensions of persons and environments? What is included and what is excluded? What dimension(s) is/are emphasized? Does it account for things that other theories have overlooked or been unable to account for?

Consistency with social work's emphasis on diversity and social justice. Can the theory help us understand uniqueness and diversity? How inclusive is it? Does it avoid pathologizing members of minority groups? Does it assist in understanding power arrangements and systems of oppression? Can it be used to promote social justice?

Usefulness for social work practice. Can principles of action be derived from the theory? At what levels of practice can the theory be used? Can it be used in practice in a way that is consistent with the NASW Code of Ethics?

Criteria for Evaluating Research

Corroboration. Are the research findings corroborated by other researchers? Are a variety of research methods used in corroborating research? Do the findings fit logically with accepted theory and other research findings?

Multidimensionality. Does the research include multiple dimensions of persons, environments, and time? If not, do the researchers acknowledge the omissions, connect the research to larger programs of research that include omitted dimensions, and/or recommend further research to include omitted dimensions?

Definition of terms. Are major variables defined and measured clearly and logically? Are they defined and measured in such a way as to avoid bias against members of minority groups?

Limitation of sample. Does the researcher specify the limitations of the sample for generalizing to specific groups? When demographic groups are compared, are they equivalent on important variables?

Influence of setting. Does the researcher specify the attributes of the setting of the research, acknowledge the possible contribution of the setting to research outcomes, and present the findings of similar research across a range of settings?

Influence of the researcher. Does the researcher specify the attributes of the researcher and the possible contributions of the researcher to research outcomes?

Social distance. Does the researcher attempt to minimize errors that could occur because of literacy, language, and cultural differences between the researcher and respondents?

Suitability of measures. Does the researcher use measures that seem suited to, and sensitive to, the situations being researched?

Exhibit 2.4   Standards for Evaluating Theory and Research

SOURCE: Reprinted with permission from Hutchison, 2003a.

Although much has been written in recent years about the limitations of science, science remains "humankind's most powerful means of attaining the best knowledge possible" about human behavior (Kirk & Reid, 2002, p. 15). Our commitment to search for the best possible evidence takes us to the high ground of science. Science can never predict all of the factors that influence a situation, however, and it is important for social workers to recognize the limits of science and navigate through the uncertainties. Science looks for patterns of occurrence and associations between causal factors for large groups and populations, not for the course of a troubling situation in the life of a particular individual, family, community, or organization. It is by nature, *probabilistic,* telling us about likelihood but not certainty. For example, science can tell us that children who are abused are more likely than children who are not abused to engage in community violence in adolescence. But most children who are abused are never involved in community violence, and science cannot tell us with certainty whether a particular abused child will become engaged in community violence. Longitudinal research demonstrates that there are large individual differences in responses to both negative and positive life circumstances, and consequently, programs designed to improve individual and social situations will not always have the same effects (Werner & Smith, 2001). That is, we know that an intervention that works with one individual may not work or work as well with a seemingly similar individual.

Both theory and research should be recognized as both helpful and important yet also partial, imperfect, tentative, and open to scrutiny. This means that every act of social work intervention should be guided by available theory and research but recognized as an informed trial, a process of discovery, full of ambiguities and uncertainties (Kirby & Paradise, 1992). Social work is a good profession for people who are committed to a constant search for the best possible evidence, but it is no place for people who yearn for "an assembly-line series of tasks" (Kirk & Reid, 2002, p. 10). It is a place for knowledgeable professionals who are ready to be flexible and responsive to unique circumstances. Throughout this book, we will help you assess both the strengths and limitations of the existing general knowledge base as found in the social and behavioral sciences.

Social workers draw on two types of social and behavioral science knowledge. One type is theory and research about approaches to social work intervention, about what techniques help to bring about change. This type of scientific knowledge is the focus of intervention (practice) courses in the social work curriculum. The other type of social and behavioral science knowledge is theory and research about human behavior. This type of scientific knowledge is the focus of the Human Behavior in the Social Environment (HBSE) curriculum in schools of social work, and the focus of this book. This type of knowledge does not prescribe interventions but does indicate intervention possibilities (Meyer, 1993). It helps us know what to look for and consider when attempting to understand human beings, their development, and their behavior. Particularly useful is theory and research that helps the social worker "pinpoint possible modifiable factors that might be causing or exacerbating the problem" (Kirk & Reid, 2002, p. 35). Identifying such knowledge is a central purpose of the working model presented in this book.

At this point, it is important to remind the reader again that theory and research in the behavioral sciences are ever changing. Although these changes are exciting and welcomed because they continue to add to the knowledge that informs what social workers do, they also add complexity to how we should/must do practice. Throughout the book, we report on the latest theory and research available at the time the book was written. Understanding of this theory and research creates the knowledge foundation necessary to examine and synthesize new information. Behavioral science knowledge development is ongoing and cumulative, with new, and sometimes contradictory, evidence coming at times at a fast pace. It is imperative that we all develop knowledge retrieval skills that will allow us to keep up-to-date about general knowledge. To do this, we must become adept at using the databases available to us in our university libraries. We also have a variety of Web-based materials available to us, but we caution that some Web-based materials are more reliable than others. On the SAGE Publications Web site for this book, http://www .sagepub.com/hutchisonchallenges, you will find a link to a listing of some key organizations that are reliable sources of information on specific challenges of living.

Learning Activities

1. Knowledge About the Case. Working in small groups, choose one of the four life stories at the beginning of this chapter. Discuss what you know about the case. Who is involved in the situation, and how are they involved? What is the nature of the relationships of the different players? What are the societal, cultural, and community contexts of the situation? What are the contextual constraints as well as the contextual resources for bringing change to the situation? What elements of the case are maintaining the problematic situation? How has the client(s) functioned in the situation, and what attempts have been made to cope with it? What else would you want to know about the situation to develop a better understanding of the case, and how would you go about getting that information? What challenges of living seem most important in the case? Which challenges of living would you need to learn more about to feel competent to provide services to improve the situation?

2. Knowledge About the Self. Working in small groups, consider your reactions to all four life stories at the beginning of the chapter. Discussing the case scenarios one at a time, focus on the following questions: What beliefs and perceptions do you have about the type of situation and the people involved in the case scenario? How might those beliefs and perceptions cause you to overlook, discount, or misinterpret information? What emotions are aroused in you when you read about the situation? How might those emotions help and/or hinder your social work in the situation? What are your social identities in terms of race, ethnicity, social class, gender, age, religion, sexual orientation, ability/disability, and so on? How might these social identities impact your social work in the case scenario? As you discuss these questions, pay attention to how your reactions are similar and different across the case scenarios. What can you learn about yourself from this critical self-reflection?

As a group, discuss any similarities and differences in reactions among group members. What do you think contributes to these similarities and differences in perceptions and reactions?

3. Values and Ethics. Working in small groups, discuss whether you see any social justice issues in each of the case scenarios. If so, what is the nature of these social justice issues? What could you do as a social worker to address the identified social justice issues? What could and should the profession of social work do? As you think about how you might approach working in the context of each case scenario, could you draw guidance from any of the other five core social work values besides the value for social justice—service, dignity and worth of the person, importance of human relationships, integrity, and/or competence?

4. General Knowledge. Working individually, develop a comparative analysis of the patterns of occurrence of HIV/AIDS in five different countries (your choice of countries). Go to the official Web site of UNICEF (www.unicef.org). Click on Info by Country. Click on the region of the first country of interest under Countries by region. Click on the name of the country. Click on Statistics. Click on HIV AIDS. Repeat this process for five countries. Make a table comparing the incidence and/or prevalence of HIV/AIDS in the five countries.

3

Financial Impoverishment

Pamela A. Viggiani,
Nazareth College of Rochester

The Salvatierra family faces many challenges, including an ongoing struggle to avoid financial impoverishment. We might consider how financial vulnerability is interrelated with some of the other difficulties this family faces. Their story may prompt us to think about the number of individuals and families having similar financial struggles, both globally and here in the United States. Unfortunately, the Salvatierras' story presents difficulties familiar to many, because, over the last several decades, the world has experienced a rapid increase in poverty and economic inequality (Ehrenreich & Hochschild, 2002; Goode & Maskovsky, 2001; Sachs, 2005). Poverty is a destabilizing force on local, national, and global levels.

Without economic resources, communities are unable to meet the basic needs of their members, and violence and unrest are often the result (Sachs, 2005). Individuals living in impoverished communities are often jeopardized across the life course in several spheres, including biological, psychological, social, and spiritual. Impoverished children are of particular concern because their biological, cognitive, emotional, and social development is vulnerable to environmental deprivations, putting them at high risk for many of poverty's complications, including death. The World Health Organization (WHO; 2003b) estimates that 10.5 million children under the age of 5 died in developing countries in 2002. Given its consequences on global, national, and local levels, poverty and its reduction are a concern for all, so much so that the United Nations Childrens Fund (UNICEF; 2005) includes the eradication of extreme poverty as the first of its eight Millennium Development Goals (MDGs).

Historically, poverty has been defined in a variety of ways (see Exhibit 3.1 for an overview of ways of defining poverty). There is considerable debate about how much or how little material resources constitute impoverishment. Governments most often define poverty by looking at income and assets. Defining impoverishment by assessing the minimal amount of income and assets needed to subsist at a basic level (enough income

Poverty as Assets	Definition			
Absolute Poverty	A definite line indicating enough to survive at a basic level: food, clothing, shelter	Not impoverished Impoverished		
Relative Poverty	Poverty in relation to average community assets; changes over time			Not impov. Impoverished Not impov. Impoverished Not impoverished Impoverished Pt. 1 Pt. 2 Pt. 3
Extreme Poverty	Definition applied to global poverty referring to chronic hunger and no access to health care, safe drinking water, sanitation, education, housing. The World Bank uses a standard of income of U.S. $1 per day per person or less of purchasing power.			
Moderate Poverty	Definition applied to global poverty referring to a condition in which basic needs are just barely met. The World Bank uses a standard of income of between U.S. $1 and $2 per day per person of purchasing power.			

Exhibit 3.1   Definitions of Poverty

to provide food, clothing, and shelter) is referred to as **absolute poverty** (Iceland, 2003). In contrast, **relative poverty** looks at impoverishment as relative disadvantage, as one's position relative to the living standards of the majority in the society (Iceland, 2003).

Both absolute and relative measures of poverty utilize what are referred to as poverty thresholds, poverty levels, or poverty indices to define the minimal amount of income and assets necessary to be considered *not* in poverty (DiNitto, 2003). As one might expect, debate about the amount of money needed to live in a nonimpoverished state is often rancorous because it is highly politicized, with ramifications for social policy development and implementation that could result in significant amounts of public expenditure. In the United States, the debate is further complicated by cultural values that stress the essential role of individual effort, achievement, and hard work as the keys to financial success (DiNitto, 2003; Popple & Leighninger, 2003; Trattner, 1998). Given these cultural values, an absolute measure of poverty is favored in the United States, while European nations favor a relative measure (Lindsey, 2004; UNICEF, 2005).

In the United States, *poverty thresholds* are used to measure poverty (Shipler, 2004; U.S. Department of Health and Human Services [USDHHS], n.d.), applying a strategy originally developed in the early 1960s by Molly Orshansky, who worked for the Social Security Administration. The thresholds, which are updated every year by the Census Bureau (Fisher, 1997; USDHHS, n.d.), are based on the **economy food plan**, which calculates the least expensive way to buy an adequate amount of nutritionally sound food for a family. Because families were spending approximately one third of their income on food in the 1960s, the poverty thresholds were established by multiplying the amount of money needed for the economy food plan by 3 (Fisher, 1997). Orshansky's thresholds also accounted for different household compositions, including sex of the head of family, number of children, and number of older adults. The thresholds were created as a level of income inadequacy rather than adequacy, but nonetheless, the United States adopted Orshansky's thresholds as a line of adequate income (Fisher, 1997).

Orshansky's thresholds have been criticized for both overcalculating and undercalculating the number of financially impoverished persons. Those who feel that the poverty thresholds are set too high point out that they only include cash income, excluding "*in-kind benefits* such as medical care, food stamps, school lunches, and public housing" (DiNitto, 2003, p. 70). Those who feel that the poverty thresholds are set too low point out that food no longer costs one third of a family's income and argue that housing costs are far more of a concern and need to be included in any measure of poverty (DiNitto, 2003). Furthermore, they cite a number of other family characteristics that may contribute to poverty but are not factored into the poverty thresholds, factors such as chronic illness or high debt loads (DiNitto, 2003). Other scholars argue that wealth and assets, not income, are the best measures of financial status, noting that even larger numbers of families are asset poor than poverty rates based on income would suggest (Lerman, 2005). Despite considerable debate, the poverty thresholds and *poverty guidelines,* a simplification of the poverty thresholds used to help organizations determine who qualifies for a variety of social welfare programs, remain the official measures of poverty in the United States (USDHHS, n.d.).

The term *extreme poverty* is utilized when discussing poverty on the global level. **Extreme poverty** is akin to absolute poverty; it refers to the inability to meet basic needs. The world's extreme poor are described in this way: "Chronically hungry, unable to access health care, lack the amenities of safe drinking water and sanitation, cannot afford education for some or all of the children and lack . . . a roof to keep the rain out of the hut, a chimney to remove the smoke from the cook stove and basic articles of clothing, such as shoes" (Sachs, 2005, p. 20). Although one could argue that homeless persons in the United States qualify as extreme poor, Sachs (2005) suggests that the extreme poor are only found in developing countries, because developed countries (like the United States) have an infrastructure in place to tend to the basic needs of their populations. So, although homeless individuals in the United States may not have access to adequate, ongoing health care, in a health crisis they would have a hospital to go to and would receive care. In a developing nation, the hospital might not exist, at least not in any reasonable proximity to those needing its services.

To measure the number of extreme poor around the world, the World Bank has developed a measurement of income of U.S. $1 or less per day per person in purchasing power as the definition of extreme poverty (Sachs, 2005; Smeeding, Rainwater, & Burtless, 2001). Although criticized as undercounting the poor by many, the World Bank's measure has been widely accepted as at least a general figure for estimating poverty on a global scale (Pangestu & Sachs, 2004).

Another term used to define poverty on the global level is moderate poverty, a relative measure of poverty. **Moderate poverty** is defined as a situation in which basic needs, as perceived by the society in which one lives, are barely met. "The moderately poor, in high-income countries, lack access to cultural goods, entertainment, recreation, and to quality health care, education, and other prerequisites for upward social mobility" (Sachs, 2005, p. 20). However, on the global level, moderate poverty is measured by the World Bank's standard of income, as having between U.S. $1 and $2 of purchasing power per day per person.

Patterns of Occurrence

The way poverty is measured affects the numbers and percentages of people counted as impoverished. Unless otherwise noted, reported rates of poverty in the United States are based on poverty thresholds of an annual income of $9,827 for an individual and $19,157 for a family of four (U.S. Census Bureau, 2005b). Because world organizations that study poverty utilize the World Bank's measure of U.S. $1 per day per person, it is the most available and recognized count of the global poor and, unless otherwise noted, is utilized in our global incidence figures.

It is important to recognize that for some families, both in the United States and globally, poverty is persistent, but many other families have spells of poverty that are relatively short in length. It takes longitudinal research to capture this phenomenon. Indeed, some longitudinal research indicates that a majority of families in the United States will experience poverty at some time in their life course (Rank, Yoon, & Hirschl, 2003). Most of the following patterns of occurrence are based on cross-sectional, time-limited data and, unless noted, do not reveal a distinction between persistent and temporary poverty.

Living in the United States can be seen as an advantage when poverty rates are compared to those of developing nations. However, when the United States is compared to other rich, industrialized nations, it is clear that residents of the United States are at far greater risk of impoverishment (Mishel, Bernstein, & Allegretto, 2005). Often, the United States is compared to other industrialized, market-economy countries that are members of the Organization for Economic Cooperation and Development (OECD). Countries have been added to the OECD over the years, and in 2005, 30 countries were members of OECD, including the United States and these 29 other countries: Australia, Austria, Belgium, Canada, the Czech Republic, Denmark, Finland, France, Germany, Greece, Hungary, Iceland, Ireland, Italy, Japan, the Republic of Korea, Luxembourg, Mexico, the Netherlands, New Zealand, Norway, Poland, Portugal, the Slovak Republic, Spain, Sweden, Switzerland, Turkey, and the United Kingdom (UNICEF, 2005).

To compare poverty rates across countries, the Luxembourg Income Study (2000) uses a relative measure of poverty as a household that has a disposable income equaling less than one half of the national median annual income. Using this definition, the United States had the highest overall poverty rate, 17%, when compared to the 19 other countries in the OECD at the time of the study. Australia had the next highest poverty rate at 14.3%, while Finland, Norway, and Sweden had poverty rates of 6.5% and below (Mishel et al., 2005). Furthermore, when compared to like countries, the United States has the most persistent poverty, defined as people who are poor continuously over 3 years. The rate for persistent poverty in the United States is 9.5%, over twice as high as most other countries, which range from 0.8% (Denmark) to 7.8% (Portugal; Mishel et al., 2005).

Using the established poverty thresholds to measure poverty in the United States and globally, rather than the relative measure used by the Luxembourg Income Study, poverty affects 12.5% of the American population and extreme poverty affects 29.4% of the global population (United Nations Millennium Project Task Force on Poverty and Economic Development, 2004; U.S. Census Bureau, 2003). Poverty rates in the United States vary by race/ethnicity, geographical location, gender, age, and disability.

The poverty rate for whites in the United States is 8.2%, 11.8% for Asians, 24.4% for blacks, 22.5% for Latinos, and 23.2% for American Indians and Alaskan Natives (Institute for Research on Poverty, 2005; U.S. Census Bureau, 2004). Globally, 93%, about 1.1 billion, of persons living in extreme poverty live in three regions of the world, East Asia, South Asia, and sub-Saharan Africa, in countries that are almost exclusively comprised of people of color. Those living in moderate poverty reside in the aforementioned countries as well as in Latin America and the Caribbean, where just under 15% of the population is affected (Sachs, 2005).

Location of residence is also important in the United States. The poverty rate is 10.2% in the Midwest, 11.4% in the Northeast, 13% in the West, and 13.9% in the South (Bishaw & Iceland, 2003). Regional differences in impoverishment are most often related to local labor market factors, including both job availability and wage scale. Poverty rates also vary by settlement type in the United States. The poverty rate is 9.1% for those living in suburban areas, 12.1% for those living in cities, and 14.2% for those living in rural areas. Within cities, those living in central city areas or the urban core experience poverty at a rate of 17.5% (U.S. Census Bureau, 2003). The poverty rate in rural areas is often attributed to low levels of educational attainment and lack of access to jobs and other resources. The Jackson, Salvatierra, and Tran families all live in urban core areas that have experienced high rates of poverty in recent years. The Loefeler family, on the other hand, faced the challenges of limited job opportunities in their rural area after the failure of their dairy farm.

Although the data are scarce and incomplete, the available data indicate that, globally, women are slightly more likely than men to experience poverty. According to Marcoux (1997), "The average proportion of women among the poor is (approximately) 55 percent" (p. 2). He notes that this gender bias in poverty, although not extremely high, is important because it is real and is growing, especially in developing countries. In the United States, women's poverty is 38% higher than men's, and single women are 100% more likely to live in poverty than single men (Christopher, England, Ross, Smeeding, & McLanahan, 2000). The 2000 census indicates that 26.4% of all female-headed households with and without children live in poverty (Joint Center for Poverty Research, 2001).

Unfortunately, children in the United States and abroad experience higher rates of poverty than other age groups. In the United States, by U.S. definitions, 17.6% of children under the age of 18 experience poverty, while only 10.8% of adults of working age (18–64) are impoverished, and the rate of impoverishment for those over 65 is 10.2% (U.S. Census Bureau, 2003, 2005b). Globally, children are at great risk of impoverishment. According to Bellamy (2004), 1 billion children across the world live in poverty, representing one in two children. Although a large proportion of these poor children live in low-income countries, many of them also live in wealthy countries. UNICEF (2005) recently undertook a study of child poverty in rich countries, with a study of the OECD countries for which data were available. As Exhibit 3.2 demonstrates, the child poverty rates in these wealthy countries, measured, relatively, as income below 50% of the national median income, vary from 2.4% to 27.7%. Denmark and Finland both have rates below 3%, and the United States and Mexico both have rates over 20%. The UNICEF data indicate that the proportion of children living in relative poverty rose during the 1990s in 17 of the 24 OECD countries for which trend data were available. The United States was one of four countries where the relative child poverty rate showed significant decline, by 2.4%, during this period, but as you can see from Exhibit 3.2, there is much room for improvement in the United States. The other countries with a significant decline were Australia, Norway, and the United Kingdom.

People with disabilities are also disproportionately represented in poverty statistics. The Census Bureau (2005a) reports that in 2000, 17.6% of people with disabilities were poor, compared to 10.6% of people without disabilities. The poverty rate was 25.0% for disabled children between the ages of 5 and 15, compared to 15.7% of nondisabled children of the same age.

Theories of Causation

Theorizing about causes of poverty can occur at different levels of analysis. At the micro level, we can ask why particular individuals or particular families are poor. Or we can focus on the community level and ask why particular communities are poorer than other communities. At the global level, we can ask why some countries are poorer than other countries. Theories have been developed to explore poverty at all of these levels of analysis.

Country (year poverty measured)	Percentage of Children Living Below Poverty Level
Denmark (2000)	2.4
Finland (2000)	2.8
Norway (2000)	3.4
Sweden (2000)	4.2
Switzerland (2001)	6.8
Czech Republic (2000)	6.8
France (2001)	7.5
Belgium (1997)	7.7
Hungary (1999)	8.8
Luxembourg (2000)	9.1
Netherlands (1999)	9.8
Germany (2001)	10.2
Austria (1997)	10.2
Greece (1999)	12.4
Poland (2000)	12.7
Spain (1995)	13.3
Japan (2000)	14.3
Australia (2000)	14.7
Canada (2000)	14.9
United Kingdom (2000)	15.4
Portugal (2000)	15.6
Ireland (2000)	15.7
New Zealand (2001)	16.3
Italy (2000)	16.6
United States (2000)	21.9
Mexico (1998)	27.7

Exhibit 3.2   Percentage of Children Living in Poverty in 26 OECD Countries.

SOURCE: UNICEF, 2005.

NOTE: The figures in this exhibit are based on a definition of poverty as household income below 50% of the national median income. Please note that the reported data reflect measurement for different years across countries. The year of measurement is presented beside the name of the country.

Individual Theories	Genetic inferiority Expectancy theory Human capital theory
Structural Theories	Social stratification Feminization of poverty Colonialism & neocolonialism Environmental geography
Cultural Theories	Culture of poverty
Ecological Theories	Individual and structural factors both taken into account

Exhibit 3.3   Theories of Causation of Poverty

Social surveys indicate that people in the United States consistently rate individual insufficiencies as the primary factors responsible for impoverishment (Gilens, 1999). These perceived insufficiencies—laziness, lack of effort, and low ability levels—are often cited as reasons for becoming and remaining poor (Gilens, 1999). Although this view is widely held, poverty scholars have developed several theoretical frameworks for understanding the causes of financial impoverishment, including individual explanations, but also structural, cultural, and ecological frameworks. See Exhibit 3.3 for a summary of these theoretical perspectives.

Individual Theories

A controversial explanation within the individual framework maintains that *genetic inferiority* causes people to be poor. Herrnstein and Murray (1996) suggested that genetic traits such as intelligence influence an individual's ability to attain financial security. **Expectancy theory** looks at psychological conditions, rather than biological factors, that may cause poverty (Charlesworth, 1997). This theory suggests that people behave in certain ways if they have expectations that such behavior will end in the desired result (Bane & Ellwood, 1994). People who are impoverished are thought to have experienced repeated failures when trying to find their way out of poverty. These failures have caused them to lose motivation and control over their lives, and thus they are unwilling or unable to put forth the effort needed to become financially secure (Bane & Ellwood, 1994).

Human capital theory focuses on skills, knowledge, and health that allow individuals to succeed in gaining income (Becker, 1994; Karoly, 2002). An illustration of human capital theory is reflected in poverty statistics indicating that those with a high school education earn more on average than those without a high school education, and those with a college education earn more still (USDHHS, n.d.). We can see this effect in several of the life stories from Chapter 2. David Loefeler has attempted to improve his human capital, and perhaps escape poverty, by returning to school. Sondra Jackson has been able to achieve a middle-class status with her high school education, but we can imagine that she would be less concerned about falling into poverty if she had been encouraged to attend college, as she was clearly capable of doing. Her sister, Estella, is much more vulnerable with her combination of limited education and substance abuse problems. Junito Salvatierra has limited his human capital by dropping out of high school, and we can hope that he will receive some encouragement, as David Loefeler did, to continue his education. If Kim Tran's father had been able to continue his education, first in his native Vietnam and later in the United States, he would, most likely, not need to work two jobs to try to avoid poverty.

Structural Theories

Structural theories of poverty contend that there are systems in society that lead to financial inequities, including poverty (Rank et al., 2003). Theorists in this tradition propose that individual factors cannot account for the level of inequality in a society; this can be understood only by examining arrangements in political and economic institutions. A structural theory of poverty was first widely disseminated during the 19th century by Karl Marx and Friedrich Engels (1848/1982), who proposed that capitalism leads to two classes of people: the bourgeois and the proletariat, the owning class and the working class, respectively. Capitalism exploits the labor of the proletariat. The bourgeois utilize their power in society to maintain control of political, social, and economic arrangements that further their interests at the expense of the proletariat.

Currently, there is a good deal of literature in the social sciences regarding the various structures that serve to privilege and impoverish groups and individual members of society (see Feagin, 2000; Gans, 1995) and a good deal of evidence to support structural explanations of poverty (see Rank et al., 2003). These structures include economic, political, educational, and other societal systems that contribute to inequality of opportunity and inequitable distribution of resources. These societal structures create an environment that favors certain individuals and groups of people over others, providing opportunity to some while denying it for others. At the same time, such structures neglect to fairly (re)distribute resources that would remedy the unequal distribution of wealth. Structural theorists pay particular attention to the failure of the labor market to provide enough jobs that pay a living wage and to the failure of social welfare policies to provide a **safety net** to prevent citizens from experiencing severe poverty (Ehrenreich, 2001; Newman, 1999; Rank et al., 2003; Shipler, 2004; Shulman, 2003).

Many people give little thought to the intricacies of unequal opportunity structures in society, but these inequalities can be quite visible to people without privilege. This was noted clearly by Kevin, a 75-year-old retired homeowner:

> You heard that saying about the guy with a rich father? The kid goes through life thinking he hit a triple. But really he was born on third base. He didn't hit no triple at all, but he'll go around telling everyone he banged the . . . ball and it was a triple. He was born there! (Oliver & Shapiro, 2000, p. 404)

Kevin's story alludes to how various components of our social structures, such as tax and inheritance law, foster the preservation and further accumulation of wealth by the wealthy.

One type of structural theory proposes that the **feminization of poverty** is a result of patriarchal structural arrangements that disadvantage women (Abromovitz, 1996; Dujon & Withorn, 1996; Mink, 1998). Rose and Hartmann (2004) describe the feminization of poverty this way:

> A kind of perverse logic perpetuates a system with a rigid division of labor both in the workplace and in the home. Employers may feel justified in discriminating against women workers if they think they will be less devoted to their jobs because of family responsibilities. They may structure jobs as part-time and dead-end for this reason and many women may accept them because they cannot find better-paying jobs. Labor market discrimination means lower earning for women; women's low earnings mean women spend more time in family care; women's commitments to family care contribute to discrimination against them. Single mothers especially suffer as they must attempt to support their families on women's lower wage levels. (p. 33)

From this perspective, black women are even more disadvantaged than white women because they experience structural disadvantages based both on patriarchy and racism. Women's risk accumulates over the life course, leaving women in late adulthood, particularly black women, at high risk of poverty. If Sondra Jackson takes on the financial care of her sister, Estella, as well as her new grandson, she may well find herself in precarious financial circumstances as she ages, even though she has been planning well for her financial future in recent years.

Structural theories have also been proposed to explain global poverty. Colonialism and neocolonialism have played a role in maintaining the wealth of some countries while impoverishing others. Historically, Western European countries extensively colonized Asian, African, and Central and South American countries for the purpose of exploiting raw materials and native laborers; this is what we mean by **colonialism**. Colonialism strengthened the colonizing countries' economies and weakened the economies of the colonized. In addition, colonial governments took power away from local governance and prevented the localities from establishing stable political systems. After the colonized countries established their independence, the United States and other Western powers established a new institutional framework that called for free trade and the transformation of the formerly colonized countries into democracies (Aronowitz, 2003).

The new institutional framework, often referred to as **neocolonialism**, has produced such organizations as the World Bank, the International Monetary Fund (IMF), and the World Trade Organization (WTO). The United States and Western European countries provide leadership to these organizations that regulate relations between countries. The result is a division between countries that dominate and countries that are dominated and dependent, a reproduction of the arrangements under colonialism (Aronowitz, 2003). In short, the structures of neocolonialism create and maintain wealth for wealthy nations by controlling and exploiting poor nations through international bodies that make rules favoring the wealthy regarding the exchange of money and resources.

Consider the situation of the Dominican Republic, native home of the Salvatierra family. The island Hispaniola was claimed by Christopher Columbus in 1492 and became a starting place for the Spanish conquest of the Caribbean. In 1697, Spain conceded French dominion over the western third of Hispaniola, which became Haiti in 1804. The rest of the island, which became known as Santo Domingo, sought independence in 1821 but was conquered by Haiti, ruled by them for 22 years, and finally attained independence in 1844. In 1861, Santo Domingo voluntarily returned to the Spanish empire, but independence was restored in a war 2 years later. In recent years, the Dominican Republic has been quite dependent on the economy of the United States, which is the source of about 80% of its export revenues. In 2004, the economy was stabilized somewhat by a renegotiation of an IMF loan, but unemployment remains high, and there is great inequality, with families barely meeting their basic needs (Central Intelligence Agency [CIA], 2006). Elias and Claudia Salvatierra had high hopes that they could escape poverty by migrating to the United States.

Other scholars who have attempted to understand different rates of poverty in different regions of the world have proposed that regional inequalities in power and wealth are based on differences in geographical environments. Using historical analysis, Jared Diamond (1999) lays out a comprehensive theory of environmental causes of inequality. He suggests that current regional inequalities are historically based and that the history itself was highly influenced by the geo-environmental context. He suggests four sets of environmental differences that had the most impact on cultural development: (1) the available wild plant and animal species, (2) geographic barriers that could thwart migration and diffusion of cultural innovation, (3) the relative isolation of continents, and (4) continental differences in area or total population size. Diamond argues that all societies have inventive people, but some environments provide better starting materials than others. He also argues that regions of the world have experienced a shifting picture over time in terms of environmental resources for cultural development. Consequently, societies have waxed and waned in power and wealth. Current inequalities, however, are rooted in historical starting points of different societies.

Culture of Poverty Theory

The term **culture of poverty** was coined by Oscar Lewis in the 1960s (Lewis, 1968). Lewis and other social scientists utilized the term to bring attention to poor families as people of worth who develop a culture, a way of life, to adapt to the marginal circumstances in which they find themselves. Lewis rooted this culture in the class-stratified, capitalistic society. However, the term *culture of poverty* has evolved in its usage and meaning.

Some have looked at a culture of poverty from a strengths perspective and learned, for instance, of the prevalence and importance of large kinship networks in the lives of poor women and families (see Stack, 1997). Often, however, the culture of poverty is associated with deviant cultural norms, an association that may have resulted from the widespread dissemination of Senator Daniel Patrick Moynihan's 1965 report on impoverished black families. Moynihan's report popularized the phrase "culture of poverty" to refer to a culture that develops in adaptation to a lack of financial opportunity. It is characterized by a matriarchic family that produces family instability and by community attitudes and behaviors that are nonnormative and destructive. Although Moynihan's report emphasized that the socioeconomic system in the United States was the major culprit in producing family instability, his report was often misrepresented in popular media to suggest the opposite, that family instability causes impoverishment (Wilson, 1996). Thus, the culture of poverty is now most often used to refer to a set of cultural deficits in impoverished communities. The cultural traits, values, and norms most often included are present rather than future orientation, acceptance of welfare dependence, out-of-wedlock births, and single female-headed households (Edin & Lein, 1997).

It is important to understand these two distinct conceptualizations of the culture of poverty. The first conceptualization looks at a culture associated with poverty as a set of attitudes and behaviors that represent an adaptive response to societal structures that block opportunity and access to adequate financial resources (see Wilson, 1996). This conceptualization also maintains that those in impoverished communities, while making adaptations to harsh circumstances, nevertheless subscribe to dominant cultural values (Hays, 2003; Wilson, 1996). The second conceptualization proposes that those who are poor have a set of cultural attitudes and beliefs that cause their impoverishment, regardless of opportunity or access to financial resources (see Banfield, 1990). In short, they believe that poor families "live in a culture of poverty that continues for generations because they are psychologically unable to plan for (a different) future" (DiNitto, 2003, p. 81).

Ecological Framework

Sociologists like William Julius Wilson (1987a, 1987b, 1996) have put forth an ecological framework that examines the way that dimensions of person, environment, and time facilitate and maintain poverty. Wilson's study of inner-city residents illustrates the importance of historical context and particular societal structures and institutions in depriving groups of individuals, black inner-city residents specifically, of the opportunity for work, acquisition of resources, and geographical mobility. At the same time, he examines how this lack of opportunity affects individual psychological, spiritual, and physical well-being. For example, he explores the adverse effects of unemployment and underemployment on mental health and "perceived self-efficacy" (Wilson, 1996). This approach would lead us to speculate that it is quite possible that Isaiah Jackson and his peers perceived their own future as lacking in opportunity and responded by engaging in risky behavior. We might speculate that the same is true for Junito Salvatierra and his friends.

Wilson looks closely at the temporal dimension of poverty, especially in relation to life course markers. For example, poor individuals tend to leave school earlier and take on adult roles earlier than middle-class members of their cohorts. They also have a shorter life expectancy.

Wilson also focuses on poverty at the community level. He studies what he calls *new poverty neighborhoods* that have an unemployment rate of more than 50%. Wilson argues that these neighborhoods are composed of a cohort of people who share an experience that differentiates them from past residents of the same impoverished neighborhoods who, while often poor, were largely employed. He argues that the current high levels of unemployment among urban African Americans can be attributed to economic shifts over the past 3 decades. These shifts include a loss of manufacturing jobs, a spatial mismatch between jobs and workers as jobs move from urban centers to the suburbs, and a skills mismatch as available urban jobs require more highly skilled workers than those found in many urban neighborhoods. He suggests that as middle-class African American families moved to the suburbs, pockets of socially isolated, extremely poor families were left behind. Think of Sondra Jackson as she looks around her neighborhood and the danger Isaiah faces. She realizes that employers have moved their businesses to the suburbs and that jobs are hard to come by anymore in the neighborhood. She often bemoans the fact that she must get in her car to access commodities and services that were once available in the neighborhood. She also is concerned that the long-time residents who anchored the neighborhood have followed these resources to the suburbs, leaving behind mostly those who are too poor to flee and compromising neighborhood stability and safety.

Maryah Fram (2004), a social worker, has adapted the scholarship of Pierre Bourdieu to propose a structural theory of financial impoverishment. Fram's major emphasis is on macro environmental structures, mainly the capitalistic economic system. Yet Fram argues that individuals do make choices within the confines of that structure. To this end, she discusses Bourdieu's conception of **habitus,** which is defined as a "set of dispositions developed through a personal history of self-reinforcing experiences of one's social location" (p. 559). While recognizing some agency in making choices, Fram limits the power of the individual by arguing that "habitus disposes people of privilege (wealth) to act in ways that maintain privilege, while disposing members of disadvantaged groups to act in ways that perpetuate their disadvantage" (p. 559). In short, she suggests that the social and economic structures place individuals in the position of reproducing the status quo. However, she also indicates that individuals across the social hierarchy are empowered if they are made aware of how their choices are reflective of an "accumulation of messages, experiences, and symbols" (p. 559) given to them by the larger society and based on their social location rather than reflective of personal capacities.

Fram (2004) also attends to **social capital** at the mezzo environment, in the social networks of poor families, but her discussion of social capital emphasizes how social networks are positioned in the macro social structure of society. To illustrate this point, Fram uses the example of the social network of a financially impoverished mother. The network is a strength because it facilitates the mother's continued survival, and yet it has its limitations if it is unable to provide access to job and higher educational opportunities that would allow the mother to rise out of poverty.

Consider the situation of Elias and Claudia Salvatierra. When Elias and, later, Claudia came to the United States, they were lucky to have the support and assistance of Uncle Victor Manuel and his wife, Alejandra. They were provided with a place to live and connections to find jobs. Since coming to the United States, they have built a wider network of migrants from the Dominican Republic. This network has helped them out in rough patches, and they return the favor. Unfortunately, however, their network does not include people who can connect them to better paying jobs or to educational opportunities. David Loefeler, on the other hand, was lucky to have a cousin who not only provided emergency housing but also connected him to resources to continue his education. Fram (2004) intends to help social workers understand the complexity of an individual's experience of poverty while considering the inseparability of that experience "from the interests of privileged groups and the . . . processes through which such interests are expressed" (p. 572).

Multidimensional Risk and Protection

The social science literature on risk, protection, and resilience often finds that poverty is a risk factor for a host of negative developmental consequences, causing risk in all dimensions of the biopsychosocial-spiritual framework. However, poverty is not as often studied in terms of the biopsychosocial-spiritual factors that put an individual, family, community, or society at risk for poverty, or in terms of those factors that protect against it. Indeed, the relationship between poverty and other challenges of living can be quite circular in nature, with poverty serving as risk for other challenges of living and those challenges of living serving to reinforce and maintain poverty. The following discussion of risk and protection, as well as the later discussion of developmental consequences, demonstrates this circular relationship. Although financial impoverishment has not yet been examined in terms of risk and protection to the same extent that the other challenges of living in this book have been, risk factors and protective factors for financial impoverishment can be extracted from existing empirical literature. See Exhibit 3.4 for a summary of biological, psychological, social, and spiritual risk and protective factors for financial impoverishment.

Biological Risk and Protection

This section covers risk related to age, health, and disability, biological factors that prohibit or limit an individual's capacity to be economically productive. Although the poverty literature does not specifically attend to protective factors, it seems safe to say that protection lies at the other end of the continuum for the three factors discussed below.

	Risk Factors	Protective Factors
Biological	Biological age: Children Poor physical health Disability	Older biological age Good physical health Lack of disability
Psychological	Low self-efficacy Mental illness	High self-efficacy

Social	Family heritage
	Families with children
	Single-parent female household
	Low educational attainment
	Domestic violence
	Impoverished social networks
	Race, class, and gender
	   discrimination
	Labor market conditions
	Governmental policies
		Family heritage
		Childless couples
		Two-parent household
		High educational attainment
		Social networks with high
		   social capital
		Labor market conditions
		Governmental policies

Spiritual		Affiliation with religious institution Spiritual belief

Exhibit 3.4   Biological, Psychological, Social, and Spiritual Risk and Protective Factors for Financial Impoverishment

NOTE: The risk and protection factors are cyclical in nature (e.g., poverty may increase risk of depression, and/or depression may increase risk of poverty).

Age

As noted earlier, across many current sociocultural contexts, children are more likely to be impoverished than any other age group. Very young children are biologically incapable of making economic contributions and are dependent on the goodwill and resources of adults to avoid impoverishment. In addition, young children require constant care; their families must either forgo paid work to provide this care or must secure substitute care (UNICEF, 2005). In agrarian societies, older children and adolescents are economic contributors and may be valued for their economic contributions, but contemporary market-based economies require an educated workforce, and these social arrangements also increase the risk of poverty for older children and adolescents who must spend their time in school rather than providing economic resources for the family (Zelizer, 1985). You may recall that David Loefeler's and Junito Salvatierra's fathers were happy to have their sons drop out of high school so that they could make a larger contribution to the family economy. Indeed, it is still the case in the United States that adolescent labor is an important factor in helping some families rise out of poverty (Graff, 1995).

Historically, old age was a risk factor for poverty in market economies, because biological capacity for market labor diminishes for most people sometime in old age. However, the development and implementation of social security programs in all market-based economies has resulted in a major reduction in poverty among older adults in all of these societies (Lindsey, 2004). For example, in the mid-1960s, poverty rates among older adults were far above those of children in the industrialized countries but now are well below them (Schiller, 2004). It is important to note, however, that older women are at greater risk of financial impoverishment than older men. Women comprised 60% of the U.S. population over 65 in 2003, but they made up 71% of impoverished older adults (Fritz, 2005). The increased vulnerability to poverty among older women is partially biological (women live longer and have to stretch resources over a longer period) and partially social (women's employment patterns do not allow them to build adequate assets). The fact that old age no longer serves as a risk factor in wealthy countries is an illustration of the role that social policy can play in mitigating biological risk factors. This point is further illustrated by the fact that in many developing countries, old age remains a risk for poverty because older adults are often unable to participate in labor and no social security infrastructure exists (Seipel, 2003).

Physical Health

The association between poverty and poor physical health is well documented (Corcoran, Danziger, & Tolman 2004). In fact, Mullahy and Wolfe (2002) find that "no matter how health is measured, low-income people are not as healthy as those with higher incomes" (p. 279). Poor health is a risk factor for impoverishment because of health care costs and also because it limits the ability to work regularly (Williams & Lawler, 2003). As a result, half of all bankruptcies filed in the United States in 2001 were related to medical debt. And the situation is growing worse; the number of medical bankruptcies has increased 23-fold since 1981 (Himmelstein, Warren, Thorne, & Woolhander, 2005). A researcher at the WHO found that poor people in Uganda identify poor health as the most common cause of poverty (Njie, 2001). Likewise, researchers at the World Bank found that malaria served as a major risk factor for poverty in rural Kenya (Christiaensen & Subbarao, 2005). Poor health in childhood has ramifications for continued poor health and impoverishment across the life course. It is also important to note that the ill health of a child may impede parents' labor force participation (Noonan, Reichman, & Corman, 2005).

Conversely, poverty increases an individual's chance of experiencing poor health, as will be discussed later. Thus, although we know that ill health and disadvantage are related, it is sometimes difficult to untangle the exact mechanisms that contribute to this relationship or to determine which came first, ill health or impoverishment (Rogers, 2003).

Disability

Disabled individuals, as a group, have some of the lowest educational levels and highest rates of poverty in the United States. Disability is defined in a variety of ways and includes several diagnoses, diseases, and conditions. The way disability is defined affects who is included as disabled (for discussions of definitions of adult disability, see Loprest & Maag, 2001; for discussion of child disability, see National Dissemination Center for Children with Disabilities, 2002). It is important to note that the disability rights movement has argued that disability is "a problem in the relationship between the individual and the environment" (Law & Dunn, 1993, p. 2). They argue that environments, particularly built environments, can be disabling if they are inaccessible to many persons.

Research illustrates that children and adults living in poverty are more likely to be disabled than those who are living in nonimpoverished environments (Fujiura & Yamaki, 2000; Skinner, Slattery, & Lachicotte, 2002). Furthermore, disability status and receipt of Temporary Assistance for Needy Families (TANF) are related. TANF recipients represent families that are very poor because the maximum annual amount of cash assistance a family of three can receive through TANF funding is at or below $8,600 in all of the states within the continental United States (Neuberger, Fremstad, Parrott, 2003). This puts these families well below the national poverty threshold/guideline of $16,090 a year per family of three (USDHHS, 2005). The disability rate among those receiving TANF is 44%, three times the rate of disability in the non-TANF population (Skinner et al., 2002).

Disability is a risk for impoverishment for many reasons. Adults who have a disability are often unemployed or underemployed and lack access to appropriate levels of rehabilitation and medical services (United Nations, 1996). Job opportunities may be limited, in part, because of barriers they face in educational settings. People with a disability may be further disadvantaged because even if qualified for a job, they may be unable to compete for it if appropriate accommodations are not available or provided. Moreover, prevalent cultural biases may result in an employer's decision not to hire a person with disabilities (Loprest & Maag, 2001). Children with disabilities risk impoverishment because their parents often are unable to obtain adequate employment because of the unavailability of appropriate child care (Skinner et al., 2002).

High health care costs are another challenge for families with disabled members. Private health insurance is often not available if families with disabled members are not connected to the workplace. Families without private insurance who do not qualify for government-based insurance quickly find resources exhausted. Families who do have private health insurance often find it to be inadequate and/or unaffordable (Skinner et al., 2002). High out-of-pocket costs for services, medications, and equipment, coupled with limitations on pre-existing conditions, put families with disabilities at further risk of impoverishment (Batavia & Beaulaurier, 2001).

Clearly, as with general health, the relationship between disability and poverty is reciprocal and circular. The effects of poverty—poor living conditions, poor nutrition, and lack of access to basic health care—are all related to the development of disabilities (Lustig & Strauser, 2004). Once people become disabled, they risk losing a job and health benefits, face diminished future job prospects, and experience increased health care costs.

The interrelated nature of disability and poverty is apparent on the global level as well. According to a WHO report (2005a), about 600 million people live with disabilities globally, and 80% of them live in low-income countries and lack access to basic rehabi-litation services. The report also indicates that the number of impoverished people with disabilities is growing due to wars, "HIV/AIDS, malnutrition, chronic diseases, substance abuse, accidents and environmental damage" (p. 1).

Psychological Risk and Protection

As noted, certain theories of poverty emphasize the role of psychological factors in devel-oping and maintaining poverty. Because there is little empirical support for this idea, we focus less on this line of analysis and instead focus on the complex relationship between serious mental health issues and poverty. Before turning to that discussion, we do want to note that there is some evidence that low self-efficacy can serve as a risk factor and high self-efficacy can serve as a psychological protective factor in the face of other risks for poverty. One research team (Popkin, Rosenbaum, & Meaden, 1993) found that impover-ished women with a "fatalistic" attitude were less likely to be employed than impoverished women who did not hold such an attitude. Two research teams have found that high educa-tional expectations protect impoverished teens in low-opportunity communities from teen pregnancy, which could serve to avoid the perpetuation of poverty in the next generation (Driscoll, Sugland, Manlove, & Papillo, 2005; Martyn & Hutchison, 2001).

David Loefeler suffers from the most prevalent mental illnesses related to poverty, depression and anxiety. It is well documented that depression and poverty are related, but it is not always clear which came first, depression or impoverishment (Belle & Doucet, 2003; Corcoran et al., 2004; Cutrona et al., 2005). Only longitudinal research can help to untangle this puzzle. It does seem arguable that depression, whether the cause or effect of poverty, may serve to maintain financial impoverishment. David Loefeler is a good example of this. His family's experience with financial disaster may have contributed to his depression and anxiety, but it appears that depression and anxiety are interfering with his ability to get and keep employment, jeopardizing his own and his children's economic status.

Poverty and mental health are linked in all societies, regardless of their level of eco-nomic development (WHO, 2003a). Mental illness is a risk factor globally for both becom-ing and remaining impoverished. Across nations, "poverty and common mental disorders interact with one another in setting up, in vulnerable individuals, a vicious cycle of poverty and mental illness" (Patel & Kleinman, 2003, p. 614).

Depression and anxiety are cited as common illnesses in developing nations, and people with low levels of education, high levels of feelings of hopelessness, and poor physical health are most at risk of developing a mental illness in these nations (Patel & Kleinman, 2003). Other serious mental illnesses like schizophrenia and various psychotic disorders are potent risk factors associated with poverty in industrialized nations (Kaplan & Sadock, 1998). In the United States, seriously mentally ill persons had an increased risk of severe impoverishment, including homelessness, with the advent of *deinstitutionalization* in the 1970s, which resulted in many severely mentally ill individuals being released from state hospitals into communi-ties without adequate services to aid them (Kaplan & Sadock, 1998).

Social Risk and Protection

Social risk and protection factors for financial impoverishment can be categorized as micro factors (family factors), mezzo factors (social network and community factors), and macro factors (societal factors).

Micro Risk and Protection

Family heritage, family size, family structure, educational attainment, and domestic violence can serve as risk for financial impoverishment. Family heritage, family size, family structure, and educational attainment may protect against it. *Being born into an impoverished family* puts a child at risk for financial impoverishment across the life course, with disadvantages accumulating across time. A poor child has a greater likelihood than a financially secure child to be raised by parents whose energy is taken up with the stressors related to inadequate financial resources, to live in a neighborhood with substandard housing and a variety of environmental and interpersonal hazards, and to attend substandard schools (Kozol, 2005; Shipler, 2004). On the other hand, children born into wealth have the protection of being cared for by parents with economic resources, living in relatively safe neighborhoods, attending quality schools, and having the opportunity for a secure advanced education (O'Rand, 1996).

Family size also serves as either risk or protection. International data indicate that families with children are more likely to experience poverty than families without children (Children Data Bank, n.d.). Risk increases as additional children are added to the family. Over the last 30 years, however, women have been using available birth control technology and electing not to have children or to bear fewer children. Reduction in family size has provided a protective buffer against financial impoverishment, with some researchers estimating that reduced family size has cut the poverty rate by roughly one fifth since the 1960s (Gottschalk & Danziger, 1993).

Changing patterns of family structure have also produced risk. Since 1960, the percentage of children in the United States living with only one parent has tripled, representing a spectacular growth in single-parent families that is occurring in all OECD nations (UNICEF, 2005). This trend has contributed to an increase in the poverty rate, because single-parent families are more vulnerable to financial impoverishment than two-parent families (Lindsey, 2004). The trend toward single-parent families is being driven by two other trends in family structure. One of these is an increase in divorce rates, which have almost doubled in the United States since the 1960s. One researcher (Zagorsky, 2005) found that divorced respondents' wealth started dropping 4 years before divorce, and divorce resulted in an average drop of 77%, with women experiencing a slightly greater drop than men. Another researcher found that after a divorce, women and children experience an average decline in income by approximately 30%, while men experience an average hike in income of about 30% (Crittenden, 2001). The other trend is a growth in births to unmarried mothers. In 2000, two thirds of all black births and one fifth of all white births were to unmarried mothers. For single mothers, marriage serves as a protective factor to reduce poverty (Grinstein-Weiss, Zhan, & Sherraden, 2006; Zagorsky, 2005).

Although the number of single fathers is growing, the great majority of single parents continue to be women (U.S. Census Bureau, 2005b). Many single mothers work full time in the paid labor market to financially support their children while having full responsibility for their children's day-to-day care, and physical, emotional, and social well-being. This difficulty is magnified for women who are only able to find low-wage work, which tends to offer the fewest benefits and to be the least flexible and tolerant of absences and tardiness related to caretaking responsibilities. Child care expenses may consume a significant portion of family income, and for many single parents, financial gain from working is minimal or even nonexistent. This helps to explain the gender disparity in financial impoverishment (Abramovitz, 1996; Ehrenreich & Hochschild, 2002). The Children's Defense Fund (2005) estimates that the annual cost of basic needs for one parent working full time and raising two children ages 4 and 7 is $29,976. On the other hand, the annual income for one adult working at minimum wage is approximately $10,700.

Another trend in family structure is the increasing presence of women in the paid labor force. Involvement of women in the paid labor force is a protective factor for many families, allowing them to escape poverty (Lindsey, 2004).

Educational attainment of family members can also serve as either risk or protection. Education provides access to jobs, information, and resources, and there is extensive evidence that higher education leads to higher income (U.S. Census Bureau, 2002). Therefore, lower education is a risk factor for financial impoverishment, and higher education is a protective factor. Unfortunately, educational institutions may not be available to most children in low-income countries, and low educational levels in these countries are associated with higher fertility rates, HIV/AIDS infection, and continued impoverishment. The education of Kim Tran's parents was interrupted by war and migration, as is the case for many refugees to the United States. In the United States, children living in impoverished communities often have the poorest quality schools (Kozol, 1988, 1995, 2000, 2005). Children in poor-quality schools have high rates of school failure, leading to dropout and limited job opportunities, which place them at risk of continued impoverishment, further inhibiting community, family, and individual stability. We can understand why Junito Salvatierra became discouraged about school, but by dropping out of high school he has put himself and his child at risk for long-term financial impoverishment. We can hope that he will recognize this, as David Loefeler did, and find a way to pursue education.

Some researchers have found that *domestic violence* against women can interfere with a woman's ability to work, leading to poorer economic outcomes for women and their children (Holzer & Wissoker, 2001; Tolman & Wang, 2005). The annual work hours were significantly reduced for women victims of domestic violence in a sample of women in the TANF program (Tolman & Wang, 2005).

Mezzo Risk and Protection

Aspects of the mezzo level of social networks and community can serve as risk or protective factors. Urban black men in many distressed neighborhoods in the United States have become more vulnerable to impoverishment as jobs moved to the suburbs and a geographic mismatch developed between these workers and where demand for labor existed (Laester, 1997; Venkatesh, 1994).

Some researchers have examined the social capital in the social networks of residents of concentrated poverty urban neighborhoods. They have found that black males in such neighborhoods report that they lack the kinds of social contacts that could assist them in finding work (Laester, 1997; Venkatesh, 1994). One research team from the United Kingdom found that young adults in distressed urban neighborhoods have networks of family and friends who support them with the problems of growing up in poor neighborhoods, but these networks also serve to close down opportunities to escape the conditions of poverty (MacDonald, Shildrick, Webster, & Simpson, 2005). Another research team from the United States found that the social networks of inner-city black families do not increase employment rates for members of the network and, in fact, contribute to the reproduction of racial segregation in the workplace (Russell Sage Foundation, 2000). On the other hand, it is clear that social networks with enriched social capital serve to protect against poverty.

Macro Risk and Protection

At the macro level, three factors have been identified to produce risk for financial impoverishment: discrimination in education and the labor market, labor market conditions, and governmental policies. Cross-national analysis has also found that labor market conditions and governmental policies can protect against financial impoverishment.

There is evidence of *race, class, and gender discrimination* in the educational system. Racial discrimination in the educational system has a blatant and pervasive history (see U.S. Commission on Civil Rights, 1982). In the 18th and early 19th centuries, teaching slaves was illegal in most southern states. In 1885, California passed a school segregation law that allowed white public schools to exclude Chinese and Mongolian children. In 1896, the U.S. Supreme Court ruled that "separate, but equal" education was constitutional. Racial discrimination in the schools is not as blatant today, but in his book *The Shame of the Nation,* Jonathan Kozol (2005) provides convincing evidence that primary and secondary schools in urban areas are highly racially segregated and quite unequal, with students of color often receiving education in woefully substandard schools. Because of class segregation in housing, school systems tend to be segregated by economic class as well, with poor students being educated in substandard educational facilities. As higher education tuition has been rising, impoverished students find it difficult to access postsecondary education (Schiller, 2004). There is also a history of female exclusion from the educational system, but current gender discrimination is more subtle, with boys and girls being encouraged toward different types of educational curricula (Sadker & Sadker, 1994).

Racial, class, and gender discrimination also exists in the labor market. In studies which matched white and black job applicants, with comparable employment histories and skill sets, applied for the same jobs, the white applicants received significantly more job offers than the black applicants. The level of racial discrimination in hiring was higher in suburban areas than in urban areas (Bendick, Jackson, & Reinoso, 1994). In addition, employers have expressed reluctance to hire applicants from neighborhoods that are perceived to be distressed (Holzer, 1994; Skinner, 1995). In ethnographic studies, inner-city residents have reported that companies sometimes try to restrict the applicant pool by advertising only in suburban newspapers (Laester, 1997; Venkatesh, 1994). In terms of gender, men and women tend to be employed in different kinds of jobs and in different job sectors, and this results in sharply different wages for men and women. In fact, despite the expansion of women's rights, women continue to earn approximately 70 cents for every dollar men earn (Sciammacco, 1998). The wage gap leads to less lifetime earnings and less ability to accumulate wealth and establish financial stability, resulting in risk of impoverishment in old age. Although there is a gender wage gap in other OECD countries, the United States has a larger gender wage gap than Finland, New Zealand, France, Denmark, Norway, Australia, and Sweden (Waldfogel, 1998).

When a macro economic approach is taken, examining *how much poverty* there is in a society rather than *who is impoverished*, it becomes clear that *labor market conditions* can be a source of risk or protection for the rate of poverty in a society. Labor market conditions include such variables as how many jobs are in existence or being created, wage scales, and required knowledge and skills. When the economy is strong, there are sufficient jobs to maintain low unemployment. However, in terms of impoverishment, it makes a difference whether the wages in these jobs are high or low. For example, the average wages of low-income mothers have stagnated in most OECD countries (UNICEF, 2005). During the 1990s, most OECD countries faced an economic recession, but the economy was strong in the United States during this period, resulting in a high demand for labor (known as a "tight labor market"). Tight labor markets have been found to benefit groups who are usually at high risk for unemployment. Indeed, available data indicate that in areas in the United States with typically very high unemployment, the employment rate increased significantly for young, less educated black males during the 1990s, a time of economic boom and tight labor markets (Nasar & Mitchell, 1999). Child poverty rates fell during this same period in the United States (UNICEF, 2005).

Governmental policies can provide a safety net that protects against impoverishment when other conditions are risky. The discrepancy between the poverty rates in the United States and similar wealthy countries is related in large part to the relative generosity of social welfare programs across countries. **Social welfare programs** are governmental policies and programs that are intended to care for citizen needs. Most other wealthy, industrialized countries provide more generous social insurance programs than the United States, including universal family or children's allowances, more generous unemployment assistance, universal health coverage, and universal child care (Rank et al., 2003).

When comparing the United States to eight similar countries, it is apparent that social welfare programs have an impact on poverty rates. As is clear in Exhibit 3.5, pretransfer (before the addition of social welfare programs) poverty rates are similarly high across countries, but posttransfer (after the addition of social welfare programs) poverty rates illustrate a drastic reduction in poverty in the eight wealthy comparison countries, while in the United States the poverty level remains quite high (Rank et al., 2003). A child or family allowance is an example of social policies utilized in industrialized nations to positively affect child and family well-being and prevent families with children from falling into poverty. The United States is the only country among 21 similar countries that does not provide a cash child or family allowance (Clearinghouse on International Developments in Child, Youth and Family Policies at Columbia University, n.d).

Country	Pretransfer Poverty Rates	Posttransfer Poverty Rates	Reduction Factor
Canada (1994)	29	10	66
Finland (1995)	33	4	88
France (1994)	39	8	79
Germany (1994)	29	7	76
Netherlands (1994)	30	7	77
Norway (1995)	27	4	85
Sweden (1995)	36	3	92
United Kingdom (1995)	38	13	66
United States (1994)	29	18	38

Exhibit 3.5   Impact of Social Welfare Programs on Poverty Rates in Nine Countries

SOURCE: Reprinted with permission from Rank, M. R., Yoon, H. S., & Hirschl, T. A., American poverty as a structural failing: Evidence and arguments in *Journal of Sociology and Social Welfare*, 30(4), 3–29, copyright © 2003.

Another example of social welfare policy that can make a difference in the lives of women and children is child support policy, policy that regulates the child support paid by a noncustodial parent (Christopher, England, McLanahan, Ross, & Smeeding, 2000). Child support enforcement policies in the United States are underdeveloped when compared to those of other Western nations (Lindsey, 2004). In many wealthy countries, the government ensures collection of child support. However, according to 2000 Census Bureau data, $60 billion are owed in child support in the United States each year, with $17.1 actually collected (Lindsey, 2004, p. 326). There have been increased governmental efforts to collect child support as part of the Personal Responsibility and Work Opportunity Reconciliation

Act (PRWORA) of 1996, and this has aided many women in receiving essential child support payments. However, many families continue to suffer from inadequate or no child support payments (Crittenden, 2001; Hays, 2003).

Although it lags behind its peers in social welfare provision, the United States does offer one significant protection from poverty through the provision of a federal **Earned Income Tax Credit** (EITC) for low-wage working families. The EITC provides approximately as much assistance to low-income families as TANF and food stamps combined (Friedman, 2003). The EITC gives families up to $4,204 in tax refund income, allowing them to purchase much needed resources and preventing a slide into poverty (Friedman, 2003). Many states and localities supplement the federal EITC program with their own tax programs, allowing low-income families to further benefit from tax refunds.

Spiritual Risk and Protection

Although there is little literature that would indicate spiritual risk factors for financial impoverishment, spirituality and affiliation with a religious institution within the community may serve as a protective factor for those who are impoverished (Bolland, Lian, & Formichella, 2005). There is a long history in the United States of community religious institutions providing resources for families living in poverty (Cnaan, 1997). Resources that religious institutions provide range from food, meals, and clothing to child care services, housing for the poor and elderly, and job training and location (Hodgkinson, Weitzman, Kirsch, Noga, & Gorski, 1993). Religiously based organizations were considerably ahead of the federal government in responding to the growing problem of homelessness in the 1980s (Cnaan, 1997). Religious affiliation also supports the development and expansion of social networks, potentially providing impoverished people with stronger and more diverse social resources to draw upon in times of need. Finally, a belief in something more powerful than humanity provides individuals and families with a sense of hope and strength (Bolland et al., 2005).

Biopsychosocial-Spiritual Integration

The identified risk factors are overlapping; in fact, many are difficult to classify as solely biological, psychological, or social in nature. For example, we have discussed mental illness as a psychological factor, but current advances in neuroscience might indicate that it is better thought of as a biological factor, or perhaps a biopsychosocial factor. We have discussed disability as a biological factor, but the disability rights community argues that disability is constructed by the interaction of the individual with the environment, arguing for a social component to disability (Law & Dunn, 1993). Moreover, many factors are difficult to classify as either antecedents or consequences of financial impoverishment because they are in fact both, as is evident with health and disability.

Our discussion also sheds light on mechanisms of protection. Most risk factors, in the inverse, operate as protective factors. So, for example, the absence of ill health or disability is a protective factor for financial impoverishment. And, in the United States, increasing age, generally, though not always, serves to protect individuals from the risk of poverty. Older men are much less likely than older women to be impoverished (Fritz, 2005). This comes from a mix of a biological factor, shorter longevity for men, and two social factors: men's employment patterns have allowed them to enter old age with more economic resources than older women, and older men are less likely than older women to live alone.

There is evidence that the physical environment interacts with biological factors, psychological factors, and social environments to create a risk of impoverishment. Natural disasters, such as drought and major hurricanes, can significantly increase the rate of poverty for a country or region of a country (Jha, 2006).

There is strong evidence that residing in a nation with a strong social welfare system and other antipoverty strategies in place serves to protect against financial impoverishment. The UNICEF (2005) study of child poverty in rich countries demonstrates, however, that it is the unique combination of such macro social variables as family structure, labor market conditions, and governmental policy—and not one isolated factor—that produces the rate of child poverty in a society. To illustrate this point, the researchers provide an example of the situations in the United States and Norway during the 1990s. During that period, the child poverty rate was reduced by 2.4% in the United States and by 1.8% in Norway, bringing the rate to 21.9% in the United States and 3.4% in Norway. However, it was a different combination of labor market conditions and governmental policies that led to the declines in child poverty in the two countries. During the period in question, the United States was enjoying a booming economy while reducing governmental programs. Norway, on the other hand, was facing an economic recession but managed to reduce child poverty even further than the already low rate by increasing governmental supports for families. The UNICEF report also concluded that **universal social welfare programs** that target all families, such as universal family allowances, while appearing more expensive, actually do more to reduce child poverty than **residual social welfare programs**, such as TANF, that are targeted only to those most in need. They suggest that such targeted residual programs may provide little incentive to move from welfare to work. The United States favors residual social welfare programs, while European countries favor universal social welfare programs.

Consequences of Financial Impoverishment

As illustrated in Exhibit 3.6, financial impoverishment blocks access to basic resources necessary for well-being. Poverty and income inequality create instability at macro, mezzo, and micro levels. System and ecological perspectives suggest that instability at any of these levels will impact all aspects of the functioning of systems and subsystems. And indeed, empirical evidence supports this principle. Poverty-induced instability is manifested in myriad ways at all three levels. Violence, ill health, and disability are three consequences of poverty.

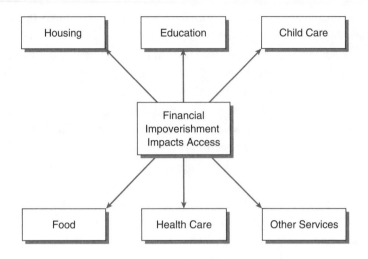

Exhibit 3.6   Impact of Financial Impoverishment on Access to Resources

Violence

Poverty and income inequality (gross economic differences between the rich and the poor) prevent societies from reaching optimal levels of social cohesion. Violence/conflict is one extreme measure of instability. As is discussed in Chapters 4 and 5, poverty has been found to be a risk factor for both community and family violence. Impoverishment itself can also be viewed as violence against humanity, because poverty, like all violence, leads to physical and emotional suffering and premature death (Van Soest & Bryant, 1995). For example, David Loefeler is of the opinion that stress related to loss of the family dairy farm is responsible for his father's early death, and he himself seems to have emotional scars from that time of high stress. Rates of violence are highest in highly impoverished nations and nations with significant inequalities. In these volatile environments, inequality is often accompanied by high degrees of conflict and **social exclusion**, or the political, economic, social, and cultural marginalization of a group of people based on a group characteristic such as class, race, or gender (Goodhand, 2001). Nations plagued by chronic poverty are also likely to experience longer periods of violent conflict, because involvement in military operations may be the only viable way of supporting oneself (Goodhand, 2001).

Violence associated with poverty is also readily transportable across borders, but the relationship between poverty and international terrorism is not direct. Many point out that terrorist organizations do not always develop in poor nations, and they are rarely led by impoverished persons themselves because poor people do not have the luxury of time or resources to plan terrorism (Ferraro, 2003; Lancaster, 2003). At least one economic analysis has suggested that living in an impoverished country is not significantly related to engagement in terrorism (Abadie, 2004). However, Sachs (2005) points out that terrorist organizations look to failed states for members. And state failure is often related to economic failure and widespread poverty. Although there is currently much debate regarding the nature of the relationship between poverty and terrorism, most agree that global poverty and inequality are interconnected with the growth of terrorism.

Turning to the United States, community violence is suffered at high rates in impoverished neighborhoods (Boney-McCoy & Finklehor, 1995; Krug et al., 2002; Simon, Mercy, & Craig, 2001). Isaiah Jackson has already become a victim to such neighborhood violence, and it appears that Junito Salvatierra is at risk of being involved in such violence, at least as a witness. In such neighborhoods, community residents suffer high rates of anxiety and depression and often feel a pervasive sense of immobilizing hopelessness as well as physical injury and trauma (Boardman & Robert, 2000). Sondra Jackson has already experienced the death of her only child and struggles to avoid the sense of hopelessness that she observes in her neighbors. Children are perhaps the most adversely affected by such violence, experiencing detrimental effects on their biological, cognitive, emotional, social, and spiritual development. Familial violence is also high for those living in poverty (Krug et al., 2002). Impoverished families often live with chronic and acute stress as well as a variety of other risk factors that predispose them to violence. Financial stress in the Salvatierra family often spills over into violence, further destabilizing a family that is already struggling to stay connected.

Poor Health

Epidemic levels of poor health are another destabilizing force with at least partial roots in financial impoverishment. The WHO (2003b) is concerned with alarmingly high levels of ill health and premature death found in impoverished communities. Communicable diseases such as HIV/AIDS, tuberculosis, and diarrheal conditions cause millions of fatalities each year. Disease prevents adults from working, parenting, and supporting children. Furthermore, death due to disease is responsible for leaving some nations without a viable workforce and without parents to raise the children. Globally, children who experience poor health and impoverishment are at high risk of death before the age of 5. It is unsettling to realize that the most pressing challenge for children in developing countries is to simply stay alive (Healthlink Worldwide, 2003).

In the United States, poverty is seen as the driving force behind growing health disparities (Krieger, Chen, Waterman, Rehkopf, & Subramanian, 2005). Impoverished families and their individual members face a greater than average risk of experiencing ill health. Ill health works to place poor families at further risk of continued impoverishment. Impoverished families and individuals often live in toxic physical environments with limited access to important health-related resources, including health insurance (Kozol, 1995, 2000). The unsafe nature of the physical and social environments of many highly impoverished communities may lead to restricted levels of activity, with negative health consequences (Mullahy & Wolfe, 2002).

The highly stressful environments in which many impoverished families live have an impact on both their physical and mental health (Wilson, 1987b). Studies suggest that chronic stress can cause changes in endocrine functioning, resulting in immune dysfunction and degenerative heart disease (Brunner, 1997; Sapolsky, 2005). Poverty has also been found to contribute to some types of mental illness. For example, household food insufficiency is associated with major depression, even when controlling for other risk variables (Heflin, Siefert, & Williams, 2005).

Impoverished children have health risks beginning during the prenatal period when they are exposed to the environmental pollution often present in impoverished neighborhoods. They are less likely to have adequate and ongoing prenatal care and are less likely to benefit from a mother who has the resources to purchase and consume a diet rich in appropriate nutrition (Mullahy & Wolfe, 2002). These factors result in many health problems, including low birth weight, infant mortality, and impaired brain development (Spencer, 2003). Such perinatal complications have been found to set up risk for a number of challenges of living throughout the life course (Werner & Smith, 2001). After birth, poor infants, toddlers, and many children continue to suffer high rates of ill health, ongoing difficulties accessing health care, hazardous environments, and inadequate nutrition.

Impoverished children suffer from more chronic and acute illnesses than their affluent counterparts (Spencer, 2003). One chronic condition associated with poverty is asthma (Halfon & Newacheck, 1993). It is thought that children living in high-stress environments, with little access to health care, substandard housing, and environmental hazards suffer from both higher prevalence and greater severity of asthma (Halfon & Newacheck, 1993; Kozol, 1995, 2000). Aside from chronic illness, children living in impoverished conditions are at a higher risk for severe childhood injury (Wen, Browning, & Cagney, 2003). Furthermore, poor children are also more likely to have high levels of lead in their blood. Lead exposure is a serious risk for poor physical, behavioral, and cognitive health (Mullahy & Wolfe, 2002). As a result of poor health, impoverished children are at risk for poor school attendance and thus low educational attainment, increasing the odds of poor health and its consequences across the life course (Bauman, Silver, & Stein, 2006).

Disability

People living in poverty often become disabled as a result of problems accompanying poverty, such as malnutrition, poor housing conditions, working in hazardous occupations, and a high exposure to violence (United Nations, 1996). Injuries in the low-wage, low-benefit meat-packing and cleaning industries are often a result of repetitive motion and hazardous workplace settings that are inadequately monitored for health and safety standards (Cooper, 2000; Ehrehreich, 2001). Individuals who suffer such injuries are rarely compensated because they either quit or are forced out of the job without compensation.

Cooper (2000) tells the story of Symery, who worked for Iowa Beef Packing (IBP) cutting meat off of backbones. Five months into his job, a month before his limited company health care package began, he slashed his palm open. Symery paid for his own medical expenses, and IBP docked his wages for his absences. After returning to work, Symery experienced a second injury that left him disabled; however, "IBP recognizes only reports of its own contract doctors, and they certified Symery as fit to work" (Cooper, 2000, p. 101). The result was that Symery had no income after the second injury. Clearly, Symery is an example of how the type of jobs that impoverished people hold put them at risk of becoming disabled and set up the complex disability-poverty relationship.

Ways of Coping

It is hard to imagine effective ways of coping with the extreme poverty found in the developing world. Yet families and children do cope. Most often the coping strategies utilized are economic in nature, because being able to obtain the basic resources necessary for survival is the foremost concern.

Children in developing nations who are left orphaned or otherwise abandoned because their families are unable to provide for them engage in many activities that help them cope and survive. One study found that Nigerian street children cope by engaging in activities that will earn them money, acting as porters, bus conductors, car washers, and trolley pushers (Aderinto, 2000). These strategies seem to help with children's survival. However, it is difficult to become and remain employed, and children are often antagonistic toward one another because survival is at stake.

Women in developing nations cope in similar ways. If they are able, they migrate to developed nations to perform the work of nannies and household help (Ehrenreich & Hochschild, 2002). These women often migrate without their families with the goal of sending money to family members for their care and support. It should be noted that the types of employment found by such women are often undocumented or unofficial, hence increasing the risk of poverty as they age. Women and families unable to migrate to developed nations cope by finding ways to sustain themselves economically, often using traditional skills. Unfortunately, families living in extreme poverty sometimes fall prey to child traffickers who often ply them with hopeful stories of the better life they can provide for children (Mokhiber, 2003).

Individuals and families within the United States utilize many coping strategies when faced with poverty. Most studies of coping strategies among poor people are conducted with low-income women, in particular women receiving TANF. This is a limitation of research in this area. However, it might be hypothesized that the coping strategies utilized by very poor women are similar to those utilized by other impoverished individuals and families.

One of the most well-documented effective coping strategies is the development and utilization of strong social networks (Cohen & Wills, 1985; Todd & Worell, 2000). Impoverished families utilize reciprocal family and friendship networks to obtain resources for survival. Social networks provide information and resources in the areas of child care, jobs, recreational activities, housing, and social welfare benefits (Strother, 2003). Social networks also provide needed emotional support even though family and friends are usually similarly poor (Strother, 2003). The Tran family seems to have bene-fited from having a larger extended family network in the United States than that of the Salvatierra family. Like many immigrant families, both families have benefited from close ethnic networks in their communities.

Many living in poverty also make effective use of the limited resources available to them, including governmental entitlement programs (e.g., TANF, Medicaid, food stamps), community aid opportunities (e.g., food pantries, clothing closets, community meals), and social supports within the community (Edin & Lein, 1997; Schulz et al., 2006). Effective utilization of such resources provides essential basic resources and additional social support for poor families and their children.

Spirituality is another widely utilized and effective coping strategy for those faced with impoverishment (Strother, 2003; Todd & Worell, 2000). Poor families often report that their belief in God and other religious beliefs provide support. A belief in something out-side of oneself appears to help alleviate some of the pressure and stress related to poverty.

Social Justice Issues

Individuals and groups within the United States and globally do not possess equal odds of experiencing poverty. Children, women, persons of color, and individuals with disabilities or health challenges are inherently vulnerable to poverty. Globally, individuals residing within impoverished nations face alarmingly high odds of death and disease. These dis-parities reveal the unjust nature of poverty and its many inextricably linked risks.

Institutional and individual levels of racism, both historical and current, have con-tributed to racial disparities in poverty rates. **Institutional racism** is racism carried out and perpetuated by sociocultural institutions (e.g., schools, banks, governmental agen-cies) that serves to exclude people of color from equal access and opportunity and serves to maintain or worsen their societal disadvantage (Pincus, 2000). It is well documented that institutional racism is related to differences in quality of education and educational attainment, obtaining and maintaining a job, income and pay, and access to resources in general. Because of the long history of institutional racism in the United States, African Americans, American Indians, and many Latinos have accumulated disadvantage across the generations, with no capacity to build a cushion of assets to get them through eco-nomic hard times.

Individual or contact racism, or the unequal treatment of persons in interpersonal relationships, results in social segregation and a lack of social networks that provide access to jobs and resources (Loury, 2002, p. 452). Occurring across time and space in ongoing "business as usual," these situations heighten the risk of impoverishment for individuals, families, and groups of color.

Cultural and structural racism also work to place people of color at high risk for impoverishment in the United States. Cultural reaction to skin color places blacks, American Indians, and Latinos at high risk of impoverishment. **Structural racism** refers to institutional ways of operating that appear to be race (gender) neutral but which, in effect, disadvantage racial minorities because of the history of institutional racism. For example, in economic downturns, organizations use the policy of seniority to determine which employees will be terminated. That appears, on the surface, to be a race-neutral policy, but in effect it serves to protect the advantage of white workers and to disadvantage workers of color, because historical institutional racism has resulted in longer longevity in the workplace for white workers (Pincus, 2000).

Some societal values and assumptions also lead to discrimination against women in the United States. Women have traditionally been charged with the primary family care work in society, meaning they are disproportionately responsible for not only child rearing but also caring for ill and aging family members (Hutchison & Charlesworth, 2000). This essential work takes place outside the paid labor market and is uncompensated yet necessary for general societal well-being and functioning. This puts women at risk for poverty if caretaking is their primary occupation, because they are often left with diminished or no personal income. But increasingly, women are performing both this unpaid labor as well as working in the paid labor force. When women juggle caretaking and paid work, their ability to advance at work may be compromised (Crittenden, 2001; Ehrenreich, 2001). The gender wage gap also contributes to lower lifetime earnings for women.

A desire to work toward economic justice requires a moral conviction that "every person counts, has human dignity, and deserves respect, equality, and justice" (Pharr, 2000, p. 451). Work for economic justice is a moral imperative. It is important to "make connections to show how everyone is interrelated and belongs in community. . . . Today's expression of violence, hatred, and bigotry are directly related to the level of alienation and disconnection felt by people. For our survival, we must develop a sense of common humanity" (Pharr, 2000, p. 451).

Practice Implications

Social workers are uniquely qualified to effectively intervene at the micro level with impoverished individuals and families, at the mezzo level with impoverished social networks and neighborhoods, and at the macro level in policy development and implementation. Our commitment to vulnerable groups, to cultural awareness, and to social and economic justice provides us with motivation to tackle the complex micro, mezzo, and macro arrangements that maintain financial impoverishment (Seipel, 2003).

When working with individuals and families, social workers will do well to draw on the literature on culturally sensitive social work practice. Key components of this literature include practitioner self-awareness of societal position (privilege), personal culture, values, and ethics that affect worldview; an awareness of cultural values, behaviors, and beliefs that influence societal structure; and the ability to work with clients occupying different societal positions and possessing different worldviews in a nonbiased fashion

(Lum, 2003a). The social work practitioner who works with financially impoverished individuals needs to avoid stereotypical assessments of clients, particularly those based on culturally dominant views that blame poor people for their poverty. Combining cultural sensitivity with a strengths-based empowerment approach to work with impoverished families will allow the social work practitioner to recognize, as well as utilize, poor clients' effective coping strategies.

At the mezzo level, social workers can work with families and individuals in communities to alter community and governmental structures that perpetuate the impoverishment of distressed communities. These strategies can be used with individuals and families within the United States as well as abroad in developing countries. Working collaboratively with community members, we can focus on "enhancing their capacity to influence the institutions that affect their lives and strengthening their participation in political and economic processes" (Ortiz, n.d., p. 6). Social workers can also work in partnership with leaders in impoverished communities to assist them to build greater social cohesion, to obtain needed resources, and to build neighborhood assets.

It is clear from the discussion in this chapter that national and global macro structures serve to maintain and increase financial inequities and poverty. Inadequate governmental social welfare policy on the national level serves both to keep impoverished people poor and to further impoverish them. Therefore, social workers need to develop and utilize macro-level advocacy skills to affect policy change on the state and national level. Haynes and Mickelson (2005) and Schneider and Lester (2001) discuss macro-level advocacy and describe models and methods for effective advocacy for change, including lobbying and working with social movements.

Schneider and Lester (2001) offer eight principles for legislative advocacy. These include identifying issues, setting goals, getting the facts, planning strategies, finding and utilizing leadership, developing relationships with decision makers, broadening the supportive base, and evaluating advocacy efforts. To be good fact finders, we must hone our research skills. As suggested by UNICEF (2005), "To change something, first measure it" (p. 5). Social workers should also become aware of the range of policies that have been proposed and implemented across national lines for reducing poverty, and with the data about the relative success of these different policies. We also must become well informed about the political culture in our localities, states, as well as the nation, and critically plan which policies are most likely to get political traction at this time.

A second approach that social workers can use on local, state, national, and global levels is either agitating for or becoming involved in social movements committed to economic justice. Haynes and Mickelson (2005) offer the 10 phases of organizing social movements found in Exhibit 3.7. Clearly, this is a simplification of the social movement process, yet the identified steps can be helpful for social workers interested in organizing. Social movements most often take years, if not decades, to result in change. However, considering the global crisis of poverty, the need to develop or to take part in such movements is clear.

A global movement has begun with the adoption of MDGs by the United Nations in 2000. The eradication of extreme poverty is one of those goals. A final report on practical strategies toward this end calls for increasing aid to developing countries from Western

Becoming aware of the problem
Raising consciousness of others
Developing leadership and using leadership
Being aware of disagreement among group members
Getting the word out/developing momentum
Suggesting solutions/debating solutions
Investigating best and most efficacious solutions
Securing political support
Paying heed to practical solutions
Implementing a compromise plan

Exhibit 3.7   Ten Phases of Social Movement Organizing
SOURCE: Based on Haynes & Mickelson, 2005.

countries and for awarding funding in the developing countries at the local level rather than the national level (Sachs, 2005). Social workers can utilize their advocacy skills to develop public awareness of the MDGs and the need for increased aid to developing nations. The United States has been challenged to give 0.7% of its gross national product (GNP) to eradicate poverty (Sachs, 2005). Social workers have the skills and professional mandate to assume public leadership in telling our government we want an end to poverty.

To make further progress on MDGs, social workers can interact and work with various international bodies, including the United Nations, World Bank, IMF, and nongovernmental organizations (NGOs; Seipel, 2003). The solution to global poverty will come from international work. Therefore, social workers should collaborate with recognized and respected international organizations. Working closely with such organizations will allow social workers to become part of the "powerful and coherent voices" intent upon fighting poverty (Seipel, 2003, pp. 205–206).

Learning Activities

1. **Knowledge About the Case.** In a small group, reread the case of Elias and Claudia Salvatierra.
   a. Discuss the biopsychosocial-spiritual factors present in their lives that might have put them at risk for financial impoverishment.
   b. Reflect on the theories of causation of poverty presented in the chapter.
      i. What theories of causation do you feel are best able to explain the Salvatierras' impoverishment? Why?

    ii. Based on the theories you selected, what might be the best micro-to-macro solutions to alleviate the poverty experienced by the Salvatierras?

    iii. Discuss what protective factors you would attempt to mobilize in order to mitigate the effects of poverty on their lives.

2. Knowledge About the Self. *Monthly Budget Exercise:* In small groups, map out a monthly budget that you feel necessary to meet the basic needs of a family of three (a mother and two children, ages 7 and 2) living in your community (if group members are from more than one community, pick one community to focus on). The monthly budget must include the following items: rent/mortgage, utilities, transportation (automobile or mass transit), health care (prescriptions, co-pays), food, other nonfood grocery items, clothing, day care, and miscellaneous needs (paper products, school trips, car insurance, car and home repairs, etc.).

    a. Compare your monthly budget results to the U.S. poverty threshold and to the average TANF cash benefit.

      i. How much more/less was your budget than the amount of those who live on the poverty threshold? On TANF?

      ii. What thoughts did you have regarding the amount your group calculated as a minimal monthly budget compared to the amount of money a family on the threshold or on TANF has to live on?

    b. What personal biases did this exercise reveal to you? Before completing this exercise, what were your feelings regarding those in poverty? After completing this exercise?

    c. As a social worker, what types of skills and competencies would you need to work with families in poverty?

    d. As a social worker, what types of governmental, community, familial, and personal resources and supports would you access to aid a family living on your minimal monthly budget? On the poverty threshold?

    e. Based on this exercise, what policy suggestions regarding poverty and its eradication do you have?

3. Values and Ethics. *TANF Exercise:* You are working with a family receiving TANF. You recently learned that the mother in the family you are working with is earning extra money under the table by babysitting for the neighbors, driving them to the store, and selling a variety of items she purchases at the local discount store for a marked-up price to neighbors. The money your client earns from these activities allows her to stretch her TANF benefit dollars enough to supply her family with some of the following: extra clothing, additional food, clean laundry, school money, and other small and/or unexpected household expenses. You are required to report any work that your client is participating in to the TANF office. If you report the earnings your client is making from her unreported work activities, you are likely to jeopardize her TANF benefit. She and her family could be sanctioned or possibly lose benefits. What would you do as the caseworker in this situation? Refer to the National Association of Social Workers (NASW) Code of Ethics to identify the standards of relevance.

4. **General Knowledge.** *Community Poverty Exercise:* Imagine that your class has been asked to undertake an activity to address poverty in your community. As individuals, small groups, or as a class, locate and utilize community resources and experts to discuss poverty rates in your community. As you work through this exercise, pay close attention to documenting trends and recent changes of importance.

    a. Collect and present data on the prevalence of community poverty in general, childhood poverty, and the poverty rate in your community compared to the most recent national statistics.

    b. Collect and present data on particularly problematic areas within your community (geographic areas, age groups at risk, racial or ethnic groups at risk). Again, compare this to the most recent national statistics.

    c. Based on the data you collected, develop a community service plan that targets those groups or areas most at risk of impoverishment. Such plans could include the following:

        i. Volunteering social work services at local agencies serving your targeted populations.

        ii. Developing additional funding or services for local agencies that work with people living in poverty.

        iii. Linking with a local advocacy group or beginning an advocacy group that works to change policies in place to help those who experience poverty or creates policies to eradicate poverty.

        iv. Linking with the groups or areas identified in (iii) and working with them to document their lives and/or to advocate for policies and programs to alleviate poverty.

4 Community Violence

Elizabeth D. Hutchison,
Virginia Commonwealth University

Community violence (CV) is a challenge for three of the families introduced in Chapter 2. The daily stress of community violence is one of the more formidable challenges faced by the Jackson family. Sondra Jackson wanted to leave the neighborhood to protect Isaiah from violence, but that was not possible, and Isaiah became a tragic victim of neighborhood violence during his adolescence. Junito Salvatierra appears to be involved in gang activity, activity that could put him at risk for becoming either a perpetrator or victim of community violence. Kim Tran has recently been drawn into home invasion acts of community violence.

In 2002, the World Health Organization (WHO) issued a *World Report on Violence and Health* and declared violence as a global public health problem (Krug et al., 2002). The WHO report defines violence as

> the intentional use of physical force or power, threatened or actual, against oneself, another person, or against a group or community, that either results in or has a high likelihood of resulting in injury, death, psychological harm, maldevelopment or deprivation. (p. 5)

The report divides violence into three broad categories: self-directed violence, interpersonal violence, and collective violence. The second category, interpersonal violence, is further divided into two categories: family and intimate partner violence, and community violence. The latter category, community violence, is the subject of this chapter. WHO defines **community violence (CV)** as "violence between individuals who are unrelated, and who may or may not know each other, generally taking place outside the home" (Krug et al., 2002, p. 6). In the 1990s, CV was declared a public health emergency in the United States (Koop & Lundberg, 1992).

Patterns of Occurrence

Although the WHO and other research groups distinguish CV from other types of violence, in reality, both in research and practice, the boundaries between different types of violence are not always clear. It is particularly hard to separate CV from family and intimate partner violence in existing data; such distinctions are not typically made in official crime and health data. Mortality data are the most dependable and uniformly collected data on violence and are useful for making regional and cross-national comparisons and for tracking trends in violence over time. However, nonfatal outcomes are far more common in incidences of CV than fatal outcomes (Krug et al., 2002). Unfortunately, data on nonfatal injuries are not as available or as reliable as data on fatal injury (Potter, 1999). Not all acts of violence result in injury that is serious enough to require medical attention, and not all who seek medical attention make a crime report. Cross-national studies show that as many as half of the victims who receive treatment for violence-related injuries do not report the incident to the police (Briggs & Cutright, 1994; Gartner, 1990). National surveys on nonfatal injuries due to violence are self-report in nature, and responses to them may be influenced by culture, for example, in some countries family honor requires killing a woman who has been raped. It is also important to note that there is much variation in the data collection capabilities of countries around the world (Krug et al., 2002).

With these limitations in mind, patterns of occurrence can be identified. We begin with international patterns of occurrence and then move to more specific discussion of the situation in the United States. The WHO report estimated that in 2000 about 1.6 million people died of some form of violence worldwide, and almost one third, 520,000, of those deaths were due to homicide (Krug et al., 2002). Rates of violence in low- to middle-income countries were about twice as high as the rates in high-income countries. Cross-national studies have found that interpersonal violence increases as the level of income inequality increases (see, e.g., van Wilsem, 2004). Elias Salvatierra recalls a story about Haitians who crossed into the Dominican Republic to escape poverty and violence in their own country. Indeed, Haiti has the highest rates of both inequality and violence of all of the Caribbean countries (Dollar, 2000).

There are some interesting regional differences in violent behavior. In the African and American regions, homicide rates are about 3 times the suicide rate, but the pattern is reversed in the European and Southeast Asian regions, where suicide rates are more than twice the homicide rates. In the Western Pacific region, suicide rates are about 6 times the homicide rates (Krug et al., 2002). There are also great differences between countries within regions. For example, in 1994 the homicide rate among males in Colombia was 146.5 per 100,000, while the rate in Mexico was 32.3 per 100,000 (Krug et al., 2002).

Males are about 3 times as likely as females to be both victims and perpetrators of homicide, but as we see with Kim Tran, we should not forget that females are involved in CV. Age is an important factor also. The highest rates of homicide perpetration worldwide are for males between the ages of 15 and 19, followed by males who are 30–44 years old. Within countries, there are higher rates of violence in urban areas than in rural areas, differences between racial and ethnic groups, and higher rates in poor neighborhoods than in wealthy neighborhoods.

Because of the disproportionately high rate of violent offending by youth, the study of CV has often focused on youth violence. It is estimated that, in 2000, almost 200,000 homicides, or 9.2 per 100,000 population, were committed by youth worldwide (Krug et al., 2002). As with general homicide rates, there were regional variations in youth-related homicide. In high-income countries in Europe, and parts of Asia and the Pacific, the youth homicide rate was 0.9 per 100,000. The overall rate for the African region was 17.6 per 100,000, and the overall rate for Latin America was 36.4 per 100,000. With the exception of the United States, where the rate was 11 per 100,000, most of the countries with youth homicide rates above 10 per 100,000 were either developing countries or countries that were experiencing rapid social and economic changes (Krug et al., 2002).

Let's turn now to the patterns of occurrence in the United States. After two decades of rising rates, violent crime in the United States declined from 1994 to 2003. The rates are still high compared to other Western countries, however. Exhibit 4.1 shows the rankings of the prevalence rates of homicide and self-reported nonlethal violence victimization among 18 Western countries, with 1 representing the highest prevalence of violence and 18 representing the lowest rate. In interpreting these data, it is important to note that the data are from different years.

In 2002, 1.6 million people in the United States visited emergency departments for assault injuries. That same year, there were 17,638 homicide deaths, 6.1 per 100,000 population (CDC, 2004a). In the United States, high-profile school shootings have received much media attention, but it is important to keep in mind that school-associated violent deaths comprise less than 1% of homicides of school-aged children and youth (Anderson et al., 2001).

Patterns of occurrence in the United States mirror the global picture. Adolescent and young adult males are disproportionately represented as both perpetrators and victims of interpersonal violence. It's likely that some knowledge of this pattern of occurrence drove Sondra Jackson's fear for Isaiah when he entered adolescence. Homicide is the second cause of death among 15- to 24-year-olds in the United States and the leading cause of death for young African American males and females ages 15–34 (Anderson, 2002). It is the second cause of death for Hispanic 10- to 24-year-olds and the third cause of death for American Indians, Alaska Natives, and Asian/Pacific Islanders of this age group (CDC, 2006c). Youth between the ages of 12 and 24 are at the highest risk of nonfatal assault (Potter, 1999), but youth in this age group are also the most frequent perpetrators of violent crime. In recent years, half of all crimes of violence, both fatal and nonfatal, are committed by 12- to 24-year-olds (Bracher, 2000). One study found that 85% of people who became involved in violent crime by the age of 27 had committed their first violent crime between the ages of 12 and 20 (Maguire & Pastore, 1999).

Self-report studies, administered by confidential interviews, suggest that there are few racial and ethnic variations in nonfatal violent behavior, but crime statistics indicate that there are racial and ethnic differences in homicide rates (Hawkins, Laub, & Lauritsen, 1998).

Country (year)	Homicide	Self-Reported Nonlethal Violence
Australia (1989, 1992)	5	4
Austria (1996)	14	16
Belgium (1989, 1992)	7	15
Canada 1992, 1996)	6	5
Denmark (2000)	12	10
Finland (1992, 1996)	2	7
France (1996, 2000)	15	9
Italy (1992)	3	17
Netherlands (1992, 1996)	13	8
New Zealand (1992)	4	1
Norway (1989)	8	13
Portugal (2000)	11	18
Spain (1989)	17	3
Sweden (1992, 1996)	10	11
Switzerland (1996, 2000)	9	14
United Kingdom (1996, 2000)	18	6
United States (1996, 2000)	1	2
West Germany	16	12

Exhibit 4.1   One-Year Victimization Ranking of 18 Western Countries for Homicide and Self-Reported Nonlethal Violence Victimization, 1989–2000

SOURCE: Based on van Wilsem, 2004, pp. 100–101.

NOTE: 1 as the Highest Prevalence Rate to 18 as the Lowest

In 1999, African American youth, ages 12–24, had a homicide rate twice that of Hispanic youth and over 12 times the rate of Caucasian, non-Hispanic youth (Krug et al., 2002). Urban residents have the highest rates of victimization, followed by suburban residents; rural residents have the lowest rates. Rates of violence are particularly high in low-income urban neighborhoods, like the one where the Salvatierra family lives. In 2003, 22% of victims of violent crime were engaged in some type of leisure activity away from their homes at the time of the violent incident, and 19% were at work or traveling to work (U.S. Bureau of Justice Statistics [USDOJ], 2003). In terms of nonfatal violent crime, Asian gangs such as the one with which Kim Tran has become affiliated are a new but growing phenomenon in some large cities, particularly West Coast cities. Robbery, particularly home invasions, tends to be the crime of choice for Asian gangs, and their victims tend to be Asian immigrant families or Asian business owners. During the home invasions, gang members tie their victims up and beat them until they produce money or other valuables (Kim, 2004; Le, n.d.).

There are regional variations in rates of both fatal and nonfatal criminal violence in the United States. For the period 1976–2002, murder rates, particularly for murder involving guns, were highest in southern regions of the United States, in the East South Central, West South Central, and South Atlantic regions. The rates were relatively low in the New England, Mountain, and West North Central regions. In 2003, the rates of violent crime, including both fatal and nonfatal violent crime, ranged from a low of 77.8 per 100,000 population in North Dakota to a high of 793.5 per 100,000 population in South Carolina (USDOJ, 2004). Exhibit 4.2 divides the 50 states into those that were high, medium, and low in violent crime in 2003.

States With High Rates[a]	States With Medium Rates[a]	States With Low Rates[a]
South Carolina (793.5)	Missouri (472.8)	Oregon (295.5)
Florida (730.2)	Massachusetts (469.4)	Nebraska (289.0)
Maryland (703.9)	New York (465.2)	Rhode Island (285.6)
Tennessee (687.8)	Arkansas (456.1)	Virginia (275.8)
New Mexico (665.2)	North Carolina (454.9)	Iowa (272.4)
Delaware (658.0)	Georgia (453.9)	Hawaii (270.4)
Louisiana (646.3)	Alabama (429.5)	Minnesota (262.6)
Nevada (614.2)	Pennsylvania (398.0)	Wyoming (262.1)
Alaska (593.4)	Kansas (395.5)	Kentucky (261.7)
California (570.3)	New Jersey (365.8)	West Virginia (257.5)
Illinois (556.8)	Montana (365.2)	Utah (248.6)
Texas (552.5)	Indiana (352.8)	Idaho (242.7)
Arizona (513.2)	Washington (347.0)	Wisconsin (221.0)
Michigan (511.2)	Colorado (345.1)	South Dakota (173.4)
Oklahoma (505.7)	Ohio (333.2)	New Hampshire (148.8)
	Mississippi (325.5)	Vermont (110.2)
	Connecticut (308.2)	Maine (108.9)
		North Dakota (77.8)

Exhibit 4.2   State Ratings of Violent Crime by High, Medium, and Low Ratings in 2003

[a]Rates per 100,000 population

SOURCE: Based on USDOJ, 2004, Table 5.

In the United States, the rate of exposure to CV, like the rate of perpetration, is highest among youth. In 2001, it was estimated that 5.5% of youth in the United States between the ages of 12 and 19 reported being victims of violent crime during the year (Brown & Bzostek, 2003). Studies have found that 50% to 96% of urban children have witnessed community violence sometime in their lifetime (Fitzpatrick & Boldizar, 1993; Gorman-Smith & Tolan, 1998; Miller, Wasserman, Neugebauer, Gorman-Smith, & Kamboukos, 1999). One study, conducted among sixth graders in two public schools in southeastern Pennsylvania during the early 1990s, found that 89% of suburban students and 96% of urban students knew someone who had been the victim of violent crime (Campbell & Schwarz, 1996). Another study examined exposure to CV among beginning college students from the four principal boroughs of New York City (the Bronx, Brooklyn, Manhattan, and Queens) and found that most of the sample had been exposed to CV, either as victim (56%) or witness (96%), when they were in high school (Rosenthal & Wilson, 2003). A study of North Carolina incarcerated youth suggests that the rate of exposure to CV is even higher in this group; almost all of the youth had witnessed some type of neighborhood violence, and 90% had been both witnesses to and victims of neighborhood violence (Martin, Sigda, & Kupersmidt, 1998).

At all ages, males are much more likely than females to be victims of CV; between the ages of 15 and 19, males are about 5 times more likely than females to be victims of homicide (Brown & Bzostek, 2003). However, in South Africa, where the murder rate is about 8 times higher than in the United States, researchers have been concerned about the rate of violence exposure among women. In one South African study of women seeking help for dealing with violent events, nearly two thirds of the sample reported at least one experience of violence outside the home in the past year (Dinan, McCall, & Gibson, 2004).

Theories of Causation

Across time, a number of theories have been proposed to explain violent behavior. Six categories of theories are prominent in recent empirical research on CV in the United States as well as globally: psychodynamic theories, biosocial theories, social process theories, cultural theories, social structural theories, and ecological theory. These theories all were developed to understand what causes interpersonal violence, but they differ in the elements that are emphasized. Exhibit 4.3 provides an overview of the central ideas of each of these theoretical perspectives.

Psychodynamic Theories

Some psychoanalytic theorists argue that all violent behavior is a response to a perceived threat to the self, a vulnerable identity (Bracher, 2000). In this view, violent behavior supports identity, which is defined as "a sense of oneself as a relatively consistent and coherent force that matters in the world" (Bracher, 2000, p. 193). When identity is

Theoretical Approach	Central Ideas
Psychodynamic	Violent behavior is a response to perceived threat to the self, a vulnerable identity.
	Violent behavior may be an attempt to protect an attachment relationship.
	Violent behavior may be caused by limited ego capacities.
	Violent behavior may be a way to build group coherence and loyalty.
Life-Course Biosocial	Two types of people engage in violent behavior.
	The life-course-persistent group engages in violent behavior across the life course.
	The adolescent-limited group engages in violent behavior only during adolescence.
	The life-course-persistent group is a small group that is responsible for a disproportionately large share of CV.
	The adolescent-limited group is a large group that is responsible for a disproportionately small share of CV.
	For the life-course-persistent group, violent behavior is rooted in biological factors and early childhood family environments.
	For the adolescent-limited group, violent behavior is rooted in the gap between biological maturity and social maturity.
Social Process	Violent behavior is developed in social interaction.
	Social learning theory. Violent behavior is learned by observation.
	Differential association theory. Violent behavior is learned and reinforced by associating with deviant peers.
Culture of Violence	Amount of CV is affected by cultural factors.
	Some cultures endorse violence as accepted method of resolving conflict.
	The United States is a society with a unique history of violence.
	There are subcultures of violence in the United States, particularly among black urban males and white southern males.
Social Structural	Individual level strain. Violence is caused by frustration about blocked opportunities, negative relationships, or stressful life events.
	Macro-level strain (MST). CV is caused by aggregate strain in the neighborhood, leads to "highly charged" environment.
	Collective efficacy. CV is caused by a lack of working trust, lack of shared belief in ability to take action, and lack of shared willingness to engage in activism.
Ecological	CV is not the result of any one factor.
	CV is the result of complex interactions of individual, social, cultural, economic, and physical environment factors.

Exhibit 4.3   Central Ideas of Major Theoretical Perspectives on Community Violence

vulnerable, violence buttresses identity by producing respect, status, recognition, or dominance. These theorists propose that a variety of risk factors, such as child abuse and neglect, poverty, and prejudice and discrimination can produce a vulnerable identity and create a need for identity-defending behavior. On the other hand, they suggest, a variety of protective factors, such as purpose and meaning, positive relationships, and high intelligence, support identity and reduce the need for violence. From this theoretical perspective, we might hypothesize that the youth in Isaiah Jackson's neighborhood engage in violent behavior to develop and defend their status and position in the neighborhood, as well as to protect the economic viability of their drug-selling business. We might also hypothesize that Junito Salvatierra's gang involvement is related to his vulnerable identity; he faced the adolescent transition at a time when he was attempting to cope with the challenge of the loss of his grandmother and the multiple demands of immigrating to the United States, reuniting with his parents, getting to know new siblings, and entering a new school environment.

Other psychoanalytic theorists (Krohn, 2000) argue that a number of different dynamics cause violence. For example, violence may be an attempt to protect an attachment relationship, or violence may be caused by limited ego capacities, such as the capacity to delay gratification, to plan, and to understand expectations. In other instances, violence may be the method by which an adolescent peer group builds group coherence and loyalty, as sometimes happens in youth gangs. It appears that the attraction of gang membership for Kim Tran is the desire for a sense of belonging that she is missing as members of her family disengage from each other.

Biosocial Theories

In recent years, it has become increasingly common to theorize that violent behavior is caused by an interaction of biological factors with social factors, sometimes called a **biosocial approach** (see Raine, Brennan, Farrington, & Mednick, 1997). This approach suggests that violent behavior occurs when biological vulnerability interacts with social vulnerability. In this tradition, Terrie Moffitt (1993) has proposed a *life course theory* of violent behavior. She argues that there are two types of people who engage in violent and other antisocial behavior.

The first type involves a small group of people who continually engage in a high level of aggressive and violent behavior across the life course and across social contexts. Moffitt calls this group the **life-course-persistent group** and proposes that their violent behavior is rooted in interactions between biological factors and early childhood family environment. More specifically, heredity and complications of pregnancy and childbirth are thought to produce deficits in the infant's nervous system. These biologically vulnerable infants often encounter deficient social environments as well, environments marked by parental rejection, family adversity, unstable family life, and family abuse and neglect. For these individuals, biological risk is compounded by social risk. Although this group is relatively small, it is responsible for a disproportionate percentage of CV.

The second type of violent person involves a much larger group that engages in aggressive and violent behavior only during adolescence. Moffitt calls this group the **adolescent-limited group** and proposes that the violent behavior of this group is driven by the gap between biological maturity and social maturity rather than by biological vulnerability and early childhood adversity. She suggests that in contemporary society, biological maturation is achieved before adult roles, statuses, rights, and responsibilities are attainable for most adolescents. In this gap, many adolescents are attracted to the delinquent style modeled by other adolescents, particularly those in the life-course-persistent group. If their preadolescent development was nonaggressive, however, these youth will develop a more conventional lifestyle when they reach adulthood. From this perspective, it seems clear that neither Junito Salvatierra nor Kim Tran are life-course-persistent offenders because there is no evidence of aggressive behavior before they reached adolescence. Likewise, there is no evidence that Isaiah Jackson was involved in aggressive behavior in his childhood, and we can speculate that he would have ceased his involvement in aggressive behavior once he reached adulthood if he had not fallen victim to neighborhood violence. We might worry that Junito's and Kim's current behaviors put them at risk of similar early death or involvement in the criminal justice system.

Social Process Theories

The social process theories propose that aggressive and violent behaviors are developed through processes of social interaction, and they analyze the processes through which such behavior comes to be enacted. Two important social process theories are social learning theory and differential association theory.

Social learning theory suggests that some children develop a pattern of cognition that supports social aggression (Huesmann, 1998). More specifically, children who observe aggressive behavior of powerful role models develop beliefs that the world is a hostile place and aggression is acceptable. Children who have observed violence across a number of contexts (e.g., parental relationships, parent-child relationships, sibling relationships, television, neighborhood) are at great risk of developing violent coping strategies. **Differential association theory** focuses on the important role of deviant peers in modeling and reinforcing aggression and violence, particularly during adolescence (Krohn & Thornberry, 2002; Sutherland, 1942). Associating with violent peers increases the likelihood of violent behavior as well as the likelihood of falling victim to violence. Isaiah Jackson has already fallen victim to violence, and there is much to worry about in relation to Junito Salvatierra's and Kim Tran's involvement with deviant peers.

Culture of Violence Theory

Some theorists propose that cultural factors affect the amount of violence in a society, noting that some cultures endorse violence as an accepted method for resolving conflicts. These theorists suggest that it is culture that explains the disparities between homicide rates and suicide rates in different regions of the world. In this same vein, some theorists have proposed that the high level of violence in the United States, relative to other Western nations, is a natural by-product of culture (Bell, 1953; Brown, 1991; Butterfield, 1995; Lipset, 1991). According to this view, the unique history of violence in the United States—the frontier tradition, Indian wars, slavery, lynching—has produced a "culture of violence." From this perspective, a violent history has become a part of U.S. identity, and CV is a "spillover of socially accepted violence" (Marshall, 2002, p. 21).

Other theorists counter that violence is not a part of dominant U.S. culture but is, instead, embraced only by some subcultures, posing a "subculture of violence" theory. In particular, a subculture of violence has been noted to explain the greater rates of violence among black urban males as well as among white southern males. The same motivation for violence, a threat to honor, is suggested for both of these groups. Some theorists have focused on the violence of black urban males and suggested a "disputatious" subculture in which a "wide variety of trivial insults and gestures are deemed sufficient to provoke violence" (Covington, 2003, p. 155; see also, Luckenbill & Doyle, 1989; Wolfgang & Ferracuti, 1967). These theorists would suggest that the CV that Sondra Jackson so feared was related to such a subculture of violence. Others have focused on disproportionate rates of violence in the South and traced it, historically, to a **"culture of honor"** that Scotch Irish immigrants brought to the region. This culture prescribed violence as the appropriate reaction to disrespect and insult, the appropriate defense of manhood and reputation (see Bailey, 2003; Greenberg, 1996; McWhiney, 1988). Some theorists have argued that black urban males, with roots in the Southeast, are the direct heirs of the white southern tradition of violence for the sake of honor (Butterfield, 1995).

Social Structural Theories

Social structural theories emphasize the role of environmental factors related to communities and large-scale social institutions in the production of violent behavior. Two social structural theories receiving attention in recent research are general strain theory and the theory of collective efficacy.

Social strain theory has a long history in the U.S. sociological study of crime. Early strain theory suggested that crime results from frustration (strain) about blocked opportunities (Cloward & Ohlin, 1960; Merton, 1938). More recently, Robert Agnew (1992, 1999) has proposed a *general strain theory* (GST) that focuses on the strain caused by negative relationships or stressful life events. Agnew has drawn on individual-level strain theory to propose a **macro-level general strain theory (MST)**. The major thesis of MST is that the aggregate level of strain within a neighborhood affects the level of violence in the neighborhood (Agnew, 1999; Warner & Fowler, 2003). Neighborhood characteristics, such as poverty, inequality, residential mobility, overcrowding, and social marginalization, increase the level of neighborhood strain. Increased neighborhood strain increases the likelihood that residents will experience negative emotions, such as frustration and anger, producing a highly charged environment that results in aggression and violent crime. Perhaps Sondra Jackson perceived a highly charged environment in her neighborhood when she said that it was not what it used to be. It appears that Junito Salvatierra is acting out of a sense of both individual-level strain and macro-level strain as he tries to find his place in the United States. Kim Tran appears to experience individual-level strain, but it is unclear how much macro-level strain she experiences. This is something that we would want to explore with her.

There is also a long history of theorizing that violence and other health-related problems are associated with social disorganization that comes with such neighborhood conditions as persistent poverty, rapid population growth and changing composition, and a transient population (Shaw & McKay, 1942). It was thought that such neighborhoods lose their capacity to achieve social control over their environment. In this tradition, Robert Sampson (2003) has presented a theory of **collective efficacy** that proposes that the level of CV is associated with "the capacity of residents to achieve social control over the environment and to engage in collective action for the common good" (p. S56). Collective efficacy involves a working trust, a shared belief in the neighborhood's ability for action, and a shared willingness to intervene to gain social control. Sampson and colleagues propose that CV decreases as community collective efficacy increases (Sampson, Morenoff, & Earls, 1999; Sampson, Raudenbush, & Earls, 1997). It appears that the neighborhood that Sondra Jackson lives in has been low in collective efficacy in recent years. We might also want to explore the level of collective efficacy in the neighborhoods where Junito Salvatierra and Kim Tran live.

Ecological Theory

In recent years, ecological theory has become the preferred conceptual model among many researchers who study CV. It was the framework for the WHO report on violence and health (Krug et al., 2002), and it is the framework for this book. According to ecological theory, no single factor explains which people will become violent or which communities will experience high rates of violent crime. Violence results from a complex interplay of individual, social, cultural, economic, and physical environment factors (Krug et al., 2002; Potter, 1999). Certainly, the situations of Isaiah Jackson, Junito Salvatierra, and Kim Tran are multifaceted, and we can easily see their behavior as multidetermined.

_____ **Multidimensional Risk and Protection**

Biological Risk and Protection

Researchers have identified a number of biological factors that are associated with increased risk of violent behavior, including low heart rate; central nervous system problems; and hormones, neurotransmitters, and toxins. Little attention has been paid to biological factors that may serve as protection against involvement in violent behavior, but there is some evidence that high heart rate and high cortisol levels serve as protection in the face of risk factors. Recent research on biological risk factors for violence have examined the interactions of biological and social factors and noted that a social factor can influence violent behavior through a biological mechanism, and vice versa (Raine, Brennan, Farrington, & Mednick, 1997). For example, physical abuse of a child can cause brain dysfunction, which can be a risk for violence. On the other hand, brain dysfunction can lead to low economic status, another risk factor for violence. Please keep the complexity of these interactions in mind as you read about risk and protection.

Biological Risk Factors

Three categories of biological risk factors have been identified in the research on community violence.

Low Heart Rate. One of the most consistent findings in the literature on biology and violence is the correlation between low resting heart rate and violent behavior (Farrington, 1987, 1997; Kindlon et al., 1995; Ortiz & Raine, 2004; Raine, 1993; Raine, Reynolds, Venables, & Mednick, 1997; Raine, Venables, & Williams, 1990; Wadsworth, 1976). Controlling for a number of other variables, Farrington (1997) found that only two variables, poor concentration and low heart rate, were independently related to violent behavior over six different analyses in a longitudinal study of 411 London males. This led Farrington to assert that low heart rate "may be one of the most important explanatory factors for violence" (p. 99). The mechanism by which low heart rate is associated with violence is not yet clear, but there are two main theoretical interpretations of the connection. One interpretation centers on a reported correlation between low heart rate and fearlessness and argues that violent behavior requires a degree of fearlessness. The other main interpretation is that violent individuals are seeking stimulation in order to increase their low levels of arousal. It has also been suggested that low heart rate may be a marker for some other biological process, such as brain dysfunction (Raine, Reynolds, et al., 1997). Heart rate is thought to "have its roots in genetics or non-genetic, early biological influences" (Raine, Reynolds, et al., 1997, p. 123). It is also important to note that low heart rate has been found in children who have witnessed parental violence (Gottman & Katz, 1989) and children whose parents divorced in the first 4 years of the child's life (Wadsworth, 1976).

Central Nervous System Problems. A number of researchers, using different measures of central nervous system (CNS) dysfunction, have explored connections between CNS problems and violent behavior. Some researchers have studied **perinatal complications**, such as low birth weight, pregnancy complications, and delivery complications, and found them to be associated with violence (Brennan, Mednick, & Raine, 1997; Hodgins, Kratzer, & McNeil, 2001; Piquero & Tibbetts, 1999; Raine,

Brennan, & Mednick, 1994; Werner & Smith, 2001). Two studies have found the number of perinatal complications to be correlated with later arrest for violent crimes but not for other types of delinquent or criminal behavioral (Kandel & Mednick, 1991; Lewis, Shanok, & Balla, 1979). Perinatal complications are hypothesized to lead to CNS damage, which leads to problems in regulating behaviors, and this is thought to be the mechanism by which perinatal complications contribute to violent behavior. There is also strong evidence that maternal cigarette smoking during pregnancy disrupts CNS development and predisposes offspring to life-course-persistent offending (Gibson & Tibbetts, 2000; Levin, Wilkerson, Jones, Christopher, & Briggs, 1996; Piquero, Gibson, Tibbetts, Turner, & Katz, 2002).

Some research teams have used **minor physical anomalies (MPAs)** as observable indicators of CNS dysfunction and found that males with high numbers of MPAs have higher rates of violence than other groups (Arseneault, Tremblay, Boulerice, Séguin, & Saucier, 2000; Brennan et al., 1997). MPAs are very minor structural deviations found in many areas of the body; common examples are asymmetrical ears, curved fifth fingers, wide-set eyes, and a large gap between the first and second toes. They indicate disruption in fetal development and are not uncommon in the general population. When large numbers of them are present in one infant, however, they are thought to be an indicator of problems in CNS development, because they occur in areas of the body that are developing at a time of major brain development, toward the end of the first trimester of pregnancy. They may have a genetic basis but also may be influenced by environmental factors (Raine, 2002b).

Other research teams have focused particularly on damage to one part of the brain, the prefrontal cortex, in relation to violent behavior. The **prefrontal cortex** is in the frontal lobe of the brain, the part of the brain responsible for motivation, attention, and sequencing of actions. One section of the prefrontal cortex is responsible for inhibition, or conscious control of actions, and damage to this section is thought to be associated with violent behavior. Several researchers have found lower prefrontal glucose metabolism in violent offenders compared to controls matched by age and sex (Raine, Buchsbaum, et al., 1994; Raine Stoddard, Bihrle, & Buchsbaum, 1998; Volkow et al., 1995). Another study has suggested that the increased social demands of late adolescence can overload a late-developing prefrontal cortex, which is still developing into the 20s and beyond, and result in loss of inhibition to violence (Raine, 2002b). Although we have no biological evidence of this, we might well wonder if the multiple challenges in the lives of Isaiah Jackson, Junito Salvatierra, and Kim Tran pose too serious a challenge to their still developing prefrontal cortexes.

Based on animal studies, Gary Kraemer (1997) argues that it is unlikely that violent behavior is related to only one brain system. He proposes, instead, that violent behavior is associated with disorganization among several brain systems. Research with rhesus monkeys indicates that a disorganized CNS leads to a failure to regulate behaviors. Furthermore, it indicates that the infant's nervous system requires attachment to a dependable and nurturing caregiver to develop normal regulatory systems.

In other words, the CNS needs to be socialized through affiliation and connectedness (Clarke, 1993). Based on this research, Kraemer (1992) proposes a **psychobiological attachment theory (PAT)** in which disruptions in early attachment lead to disruptions in neurobiological regulatory systems. When early attachment is disrupted in monkeys, the young monkeys "do not follow the rules . . . at both behavioral and biological levels of analysis" (Kraemer, 1997, p. 224).

Hormones, Neurotransmitters, Enzymes, and Toxins. Research on the links between hormones and violent behavior has focused in the main on testosterone, a steroid hormone produced by the testes and adrenal glands and responsible for the development of male sex characteristics. There is considerable evidence that high testosterone levels are associated with violent behavior in adults but not in children and adolescents (Harris, 1999; Mazur & Booth, 1999; Raine, 2002a; Tremblay et al., 1997). The relationship between testosterone and aggressive behavior is bidirectional; high levels of testosterone lead to aggression, and experiences of triumph increase testosterone, while experiences of failure reduce testosterone (Mazur & Booth, 1999). Researchers have also investigated the link between violent behavior and the level of another hormone, cortisol, often called the stress hormone because it can increase due to any type of physical or mental stress. A low level of cortisol in preadolescents has been found to correlate with aggressive behavior later in adolescence (McBurnett, Lahey, Rathouz, & Loeber, 2000; Shoal, Giancola, & Kirillova, 2003). It appears that both genetics and chronic stress contribute to cortisol levels (Shoal et al., 2003). It is important to note that although researchers are finding these types of correlations, there is much that they still do not know about why these correlations occur.

Researchers have also examined the ways that *neurotransmitters* (chemicals that act as messengers between cells in the brain and nervous system), *enzymes* (proteins that act as a catalyst for specific biochemical reactions), and *toxins* (poisonous substances that can cause disease) are related to violent behavior. One particular neurotransmitter, serotonin, has been found, in both animal and human studies, to regulate aggressive behavior. One epidemiological study examined the relationship between whole blood serotonin and violent behavior and found a relationship for men but not for women. The mean serotonin level was higher for violent men than for nonviolent men (Moffitt et al., 1997). Levels of one particular enzyme, monamine oxidase A (MAOA), have been implicated recently in violent behavior in males who were abused as children (Caspi et al., 2002). MAOA metabolizes several kinds of neurotransmitters and renders them inactive, thereby helping to keep communication between neurons working efficiently. When males who were severely abused as children have *low* levels of MAOA, which are controlled by one gene on the X chromosome, they are about 3 times more likely than maltreated boys with *high* levels of MAOA to be convicted of violent crime. At least one study has examined the role of two toxins, lead and manganese, in violent behavior and found that countries with the highest rates of lead and manganese also had the highest rates of violence (Masters, Hone, & Doshi, 1998). The exact mechanisms involved in these correlations are not yet well understood, and more research is needed in this area.

Alcohol and Other Drugs. Adolescent violence is associated with misuse of alcohol and other drugs (Ellickson, Saner, & McGuigan, 1997; Woodward & Fergusson, 2000). It seems that abuse of alcohol and other drugs sometimes precedes youth involvement in CV, and sometimes the two deviant behaviors simply co-occur. Substance abuse can affect CNS functioning in such a way as to undermine behavioral inhibition, connoting a possible biological mechanism for the correlation of substance abuse and CV. Another possible explanation for the correlation is that CV is often tied up with protection of territory in the illegal drug trade. Still another possible explanation is that CV is often tied up with a more general delinquent lifestyle that includes such other behaviors as abusing substances and being truant from school. These later two explanations would not indicate a biological risk mechanism. It is not clear which of these explanations most accurately describes the co-occurrence of substance abuse and CV in the story of Isaiah Jackson, but his death is thought to be related to the drug culture in his neighborhood.

Biological Protective Factors

There have been less than a handful of studies that examined biological protective factors in relation to violent behavior. Some of these studies have found that antisocial adolescents who desist from violent behavior as adults have significantly higher heart rates than those who do not desist (Farrington, 1997). It would also appear that high levels of the MAOA enzyme serves as a protective factor for males who were severely abused as children (Caspi et al., 2002). Good right hemisphere brain function has also been found to protect physically abused children against violence (Raine et al., 2001).

Psychological Risk and Protection

Research has identified a number of psychological risk factors for violent behavior, which can be categorized as personality factors or cognitive factors. There has been little empirical attention to psychological protective factors, but one cognitive protective factor has been found, and it is possible, in a few other instances, to think of protective factors as the counterpoint to risk factors.

Personality Risk Factors

Personality is multidimensional and can be configured in many different ways, and consequently the research findings on the links between personality and violence are sometimes contradictory. That said, several personality dimensions have been found to be associated with aggressive and violent behavior: impulsivity; sensation-seeking; low empathy; low cooperativeness evidenced by intolerance, mistrust, dislike of people; poor emotional regulation; and restlessness (Cloninger, Svrakic, & Svrakic, 1997; Farrington,

1989; Henry, Caspi, Moffitt, & Silva, 1997; Lahey, 2004; Lynam et al., 2000; Scarpa, 1997). These personality dimensions are thought to be the combined product of genetics and environment. Whether any of these personality dimensions serve as risk for violence depends on the way it is configured with other personality dimensions. There is little indication that these personality characteristics describe the personalities of either Isaiah Jackson, Junito Salvatierra, or Kim Tran, and this suggests again that whatever aggressive activity these youth were involved in was of the adolescent-limited rather than the life-course-persistent type. It is quite possible, however, that these personality factors could be found in some members of Junito's or Kim's gangs or in the youth who murdered Isaiah.

Cognitive Risk Factors

Two types of cognitive factors serve as risk for violent behavior. First, low cognitive abilities, such as low general intelligence, low language development, learning problems, and concentration problems, have been found to be risks for violence (Donnellan, Ge, & Wenk, 2000; Farrington, 1989; Lahey, 2004; Lipsey & Derzon, 1998; Piquero & White, 2003). Second, some types of cognitive attributions, perceptions, beliefs, and attitudes are associated with aggressive behavior. Aggressive individuals tend to perceive hostility in others when it does not exist. They are likely to hold beliefs that approve of aggression as a way to solve problems and have contempt for criminal justice personnel and disrespect for conventional law. They also engage in aggressive fantasies, which serve as rehearsal for aggressive behavior. Longitudinal research indicates that aggressive attributions and scripts crystallize during early to middle childhood and are stimulated by observing violence in real life or in the mass media (Guerra, Huesmann, & Spindler, 2003; Huesmann, 1997; Huesmann & Guerra, 1997; Kroner & Mills, 1998; Zelli, Dodge, Laird, & Lochman, 1999; Zelli, Huesmann, & Cervone, 1995). Again, there is no evidence that these cognitive factors were related to any aggressive behavior in which Isaiah Jackson, Junito Salvatierra, or Kim Tran might be involved.

Psychological Protective Factors

High IQ has been found to serve as a protective factor against criminal behavior among adolescent and young adult males who are otherwise at high risk for violence (Kandel et al., 1988; Piquero & White, 2003; White, Moffitt, & Silva, 1989). The research on psychological correlates of violence suggests other factors that may also serve as protection in the face of other risks, including empathy and good emotional regulation.

Social Risk and Protection

The social world is multidimensional, and both risk and protective factors have been identified in the family, peer/school, community, and societal dimensions.

Family Risk Factors

A number of family risk factors have been found to be associated with violent behavior. First, violence is associated with low family socioeconomic status (SES), chronic family stress, unstable family environment, family conflict, and family breakup and disruption (Farrington, 1989; Ferris & DeVries, 1997; Hawkins, Herrenkohl, et al., 1998; Henry et al., 1997; Kipke, 2004; Lipsey & Derzon, 1998; Moss, Vanyukov, Yao, & Kiriflova, 1999; Raine, Brennan, & Farrington, 1997; Wright, Caspi, Moffitt, Miech, & Silva, 1999). We see all of these risk factors in the life of Junito Salvatierra and several in the life of Kim Tran. In the United States, Junito's parents are struggling financially and seem to be under chronic stress. His mother and grandparents have attempted to provide a stable family environment, but he has had to face many family disruptions in his short life. Currently, he lives with the intense conflict, and occasional violence, between his parents. Kim's family has managed to become economically stable by working long hours, but in recent years there has been a great deal of family conflict, and family members have disengaged from each other. Although Sondra Jackson was a competent parent, she was not able to protect Isaiah from the chronic stress of living in a violent neighborhood, even though she was highly motivated to do so.

Second, parental involvement in criminality and substance abuse are risk factors for offspring violence (Farrington, 1989; Hawkins, Herrenkohl, et al., 1998; Lipsey & Derzon, 1998; Shoal et al., 2003). Third, several aspects of parenting style also serve as risk for violent behavior in offspring. These include harsh and punitive discipline, lack of supervision, maternal rejection, child abuse and neglect, and poor attachment between parents and children (Caspi et al., 2004; Kraemer, 1997; Lipsey & Derzon, 1998; Raine, Brennan, & Farrington, 1997; Scarpa, 1997; Widom, 1989). Isaiah Jackson does not appear to have experienced any of these risk factors, but Junito Salvatierra and Kim Tran have experienced some of them. After Junito came to the United States, both parents worked long hours and he often lacked supervision. He seems to have developed a good early attachment relationship with his mother and grandparents, but this never seemed to happen with his father. The family disruptions related to different timing in immigration and to the death of his grandmother appear to have left him adrift in terms of attachment relationships. His father has an untreated substance abuse problem. Like the Salvatierra family, Kim's family has not been able to provide adequate supervision and support during her adolescent years.

Finally, having an antisocial sibling also is a risk factor for violent behavior (Conger, 2004). This risk factor does not appear in the stories of either Isaiah Jackson, Junito Salvatierra, or Kim Tran, but Junito's current behavior could serve as a risk for his younger siblings.

Peer/School Risk Factors

Deviant peers and gang membership have been found to have a powerful influence on the development of violent behavior during adolescence, particularly for adolescent-limited violence (Conger, 2004; Fergusson, Horwood, & Nagin, 2000; Lipsey & Derzon, 1998; Stewart, Simons, & Conger, 2002). This risk factor has been present in the lives of Isaiah Jackson, Junito Salvatierra, as well as Kim Tran. The quality of the school experience is also associated with violent behavior. Low bonding with school, truancy, and academic failure are risk factors (Farrington, 1989). Junito Salvatierra was a strong student in his native Dominican Republic, but he has not been able to make the adjustment to schooling in the United States. He fell behind, began to skip school, received some failing grades, and ultimately dropped out of school. Kim Tran, on the other hand, continues to do well in school even as she experiments with a delinquent lifestyle.

Community Risk Factors

Several aspects of community life have been found to be associated with CV, including concentrated poverty and residential instability (Peterson, Krivo, & Harris, 2000; Sampson, 2003). Junito Salvatierra lives in a concentrated poverty neighborhood with high residential instability, and residence in the neighborhood in which the Jackson family lives has grown increasingly less stable during the past decade. A high concentration of bars in a neighborhood has also been found to be associated with an increased level of CV in the neighborhood (Peterson et al., 2000). Sampson (2003) has found empirical support for his theory that low collective efficacy, or the capacity of the community to develop a working trust and shared willingness to intervene in social control, is associated with higher rates of CV. We do not know much about the collective efficacy in the neighborhood in which Isaiah Jackson lived, but Sondra Jackson's concerns about her neighborhood suggest a lack of collective efficacy. We know even less about the collective efficacy in the neighborhoods where Junito Salvatierra and Kim Tran live.

Societal Risk Factors

At the societal level, racial and ethnic discrimination serves as a risk factor for violence among the targets of discrimination. One study found that among black males in a concentrated poverty neighborhood, exposure to racial discrimination increased the probability of violent behavior (McCord & Ensminger, 2003). Without the details, we can only speculate about the possibilities of racial and ethnic discrimination faced by Isaiah Jackson, Junito Salvatierra, and Kim Tran. This is a possibility that we would want to be open to hearing. Television watching has also been found to be associated with violent behavior; a significant association has been found between the time spent watching television in early adolescence and later violent behavior (Herrenkohl et al., 2003; Johnson, Cohen, Smailes, Kasen, & Brook, 2002).

Social Protective Factors

Researchers have also identified a number of social protective factors for violent behavior. In the family dimension, high family income, good family communication, intact family, consistent parental behavioral monitoring and discipline, and a good marriage in adulthood protect in the face of other risk factors (Aspy et al., 2004; Catalano & Hawkins, 1996; Conger, 2004; Herrenkohl et al., 2003; Werner & Smith, 2001). In the dimension of peers and school, nondeviant friends and a strong bond with school are protective factors (Aspy et al., 2004; Catalano & Hawkins, 1996; Herrenkohl et al., 2003; Werner & Smith, 2001). At the community level, nonparental role models, neighborhood affluence, community collective efficacy, and community recreation centers are protective factors (Aspy et al., 2004; Peterson et al., 2000; Sampson, 2003).

One interesting experiment in the United States involved moving families from high-poverty neighborhoods to low-poverty neighborhoods; one result was lower violent offending among juveniles (Katz, Kling, & Liebman, 2001; Ludwig, Hirschfield, & Duncan, 2001). We can wonder if Isaiah Jackson might still be alive if Sondra had been able to realize her dream to move out of the increasingly disorganized neighborhood in which they lived. At the societal level, cross-national studies have found an association between higher national social welfare expenditures and decreases in violent crime (Briggs & Cutright, 1994; Messner & Rosenfeld, 1997). The United States lags behind most European countries in the percentage of the gross domestic product (GDP) spent on health, education, and welfare. For example, in 1994, the United States spent 10.9% of the GDP on health, education, and welfare compared to 31.5% in the Netherlands, 30.6% in Sweden, 25.7% in Finland, 21.7% in Norway, and 21.1% in Denmark (Bradshaw, Healey, & Smith, 2001, p. 189).

Spiritual Risk and Protection

Although collective violence has often been associated, over historical time, with religious conflict, there is no evidence that spirituality or religion is a risk factor for CV. On the other hand, a number of longitudinal studies have found that strong bonding with a religious institution is a protective factor, lowering the probability of later violence among aggressive children (George, Larson, Koenig, & McCullough, 2000; Herrenkohl et al., 2003; Smith & Carlson, 1997; Werner & Smith, 2001). James Garbarino (1999) writes that a strong sense of meaning and purpose can serve as a spiritual anchor for troubled youth. We know that religion was a major source of comfort and support for Isaiah Jackson's grandmother and Kim Tran's extended family, but we don't see evidence that Isaiah had or that Junito Salvatierra or his parents have a strong spiritual anchor. Kim has fond memories of Buddhist traditions, but her family has lapsed in their practice of these traditions.

Biopsychosocial-Spiritual Integration

Exhibit 4.4 summarizes the empirical evidence regarding biological, psychological, social, and spiritual risk and protection summarized in the preceding discussion.

This discussion demonstrates that some factors that are associated with violence can be classified rather unambiguously as either biological (heart rate), psychological (attitudes and beliefs), social (community collective efficacy), or spiritual (purpose and meaning). However, sometimes, because of the transactional nature of biological, psychological, social, and spiritual dimensions, it can be difficult to decide to which category a factor belongs. For example, is IQ, which has a substantial genetic component, a psychological or a biological factor? Is attachment a social, psychological, or perhaps even a biological factor?

Even when factors can be easily classified in one dimension or another, it is clear that, just as the ecological theory would predict, there are many reciprocal linkages among factors across dimensions. A few examples help to clarify this point. For example, genetics (biological) is thought to play a substantial role in heart rate, which is associated with both impulsive and aggressive personalities (psychological). Given the shared genetics between parents and children, we might expect that many children with low heart rates will be reared in homes where at least one parent has impulsive and aggressive behavior, perhaps leading to an adverse family environment (social).

For another example, research indicates that perinatal complications (biological), CNS problems (biological), poor emotional regulation (psychological), and a number of measures of adverse environments (social) are associated with violence. There is also good evidence that adverse environmental conditions such as poor nutrition (social) can contribute to perinatal complications (biological), that perinatal complications (biological) can contribute to CNS problems (biological), that CNS problems (biological) can contribute to poor emotional regulation (psychological), that adverse environmental conditions such as child abuse (social) can contribute to both CNS problems (biological) and poor emotional regulation (psychological). Contemporary research on the brain's susceptibility to environmental influences throughout life (known as brain plasticity) must be taken into consideration when examining the role of the brain and the nervous system in behavior.

For a final example of reciprocal linkages among factors across dimensions, we might expect that children who are reared in hostile families and violent neighborhoods (social) will often come to see the world as a hostile place and to approve of violence as a way to solve problems (psychological). This will predispose them to produce hostile families and violent neighborhoods.

Unfortunately, the types of interconnections of biological, psychological, and social factors discussed above result in a concentration of risk factors among some population groups, especially ethnic minorities living in concentrated poverty urban neighborhoods. There are linkages across dimensional lines as discussed above, but there is also a likelihood of co-occurrence of a number of social risk factors, such as low SES, chronic stress, unstable family environment, family conflict, unsupportive school environment, and an impoverished neighborhood environment. The co-occurrence of risk factors leads to a pileup of stress. This has been described as cumulative risk, and researchers have found that higher numbers of risk factors result in more problems of living. One longitudinal

	Risk Factors	Protective Factors
Biological	• Low heart rate • Perinatal complications • Maternal smoking during pregnancy • Minor physical anomalies • Prefrontal cortex damage • Disorganization among brain systems • High testosterone levels • Low cortisol level in preadolescents • High serotonin level in men • Low level of MAOA enzyme among severely abused males • High environmental levels of lead and manganese • Alcohol and other substances	• High heart rate • High levels of MAOA enzyme in severely abused males • Good right hemisphere brain function among abused children
Psychological	• Personality factors of impulsivity, sensation-seeking, low empathy, and low cooperativeness • Low cognitive abilities • Belief that the world is hostile • Belief that aggression is the way to solve problems • Contempt for criminal justice personnel • Aggressive fantasies	• High IQ • Empathy • Good emotional regulation
Social	• Low family income • Chronic family stress • Unstable family environment • Family conflict • Family breakup and disruption • Parental involvement in criminality and substance abuse • Harsh and punitive discipline • Lack of supervision • Maternal rejection • Child abuse and neglect • Poor parent-child attachment • Antisocial sibling • Deviant peers • Low bonding with school • Concentrated poverty neighborhood • Residential instability • High concentration of bars in neighborhood • Low collective efficacy • Racial and ethnic discrimination • Extensive time watching television	• High family income • Good family communication • Intact family • Consistent parental behavioral monitoring • Good marriage in adulthood • Nondeviant peers • Strong bond with school • Nonparental role models • Neighborhood affluence • Community collective efficacy • Community recreation centers • Social welfare programs
Spiritual		• Strong bonding with religious institution • Strong sense of meaning and purpose

Exhibit 4.4   Biological, Psychological, Social, and Spiritual Risk and Protective Factors for Community Violence

study (Moffitt, 1990) found that a group of youth with both neurological problems and family adversity were 4 times more aggressive than other groups. Another study (Raine, Brennan, & Mednick, 1994) found that the combination of childbirth complications and maternal rejection led to a disproportionate increase in violence.

A National Youth Survey conducted in the United States found that about three quarters of those who had committed serious violence during adolescence discontinued violent behavior after 1–3 years (USDHHS, 2001b). This and other studies provide support for Moffitt's life course theory that there are genetic risk factors for life-course-persistent violence and other antisocial behavior but not for adolescent-limited antisocial behavior. For the adolescent-limited typology, association with deviant peers is the most significant risk factor (Moffitt, Caspi, Harrington, & Milne, 2002). This seems to be the case for Isaiah Jackson, Junito Salvatierra, and Kim Tran.

Consequences of Community Violence

CV has tremendous financial, health, and social costs for individuals, families, and communities. There are health care costs, law enforcement costs, legal costs, and economic costs related to lost worker productivity. It is very hard to get exact figures on the financial costs of CV, but the Children's Safety Network Economics & Data Analysis Resource Center (2000) estimates that the direct and indirect costs of youth violence, including medical costs, lost productivity, and administrative costs to the criminal justice system, exceed $158 billion every year.

In terms of social costs, researchers have been interested in the outcomes of CV for those who are the victims rather than perpetrators. The research on the consequences of exposure to CV suggests that there are both general consequences that tend to be shared across groups as well as some differential consequences, some different ways in which different groups are impacted. We will turn first to discussion of the general consequences.

There is evidence that CV affects both family and individual functioning in a variety of ways. CV can increase stress on the family and contribute to general family instability and disorganization. Both parents and children are affected by exposure to CV. Living in a neighborhood with high levels of CV is associated with an increased level of spousal conflict (Osofsky, Wewers, Hann, & Fick, 1993). High levels of parental distress can lead to less sensitive and consistent caregiving, and this can contribute to disruption in parent-child attachment (Cicchetti, Toth, & Lynch, 1995; Linares et al., 2001; Lynch & Cicchetti, 2002). It can also lead both children and parents to feel less confidence in the capacity of parents to protect children from harm (Lynch & Cicchetti, 2002). Sondra Jackson reports that she lost confidence in her ability to protect Isaiah from CV in the neighborhood in which they lived.

Although exposure to CV seems to have less deleterious effects on children than being a victim of CV, there are a number of negative child outcomes associated with exposure to

CV. A nationwide survey of high school students in 2003 found that about 6% of respondents reported failure to go to school on 1 or more days in the past 30 days because they felt unsafe at school or on the way to and from school (CDC, 2004e). Children exposed to CV have been found to have difficulties in exploring and mastering their environments, in forming secure and trusting relationships, and in regulating their emotions (Osofsky, 1995). They have been found to demonstrate regressive behaviors such as enuresis and thumb sucking (Dubrow & Garbarino, 1989). There is evidence that some children repeatedly exposed to CV become habituated to it and begin to develop beliefs and attitudes that normalize the use of violence to solve problems (Guerra et al., 2003). They have been found to engage in more aggressive antisocial behavior and to have problems at school, such as school suspension and placement in classes for emotionally disturbed students and in special education classes (First & Cardenas, 1986). One recent study also found that increased exposure to CV predicted a higher number of asthma symptom days, indicating an impact on physical as well as mental health (Wright et al., 2004).

On the other hand, one research team recently found that although adolescents living in violent neighborhoods are at risk for depression, violent adolescent boys who live in unsafe neighborhoods where they are exposed to high levels of violence do not get as depressed as youth who are not violent (Latzman & Swisher, 2005). The researchers suggest that these findings indicate that being aggressive in a violent context may be an adaptive strategy that protects against depression.

Much of the research on the consequences of CV has looked only for general consequences and not explored different consequences for different groups. Some researchers, however, have examined differential consequences and found different consequences based on levels of CV exposure, on whether one was victim or witness, on relationship between victim and perpetrator, and on age, gender, level of family conflict, and community characteristics. The factors that affect the impact of community violence on children are summarized by Gorman-Smith and Tolan (2003). As the amount of violence exposure increases, so does the number and intensity of psychological symptoms (Dinan et al., 2004; Rosenthal, 2000). In addition, there are some differences in consequences related to whether one witnesses CV or is the victim of CV. One study found that witnessing CV, but not victimization, is associated with aggressive cognitions; on the other hand, victimization is more closely linked than witnessing with problems in emotional regulation (Schwartz & Proctor, 2000). Another study found that **internalizing symptoms** (withdrawal, somatic complaints, anxiety, depression) are more likely in children who witness CV, and **externalizing symptoms** (aggression, delinquency) are more likely among those who are victimized (Shahinfar, Fox, & Leavitt, 2000). Rosenthal (2000) found witnessing to be slightly more related to anger and victimization more related to depression. O'Donnell and colleagues (O'Donnell, Schwab-Stone, & Muyeed, 2002) found that children who witness CV are less likely than children who are victimized to have low future expectations, to misuse alcohol and other drugs, to report physical symptoms and symptoms of depression and anxiety, and to engage in antisocial behavior. More distress is felt if the victims and/or perpetrators are family members or other familiar people (Jenkins & Bell, 1994; Martinez & Richters, 1993).

There is some evidence that children are particularly vulnerable to exposure to violence in the first 3 years of life because of the resulting serious and perhaps permanent damage to the brain (Perry, 1997). Young children tend to exhibit passivity and regressive symptoms in response to violence, and in middle childhood, children are more likely to be aggressive and to have somatic complaints and school problems (Garbarino, Dubrow, Kostelny, & Pardo, 1992; Guerra et al., 2003). A South African study of adult women exposed to CV found that the younger women display more traumatic symptoms than the older women (Dinan et al., 2004).

One study of African American elementary school children whose parents had been victims of CV found gender differences in the children's behavioral responses. The females were found to have more internalizing symptoms than the males, and the males were found to have more externalizing symptoms (Dulmus, Ely, & Wodarski, 2003).

The consequences of exposure to CV also seem to vary with the level of family conflict. One study found that in families with low conflict, higher levels of witnessed violence are associated with increases in antisocial behavior over time. This may well have been the situation for Isaiah Jackson. In families where there are relatively high levels of parent-child conflict, witnessing CV makes no additional contribution to antisocial behavior (Miller, Wasserman, et al., 1999). This suggests the potency of parent-child conflict as a risk factor.

Reactions to exposure to CV also are influenced by characteristics of the neighborhood. In particular, social support and social cohesion among neighbors and a high level of participation in formal and voluntary organizations are aspects of community that can buffer the impact of CV (Sampson, 2003; Sampson, Raudenbush, & Earls, 1997).

Ways of Coping

There is much evidence of the health hazards of exposure to CV, but there has been little research about the ways that individuals, families, and communities attempt to cope with CV. There is a limited research literature on this topic, however, and we review the results of that literature as it pertains to children and youth, adults, and communities (see Exhibit 4.5 for a summary). Children, youth, and their families cope in a variety of ways, some of which work better than others. Indeed, some attempts to cope become health hazards themselves, and some coping efforts increase the CV problem (Irwin, 2004).

Recent research identifies several strategies used by children and youth to cope with CV. We classify them here as avoidance, seeking support, confrontation, cognitive strategies, and religiousness. Avoidance may involve avoiding both places and people (Irwin, 2004; Sweatt, Harding, Knight-Lynn, Rasheed, & Carter, 2002). It may mean staying away from particular places that are known to be dangerous, even if that means going several blocks out of the way to get from home to school to avoid the corner where drugs are sold. If you are a gang member, it may mean avoiding neighborhood spaces controlled by rival gangs. It may mean no playing outside, and sometimes it means hardly leaving the apartment

Avoiding places and people
Seeking support
Confrontation
Cognitive strategies: becoming street smart, cognitive reappraisal, thought blocking
Religion and/or spirituality
Self-soothing activities (e.g., listening to music)
Safety measures
Political activism and neighborhood organizing

Exhibit 4.5   Ways People Attempt to Cope With Community Violence

or building. Sondra and Freda Jackson encouraged Isaiah to use avoidance as a coping strategy for the violence in their neighborhood, asking him to come straight home from school and trying to prohibit him from being outside. Avoidance also means avoiding strangers and people who are known to be dangerous. For some children and youth, avoidance means staying away from gangs and drugs, and for others it means staying away from members of rival gangs.

Children and youth also seek out emotional support to help them cope with CV. One study found that approximately three fourths of the middle school research participants talked to someone about their exposure to CV; mothers were the most frequent sources of support, but children and youth also talked to fathers and grandparents as well as police officers, neighbors, religious leaders, pets, and stuffed animals (Campbell & Schwarz, 1996). Some children and youth turn to friends for support, but one study found that this is more likely to be the case for children and youth from the most violent neighborhoods (Irwin, 2004). Children and youth who live in neighborhoods with high rates of violent crime are more likely than other children and youth to report that it is important to have friends who are willing to fight with or for them. Females report needing friends who will protect them from rape and sexual exploitation. This need for protection becomes one motivation to join gangs. Indeed, for Junito Salvatierra, protection may be as serious a motivation to join a gang as a need to belong. That does not appear to be the case for Kim Tran, who appears to be motivated by a need to belong.

Friendship and gang membership developed for this purpose have mixed results; they provide protection but also obligate one to return the favor and to commit to confrontation as a coping strategy. Youth in some high crime neighborhoods report that to stay safe, it is imperative that they establish dominance, power, and status. They must earn and maintain status by fighting (Sweatt et al., 2002). Some youth carry weapons as a strategy for staying safe (Irwin, 2004).

Cognitive strategies may also be used to cope with CV. In neighborhoods with rival gangs, some youth cope by becoming well informed about historical and contemporary antagonisms (Sweatt et al., 2002). One research team found positive reappraisal, or attaching a positive meaning to events, to be the most common strategy used by children and youth to cope with CV (Rasmussen, Aber, & Bhana, 2004).

Children and youth also use religion and spirituality as resources for coping. They may attend religious services and other religious activities; engage in personal religious practices such as praying, watching or listening to religious programs on TV or radio, or reading religious literature; or they may engage in other activities of a spiritual nature that help them feel connected to other people and the universe. In one study, African American youth reported higher levels of religiousness than other youth, and girls reported higher levels than boys (Pearce, Jones, Schwab-Stone, & Ruchkin, 2003). In this study, higher use of personal religious practices was associated with lower rates of conduct disorder under conditions of high CV exposure.

The limited research on how adults cope with CV has focused on the strategies of African American women in high-crime neighborhoods. A primary finding is that, for these women, keeping themselves and others, particularly their children, safe is a core concern (Jenkins, 2002). This seems to have been the case with Sondra Jackson. We look first at how women attempt to keep themselves safe. Based on in-depth interviews with 25 mothers in a violent Chicago public housing development, Wolfer (2000) identified three types of coping strategies used by the women. The first method was *getting away* from the CV, by staying indoors or by leaving the neighborhood for day trips or overnight visits. Sometimes self-imposed isolation led to inactivity, boredom, and overeating, behaviors that jeopardized their health. The second method was *getting along*, by attempting to limit their interactions with dangerous people or situations. If they could not accomplish this, they tried to minimize the level of conflict, and when this didn't work, they fought back or called the police. The third method was *getting through*, by using a variety of coping strategies. The most common strategies were prayer, blocking thoughts of CV, or engaging in self-soothing activities such as listening to gospel music. A few women used alcohol or drugs to manage their emotional distress. Similar methods of coping were found by two other research teams (Hill, Hawkins, Raposa, & Carr, 1995; Mohr, Fantuzzo, & Abdul-Kabir, 2001). Hill and colleagues (Hill et al., 1995) found that black mothers with higher education and income used political activism as a coping strategy. Such activism might help to build collective efficacy in the neighborhood. Although Sondra Jackson has many demands on her time, she might feel empowered by joining in activism with other neighbors to develop some sense of community cohesion and control. The same is true for Claudia Salvatierra.

The mothers in these studies were also concerned about keeping their children safe. One way they did this was to focus on safety measures, sometimes becoming overprotective and using extreme safety measures such as refusing to let their children play outside or having the child sleep in the bathtub out of the way of stray bullets (Overstreet, 2000). Another way they tried to keep their children safe was by using corporal punishment to control and discipline their children, hoping to prevent them from getting into trouble in the neighborhood (Sanders-Phillips, 1997). Some mothers tried to keep their children safe by keeping open lines of communication with them, and others involved their children in religious and recreational activities (Mohr et al., 2001).

Although there is little research to address the issue, there is some evidence that neighborhoods and communities also attempt to cope with CV. Sometimes neighborhood residents join in political activism and neighborhood organizing to make communities safer (Sampson, 2003). Two programs that have grown out of these efforts are the Neighborhood Watch Program, through which residents attempt to reclaim high-crime neighborhoods, and Citizen Corps, a program that attempts to build on community strengths and citizen participation. It would be helpful to know whether any of these programs are active in the neighborhoods where the Jackson, Salvatierra, and Tran families live.

Social Justice Issues

CV does not often get examined in terms of social justice. The available evidence tells us that minority youth in concentrated poverty neighborhoods are the most likely perpetrators as well as victims of CV. The analysis in this chapter suggests that adverse social environments play a large role in the production of CV, contributing to perinatal complications, disturbance in CNS development, and disrupted attachments at home and school. Cross-national research indicates that violent crime increases with the level of social inequality (Beckett & Sasson, 2000; Zimring & Hawkins, 1997), and despite limited research on the topic, there is some evidence that exposure to racial discrimination increases the likelihood of violent behavior (McCord & Ensminger, 2003). The latter finding would suggest that we should be careful to talk about racism, rather than race, as the risk factor for CV. Indeed, the injustices associated with CV should be considered in the context of both historical and contemporary systems of racial oppression and discrimination, from slavery to legal supports for segregation, to the current discrimination in housing, employment, and education, along with police brutality and racial profiling (Kuther & Wallace, 2003).

Our recent societal response to crime has done just the opposite, however; it has emphasized "getting tough on crime" and demonized the low-income minority youth who assault and kill (Zimring & Hawkins, 1997). After a run of high school killings by white middle-class youth in the 1990s, Alvin Poussaint, Harvard psychiatrist, commented: "When white middle-class kids kill, there is always a public outcry of why and a search for what went wrong, but when inner-city minority kids kill, the public is warned of demons and superpredators" (as cited in Garbarino, 1999, p. 4). The class and race bias in this response also feeds the kind of public policy that allows growing inequality and enforces harsh penalties for crime. It is important to note that other Western democracies that treat violent, as well as nonviolent, criminals less punitively than the United States have much lower homicide rates (Beckett & Sasson, 2000).

There seems to be resistance in the United States to recognizing that many perpetrators of CV are themselves victims of social oppression and violence. Until that is faced, we cannot struggle with the hard question of how to prevent victims from becoming perpetrators, and when they do, how to treat victims who have become perpetrators. In a discussion of attachment and aggression, Kraemer (1997) argues that research should focus on finding therapeutic approaches that are successful with disorganized nervous systems. He is skeptical of the idea that "pharmacological fixes" will be the answer, because animal research indicates that the problem is not just in one neurobiological system; it is in the organization among systems. Kraemer suggests that our current solutions may, indeed, be aggravating the problem, a position taken by Jerome Miller (1996) in his book *Search and Destroy: African American Males in the Criminal Justice System.* There is a tendency to think of violent behavior as motivated behavior that can be controlled by punishment, and if punishment doesn't work, harsher punishment is recommended. If, however, aggressive behavior comes from disrupted attachment and disorganized nervous systems, as is clearly the case with rhesus monkeys, isolating violent individuals and housing them with other violent individuals is contraindicated.

One challenge for the criminal justice system is to attend to the rights and needs of both victims and perpetrators. In recent years, public criminal justice policy in the United States has been based on **retributive justice**, which focuses on paying one's "debt to society," matching the severity of the punishment to the seriousness of the offense. Across the world, another approach, called *restorative justice,* is gaining favor and seems to have benefits for victim, community, and perpetrator. **Restorative justice** treats crimes as wrongs against individuals and communities, rather than against society. The emphasis in restorative justice programs is on making amends. In some cases, it brings victims and offenders together in a way that allows victims to state their injury and what they need in the way of compensation, whether that means an apology or a plan for the offender to work with the victim and community to make some reparation. In the process, offenders are asked to take responsibility for their actions and the harm they have caused. Sometimes, community conferences are held to allow victims, offenders, and community members to engage in mutual planning (Anderson, 2004; Beckett & Sasson, 2000). At least 15 states in the United States have legislation to promote restorative justice in the juvenile justice system, but there is some evidence that citizens in the United States are more wedded to the concept of retributive justice than citizens in other Western nations (Roberts & Stalans, 2004). The evidence to date suggests that one of the side benefits of restorative justice programs is reduced recidivism (Anderson, 2004).

Practice Implications

Both in the United States and in other Western nations, concerted efforts have been under way to find effective strategies for preventing and remediating CV. On the international level, that was the focus of a WHO report in 2002 (Krug et al., 2002). In the United States that was the focus of a National Institutes of Health (NIH) State-of-the-Science Conference in October 2004 (National Institutes of Health [NIH], 2004). Both of these initiatives have been concerned with identifying those practices with the strongest empirical evidence of success, and there is a great deal of agreement about the nature of these practices:

- Successful programs target empirically identified risk and protective factors.
- Successful programs address both individual and contextual factors.
- Successful programs are multifaceted and involve efforts of multiple parties.
- Successful programs are intense and long term in nature.
- Successful programs are developmentally appropriate, targeting the risk factors that are particularly salient at different developmental periods.

The major difference between the WHO report and the NIH conference is that the WHO is much more deliberate in calling for changes at the societal level.

Exhibit 4.6 presents the strategies recommended by the WHO for each developmental period from prenatal development through young adulthood, organized by strategies at the individual, family/peer, community, and societal levels. There is some evidence to support all of these strategies, but those with the strongest empirical support with controlled studies are marked with an "[a]". As Exhibit 4.6 demonstrates, programs, such as home visitation and parent training, aimed at improving the quality of parenting during infancy and early childhood can be very effective strategies for preventing later violence. Infant intervention programs that attempt to establish an early base of biopsychosocial skills are also potentially effective. Exhibit 4.6 also demonstrates the potential value of social development programs from early childhood through adolescence; these programs use a variety of strategies to build emotional regulation and social skills. One highly effective social development program to reduce bullying was piloted in Bergen, Norway, and is now being reproduced in England, Germany, and the United States (Olweus, Limber, & Mihalic, 1998). During adolescence, both mentoring programs and family therapy have been found to be particularly successful in long-term reduction of violent and delinquent behavior.

Exhibit 4.6 provides evidence that a number of strategies are effective with adolescents. Recent research has also found that a number of violence prevention strategies used with adolescents are ineffective, and some may even aggravate the problem of youth violence (Krug et al., 2002; Mendel, 2000). Programs that have been found to be ineffective are individual counseling, probation or parole programs that attempt to frighten youth by exposing them to the brutalities of prison life, residential programs in psychiatric or correctional institutions, training in the safe use of guns, military-like training programs, trying young offenders in adult courts, peer mediation or peer counseling, gang prevention programs, and gun buy-back programs (Mendel, 2000; Sherman et al., 1997). Some recent research indicates that programs that put deviant youth together may increase aggressive and violent behavior, particularly if the situation involves inadequate supervision by adults (Poulin, Dishion, & Burraston, 2001).

In the United States, several types of violence prevention programs have been attempted. A number of these programs look promising, but four have received the best empirical support to date: Life Skills Training, Functional Family Therapy, Multisystemic Therapy, and the Incredible Years Series programs (Elliott, 2004). Each of these programs is described briefly.

Developmental Period	Individual	Family/Peer	Community	Societal
Prenatal	• Preventing unintended pregnancy • Increasing access to prenatal care		• Monitoring lead levels and removing toxins	• Deconcentrating poverty • Reducing income inequality
Infancy (0–3 years)	• Increasing postnatal care	• Home visitation[a] • Parent training[a]	• Monitoring lead levels and removing toxins • Increasing the availability and quality of child care facilities	• Deconcentrating poverty • Reducing income inequality
Early childhood (3–5 years)	• Social development programs[a] • Preschool enrichment programs[a]	• Parent training	• Monitoring lead levels and removing toxins • Increasing the availability and quality of preschool enrichment programs	• Deconcentrating poverty • Reducing income inequality • Reducing media violence • Public information campaigns
Middle childhood (6–11 years)	• Social development programs[a]	• Mentoring programs • Home-school partnership programs	• Creating safe routes for children in the neighborhood • Improving school settings • After-school programs • Extracurricular activities	• Deconcentrating poverty • Reducing income inequality • Reducing media violence • Public information campaigns • Reforming educational systems

Developmental Period	Individual	Family/Peer	Community	Societal
Adolescence (12–19 years)	• Social development programs[a] • Providing incentives for high-risk children to complete secondary school[a] • Academic enrichment programs	• Mentoring programs[a] • Family therapy[a] • Temporary foster care	• Creating safe routes for children in the neighborhood • Improving school settings • Extracurricular activities • Training health care workers to identify and refer high-risk youth • Community policing • Reducing alcohol availability • Improving access to health care	• Deconcentrating poverty • Reducing income inequality • Reducing media violence • Public information campaigns • Reforming educational systems • Enforcing laws prohibiting gun sale to youths • Promoting safe and secure storage of firearms • Strengthening and improving police and judicial systems
Young adulthood (20–29 years)	• Providing incentives to pursue courses in higher education • Vocational training	• Programs to strengthen ties to family and to jobs and to reduce involvement in violent behavior	• Establishing adult recreational programs • Community policing • Reducing alcohol availability • Improving access to health care	• Deconcentrating poverty • Reducing income inequality • Public information campaigns • Promoting safe and secure storage of firearms • Strengthening and improving police and judicial systems • Establishing job creation programs for chronically unemployed

Exhibit 4.6 Strategies for Violence Prevention by Developmental Period and Ecological Context

[a]Strategies with the strongest empirical support from controlled studies.

SOURCE: Based on Krug et al., 2002, Tables 2.3 and 2.4.

Life Skills Training

The Life Skills Training (LST) program was developed as a school-based substance abuse prevention program, but it also has been shown to reduce violent and aggressive behavior (Life Skills Training, 2002). It was developed in the late 1970s and has been extensively evaluated for over 20 years in over a dozen major federally funded studies by researchers at Cornell University's Institute for Prevention Research. LST provides a structured school curriculum for both elementary and middle school children. The elementary school curriculum provides 24 class sessions of approximately 30–45 minutes each conducted over a 3-year period. The middle school curriculum provides 30 class sessions of approximately 45 minutes each conducted over 3 years. There are three components to the LST curricula. The first component includes drug-resistance skills, including factual information on alcohol and other drugs and resistance skills for dealing with peer and media pressure. The second component includes personal self-management skills, including self-knowledge, goal setting and tracking, problem solving, stress reduction, and positive reappraisal. The third component includes general social skills such as overcoming shyness, effective communication, assertiveness skills, and nonviolent conflict resolution.

Functional Family Therapy

Functional Family Therapy (FFT) is a family intervention for high-risk youth ages 10–18 and youth in the juvenile justice system (Functional Family Therapy, 2003). FFT was developed as a clinical model 30 years ago, has been evaluated extensively in federally funded projects, and is considered a model program for seriously delinquent youth. The primary focus of FFT is to motivate families to change by uncovering their unique strengths, to help families build on their strengths, and to offer families specific ways to improve. The program is both systematic and individualized, organized around three specific intervention phases. Phase 1 focuses on engagement and motivation, working to increase hope, decrease resistance, and build a working alliance. Phase 2 focuses on behavior change, and Phase 3 focuses on generalizing the behavior change to relationships with other social systems. Assessment is multidimensional, including cognitive and emotional development of the adolescent, parental style, and the presence or absence of risk and protective factors across individual, family, and community dimensions. The intervention typically lasts for 8–10 one-hour sessions but may last for 30 sessions in more difficult situations.

Multisystemic Therapy

Multisystemic therapy (MST) is an intensive family- and community-based intervention that attempts to address the multiple determinants of serious aggressive behavior in juvenile offenders (Multisystemic Therapy, 2004). MST was developed in the late 1970s during a time of dissatisfaction with the effectiveness of traditional mental health services with serious juvenile offenders; the program has been and continues to be evaluated extensively. The purpose of MST is to produce behavior change in the youth's natural environment, drawing on the strengths of each system, including family, peers, school, neighborhood, and the indigenous support network. Goals include improving parental discipline practices, enhancing family relationships, decreasing youth association with deviant peers, increasing youth association with pro-social peers, improving school or vocational performance, engaging youth in positive recreation, and developing an indigenous support network of extended family, friends, and neighbors. The average length of MST treatment is approximately 4 months. Because of its emphasis on drawing on strengths and building supports in several systems, it seems to hold particular promise for work with the Salvatierra and Tran families around the gang-related activity of Junito and Kim. Both youth could benefit from interventions that enhance their family relationships, decrease association with deviant peers, and build stronger support systems. Junito could also benefit from interventions to improve his school performance.

The Incredible Years Series

The Incredible Years Series (IYS) is a set of three coordinated curricula for parents, teachers, and children that attempts to promote social and emotional competence in young children ages 2–8 and to prevent, reduce, and treat conduct problems (Webster-Stratton, 2000). IYS has been used and evaluated for the past 20 years. In all three programs, trained facilitators use videotape vignettes to stimulate group discussion and sharing of ideas. The parent training program focuses on parenting skills such as how to play with children; ways to promote children's cognitive, language, social, and academic skills; using incentives; limit setting; and methods for handling misbehavior. An ADVANCE program focuses on communication skills, and the SCHOOL program emphasizes ways that parents can help children be successful at school. The basic program lasts for 12 weeks, and supplementary programs are of varying lengths. The 48-hour training program for teachers emphasizes effective classroom management skills. The training program for children focuses on emotional intelligence, empathy, friendship skills, anger management, interpersonal problem solving, and how to be successful at school.

_____ **Learning Activities**

1. **Knowledge About the Case.** Reread the story of the Salvatierra family at the beginning of Chapter 2. Imagine that the family lives in a neighborhood in your community. Working in teams of 3–4, select a neighborhood in your community where you will imagine the Salvatierras live; if at all possible, select a neighborhood that shares some characteristics with the one where they live. Next, imagine that you are a youth worker at the

community center in this neighborhood and have been assigned to develop a violence prevention program for the neighborhood. Working together, research CV in the neighborhood. Locate and utilize community resources and experts to discuss violence in the neighborhood. Collect and present data on the prevalence of CV in the neighborhood. Collect and present data on the victims and perpetrators of violence in the neighborhood. Collect information about efforts, if any, the neighborhood has made to combat community violence. What groups are involved in such efforts? Based on the discussion of implications for practice in this chapter, and your findings on community violence in the neighborhood, outline a prevention program for the neighborhood.

2. Knowledge About the Self. Reread the story about Kim Tran at the beginning of Chapter 2. After you have finished reading the story, spend 5 minutes writing about your reactions to Kim's recent involvement in home invasion activity. Write about your emotional reactions and your attitudes and beliefs about that aspect of Kim's story. Also write about your social location and how that location influences your reactions. In addition, write about how your emotional reactions, attitudes and beliefs, and social location might help or hinder your ability to engage Kim if she confided in you about this activity when she came to your neighborhood health clinic asking for birth control information. Read what you have written. Was there anything in what you wrote that was surprising to you?

3. Values and Ethics. Reread the story about Sondra Jackson at the beginning of Chapter 2. Assume you are the child protective services (CPS) social worker assigned to talk with her about becoming the caregiver for her new grandson. Working with a small group of 3–4 classmates, talk about whether the violence in the neighborhood where Sondra lives should have any influence on your decision about having Sondra become the caregiver for this child. As you talk, review the core values and ethical principles of the National Association of Social Workers (NASW) Code of Ethics and discuss whether any values or principles seem particularly relevant to this situation. What questions get raised for you as you review the values and principles?

4. General Knowledge. In a small group, reread the story of the Jackson and Tran families from Chapter 2. Also review the theories of community violence in this chapter. Discuss which theory or theories best explain Isaiah's violent death. Discuss your reasons for selecting this particular theory or theories. Next, discuss which theory or theories best explain Kim Tran's involvement in the home invasions. Discuss your reasons for selecting this particular theory or theories. It is clear that neither Isaiah nor Kim have a life-course-persistent pattern of violent and other delinquent behavior. For homework, search social work and behavioral science databases to see if you can find new research on the risk factors for adolescent-limited violent behavior. Reconvene with your small group and discuss what you have found. Also discuss whether any new findings are helpful to understand how Isaiah became a victim and Kim became a perpetrator of CV.

5

Child Maltreatment

Leanne W. Charlesworth,
Nazareth College of Rochester

D avid Loefeler describes his father as "ruling the house with a heavy hand" and himself as a frequent target of violent outbursts. Have you thought about what exactly David means by this and what role his family environment may have played in shaping his development? In thinking about Kim Tran, have you considered the unique aspects of parenting an adolescent or contemplated how Kim's multigenerational family system has shaped Kim's life course thus far? Have you wondered how Sondra and Estella Jackson fared when their parents were unable to closely supervise them and how Isaiah's son will fare in the future, given his mother's apparent struggle with substance abuse? What are your feelings about the issues facing and decisions made by Junito Salvatierra's parents during his early childhood and adolescent years? In each of these scenarios, questions are raised about the nature and implications of the care received by children.

Indeed, children are inherently dependent upon the care of others. Across historical and cultural context, this dependency creates heightened vulnerability. Although most adults respond to such vulnerability by protecting and nurturing the young, historical documents suggest that children have experienced trauma, abandonment, and death inflicted by caregivers in most societies throughout time (Ashby, 1997; Ten Bensel, Rheinberger, & Radbill, 1997).

Discussion of child maltreatment must begin with the acknowledgment that child abuse and neglect are **socially constructed** phenomena, meaning that the historical context shapes values and beliefs regarding children and their development, and at any one point in time, different cultures possess unique and evolving beliefs about children's rights and needs. Consider, for example, views of children's rights and needs in your current community context versus those that might have existed in war-torn Vietnam or in David Loefeler's family context. It is widely accepted that historically and culturally shaped beliefs directly shape parenting and other aspects of children's care (Agathonos-Georgopoulou, 1992; Fass & Mason, 2000; Janko, 1994; Korbin, 1981, 1997, 2002; Krug et al., 2002).

And yet, as the World Health Organization's (WHO) report on violence and world health points out, in the midst of diversity there is some level of cross-cultural agreement regarding the care and development of children. For example, the WHO report indicates that virtually all cultures agree that sexual and severe physical abuse of children should not occur. Focusing on such universals, the WHO utilizes the following definition of child maltreatment:

> Child abuse or maltreatment constitutes all forms of physical and/or emotional ill-treatment, sexual abuse, neglect or negligent treatment or commercial or other exploitation, resulting in actual or potential harm to the child's health, survival, development or dignity in the context of a relationship of responsibility, trust or power. (Krug et al., 2002, p. 59)

The United States federal government first publicized an official, national definition of child maltreatment through the 1974 Child Abuse Prevention and Treatment Act (CAPTA). CAPTA provides minimum standards for state and local governmental definitions of child maltreatment. Under CAPTA, child maltreatment is defined as follows:

> Any recent act or failure to act on the part of a parent or caretaker, which results in death, serious physical or emotional harm, sexual abuse, or exploitation, or an act or failure to act which presents an imminent risk of serious harm. (National Clearinghouse on Child Abuse & Neglect Information, 2005)

There are distinct types of child maltreatment, and each type possesses its own unique definitional challenges. Four commonly recognized child maltreatment types are physical abuse, sexual abuse, psychological or emotional abuse, and neglect. Each of these commonly recognized types consists of distinct subtypes. For example, child neglect may be conceptualized as including the subtypes of physical neglect, educational neglect, medical neglect, and emotional neglect. State definitions of physical abuse, sexual abuse, psychological or emotional abuse, and neglect vary quite widely, and some states do not officially define all maltreatment types. The National Clearinghouse on Child Abuse and Neglect Information has developed a set of definitions capturing common elements across states. These definitions are presented in Exhibit 5.1, along with definitions recognized by the WHO.

In addition to the definitional challenges that emerge when we consider each distinct maltreatment type, another important issue to consider is the role of harm to the child. Should *potential* for harm or injury to a child be sufficient to qualify as maltreatment, or must a child suffer *actual harm?* In other words, is there a difference between a child who is beaten but sustains no obvious physical injuries and a child who receives the same beating but sustains serious **cognitive damage** that impairs brain functioning and diminishes capacity for judgment and reasoning?

Physical Abuse	Sexual Abuse	Psychological/Emotional	Neglect
United States			
Physical injury (ranging from bruises to severe fractures or death) as a result of punching, beating, kicking, biting, shaking, throwing, stabbing, choking, hitting (with a hand, stick, strap, or other object), burning, or otherwise harming a child	Activities by a parent or caretaker such as fondling a child's genitals, penetration, incest, rape, sodomy, indecent exposure, and exploitation through prostitution or the production of pornographic materials	Pattern of behavior that impairs a child's emotional development or sense of self-worth. This may include constant criticism, threats, or rejection, as well as withholding love, support, or guidance	Failure to provide for a child's basic needs; potentially including physical (e.g., failure to provide necessary food, shelter, or supervision); medical (e.g., failure to provide necessary medical or mental health treatment); educational (e.g., failure to educate a child or attend to special education needs); and emotional (e.g., inattention to a child's emotional needs, permitting the child to use alcohol or other drugs)
International (World Health Organization)			
Those acts of commission by a caregiver that cause actual physical harm or have the potential for harm	Those acts where a caregiver uses a child for sexual gratification	Failure of a caregiver to provide an appropriate and supportive environment, and includes acts that have an adverse effect on the emotional health and development of a child	Failure of a parent to provide for the development of the child—where the parent is in a position to do so—in one or more of the following areas: health, education, emotional development, nutrition, shelter, and safe living conditions

Exhibit 5.1   Definitions of Physical Abuse, Sexual Abuse, Psychological/Emotional Abuse, and Neglect

SOURCE: Based on Krug et al., 2002, and U.S. Department of Health and Human Services, Administration for Children & Families (USDHHS, ACF), 2006b.

A final significant and related definitional challenge is the handling of caregiver intent. Is it necessary that an injury or other detrimental impact was intended or *purposeful*? Or should a parent or caregiver be held responsible simply if potential or actual harm occurs, *regardless of intent*? Imagine that young children suffer serious injury as a result of setting an accidental fire while home alone. The caregiver would never have purposefully harmed his or her children, and the caregiver is devastated. Is the caregiver an abusive or neglectful caregiver, despite the absence of intent?

Our case scenarios further illustrate these definitional challenges. Junito Salvatierra has struggled emotionally, socially, and perhaps spiritually since arriving in the United States. It seems fair to say that his emotional needs have not been met. Perhaps the same could be said for Kim Tran. In the absence of caregiver intent or serious harm, are these instances of child maltreatment? And how should we handle issues of caregiver substance abuse or mental health challenges in determining adequate care and issues of intent?

A plethora of existing literature focuses on child maltreatment definitional issues (Glaser, 2002; Haugaard, 2000; Korbin, Coulton, & Lindstrom-Ufuti, 2000; National Research Council, 1993; Straus & Kantor, 2005). Our discussion has only skimmed the surface of the challenges inherent in attempting to define child maltreatment as a whole as well as each specific type of maltreatment. Straus and Kantor (2005) suggest that one uniform set of definitions may be inappropriate and unnecessary. Definitions must be shaped by their context and purpose. Definitions used for prevalence research may inevitably and wisely differ from definitions used for treatment purposes.

In the last few decades, substantial progress has been made in creating an empirically grounded child maltreatment knowledge base (Leventhal, 2003). Ultimately, our ability to establish a clear understanding of the prevalence of child maltreatment in any given place at any point in time as well as our ability to compare and track trends across time and place is compromised by these perhaps unsolvable definitional issues. And definitional issues have a ripple effect on other areas, including our understanding of causes (etiology) and processes of maltreatment.

Patterns of Occurrence

In the United States today, the two widely recognized national data sources used for tracking child maltreatment trends are the official statistics of the National Child Abuse and Neglect Data System (NCANDS) and the National Incidence Study (NIS) of Child Abuse and Neglect (UNICEF, 2003; Thomlison, 2004). NCANDS statistics are derived from data on officially recorded cases referred to and tracked by local and state child protective service (CPS) agencies. NCANDS data are widely seen as a standardized, reliable source of information about child abuse and neglect in the United States. As of 2006, the fourth National Incidence Study of Child Abuse and Neglect (NIS-4) is under way but not yet completed (USDHHS, ACF, n.d.). The third NIS was completed in 1993. The NIS has created a "harm standard" under which children identified in the study are considered maltreated only if they have already experienced some form of abuse or neglect.

Complexities and Limitations Within Available Data

In addition to NCANDS and NIS data, there are many other types of completed and ongoing child maltreatment research projects widely drawn upon in the United States to study incidence and prevalence as well as various other aspects of child maltreatment. Retrospective survey-based studies of child maltreatment typically ask adults about their experiences as children. Other studies use the contemporaneous self-reported data of children, adolescents, and caregivers. Estimates derived from self-reported information from the general population or specific target populations generally produce much higher incidence and prevalence estimates than official data collected by child welfare and other governmental systems.

There is consensus in the United States and across the globe that official child maltreatment data generally underestimate the true prevalence of child abuse and neglect (Centers for Disease Control and Prevention, National Center for Injury Prevention and Control [CDC, NCIPC], 2005; Krug et al., 2002). Moreover, in the United States, some believe that the child welfare system itself and related official victimization data overrepresent incidence among children of color (Billingsley & Giovannoni, 1972; Gil, 1970). Many believe that insufficient attention is paid, in official incidence data, to the linkages between child maltreatment, poverty, and race. Families belonging to privileged groups may play a more significant role in shaping definitions of maltreatment and may possess a heightened ability to avoid contact with CPS agencies and other forms of public intrusion into family life. Certain types of child maltreatment such as psychological or emotional maltreatment may be seriously underestimated across all groups, particularly high-income families (Edwards, Holden, & Felitti, 2003; Glaser, 2002).

In a global context, these issues remain relevant but reach new levels of complexity. At the global level, **sex trafficking**—the movement of individuals across borders for the purpose of sexually exploiting them—is increasingly recognized as a threat to all children but particularly girls (Roby, 2005; United Nations Office on Drugs and Crime, 2006). All forms of violence against children in some developing or war-torn countries are so widespread and yet poorly documented that such countries are excluded from cross-nation analyses. We have not yet begun to address child maltreatment from the same starting point in many other nations in part because the violence and other challenges to healthy development facing children in these nations are overwhelming. Moreover, many countries do not have legal or social systems with specific responsibility for recording or responding to reports of abuse and neglect (Krug et al., 2002).

Identifying accurate child maltreatment trends in the United States and globally is challenging for these and many other reasons. Psychological, or emotional, maltreatment is not well understood or consistently defined and thus is more likely to be underrecognized and underestimated in official data sources. Many experts also believe that official data seriously underestimate the incidence and prevalence of child sexual abuse. In fact, depending on the definitions and research methodology employed, child sexual abuse prevalence rates range from 1% to 19% for men and 1% to 45% for women (Krug et al., 2002). Such disparities suggest that it is only through multiple methodologies and data sources that we can begin to approach an accurate understanding of the extent of child abuse and neglect as a social problem.

An additional, obvious challenge to estimating child maltreatment prevalence is the inherent nature of the social problem. Embarrassment and shame, **defense mechanisms**—unconscious thought processes that minimize psychological threat—utilized by families, the need to balance children's needs with parental rights, and the often conflicting societal values of family privacy and child protection combine to act as powerful deterrents to detection and accurate measurement.

Also, accurate historical analysis of international trends in child maltreatment is challenging if not impossible due to the lack of comparable data across nations over time. Using the United States as an example, the United Nations Childrens Fund (UNICEF) points out that the number of reported child maltreatment cases has increased almost five-fold in the last 20 years. This trend, however, could represent a significant change in actual levels of maltreatment, effects of increased rates of substance abuse, or just as likely, a significant change in public and professional awareness of the phenomenon, changes in definitions of what constitutes maltreatment, and significant changes in reporting systems and procedures as well as other aspects of agency practice or some combination of all of these factors (Tzeng, Jackson, & Karlson, 1991; Wang & Daro, 1997). With these issues in mind, we review available data on child maltreatment prevalence and incidence over time.

Trends in Patterns of Occurrence

Beginning with child fatality trends, the U.S. Department of Health and Human Services (USDHHS; 2005) reported that in 2003, approximately 1,500 children died from abuse or neglect in the United States, representing an incidence rate of 2 deaths per 100,000 children. In recent years, child fatality trends have held relatively stable, hovering close to these figures. A minority of fatality victims have had either brief or intensive prior involvement with CPS agencies. In 2003, 10.7% of fatality victims' families had received family services in the prior 5 years, and 2.8% had been reunified with their families after foster care placement within the past 5 years. In 2005, the USDHHS asserted that because child fatality data may often be collected by other governmental agencies such as public health departments or **child fatality review boards** (established and administered by localities to investigate the causes of child death), child fatality data may be somewhat more comprehensive and accurate than other types of abuse and neglect data.

Turning to maltreatment in general in the United States, official data suggest that while reporting of suspected maltreatment has steadily increased, actual victimization may have declined recently. NCANDS data indicate that in 2003, CPS agencies across the nation received 2.9 million referrals, or reports, of suspected child abuse or neglect. This figure represents a reporting rate of 39.1 per 1,000 children. CPS agencies accepted approximately two thirds of these 2.9 million reports for investigation or assessment purposes. Ultimately, CPS agencies identified approximately 906,000 children as "confirmed" victims of abuse or neglect in 2003, representing approximately 31.7% of all children whose reports were investigated or assessed (U.S. Department of Health and Human Services, Administration on Children, Youth, and Families [USDHHS, ACYF], 2005).

Although the CPS investigation rate (the proportion of all children experiencing a CPS assessment or investigation) has significantly increased in the last decade (from a rate of 36.1 per 1,000 children in 1990 to 45.9 in 2003), the official victimization rate has decreased from a 1990 rate of 13.4 confirmed victims per 1,000 children to a 2003 rate of

12.4 (USDHHS, ACYF, 2005). In recent years, the official victimization rate has remained relatively stable, at approximately 12 per 1,000 children.

Child neglect is consistently the most common form of documented maltreatment. In 2003, 63.2% of the 906,000 officially confirmed or documented child maltreatment victims were found to be victims of neglect, 18.9% were found to be victims of physical abuse, 9.9% were found to be victims of sexual abuse, and 4.9% were found to be victims of psychological or emotional maltreatment. Approximately 16.9% of victims experienced types of maltreatment commonly classified as "other" (such as "abandonment" or "congenital drug addiction"). These combined percentages surpass 100 because victims typically experience more than one type of abuse or neglect simultaneously and therefore are appropriately included in more than one category. These 2003 figures are representative of maltreatment subtype trends over time; victims of child neglect consistently account for more than one half of all child maltreatment victims (see Exhibit 5.2; USDHHS, National Center on Child Abuse and Neglect [NCCAN], 1996; USDHHS, ACYF, 2004, 2005).

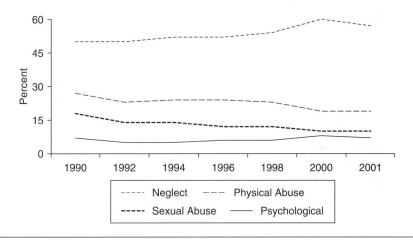

Exhibit 5.2   Percentage of Victims by Type of Maltreatment, 1990–2001

NOTE: The percentages total more than 100% of victims because children may have been victims of more than one type of maltreatment.

SOURCE: USDHHS, ACYF, 2003.

As noted, many researchers feel that official victimization rates are artificially low, and empirical evidence provides support for this view. Under Harm Standard definitions established by the Third National Incidence Study of Child Abuse and Neglect (NIS-3), CPS agencies investigated only 28% of children deemed at risk of harm. In the United States, NIS data suggest a steadily increasing number of children identified as maltreated, particularly children identified as emotionally maltreated (Sedlak & Broadhurst, 1996).

Additional evidence supporting the assertion that official data underestimate the prevalence of child maltreatment is found in the work of Murray Straus (see Straus,

Hamby, & Finkelhor, 1998). Straus's 1995 survey of parents used the Conflict-Tactics Scale and classified the following actions as physically abusive: hitting the child with an object other than on the buttocks, kicking the child, beating the child, and threatening the child with a knife or gun. Based on this survey, Straus estimates a much higher physical abuse rate of 49 per 1,000 American children, compared to the official government rate that averages in the mid to low teens.

Using the Conflict-Tactics Scale, international comparisons have been analyzed and are presented in Exhibit 5.3 (Krug et al., 2002). Such international comparisons have confirmed that attitudes toward moderate forms of physical discipline vary widely across countries. For example, while spanking a child on the buttocks with one's hand is a commonly used type of physical punishment across countries, cultural acceptance of slapping a child on the face or head appears to vary more widely (Krug et al., 2002, p. 63). Similar diversity exists in use of verbal or psychological punishment. Although parents in many cultures appear to utilize shouting at their children as a common punishment tool, cultures vary widely in the use of strategies such as threats of "evil spirits" or threats of "kicking the child out of the household."

Estimated incidence (%) rates of various punishment types in last 6 months as reported by mothers					
	U.S.A.	Chile	Egypt	India[a]	Philippines
Physical punishment					
Hit child with object, not on buttocks	4	4	26	36	21
Kicked the child	0	0	2	10	6
Hit child on buttocks with object	21	18	28	23	51
Slapped child's face or head	4	13	41	58	21
Shook the child	9	39	59	12	20
Verbal or psychological punishment					
Yelled or screamed at the child	85	84	72	70	82
Called the child names	17	15	44	29	24
Cursed at the child	24	3	51	—	15

Exhibit 5.3   International Comparisons of Punishment Types

[a]Only rural parts of India included.

SOURCE: Based on Krug et al., 2002, Tables 3.1 and 3.2.

The use of physical, or corporal, punishment in institutions such as day care centers and schools varies widely across countries as well. Although some countries have passed legislation making corporal punishment illegal in homes as well as institutions, corporal punishment is legal in schools and other institutions in 65 countries and in homes in all but 11 countries in the world (Krug et al., 2002).

Turning to child neglect, definitions vary so widely that international comparisons are close to impossible. Reporting of child neglect is not mandated in some countries. Moreover, some countries, including the United States, specifically exclude conditions associated with poverty (e.g., housing issues) from legal definitions of child neglect, and other countries explicitly include financial impoverishment and hunger within their neglect definitions (Krug et al., 2002).

Many have pointed out that child maltreatment does not discriminate based on age, sex, socioeconomic status (SES), sexual orientation, race or ethnicity, disability or ability, or religion. In other words, child abuse and neglect impact children and families across socioeconomic levels and other aspects of group identity. And yet, there are certainly important differences to note in these areas. We examine the most heavily studied areas: differential rates of maltreatment according to age, gender, poverty status, and ethnicity or race.

Age

For child maltreatment as a whole, victimization rate and age are inversely related, with young children consistently accounting for the highest percentage of victims. For example, in 2003 in the United States, the rate of victimization for children under 3 years of age was 16.4 per 1,000 children, compared to a victimization rate of 5.9 for children ages 16 and 17 (USDHHS, ACYF, 2004, 2005).

Examining specific types of maltreatment, the following patterns emerge. Fatal cases of physical abuse and neglect are most likely among young infants, and this appears to hold true across countries and cultures. In 2000, approximately 57,000 deaths of children under age 15 worldwide could be attributed to homicide. Globally, homicide rates for children under 5 years of age were more than double those of children ages 5 to 14 (Krug et al., 2002). In the United States in 2003, 78.7% of children who were killed by parents or other caregivers were under 4 years of age. Consistently in the United States, children under 1 year old are those most likely to be killed by parents or other caregivers (USDHHS, ACYF, 2004, 2005).

UNICEF (2003) points out that across the globe, there is consistent data supporting infant vulnerability to fatal physical abuse. There are inherent and obvious biological vulnerabilities of infants: their physical development allows them to be more easily lifted, dropped, thrown, or shaken, and relatively little force is required to cause serious or fatal harm. The weakness of their neck muscles heightens the risk of cerebral trauma, the leading cause of assault deaths for infants. Moreover, age-specific vulnerability continues even after the actual assault or abuse: infants and young children cannot easily describe events or articulate injuries, nor are they necessarily in contact with or able to easily seek the help of others.

UNICEF also argues that another relevant cross-cultural commonality is that all parents of newborns are faced with the

huge and sudden responsibilities of caring for a dependent and demanding human being. Along with the curtailment of previous freedoms, and possible new pressures on relationships and finances, they may also have to contend with feelings of exhaustion, inadequacy, and possibly depression. All of these well-known pressures are coped with and kept in perspective by the majority of new mothers and fathers, but they can prove too much for parents who are ill-prepared, ill-equipped, and under-supported. (UNICEF, 2003, p. 11)

As children age, they grow less physically vulnerable, more capable of strategizing to avoid, resist, or otherwise evade assault or abuse, and more capable of recovering from assault, running from or otherwise avoiding danger, and appealing to others for help (Thomlison, 2004; UNICEF, 2003). Simultaneously, the pressures and stressors associated with parenting typically subside. UNICEF (2003) also points out that "truly violent or psychotic parents will have struck before a child reaches the age of four or five" (p. 12).

The peak age of susceptibility to nonfatal physical abuse, however, varies across countries. For example, in China rates of nonfatal physical abuse are highest for children between 3 and 6 years of age, whereas in the United States, children appear most susceptible to physical abuse between the ages of 6 and 12. Some speculate that in the United States at least, this association may be due to increased likelihood of public detection through school contact during these years. In the United States and across the globe, although young children are often victims of sexual abuse, sexual abuse rates generally tend to rise rapidly during and after the onset of puberty, with the highest rates consistently correlated with adolescence (Krug et al., 2002).

Sex

In the United States, overall child maltreatment victimization has been slightly higher among girls than boys. Available data suggest that girls are consistently at higher risk of sexual abuse than boys (USDHHS, ACYF, 2004, 2005). In many countries, girls are at higher risk than boys not only for sexual abuse and exploitation but also for infanticide as well as nutritional and educational neglect. Across the globe, 60% of children ages 6 to 11 who are not in school are girls, and in some countries it is still commonly accepted that girls do not receive schooling (UNICEF, 2003). On the other hand, in many countries around the world, boys are at greater risk of harsh physical punishment than girls.

In the United States, boys appear to be slightly more likely to be both seriously harmed and killed by parents or other caregivers than girls. In 2003, there were 17.7 officially recorded male infant abuse and neglect-related deaths per 100,000 children, compared to 14.1 female infant deaths. In fact, data across time suggest that child abuse and neglect fatality rates are higher for American boys than girls regardless of age (USDHHS, ACYF, 2004, 2005).

Poverty

Financial impoverishment is highly correlated with a wide variety of challenges to individual and family well-being, including child maltreatment. Child neglect in particular is strongly associated with financial impoverishment. In the NIS-3, low-income children were over 20 times more likely to be seriously injured from maltreatment than middle- and upper-income children (Sedlak & Broadhurst, 1996). Extreme poverty increases risk substantially. In the NIS-3, children in the lowest-income families were over 50 times more likely to be educationally neglected and 18 times more likely to be sexually abused than children from higher-income families. Also salient in the international context is the income level and regional location of the area in which the child resides. Fatality rates are 2 to 3 times higher for children residing in low- to middle-income countries when compared to rates in most high-income countries (UNICEF, 2003).

A comparison of middle- and high-income countries alone suggests that other poverty-related issues such as the level of inequality and violence may also be relevant to rates of child maltreatment. Comparing a variety of types of data in several distinct areas, UNICEF (2003) finds that, among developed nations, the United States consistently falls within a small group of countries performing the "worst" on several different measures of child well-being. Cross-nation comparisons indicate there may be an association between adult homicide and child maltreatment rates. Among industrialized nations, the United States, Mexico, and Portugal have the highest rates of child deaths attributed to maltreatment as well as the highest rates of adult homicide.

Race and Ethnicity

Trends in the relationship between race and ethnicity and officially documented child victimization appear consistent across time. Of all documented maltreated children each year, white children constitute the majority. Specifically, in 2003, 54% of all documented victims were white, 26% were African American, and 12% were Hispanic (USDHHS, ACYF, 2004, 2005). In 2003, white children also comprised the majority of fatality victims, accounting for 43.1% of all fatalities.

However, African American and Native American or Alaska Native children appear to have disproportionately high rates of documented victimization, within CPS systems, compared to children belonging to other racial and ethnic groups. That is, African American and Native American or Alaska Native children represent a higher proportion of officially documented victims than is statistically expected, given their representation in the general population. In 2003, NCANDS reported victimization rates of 11.0% for white children, 21.3% for American Indian or Alaska Native children, 9.9% for Hispanic children, and 20.4% for African American children. Caution is warranted in interpreting such data because of the complexities and inconsistencies related to racial and ethnic group categorization, as well as issues of institutionalized racism and oppression. Thomlison (2004) points out that the NIS studies and other research that controls for poverty and related factors suggest that race, ethnicity, and culture are not correlated with actual rates of child maltreatment in the general population. The conclusion is that although children of color are disproportionately represented within the child welfare population, studies that are cognizant of the relationship between culture and parenting practices, that control for the role of poverty, and that examine child maltreatment in the general population find no association between a child's race or ethnicity and likelihood of child maltreatment. Thus, it is likely that the disproportionate representation of children of color within the child welfare system is caused by the underlying relationship between poverty and race or ethnicity.

A few race and ethnicity differences may exist, however, in specific types of maltreatment. According to Thomlison (2004), a limited amount of evidence suggests that white, non-Latino girls are more vulnerable to sexual abuse in the early childhood years, while African American girls appear more vulnerable to sexual abuse in the pre-teen, or late middle childhood, years. Overall, however, the lifetime prevalence of child sexual abuse appears to be roughly equivalent across ethnic groups. Careful research regarding actual (rather than officially substantiated) maltreatment differences according to race or ethnicity is very limited, and thus our understanding of such phenomena is in its infancy (Behl, Crouch, May, Valente, & Conyngham, 2001; Cross & Miller, 2006; Finkelhor, 1994).

Theories of Causation

Why does a parent or other caregiver abuse or neglect a child? There are many different approaches to answering this question. It is important to first understand that although child maltreatment is often thought of as existing on a continuum of parenting behaviors, with optimal parenting frequently leading to optimal or ideal development at one end and severely abusive or neglectful parenting leading to serious injury or death at the other, this continuum has been criticized as an inaccurate conceptual framework. That is, although severe maltreatment and child fatalities receive a significant amount of public attention and concern, this type of maltreatment is not only rare but also may represent a quite distinct type of parent or caregiver.

Richard Gelles (1997) has argued that parents and other caregivers who severely abuse, torture, or murder children are categorically distinct from other caregivers, including most maltreating caregivers. Indeed, UNICEF (2003) recently pointed out that most child fatalities do not result from a gradual progression or worsening of abuse or neglect over a period of time. UNICEF asserts that research in the United States, Canada, the United Kingdom, and Sweden indicates that only approximately half of child fatalities appear to be preceded by less severe abuse or neglect and that a major cause of child fatalities is caregiver psychosis or other forms of serious mental illness. UNICEF concludes that while it is very important for us to recognize that escalation occurs in many cases, evidence also supports the existence of an important "divide between those who kill children and those who abuse without causing death" (p. 13). Turning to child welfare policy and practice, this finding leads child protection advocates such as Gelles and others to argue that severe forms of physical abuse, including child homicide, should be considered separately from other types of maltreatment for theoretical and practical purposes.

This discussion illuminates the fact that the nature and causes of maltreatment are diverse, complex, and dynamic. Most child maltreatment prevention and intervention work across the micro to macro continuum is today guided by concepts and principles associated with the life course and social systems, or ecological, perspectives. The ecological or systems perspective, applied to child maltreatment, suggests that maltreatment is caused by complex interactions among micro-, mezzo-, and macro-level systems. The life course perspective recognizes the role of complex transactions within and across systems while emphasizing the important impact of time (Hutchison, 2003b). Applied to child maltreatment, the age or developmental phase of the individuals involved is the immediately apparent relevant dimension. Runyan and Litrownik (2003) describe their ongoing, longitudinal studies of maltreatment as guided by *ecological-developmental theory,* calling for incorporation of "age-specific risk and protective factors at the child, parent, family, neighborhood, and cultural levels" (p. 1).

A Multidimensional Approach to Understanding Child Maltreatment

The use of ecological-developmental theory to explain child maltreatment is relatively recent. In the United States in the 1970s and early 1980s, James Garbarino (Garbarino & Crouter, 1978) and Jay Belsky (1980, 1984) began to apply the ideas of developmental psychologist Urie Bronfenbrenner (1977, 1979) to an examination of the etiology of child maltreatment. Bronfenbrenner drew upon the concepts and principles of systems perspective theorists in his development of a framework for understanding the nested and inextricably linked developmental contexts of children and families. Garbarino and Belsky applied these concepts to analyze the causes and maintenance of child maltreatment as well as to identify potential prevention and intervention points. The ecological framework had become the dominant theoretical approach to understanding child maltreatment as a social problem (Krug et al., 2002).

Within this framework, the maltreated child is understood as an individual system developing within the contexts of family, community, and society. These contexts, or systems, interact in a dynamic fashion across time, with particular focus on the child's conception or infancy through adolescence. The individual child as a system—with a particular set of dynamic traits and developmental processes—transacts with the family system and its own set of system characteristics and processes across time to create child maltreatment risk, protection, and resilience. The child and family exist within a community context, and the community exists within a societal context. As we will see, risk and protective factors exist at each level, and individual, family, community, and societal-level risk and protective factors change across time.

One of the most important foundational ideas of a multidimensional perspective is recognition of the potential relevance of multiple theoretical perspectives (Hutchison, 2003c). Many publications focused on child maltreatment in particular and family violence more generally (Barnett, Miller-Perrin, & Perrin, 1997; Cicchetti & Carlson, 1989; Tzeng et al., 1991; Winton & Mara, 2001) identify and analyze the wide variety of theoretical perspectives relevant to understanding child maltreatment's causes and consequences. Many disciplines other than social work—such as sociology, medicine, psychology, and law—study child maltreatment within a particular disciplinary **paradigm**, or frame of reference. As others have discussed, there are many reasons that the ecological framework alone is insufficient. Two of these reasons are linked and of considerable importance.

First, child maltreatment is an extremely complex phenomenon, and at least four specific subtypes of maltreatment exist. Some have pointed out that there are inextricable linkages between these subtypes. For example, some argue that psychological or emotional maltreatment always exists when any other subtype is present. Consider for a moment David Loefeler's situation. Although he only mentions his father's physical outbursts, we could consider David a victim of both physical and emotional maltreatment. And yet others have pointed out that each type of maltreatment possesses distinct features and therefore deserves its own theoretical explanations.

A related argument for the existence and continued development of specific theories is the limitations of the ecological framework in the areas of intervention and treatment. That is, the ecological approach is most useful for understanding, or assessment, purposes but falls short in the area of suggesting *specific* intervention ideas with specific children, caregivers, or family systems. So, for example, while such a framework may help us understand the factors contributing to the dynamics within Sondra Jackson's, Kim Tran's, Junito Salvatierra's, or David Loefeler's families of origin, it may not be as helpful in suggesting intervention strategies to employ with each family as a whole or individual family members. Many theories are more focused on intervention, but caution must be used when applying such theories for general explanation purposes. In sum, the ecological-developmental approach to understanding causes of child maltreatment has not always dominated theoretical work in the field of child maltreatment, nor is it the only current theoretical perspective of relevance.

Theories of Child Maltreatment in Historical Context

Mark Winton and Barbara Mara (2001) identify 12 theories frequently employed to understand the causes and dynamics of child maltreatment and then classify these theories into three broad "models." The three models and their associated theories are summarized in Exhibit 5.4. Tzeng et al. (1991) cast the net more widely and identify 46 theories used to explain maltreatment causative factors and processes. They then classify these theories into nine paradigms. The authors situate these paradigms on three continua useful to understanding their relationships and essential principles. Exhibit 5.5 provides a visual illustration of these continua as well as the basic beliefs of each paradigm. The individual determinants paradigm, focusing on caregiver personal traits as major causative factors, was in fact the first dominant paradigm in the field of child maltreatment and is generally associated with the disciplines of medicine, psychiatry, and psychology.

Model	Psychiatric, Medical, Psychopathology	Social-Psychological	Sociocultural
Associated Theories	Medical/biological, sociobiological/ evolutionary, psychodynamic/ psychoanalytic	Social learning theory, intergenerational transmission theory, exchange theory, symbolic interaction theory, structural family systems theory	Ecological theory, feminist/conflict theory, structural-functional/ anomie/strain theory, cultural spillover theory

Exhibit 5.4   Theoretical Models of Child Maltreatment

SOURCE: Based on Winton & Mara, 2001.

Consistent with this work, Hillson and Kuiper (1994) classify theoretical explanations of child maltreatment into three historical eras. They argue that first-generation models of child maltreatment, prominent mainly in the 1970s and associated with the psychodynamic perspective, assumed that a single factor could be responsible for the onset and maintenance of child maltreatment. The factor itself could have been individual (child or caregiver) or environmental in nature. However, because no single child, adult, or environmental characteristic clearly emerges as consistently predictive of maltreatment, empirical evidence did not support this focus.

Second-generation models emerged in the 1980s and strived to explain and integrate the multiple causative factors of relevance to understanding child maltreatment. Hillson and Kuiper (1994) argue, however, that although second-generation models provided helpful thinking regarding the ways in which multilevel factors interact to potentially lead to child maltreatment, they failed to provide a sufficient degree of detail regarding the specific nature, level, or combination of factors necessary to actually stimulate the onset of maltreatment.

	Continuum Extreme	*Midpoint*	*Continuum Extreme*
Paradigm	*Individual Determinants*	*Individual-Environment Interactions*	*Sociocultural Determinants*
Beliefs	Characteristics or factors within the individual cause maltreatment	Maltreatment results from multiple, interacting variables internal and external to the individual	Factors external to the individual cause or directly and indirectly facilitate maltreatment
Paradigm	*Offender Typologies*	*Family Systems*	*Parent-Child Interactions*
Beliefs	Perpetrator flaws, identified through psychoanalytic concepts, are one major cause of maltreatment; social norms, situational variables, and child characteristics are also relevant	Individual personality factors, stressors, and cognitive processes shape and are shaped by family structure, values, and dynamics; family system's interactions with other systems also relevant; ultimately, family system dynamics lead to abuse	Disturbed early parent-child relationship creates susceptibility, along with characteristics of the parent, child, and their environments
Paradigm	*Sociobiological*	*Ecological*	*Learning/Situational*
Beliefs	Genetic factors shape human behavior; parents and caretakers may make parental care calculations based on desires or assumptions regarding child's ability or fitness to pass on genetic materials	Inter- and intrasystem processes within individual, family, community, and societal-level systems are relevant; emphasizes the importance of multilevel factors such as individual socialization, cognitive and perceptual processes; family interactions, values, parenting practices, and stressors; social support systems and social isolation; community-level stressors; sociocultural stressors and beliefs such as sanctioning violence	Emphasizes role of modeling, cognitive expectations, and situational factors; intergenerational cycles of maltreatment explained by exposure to aggressive models; focuses on role of frustration, aggressive cues, rewards and punishments, and assumes external locus of control increases risk

Exhibit 5.5   Theories of Child Maltreatment: Major Paradigms

SOURCE: Based on Tzeng et al., 1991.

Hillson and Kuiper (1994) therefore call for a new category of models: contemporary or third-generation models. They draw on Milner's (1993) **information-processing theory** of child maltreatment, which focuses on information flowing from the external world through the senses to the nervous system, and Lazarus's ideas regarding coping (Lazarus, 1993) to propose a new stress and coping model of child maltreatment. This "third-generation" model proposes that most individual factors (at the caregiver, child, and environmental levels) identified in first- and second-generation models are indeed relevant to child maltreatment. However, such factors are not easily classified as either "potentiating" (risk) or "compensatory" (protective) because of the critical role of cognitive appraisal.

The manner in which a particular individual perceives, interprets, or "appraises" a factor—its meaning for a particular individual within a particular context—determines the factor's role or impact in a particular situation. Such cognitive "appraisals" are classified for analytical purposes as primary and secondary. Primary appraisal refers to the process during which an individual attempts to understand or decide whether a particular factor poses some sort of threat to well-being. Secondary appraisal refers to the individual's review of resources available to cope with a perceived threat.

In this model, at the time of or after the individual goes through the primary and secondary appraisal processes, coping behaviors begin. The authors note that some coping strategies, such as the use of substances to relieve anxiety, may in and of themselves contribute to child maltreatment.

Assessment of Recent Theoretical Developments

Hillson and Kuiper's (1994) stress and coping model of child maltreatment is relevant and thought provoking. We must remind ourselves, however, that important differences across caregivers exist in the actual stressor being appraised. That is, across caregivers, families, and groups, there are significant differences in objective events or experiences. Moreover, there is a significant role for cumulative risk, or accumulation of "potentiating" factors, in shaping the likelihood of maltreatment. Hillson and Kuiper acknowledge these limitations and the fact that their model represents movement away from the necessary breadth associated with second-generation models. Because there is widespread agreement today that child maltreatment is a multidimensional phenomenon, the authors conclude that the ongoing use of ecological assessments of risk and protection at each level of influence is critical. Moreover, multidimensional assessment should be particularly attentive to all risk and protective factors specifically identified as relevant to child maltreatment. Yet Hillson and Kuiper argue that "even more central, however, is the need to assess the caregiver's primary and secondary appraisals, as the model suggests that these cognitions may ultimately prove to be the most significant determinants" (p. 280).

We agree that a multidimensional approach to understanding child maltreatment is critical in that it helps us understand the diverse types of maltreatment that exist and the complexities of maltreatment processes. Many of the theories employed to explain or analyze child maltreatment over time have been criticized for limited utility or contradictory empirical evidence. Some theories are relevant to understanding only a limited number of maltreatment cases, and some are relevant to understanding only one type of maltreatment.

David Finkelhor (1984), for example, explored causes of and treatment for child sexual abuse and developed a "four-preconditions model" of child sexual abuse (p. 54). This model is widely embraced as useful for understanding child sexual abuse and yet makes little sense when applied to child neglect. Not only do child maltreatment types differ significantly, but individual cases of the same type of maltreatment often possess very unique qualities. It is important to remember that there will often be significant differences in the causal processes associated with particular cases of child maltreatment.

Empirical investigations of Hillson and Kuiper's recent theoretical work will expand our understanding of the model's comprehensive utility across maltreatment types and contexts. Today we recognize that although children, caregivers, and families experiencing child maltreatment may share many characteristics, they are also very diverse. At this point, use of multiple theoretical perspectives, particularly the life course, ecological, systems, and stress and coping perspectives, seems to be particularly helpful for understanding situations of child maltreatment.

Multidimensional Risk and Protection

We have discussed the finding that multilevel risk and protective factors interact to facilitate or prevent child maltreatment. Sandler, Wolchik, MacKinnon, Ayers, and Roosa (1997) point out that thinking about the linkages between ecology and stress should draw attention to the dynamic nature of risk and protective factors. It is important to think about the duration, chronicity, and intensity of factors, as well as their interaction with the individual's developmental phase and the simultaneous presence of other risk and protective factors. Although many analyses focus on identifying relevant factors at the individual, family, community, and societal levels, our analysis is somewhat unique in that we will classify known risk and protective factors through use of the biopsychosocial-spiritual framework. Our discussion, summarized in Exhibit 5.6, draws heavily upon several recent reviews of child maltreatment risk and protection (see Krug et al., 2002; Thomas, Leicht, Hughes, Madigan, & Dowell, 2003; Thomlison, 2004).

Biological Risk and Protection

Many individual-level, biologically based maltreatment risk and protective factors have been identified. Focusing first on the child, as noted, age and sex are associated with risk and protection but in different ways for distinct types of maltreatment. For example, in the United States, younger children are most likely to be neglected, but risk for sexual abuse appears to generally increase with age; female children and adolescents appear

	Risk Factors	Protective Factors
Biological	• Age of child (young for neglect, older for sexual abuse) • Sex of child (female for sexual abuse) • Premature birth • Child health problems • Child developmental delay or disability • Age of caregiver (young) • Sex of caregiver (male for sexual abuse and severe physical abuse) • Caregiver substance abuse	• Good health of child • Absence of disability and developmental delay in child
Psychological	• Difficult child temperament/disposition • Caregiver mental health challenges • Caregiver poor social skills • Caregiver antisocial tendencies • Caregiver low self-esteem • Caregiver poor impulse control • Caregiver high stress levels • Caregiver lack of child development knowledge	• Above-average intelligence of child • Easy child temperament • Child internal locus of control & active coping style • Positive self-esteem of child & caregiver • Good social skills of child & caregiver • Caregiver reconciliation with own history of child maltreatment • Caregiver knowledge of child development • Caregiver impulse control
Social	• Poor child-caregiver attachment • Child behavior problems • Low parental educational level • Social isolation/limited social support • Caregiver with childhood history of abuse • Low family income • Single-parent family • Domestic partner violence • Large nuclear family size • Community with high levels of unemployment, poverty, population turnover, inadequate housing • Community violence	• Good child-caregiver attachment • Child with good peer and adult relationships • Extended family support • High parental education • Middle to high family income • Access to health care and social services • Stable parental employment • Adequate housing • Neighborhood with high-quality schools • Two-parent family • Social support
Spiritual	• Religious beliefs that value child obedience and corporal punishment	• Family participation in religious faith • Social support from religious community

Exhibit 5.6   Biological, Psychological, Social, and Spiritual Risk and Protective Factors for Child Maltreatment

more likely to suffer from sexual abuse than males. Other salient biologically based child characteristics that may serve as risk factors include premature birth, health problems or chronic illness, and developmental delay or disability. For example, Sondra Jackson's grandson may be identified as an "at risk" child. On the other hand, for children, biologically based protective factors include good health and the absence of disability or developmental delay.

Biologically based caregiver characteristics of relevance include sex and age. Younger caregivers are at higher risk of becoming abusive or neglectful. Although female caregivers constitute the majority of maltreatment perpetrators, once time spent with the child is statistically controlled, being a male emerges as a more significant risk factor for maltreatment. Specifically, males appear more likely than females to commit sexual abuse and severe or fatal physical abuse. As noted in Chapter 4, recent research suggests that several additional biological characteristics (specifically, heart rate, central nervous system functioning, hormones, neurotransmitters, enzymes, and toxins, as well as alcohol and other substances) may serve to increase or decrease risk of violent behavior, but the specific relationships between most of these factors and child maltreatment have not yet been thoroughly investigated. One exception is parental substance abuse, which has been found to be a risk factor for child maltreatment (see Ryan, Marsh, Testa, & Louderman, 2006).

Psychological Risk and Protection

A number of risk and protective factors are difficult to classify because traits previously viewed as solely psychological in nature are now increasingly recognized as biologically, socially, spiritually, *and* psychologically based. For purposes of analysis, we discuss some of these factors as psychological risk factors. Focusing first on the child, these factors include difficult temperament and difficult disposition or mood. Protective factors for children seem to include above-average intelligence, "easy" temperament, internal locus of control, a positive disposition, positive self-esteem, possession of interests facilitating positive self-regard, an "active" coping style, good social skills, and a balance between seeking help and self-reliance. Our image of Sondra Jackson as a child seems to fit this profile.

Turning to caregivers, significant risk factors include mental health challenges, poor social skills or antisocial tendencies, low self-esteem, poor impulse control, high stress levels, and lack of child development knowledge or inappropriate child behavior expectations. In most cases, the absence or inverse of these risk factors serves to decrease risk of perpetrating maltreatment. For caregivers with a history of child maltreatment, reconciliation with their own childhood history of abuse or neglect appears to serve as a protective factor.

Social Risk and Protection

Micro to Mezzo Risk and Protection

A variety of social risk and protective factors have been identified. Poor infant-caregiver attachment serves as a potent risk factor. In addition, children with behavior problems or problematic social skills are at elevated risk. As would be expected, then, children with good peer and adult relationships seem to be at lower risk.

Among caregivers, secure child-caregiver attachment serves as a consistent, significant protective factor. Caregiver or family expectations of pro-social behavior also function as a protective factor. Low educational level, social isolation or limited social support, low family income, and single-parent status all serve as risk factors. Some research evidence suggests that maltreating mothers have fewer friends, less contact with the friends they possess, and lower ratings of support received from friends. Caregivers with a childhood history of maltreatment are at heightened risk. The presence of intimate partner, or domestic, violence in the home also increases the risk of maltreatment to children. Large families, particularly in the context of overcrowded or otherwise inadequate housing, appear to be at heightened risk. Moreover, living in a community with high levels of unemployment, poverty, population turnover, overcrowded or inadequate housing, and low levels of *social capital* appears to elevate risk.

Protective factors within families in general appear to be extended family support and high parental education. Also, families with diminished risk generally are of middle to high SES; have consistent access to quality health care and social services, stable parental employment, and adequate housing; and reside in neighborhoods with high-quality schools. Generally, two-parent families appear to experience less risk perhaps largely due to enhanced financial stability. Also, again for both children and caregivers, the presence of supportive adults outside the family who serve as sources of support and role models or mentors seems to help protect families from maltreatment.

Macro Risk and Protection

Poverty is a serious risk factor associated with all maltreatment types but particularly child neglect. Violence in general, including community-level violence, is an important risk factor, as is concentrated unemployment. Others have suggested that narrow legal definitions of maltreatment, social or cultural acceptance of or support for violence (e.g., in the media), and political or religious views supporting noninterference with family life may also be associated with heightened risk of maltreatment.

Spiritual Risk and Protection

In general, religion, or spirituality, has been found to function as a protective factor for families (Brodsky, 1999; Mowbray, Schwartz, & Bybee, 2000). Indeed, family participation in a religious faith has specifically been identified as a child maltreatment protective factor. According to Shor (1998), examples of the ways in which religion may support family well-being include "protecting the sanctity and importance of the family, providing clear norms and behavioral guidelines, and facilitating a parental support system" (p. 400). One important component of religious involvement is often social support, and this operates in most cases as an important protective factor for caregivers and children.

On the other hand, risk is reportedly elevated when religion prescribes acceptance or valuing of obedience and corporal punishment (Shor, 1998). Religious or spiritual beliefs interact with beliefs regarding children and child rearing. Religion has been identified as a significant predictor of caregivers' beliefs regarding the role of corporal punishment and, more generally, "expectations of their children's behavior, their perceptions of what is considered appropriate and inappropriate child behavior and which child-rearing practices are acceptable/not acceptable" (Shor, 1998, p. 407). However, Jones Harden and Nzinga-Johnson (2006) caution against oversimplifying the relationships between religion and parenting. Religion and spirituality are multidimensional constructs. For example, religious beliefs may shape whether a community is more **collectivist**, prioritizing group rather than individual goals and needs, or **individualistic**, emphasizing individual goals and needs, in nature. Shor (1998) argues that neither the collectivist nor individualistic orientation of a religious community is in and of itself a risk or protective factor. It is the way in which a family or community interprets religious beliefs and uses this belief system in parenting practices that matters most. So while some interpret a religious principle as discouraging the use of physical punishment with children, others may use the same principle to support or rationalize abusive behavior for perceived acts of disobedience (see Mahoney, Pargament, Tarakeshwar, & Swank, 2001). Diversity in interpretation may also occur in the area of family privacy and parental rights. Whether family religiosity or spirituality emerges as a risk or protective factor for maltreatment varies, depending on the particular nature of the individual caregiver's beliefs and involvement with a faith community.

Biopsychosocial-Spiritual Integration

The linkages across the biological, psychological, social, and spiritual dimensions are evident. Perhaps both embedded within and distinct from these dimensions, the physical environment is an additional, often underemphasized influence on behavior. Diverse aspects of the physical environment, including both natural and built environments, may threaten or support child and family well-being (Bell, 2005; Hutchison, 2003d; Rotton & Cohn, 2004). For example, many believe that it is good for children to play outside; recent evidence suggests that regular exposure to the natural environment may indeed play an essential role in supporting positive child behavior and development (Kuo & Taylor, 2004, 2005; Taylor, Wiley, Kuo & Sullivan, 1998). And turning to the built environment, research suggests a relationship between family well-being and housing as well as other neighborhood conditions (Ernst, Meyer, & DePanflis, 2004; Freisthier, Merritt, & Lascala, 2006). There is ample evidence that the physical environment directly and indirectly interacts with the biological, psychological, social, and spiritual realms. Factors in all dimensions can be transient or enduring, and the presence and levels of particular factors shift throughout the life course (Thomlison, 2004).

Thorough consideration of the processes involved with virtually any risk or protective factor reveals the potential linkages and transactions between the biological, psychological, social, and spiritual dimensions. For example, consider the idea that a child's temperament may serve as a risk or protective factor for maltreatment. Temperament, or a child's "innate disposition," is widely viewed as consisting of multiple components such as activity level, adaptability, initial reaction to new stimuli, and intensity of reaction (Woody, 2003, p. 133). There are disagreements, however, about whether temperament is genetically determined, innate, and stable over time (biological) or shaped by environment and shifting across time (psychological and social). Woody (2003) points out that a caregiver's perception of his or her child's temperament plays a much more critical role in predicting the development of child behavior problems than any objective aspects of a child's personality. Bugental and Happaney's (2004) examination of similar issues in the context of child maltreatment provides similar evidence. As a maltreatment risk or protective factor, then, "child temperament" is not easily categorized as simply biological, psychological, social, or spiritual in nature. It is instead a construct created by interplay among these dimensions.

Similarly, our discussion of female gender as a risk factor for poverty (see Chapter 3) indicates that gender is a biologically based trait that gains meaning in social context. Turning to child maltreatment, research suggests that girls face higher risk than boys of sexual abuse victimization. This is true not simply because the biological aspects of being female create heightened susceptibility. Instead, girls' elevated risk of sexual victimization from infancy through adulthood results from the ways in which biological, psychological, and social dimensions of gender shape sexuality and conceptions of what it means to be a girl or a boy, a woman or a man. Indeed, gender emerges as relevant to risk of victimization and perpetration of distinct types of maltreatment because of its complex biological, psychological, social, and spiritual components. Risk and protective factors may be classified as primarily biological, psychological, social, or spiritual for our analytical purposes, but in reality any risk or protective factor is comprised of contributions from all dimensions and their ongoing interactions.

Consequences of Child Maltreatment

The impact of child maltreatment on an individual child varies, based on a number of factors, including but certainly not limited to the type of maltreatment, the age of the child, and many other child, family, and community characteristics. In their review of literature on child maltreatment outcomes, Haugaard, Reppucci, and Feerick (1997) find considerable empirical evidence that many variables influence maltreatment outcomes. For example, what is the nature of the relationship between the perpetrator and victim? Is family functioning highly and chronically dysfunctional and detrimental to child well-being, or do aspects of the family environment offer some level of stability and protection for the child? Does one type of abuse or neglect occur in isolation or simultaneously with one or more other types of maltreatment? When in the child's development does the maltreatment begin and end? What is the specific nature of the maltreatment, at what developmental point, and at what level of intensity and duration? How do others in the child's micro and mezzo environments react? How do these various factors interact with this individual child and his or her particular set of vulnerabilities and competencies?

Added to this list are factors such as the child's gender and a host of other often overlooked issues such as whether and when reporting of the maltreatment occurred and the investigation or response experience. Consideration of the wide variation that exists within the term *maltreatment* and the role of these many additional variables of relevance suggests that specifying outcomes in a straightforward manner is simply impossible. However, as a whole, children who experience child abuse and neglect of any type are at risk of a wide variety of negative developmental outcomes, and the detrimental impacts of maltreatment may interact in a synergistic and cumulative fashion. For example, how is David Loefeler's life illustrative of such synergy, or risk accumulation?

The Centers for Disease Control and Prevention, National Center for Injury Prevention and Control (CDC, NCIPC; 2005) published a recent overview of child maltreatment consequences, pointing out that experiencing maltreatment as a child is associated with an overwhelming number of negative health outcomes as an adult. These outcomes include an increased likelihood of smoking, using alcohol and other substance abuse, disordered eating, severe obesity, depression, suicide, sexual promiscuity, and susceptibility to certain chronic diseases.

Experiencing maltreatment during infancy or early childhood may have particularly severe consequences because it has been linked to changes in brain functioning and associated physical, cognitive, and emotional outcomes. Nonfatal consequences of physical abuse during infancy include cognitive, motor, and visual impairment. Moreover, victims of child maltreatment are more likely to be revictimized throughout the life course and are more likely to victimize their own children. Indeed, a significant body of research indicates that maltreatment heightens risk of problematic social functioning in many areas, including violence in intimate relationships (CDC, NCIPC, 2005). We see evidence of this type of impact in David Loefeler's life, although we do not know whether he has recreated the cycle of violence in his own family system.

Victims of maltreatment in general have a higher likelihood of academic problems than nonvictims. There is some evidence that neglected children are most likely to suffer in the cognitive development domain and consequently are the victims most likely to suffer from poor school performance. Associations between maltreatment and academic performance have led to the empirically grounded speculation that maltreatment is ultimately associated with lower levels of educational attainment and therefore heightened risk of financial impoverishment (Haugaard et al., 1997).

Indeed, direct costs of maltreatment to society, such as support for direct responses within the health, judicial, and legal systems, have recently been estimated at an annual cost in the United States of $24 billion each year. Some speculate that because child maltreatment is indirectly responsible for a variety of other challenges of living that also receive public attention and funds, including indirect costs would drive this figure much higher. It seems close to impossible to speculate about indirect costs, but those who have done so estimate that the annual indirect costs fall near $69 billion each year in the United States (CDC, NCIPC, 2005).

As noted, the consequences of maltreatment simply are not monolithic phenomena. For example, abuse and neglect often impact social functioning, but for some children the specific resulting issues are *externalizing disorders,* while for other children the outcomes are *internalizing disorders.* Generally, physically and sexually abused children are more likely to exhibit both internalizing and externalizing disorders than children who have not been physically or sexually abused. Physical aggression appears most likely among physical abuse victims, with sexual aggression or promiscuity more likely among victims of child sexual abuse. Victims of repeated and violent sexual abuse are more likely to experience **dissociative disorders**, characterized by sudden, temporary changes in normal functions of consciousness, identity, and memory, than nonvictims or victims whose sexual abuse is less violent or frequent (Haugaard et al., 1997).

There is conflicting evidence regarding which type of maltreatment produces the most severe outcomes (Haugaard et al., 1997). At least one study suggests that sexually abused children exhibit higher rates of self-injurious and suicidal behavior than physically abused or neglected children. On the other hand, several studies have found that of all victim types, sexually abused children are actually most likely to report healthy levels of social competence and the absence of problematic consequences or symptoms altogether. In fact, after reviewing the proportion of literature devoted to research and treatment focusing on physical abuse, sexual abuse, and neglect, respectively, Haugaard et al. (1997) conclude that because "physical abuse and neglect can be just as damaging, if not more damaging, than sexual abuse, it is unclear why there is such little emphasis on therapy with physically abused and neglected children" (p. 89). Margaret Smith and Rowena Fong (2004) raise a similar question about neglected children, arguing that the consequences of neglect are at least as serious as the consequences of physical and sexual abuse.

In general, inconsistent consequences are observed largely because child maltreatment itself is an inconsistent, or complex, phenomenon. Also, different theoretical perspectives are drawn upon to guide this body of research. Haugaard et al. (1997) classify theoretical approaches to understanding the nature and processes of child maltreatment impacts into biological, psychoanalytic, learning, attachment, and cognitive explanations. In isolation, each perspective provides an insufficient explanation for the range of outcomes observed. However, each perspective possesses some degree of empirical support.

Ways of Coping

A body of research now supports the idea that although exposure to serious stress is a common part of growing up in the United States (and even more common in some parts of the world), positive development in the face of adversity is also possible (Sandler et al., 1997). It is worthwhile, then, to consider what types of coping may promote positive development. As we do so, however, we should note that the type of coping possible and likely is impacted by, among other qualities, the age and abilities of the children and caregivers involved. For example, Jones (1997) points out that cognitive reappraisal of the situation (focused on "making sense" of what is happening and rejecting self-blame) and use of social support will, of course, be less possible among very young children.

Many potentially effective approaches to coping with child maltreatment have been identified. Abilities such as recognizing danger and adapting, distancing oneself emotionally from intense feelings, and projecting oneself into a "better" time and place have been identified as potentially helpful coping strategies in certain scenarios (Thomas et al., 2003). Use of psychological avoidance seems to be particularly helpful as a short-term coping strategy for situations of severe abuse; however, dissociation has also been identified as a risky coping strategy in terms of potential long-term outcomes associated with overreliance on this strategy (Chaffin, Wherry, & Dykman, 1997).

The child's and caregiver's ability to engage in mutually positive interactions or create certain positive aspects of their relationship may be a critical coping strategy for both child and caregiver (Haugaard et al., 1997). In sexual abuse scenarios, research consistently finds that the reaction of the nonoffending caretaker is crucial (Bolen & Lamb, 2004; Hill, 2005; Lovett, 2004). Supportive reactions among nonoffending caretakers seem to play a potentially critical role in facilitating positive adaptation among victims.

Existing research, although incomplete, seems to support the idea that for many families, the "parenting of maltreating parents is not monolithically bad. . . . There is a range of overall parenting skills among maltreating parents" (Haugaard et al., 1997, pp. 87–88). Haugaard et al. (1997) suggest that children are sometimes able to evoke more "**developmentally appropriate parenting**" (p. 88), parenting that reflects understanding of and responsiveness to the child's developmental stage-related needs and abilities in each developmental domain. They further suggest that those children who are more adept at engaging their parents or other adults and whose behaviors are less troublesome to adults may receive better overall caretaking. They conclude that "given the apparent strength of the relationship between supportive caretaking and adaptation to maltreatment, any child behaviors that encourage more parental support are likely to have an indirect influence on the child's adaptation" (p. 88). Continued attempts to engage in positive interactions and to maintain positive relationships with primary caregivers as well as other adults represent important coping efforts on the part of the maltreated child. The child's desire to make these attempts and his or her ability to succeed in this endeavor, however, may often reflect not only child characteristics but also characteristics of the family system as a whole. In addition, the environment of the family may or may not provide adequate resources and support to the child and family. Thomlison (2004) points out that "the child's adaptive or maladaptive response to harmful experiences may then depend on whether the parenting environment has adequate social and economic resources to change childcare patterns" (p. 95).

Engaging in activities and cognitions that support self-esteem is also consistently identified as a helpful coping strategy (Thomas et al., 2003). Retrospective research with child maltreatment survivors supports this idea; many individuals seem to believe their positive self-talk and, more important, their ability to develop and maintain a true belief in their inherent value as a human being was an effective coping strategy. Research with survivors suggests that externalizing blame for the maltreatment is a helpful coping strategy as well. Some have speculated that ego "overcontrol" or a calculated and controlled way of interacting may also function as a coping mechanism for some maltreated children (Haugaard et al., 1997). We can imagine that for David Loefeler, learning ways to carefully avoid and defuse his father's anger may have served as an effective short-term coping strategy.

Engaging in spiritual activities or generally focusing on spiritual development has also been identified as an often helpful coping strategy (DiLorenzo, Johnson, Bussey, 2001). Spiritually focused coping may be particularly helpful for those caregivers struggling with substance abuse. There is a strong relationship between spirituality and social support, and thus it is difficult to determine the specific role spirituality plays in shaping positive outcomes for caregivers.

Although existing coping research has limitations, it suggests that at least a few coping strategies are consistently associated with heightened odds of long-term recovery and resilience. These include rejecting self-blame as well as engagement in positive thinking and activities focused on maintaining a sense of self-esteem or self-efficacy. Also, efforts focused upon developing or maintaining social relationships appear to be critical. Across types of maltreatment, development and maintenance of positive relationships and social support networks, for both children and caregivers, appear to help prevent the onset, escalation, return, and detrimental impacts of abuse or neglect.

Social Justice Issues

Social justice focuses upon issues of equal protection and opportunity. Developmentally speaking, children simply are not equal to adults. Though recognizing the potential resilience of children is important, we must also be cognizant of the fact that children are fragile. Because they are still developing in all **developmental domains**, including physical/motor, emotional/psychological, social, and cognitive domains, their experiences play a critical and profound role in shaping subsequent capacity and functioning. Thus, all children need a heightened level of protection to ensure healthy development or "equal opportunity." As a nation and a world, we recognize in the abstract that children should be protected from abuse and neglect. But at any point in time, children suffer and benefit unequally from action or lack thereof in the area of child protection.

In the United States, child maltreatment is intertwined with poverty, and poverty is intertwined with gender and race. Experiencing poverty as a child is a significant developmental risk factor (Drake & Zuravin, 1998; Gershoff, 2003). The combined experience of chronic poverty and maltreatment contributes to an extremely potent chain of risk. Financially impoverished children in general and children of color particularly are disproportionately represented among documented maltreatment victims (see Courtney & Skyles, 2003; Hines, Lemon & Wyatt, 2004). Given our knowledge regarding the developmental outcomes associated with such victimization, child maltreatment begins to take shape as a social justice issue. Far too often, however, the relationships between inadequate support for vulnerable families and social problems such as violence and substance abuse are not addressed.

Reform of the child welfare system is often discussed as a logical first step toward enhancing protections for children and supports for families. The Childrens Bureau's system of Child and Family Services Reviews has made important strides toward child welfare system improvement and offers promise as an ongoing monitoring strategy (USDHHS, ACF, 2006a). **Child and Family Services Reviews** (CFSR) are federal reviews of state child and family service programs to investigate compliance with existing laws and regulations. However, this approach to system improvement faces many barriers, and there are many problematic issues needing attention in the areas of child welfare policy, programs, and practices (Courtney, Needell, & Wulczyn, 2004; Karson, 2001; U.S. General Accounting Office, 2004).

An important ongoing challenge and call to action is the disproportionate representation of children of color in the child welfare system. Also, many have pointed out the need to devote more funds to prevention and support services for families. As a nation we have allocated far more funding over time to support maltreatment investigation and foster care placement compared to funds for supporting families in a more comprehensive, preventative fashion (Lind, 2004; Pecora, Whittaker, Maluccio, & Barth, 2000).

In addition to the urgent need for attention to the inadequacies within our child welfare systems and the linkages between poverty and child maltreatment, some argue that there is a relationship between our nation's view of children's rights in general and child abuse and neglect. In 1989, the United Nations adopted the Convention on the Rights of the Child. The convention attempts to protect children's rights by rejecting "**cultural relativism** in favor of universal human rights that transcend cultural, religious, historical, and economic differences in order to set a minimum standard of protection and respect to which all children are entitled." An explicit and important focus of the convention is the requirement that children be protected against "all forms of physical and mental violence . . . while in the care of parent(s), legal guardian(s), or any other person who has the care of the child" (UNICEF, 2003, p. 3). Today, the United States and Somalia are the only two countries in the world that have not ratified the convention. Ratifying the convention indicates agreement to work toward implementation of the rights of children as identified in the document and to make periodic progress reports to the United Nations (Walker, Brooks, & Wrightsman, 1999).

The United States supports the spirit of the convention and is perhaps a leader in certain areas of child welfare such as documentation and tracking systems (see United States of America, 2005). Yet it is unfortunate that the United States has not joined other nations who have taken a lead in symbolically declaring children's rights and well-being a top national priority. Unfortunately, many nations perceive the United States' failure to ratify the convention as symbolic of the poor standing of children's rights and needs within our nation's priorities.

As a nation we have failed to fully join an international movement striving to understand and confront the ways in which poverty and a "culture of violence" seem to support child maltreatment. Our empirical knowledge of the causes and consequences of child abuse and neglect is quite comprehensive. And yet we have been unable to take the steps necessary to prevent child maltreatment to the extent that seems theoretically possible.

Practice Implications

Our discussion has implications for micro-, mezzo-, and macro-level social work practice. Sufficient evidence underscores the profound importance of macro-level change. Because of the strong relationship between poverty and maltreatment, strategies focused upon financial impoverishment ultimately will link to child maltreatment. Consider, for example, the different life that Junito Salvatierra may have led if his family possessed financial security. Other macro-level targets include our cultural norms and values, particularly culture of violence attitudes, beliefs, and behaviors. At the mezzo level, successfully confronting community violence and financial impoverishment will have positive implications for child maltreatment as well (see Edleson, Daro, & Pinderhughes, 2004). Also at the mezzo level, efforts to improve the functioning of child welfare agencies and systems must continue with sufficient attention and resources.

Prevention and intervention efforts at the mezzo and macro levels can play an essential, long-term role in confronting child maltreatment. Recently, the USDHHS's Office on Child Abuse and Neglect implemented a new child abuse prevention initiative, representing a continuation of federal and local abuse and neglect prevention efforts. One product associated with this initiative was the publication of a report titled *Emerging Practices in the Prevention of Child Abuse and Neglect* (Thomas et al., 2003). A public health framework dominates prevention conceptualization across disciplines. This framework identifies three major types of prevention efforts.

Primary prevention efforts are universal in scope and target the general population; applied to child abuse and neglect, such efforts can be thought of as attempting to prevent maltreatment from ever occurring. **Secondary prevention** programs target individuals or families identified as at heightened risk of maltreatment; this type of prevention work focuses on early identification in an attempt to limit the extent or severity of the maltreatment. Finally, **tertiary prevention** programs target families in which maltreatment has already occurred or is occurring; this type of prevention generally focuses on stopping the maltreatment, facilitating recovery from its effects, and developing supports and strengths to prevent its return (Thomas et al., 2003). The *Emerging Practices* report identifies illustrative examples of each category, summarized in Exhibit 5.7. The authors of the report point out that many organizations active in prevention work are simultaneously engaged at all three levels.

And yet, after examining available data on the effectiveness of prevention approaches, the authors of the *Emerging Practices* report agree with many other prevention researchers (Daro & Donnelly, 2002; Harder, 2005) that all prevention models and strategies are "in need of more rigorous study" (Thomas et al., 2003, p. 57). With the limited data and information available, the authors conclude that home visiting programs, parent education programs, and child sexual abuse awareness programs all have the potential to improve family functioning.

Most home visiting programs focus on the interactions and relationship between a staff member (e.g., a counselor, social worker, teacher, or other professional or paraprofessional)

Primary Prevention (Universal)	Secondary Prevention (Targeting Risk)	Tertiary Prevention (Facilitating Recovery)
Public service announcements that encourage positive parenting	Respite care for families that have children with special needs	Parent support groups that help parents transform negative practices and beliefs into positive parenting behaviors and attitudes
Parent education programs and support groups that focus on child development and age-appropriate expectations and the roles and responsibilities of parenting	Parent support groups that help parents deal with their everyday stresses and meet the challenges and responsibilities of parenting	Parent mentor programs with stable, nonabusive families acting as role models and providing support to families in crisis
Family support and family strengthening programs that enhance the ability of families to access existing services and resources and support interactions among family members	Parent education programs located in high schools, for example, that focus on teen parents, or within substance abuse treatment programs for mothers and families with young children	Intensive family preservation services with trained professionals that are available to families 24 hours per day for a short period of time (e.g., 6–8 weeks)
Public awareness campaigns that provide information on how and where to report suspected child abuse and neglect	Home visiting programs that provide support and assistance to expecting and new mothers in their homes	Mental health services for children and families affected by maltreatment to improve family communication and functioning
	Family resource centers that offer information and referral services to families living in low-income neighborhoods	

Exhibit 5.7   Child Abuse and Neglect Prevention

SOURCE: Based on Thomas et al., 2003.

and parent or family as a whole as the main vehicle through which changes in parental knowledge and practice are expected and facilitated. Ongoing evaluation research suggests that sufficient service intensity, duration, and quality are essential for intervention success and yet are only a few of the factors that may shape the impact of such programs (Olds, 1997, 2003).

Family support programs typically focus on prevention of child abuse and neglect through a variety of community-based, universally available education and prevention services for families. These programs generally have been found most effective in producing positive family gains and enhancing social, emotional, and cognitive outcomes for children when they facilitate peer support among caregivers, utilize groups, and use effective early childhood education strategies for improving cognitive skills (Layzer, Goodson, Bernstein, & Price, 2001). At this point in her life, do you believe Analiz, the mother of Junito Salvatierra's child, could benefit from a home visiting or family support program? What types of agency, program, or staff characteristics would most effectively support Analiz's parenting?

A relevant best practices issue is family engagement. Many families served by child and family service programs are difficult to engage due to transient living arrangements, frequent scheduling conflicts, lack of telephones, and a long history of unsuccessful involvement with service agencies. Many suggestions included in the *Emerging Practice* report represent effective social work practice more generally. Identified essentials include skill in community needs assessment and outreach, cultural competence, relationship building, and provision of services and resources identified as worthwhile by clients. Also, focusing primarily on child neglect, the USDHHS (2004) recently disseminated recommendations regarding various aspects of effective child and family service program functioning (summarized in Exhibit 5.8). Which of these issues or recommendations are most relevant to your thoughts regarding Analiz's needs?

Use a collaborative, strengths-based, family empowerment approach
Focus on the relationship between staff and caregivers
Offer staff ongoing training
Use multidisciplinary teams in working with families
Build collaboration with community partners
Offer a combination of out-of-home and in-home services
Form advisory committees that engage all stakeholders
Continuously assess strengths/needs of family and members, community/environment
Be prepared to address crises immediately
Customize services and be flexible, combining prevention, intervention, and treatment
Be flexible with the curriculum in parenting education and support groups
Focus on poverty issues, recognize related needs, and engage in advocacy
Offer or refer to a broad array of services
Address children's needs on-site or through referral
Offer services for older youth
Provide intensive, long-term services
Deliver follow-up or after-care services

Exhibit 5.8   Effective Approaches to Addressing Child Neglect

SOURCE: Based on USDHHS, 2004.

Finally, **family preservation programs** focus on preserving or reunifying high-risk families and often offer intensive services to families at imminent risk of child removal due to abuse or neglect. A recent evaluation of family preservation programs (Westat, Chapin Hall Center for Children, & James Bell Associates, 2002) suggests that the functions, target group, and characteristics of services in such programs need to be reexamined. Agreeing with others in the field, the evaluators believe that child placement prevention should not be the sole priority or primary goal of family preservation services. Instead, the focus should be on the general improvement of family and child functioning. In particular, the evaluators question whether a short-term, crisis-oriented approach fits the needs of most high-risk, multiproblem families. For example, how effective would a short-term, crisis-oriented approach be with a family such as David Loefeler's family of origin? The somewhat recent assertion is that family preservation programs should be thought of as one important part of the continuum of child welfare services, unlikely to alone function as a panacea. An additional suggestion is the development of a series of small "preservation" programs with specific areas of expertise and specialized services (e.g., programs and services targeting families with substance abuse issues or targeting young, isolated mothers) rather than the use of all resources to support general, undifferentiated efforts.

A recent outcome of extensive work in the child welfare service and system improvement area is a publication titled *Tough Problems, Tough Choices: Guidelines for Needs-Based Service Planning in Child Welfare* (Field & Winterfeld, 2003). This publication is designed to provide a framework for service planning for several specific types of child abuse and neglect. The guidelines provide extensive topic-specific information and comprehensive decision-making trees. The authors are quick to point out that they are focusing on decision making after risk assessment has occurred. A separate and extensive risk assessment literature exists in the child welfare field (see Gambrill, 2005; Leschied, Chiodo, Whitehead, Hurley, & Marshall, 2003; Shlonsky & Wagner, 2005).

While these guidelines can be used by individual professionals, the preferred decision-making method in child welfare is a team approach, consisting of the family, the caseworker, allied agency staff, and at least one other child welfare agency representative. A team of this nature is thought to be more capable of making objective decisions. That is, a team approach enhances the ability to "identify and isolate personal value judgments that can cloud and misdirect individually made casework decisions" (Field & Winterfeld, 2003, p. 4).

There are many resources for supporting culturally competent, evidence-based child welfare practice (see Dubowitz & DePanfilis, 2000; Faller, 1999; Samantrai, 2004; Thomlison, 2003). A recent report by the Kauffman Best Practices Project (Chadwick Center for Children and Families, 2004) focuses on **best practices** in the area of clinical services for children and parents confronting physical and sexual abuse. This project has identified three micro-level treatment protocols as possessing the highest level of theoretical, clinical, and empirical support: trauma-focused cognitive-behavioral therapy (CBT), abuse-focused cognitive-behavioral therapy (AFCBT), and parent-child interaction therapy.

Trauma-focused cognitive-behavioral therapy (TFCBT) is a treatment for posttraumatic stress disorder (PTSD) symptoms in sexually abused children. TFCBT is based on learning and cognitive theories and focuses on "correcting maladaptive beliefs and attributions related to abusive experiences" as well as "reducing negative emotional and behavioral responses" (Chadwick Center for Children and Families, 2004, p. 9). TFCBT also focuses on providing support and skills to nonoffending caregivers to enable them to cope effectively and to respond appropriately to abused children. Imagine, for example, that Freda discovered that Estella, as a child, was being sexually abused while in the care of neighbors. What types of support would both Estella and Freda have needed at that point in their lives?

An additional intervention, AFCBT, is an approach to working with abused children and their offending caregivers that incorporates behavioral principles presented in learning theory. AFCBT is most appropriate for situations in which enhancement of specific intrapersonal and interpersonal skills would be helpful. In particular, parents with poor behavior management skills, who rely heavily on physical punishment methods of child discipline, and parents with high levels of other negative interactions with children are appropriate for AFCBT. Children with externalizing behavior problems, including aggression with peers, are appropriate for AFCBT. Like TFCBT, AFCBT is not appropriate for all situations and may be contraindicated for children or parents with serious psychiatric issues or other challenges (such as cognitive impairment or substance abuse) that may compromise the ability to learn and consistently implement new skills.

Parent-child interaction therapy (PCIT) developed as a result of several empirically supported observations. A coercive interaction pattern (such as using aggression to acquire child compliance and a general overreliance on punishment) seems to frequently become ingrained within the family system, emerging as a stable form of responding to parent-child conflict. PCIT appears particularly effective when the goals are improved parenting skills, decreased child behavior problems, and improvement in the quality of the parent-child relationship. PCIT is a very specific, coached behavioral parent-training model. Many components of PCIT are common among cognitive-behavioral interventions: parents are provided with both general and specific information, time and attention is devoted to skill acquisition progressing toward mastery with use of "homework" and other tools, and attention is given to generalization to other children and settings. The ideal method includes immediate prompts to a parent while the parent is interacting with the child through face-to-face coaching or use of technology such as an earpiece (Chadwick Center for Children and Families, 2004).

It is beyond the scope of the present discussion to identify and thoroughly address best practices in prevention and intervention, in all areas of maltreatment, and for all victims, caregivers, and families. However, a solid albeit dynamic knowledge base exists in each of these areas, and this knowledge is necessary for competent practice in the field of child maltreatment. Relevant to this conversation about *best practices* is the Kaufmann Project's interest in the topic of information dissemination. A "wide gulf in time exists between the development of a best practice and the adoption of it in everyday practice across the nation" (Chadwick Center for Children and Families, 2004, p. 20). Following this logic, the project identifies the following prerequisites to best practices implementation: awareness of the best practice, belief in the efficacy of the practice itself as well as personal efficacy in learning and applying the practice, the decision to change practice behavior, preparation for applying the practice by learning knowledge and skills necessary to deliver the practice as intended, clients willing to accept the practice, funding sources willing to support the intervention, and finally, successful experience in delivery of the best practice. In order to meet these prerequisites, agencies must function as learning organizations, capable of constant learning, change, and innovation, and practitioners and supervisors must embrace evidence-based practice and collaborate to form effective support networks or *communities of practice.*

What is most important for us to remember is that knowledge regarding best practices in the field of child maltreatment exists. There is a strong and ever-expanding body of empirically based information about effective prevention, assessment, and intervention strategies, and we must stay abreast of and apply these strategies. To be effective as professionals, we must recognize the need for continuous learning and seek, contribute to, disseminate, and implement available knowledge.

Learning Activities

1. Knowledge About the Case. Imagine that you meet David Loefeler when he is 11 years old. He has been referred to you by his teacher, who seems unsympathetic toward and very frustrated with David. David's school attendance and academic performance are poor. His problematic behavior, including aggression toward other boys, seems to have gradually escalated during the last several months. David's teacher explains that he has never met David's father, and his mother seems extremely shy and uninvolved in David's life. Review Exhibit 2.1 and its list of key Knowledge About the Case questions. Working in small groups, brainstorm answers to these questions, applying them to David's case. Consider whether there are additional questions you would consider essential to answer in formulating a comprehensive assessment and potential intervention plan.

2. Knowledge About the Self. As the next chapter in Sondra's "story" unfolds, she learns that 14-year-old Angel Smith has told hospital and child welfare staff members that Isaiah Jackson is the father of her child, whom she has named Isaiah as well. You are the child welfare social worker assigned to Isaiah Jackson Jr. Isaiah Jr. was born at 30 weeks gestation and tests indicate intrauterine exposure to cocaine; he remains hospitalized in a neonatal intensive care unit but should be discharged within approximately 2 months. Angel presents herself as a confident young woman determined to care for her infant son. Angel's mother works full time, and although she indicates that she had been recently estranged from her daughter, she states that Isaiah Jr. and Angel will live with her and she will provide for both financially. In your opinion, Sondra seems to be in shock. Her initial reaction was to request a paternity test. After the results confirmed Sondra's biological relationship to Isaiah Jr., Sondra has seemed quiet and reserved. She has calmly stated that she will take care of her grandson but has otherwise expressed little emotion. As you consider how to proceed, consider your own perceptions of and beliefs regarding Angel and Sondra. Do you have a strong emotional reaction to any of the individuals involved in this situation? What personal values, beliefs, and emotions shape your initial reactions to this situation? How do your personal characteristics, including your past and present experiences, gender, ethnic background, culture, and SES, shape your potential thoughts, emotions, and actions in this situation? Independently write down your responses to these questions. Include any descriptive words or thoughts that come to mind, in a brainstorm or freewrite fashion. When you have finished, share and explain what you have written down to a partner. Together with your partner, discuss ways that you could ensure this knowledge about the self helps rather than hinders competent and ethical practice in this situation.

3. **Values and Ethics.** You meet Kim Tran exactly 1 year after her "story" ended. At 18, she is now the mother of an apparently healthy 4-month-old daughter, Ann. Kim is living in one of your organization's transitional housing units. She has confided in you that she loves Ann, but she frequently finds herself tired of the baby's constant demands. She confesses that last Saturday night, she left Ann alone for several hours so that she could hang out with some old friends. You have noticed that she pays little attention to Ann when you are with her and often seems annoyed when Ann cries. You are concerned about Ann's well-being, but you also know that involvement with CPS could lead to Kim's eviction. Kim told you during a prior conversation that her mother has made it clear that she and the baby are not welcome in her parents' home. You are also well aware of the shortage of adequate foster care placements for infants in Orange County. In small groups, carefully consider the core values of the National Association of Social Workers (NASW) Code of Ethics and identify the major ethical principles or standards relevant to this situation. What ethical dilemmas exist in this scenario? How could you proceed in an ethical fashion?

4. **General Knowledge.** This chapter identifies the four major types of child maltreatment as neglect, physical abuse, sexual abuse, and psychological or emotional abuse. Assign each type of child maltreatment to a small group. Each group's homework is to use the information presented in the chapter, along with other academic sources, to identify major changes in the last 50 years in social scientists' beliefs regarding best practices in working with children and families identified as experiencing this particular type of maltreatment. This work should include identification of the theory or theories guiding historical and contemporary intervention in this particular area. Each group should pay particular attention to changes in thinking regarding best practices in this area and should attempt to identify the rationale behind such changes.

6

Traumatic Stress

Holly C. Matto,
Virginia Commonwealth University

E lias, Claudia, and Junito Salvatierra migrated from the Dominican Republic (DR) to the United States. Although the migration experience was different for each of them, it seems safe to say that all three of them found the process of migration to be quite stressful, and perhaps even traumatic. Given his age and the many losses associated with his migration, we might suspect that Junito was particularly traumatized by his experience with migration. Stress can be defined as any event in which the situational demands tax the adaptive resources of an individual. Stress that is so severe as to overwhelm the coping capacities is referred to as traumatic stress. Trauma creates an intense impact on the physical and psychological systems, distorting trust in predictable outcomes, leading to intense feelings of helplessness (Brewin, 2003). Traumas affecting immigrants may be caused by significant separations from family that create prolonged grief reactions, particularly for refugees who are escaping violence in their country of origin and may not know about the safety of relatives left behind (Abe, Zane, & Chun, 1994).

The chronicity, severity, and proximity that characterize an individual's relationship to the trauma experience will influence trauma response patterns and symptom development. Terr (1991) identifies two types of trauma, Type I and Type II, each of which may lead to differential symptom severity and duration. **Type I trauma** is characterized by one event, whereas **Type II trauma** is a product of a series of events, such as ongoing, chronic abuse. Webb (2004b) discusses other trauma typologies such as "danger traumas," which are life-threatening, "loss traumas," which are defined by the loss of loved ones or loss of status, and "responsibility traumas," which are self-destructive acts.

We can see in Elias's and Claudia's story how loss traumas may manifest in children and adolescents. Junito experiences ongoing loss trauma associated with the parental separation that initially occurred when he was 6 years old and culminated in his reunification with his biological parents again when he was almost 14, after his grandmother, the significant caretaker during his latency years, died of cancer. Junito, at an early age, is faced with multiple losses. He experiences the intense loss related to the early separation with his parents, then the loss of his primary caregiver (grandmother), both of which are later layered with the loss of friends, loss of academic and place attachment and loss of country, and loss of language and other culturally familiar pieces of his life, when he makes the transition to the United States. These cumulative losses suggest that Junito is at risk for developing trauma-related symptoms, which may be exacerbated by grief reactions. At age 14, Junito is also struggling with his own identity formation, which is intensified by entering into a new family system and cultural world. In addition, family role changes occur at the same time Junito is trying to solidify role commitments related to friends and school. Junito is suddenly responsible for taking care of his younger sisters, whom he had not previously met, simultaneously with the dramatic loss of his grandmother's caretaking role. He is being asked to be a caretaker while perhaps feeling abandoned by others who were charged with caring for him.

Traumatic stress can lead to **disorders of extreme stress** (DES), which is the focus of this chapter. Van der Kolk, Hopper, and Osterman (2001) and Van der Kolk, Roth, Pelcovitz, Sunday, and Spinazzola (2005) at the Trauma Center in Boston define DES as impairment in six areas of functioning, to include disruption in affect regulation, attention, self-perception, interpersonal relationships, meaning schemas, and **somatization**. People with DES often have experienced chronic and intense traumatic events such as physical and sexual assaults and natural disasters or have witnessed intimate and/or community violence. Abused children, people living in families with domestic violence, refugees, and people who have experienced physical trauma all *may* develop DES.

Although **posttraumatic stress disorder (PTSD)** is not a necessary precondition for a DES diagnosis, both diagnoses share common factors. Two commonalities between DES and PTSD are intense avoidance and suppression of trauma-related memories (often through chronic substance abuse) with accompanying numbing and affect constriction and the predominant use of **dissociation** (a detachment of the mind from one's emotions and/or body) to cope. PTSD symptomatology typically emerges from experiencing an event where human physical safety is compromised and fear and helplessness are central organizing emotions. PTSD symptomatology includes a reexperiencing of the traumatic event, avoidance of trauma reminders, lack of pleasure and detachment, and often includes hyperarousal that interferes with sleeping and concentration. The specific diagnostic criteria for PTSD as found in the *Diagnostic and Statistical Manual of Mental Disorders, Fourth Edition (DSM-IV*; American Psychiatric Association [APA], 2000, pp. 467–468) are illustrated in Exhibit 6.1. PTSD symptoms in children manifest as agitation, impulsivity, anger expression, separation anxiety, attention problems, and mood disturbances (Foster, Kuperminc, & Price, 2004).

In summary, the three main domains characteristic of PTSD, which is a disorder that may or may not result from extreme stress (traumatic) experiences, are intrusive reexperiencing, avoidance of trauma stimuli, and physical hyperarousal and intense reactivity.

Category	Specific Criteria
A The person has been exposed to a traumatic event in which both of the following were present:	1. The person experienced, witnessed, or was confronted with an event or events that involved actual or threatened death or serious injury or a threat to the physical integrity of self or others. 2. The person's response involved intense fear, helplessness, or horror.
B The traumatic event is persistently reexperienced in one (or more) of the following ways:	1. Recurrent and intrusive distressing recollections of the event, including images, thoughts, or perceptions 2. Recurrent distressing dreams of the event 3. Acting or feeling as if the traumatic event were recurring (includes a sense of reliving the experience, illusions, hallucinations, and dissociative flashback episodes, including those that occur on awakening or when intoxicated) 4. Intense psychological distress at exposure to internal or external cues that symbolize or resemble an aspect of the traumatic event 5. Physiological reactivity on exposure to internal or external cues that symbolize or resemble an aspect of the traumatic event
C Persistent avoidance of stimuli associated with the trauma and numbing of general responsiveness (not present before the trauma), as indicated by three (or more) of the following:	1. Efforts to avoid thoughts, feelings, or conversations associated with the trauma 2. Efforts to avoid activities, places, or people that arouse recollections of the trauma 3. Inability to recall an important aspect of the trauma 4. Markedly diminished interest or participation in significant activities 5. Feeling of detachment or estrangement from others 6. Restricted range of affect (e.g., unable to have loving feelings) 7. Sense of a foreshortened future (e.g., does not expect to have a career, marriage, children, or a normal life span)
D Persistent symptoms of increased arousal (not present before the trauma), as indicated by two (or more) of the following:	1. Difficulty falling or staying asleep 2. Irritability or outbursts of anger 3. Difficulty concentrating 4. Hypervigilance 5. Exaggerated startle response
E Duration of the disturbance (symptoms in Category A, B, C, D) is more than 1 month	
F The disturbance causes clinically significant distress or impairment in social, occupational, or other important areas of functioning	

Exhibit 6.1   *DSM-IV* Diagnostic Criteria for Posttraumatic Stress Disorder

SOURCE: Reprinted with permission from the *Diagnostic and Statistical Manual of Mental Disorders, Fourth Edition, Text Revision*, copyright © 2000, American Psychiatric Association.

Patterns of Occurrence _____

Some estimates suggest that approximately 21%–39% of adults report having experienced at least one traumatic event in their lives (e.g., victim of crime, accidents, natural disasters; Webb, 2004a), while others estimate the number to be over half of the U.S. population (50% to 60%), with only 5%-10% developing PTSD (Ozer, Best, Lipsey, & Weiss, 2003). Others estimate that PTSD develops in about 25% of individuals who have been exposed to extreme stress (Perrin, Smith, & Yule, 2000). Between 5% and 35% of refugees have experienced torture (Baker, 1992), with many living as immigrant survivors in the United States without coming to the attention of the formal mental health system. Other studies have shown that half of refugees seeking political asylum have PTSD (Cervantes, Salgado de Snyder, & Padilla, 1989). Estimates suggest that up to 70% of Southeast Asian refugees who are in the mental health care system are diagnosed with PTSD, and one third to two thirds of refugees from Central America have the disorder (USDHHS, 2001a). African Americans are more likely to be exposed to violence as compared to whites, regardless of age, with one quarter of black youth developing PTSD after violence exposure. Native American Indians are twice as likely as the general population to be victims of violence, with over one fifth (22%) experiencing PTSD (USDHHS, 2001a). A recent meta-analysis showed that the kinds of traumas males are most likely to experience include physical assaults, accidents, and combat-related traumas, while it is more likely that females will experience sexual traumas (Tolin & Foa, 2002).

The *National Comorbidity Study* (Kessler, Sonnega, Bromet, Hughes, & Nelson, 1995) shows that the rate of occurrence of PTSD in the general population is 7.8%, with 84% of people with PTSD reporting another mental health condition occurring at some point in their lives. The most consistent co-occurring disorders with PTSD include substance abuse, anxiety disorders, and depression. About one third (34.5%) of males and one quarter (26.9%) of women who have PTSD will also abuse or be dependent on drugs during their lives as compared to 15.1% of men and 7.6% of women without this diagnosis (Kessler et al., 1995). For men with PTSD, the highest prevalence of co-occurring disorders is alcohol abuse, depression, conduct disorder, and drug abuse. Women with PTSD show the highest co-occurring disorder prevalence with depression, anxiety disorders, alcohol abuse, and drug abuse (Kessler et al., 1995).

The prevalence of PTSD in adolescence is 6.3% in non-treatment-seeking adolescents living in the community as compared to a PTSD diagnosis of 19.2% in adolescents seeking help for substance dependence (Deykin & Buka, 1997; Giaconia et al., 1995). Prognosis is most problematic when PTSD occurs during early childhood or adolescence. In a large longitudinal study of young adults, researchers found PTSD was associated with a significant increased risk of drug abuse and dependence (Chilcoat & Breslau, 1998).

In terms of occupational breakdown of PTSD prevalence rates, some estimates show rates of 7% in law enforcement populations with symptom severity contingent upon extent of exposure to the violence and whether the violence resulted in a child's death or the death of a colleague (Rallings, 2002). And studies show that 9% of emergency medical service personnel exhibit psychiatric symptoms related to their work (Stamm, 1997). As is true in the general population, increased exposure to the traumatic experience is associated with increased distress in emergency services personnel, with dissociation symptoms particularly related to extent of exposure (Weiss, Marmar, Metzler, & Ronfeldt, 1995). Negative coping and stress, but not trauma history, predicted PTSD symptoms in mental health professionals, whereas stress and trauma history were both significant predictors of PTSD in law enforcement personnel (Follette, Polusny, & Milbeck, 1994).

One study found lifetime prevalence rates for psychiatric diagnoses in the military to be 40% and 1-year rates to be 21%. Military women were 5 times more likely than military men to have a PTSD diagnosis, with rape as the predominant trauma in half of those women (Hourani & Yuan, 1999). Other studies have found that military personnel have higher premilitary rates of trauma than community samples, with the physical, interpersonal, and environmental stressors that come with being in the military adding to the total stress burden that military personnel face when they experience trauma during active duty (Whealin, Morgan, & Hazlett, 2001). For additional reading on occupational differences in exposure and response to traumatic stress, see Violanti and Paton (1996).

The next sections in this chapter examine theories that attempt to explain the development of DES and/or PTSD following the experiencing of traumatic stress, as well as the biopsychosocial and spiritual risk factors that predict the development of DES and PTSD symptomatology and the protective factors that help to mitigate the risks after exposure to traumatic stress.

Theories of Causation

A number of theories across multiple dimensions have been proposed to explain disorders of traumatic stress. They are presented below and summarized in Exhibit 6.2.

Interpersonal Neurobiology

Interpersonal neurobiology (Siegel, 2001; Solomon & Siegel, 2003) is an emerging theoretical framework that combines attachment theory and cognitive neuroscience research, proposing that there is interdependence between the brain and interpersonal relationships that influences the developing mind. The environment and its associated relational experiences "get into the brain" and lead to functional and structural changes. Researchers continue to examine the plasticity of the human brain, with science demonstrating that new neurons and new neuronal connections can develop throughout the life course through relationships (Siegel, 2001). The interpersonal neurobiology literature suggests that relationships to caregivers, family, and community are the organizing foundation for internal (brain, mind, and body) regulation and for mental health.

	Tenets	Representative Citations
Interpersonal Neurobiology	Brain changes result from attachment relationships. Trauma that disrupts attachment processes also disrupts brain functioning and self-regulation capacity.	Siegel, 2001; Solomon & Siegel, 2003
Dual Representation Theory	Memory is encoded in two capacities— as verbally accessible memory (VAM) and as situationally accessible memory (SAM). Trauma memories may be encoded as sensory material, with much of the experience inaccessible to verbal retrieval.	Brewin, 2001, 2003; Brewin, Dagleish, & Joseph, 1996.
Psychodynamic Theory	Trauma impairs self-system functioning and ego capacity, often resulting in the use of primitive defenses and in dissociative symptomotology.	Lindy & Wilson, 2001
Cognitive-Behavioral Theory	Beliefs, emotions and behavior are interdependent, and trauma disrupts beliefs about the self and world, therefore affecting emotions and subsequent behavioral response.	Zoellner, Fitzgibbons & Foa, 2001
Constructivist Self-Development Theory	Cognitive schemas are distorted by the trauma experience (e.g., around trust, safety) and need to be restored.	McCann & Pearlman, 1990; Pearlman & Saakvitne, 1995
Social Disorganization Theory	There is a high risk of violence exposure and subsequent trauma reactions in communities with a deteriorating infrastructure.	Wilson, 1987b, 1996

Exhibit 6.2   Theoretical Explanations of Disorders of Traumatic Stress

Specifically, the orbitofrontal cortex may be affected as a result of trauma. The **orbitofrontal cortex** is an integrative brain structure that facilitates linkages between the limbic/emotional structures and higher-order cortical structures. It is responsible for adaptive capacities such as affect regulation (Schore, 1994), social cognition, self-awareness, and response flexibility (Solomon & Siegel, 2003) and is developed through interpersonal attachment processes. These adaptive capacities are thought to be developed through "contingent communication" patterns (sender-receiver match) and relational attunement (Siegel, 2003). Trauma can disrupt the attachment process by decreasing the opportunities for contingent communication and thus can impair relationship formation and the brain structures that rely on such relationships. Early childhood trauma can impact self-awareness even before cognitively conscious memory structures are developed (Solomon & Siegel, 2003), and research has shown that PTSD may involve problems in orbitofrontal cortex functioning (Bremner, 2005).

Disorders of extreme stress develop from intense and/or chronic stress exposure, partic-ularly from interpersonal trauma, and interpersonal traumatic experiences are more likely than other types of trauma to lead to symptom development (Van der Kolk et al., 2001).

Dual Representation Theory

Dual representation theory (Brewin, 2001, 2003; Brewin et al., 1996) has become a well-developed theoretical framework for understanding PTSD, positing that there are two memory systems that process experience: (1) the declarative or explicit system and (2) the nondeclarative or implicit system. Each develops and functions quite differently. Explicit or or **declarative memory**, is verbally accessible memory (VAM) with conscious recall and is dependent on the frontal lobe and **hippocampus** (the brain structure responsible for factual memory and putting experience into appropriate time and place context and for the conscious recall of facts and events associated with memory). This type of memory accounts for factual and autobiographical memories and places events, feelings, and sequencing in context. Episodic memory, characterized by self-knowing processes and narrative coherence (self across time, past, present, future), requires hippocampal activa-tion (Brewin, 2001, 2003). Implicit **nondeclarative memory**, is situationally accesible memory (SAM), does not require conscious processing and is independent of the hip-pocampus or other structures of the executive frontal lobe. This type of memory is sensory based (e.g., images, auditory, and physical sensations), with no verbally or cognitively accessible material. Dual representation suggests that traumatic experiences disrupt the way information is processed, such that the trauma is not verbally encoded but is processed as sensory data, rather than cognitively conscious information. Therefore, the theory suggests that traumatic symptoms, such as flashbacks and physiological responses to trauma reminders, are caused by this distinct way trauma information is processed.

Psychodynamic Theory

A psychodynamic understanding of trauma focuses on the intrapsychic structures impacted by the traumatic experience, suggesting that primitive defenses, such as dissoci-ation, denial, and somatization, develop in response to the trauma on the self that causes internal self-system disorganization and ego impairment (Lindy & Wilson, 2001). Thus, PTSD develops from self-system impairment and problems in affect regulation, in a con-text where the individual's sensory modalities are all on high alert (Lindy & Wilson, 2001). One's ego capacity for emotional awareness and affect modulation are disrupted, and the helping professional then becomes the container for these strong emotions, with the goal of assisting the individual to develop or redevelop self-soothing capacities that have been compromised by the trauma (Lindy & Wilson, 2001). In other words, the helping relationship itself becomes a medium for modeling new ways of handling strong emotions to ultimately strengthen a person's core coping capacity (i.e., developing "ego strength"). From a psychodynamic orientation, clients may engage in what looks like risky behaviors (e.g., putting oneself back in environments or relational situations that mimic the original trauma event) as an unconscious attempt to regain mastery over the original trauma experience. The goal in work with such clients is to begin to bring such experiences back into awareness and to model more adaptive strategies to deal with life's challenges in a way that does not trigger a regression back to earlier maladaptive behavioral responses.

Cognitive-Behavioral Theory

Cognitive-behavioral theory focuses on the interdependencies between events, thoughts, emotions, and behaviors, suggesting that trauma may change core schemas that lead to rigid beliefs about the self and world (Zoellner et al., 2001). Behavioral consequences related to trauma experiences result from these distorted beliefs that may be developmentally prescribed. For example, a common reaction to trauma by younger children in an early egocentric stage of cognitive development is self-blame. Self-blame attributions may lead to feelings of helplessness and depression that may, in turn, lead to social and academic withdrawal. A client's beliefs about the predictability and safety of the world, and beliefs about one's own ability to control life circumstances, may be changed after trauma. Clients may generalize these beliefs to other areas of their lives and subsequently may lose confidence in making seemingly simple and unrelated daily decisions (e.g., establishing appropriate interpersonal boundaries, assessing environmental safety from social context cues).

Constructivist Self-Development Theory

Constructivist self-development theory (CSDT) draws from cognitive-constructivism, social learning theory, developmental theory, and psychodynamic theory, proposing that people construct meaning about the traumatic experience that then becomes their reality (McCann & Pearlman, 1990; Pearlman & Saakvitne, 1995; Saakvitne, Gamble, Pearlman, & Tabor Lev, 2000). A person's developmental stage is critical to assess because the developmental tasks a person faces will influence derived meaning systems and adaptive capacity. CSDT seeks to restore more functional cognitive schemas out of the ones disrupted by the trauma experience, with schemas organized around themes of safety, trust, esteem, intimacy, and control.

Social Disorganization Theory

Social disorganization occurs within a community when the community infrastructure and its resources diminish in the presence of structural changes such as resident retreat, increasing crime, and business withdrawal. Resultant decreased socioeconomic heterogeneity and community marginalization and detachment from mainstream institutions (e.g., from vibrant businesses, banks, health care systems) leads to a problematic macro infrastructure and the development of micro behaviors, or what William Julius Wilson refers to as "rational" responses to destructive and deteriorating community conditions. Social disorganization occurs at multiple levels. Simultaneous to the downward socioeconomic status (SES) compression and middle income flight that is often found in communities with high violence exposure, individuals within such communities are impacted by the social disorganization, resulting in micro-level self-system organizational impairments that may reflect the larger macro conditions (see Wilson, 1987b, 1996). As Junito's story continues to unfold, we might begin to wonder how the macro structural elements of the neighborhood and community where he lives are impacting the longer-term developmental and behavioral outcomes for Junito (e.g., his academic disengagement and his growing involvement in drug dealing and gang activity).

Multidimensional Risk and Protection

Biological Risk and Protection

The biological risk and protection literature has grown rapidly and substantially in recent years and offers significant advancements to our understanding of how trauma affects biological structure and functioning, often leading to DES and/or PTSD (see summary of biological risk and protection factors in Exhibit 6.3). Studies have found pronounced differences in hemispheric brain functioning and integration in people who have experienced trauma compared to those who have not experienced trauma. Individuals with childhood maltreatment histories showed significant differences in left hemisphere frontal lobe problems but not in right-sided problems, suggesting that childhood abuse is associated with problems in left hemisphere development (Teicher et al., 1997). When asked to retrieve a "neutral" (nontrauma) memory, adults with trauma histories showed predominant left hemisphere processing, whereas when asked to retrieve a trauma memory, right hemisphere processing dominated (Schiffer, Teicher, & Papanicolau, 1995). Trauma triggers tend to activate the right hemisphere limbic system, but not the left, in people with PTSD (Rauch et al., 1996). In addition, childhood trauma is associated with problems in right-left hemispheric integration, with studies showing that children with histories of abuse or neglect had a 23%–31% decrease in the corpus callosum (a brain integrative structure) as compared to children without such histories. Interestingly, the researchers found significant gender differences, with child neglect affecting more regional diminution of the corpus callosum in boys and sexual abuse affecting size reduction in girls (Teicher, 2002; Teicher et al., 1997).

Traumatic events can also cause impairment in the body's chemical regulation. "Early life events that increase stress reactivity result in greater exposure to stress hormones and thus greater vulnerability for stress-induced illness over the lifespan" (Francis & Meaney, 2002, p. 765). This can impact the developing neural systems that regulate stress response. For example, early childhood physical or sexual abuse can cause changes in corticotropin-releasing hormone (CRH) that leads to poor psychosocial functioning and mental health risk, such as the onset of major depression, in adulthood (Claes, 2004). Gamma-aminobutyric acid (GABA), a chemical that facilitates emotional regulatory control and self-soothing capacity, may be impaired in abused children (Teicher, 2002). Excessive cortisol production, as is the case in extreme stress conditions, can increase the risk of neuronal death. One study, examining the effects of trauma on military populations,

	Risk Factors	Protective Factors
Biological	• Right-left hemispheric disintegration • Changes in stress hormones • Decreased GABA	• Neuropeptide-Y • Strong neuronal activity in hippocampus and prefrontal cortex
Psychological	• Trust impairment • Decreased ability to self-soothe • Attention deficits • Depression • Anger • Low self-efficacy • External locus of control	• Internal locus of control • Coherence in sense of self across time • Coping self-efficacy
Social	• Weak social support network • Community violence • Lack of social bonding/isolation	• Cultural rituals • Culture-specific roles and continuity in roles • Collective support
Spiritual	• Isolation • Lack of hope • Despair	• Connection to higher power • Sense of belonging in religious institution • Hope • Sense of community • Finding meaning in the trauma

Exhibit 6.3   Biological, Psychological, Social, and Spiritual Risk and Protective Factors for Disorders of Traumatic Stress

found that neuropeptide-Y (NYP), which often exists in concentration levels in the **amygdala** (a brain structure that is responsible for assigning "emotional value" to an event), served as a protective factor against distressing symptoms related to trauma exposure in soldiers undergoing acute stress conditions (Morgan et al., 2000). Other military-based population studies have found that perception of stress is directly related to physical stress response (i.e., hypothalamic-pituitary-adrenal [HPA] activation; Whealin et al., 2001).

However, although neural connections can be destroyed by stress hormones, the brain remains plastic and amenable to modification and structural reorganization throughout the life course. Researchers are beginning to conduct studies that test the impact of psychosocial and pharmacological interventions on brain change.

Studies have found smaller hippocampi in people with PTSD. This has a significant impact on declarative (cognitively conscious) information processing and may increase responsivity to sensory-based stimuli related to the trauma, without the requisite ability to cognitively regulate such responses (Siegel, 2001). The hippocampus develops at around 18 months, so if a high-stress environment curtails development of this structure during this critical period of development, the child may have reduced regulatory capacity to contextualize and cognitively control emotions related to the stress event (Siegel, 2001; Teicher, 2002).

Traumatic experience representations may be stored in multiple parts of the brain as "engrams" or mental images. "Remembering is not merely the reactivation of an old engram; it is the construction of a new neural net profile with features of the old engram and elements of memory from other experiences as well as influences from the present state of mind" (Siegel, 2001, p. 1000). Thus, the most recent social neuroscientific evidence suggests that trauma, which deactivates the cognitive processing capacities in the brain (e.g., frontal lobe regions and hippocampus), may relegate memory processing to implicit sensory representations that may later be activated by sensory stimuli that become sensory responses, not under conscious cognitive control.

Trauma may create memories that are not amenable to integration and that are left as sensory fragments. Studies have found that narrative memory was incomplete or fragmented for 41% of children who had been severely abused (Burgess, Hartman, & Baker, 1995) and that trauma memories are often reactivated by sensory input. Roe and Schwartz (1996) found that 60% of their abused inpatients reported their first recovered memory in the form of a somatosensory flashback, and Cameron (1996) found sexual abuse survivors to have prominent sensory memories, with narrative coherence only coming with later therapeutic work.

One recent study by Gil, Caspi, Ben-Ari, Koren, and Klein (2005) found that explicit memory of the traumatic event, as measured by verbal recall of the trauma details, in a sample of traumatic brain-injured patients was related to increased PTSD symptomotology at 6-month follow-up (23% with the memory showed PTSD at follow-up versus 6% without any verbalized memory). These results, with a traumatic brain-injured population, suggest that there could be harmful effects associated with the presence of explicit memory of the physical trauma experience. These findings could also suggest that explicit recollection only, without concomitant implicit processing work, may contribute to an exacerbation of PTSD symptomotology. Although these researchers did not employ implicit memory measures, additional investigation of the differential impact between explicit and implicit memory, and their interaction, on PTSD symptom development is of significant clinical interest for directing psychosocial treatment interventions.

Thus, traumatic experience occurring through person-in-environment transactions across the life course can alter the "neural network profile," its synaptic connections and communication patterns, which has profound implications on a developing person's cognitive, emotional, behavioral, and interpersonal functioning.

Psychological Risk and Protection

A number of psychological risk and protection factors have been identified in the research literature on traumatic stress disorders (see summary in Exhibit 6.3). McCann and Pearlman (1990) conceptualize traumatization through a developmental framework (CSDT) that is influenced by self and other constructions related to the trauma experience. Perceptual disturbances of the self and severe trust impairment are prominent and may be a risk factor for later problematic interpersonal relationships, poor boundaries, underdeveloped safety plans, and limited bodily awareness. People who experience extreme trauma may become easily overwhelmed and may not have the **self-regulation capacities** necessary to self-soothe or may find destructive means to attempt self-soothing behaviors. Other consequences include difficulty with anger management, focal attention deficits, and engaging in risk-taking behaviors. Generally, individuals who are more vulnerable to PTSD symptom development after exposure to extreme stress are those with previous trauma histories, deficits in psychological adjustment prior to the trauma exposure, and those for whom the trauma was life-threatening and who experience immediate dissociation after the traumatic event (Ozer et al., 2003).

For example, depression and anger were found to be significant risk factors for a continuing course of PTSD symptomotology in a longitudinal study of Vietnam veterans (Koenen, Stellman, Stellman, & Sommer, 2003). And in their study of international peacekeeping military personnel who served on missions in Cambodia, Lebanon, and the former Yugoslavia, Dirkzwager, Bramsen, and Van der Ploeg (2005) found that PTSD symptoms were related to higher levels of traumatic exposure during deployment, as well as to subjective appraisals of the traumatic situation, such as feeling a sense of diminished control and experiencing powerlessness over a mission perceived as meaningless and yet also life-threatening. A prospective study of new firefighters found that pretraining baselines of high hostility and low self-efficacy accounted for 42% of the variance in PTSD after 2 years of firefighting (Heinrichs et al., 2005). Low perceived self-efficacy, or external locus of control, has also been found to be a risk factor for PTSD among military personnel (Ginzburg, Solomon, Dekel, & Neria, 2003) and in children and adolescents who experienced an industrial fire (March, Amaya-Jackson, Terry, & Costanzo, 1997).

Psychological impairment related to the trauma experience, such as poor concentration, can be a risk factor for social impairment if attention deficits cause school disengagement and formation of problematic peer relations. We see Junito struggling with some of these risks. He remembers much grief and loneliness associated with parts of his early childhood immediately after his parents' departure. This grief and loneliness that he was able to manage through new relationships is now activated again by his current cultural transitioning, impacting his academic engagement and suggesting that the reactivation of earlier trauma can occur at a later time in development.

The importance of a person's developmental level at the time the trauma occurs, and the nature or circumstances and characteristics (e.g., nature of relationship with the perpetrator[s], timing of the event) around the traumatic event, are important to assess. Age and developmental stage may influence the way a person will be able to adapt, because adaptational opportunities and coping resources may be developmentally sensitive (Solomon & Siegel, 2003).

Dissociation is frequently associated with PTSD and is characterized by a disintegration in experience, where the trauma exists apart from the rest of consciousness. Disintegrated pieces of the trauma narrative may take the form of sensory information (e.g., visual, auditory, somatic, emotional) and, as such, may not be captured verbally. Narrative organization (ability to successfully piece together elements of the trauma experience into a whole and to integrate the trauma experience into one's larger life narrative) is associated with less trauma-related psychopathology (Foa, Molnar, & Cashman, 1995). In addition, increased arousal levels can disrupt one's cognitive meaning system, and individuals may begin to lose a sense that life has purpose.

Cicchetti and Rogosch (1997) found different predictors of adaptive outcomes in maltreated versus nonmaltreated children, where supportive relationships and ego resilience contributed to positive outcomes in nonmaltreated children, and self-system processes, ego resilience, and ego overcontrol were protective factors related to resilient functioning in maltreated children. This adds to the fundamental notion that disruptions in self-organization (e.g., disintegration of trauma narrative, poor regulatory capacity) is a signature of trauma's impact and that self-system preservation opportunities (e.g., shoring up emotional management skills, developing coherent self-constructions linking past, present, and future selves, and nurturing supportive interpersonal relationships pre- and posttrauma) serve as important protective factors to psychological trauma-related outcomes. Although self-efficacy and locus of control have been more pointedly studied as risk factors rather than as protective factors to buffer against traumatic stress disorders, there is beginning suggestion in the research literature that internal locus of control and coping efficacy serve as buffers when experiencing traumatic stress (Langley & Jones, 2005; March et al., 1997).

We see significant ego strength in Elias's resourcefulness and determination in seeking out a better life for his family, his perseverance in acting on these values, and his problem-solving abilities when faced with challenges and obstacles along the way. Elias expects the same ego strength from his son, Junito, and he recommends working at the mechanic shop, rather than school, as a way to learn these self-determination skills. As social workers, it is important to examine the potential unintended consequences (e.g., in this case, Junito's disengagement from school) that may go along with a family's solutions to adapt to adversity and to help families creatively make decisions that embrace and expand upon such existing strengths.

Social Risk and Protection

Social arrangements can produce both risk and protection following exposure to traumatic stress (see Exhibit 6.3 for a summary of social risk and protection factors). Some scholars in the field of trauma work suggest that the individually based clinical framework that comes from the psychiatric model of PTSD is not enough when working with trauma survivors, arguing that treatment needs to be conducted from a larger community context (Farwell & Cole, 2002). Given that a consequence of violence is an erosion of collective community connections and cohesion and the emergence of unreliable social institutions (particularly seen after widespread political violence in unstable regions around the globe), intervention at the community level and mobilization of social supports is critical (DeVries, 1996; Farwell & Cole, 2002). DeVries (1996) discusses the consequence of violence on a larger societal level, suggesting that resulting trauma responses are not only individual experiences but become integrated and embedded into the larger community story. Advocated is the need to acknowledge and address the larger social suffering that contextualizes the trauma experience. A grieving community can work together to restore social networks and to creatively restore a sense of justice at the sociopolitical or economic level.

Culture provides for a context within which the trauma takes place, whereby historical continuity and culture-specific social roles can help members navigate through a collective trauma. However, severe traumatic experiences at the societal level, such as natural disasters and genocide arising from civil war, lead not only to individual suffering and symptoms but also to collective loss of cultural rituals and loss of a sense of place. Previous roles and statuses change and no longer provide order and predictability. The resultant cultural disorganization severs access to structure and to collective support, limiting opportunities to collectively participate in the grief process. Individuals are splintered from the whole and left to suffer and grieve on their own or in smaller groups at the same time the traumatic impact may be ongoing and unrelenting (DeVries, 1996). This has been tragically witnessed in the current humanitarian crisis in the Darfur region at the Sudanese and Chad border in Africa caused by the widespread violence and mass murders, rapes, and burning that have killed more than 200,000 people and displaced 2 million more.

Therefore, it is critical to examine not just how the trauma has impacted individual development in isolation, or as in the Darfur crisis how it has impacted individual daily survival, but also how the trauma has influenced, altered, or changed the larger cultural structure, and, reciprocally, how a change in a culture's resources, meanings, roles, and rituals further influence the consequences and opportunities to move beyond the trauma experience at the individual level. "The avenues of vulnerability resulting from trauma follow the routes vacated by culture: Paranoia substitutes for trust; aggression replaces nurturance and support; identity confusion or a negative identity substitutes for a positive identity. Social bonding becomes a regression to nationalism and tribalism, thereby permitting individuals to deny the experienced losses or to defend themselves against expected additional losses" (DeVries, 1996, p. 408). After trauma, order is necessary not only for individual emotional regulation but for order in social relationships and cultural reconnection.

As has been discussed, trauma can disrupt social relationships and attachment processes, which can impair brain structures responsible for emotional and social functioning (i.e., orbitofrontal cortex) and regulation. Attachment is universal across cultures and fundamentally functions to (a) protect and create security, (b) regulate affect and arousal, (c) facilitate affect expression and communication, and (d) provide a base for exploration (Webb, 2004a). Estimates of trauma's effect on attachment is alarming, with 80% of children who have experienced trauma showing disorganized attachment patterns (Carlson, Cicchetti, Barnett, & Braunwald, 1989), creating, among other problems, an inability to self-soothe in the presence of even minor stressors. "Social interactions are one of the most powerful forms of experience that help shape how the brain gives rise to the mind" (Solomon & Siegel, 2003, p. 18). Neighborhood violence is associated with poor attachment, in addition to aggression and internalizing disorders in school-age children, with low levels of coparent conflict a specific protective factor for girls and a moderator of both depression and aggression (Forehand & Jones, 2003; Osofsky, 1995). However, research shows that new healthy attachment patterns can be developed, despite trauma's early effects. "Earned secure" adult attachment patterns (Roisman, Padron, Sroufe, & Egeland, 2002) are characterized by those adults who, despite traumatic childhoods, have been able to later develop coherent narratives.

A weak social support system has been found to be one of the strongest predictors that an individual will develop PTSD after trauma exposure (Brewin, Andrews, & Valentine, 2000; Ozer et al., 2003), and social support has been shown to moderate the effects of stress on health outcomes (Schmeelk-Cone & Zimmerman, 2003). For example, less community involvement and a perception of negative community attitudes toward those veterans returning from Vietnam predicted longitudinal continuation of PTSD symptomotology in a large random sample of men (Koenen et al., 2003).

Therefore, DES may increase isolation from others, with the overall traumatic impact even stronger when it occurs in the context of disrupted interpersonal relationships, creating additional risks to an individual's ability to adapt posttrauma. We can see that Elias and Claudia place strong emphasis on social connections to extended family and value a shared responsibility and commitment to providing the instrumental, and perhaps emotional, support needed of various family members across the life course. However, as Junito arrives in the United States, these relationships with Victor Manuel and Alejandra have already become strained, Claudia has become increasingly isolated, and Elias's drinking has become more problematic, further distancing family members from each other. Junito has abruptly left the warmth, protection, and familiarity of his childhood, entering into a new uncertain and relationally turbulent social climate. All of this is happening simultaneously with his own entrance into early adolescence, a time of significant physical, emotional, and interpersonal change. As Junito continues to grow as an adolescent, he struggles to carve out a social niche for himself and begins exploring ways of gaining intimacy in relationships outside the immediate family.

Spiritual Risk and Protection

Torture and other traumatic experiences often bring with them raw confrontation with faith and spirituality. Sister Dianna Ortiz's (as cited in Engstrom & Okamura, 2004) torture experiences were captured in her own search for spiritual meaning and a questioning of her faith, as she wrote, "God, I don't know who to turn to. I don't even believe in you but yet I talk to you. . . . I don't want to remember the details of this nightmare. Please, God, take away these memories" (p. 295). Spiritual crises, such as those described above, that arise from traumatic experiences may undermine relational attachment to important social support and systems (e.g., family and community). Spiritual risk and protection factors for DES are summarized in Exhibit 6.3.

The literature shows that spirituality can be a protective factor in dealing with life stress and that church provides a place of belonging, value, and acceptance, where African

American children can learn about their history and be exposed to hope and a sense of community (Haight, 1998). It is in our social work that we help our clients explore the meaning in the trauma, and it is in this collaborative work that a potentially deeper connection to others and to something beyond the self or to a higher power may occur. A spiritual-based social work practice approach with those who have experienced trauma focuses on helping the client to access inner resources and to develop a commitment to a healing process through cultivation of a contemplative attitude and a mindfulness and openness to achieving a wider consciousness of the meaning of suffering (Webb, 2004a). Hodge (2005b, p. 82) discusses the use of spiritual life maps to assess spiritual resources and to help clients in documenting spiritual turning points in their lives.

Although we do not gain much direct insight into the spiritual world of Elias and Claudia's family, we can see that Elias may have found special inner strength through his commitment to family. His current experience of "failing" his family and the pain of witnessing the struggles they are experiencing may have contributed to his drinking episodes and current spiritual depletion. It would be instructive, in further work with this family, to explore where each member gets his or her inner strength and to construct a spiritual timeline of key turning points where each individual, as well as the family as a whole, has felt more connected, more hopeful, and has experienced more faith than at the present time. This tool may lead to a concrete visualization for the family of the spiritual resources they have been able to leverage over time and may encourage discussion of current opportunities to reintroduce cognitive, affective, and behavioral manifestations of the spiritual dimension back into their lives.

Biopsychosocial-Spiritual Integration

The literature shows that it is the combination and accumulation of multidimensional risk factors across developmental time periods that mark significant risk. New research demonstrates how trauma experiences affect information processing (via the environment acting on biological and subsequent psychological dimensions) and how interpersonal relationships and social supports can help develop the neurobiological structures necessary for fostering resiliency. A consistent theme in the literature is that trauma tends to impact the integrative functions of the brain, leading to memory fragmentation, self-system disorganization, and impaired social relationships. Social workers need to examine where and how social support and new relationship opportunities might be introduced in order to effect change in these core neurobiological regions that may lead to increased adaptive capacity after trauma exposure. For example, social workers might examine how Junito's self-organizing disturbances related to loss trauma might interact with his current early adolescent developmental task of identity formation. New research initiatives that examine the permutations of cumulative risk and protective factors tracked to specific developmental time periods would profoundly enhance understanding of how and when to direct our social work interventions.

Consequences of Traumatic Stress

Primary consequences of early traumatic stress, such as childhood abuse, include depression, anxiety, attention deficit disorder, behavioral or conduct problems, and substance abuse (Foster et al., 2004; Teicher et al., 1997). And having a history of childhood abuse and neglect specifically puts individuals at risk for developing PTSD, when confronted with subsequent traumatic stressors (Bremner, Southwick, Johnson, Yehuda & Charney, 1993; Widom, 1999), because individuals are more prone to self-regulation disturbances that undermine coping capacity.

A number of physical problems have been linked to trauma experiences. Studies have found that women with chronic childhood sexual abuse have impaired immune systems and a significant increased risk for heart disease, stroke, diabetes, and cancer in adulthood. Women with childhood sexual abuse histories often have more medical problems and medical service usage than non-trauma-exposed women (Felitti et al., 1998; Foa, Keane, & Friedman, 2000; Wilson, Calhoun, & Bernat, 1999). Social work assessment, therefore, should include a very detailed account of a client's physical health status and should include referrals to appropriate medical specialists when assessment indicates additional specialized knowledge. Furthermore, the advances being made in mind-body medicine related to trauma work will be of significance to social work practitioners. Social workers will need to make a commitment to keeping up with this growing knowledge base to enhance service delivery to this client population.

Traumatic stress may set the stage for later problematic interpersonal relationships, poor boundaries, underdeveloped safety plans, and limited bodily awareness. Other consequences include difficulty with anger management, focal attention deficits, and engaging in risk-taking behaviors. Engstrom and Okamura (2004) discuss the all-encompassing nature of torture experiences that go beyond physical and psychological consequences. Torture experiences disrupt social capacity and impair workplace relationships; they erode spiritual connectedness and alienate communities.

Factors affecting trauma response are varied and include a person's age, cognitive development, personality characteristics, previous and current losses, and coping strategies (Webb, 2004a). Also, the nature of the relationship between the victim and perpetrator in interpersonal trauma, and the frequency, duration, and severity of the trauma experience (e.g., multiple vs. single occurrence), will differentially influence trauma response (Cusack, Falsetti, & De Arellano, 2002). Abe et al. (1994) found that Southeast Asian refugees with PTSD symptomotology showed more somatic symptoms, were more depressed, showed higher signs of psychopathology, were less interested in maintaining cultural ties and identity, and reported significantly more intense anger as compared to a matched group of refugees without a PTSD diagnosis. The study showed that postmigration adjustment (such as social support), rather than premigration factors, was most important in differentiating the two groups. Other studies have shown that 20% of PTSD symptoms in asylum seekers were explained by premigration factors such as earlier traumas, while 14% were explained by postmigration factors such as adjustment problems, lack of health care, and additional losses (Silove, Steel, McGarry, & Mohan, 1998). The posttrauma adjustment process may be complicated by intense grief reactions, with traumatic grief characterized by fear (Webb, 2004a). The most common symptoms found in torture survivors who have come to the United States in immigration waves escaping political upheaval and civil war (e.g., Vietnam, Cambodia, Laos, El Salvador, Guatemala) include depression, anxiety, and PTSD, along with substance abuse (Wilson, Friedman, & Lindy, 2001).

Studies of Cambodian adolescent refugees show that while depressive symptomotology tended to abate over time, PTSD symptomotology persisted (Kinzie, 2001). Females are more likely to develop PTSD symptoms as compared to males after experiencing trauma (Breslau et al., 1998; Horowitz, Weine, & Jekel, 1995; Tolin & Foa, 2002), to have symptoms precipitated by sexual or physical abuse, and to have more drug-related problems associated with PTSD symptomatology as compared to men (Stewart, Ouimette, & Brown, 2002). Girls who are victims of violence are more likely to report psychological symptoms than boys and are more likely to present with internalizing symptoms, while boys are more likely to present with externalizing symptoms (Horowitz et al., 1995). Adolescents with a trauma history (e.g., assaults, witnessing violence) and those with PTSD are at increased risk for substance abuse (Kilpatrick et al., 2000). Other co-occurring disorders in children with PTSD include attention deficit and conduct disorders (Saigh, Yasik, Sack, & Koplewicz, 1999), and children who present with PTSD symptoms will most frequently show reexperiencing problems (Fitzpatrick & Boldizar, 1993).

Ways of Coping

Emotional processing theory posits that both cognitive content and cognitive processing are important in PTSD development (Foa & Kozak, 1986), with adaptive cognitive coping buffering the onset and severity of PTSD symptomatology after trauma exposure. Other studies show that dissociation after the trauma experience is the most significant and profound predictor of PTSD symptomatology (see Ozer et al., 2003). Some researchers have found that *initial* rather than *delayed* emotional reactivity promotes quicker recovery from PTSD (Zoellner et al., 2001). Associations between the trauma stimulus, trauma response, and meaning attributed to the trauma contribute to adaptive or maladaptive coping, suggesting that how a person copes will be influenced by pretrauma schemas and posttrauma reactions from others. Other studies have found that changes in the problematic cognitions related to the trauma (e.g., attributions of self-blame) improve overall psychosocial functioning and that cognitive coping is an important contributor to well-being after trauma (Ehlers, Clark, Hackmann, McManus, & Fennell, 2005). More successful cognitive coping, in part, comes from not generalizing the beliefs associated with the trauma event to other global areas of one's life (Tolin & Foa, 2002).

Gustafsson, Persson, and Amilon (2002) identified 11 cognitive coping strategies that individuals who have experienced physical trauma (traumatic hand injury) employed in early recovery: comparing the trauma with a worse situation, positive thinking, relying on personal capacity, keeping the problem at a distance, distracting attention by keeping cognitively busy, accepting the situation and making do, seeking emotional and instrumental social support, maintaining control, creative problem solving to figure out ways to manage new difficulties, pain relief through medicine as well as through cognitive distraction, and active processing of the trauma experience through analysis and explanation (p. 597). While their study did not examine the effectiveness of these various cognitive strategies in practice, it offers some preliminary insight into what kinds of cognitive strategies might be employed in the early stages of recovery from a physical trauma.

Work has been done on how religious/spiritual coping helps individuals manage traumatic stress. Pargament and colleagues (Pargament, Smith, Koenig, & Perez, 1998) describe positive (e.g., secure attachment to God, belief that life has meaning, spiritual connectedness, seeking spiritual guidance, religious reappraisals) and negative (e.g., punishing appraisals related to God, individual rather than connected coping, spiritual discontent) patterns of religious coping methods, with their work showing that people who have experienced a serious trauma or who are coping with a serious medical illness more frequently use positive religious coping methods as compared to negative methods, although there is a tendency to combine strategies (p. 712). Positive coping strategies were associated with reduced psychological distress and improved psychological and spiritual functioning, while the negative strategies were related to poor emotional health.

Utilizing the Pargament et al. (1998) theoretical framework, Ai, Peterson, and Huang (2003) examined the effects of religious/spiritual coping strategies on the cognitive resources (attitudes) of Muslim refugees from Kosovo and Bosnia who have resettled in the United States. Their research showed that increased hope, a salutary attitudinal resource, was associated with decreased use of negative religious/spiritual coping strategies, while optimism was associated with increased positive religious/spiritual coping strategies. In addition, those individuals who exhibited more intense trauma symptoms tended to use more negative coping strategies that ultimately decreased their sense of hope.

Action-oriented approach strategies, such as problem solving and asking for social support from others, moderate the relationship between violence exposure and PTSD symptomatology in children (Kliewer, Lepore, Oskin, & Johnson, 1998), with less active coping strategies employed by adolescents who are under chronic stress (Schmeelk-Cone & Zimmerman, 2003). In their sample of African American inner-city youth, Dempsey, Overstreet, and Moely (2000) found that cognitive reexperiencing PTSD symptomatology *increased* when using "cognitive distraction," an avoidant coping strategy (i.e., thinking about something more positive), for those with high trauma exposure, whereas cognitive distraction seemed to *decrease* reexperiencing symptomatology in the low exposure group. Conversely, use of an avoidant behavioral coping strategy (i.e., withdrawal, avoidance of activity) was associated with lower levels of PTSD arousal (e.g., decreased startle response; decreased **hypervigilance**, which is a state of intense preoccupation with surrounding stimuli and a heightened alertness to one's environment) in the high trauma exposure group but was associated with higher arousal symptoms in the low trauma exposure group.

Therefore, this literature, along with the biological risk and protection literature, suggests that an integrated treatment protocol that allows for cognitive processing, but in the context of behavioral (sensory-somatic) control, may be particularly indicated for individuals with high trauma exposure. Thus, a variety of coping strategies need to be taught and implemented in order to achieve successful adaptation, depending on trauma exposure severity. Implementation of cognitive avoidance strategies with lower, but not higher, levels of trauma severity, and behavioral avoidance at higher, but not lower, levels of trauma severity, may improve functioning status after trauma. This research also suggests that behavioral avoidance strategies may be more helpful when the stressor is highly uncontrollable and that cognitive distraction strategies may be less beneficial when stressors are more severe as the individual may need to process, not cognitively avoid, the material. Exhibit 6.4 provides an overview of strategies used to cope with traumatic stress.

Cognitive	Spiritual	Sociocultural
Avoid generalizing beliefs related to trauma to other areas of life	Maintain belief that life has meaning	Reestablish symbolic places
Problem solve to manage new challenges	Seek spiritual guidance	Reinstate cultural rules and roles
Maintain control in aspects of life that are controllable	Increase sense of hope and optimism	Seek emotional and instrumental support
Use cognitive distraction for those with lower levels of trauma exposures and behavioral avoidance for higher levels of trauma exposure	Utilize positive, rather than punitive and negative, religious coping strategies	Connect with the larger cultural story related to the trauma as well as the individual trauma narrative

Exhibit 6.4   Strategies to Cope With Trauma

Social Justice Issues

Early stressful experiences, such as living in a violent community or being exposed to chronic interpersonal violence, impacts the growth of the brain and the mind, which are particularly vulnerable at sensitive developmental periods when critical areas of brain growth are scheduled to occur. The differentiation of the brain to form specialized functions occurs early in life. This process is dependent upon interpersonal experiences that provide sensory stimulation to facilitate brain growth in early life, with significant pruning of neurons and their connections taking place later in adolescence. An important social justice concern is how developmental opportunities and access to experiences (e.g., having play activities constrained by living in a drug-infested and dangerous neighborhood) that significantly shape brain development are differentially afforded individuals by their race, ethnicity, SES, or other ascribed statuses.

Perhaps from a public health perspective, not only should differential access to and quality of mental health services be examined as indicators of health disparities, but environmental conditions and their impact should be of concern to researchers and social workers working to recognize and eliminate health disparities. Doing so might lead to important work in developing "ethnic-sensitive" interventions (Haight, 1998) at both the macro and micro levels. Disempowerment comes from "inequality of agency," with empowerment coming through a renewed ability to negotiate, control, and influence resources and information (Narayan, 2005). Becoming empowered over one's trauma experience by taking back control internally, externally, communally, and by facing the injustices that were committed, with support, can lead to enhanced sense of purpose and a deeper commitment to one's spirituality (Wilson & Moran, 1997).

Practice Implications

There are both micro and macro practice approaches in trauma work that are linked to the risk and protection literature. Exhibit 6.5 provides examples of evidence-based approaches to treating traumatic stress. First, a comprehensive assessment is critical in trauma treatment. Bessel Van der Kolk's Traumatic Antecedents Questionnaire (2006) is a 42-item self-report measure that assesses frequency and severity of exposure to traumatic and adaptive experiences in early childhood, middle childhood, adolescence, and adulthood. Eleven domains are assessed: competence, safety, neglect, separation, family secrets, emotional abuse, physical abuse, sexual abuse, witnessing trauma, other trauma (e.g., natural disaster, serious accident), and exposure to drugs and alcohol. Geographic and emotional proximity to the traumatic events and its context should be examined. Fabri (2001) suggests that clinicians become knowledgeable about the historical and current political, civil, and human rights events that have occurred in their clients' countries of origin. In addition, social workers need to work at the community level to help heal the larger distressed relationships that occur as a result of chronic stress conditions and high trauma exposure (Chambon et al., 2001), but they must also work to build on the existing strengths ready to be leveraged within the community (e.g., to identify indigenous resettlement services already operating in a community). When working cross-culturally, Kinzie (2001) notes the need to emphasize education, community, and medical referrals, and not just provide psychotherapy.

At a more micro practice level, researchers have developed treatment interventions to respond to the lack of representational integration that occurs during trauma experiences and to utilize strategies that activate, attend to, and integrate fragmented representations in the service of creating a more comprehensive narrative (Solomon & Siegel, 2003). As part of the traumatic memory inventory (TMI; van der Kolk & Fisler, 1995), questions are asked about the sensory modalities experienced during the trauma experience: for images, "What did you see?"; for sounds, "What did you hear?"; for smells, "What did you smell?";

Treatment Approach	Goals/Methods	Representative Citations
Structured Sensory Intervention for Children, Adolescents, and Parents	Combines drawing and cognitive restructuring to reduce PTSD symptoms in children and adolescents	Steele & Raider, 2001
Seeking Safety	Simultaneous treatment of substance abuse and PTSD in adult dual diagnosis populations, using cognitive-behavioral therapy (CBT) program that includes education, exposure to trauma memory, and skills training	Najavits, Weiss, & Liese (1996); Najavits, Weiss, Shaw, & Muenz (1998)
Multimodal Trauma Treatment (MMTT), now called Trauma-Focused Coping (TFC)	Group CBT modality (cognitive restructuring and behavioral exposure) administered in schools for children and adolescents who have developed PTSD from a single-incident trauma	Amaya-Jackson et al., 2003; March et al., 1997
Posttraumatic Child Therapy (PTCT)	Parson's trauma treatment model for African American, Latino, and Caucasian children experiencing urban violence traumatic stress syndrome (UVTS) that includes child and family education, emotional expression, symptom management, coping skill development, and attachment development	Parson, 1994, 1997

Exhibit 6.5   Examples of Evidence-Based Approaches to Treating Traumatic Stress

for tactile or bodily sensations, "What did you feel in your body?"; and for emotions, "What did you feel emotionally?" This information is collected to piece together how individuals initially remembered the trauma while they are most bothered by the memory and/or at the height of the reexperiencing. The TMI allows for detailed exploration of memory characteristics linked to a specific memory context.

Steele and Raider (2001) present a structured sensory intervention for traumatized children, adolescents, and parents that engages the traumatized client in a structured therapeutic drawing activity that facilitates a safe reexperiencing of the traumatic experience, development of a trauma narrative, and cognitive restructuring of the trauma narrative. Specifically, the I Feel Better Now! program for children ages 6–12 has been implemented nationally in various treatment facilities and schools. Formal empirical testing of this approach with children, and expanded work to include adolescents up to 18 years old, has shown effectiveness in reducing PTSD symptomatology. Integrated dual processing protocols have been highly touted as facilitating change by activating the relevant brain regions necessary for creating a more coherent trauma narrative (Matto, 2005a, 2005b). "Journal writing, guided imagery, and exercises for 'drawing on the right side of the brain' have proven helpful to catalyze such a new form of bilateral resonance" (Siegel,

1999, p. 237). Multimodal treatment strategies that target a variety of sensory modalities have been found to facilitate trauma narrative retrieval and new narrative coherent construction. Some believe that without a visual image to anchor an experience as belonging to its correct contextual location (in the past), traumatized individuals are prone to trauma-related sensory experiences in the present.

Lisa Najavits's Seeking Safety protocol, which has been designed to address the needs of clients with dual diagnosis (substance abuse and PTSD), has also shown much success (Najavits et al., 1996; Najavits et al., 1998). This manualized CBT program was developed through the National Institute on Drug Abuse (NIDA) Behavioral Therapies Development Program and is designed to treat both PTSD and substance abuse at the same time. The program has been successfully applied to various treatment populations such as women in prison, women veterans, and clients in substance abuse treatment facilities. Cognitive processing therapy (Resick & Schnicke, 1992), which requires educating the patient about PTSD, exposing the client to traumatic memories via structured writing exercises, and implementing cognitive therapy techniques to rework beliefs related to the trauma, has also shown to decrease PTSD symptomatology and improve psychosocial functioning.

Other types of exposure therapies, where a client is reintroduced and exposed to traumatic memories, have shown effectiveness in improving psychological functioning in PTSD patients (Zoellner et al., 2001). Imaginal exposure, which requires the client to recount details of the traumatic event to encourage emotional engagement and, therefore, narrative transformation, has been consistently shown across studies to be effective at reducing PTSD symptomatology (Foa et al., 1995). Expression of anger and fear after trauma results in quicker recovery (Zoellner et al., 2001). It appears that Junito has had little opportunity during his life course to process the anger and fear he experienced as a result of the separation trauma from his biological parents. In many Latino cultures, the good of the larger collective family unit supersedes the interests of the individual (Lum, 2003b). From this perspective, it is likely that Elias and Claudia embraced this larger family goal in their decision to separate from Junito and move to the United States while still recognizing the sacrifices required of the individual family members.

Social workers could effect change in multiple ways in addressing the traumatic stress and grief/loss reactions experienced by the Salvatierra family. A social worker might link Claudia with resources to develop skills to improve her agency and mastery in a new culture, such as linking her up with an informal networking group held at a local elementary school that teaches women English skills and educates women on accessing resources within their new culture. It would be important to examine how the intermittent domestic violence in the family, between Elias and Claudia, that began before Junito's arrival in the States but continues to sporadically persist might be influencing Junito's own sense of trust, safety, and bonding in the family and his developing identity. In addition, although Junito is at lowered risk for developing more intense trauma symptomatology, given his premigration psychological status (excelling academically, positive attachment to prosocial peer support network), we know very little about the immediate neighborhood in which Junito is currently growing up and are at least peripherally aware of the symbolic community (the gang community) to which he has been introduced. If he continues engagement in this peer community, there is a risk he will be increasingly exposed to violent acts and potentially abusive relationships. Allowing an opportunity for Junito to begin processing and giving expression to his current grief related to his grandmother's death may be beneficial in helping him develop the skills needed to regulate negative affect associated with this loss experience and may protect against an unconscious urge to work through his grief by attempting to master new traumatic experiences or to find new intimacy through gang affiliation. Finally, helping Elias to learn more productive self-regulation skills simultaneous to addressing the real structural constraints that might be impacting his employment opportunities and economic stability may offer alternatives to his anger expression within the family.

Learning Activities

1. Think of a family member, former client, or other person you know well, and write down the losses this person has experienced in his or her life (**knowledge about the case**). In your estimation, based on knowledge from this chapter, was this a "traumatic" experience and did he or she experience traumatic reactions (**general knowledge integrated with knowledge about the case**)? If yes, in what ways? If no, why would it not be characterized as traumatic, and what might have prevented the development of such trauma reactions (**general knowledge**)? Identify any significant or unique sociocultural aspects that occurred in this person's life that may have led to his or her current emotional and mental functioning after experiencing loss (**values/ethics/social justice concerns**). This assignment asked you to analyze a person whom you knew well. How do you think your own thinking, emotions, and biases from subjective experiences with this person may have influenced your analysis (**knowledge about self**)?

2. Take one character from the Salvatierra family and identify the losses and trauma reactions he or she experienced, taking into consideration the sociocultural and social and economic circumstances within which this family is embedded (**knowledge of case and values/ethics/social justice implications**). Rewrite a portion of this family member's life story to facilitate a different biopsychosocial-spiritual ending to the losses/trauma the member experienced. What area did you focus on first? Why? What areas did you leave out? Why? What ethically guided you in this direction (**knowledge of self and own thinking integrated with knowledge of case and values/ethics**)? What knowledge, from the risk/protection literature presented in this chapter, helped to inform your decisions (**general knowledge**)?

3. Imagine that you are a social worker working with the Burak family, which has just immigrated to your area from Sudan. The Buraks are a large and intact family, with an extended contingent of kin successfully able to flee their country—though a few relatives

who were detained at the Congo border have been left behind. As a result of several recent raids and years of unpredictable brutal violence perpetuated by the government that plagued their small town before being able to escape to freedom, the Burak family is experiencing extreme difficulty in adjusting to a new life in the United States. After your initial visit with the family, you believe many family members are suffering from PTSD.

Get into small groups based on the following life course groupings: early childhood, adolescence, middle adulthood, older adulthood. Spend 25 minutes identifying the PTSD symptoms and trauma reactions that are demonstrated by the family member(s) in your age cohort (base your responses on the differential reactions found in the trauma literature) **(general knowledge).** Starting with the early childhood group, present to the next consecutive life course group what your group anticipates to be the biopsychosocial-spiritual risks that your family member(s) will experience as he or she enters into the next life course phase. What are the cultural considerations that should be noted in your risk assessment **(general knowledge integrated with case knowledge of family members, with focus on values/ethics of assessment related to cultural considerations)**? Check in with the responses of the next life course group to compare/contrast your group responses. What do you notice as differences? Where might these differences in response among your classmates originate, if you each are working from a similar general knowledge base **(knowledge of self and values/ethics)**?

As a class, identify the protective influences, at multiple levels, that a social worker might leverage to prevent these risks from developing at each next stage. As a social worker, what would be your *initial* plan for this family? Describe how this initial plan is in line with the National Association of Social Workers (NASW) Code of Ethics **(knowledge of case and general knowledge, as well as values and ethics to guide your plan).**

7

Substance Abuse

Holly C. Matto,
Virginia Commonwealth University

A s you think back to Junito Salvatierra, you will recall an emerging theme of intergenerational substance abuse in the family, with its attendant emotional and interpersonal consequences. You might be concerned about Junito's use, wondering what factors have contributed to these behaviors, as well as wanting to identify where the most effective areas of intervention might be to change this early pattern you see developing. You might also be wondering about how Junito's sisters, Sergia and Isabel, will be affected and what their decisions around substance use will be as they get older.

According to the Robert Wood Johnson Foundation (RWJF), substance abuse is the nation's number one health problem (Ericson, 2001). The *Diagnostic and Statistical Manual of Mental Disorders, Fourth Edition (DSM-IV;* APA, 2000) and International Classification of Diseases (ICD-10; World Health Organization [WHO], 2005b) define **substance abuse** disorders as use that occurs in larger quantities than intended, with a strong desire or compulsion to use, a neglect of alternative interests, significant impairment in social, occupational, and recreational activities, continued use despite these adverse consequences, and development of **tolerance** (a body's need for higher dosages of the drug to achieve the same effects) and **withdrawal** (the body's physical reaction to stopping use of a drug when a person has become drug dependent) symptomotology with prolonged substance use. Drug *abuse* is typically defined as voluntary use with psychosocial consequences, while drug *dependency* is characterized by a physiological need for the drug that leads to compulsive drug use and is often considered a medical disease. Exhibit 7.1 shows the specific *DSM-IV* criteria for both **substance dependence** and substance abuse.

Substance Dependence Specific Criteria	
A maladaptive pattern of substance use, leading to clinically significant impairment or distress, as manifested by three (or more) of the following, occurring at any time in the same 12-month period:	1. Tolerance 2. Withdrawal 3. The substance is often taken in larger amounts or over a longer period of time than was intended 4. There is a persistent desire or unsuccessful efforts to cut down or control substance use 5. A great deal of time is spent in activities necessary to obtain the substance, use the substance, or recover from its effects 6. Important social, occupational, or recreational activities are given up or reduced because of substance use 7. The substance use is continued despite knowledge of having a persistent or recurrent physical or psychological problem that is likely to have been caused by the substance
Substance Abuse Specific Criteria	
A maladaptive pattern of substance use leading to clinically significant impairment or distress, as manifested by one (or more) of the following, occurring within a 12-month period:	1. Recurrent substance use resulting in a failure to fulfill major role obligations at work, school, or home 2. Recurrent substance use in situations in which it is physically hazardous 3. Recurrent substance-related legal problems 4. Continued substance use despite having persistent or recurrent social or interpersonal problems caused or exacerbated by the effects of the substance

Exhibit 7.1   Substance Use Disorder *DSM-IV* Diagnostic Classification

SOURCE: Reprinted with permission from the *Diagnostic and Statistical Manual of Mental Disorders, Fourth Edition, Text Revision,* copyright © 2000, American Psychiatric Association.

Patterns of Occurrence

The International Council on Alcohol and Addictions (ICAA), an international non-governmental organization focusing on drug addiction (www.icaa.ch), estimates that there are 140 million people who are alcohol dependent, with an estimated 200 million people using illicit drugs worldwide. The World Health Organization's (WHO) global estimates on drug use show that 2 billion people use alcohol, 1.3 billion smoke cigarettes, and 185 million use illicit drugs. These substances combined account for 12.4% of all deaths worldwide (WHO, 2002). The United Nations Office on Drugs and Crime's *World Drug Report* (United Nations Office on Drugs and Crime [UNODC], 2005) estimates global prevalence rates for all illicit drugs used in the previous year at 5% of the worldwide population ages 15–64. In 2003–2004, global prevalence rates for cannabis were 4.0% (160.9 million), amphetamines 0.6% (26.2 million), ecstasy 0.2% (7.9 million), cocaine 0.3% (13.7 million), and opiates 0.4% (15.9 million; UNODC, 2005).

In Europe, the prevalence of problem drug use during the previous year, with estimated numbers taken at various times across countries during the period 1995–2000, was between 2.6 (Ireland) and 12.5 (Luxembourg) per 1,000 in the population ages 15–64 years old (European Monitoring Centre for Drugs and Drug Addiction [EMCDDA], 2003). According to the European Monitoring Centre for Drugs and Drug Addiction (EMCDDA)'s *2004 Statistical Bulletin,* the lifetime prevalence of drug use among all adults (as percentage of 15–64 year olds) in European countries, estimated in years 2000–2003, was between 5.7 (Hungary) and 31.3 (Denmark) for cannabis; 0.6 (Finland) and 6.2 (England and Wales) for cocaine; 0.5 (Portugal) and 12.3 (England and Wales) for amphetamines; 0.2 (Sweden) and 6.6 (England and Wales) for ecstasy; 0.6 (Slovakia) and 9.3 (England and Wales) for hallucinogens; and 0.0 (Italy) and 6.2 (England and Wales) for LSD. Other general population studies that examined six countries found the prevalence of alcohol use was highest in the Netherlands, then in descending order, the United States, Canada, Brazil, Germany, and Mexico (Vega et al., 2002).

In the United States, results from the 2004 National Survey on Drug Use and Health (NSDUH; Substance Abuse and Mental Health Services Administration [SAMHSA], 2005) showed that 7.9% of Americans ages 12 years and older, or 19.1 million people, were current illicit drug users (had used an illicit drug in the past month), with marijuana prevalence rates the highest at 6.1% of the population (14.6 million people) using marijuana within the past month. Estimates of other illicit drug use in 2004 included 450,000 ecstasy users, 2.0 million cocaine users, and 166,000 heroin users. In the United States, 40% of people admitted to treatment facilities reported cocaine as their primary drug of abuse, with primary heroin admission estimates ranging from 62% to 82% in various U.S. cities (SAMHSA, 2005). NSDUH data (SAMHSA, 2005) show the following rates by race/ethnicity for current illegal drug use among youth ages 12–17: 26.0% American Indian/Alaska Native; 12.2% of those who identified with two or more races; 11.1% white; 10.2% Hispanic; 9.3% black; and 6.0% Asian.

According to the NSDUH data (SAMHSA, 2005), there were 121 million people in the United States age 12 or older (50.3% of the population) who were current drinkers in 2004, 22.8% (55 million) binge drinkers, 6.9% (16.7 million) heavy drinkers, and 29.2% (70.3 million people) tobacco users. Young adults ages 18–25 years old showed the highest prevalence of binge and heavy drinking, with rates peaking at age 21, and showed the highest rate of past month cigarette use (39.5%) as compared to all other age cohorts. Race and ethnicity alcohol use estimates for youth ages 12–20 were as follows: 16.3% of Asian, 19.1% of black, 24.3% of American Indian/Alaska Native, 26.4% of those who identified with two or more races, 26.6% of Hispanic, and 32.6% of white (SAMHSA, 2005).

One study found that close to half of women who were Cuban American, Mexican American, and Puerto Rican abstained from alcohol, with only 3% or less reporting heavy drinking (Collins & McNair, 2002), and other studies have found that African Americans are not as likely as white adolescents to abuse alcohol (Loue, 2003), with lower substance use rates in adolescence and early adulthood as compared to other racial/ethnic groups. Hispanic high school seniors tend to show the highest rate of cocaine, crack, and heroin use. Still other studies have shown that racial/ethnic differences in prevalence rates for crack cocaine, in particular, wash out after social and environmental determinants (e.g., neighborhood social conditions) are equated (Lillie-Blanton, Anthony, & Schuster, 1993).

Results from the recent Monitoring the Future study (Johnston, O'Malley, Bachman, & Schulenberg, 2004), which tracks drug use trends with annual surveys administered to 8th, 10th, and 12th graders nationwide, show that 54% of 12th graders have tried cigarettes and one quarter (24%) consider themselves current smokers. Over three quarters (77%) of students have consumed alcohol by the end of high school, and 46% have consumed alcohol before the end of 8th grade, with 58% of 12th graders reporting having been drunk at least once. Half of students (51%) today will have tried an illicit drug by the end of high school and 30% by the end of 8th grade, with one fifth of students reporting drug use during the 12 months prior to the survey. In adolescence, drinking may be manifested as one behavior of many problem behaviors, or the substance use may just be part of the adolescent's course of development, with consumption as time-limited and developmentally appropriate (Zucker, 1994).

Research shows that two thirds of problem drinkers are men, and women are less likely to use/abuse drugs than men, with women making up less than 40% of the drug abusing population (Wasilow-Mueller & Erickson, 2001). In 2004, NSDUH data (SAMHSA, 2005) showed male youth (ages 12–17) decreased their marijuana use between 2002 to 2004 (9.1%, 8.6%, 8.1%), while marijuana use rates for female youth remained flat across these 3 years (7.2%, 7.2%, 7.1%). In addition, more males (27.7%) than females (22.3%) aged 12 and older used tobacco, but for the subset of youth ages 12–17, the trend reversed, and more girls (12.5%) smoked as compared to boys (11.3%).

Gay, lesbian, bisexual, and transgender (GLBT) youth show higher use of substances compared to heterosexual youth (Cochran, Keenan, Schober, & Mays, 2000). Rosario, Schrimshaw, and Hunter (2004) studied female and male adolescents ages 14–21 and found the coming-out process for both genders was associated with changes in alcohol and marijuana use. Initial involvement in the coming-out process was related to an increase in substance use, with later continued involvement in gay-related activities associated with a decrease in substance use.

Theories of Causation

You have just read about substance use prevalence rates and different patterns of use across various groups, and you are probably beginning to think about possible explanations of why one person or group initiates and sustains patterns of use and others show limited experimentation with substances. As you might expect, there is not one set of etiological explanations for substance use; rather, there are a variety of biological, psychosocial, and environmental theories of causation (see Exhibit 7.2 for a summary of these perspectives).

Genetic/Biological

Research that has examined the etiology of drug use estimates that 40%–60% of risk for substance abuse is due to genetic factors (Hesselbrock, 1995; Kendler, Neale, Heath, Kessler, & Eaves, 1994), showing that children of substance abusers are at increased risk

	Tenets	Representative Citations
Genetic Model	Family history of substance abuse creates vulnerability to substance abuse in offspring	Chassin Pitts, DeLucia, & Todd, 1999; Goodwin, 1988; Hesselbrock, 1995; Kendler et al., 1994
Cognitive-Neurobehavioral Model	Substance abuse heightens subcortical reactivity and diminishes executive cognitive functioning leading to continued substance use	Giancola & Moss, 1998
Conditioning Theories	Cue-response patterns lead to drug use propensity	Childress et al., 1999; Schneider et al., 2001; Sell et al., 2000
Associational Model	Negative affect influences incentive value attributed to behavior and can lead to increased substance use	Baker Piper, McCarthy, Majeskie, & Fiore, 2004
Personality Traits	Personality traits such as antisocial characteristics, sensation-seeking, and impulsivity may lead to drug use behaviors	Hesselbrock Hesselbrock, & Epstein, 1999
Coping Theories	Coping style, such as avoidant or emotion-focused coping, rather than problem-focused coping, may lead to continued drug use	Avants Warburton, & Margolin, 2000
Social Cognitive Theory	Poor coping processes, such as diminished self-efficacy, is influential in the initiation and perpetuation of substance abuse	Bandura, 1986; Larimer Palmer, & Marlatt, 1999; Marlatt & Gordon, 1985; Witkiewitz & Marlatt, 2004
Unified Theory of Behavior	Behavioral intention is determined by six factors, including attitudes, social norms, self-concept, self-efficacy, affect/emotions, and beliefs	Jaccard, Dodge, & Dittus, 2002
Sociocultural Theories	Social affiliations and familial relationships influence initiation and perpetuation of substance abuse; the sociopolitical and economic context, as well as racism and discrimination, lead to increased vulnerability to substance use among women and minority groups	Hirschi, 1969; Rhodes & Johnson, 1997; Roberts, Jackson, & Carlton-Laney, 2000; Schiele, 2000; Sher, 1991; Sutherland, 1947

Exhibit 7.2   Etiological Explanations

of developing a substance abuse problem as adolescents (Chassin et al., 1999; McGue, 1994). A family history of substance abuse is a risk factor for use in young adulthood (Quigley & Marlatt, 1996), with children of alcoholics 3–4 times more likely than children of nonalcoholic parents to engage in problematic drinking later in life (Goodwin, 1988; Schuckit & Sweeney, 1987).

Although twin and adoption studies show a significant genetic component to drug addiction, this leaves an incomplete picture of causation. For example, even within the biological domain of gene transmission, there are outcomes that require environmental interaction. While the *template* gene function creates a "passing down" of certain genes that may increase one's propensity to abuse substances (although no "addiction gene" has been found to date), the *transcription* function, or the propensity for a gene to express itself through protein synthesis and to form synaptic connections that strengthen specific neural patterns, may be influenced more by environmental factors (Kandel, 1998; Kendler, Heath, Neale, Kessler, & Eaves, 1992).

Giancola and Moss (1998) discuss a **cognitive-neurobehavioral model of alcoholism** that focuses on executive cognitive functioning (ECF) capacities such as planning, self-monitoring, self-correction, evaluation, and modification of behavioral implementation. The model suggests that capacity disruptions occur when there is dysfunction in the prefrontal cortex of the brain, which causes problems in connections to the limbic-memory system and subcortical regions associated with arousal, physiologically based emotion, or affect, and motivation. Therefore, alcoholism may lead to heightened reactivity of this subcortical circuitry with a disconnect from the regulatory prefrontal structures that may lead to problems in behavioral control.

Treatment models, such as the Minnesota Model, have been developed based on a medical or "**disease concept**" approach to addiction, and prescribe abstinence to rid the body of drug toxins and to restore and maintain the body's natural chemical balance. The disease model is the predominant approach that many inpatient and hospital-based substance abuse treatment programs in the United States take to treating drug addiction.

Psychosocial

In addition to a physiological approach to understanding substance abuse, many psychosocial theories of causation offer further explanation. One such theoretical approach, *conditioning theories,* bridges the biological and cognitive domains. **Conditioning theories** (see e.g., Childress et al., 1999; Schneider et al., 2001; Sell et al., 2000; Weiss & Porrino, 2002) suggest that drug-related behaviors are linked to specific cues that may trigger a physiological reaction that heightens the **craving** response, an intense urge to drink or drug, and ultimately drives the drug use behavior. Cues may be interpersonal in nature (e.g., seeing old friends that you used to get high with), environmental (e.g., walking down a street where you used to use drugs; seeing the road signs for the turnoff to Baltimore City), or may be sensory (e.g., encountering images, smells, or sounds that occurred during drug experiences).

A **stress vulnerability model** of addiction integrates biological research into these conditioning models and can be helpful in more fully understanding the conditioning process and its effects. For example, stress vulnerability research has shown that the hippocampus, an important brain structure for integrating information across different brain regions and integrating stimuli (i.e., visual, auditory, and spatial; Kesner, Gilbert, & Barua, 2002), may become impaired during high-stress situations. If, indeed, substance abuse experiences impair the cognitive and integrative functions of some brain structures like the hippocampus, these sensory stimuli may be left as fragmented and displaced, vulnerable to activation by environmental cues, increasing the risk for relapse.

Baker, Piper, McCarthy, Majeskie, and Fiore (2004) present an *associational model* of drug addiction with negative affect at the core of the model. The model draws on information-processing theory, which examines the relationship between cognitions and emotions, to understand constrained behavioral response patterns. These researchers suggest that affective reactions, both conscious and cognitively unconscious, influence the incentive value attributed to behavior. Coping responses may be influenced by strong negative emotions that arise, leading to resumed drug use behaviors. The cognitive processes needed to resist drug use in the presence of strong emotions may not be available.

Personality traits have also been implicated in facilitating and maintaining drug addiction. For example, antisocial traits, sensation seeking, and impulsivity may lead to drug use behaviors (Hesselbrock et al., 1999). Patterson and Newman's model of disinhibition (1993) addresses personality traits most often cited as risk factors for substance abuse such as neuroticism (emotional reactivity and anxiety), extraversion, and disinhibition. However, while it is believed that these traits may make an individual more prone to drug use behaviors, it is the interaction of these traits with peer, family, and other system relationships that will ultimately influence pathways into problematic drug use.

Theories of coping have also been used to understand substance abuse. Coping deficits in managing emotions, such as boredom, anger, and anxiety, may lead to self-medication through drug use. The coping literature suggests that assessment of the coping *focus* (e.g., whether a person focuses on the problem or on the emotional climate of a situation), as well as the *method* one uses to cope (e.g., whether cognitive or behavioral resources are mobilized), will be important in understanding how one fully responds to a distressing situation. Researchers have found linkages between coping methods and substance abuse behavior, with avoidant coping (e.g., cognitive avoidance, resigned acceptance) related to continued drug use (Avants et al., 2000). Lazarus and Folkman's (1985) model of appraisal-focused (cognitively working through beliefs about the situation), emotion-focused (emotional discharge), and problem-focused (using approach strategies such as actively seeking support) coping domains is useful in assessing and understanding why drug use begins and why it may persist despite a desire to stop, with emotion-focused coping styles, as compared to problem-focused coping, more likely to be seen in those who abuse substances.

Social learning theory (Bandura, 1986) has also been used to understand drug use, suggesting that **self-efficacy** (perceived ability to resist drug use) and expectancies (perceived advantages and disadvantages of drug use) may explain entry into and continued use of substances. Causation may be reciprocal here, where an individual's self-efficacy and coping repertoire become increasingly diminished with continued use of substances. With continued use of substances, negative consequences increase (such as guilt, anxiety, problematic relationships), at which time continued use is negatively reinforced (to remove these negative consequences), strengthening a sustained pattern of drug use, which, in turn, continues to undermine self-efficacy and other problem-solving coping capacities.

Cultural Perspectives

A feminist perspective as applied to substance abuse etiology posits that the sociopolitical and economic context within which women are embedded influences the development of substance use disorders. In a context where women are more likely to be the primary caretaker for children and/or other family members, have limited financial independence, be a victim of domestic abuse and control, and hold weak labor market attachment, psychosocial stress is more likely to mount and, with that, put the woman at increased risk for substance abuse. And if a problem with substances does develop, shame, stigma, financial hardship, and child care responsibilities often pose significant barriers to women's treatment seeking (Rhodes & Johnson, 1997).

In addition, the effect of sexism and racism on substance abusing persons who are members of more than one vulnerable group (e.g., being a woman, being African American, and being addicted) may lead to entrenched oppression that manifests through continued substance abuse in order to cope (Comas-Diaz & Greene, 1995; Rhodes & Johnson, 1997). Women specifically and other culturally vulnerable groups in general have been confronted historically and contemporaneously with "dependency" (e.g., financial, psychological) resulting from collective disempowerment (Lengerman & Niebrugge-Brantley, 2000). Therefore, substance abuse, from a feminist approach, may be viewed as another example of women's socially constructed and structurally linked dependency.

Similar to the focus on oppression as causal agent in sustaining substance dependency from a gendered analysis of this challenge in living, the **Afrocentric perspective** (see Roberts et al., 2000; Schiele, 2000) orients understanding of substance abuse around sociopolitical and economic oppression and exploitation, resulting in spiritual disconnect. Collectiveness and spirituality, traditionally protective factors from an Afrocentric worldview, become eroded through transactions within an oppressive society, and as these traditions deteriorate and individuals become more isolated and alienated from one another, substance abuse takes on more power, both at the individual as well as community levels (Schiele, 2000).

Environmental

Sociological theories have contributed to our understanding of drug addiction through the application of *deviance* and *subculture* models (Johnson, 1980), suggesting that deviant behavior may precede drug use and that affiliation with drug-using peers defines one's group culture (also see Sutherland's [1947] differential affiliation theory). Including an intergenerational family component to this environmental approach, Sher's (1991) *deviance proneness* model suggests that parental alcoholism leads to poor parenting behaviors, which create a pattern of behavioral undercontrol (e.g., impulsivity) in their children, resulting in school failure and increased affiliation with deviant peers, leading to the development of substance use. Similarly, Hirschi's (1969) *social bond theory* proposed four factors that promote conformity to conventional norms and decrease the likelihood of developing a deviant life course trajectory. The four elements are: (1) attachment to significant members in one's social system and to social institutions, (2) commitment to social activities that promote positive outcomes such as educational or employment opportunities, (3) involvement or time invested in these conventional behaviors, and (4) beliefs that uphold society's antideviant values and norms. A better understanding of how specific social influences facilitate these social bonding processes might help in developing multilevel clinical strategies that prevent early entry into substance use.

A newer way of conceptualizing the impact of the environment on drug addiction is to think of "addiction" and "recovery" as distinct communities in and of themselves, with their own unique language, symbols, rituals, interpersonal affiliations, and behaviors (see Matto, 2004; Matto, Miller, & Spera, 2005). This contextualized approach is different from traditional subculture models in that the emphasis is on addiction and recovery as *communities of engagement* and on assessing and addressing the strength of an individual's attachment to those respective communities through social context factors, rather than focusing on the individual's affiliation with a deviant societal subculture. This community attachment model suggests that cognitive, affective, and behavioral attachment to such communities can be changed (e.g., reaching greater attachment to recovery versus addiction community) through leveraging salient social context referents and addressing individual-community transactional processes that are influencing cognitive and affective dimensions, and can be used to produce behavioral change.

Biopsychosocial Model

Most substance abuse treatment agencies view drug addiction as a biopsychosocial disorder, which has a physiological component and psychosocial consequences. Proponents of this biopsychosocial model adhere to the belief that there are multiple causes, consequences, and solutions to addiction, and they attempt, in theory, to focus on all dimensions. One new theoretical framework that offers a comprehensive and integrated approach to understanding health behaviors from a biopsychosocial approach, and that is currently being applied to drug addiction, is the *unified theory of behavior* (UTB). The UTB has evolved from other theories such as Ajzen and Fishbein's theory of reasoned action, Bandura's social learning theory, and Triandis's theory of subjective culture. The UTB hypothesizes six determinants of behavioral intention (e.g., intention to stop using drugs) that integrate biological and psychosocial dimensions: (1) attitude toward the behavior (favorable or unfavorable), (2) social norms (what significant others think about performing the behavior), (3) self-concept (is the drug-using or drug-stopping behavior consistent with the person's self image?), (4) affect and emotions, (5) self-efficacy, and (6) beliefs and outcome expectations (negative and positive). The theory also postulates four immediate determinants of behavioral change that directly influence actual behavioral implementation, in addition to whether the individual *intends* to perform the behavior. These are: (1) knowledge and skills needed to perform the behavior, (2) environmental constraints (barriers to implementing behavior change), (3) salience of the behavior to the individual, and (4) habits and automatic processes (see Jaccard et al., 2002, for conceptual model description).

It is not likely that one set of explanations is sufficient for understanding drug addiction. For example, developmental changes, environmental stressors, social circumstances, and learned experiences can affect gene expression. Not only is parental substance use a risk factor for children's substance use (a genetic predisposition), but parental attitudes that are favorable toward substance use is a significant risk factor as well (Hawkins, Catalano, & Miller, 1992). And family dysfunction is related to a variety of problematic outcomes such as child maltreatment, domestic violence, and HIV/AIDS (Miller & Weisner, 2002), including substance use. In some cases it may be that family dysfunction contributes to other consequences, such as domestic violence, that cause a child to develop problematic coping and poor peer relations that later leads to a substance abuse disorder. The paths are both direct and indirect, and a social worker must be committed to a multidimensional assessment process that carefully examines all areas, rather than assuming causation from one factor (e.g., from only asking about a family history of drug addiction).

In summary, we can think of factors associated with substance abuse within etiological clusters that encompass biological, psychological, social (e.g., family and interpersonal relationships), and environmental domains. The rest of this chapter focuses on risk and protection in these domains, including spiritual risk and protection, to help in understanding how social workers might intervene across the life course and across systems within which the individual is contextually embedded.

Multidimensional Risk and Protection

Biological Risk and Protection

Exhibit 7.3 summarizes the biological risk and protective factors related to substance abuse. Individuals who are genetically vulnerable to substance abuse through a family history of addiction may progress more quickly from use to abuse to dependency than those for whom there is no family history of substance abuse. Drug progression may come about from use that helps to normalize brain chemistry that has been altered by genetics (Wasilow-Mueller & Erickson, 2001). For example, dopamine dysfunction has been associated with diminished frontal lobe inhibitory control and a lack of responsiveness to non-drug-related rewards (Volkow, Fowler, Wang, & Swanson, 2004). Recent research shows that drugs such as cocaine, amphetamines, morphine, alcohol, and nicotine may increase dopamine release. During this process, the receptors that stimulate the release of dopamine contribute to what scientists call long-term potentiation (LTP; or you can think of this as "learning transfer") in the brain, causing the cells to release dopamine at even higher levels when the brain is exposed to the same stimulus in the future. In other words, LTP results in increased dopamine release with subsequent exposure to the drugs. Interestingly, these same researchers have found that stress itself tends to contribute to LTP in a similar way as drugs, increasing dopamine release in the brain, suggesting that stress can trigger pathways back to drug-taking behaviors in people who are substance users (Saal, Dong, Bonci, & Malenka, 2003). Scientists are continually working to better understand how this learning process that occurs among brain cells influences relapse potential and the role that stress plays in triggering urges to use drugs.

	Risk Factors	Protective Factors
Biological	• Family history of substance abuse • Increased limbic system activation • Biological deficits in executive cognitive functioning (ECF)	• Well-developed hippocampus and prefrontal brain regions
Psychological	• Affect dysregulation • Behavioral undercontrol (impulsivity) • Reward-seeking personality • Sensation-seeking personality • Low self-efficacy • Low self-esteem • Positive outcome expectancies of drug use • Negative emotional states (e.g., anger, boredom)	• High self-efficacy • Good problem-solving skills • Emotional regulation capacity
Social	• Neighborhood disorganization • Low family bonding/attachment • Family conflict • Early childhood abuse • Family drug behaviors • Peer rejection • Childhood physical and/or sexual abuse • Academic disengagement • Witnessing violence • Strained interpersonal relationships • Drug availability through peer or neighborhood influence	• Family bonding/attachment • Involvement in prosocial activities • Effective familial communication • Prosocial peer membership • Perceived social support • Access and connections to community resources
Spiritual	• Lack of engagement in fellowship community • Negative religious coping	• Participation in religious institutional practices • Rituals • Individual relationship with a higher power

Exhibit 7.3 Biological, Psychological, Social, and Spiritual and Risk and Protective Factors for Substance Abuse

Deficits in self-regulation, particularly in the dysregulation of negative emotions, is a significant factor in developing substance abuse disorders. Current neurobiological research shows why this might be the case. The time between ages 8 and 18 is the second critical developmental period for the prefrontal cortex region, the brain structure that is important in emotional and behavioral regulation, planning capacities, and problem-solving abilities (Giancola & Moss, 1998). Deficits in this executive cognitive functioning structure is a risk factor for substance abuse. Experiencing extreme psychosocial stress, such as growing up in adverse environmental or family conditions, may lead to problems in prefrontal cortical development and, thus, problems in affective, cognitive, and behavioral regulation (Fishbein, Hyde, Coe, & Paschall, 2004). In fact, some researchers suggest that parental substance abuse may account for the development of behavioral disturbance in a child only when the parent's substance abuse occurs during the sensitive developmental time period when the executive cognitive functioning capacities are being developed (from age 6 or so into adolescence; Giancola & Moss, 1998).

Therefore, psychosocial and environmental stress may pose biological risk. People diagnosed with mood disorders such as depression and bipolar disorder show similar dysfunction in the prefrontal cortex (Anand & Shekhar, 2003). This, in conjunction with the high **comorbidity** shown between mood and substance use disorders, suggests there may be a "stress vulnerability" explanation to substance abuse whereby stress impacts the body's physiological response system leading to increased drug craving and use. Shaham, Erb, and Stewart (2000) state, "It is also possible that chronic exposure to drugs selectively increases the vulnerability of the individual to stress-induced relapse during a drug-free period. Former opioid users show increased autonomic responses to a physical stressor during a drug-free state" (p. 25). Researchers studying biological precipitants to drug use have found that drug use behavior is governed by automatic processes, such as implicit memory activation associated with drug cues (Goldman, Brown, Christiansen, & Smith, 1991; Stacy, Ames, Sussman, & Dent, 1996; Tiffany, 1990). Controlled studies have found increased limbic activation (affective activation) associated with craving response following observation of cocaine videos and decreased hippocampal (the structure responsible for conscious and contextual processing) activation during craving, indicating that conscious cognitive processing is weakened, while physiological and emotional activation is more prominent at these times (Childress et al., 1999). White and Swartzwelder (2004) found that alcohol impairs hippocampal functioning, thus impairing explicit memory capacity. Adolescents may be more vulnerable than adults to the effects of substances on these structural impairments and memory deficits, with research showing that adolescence is a distinct stage from adulthood in the effect of substances on brain development and function (Fishbein et al., 2004; Giancola & Moss, 1998).

Thus, strong prefrontal and hippocampal development can provide the top-down processing needed to modulate emotional activity and prevent behavioral disinhibition. However, these brain structures may be impaired for individuals with substance abuse disorders, and perhaps adolescent brains, in their early structural development, may be particularly vulnerable. The empirical brain imaging research is not available yet to identify the directed psychosocial treatment strategies that might facilitate specific brain structure development after impairment, but there is research that suggests that interpersonal relationships and attachment processes can serve to strengthen these key brain structures throughout the life course (e.g., see Siegel, 1999, 2001).

Psychological Risk and Protection

As addressed in the theory section, personality traits may increase a person's risk of abusing substances. A person who actively seeks out rewards and takes risks has a greater likelihood of participating in substance-using behaviors. Once engaged in drug behaviors, people with this reward orientation are more likely to focus on the rewarding aspects associated with the behavior as opposed to the punishing aspects of drug use, and thus are more prone to sustaining these behaviors. Other researchers have found that behavioral undercontrol (lack of ability to regulate impulsivity) and lower perceived parental discipline in adolescence was significantly related to drug use in emerging adulthood (King & Chassin, 2004). Chronic affect dysregulation that may arise from early childhood abuse experiences has also been linked with substance use (Chilcoat & Breslau, 1998). Women substance abusers often experience more shame, depression, and anxiety than male substance abusers, whereas male substance abusers have higher diagnoses of antisocial personality disorders as compared to their female counterparts (Conte, Plutchnik, Picard, Galanter, & Jacoby, 1991). Substance abusers frequently have difficulty controlling anger and aggression, which is experienced equally by men and women, but studies have found that female substance abusers have more psychiatric hospitalizations as compared to male substance abusers (Davis & DiNitto, 1996). Thus, the literature suggests that undercontrol of negative emotions (such as shame, anxiety, or anger) and antisocial personality characteristics may lead to the initiation and/or perpetuation of substance use disorders across gender.

Kambouropoulos and Staiger (2004) found that a sensation-seeking personality trait was associated with a change in affect that motivates behavior, such that sensitivity to reward was linked to positive urge to drink and behavioral motivation for drug use. Thus, sensation seeking as a personality trait tends to create affect change, which then leads to behavioral change and an increased urge to drink. These authors found no relationship between trait anxiety and change in affect or desire to drink but found that individuals tended to become more frustrated and intolerant of nonrewarding situations, and this was associated with urge to drink. The authors concluded that both rewarding/positive and aversive/negative motivational processes were related to **cue reactivity**, physiological and psychological reactions that are directly related to drug/alcohol cues, in their sample of social drinkers.

Oriented around high-risk situations, Marlatt and colleagues (Larimer et al., 1999; Marlatt & Gordon, 1985; Witkiewitz & Marlatt, 2004) propose in their relapse prevention (RP) model of addiction that several key cognitive processes are determinants of relapse when faced with high-risk situations: low self-efficacy, positive and negative outcome expectancies about the consequences related to drug use, cravings, negative emotional states, and problematic coping skills. High self-efficacy has consistently been found to be a protective factor in mitigating the negative consequences of substance use and in preventing relapse. The RP model suggests that outcome expectancies, particularly anticipated positive changes in social life, may mediate the relationship between coping skills and substance use behavior in adolescence (Smith, McCarthy, & Goldman, 1995). Smith (1994) found expectancies accounted for 22% of the variation in drinking behavior in a longitudinal design with an adolescent sample. Other studies have found that positive and negative expectancies account for 35% of the variance in future drug use, with positive expectancies accounting for the majority of the explained variance (Stacy, Widaman, & Marlatt, 1990). Expectancies related to alcohol use have been found to develop as early as third grade (Kraus, Smith, & Ratner, 1994), suggesting that cognitive-based prevention programs should include elementary school children.

Thus, as summarized in Exhibit 7.3, common psychological risk factors include expecting positive results related to drug use and experiencing negative emotional states (depression, frustration, anger, anxiety, boredom). Behavioral undercontrol (impulsivity, aggressiveness) increases the odds of an adolescent developing a substance use disorder in adulthood (King & Chassin, 2004). Protective factors include problem-focused coping skills, high self-efficacy, and emotional regulation capacity. Protective factors for youths ages 12–14 who were at risk for substance use specifically included knowledge/beliefs about alcohol and drug use, communication, bonding, and the family's capacity to seek help in the community when they experienced problems (Johnson et al., 1998).

Social Risk and Protection

Social risk and protective factors for substance abuse are summarized in Exhibit 7.3. Hawkins et al. (1992) provide a review of social risk factors for substance abuse, such as neighborhood disorganization, family drug behaviors, family conflict, poor bonding practices and lack of family cohesion, academic disengagement, and peer rejection. Female substance abusers are more likely to have problematic family relations and a family history of drug use as compared to male substance abusers, and perhaps as a result, research shows that social risks are highest for female substance abusers, leading to more significant social/interpersonal problems as compared to male substance abusers (Davis & DiNitto, 1996). Although rates vary by study design, estimates of up to three quarters of women in inpatient substance abuse treatment facilities have histories of childhood physical and/or sexual abuse, compared to one third of women in the general population (Kilpatrick, Edmunds, & Seymour, 1992; Miller & Downs, 1993; Rohsenow, Corbett, & Devine, 1988; Teets, 1995; Wasilow-Mueller & Erickson, 2001; Windle, Windle, Scheidt, & Miller, 1995).

Social protective factors include strong family attachment (emphasizing the importance of father-son bonding as protection against risk), strong communication, perceived support, an adolescent's confiding in a family member, and strong prosocial peer membership (Beauvais & Oetting, 1999; Hawkins et al., 1992; Stronski, Ireland, Michaud,

Narring, & Resnick, 2000). Social systems offer the opportunity for persuasion, modeling, and development of social norms that may guide behavioral decision making around substance use. "Having or creating a support system for engagement in a behavior seems to be an important element in initiation, modification, or cessation of behaviors" (DiClemente, 2003, p. 35).

A social stress model (Rhodes & Jason, 1990) of addiction emphasizes individual and family coping competence, positing that adolescent drug abuse is related to relationships with others in the environment and within social systems. One study found that witnessing violence was the most salient predictor of adolescent substance use (Kilpatrick et al., 2000). Stress and associated risk will be buffered by positive attachments, coping skills, and community resources, and therefore it is critical to call upon the community, peers, family, and school in shoring up protection against substance use. For example, there is a strong relationship between low assertiveness in adolescence, a problematic family environment, and substance use severity. In addition, weak sibling and parental relationships and a lack of support and encouragement from parents are all related to higher substance use.

Researchers have tested how developmental processes such as individuation during adolescence act as mediators of substance use (McQueen, Getz, & Bray, 2003), with studies showing contradictory results. The acculturation process during adolescence, when minority youth are learning to incorporate the beliefs, values, and technologies of their new cultural world, may impact individuation, which may influence substance use, as higher levels of acculturation have been associated with greater substance abuse risk (Gfroerer & De La Rosa, 1993; Vega, Aldrette, Kolody, Aguilar-Gaxiola, 1998). Other studies have found that some cultural groups who adopted more of American culture (via perceptions and attitudes) have higher resistance to substance abuse, suggesting that acculturation may serve as a coping mechanism for some individuals (Szalay, Strohl, & Doherty, 1999). The way that Murray Bowen defined his original concept of individuation—as a process where an adolescent begins to pull away from the family in pursuing his or her own interests while simultaneously remaining connected in a meaningful way to the core family unit—is a developmentally normative process. How this process actually plays out among members in the family may be different across cultures. Migration histories, for example, that cause separation from parents and that occur at the same time as this individuation process in adolescence may exacerbate problem behaviors, as research has shown that separation from parents, including emotional distancing, during this developmental period is a consistently significant predictor of adolescent alcohol use (Bray, Adams, Getz, & McQueen, 2003).

Change in social roles associated with the adulthood transition may serve as a protective factor and may decrease substance use (Quigley & Marlatt, 1996), as individuals "age out" of using behaviors that are replaced by new emotional and behavioral commitments to family, education, or work. However, social role changes unaccompanied by adequate resources that would help an older adolescent take on and successfully manage these new roles can produce or sustain problem behaviors. Junito's story informs us of this as we see him struggling with his late adolescent options. School engagement has been frustrating for him, particularly as he compares his current failures to his previous academic successes, and the work in the mechanic shop has not given him the security of being able to sufficiently provide for his new family. Similar perhaps to his father's driving resourcefulness, Junito resorts to innovative means of adapting to these limited options (e.g., making new connections to sell drugs).

It is important to assess culturally specific stress that might be related to substance abuse to include acculturative stress, minority stress, socioeconomic stress, and context stress, which might compromise role availability and acquisition (Dougherty, James, Love, & Miller, 2002). Junito, at age 14, immigrated to the United States from the Dominican Republic, leaving as a result of the death of his grandmother. The move brought with it anticipation and anxiety about reunification with his biological parents and new siblings, as well as acculturative stress associated with adjustment to a new country, neighborhood, language, school, and peer groups without the familiarity and predictability he had known.

Consistent with the pattern that we see forming with Elias and his family, interpersonal relationships frequently suffer first with an individual's increased substance abuse. In their sample of college students, Szalay et al. (1999) found that drugs serve an important social function for substance users, for whom interpersonal relationships are often described as problematic. Academic and family problems were second to troubling interpersonal relationships, and drug users commonly experienced strained relationships with family, friends, and significant other/partner, and more academic problems as compared to nonusers. Researchers have found that support from others that is related to a specific behavior (e.g., drinking or abstaining) is more important than just a general feeling of support from others (DiClemente, 2003). A significant protective factor is functional social support and perceived quality of support from nonabusers, in addition to drug-free social norms within the school, peer groups, and larger community. Some researchers have found that changing these perceived norms is more influential than behavioral programs that train adolescents to refuse drugs in substance use prevention (Hansen & Graham, 1991).

Spiritual Risk and Protection

In an extensive review of the literature on addiction and spirituality, Cook (2004) found 13 spiritual concepts used to define spirituality: relatedness and transcendence (most common), humanity, core/force/soul and meaning/purpose, authenticity/truth, values/worth, nonmateriality, nonreligiousness, wholeness/health, self-knowledge, creativity, and consciousness/awareness (p. 543). Other definitions include "finding freedom from suffering," growth, change process, being fully alive and present in the moment, "finding a way to live with incongruity and to embrace paradox" (Cook, 2004). See Exhibit 7.3 for a summary of the risk and protection factors related to substance abuse.

One large study found a strong association between religious affiliation/participation and the value of abstaining from drug use in a sample of African American women (Collins & McNair, 2002). Church attendance was shown to serve as a protective factor against the use of drugs/alcohol in youth who did not complete high school and who were not attached to the labor market (Zimmerman & Maton, 1992). Other recent studies have found that female trauma survivors with co-occurring posttraumatic stress disorder (PTSD) and substance use disorders showed more use of positive (e.g., collaborating with God, feeling spiritual support) rather than negative (e.g., punishing appraisals such as thinking the behavior is a result of God's judgment, spiritual abandonment) religious coping strategies, but that frequency of trauma symptoms, a measure of symptom intensity, was significantly associated with negative religious coping in this dual disorder population (Fallot & Heckman, 2005). These results suggest that assessment practices should include how spiritual/religious coping is being used, what its effects are, and how other mental health conditions might influence how these coping resources are employed.

Twelve-step program principles (e.g., Alcoholics Anonymous, Narcotics Anonymous, Chemically Dependents Anonymous) are spiritually based, focusing on such activities as encouraging members to accept powerlessness in the service of regaining power over one's addiction, turning one's life over to a higher power (i.e., "We came to believe that a power greater than ourselves could restore us to sanity"). Rituals are also associated with positive health outcomes (Koenig, McCullough, & Larson, 2001), and the inclusion of ritual, along with structure, support, and obligation in 12-step programming may be why, for some individuals, fellowship within the program is important to maintaining recovery commitment. Often the spiritual message is fostered through gaining trust in something that is beyond one's own level of control and in fostering trust in a healing process, what Hodge (2005a) calls developing "salutary beliefs." These spiritual messages can be developed through supportive and trusting relationships with others in recovery.

New work is beginning to emerge on the relationship between mindfulness and substance abuse (see Marlatt et al., 2004). The conceptual and empirical differentiation between religiosity (a more formal organized approach to practicing beliefs), spirituality (a more individualized approach to practicing beliefs and engaging in one's faith), and mindfulness (practicing a meditative awareness grounded in Buddhist tradition) and their relationships to substance abuse behaviors is as yet understudied. Leigh, Bowen, and Marlatt's (2005) recent work on these relationships has found an empirical distinction between mindfulness and spirituality, and their study showed that spirituality (measured by the Spiritual Transcendence Index and Spirituality Assessment Scale) was associated with decreased substance use, whereas, in their sample of college students, mindfulness (measured by the Freiburg Mindfulness Inventory) was associated with increased substance use. Social workers should be sure to include a spirituality component to their substance abuse assessments, asking about a client's organized religious practices and participation as well as their spiritual beliefs related to where they get inner strength and their philosophy about their connection to a higher being.

Biopsychosocial-Spiritual Integration

Costa, Jessor, and Turbin (1999) provide a summary of psychosocial risk factors related to substance abuse in their longitudinal study of adolescents, such as the direct influence of peers, the indirect influence of peers as a gateway to drug availability, low expectations for success, low self-esteem, hopelessness, having using friends, high stress, low academic achievement, and proneness to dropping out of school. They also identified psychosocial protective factors that included a positive orientation to school, attitude against drug use, religiosity, positive orientation to health, positive relationships with adults, friends who can serve as models of prosocial behavior, and involvement in prosocial activities (volunteering, family activities; pp. 480–481). All risk factors were significant in predicting problem drinking, and protective factors were significant in reducing the risk of problem drinking, together accounting for 34%–39% of variation in problem drinking.

McKay (1999) has also identified significant factors associated with substance abuse relapse to include negative affect, craving, relationship difficulties, deficits in coping skills, cognitive outcome expectancies, and low self-efficacy. Risk factors found to predict continued drug use after opiate treatment were high level of pretreatment opiate/drug use, prior opiate drug treatment, no prior abstinence from opiates, depression, high stress, unemployment/employment problems, association with substance-abusing peers, short length of treatment, and leaving treatment prior to completion (Brewer, Catalano, Haggerty, Gainey, & Fleming, 1998).

Other researchers have found that children of alcoholics are at risk for substance abuse themselves through other operating mechanisms such as stress, negative emotions, and poor parental monitoring linked to parental alcoholism (Chassin & Barrera, 1993). This detailed constellation of factors represents risk and protection from biological, psychological, social, and spiritual domains that can be understood as interrelated components of an integrated and comprehensive social work assessment, which will necessarily drive treatment planning.

The UTB, presented earlier in this chapter, offers an integrated framework for understanding the process of addiction and substance use decision making. The framework suggests that drug use decisions will be influenced by behavioral intention, which itself is influenced by beliefs and expectancies (psychological), self-efficacy (psychological), attitudes (psychological), social norms (social, environmental, and psychological), self-concept (psychological), and affect and emotions (biological and psychological). In addition, the framework posits that, in addition to intention, drug use decisions are also influenced directly by habitual responses (biologically based automatic processes that require limited focal attention), requisite knowledge and skills needed to make the behavioral change (psychological), environmental constraints (social, environmental), and salience of the drug use behavior to the individual (psychological). Taken together, a thorough assessment based on these different factors gives an idea of where a client presents on the resiliency continuum and offers guidance in discovering the unique areas for treatment attention.

Resiliency is a product of the dynamic interaction between risk and protection across development and is associated with positive outcomes, despite encountering adverse life experiences (Luthar, 2003). Risk and protective factors can be robust (predict current levels of and future changes of substance use), emergent (predict future changes but not current levels of substance use), or concurrent (predict current levels but not future changes in substance use; Schulenberg, Maggs, & Hurrelmann, 1997). Concurrent risk/protective factors can be moving (where they travel with the person to each developmental stage and pose same risk/protective function) or they can be developmentally limited (where they are potent for a particular developmental time period). In addition to requiring a much more nuanced understanding of how these risk and protective factors manifest and have manifested (in the past, developmentally) for our clients, we as social work professionals need to attend to protection models as much as we've attended to risk models. Much of our child development knowledge has been based on cumulative risk models. Perhaps attention to cumulative protection across biopsychosocial-spiritual dimensions and across development is also needed and would further refine our knowledge base in the service of better helping our clients.

Consequences of Substance Abuse

The economic costs of substance abuse include treatment, prevention, health care, reduced job productivity, crime, and social welfare. The consequences of substance abuse are not only economic but affect public safety, health, and community capacity. According to the RWJF, more people die, become ill, or sustain disabilities from substance abuse than from all other health problems, with around 25% of all deaths each year related to substance use. People with substance abuse problems frequently are brought to the attention of health care professionals through health care and social systems other than primary substance abuse treatment facilities such as primary health care offices, emergency rooms, the criminal justice system, child welfare or public assistance offices, or mental health clinics (Weisner, 2002). In fact, it is estimated that 80% of those in the criminal justice system have committed a substance-related offense (Miller & Weisner, 2002).

Oesterle et al. (2004) examined the relationship between four adolescent drinking trajectories and health status in emerging adulthood at age 24, tracking a sample of 808 fifth graders who were interviewed through adolescence at ages 13–16, then in emerging adulthood at ages 18, 21, and 24. Results showed that those who increased drinking consumption throughout adolescence also reported unsafe health practices (e.g., nonuse of seat belt, unsafe driving practices) and showed increased health risk (e.g., high blood pressure, hypertension, obesity, lack of exercise) practices at age 24. Those who increased drinking only in mid-adolescence did not show significant differences in health outcomes at age 24 when compared to the other trajectory conditions. Therefore, as might be expected, it is *chronic* heavy use throughout adolescence that has the most significant health consequences in emerging adulthood.

In addition to the general developmental consequences of substance use discussed above, studies have shown differential impacts of substance use for various groups. African American adolescent females have increased self-confidence and lower substance abuse rates as compared to white female youth (Belgrave, Chase-Vaughn, Gray, Addison, & Cherry, 2000). However, the research shows that the later onset of substance use for

African Americans still comes with more problematic consequences such as health-related problems (Gil, Wagner, & Tubman, 2004). Other researchers have found that, across minority groups, substance abuse is related to low self-esteem, cultural identity struggles, and hopelessness (Collins & McNair, 2002). For example, the alcoholism mortality rate for Native Americans is 6 times that of the general population (Frank, Moore & Ames, 2000).

Gender differences in consequences of drug use are many. Women who abuse alcohol have higher rates of comorbid depression as compared to male alcohol abusers, but this difference did not hold for male and female drug abusers (Westermeyer, 2003). Physical consequences of substance use are accelerated in women through a process known as "**telescoping**," related to the differences in how women and men biologically process alcohol and drugs in the body. Women develop liver problems (e.g., hepatitis and cirrhosis) over a shorter period of time and with less quantity of substances as compared to men and are more likely to die from these diseases than male substance abusers. Female alcoholics have death rates 50%–100% higher than male alcoholics (Wasilow-Mueller & Erickson, 2001). For additional detailed information on female adolescent substance abuse and racial/ethnic differences within this population, see Guthrie, Rotheram, and Genero (2001).

There are many conditions that co-occur with substance abuse, and sometimes it is difficult to discern from the literature whether these conditions precede a substance abuse disorder, occur simultaneously with substance abuse, or are a consequence of the substance abuse. Common co-occurring disorders with substance abuse include schizophrenia, bipolar, major depression, PTSD, and obsessive-compulsive disorders. Individuals with a substance use disorder are 5 times as likely to also have a mood disorder at some time during their lives (Greenfield, 2003). Comorbidity rates across both non-treated and clinical samples are between 40% and 90% for adults and adolescents (Kessler et al., 1997; Rounds-Bryant, Kristiansen, & Hubbard, 1999). About one third (36%) of people with an alcohol disorder and half (50%) of people with a drug disorder will have another mental health condition (Bennett, 2002). Although there is variation in rates across studies, it can generally be said that mood disorders begin before substance use in only 30% of the substance abuse cases. For example, in 60% of cases, people develop substance use before bipolar disorder; 85%–95% of people only experience depressive symptoms during sustained alcohol use (DelBello & Strakowski, 2003).

Other studies have more definitively shown that mood disorders begin before substance use disorders (Kessler et al., 1997). The onset of psychiatric disorders tends to precede substance use disorder in adolescents (Hovens, Cantwell, & Kiriakos, 1994; Kessler et al., 1997), where vulnerability to a psychiatric disorder may lead to increased risk for a substance abuse disorder. For adolescents, conduct disorder or other externalizing disorders are related to more frequent alcohol use, more problematic treatment outcomes, and increased risk of treatment noncompletion (Rowe, Liddle, Greenbaum, & Henderson, 2004).

In a longitudinal study that examined substance abuse patterns in individuals ages 12–31, Bennett, McCrady, Johnson, and Pandina (1999) found that the interval between ages 21 and 28 represents the developmental period when young adults are most likely to mature out of problem-drinking status, with those continuing on with problem drinking reflecting a "developmentally persistent" pattern of substance use. The research showed that the developmentally persistent group was differentiated from other substance use trajectories by gender (predominantly male), cognitive factors (high in disinhibition), and behavior (high in other problem behaviors). Decreases in problem drinking across the adolescent to young adulthood transition is associated with taking on normative roles in adulthood such as work and family responsibilities and developing self-regulatory capacity (Jessor, Donovan, & Costa, 1991; Moffitt, 1993).

A social worker working with Junito might be concerned about his longer-term developmental trajectory and his ability to "mature out" of substance use, given his gender, eroding academic attachment, and intense feeling of being overwhelmed, which the literature shows could lead to other risky behaviors if he grew more deeply hopeless. A social worker would also explore the strengths that contributed to Junito's earlier academic success in his country of origin, which can now be revisited in order to help him reorient to earlier positive experiences and capabilities.

Ways of Coping

The substance abuse literature indicates a variety of ways that people attempt to cope with a substance abuse disorder (see Exhibit 7.4 for a summary). Schulenberg et al. (1997) identify several models that describe the developmental transition into substance abuse. The *overload model* suggests that developmental transitions along the life course may impair coping capacities that lead to substance use. The *developmental mismatch model,* characterized by life's risk and opportunities, suggests that it is in the match between the individual and his or her ecological context at the time of the developmental transition (e.g., individual developmental needs and the ecological context resources) that will indicate how well and the way in which one copes. The *increased heterogeneity model* suggests that developmental transitions serve as moderators of risk, in that developmental crises lead to later problems that lead to unhealthy adaptive capacity and different life trajectories over time. For example, as poorly adjusting adolescents continue to experience additional transitions, their chances at successfully leveraging positive coping strategies to negotiate the transition become increasingly challenged, which may further increase the risk of substance use. The *transition catalyst model* posits that risk taking is normative in maneuvering through adolescent transitions (e.g., autonomy, identity expansion and formation; p. 5). This would be compatible with the time-limited and developmentally appropriate use of substances in adolescence—what many might refer to as an "experimental" phase.

Niaura (2000) presents a dynamic regulatory model of drug relapse that integrates biological and psychological dimensions of risk, suggesting that drug cues activate attentional processes, craving, and positive outcome expectancies along with physiological responses. Relapse can be prevented by identifying and attending to the cues in new ways. The availability of coping skills posttreatment was a significant predictor of drug use

Cognitive	Spiritual	Sociocultural
Analysis of positive and negative consequences of substance use	Praying	Utilizing sober social support network
Regulation of impulsivity	Relying on a higher power	Good ecological niche or fit between needs and resources
Successful negotiation of developmental transitions	Staying spiritually connected	Attending self-help meetings
Good problem-solving abilities and behavioral refusal skills	Practicing meditation and mindfulness	Strengthening parenting discipline and family cohesion

Exhibit 7.4   Coping Strategies

outcome, regardless of type of treatment received (Litt, Kadden, Cooney, & Kabela, 2003). Problem-solving coping strategies are more likely to be used by individuals who are able to abstain from substance use as compared to those who relapse (Myers & Brown, 1990a, 1990b). King and Chassin (2004) found that lower-perceived parental discipline and inability to regulate impulsivity mediated the relationship between parental substance use and emergence of a substance use disorder in early adulthood. Findings suggest that intervening in families to strengthen behavioral control and parenting discipline in families where there is at least one parent with a substance use disorder can significantly reduce the odds of the child developing a substance use disorder later in the life course, suggesting that psychosocial interventions may be able to interrupt existing biological influences.

More specifically, Rohsenow, Martin, and Monti (2005) examined specific coping strategies that facilitated a reduction in cocaine use, after residential treatment, in a sample of cocaine-dependent individuals. They found that several urge-specific coping skills were associated with reduction in cocaine use at 6-month follow-up, which include "behavioral skills (finding alternative behaviors, escape, employing behavioral refusal skills, problem-solving, relaxation, and attending meetings and accessing social support); cognitive skills (thinking about the positive and negative consequences of staying sober and using, distraction, and inner strength messages); and spiritual (praying and relying on a higher power)" (p. 216). Inner-strength messages and seeking social support were not influential in the first 3-month follow-up but were found to be effective between 3 and 6 months. Substituting nondrug consumption for cocaine consumption, challenging negative thoughts, and self-punishing thoughts were not effective. General lifestyle changes were also found to be effective in reducing cocaine use at 6-month postresidential treatment. Effective lifestyle changes included engaging in clean ways of having fun, keeping busy, relaxing and meditating, reducing the amount of money the individual has access to, living with sober people, spending time with sober-supportive people, working toward future goals, reminding oneself that one is a sober person, thinking of the consequences of drug use and sobriety, and maintaining a spiritual connection. Keeping busy, thinking of negative consequences, and living with sober people were only effective during the first 3 months posttreatment (they maintained same gains from 3 to 6 months but showed no additional contribution during this later time frame), whereas thinking about positive consequences made additional contributions to reducing cocaine use throughout the 6-month time frame.

The substance abuse literature shows that responsibility for child care is a significant problem for women coping with sobriety, and there is often significant guilt related to the parenting role. Thus, high reactivity to stress may be a precursor to using substances as a way to cope (Sheppard, Smith, & Rosenbaum, 1988). It is critical to help clients learn how to adapt to these internal and external stressors, to manage emotions, and to connect to supports and resources in order to control stress reaction. Because affect dysregulation caused by the stressor, not the stressor itself, may lead to increased substance use as a way to cope, strategies that help strengthen attention, planning, cognitive flexibility, and self-monitoring capacities, in the presence of intense emotional experience, may be particularly effective in prevention and coping efforts.

Social Justice Issues

The stress vulnerability model of addiction that helps to explain reactivity patterns and treatment models that focus on managing affective material (e.g., emotional management programs) do not address the larger societal and structural issues that may be contributing to a community's disproportionate use of addictive substances. As social workers, we are constantly called to examine the range of intended and unintended consequences of our beliefs and to identify what sources inform our conceptual frameworks. Indeed, how we choose to view the etiology of substance use will determine how we treat the problem and to whom we ascribe responsibility for further action. For example, if we view substance abuse as a disease, do we risk minimizing the larger socioeconomic opportunity structures that might be implicated in perpetuating the addictive behaviors and lose out on a more comprehensive treatment strategy for our client? If we view substance abuse as a criminal act, who or what groups might be unfairly targeted by our criminal justice system?

As social workers, we may, at some point, find ourselves experiencing a conflict between our own professional and personal ethical framework and that of our work environment. For example, we may personally and professionally believe in helping clients maximize self-determination and exercise choice in treatment planning through collaborative decision making, and yet we may work in a treatment agency that emphasizes a clinician's hierarchical role, deemphasizes collaborate treatment planning, and prioritizes the clinical team's recommendations over client input, since "what the client has tried in the past has not worked." Some social workers have explored alternative treatment philosophies, such as harm reduction approaches, that seek to address and respond to these conflicts (Brocato & Wagner, 2003). Given the complexity of how substance abuse manifests in clients' lives, a social justice perspective would suggest that we have an ethical responsibility to acknowledge and address substance abuse from multiple vantage points that enhance individual agency and organizational capacity to give clients the opportunity to translate choice into action.

The current literature provides compelling evidence that psychosocial conditions pose biological risk and that biological risk can lead to psychosocial developmental challenges, which may lead to problematic behavioral outcomes like substance abuse. Therefore, the differential impact associated with environmental opportunities and constraints (see Shonkoff & Phillips, 2000) afforded to different racial/ethnic and socioeconomic groups contributes to growing health disparities. At a biological level, this may be seen in differential environmental opportunities for hippocampal development, as studies have shown stronger hippocampal growth (some estimates of 15% greater growth) in enriched as opposed to impoverished environments (Curtis & Nelson, 2003).

Enriched environments have been shown to produce neurochemical and neuroanatomical advantages, such as increased brain efficiency and plasticity. Studies have shown the importance of physical interaction with the environment for brain change and learning to occur (Curtis & Nelson, 2003). Researchers are working to better understand how the environment influences gene expression and thus how gene expression through environmental interaction affects the development of substance abuse disorders. New research needs to examine how prevention models operating at multiple system access points (individual, family, and community) might disrupt stress vulnerability at early onset, chronic, and ongoing dependency stages, across ages, racial/ethnic groups, and gender.

Practice Implications

As social workers, we have spent a great deal of energy focusing on the psychosocial determinants of risk and protection in various challenges of living and have not directed as much attention to the biological dimension, although continuing to espouse a "biopsychosocial" foundation from which we practice. Bridging the biological and socioenvironmental dimensions of our model in a more intentional and informative way may be particularly useful for understanding, assessing, and treating substance abuse disorders.

In addition, we might begin to work toward greater convergence between our explanatory (e.g., risk/protection factor) research and our clinical or intervention research. Practicing social workers can stand to benefit from utilizing this risk/protection explanatory research to inform and advance treatment interventions. Videka (2003) makes a recommendation along these lines in advocating for a blended methodological approach that includes information flow from both epidemiological and efficacy research approaches. "What is needed now is a new generation of studies that examine the moderating effects of epidemiological risk and protective factors on processes with the outcomes of interventions" (p. 181).

Along these lines, Masten (2004) provides an integrative perspective on risk and resilience, related to adolescent development, that offers social workers a multidimensional framework for assessment and intervention practices. In particular, Masten discusses regulatory capital that consistently differentiates at-risk youth from resilient youth and includes executive functioning, emotional regulation, attachments to adults who monitor and support youth, relationships with peers who effectively regulate interactions, bonding to prosocial socializing and community organizations, and sociocontextual opportunities for regulatory capacity building (p. 315). There are many exciting and creative multilevel prevention and intervention strategies that can be developed to increase regulatory capital, based on this research. For example, intervening at multiple system levels could include examining education or vocation-focused mentorship opportunities for Junito within the Latino community, shoring up support within Junito's religious institution, participating as a family in culturally congruent family-focused programs that provide skills training in parent-child communication and parental monitoring and supervision, coordinating services with the school to provide appropriate resources that promote academic engagement, as well as helping Junito to develop individual strengths such as problem-focused coping, self-efficacy in high-risk situations, and emotional management skills (see USDHHS, National Institute on Drug Abuse's [NIDA] *Preventing Drug Use Among Children and Adolescents,* 2003 for more details).

Other factors associated with resilient youth are religious faith and affiliations and beliefs that life has meaning and purpose. Neighborhoods high in social capital, such as those with structure, positive expectations of youth culture, and support, are associated with less youth problems (Sampson, et al., 1997).

Winters (2001) suggests several core domains in adolescent substance abuse assessment that are useful in directing treatment intervention. Assessment domains should include (a) drug abuse problem severity (history of use, quantity, frequency, duration of symptoms), (b) reasons for use and biopsychosocial consequences of use, (c) risk and protective factors to include personal adjustment (learning abilities, psychological status, delinquent behavioral risks), (d) peer environment (peer drug use, peer norms, repertoire of role models), (e) home environment (parenting practices, family cohesiveness, parental drug use behaviors and attitudes, abuse, sibling substance use, family norms and expectations about drug use), and (f) community and neighborhood characteristics (socioeconomic status, crime statistics; p. 87). In addition, perception of neighborhood norms related to drug use and recovery behaviors, employment and non-drug-related opportunities, neighborhood opportunities for obtaining social and psychological capital (e.g., peer group attainment, self-efficacy, personal respect, monetary rewards, social power) from non-drug-related activities should be included in a multidimensional assessment.

A client's readiness for behavior change cannot be overstated. Awareness and acceptance of the problem often precedes readiness for action. Prochaska and DiClemente's (1983) **transtheoretical model** (TTM) of change provides a stage sequential framework for understanding the readiness to change process (see Exhibit 7.5 for an overview of this and other evidence-based treatment approaches). In their model, a client is in the (a) *precontemplation* stage when there is no problem recognition/acknowledgment and no intention of changing, (b) *contemplation* stage when one considers change but has no plan, (c) *preparation* stage when the client is ready to change and takes action steps, (d) *action* stage when steps to change have been taken, and (e) *maintenance* stage when one is actively working to maintain gains made. Assessment of a client's readiness to change can offer treatment recommendations that are in line with the client's pace of change. Helping clients to weigh the risks and benefits of their substance use and examine the consequences of continuing to use versus stopping use can be one way of gauging where a client is in the commitment to change. Some clients may not agree that their substance use is a problem for them but have come to your attention because their family has encouraged them (or has given them an ultimatum) to seek help. Outpatient family education sessions may be helpful here to engage the entire family around the "problem" and to understand the family's influence in the process.

Practice Approach	Goals/Methods	Representative Citations
Transtheoretical Model (TTM)	This readiness-to-change model suggests that clients go through five stages in making behavioral changes: precontemplation, contemplation, preparation, action, and maintenance. Relapse is a final sixth stage in the model.	Prochaska & DiClemente, 1983
Community Reinforcement and Family Training (CRAFT)	This approach is used by family members who wish to engage a loved one and help him or her commit to treatment for a substance abuse problem.	Meyers, Miller, Hill, & Tonigan, 1999; Myers, Miller, Smith, & Tonigan, 2002
Motivational Interviewing (MI)	MI utilizes a nonconfrontational approach that emphasizes collaboration with clients, empathy, and client choice. Decisional balance (weighing the advantages and disadvantages of behavior change) is a key technique used in this approach.	Burke, Arkowitz, & Menchola, 2003; Miller & Rollnick, 2002
Cognitive-Behavioral Therapy (CBT)	This approach helps the client link thoughts, emotions, and behaviors through a functional analysis of the positive and negative consequences of drug use, develop planning capacities to manage triggers, and modify interpretations and beliefs about oneself and drug use.	See review article by Carroll, 1996
Relapse Prevention Model (RP)	RP targets skills development to help clients successfully negotiate high-risk situations related to their drug/alcohol use.	Marlatt, 1985

Exhibit 7.5   Examples of Evidence-Based Approaches to Treating Substance Abuse

Bernstein et al. (2005) found that a single contact by a peer educator with cocaine and heroin users who were not in substance abuse treatment but who were seeking services in a medical setting was effective at reducing drug use at 6-month follow-up, suggesting that the tenets of brief motivational interviewing can be employed in service settings other than primary substance abuse treatment agencies to get drug users on the path toward abstinence. Another family-oriented treatment engagement model that has shown promising evidence-based support is the Community Reinforcement and Family Training (CRAFT) approach (Meyers et al., 1999; Meyers et al., 2002; Miller, Meyers, & Tonigan, 1999). The approach is used when the family member has not yet made a commitment to treatment, and the broad goal is to help facilitate family members to engage their loved one in treatment through reinforcing abstinent behavior. Using a nonconfrontational approach, CRAFT emphasizes timing as a critical motivating element in engaging the treatment refuser, and teaches family members skills in helping to support their loved one's commitment to seek treatment.

For clients who are ready to engage in a formal treatment process themselves, experiential rather than cognitive-behavioral strategies might be more appropriate in the early stages before one has committed to changing thoughts related to substance-using behaviors, whereas behavioral strategies may be more appropriate at later stages, when a client is looking for problem-solving help in taking action to change (Prochaska, DiClemente, & Norcross, 1992).

Developmental scaffolding with its inherent flexibility and plasticity can lead to diversity in outcome and different developmental pathways by different "interventions" at various points in the life course that build on either the adaptations and competencies or vulnerabilities that have accumulated to that point in time (Yates, Egeland, & Sroufe, 2003). New research should examine issues of developmental sensitivity and attend to accumulative protection with the same research vigor as we have attended to accumulative risk. In understanding these nuances, we can uniquely tailor our treatment plans to the specific needs of our clients. For example, Fishbein et al.'s (2004) evidence suggests that some substance-abusing adolescents might need more intensive cognitive therapy than may be traditionally offered and/or needed for other types of youth in treatment who do not have such cognitive deficits. Intervening early is important. Schulenberg, Maggs, Steinman, and Zucker (2001) discuss the role of prevention in adolescence as critical in deterring the development of long-term consequences in adulthood, because adolescence is a time when life choices are made that lead to subsequent educational, occupational, and relational opportunities.

For example, it will be particularly beneficial to intervene with Junito and his family before Junito enters emerging adulthood, as the literature suggests that other health risks are likely to develop if he continues his substance use pattern into young adulthood. Helping Junito develop normative roles (such as engagement in work, family, community service, religion, education), with adequate supports and resources, can lead to decreased use.

Marlatt's (1985) **relapse prevention model** also provides a useful framework for substance abuse treatment, where high-risk situations lead to effective or ineffective coping responses that influence self-efficacy and impact drug use. Thus, understanding a person's unique high-risk situations can lead to awareness and strategies to decrease vulnerability. Rowe et al. (2004) found that multidimensional family treatment and cognitive-behavioral therapy (CBT) are effective treatments for adolescent substance abusers with externalizing disorders. However, adolescents with comorbid psychiatric problems, as compared to a substance use only group, had poorer 6- and 12-month post-treatment follow-up outcomes related to drug abstinence. These findings, in conjunction with the Fishbein et al. (2004) findings, suggest that there may be a subset of adolescents with comorbid substance abuse and psychiatric diagnoses (i.e., those with prefrontal cortex deficits who have difficulty integrating cognitive and emotional material) for whom a more specialized type of CBT might be indicated.

Understanding cultural differences and drawing upon cultural strengths in working with people struggling with substance abuse needs to be emphasized. Loue (2003) discusses the Latino concept of machismo, where it may not be acceptable to ask for help because one may risk disgracing the family. In many cultures, "needs" are viewed as family and community needs, rather than individual needs. And there is often a pronounced value and respect for elders. Knowing these cultural strengths, a social worker may be able to work with clients in a culturally congruent manner, perhaps developing relationships with older adults who are in recovery and creating a "family unit" within the recovery community so that sharing becomes culturally acceptable. Along these lines, it is important that social workers working with clients experiencing alcohol and other drug use disorders understand the role of women in the client's culture. It is important to check out with clients their expectations about gender role practices and beliefs, particularly as it might conflict with a social worker's own treatment philosophy (e.g., advocating that a female client become empowered to leave her substance-abusing husband may be culturally incompatible).

In addition, the client may value talking about health problems more than talking about mental health problems, which has implications for how the social worker might construct language around the problem, perhaps focusing on the physical consequences of the addiction in the early relationship development process. In addition, the common 12-step and medical model principle of "accepting powerlessness" over one's addiction may not be culturally (or spiritually) congruent to some treatment seekers who are socialized to keep emotions suppressed and to take control of situations and interpersonal relationships. Furthermore, compatible with any multidimensional assessment, a social worker needs to assess for migration and acculturation history and past trauma experiences that may be complicating addictions treatment in order to better understand how a client's cognitive and affective connection with the cultural community might be appropriately leveraged to facilitate recovery.

Research has shown that the stronger a person's perception that other significant people in his or her life associate the treatment seeker with a drug identity, and the weaker these significant others' association of the treatment seeker with a recovery identity, the more severe the treatment seeker's self-assessed drug-use severity (Matto et al., 2005). This suggests that significant social context referents (e.g., family, peers, community) may have important influence on the addiction recovery process. In better understanding the unique social context constellation of influence for each treatment seeker, social workers may be able to directly and indirectly intervene within the larger ecological context to gain leverage in strengthening a treatment seeker's attachment to a recovery-related community. By leveraging the power of social context change influences within one's environment, more informal preventive service delivery systems may begin to develop. And in the long run over time, data from aggregate studies might facilitate the development and design of community- and culturally specific "fellowship" models that utilize indigenous community supports to help facilitate recovery and to build stronger, healthier communities.

Learning Activities

1. The SAMHSA Center for Substance Abuse Treatment (CSAT) addiction counseling practice competencies specifically include (a) clinical evaluation, (b) treatment planning, (c) referral, (d) service coordination, (e) counseling, (f) client, family, community education, (g) documentation, and (h) professional and ethical responsibilities. (SAMHSA, Center for Substance Abuse Treatment, 1998).

What, in your estimation, is missing from the above listed practice competencies from a social work perspective **(values/ethics analysis and general knowledge)?** How does social work's professional competencies integrate with these SAMHSA practice competencies **(values and ethics)?** Where do you see social work playing a significant role? In what ways? What contributions will social work make to an overall service plan for substance abuse clients, drawing on this practice competency framework? Insert the element of time into the above referenced practice competencies—what would a service delivery/ case management plan look like? What would be difficult for you personally, as a social worker, in implementing this service delivery plan **(general knowledge, values/ethics, knowledge of self)?**

2. Get into four small groups, each representing a different biopsychosocial-spiritual dimension. As a group, spend 25 minutes developing a dimension-determined argument of risk/protection to present to the other three dimensions (e.g., biologically determined; socially determined). Try your best, as a group, to *only* focus on your specific dimension without introducing aspects of the others into your argument **(general knowledge).**

- What were the challenges your group faced in composing the argument **(knowledge of self, values/ethics)?**
- How did your group's argument contribute to understanding the nature of substance abuse and how to help individuals, families, and communities struggling with addiction?
- What are the strengths and limitations of the existing risk/protection literature on your dimension in understanding and helping people struggling with addiction **(general knowledge)?**

As a class, what are the important aspects of each dimension's argument that can be integrated to provide a more accurate and holistic understanding of substance abuse as a challenge of living?

3. Social justice is a core set of principles that guides social work practice and the profession. In this chapter, you have been introduced to various multilevel theories about substance abuse etiology and progression and were exposed to the notion that larger structural issues may influence who develops addiction, who gets treatment, and what type of "treatment" is offered. What is your own philosophy about how substance abuse develops and about who is responsible for treating the problem **(knowledge of self, values/ethics)?** Do you fundamentally believe substance abuse is a disease or a social condition? Do you believe certain groups of individuals, families, or communities (geographic locations) are disproportionately more vulnerable to developing addiction than others **(values/ethics, knowledge of self, knowledge of case/population)?** Which groups, in what ways, and why? What are the larger structural issues that might perpetuate substance abuse and influence treatment options **(general knowledge)?**

4. You have a $1 million grant to "alleviate the problem of substance abuse" in your county. Would you use the money to focus on prevention or intervention **(draw on values/ethics, knowledge of self, and general knowledge to make your case)?** Would you target specifically or target universally? Who would likely be the beneficiaries **(values/ ethics)?** Is your money going toward short-term acute solutions or long-term, steady remediation, what are the likely unintended consequences of choosing one over the other, and how does the decision personally sit with you **(values/ethics, knowledge of self, general knowledge, knowledge of case—e.g., substance abuse population in your community)?** What are important components of your program/approach at individual, family, and/or community levels, drawing on this risk/protection literature **(knowledge of case—e.g., substance abuse population—general knowledge)?**

8

Obesity

Marcia P. Harrigan,
Virginia Commonwealth University

In the case of Elias and Claudia Salvatierra, you may recall that over time Claudia became obese, gaining over 60 pounds since her arrival in the United States. However, to our knowledge, obesity was never presented as a concern of Claudia's, even though Elias made derogatory comments about her weight. Nevertheless, Claudia may be beginning to live with some consequences of her obesity, perhaps both biological and psychosocial consequences. In this chapter, we continue to examine risk and protection, with the focus on obesity.

Within the last 10 years, obesity has become the number one newly recognized public health concern. Today one out of three people in the United States is overweight or obese, a rising trend that extends well beyond the U.S. border. One need only pick up a major newspaper or popular magazine to find newly reported research related to the incidence and causes of, as well as interventions for, obesity. These trends are so alarming that some predict that for the first time in all developed countries during modern times, life expectancy may actually decrease, should obesity prevalence continue to rise (Mizuno, Shu, Makimura, & Mobbs, 2004). In fact, in March 2006, the U.S. surgeon general predicted that the obesity epidemic will become a bigger threat than terrorism if progress is not made to reverse the current trend (Associated Press, 2006).

There are cultural and ethnic variations as well as gender differences about the meaning or perception of normal weight, body size preference, and at what point a person may be perceived as "obese" (Cachelin, Rebeck, Chung, & Pelayo, 2002; Thompson & Story, 2003). In the United States, the prototype continues to be the slim figure paradoxically juxtaposed against "super size it!" in the fast-food industry. Many people continue to view obesity as a psychological issue rooted in unmet emotional needs or a character flaw, merely a lack of self-control. From this perspective, the solution is frequently conveyed with the quick-fix adage, "Eat less; move more." Embracing this simplistic perspective, helping professionals, including social workers, often join the rest of society in responding negatively to persons who are obese (Puhl & Brownell, 2001; Schwartz, Chambliss, Brownell, Blair, & Billington, 2003). This prejudice, or "fat bias," impacts our behavior toward obese clients, ultimately becoming a barrier to helping relationships. Given the obesity epidemic, social workers will encounter more and more clients challenged by obesity, demanding the use of new and rapidly expanding knowledge to guide our work in a broad range of settings (Eliadis, 2006).

Most researchers, both in the United States and in other countries, have adopted the definition of obesity established by the National Institutes of Health (NIH) and endorsed by the World Health Organization (WHO). This definition uses the **body mass index (BMI)**, which is numerically calculated based on height and body weight, using either pounds and inches or kilograms and meters. The formulas are as follows:

BMI = body weight (standard or kilograms)/height (standard or meters)^2

OR

BMI $= kg/m^2$

Using pounds and inches, the formula to calculate BMI is

BMI $=$ Weight (pounds)/height (inches)$^2 \times 703$

To calculate BMI online, see www.nhlbisupport.com/bmi/bmicalc.htm.

A BMI score of less than 18 is considered underweight, 18–24.9 is considered normal weight, 25–29.9 is considered overweight, 30–39.9 is considered obese, and BMI > 40 is considered morbidly obese (see Exhibit 8.1). The cut point designating **obesity** as BMI ≥ 30 was established by NIH because of the increasing negative health consequences as weight rises in relation to height. Although not everyone with BMI ≥ 30 experiences health problems, most do, particularly persons who meet the criteria for metabolic syndrome, which is described later. Researchers are asking whether or not these definitions of obesity using BMI and **waist circumference (WC)** cutoffs are applicable to all populations (Chen, Ho, Lam, & Chan, 2006; Dhiman, Duseja, & Chawla, 2005; Kim et al., 2005). There is a preliminary recommendation of BMI cutoff of 25.0 for obesity for South Korean females aged 8–18 (Kim et al., 2005), but it has been suggested that the NIH BMI cutoffs appear appropriate for Chinese women (Chen et al., 2006).

In spite of the widely accepted use of BMI ≥ 30 as the definition of obesity, other factors must also be considered. For example, the BMI ratio does not consider the proportion of body fat to muscle tissue, the latter weighing more per mass unit. Research has shown that persons with more fat tissue in the abdominal area have increased risk of negative health consequences compared to those of a similar height and weight but with fat distributed more evenly on the body. In response, NIH guidelines to determine obesity for persons

< 18	Underweight
18–24.9	Normal Weight
25–29.9	Overweight
30–39.9	Obese
> 40	Morbidly Obese

Exhibit 8.1   Body Mass Index Cut Points

with a BMI greater than 25 now include WC that is over 40 inches (102 cm) for men and 35 inches (88 cm) for women (NIH, 1998). **Waist-to-hip ratio (WHR)** is another indicator used to establish risk from overweight and obesity (Ostman, Britton, & Jonsson, 2004). For men and women, the WHR ≥ 1.0 is considered a risk for negative health outcomes. A desirable WHR is 0.90 or less for men and 0.80 or less for women (NIH, 1998).

These various cut points for BMI and WHR reflect the point at which fat tissue leads to adverse metabolic effects. Most recently there has been increased attention to what is termed the *metabolic syndrome* related to obesity because it increases, more so than obesity, the risk of life-threatening illnesses. Most researchers agree that **metabolic syndrome** is comprised of two major symptoms: large waist circumference in relation to height and insulin resistance along with two additional symptoms of elevated blood pressure (hypertension) and hyper- or dyslipidaemia (elevated fat in the blood; Bray & Bouchard, 2004b; Roche, 2004; Wisse, 2004). Some ethnic groups have a high prevalence of metabolic syndrome but not obesity, a situation that has stimulated research to identify the risk factor(s) that may be the most predictive of metabolic syndrome. In a study of over 8,200 Japanese men and women, Hsieh and Muto (2006) found that the weight-to-height ratio (W/Ht ≥ 0.05) was the preferred indicator, rather than BMI and WC, to screen Japanese people for metabolic syndrome.

When applied to children, the definition of obesity must consider several factors other than BMI. Some define obesity for persons between the ages of 2 and 19 by using population data represented as percentiles. Children in the 95th or higher percentile for weight are considered to be overweight, and the 97th percentile is used as the cut point for obesity. Others suggest that a child's sexual maturation also should be taken into account because the typical increase in weight at the onset of puberty does not indicate obesity risk over time for most children (Himes et al., 2004).

Patterns of Occurrence

The almost universal use of BMI with established cut points to designate obesity facilitates global comparison of obesity rates and consequences. Once considered an outcome of the affluence of industrialized nations, obesity is now found in most countries, including the developing nations. This pattern has led the WHO to coin the term "**globesity**" to convey the global nature of the problem (Mason, 2005).

Some Global Patterns of Occurrence

The WHO has declared childhood obesity a global epidemic extending well beyond affluent countries. England has shown a threefold increase over 10 years, Egypt a fourfold increase over 18 years. Even the incidence of obese children in developing countries, including Brazil, Ghana, and Haiti, has substantially increased (Ebbeling, Pawlak, & Ludwig, 2002; Schmidt, 2003).

There is higher health risk at all levels of BMI for Chinese and South Asian people, and it is speculated that this remains so regardless of resident country (Seidell & Rissanen, 2004). In their overview of global obesity, Seidell and Rissanen (2004) concluded that there is no difference by gender for white populations in Western and Northern Europe, Australia, and the United States. However, women have a prevalence rate 1.5–2.0 times that of men in countries with a low gross national product such as Central and Eastern Europe, Asia, Latin America, and Africa. Although women are more likely than men to be obese regardless of age in poor countries, only older women report higher rates of obesity than men in affluent societies.

Children and Obesity in the United States

The percentage of children in the United States who are obese has doubled in the last 20 years (Federal Interagency Forum on Child and Family Statistics, 2003; National Library of Medicine [NLM], 2005). For all children ages 6–18, 15% are at least over-weight, a statistic that climbs to 26% for Hispanic children. Using BMI and skinfold mea-sures, one group of researchers examined the prevalence of overweight in children and youth between the ages of 6 and 18 who were of predominantly El Salvadoran ancestry. Their data indicated that the rate of overweight among this sample was twice the national average of all U.S. children and 1.7 times greater than that of Mexican American children (Mirza et al., 2004). While not focused totally on obesity, data from the National Longitudinal Study of Adolescent Health revealed some interesting socioeconomic status (SES) and ethnic disparity patterns for overweight adolescent females. As SES increases, so does overweight prevalence for African American females, whereas overweight preva-lence decreases as SES increases for white, Hispanic, and Asian U.S. teens (Gordon-Larsen, Adair, & Popkin, 2003). These findings raise concern about whether ethnic-specific waist circumference cut points should be established for identifying at-risk children and adolescents. One set of researchers found that Mexican American boys and girls, ages 2–18, have higher WC than either African American or European American boys and girls. African American boys were found to have lower WC than boys of other ethnic groups. Mexican Americans also showed a higher rate of growth of WC with age than the other groups. These researchers emphasize that it is yet to be determined whether these ethnic differences indicate greater risk for Mexican American children and youth and suggest that further research is needed to address this question (Fernandez, Redden, Pietrobelli, & Allison, 2004).

Adults and Obesity in the United States

Obesity among adults in the United States has doubled in the past 20 years, from a prevalence of 15% in 1976–1980 data to a prevalence of 32% in 1999–2000 data (North American Association for the Study of Obesity, 2006). For adults without a history of obesity, the most pronounced weight gain occurs between the ages of 25 and 44, when women gain an average of 4 kg (9 pounds) and men 7 kg (15 pounds). For women, weight tends to increase until the age of 50, when it will gradually begin to decrease. This pattern occurs one decade later for men, with weight decline beginning around age 60 (Mizuno et al., 2004; Sadock & Sadock, 2003).

Older Adults and Obesity in the United States

After age 60 it is rare that a person becomes obese for the first time in the life course. In 2000, 32% of persons in the United States over age 60 were obese. Using data from five nationally representative surveys of U.S. adults, Arterburn, Crane, and Sullivan (2004) predict that by the year 2010 the proportion of older adults who are obese will rise to 37.4%. This prediction reflects the fact that obesity is increasing among younger cohorts, and as these cohorts age, the proportion of older adults who are obese will increase.

Other Patterns of Obesity in the United States

Obesity occurs in all age groups, races, and genders, but a disproportionate obesity burden is borne by persons of lower income and education levels, where it is 6 times more prevalent (Mizuno et al., 2004; Sadock & Sadock, 2003; Song et al., 2004). People with chronic and severe mental illnesses also are more prone to being overweight and obese (Vieweg et al., 2004). The North American Association for the Study of Obesity (NAASO) provides detailed obesity statistics from national studies over time to highlight national trends.

Theories of Causation

Several theoretical approaches have been advanced to explain obesity. These may be categorized as anthropological, biological, biosocial, psychological, social, and ecological. Exhibit 8.2 provides an overview of the major tenets of these theoretical perspectives.

Anthropological Theory

Humans have always had an appetite for meat and sweets (proteins and glucose), which are essential for survival. Our prehistoric ancestors ate meat lower in fat because there were no domesticated meat sources, which have higher fat content. They found scarce sources of glucose while at the same time expending enormous amounts of energy

Theoretical Perspective	Central Ideas
Anthropological	• Human physiology is relatively changed over time. • Humans became less active over time. • Humans consume more energy-dense, processed foods over time.
Biological	• Obesity occurs when ingested calories exceed energy output. • Obesity-related genes, markers, and chromosomal regions contribute to obesity. • Proteins, hormones, and other chemicals contribute to obesity.
Biosocial	• Obesity is caused by undernutrition in utero and early childhood, followed by a period of abundant nutrition.
Psychological	• Low self-esteem and depression put a person at risk for obesity.
Social	• Eating and exercise are influenced by social modeling. • Eating preferences are shaped by reinforcements. • Eating preferences are shaped by association with the social/emotional climate while eating. • Changing lifestyles, involving changes in family meal time and changes in activity level, are contributing to societal obesity. • Food insecurity contributes to obesity. • Food production high in sugar and fat contribute to obesity.
Ecological	• Biological factors, behavioral factors, and environmental factors contribute to obesity.

Exhibit 8.2   Central Ideas of Theoretical Perspectives on the Causes of Obesity

to hunt and gather food supplies. With the invention of agriculture, food sources and an increased number of food types became more available.

Human physiology is relatively unchanged across time, but people became less active over the last several million years while at the same time consuming more energy (calorie)-dense, processed foods. In essence, our body today remains genetically unprepared to live in modern society where food is abundant and available; rather, the human body today functions as it did in prehistoric times, which were fraught with frequent famine. Consequently, according to this theory, our bodies are genetically programmed to eat as much food as is available, to rest when activity is not demanded, and to choose foods that are higher in calories, fat, and sugar (Schmidt, 2003). In an industrialized society, these nutrients are easily and cheaply produced, but people overeat as if the available food may become scarce or unavailable.

This theory appears to contradict other biological evidence that if left to their own choices, infants, and perhaps children up to the age of 3, will eat to satiation, and over time intake will reflect a balanced diet (Birch, Johnson, & Fisher, 1995; Satter, 1995, 1996). So the question must be asked: What accounts for the change in a balanced food intake between infancy and later periods? The answer to this question lies with other factors that together weave the complex fabric of obesity.

Biological Theories

Several different biological mechanisms have been proposed to play a causal role in obesity, including nutrition; genetics; and proteins, hormones, and other chemicals.

Nutrition

Nutrients required by the body roughly fall into three categories: fats, carbohydrates, and protein. Because carbohydrates and proteins cannot be stored, the body converts these nutrients to fat when the energy output is less than the food intake. The energy unit is the calorie, and established guidelines indicate how many calories are needed to support how many pounds of weight in relation to the amount of physical activity. When ingested calories exceed energy output, the result is fat storage. It is this biological process that leads to the simplistic solution to obesity, suggesting that less food intake and more energy output, such as increasing exercise, will balance the equation and lead to weight loss and a resulting normal weight. For many, perhaps most, people, there is ample evidence that this theory, in fact, holds, but for some persons who are obese, this does not occur easily, if at all. The reasons for this are rapidly unfolding as researchers clamor to discover the multiple and complex bodily processes related to obesity (Bray & Brouchard, 2003b).

Genetics

In 1995 scientists discovered a gene that regulates the secretion of **leptin**, a chemical that signals the brain that there is sufficient fat in the body (Bouchard, Perusse, Rice, & Rao, 2004). There is a prevalent belief that multiple genes are involved in the production of obesity. More than 300 obesity-related genes, markers, and chromosomal regions have been linked with human obesity phenotypes (Chagnon et al., 2003). Results from one recent study of 816 participants found that chromosome 2p22 has genes that influence several obesity-related phenotypes, including macronutrients such as saturated fat intake (Cai et al., 2004). Together with perinatal factors, these genes may predispose a person to obesity (Ebbeling et al., 2002). However, these significant discoveries of genetic differences that can result in obesity appear to apply to only an estimated 5% of all persons who are obese (Boston, 2004).

Proteins, Hormones, and Other Chemicals

Researchers no longer consider fat cells, called **adipocytes**, to passively store fat, but rather they see them as acting in complex and dynamic ways that influence a wide range of bodily functions. The proteins, hormones, and other chemicals that fat cells release affect the brain, liver, muscles, reproductive organs, and the immune system. Most recently, scientists have found that fat cells influence the production of new fat cells, one of the reasons why weight gain after a certain point spins out of control, well beyond the weight gain expected from calories ingested in relation to those expended (Bray &

Bouchard, 2004a, 2004b). Fat tissue functions much like other organs that influence a wide range of bodily functions, and to understand this process it is important to know how fat cells develop and something about the newly discovered chemicals and how they function.

The cycle of hunger, eating, and digestion involves a complex interplay of signals that are biochemical (e.g., hormones and enzymes), neurologic (e.g., nerve stimulation), and mechanical (e.g., feeling of fullness when stomach is full). The hunger hormone, called **ghrelin**, stimulates appetite, telling the brain that it is time to eat. After food is ingested and leaves the stomach, **cholecystokinin** (the CCK hormone) produced in the small intestine signals that the meal is over and triggers the release of digestive enzymes from the gall bladder and pancreas. This is the point of satiation. **Satiety** refers to the inhibition of food consumption between meals; it is thought to have biological, cognitive, and environmental determinants (Blundell & Stubbs, 2004).

In 1994 the hormone leptin was discovered and found to signal the brain about the amount of fat in the body and to suppress appetite once a certain level is reached. The gene that regulates leptin recently has been found to express itself in the adipocytes as well as the brain, but how this neurobiological process specifically impacts obesity is not understood yet. Some researchers believe that for persons who are obese, the brain is resistant to leptin, so that appetite is not suppressed when sufficient fat levels are reached (Eikelis & Esler, 2005).

Since 1994 several other compounds have been found to influence one's weight. The protein **adiponectin** is produced by fat cells, blocks production of blood glucose in the liver, and increases muscle activity to make energy. The human body protects against the use of stored fat, however, making weight loss difficult. The leptin level decreases when fat is used for energy, and the body interprets this as a signal of starvation and responds by expending less energy while signaling the brain that more food needs to be ingested to replenish the fat that was used.

Researchers know that all of the recently identified substances found in fat tissue work together in complex ways to influence most body organs and processes. We also know that these fat cell compounds work to protect the body. However, when produced in excess amounts, or when the neuro-pathways are interrupted, problems arise. How these substances work together and why these processes may vary from person to person is not fully understood. While understanding of the neuro- and biochemistry of obesity unfolds, other research is pointing to the role of cognition and environmental factors.

Biosocial Theories

Using global population data, a relationship between early nutrition (in utero and early infancy) and adult obesity has led to the **fetal origin hypothesis**. In countries where there has been chronic malnutrition prior to a period of adequate nutrition, rapidly increasing childhood weight is found. Childhood overweight or obesity leads to adult obesity, but there are greater negative consequences for adults who had a period of undernutrition prior to a period of abundant nutrition, leading to overweight or obesity, than for obese adults who have not had this early life malnutrition. Because the negative outcomes such as heart disease are more prevalent in populations with early life malnutrition, obesity alone ceases to explain these differences in negative health outcomes (Barker, 2004).

Psychological Theory

Researchers also search to establish a link between obesity and depression, self-esteem, and other psychological factors (Carpenter, Hasin, Allison, & Faith, 2000; Dixon, Dixon, & O'Brien, 2003; Faith, Matz, & Jorge, 2002; Onyike, Crum, Lee, Lyketsos, & Eaton, 2003; Palmer, 2003). This line of inquiry has become more sophisticated, moving from literature that is theoretical to large cross-sectional studies focusing on the relationship between psychological factors and obesity. Some scholars propose that depression is a risk factor for obesity (Barefoot et al., 1998; Pine, Goldstein, Wolk, & Weissman, 2001) or that antidepressant medications contribute to obesity (Fava, 2000). On the other hand, other scholars propose that depression is a consequence, not cause, of obesity (Carpenter et al., 2000). Others simply propose that depression and obesity co-occur (Onyike et al., 2003). There is limited longitudinal research to examine this relationship, but the existing research, though sometimes contradictory, indicates that there is a complex bidirectional relationship between depression and obesity that differs across groups (Richardson et al., 2003).

Social Theories

Several theories, focusing on different levels of social life, have proposed a relationship between obesity and the social environment. Four are discussed here.

Social Learning Theory

Several different social learning mechanisms are proposed to play a role in the development and maintenance of obesity. Some obesity scholars have drawn on Albert Bandura's (see Bandura, 1977) concept of *social modeling* to suggest that eating and exercise patterns are influenced by role models. The most commonly studied role models are parents (Benton, 2004), but attention has also been paid to media role models (Golan & Crow, 2004) and older peers (Wardle & Watters, 2004). Other scholars have proposed that food preferences in children are shaped by *reinforcements* (see discussion in Benton, 2004). They suggest that when one food is used as a reward for eating another food ("you can have dessert if you eat your peas"), preference for the food used as reward (dessert) is enhanced and the attractiveness of the food for which the reward was offered (peas) is diminished. It is also proposed that eating preferences are developed by *association,* wherein children develop a preference for foods that are eaten in positive emotional atmospheres and lose interest in foods that are eaten in a negative emotional atmospheres (see discussion in Benton, 2004).

Changing Family Lifestyles

Sociologists also point to changes in family lifestyles as contributors to the increase in obesity, including changes in family mealtime, reduction in physical activity, and increase in sedentary behaviors (see Golan & Crow, 2004). Plentiful fast foods, high in fat and sugar, are "convenient" for the fast-paced American family lifestyle. Furthermore, food consumption may become a solitary event where people eat whatever they want and whenever they so desire. Communication technology also influences family life behavior. The amount of time that children and youth spend watching television or playing video games has led to a more sedentary lifestyle that is juxtaposed with advertisement of energy-dense foods and increasing portion sizes. In communities where violence and poverty are the norms, this sedentary lifestyle is further reinforced when the safety of being inside overrides outdoor activity (see Chapter 4 on community violence). Transportation technology and the design of the built environment have led to less walking and more riding (Finkelstein, Ruhm, & Kosa, 2004).

Food Insecurity and Poverty

Obesity as a result of inadequate food supply sounds paradoxical. In fact, the linking of obesity to food abundance, and malnutrition and underweight to insufficient food supplies, was the prevailing belief until 1995, when Dietz proposed a relationship between episodic food shortages and obesity (Dietz, 1995). He introduced the concept of "**food insecurity**," defined as "limited or uncertain availability of nutritionally adequate and safe foods; or limited or uncertain ability to acquire acceptable foods in socially acceptable ways" (Townsend et al., 2001, p. 1739). Further studies support Dietz's position that food insecurity exists among the poor and is related to obesity (Frongillo, 2003; Kendall, Olson, & Frongillo, 1996; Nestle & Guttmacher, 1992; Rose, 1997; Rose, Basiotis, & Klein, 1995), albeit a view not favored by all policymakers. A review of this line of inquiry until 2003 is provided by Frongillo (2003).

The Economic Explanation of Obesity

When economics are used to explain obesity, we find ourselves immediately in the political arena and in the midst of considerable debate. On one side are those who argue that foods high in sugar, particularly corn syrup, are not only cheaper but are made available to low-income families because of government-subsidized corn crops. Critics also place partial blame on an economic system that continues to support food production that is high in fat and sugar, foods that are more available in inner-city areas and have lower cost than healthier foods such as fresh fruits and vegetables (Fields, 2004). At the heart of this argument is the fact that many schools increase access to these foods by supporting vending machines. While various advocacy groups oppose school vending machines, and changes are beginning to occur in the use, food costs, and contents of vending machines, the paradox is that some schools depend on vending machine profits to support important school programs that are vulnerable to cuts when there is a revenue shortfall (Center for Science in the Public Interest, 2004). And ironically, when school programs are cut, they are likely to be those related to physical activity and after-school programs such as sports and other activities related to obesity prevention and intervention.

An Integrative Model to Understand Obesity

The rapidly expanding literature on obesity is vast, with at times contradictory or confusing information. The current focus is on rapidly emerging biological explanations, with the study of environmental influences following close behind. What is common is the convergence of thinking across the many disciplines concerned with obesity that no one theory or discipline can explain this complex phenomenon. Australians Swinburn and Egger (2004) have proposed a model of obesity to be used as a framework for prevention and intervention. Their proposed **ecological model** allows for the simultaneous examination of individual and environmental perspectives.

Swinburn and Egger's ecological model is based on the theory of energy balance, whereby obesity occurs when the rate of energy (food) intake is greater than the rate of energy (food/fat) expenditure, resulting in energy (fat) storage. Three major influencing factors are considered in this ecological model: biological factors (genes, hormones, age, gender, ethnicity, and drugs), behavioral factors (sedentary lifestyle and overconsumption of food), and environmental factors (physical, economic, political, and sociocultural factors). Emphasis on the environmental subcategories is important, especially to social workers who are likely to target interventions in this area.

The physical environment refers to available foods and access to physical activities, education, technological innovations, information, and food labels. The economic environment includes all financial factors such as costs of obesity in comparison to costs of interventions, as well as profit that is, or could be, impacted by various approaches to obesity (consider the economic costs to the fast-food industry should they face the demise of the super size it). The policy environment refers to policies at all levels, including laws and other mandates that impact behavior related to obesity, such as legislation for food labeling, advertising regulation, appropriations for research, prevention, and intervention, and environmental zoning. The sociocultural environment includes the attitudes, perceptions, values, and beliefs of a person or group that can lead to obesity. This model can serve as a checklist of factors to explore in terms of risk and protection.

_____ Multidimensional Risk and Protection

Exhibit 8.3 provides a summary of the biological, psychological, social, and spiritual risk and protective factors currently identified in the literature on obesity.

	Risk Factors	Protective Factors
Biological	• Heredity • Psychotropic medications • Selected and rare illnesses • Successive pregnancies • Over 10 lbs. at birth • Overweight or obese as child or adolescent • Diet of energy-dense foods • Alcohol use • Possibly food substitutes • Smoking cessation	• Breastfed as infant • Diet balanced between energy intake and energy output • Physical activity/exercise
Psychological	• Negative emotions • Depression	• None identified
Social	• Overcontrolling or democratic parent style, culture specific • Parental modeling • Sedentary lifestyle • Built environment that discourages physical activity • "Super size-it" culture • Readily accessible energy-dense, lower-cost foods • Food insecurity • Immigration • Sexual abuse	• Positive parent-child relationship • Parental modeling of good food choices • Energy balanced eating patterns established early in development • Regular physical exercise/active lifestyle • Built environment that encourages physical activity
Spiritual	• None identified	• None identified

Exhibit 8.3   Biological, Psychological, Social, and Spiritual Risk and Protective Factors for Obesity

Biological Risk and Protection

Research related to the biological factors that influence obesity is clearly in its infancy. Current studies are too seldom connected across disciplinary lines, are largely based on animal studies that may or may not apply to humans, and are frequently conducted without incorporation of the environmental or external factors that are increasingly recognized to heavily influence the biology of obesity. Consequently, the following discussion of risk and protective factors should be considered as very preliminary findings without assigning a direct linear cause of obesity (Blundell & Stubbs, 2004).

Heredity is a known risk factor for obesity, but it is difficult to sort out the hereditary influence from the social learning contribution/influence. For example, children whose parents are obese are 10 times more likely to be obese. Studies vary in findings about the proportion of obese children who become obese adults, but there is an established relationship, especially if children's parents are obese (Barker, 2004; NIH, 1998; NLM, 2005).

The mapping of the human genome opens a new door for understanding and treating obesity. Preliminary evidence has pointed to several genetic markers located on the human chromosome 2p22 that influence a variety of nutrient intakes such as fat and proteins (Cai et al., 2004). At the time this chapter was written, there were seven identified genetic disorders related to obesity (Bray, 2004). However, these genetic anomalies are rare. Again, it is believed that only an estimated 5% of cases of obesity may be explained by genetics.

Major mental illnesses, largely thought to have a biological basis, pose risk of obesity. For example, persons diagnosed with schizoaffective disorder, bipolar type, are at greater risk for metabolic disorder, which typically results from obesity (Basu et al., 2004). The psychopharmacologic agents used to treat mental illness are the primary link between mental illness and weight gain. Antipsychotic medications such as Zyprexa, mood stabilizers such as lithium, and antidepressants such as Prozac result in weight gain as a common side effect, due either to fluid retention or to increased caloric intake related to increased appetite, particularly for carbohydrates (Bray, 2004; Sadock & Sadock, 2003; Virk, Schwartz, Jindal, Nihalani, & Jones, 2004). Other drugs such as cortisone, which is used to boost the body's immune system, also place a person at risk of weight gain. Weight gain resulting from cortisone is found typically in the trunk area, and this may be associated with increased negative health consequences.

Obesity also is a consequence of other, typically rare, illnesses. Multiple congenital anomaly/mental retardation syndromes, such as Prader-Willi Syndrome, are associated with intrinsic obesity (Gunay-Aygun, Cassidy, & Nicholls, 1997). Cushing's disease, caused by dysfunction or tumors of either the pituitary or adrenal glands, endocrine system dysfunction such as hypoactive thyroid, and Frohlich's syndrome are examples of other biological dysfunction or diseases for which obesity is one of the many symptoms.

Weight gain associated with pregnancy also poses risk of obesity. On average, women begin a subsequent pregnancy 2.5 kg (or 5.5 pounds) heavier than the previous one (Sadock & Sadock, 2003). In a large (N = 2,035) study of women, the risk of obesity increased about 7% with each live birth after controlling for SES, age, marital status, BMI at age 18, use of oral contraceptives, hysterectomy status, physical activity, age of menarche, and the current use of hormone therapy (Bastian, West, Corcoran, & Munger, 2005). Claudia Salvatierra is a good example of this. She started a progressive weight gain after Junito's birth; she gained considerable weight with her pregnancy with Sergia and Isabel and has continued to gain weight.

Developmental stage may also pose risk for obesity. There appear to be three critical developmental periods that are related to adult obesity: prenatal period, childhood, and adolescence. Birth weight over 10 pounds and overweight and obesity in childhood and adolescence place a person at greater risk for adult obesity (Barker, 2004).

There are several other risk factors that bridge the biological and social dimensions, and the interactive effects across the various dimensions are still unknown. For example, Ebbeling et al. (2002) report that indulgence in energy-dense foods with high glycemic index, such as those found in fast-food enterprises, results in a rapid increase in blood sugar and insulin, which is then followed by a sharp decline and hunger. These foods induce a sequence of hormonal activities that stimulate hunger, leading to overindulgence and more frequent eating and, consequently, in more energy input in relation to output. Obesity is the ultimate result.

Energy-dense foods are also more cost effective for the food industry compared to other foods, such as fresh fruits and vegetables, that are more satisfying because they have a slower release of energy. Therein lies a social risk factor. Besides being less expensive, energy-dense foods also have a longer shelf life, are less prone to spoilage, and because they typically do not need refrigeration, they are easier to transport as well. Consequently, these foods comprise a larger proportion of food selections in the smaller stores typically found in areas where there is lower household income.

The ingestion of dietary fats also serves as a risk factor for weight gain, leading to obesity. This is particularly so when there is a genetic predisposition for weight gain in women. Foods high in fat content are more energy dense and therefore weigh less than other food sources with equal amounts of energy. It is speculated that fat ingestion results in more weight gain because it does not produce the same degree of fullness sensation as do less energy-dense foods such as fruits and vegetables (Bray, 2004; NIH, 1998; NLM, 2005). However, it is also known that not all people with high fat intake, even holding energy output constant, gain weight. Researchers continue to search for what complex interplay of factors results in obesity for some individuals but not in others.

Alcohol is a well-established risk factor for obesity because it contains almost twice as much energy as do carbohydrates and proteins per unit and is metabolized quickly in the body. Also, other food that is ingested at the same time as alcohol is digested and stored more rapidly as fat (Bray & Bouchard, 2004b; NIH, 1998; NLM, 2005). These outcomes related to alcohol and weight gain vary by gender, although there is insufficient explanatory research as to why this is so.

Food substitutes have also been suspect in understanding obesity. However, insufficient data exist to support several hypotheses that food substitutes (e.g., for sugar and fat) act as either protective or risk factors for obesity. Some researchers have provided evidence that these food substitutes stimulate intake of either similar foods or high-energy foods. Other researchers have found the opposite, that using food substitutes suppresses the desire for foods that lead to weight gain. Still others show evidence that both situations can occur depending on when the food substitute is ingested in relation to other foods, how much is ingested in a given period of time, and the type of food being ingested, such as liquid or solid (Blundell & Stubbs, 2004).

Smoking cessation is another risk factor for weight gain. In twin studies, for example, those no longer smoking had a 27% greater incidence of obesity than their currently smoking twin (Flegal, Troiano, Pamuk, Kuczmarski, & Campbell, 1995).

Protective Factors

Breast-feeding protects against childhood obesity, although the reasons are not clearly established. Several theories have been posited to explain this protective factor. One is that breast-feeding promotes more self-regulation of intake. Another theory is that breast milk provides hormonal or growth factors that permanently change the child's metabolism (Barker, 2004). In a study of 11,000 German children in the first grade, those who were solely breast-fed for at least 1 year reported only an 0–0.8% rate of obesity compared to 4.8% obesity rate for children who had no or little breast-feeding (Von Kries et al., 1999). A large longitudinal study in the United States (N = 73,458 white and black low-income children) provided further evidence that breast-feeding was a protective factor for obesity at age 4 years, with protection varying by race, smoking behavior of mother, and breast-feeding length of time. Protection was found only for white children whose mothers did not smoke and who were breast-fed for at least 16 weeks without formula supplements or for at least 26 weeks with formula supplement (Bogen, Hanusa, & Whitaker, 2004).

Energy input and output factors can protect against obesity. Well-balanced diets with total daily calories equal to energy expended will result in either obesity prevention or weight reduction. Establishment of early eating patterns that reflect a wide variety of foods has been found to be a protective factor (Birch & Fisher, 1998). Research findings about this biological protective factor are not straightforward, however. One study that examined the relationship between physical activity and diet for 200 preadolescent African American girls revealed that income was inversely related to the proportion of calories ingested from fat, data that would support a social risk factor. However, when the data were analyzed to control for household income, material possessions, and total caloric intake, the data showed that greater physical activity was related to lower ingestion of dietary fat (Jago et al., 2004). This finding supports the widely held belief that energy input and output balance protects against obesity. Yet, another study conducted by the same research center to further examine this relationship found no significant relationship between physical activity and dietary variables or between physical activity and/or diet and BMI. This seemingly contradictory finding could have resulted from a smaller sample size (N = 127) with short duration or the inclusion of more than one type of intervention (Thompson et al., 2004). Finally, another research team concluded that the relationship between obesity and physical functioning in older women is not well understood. Their study revealed, however, that physical activity, and not obesity, is more important in predicting future overall physical functioning (Brach, VanSwearingen, FitzGerald, Storti, & Kriska, 2004).

Psychological Risk and Protection

Earlier we suggested that mental illness increasingly is thought to be based, at least partially, in biology and is discussed as a biopsychosocial phenomenon. We are discussing mental illness here as psychological risk factor because of attention to the emotional aspects of mental illness. The relationship between depression and other psychiatric conditions, such as obsessive-compulsive disorders, and obesity is well established. Likewise, it is widely accepted that there is a transactional relationship between emotion and weight gain, with negative emotions contributing to weight gain and weight gain contributing to negative emotions. Sometimes it is very hard to tease out the nature of these transactions.

Using longitudinal data, children with childhood depression have been found to have higher BMI in a 10- to 15-year follow-up than comparison children without childhood depression (Pine et al., 2001). In a sample of 9,374 adolescents, depression at baseline was a risk factor for obesity at 1-year follow-up (Goodman & Whitaker, 2002). This predictive relationship remained, even when the researchers controlled for baseline obesity, age, race, gender, parental obesity, number of parents in the home, SES, smoking, self-esteem, conduct disorder, and physical activity. Other longitudinal studies have found that there are gender differences in the relationship between adolescent depression and later obesity. Longitudinal data from 1,037 people born between 1972 and 1973 in New Zealand indicate that adolescent depression increases the risk for early adulthood obesity in females but not in males (Richardson et al., 2003).

Cross-sectional research also indicates a relationship between depression and obesity. These data must be interpreted with caution, however, because the direction of the relationship—which came first, the depression or the obesity?—cannot be ascertained with cross-sectional research. Data from the Third National Health and Nutrition Examination Survey supported the idea that obesity is associated with depression, particularly for persons with severe obesity (Onyike et al., 2003). But gender also appears to influence the relationship between obesity and major depression. In a national study of 40,086 African American and white participants, increased BMI was related to both major depression and suicide ideation for women; among men, however, lower BMI was associated with major depression as well as suicide ideation and attempts (Carpenter et al., 2000).

Some researchers present conflicting results pointing to the need to continue to unravel how depression and obesity are related (Goodman & Whitaker, 2002; Richardson et al., 2003). With the use of bariatric surgery to treat obesity, many thought that the rapid and successful weight reduction would also treat the related depression. In fact, in a study of 487 women who underwent bariatric surgery, Dixon et al. (2003) reported that weight loss was related to significant and sustained declines in depression scores over the 4-year period of study. Improvement in depression scores was particularly strong for younger women with greater weight loss. However, recent research indicates that this is not the case for many who undergo this surgery. In fact, without psychosocial intervention, the weight loss is likely to be reversed if the only change in food behaviors is an adaptation to the new physical limitations on food intake imposed by the surgery. Binge eating before surgery may turn into what is referred to as postoperative "grazing" behavior (Saunders, 2004a, 2004b). This finding lends support to the notion that underlying depression or other unmet emotional needs present risk of obesity. Obviously, more research is needed to better establish the risk that depression poses and how depression interacts with other factors to produce risk.

Social Risk and Protection

A number of social risk factors for obesity have been found, including parenting style, parental modeling, food selection, sedentary lifestyle, aspects of the built environment, the super size it culture, food insecurity, immigration, and child sexual abuse. Protective factors center on eating, exercise habits, and potential governmental regulations.

Overcontrolling parental behavior in relation to feeding children has been shown to influence children's food intake and ultimately their weight. Food restriction can lead a child to eat too much, too rapidly, and to other negative eating behaviors (Benton, 2004; Johnson & Birch, 1994; Satter, 1996). Conversely, a positive parent-child relationship related to food, coupled with consistent mealtime habits, may serve as a protective factor (Satter, 1995, 1996). There may be cultural variation in this relationship, however. In a study of Chinese American children and their mothers, Chen and Kennedy (2005) found that age (older), poor family communication, and a democratic parenting style contributed to increased BMI. What stands out is that the relationship between parenting style and obesity may vary by culture.

Research also shows that parental modeling is critical in the socialization of children's eating behaviors, at least until the age of 10, when other social and environmental factors become more influential (Benton, 2004). While mothers remain the primary person to prepare food, researchers have found that fathers may have the most influence on what children choose to eat. But food intake based on modeling behavior does not happen overnight. A variety of foods introduced early in life results in greater variety of preferred foods as a child becomes older and therefore in greater likelihood of preferring foods from all food groups, a characteristic of food intake by persons of normal weight. Also, research has shown that on average it takes 5–15 introductions of a new food before a child will "like" it (Birch & Fisher, 1998).

Trans fats, which pose risk of weight gain, are used in food production to preserve shelf life without using refrigeration, thus lowering food cost. Consequently, foods using trans fats tend to be more available in low-income communities. This may explain, in part, why those in lower SES are more likely to be obese. The 2006 FDA regulations require that food nutrition labels include the presence and amount of trans fats. While this labeling will not be required of restaurants, the anticipated increase in public awareness of nutrition in relation to obesity and other health problems has spurred the restaurant industry to begin to eliminate foods containing trans fats (Food and Drug Administration [FDA], 2006).

A sedentary lifestyle is perhaps the most consistently cited social risk factor for obesity, and conversely, an active lifestyle established early in the life course serves as a protective factor (Bray, 2004; CDC, 2003b; NIH, 1998; NLM, 2005). As obesity has increased in children, other related trends have been documented to place children at risk. For example, between 1995 and 2001, there was a 33% decrease, from 18.3% to 12%, in the number of children who attend daily exercise classes. During the same time period, data indicate that about 25% of children watched 4 or more hours of television per day on average, a group that also has a significantly higher BMI compared to children who watch 2 hours or less (Schmidt, 2003). Television is a sedentary activity that frequently is paired with increased eating, particularly foods high in sugar and fat. Compounding this risk is advertising of snack foods aimed primarily at children (Ludwig & Gortmaker, 2004).

In response to urban sprawl, the built environment has come to the forefront as a potential risk and protective factor. As a risk factor for obesity, the built environment can contribute to less physical activity, such as walking, by placing the workplace and shopping venues at long distances from residences or by failing to provide areas such as parks that are conducive to physical activity. For example, most trips are made in cars, 90% of all trips by adults and 70% for children. In 1969 twice as many children as today walked or biked to school (Schmidt, 2003). Obviously, physical activity burns more body energy compared to a sedentary activity such as driving a car. And easier access to attractive, safe, and comfortable sites for physical activity has shown to increase activity. However, there is little data that link the built environment specifically to obesity. One study reported data to support the idea that activity levels do increase when it is feasible to walk or bike in neighborhoods that are dense but interspersed with schools, stores, and businesses. Federal agencies such as the National Institute of Environmental Health Sciences (NIEHS) have recently directed research funds to further examine the relationship between the built environment and obesity. Finally, the Institute of Medicine (IOM) is completing two major studies that include the built environment as one of many risk factors for childhood obesity (Schwartz et al., 2003). It is hoped that the results of these studies will point to interventions aimed at designing environments that protect against obesity.

The super size it phenomenon is a social trend that also places persons, especially children and youth, at risk. For example, in 1980 the average cheeseburger contained 333 calories, whereas today an average cheeseburger contains 590 calories. Rolls (2000) reports that fewer energy units or calories are consumed when low-density foods are served regardless of fat content. But age appears to play a role. When preschool children were given different sized portions and the consumption amount measured, younger children's energy intake did not change, whereas older children ate more when larger portions were given (Rolls, Engeli, & Birch, 2000). This highly politicized source of larger and more energy-dense food portions is also underresearched, although it is known that fast food is one of the less expensive energy-dense types of food. Most recently, the fast-food industry has begun to offer greater variety in its menus to include lower fat and higher fiber foods; they also have begun to publicize the nutritional content of their products.

On the other hand, living with food insecurity has also been found to put people at risk for obesity. In a population study of women of child-bearing age and school-age children, Olson (1999) found that, controlling for income level, household food insecurity correlated with higher BMI. Another study, based on national data from 1994 to 1996, concluded that food insecurity for women was related to becoming overweight across all levels of food insecurity except severe (Townsend et al., 2001). These researchers called attention to the cycle of food stamp provision that results in food abundance early in a given month followed by severe food limitations for the last week of the month. It is during the weeks of abundance that energy-dense foods are consumed in large quantities, reminiscent of our earlier anthropological discussion to explain obesity. Research continues to explore the food insecurity hypothesis using different instruments to measure the concept (Kaiser, Townsend, Melgar-Quinonez, Fujii, & Crawford, 2004), sampling different populations (Kaiser et al., 2002; Olson, 1999), and applying to countries beyond the United States (Gulliford, Mahabir, & Rocke, 2003).

Immigration and length of U.S. residence also serve as risk factors that vary among groups within the United States. One group of researchers used the 1998 National Health Interview Survey data to examine obesity rates of Hispanic immigrants in relation to the amount of time living in the United States. Exhibit 8.4 shows the gradual increase in obesity rates for these 2,420 foreign-born Hispanic adults aged 18 or more (Kaplan, Huguet, Newsom, & McFarland, 2004). There was a fourfold increase in obesity rates for immigrants residing in the United States for 15 or more years when compared to those in the United States for 4 years or less. Based on interview data from 357 Mexican American women, a second study also linked obesity to the length of time in the United States (Ayala et al., 2004). In addition to length of time in the United States, the high rate of obesity in this sample (42%) was also explained by less integration into Anglo culture and by unemployment. This pattern was found to be slightly different in a third study that compared 500 Korean adults in Seoul to 2,830 Korean Americans in California. These researchers concluded that higher levels of acculturation exposed the respondents to a greater risk of obesity, among other health risks, but there were gender differences in the type of health risks encountered. Specifically, acculturated women were more likely to smoke and drink, while acculturated men were more likely to become obese (Song et al., 2004). Although the ethnic groups varied, as well as the factors related to obesity, what remained constant across all three studies is that most immigrants who lived in the United States showed increased risk of obesity.

Time residing in U.S.	% with BMI > 30
0–4 Years	9.4
5–9	14.5
10–14	21.0
> 15	24.2

Exhibit 8.4   Proportion of Hispanic Immigrants with BMI > 30 by Years Residing in the United States

SOURCE: Based on Kaplan, Huguet, et al., 2004.

Based on research using retrospective and self-report data, childhood sexual abuse has been identified as a potential risk factor for obesity. Gustafson and Sarwer (2004) reviewed this literature and concluded that there is at least a modest relationship between childhood sexual abuse and obesity. They recommended further consideration of the role that depression and negative emotions may play in eating behaviors of adults who were sexually abused as children and also further consideration of the possibility that obesity is an adaptive consequence of sexual abuse.

Claudia Salvatierra emigrated from the Dominican Republic (DR) to the United States, where over time she gained more than 60 pounds. It is hard to say what combination of factors may have led to this weight gain. Perhaps there was a greater abundance and greater convenience of high-density foods. Perhaps there was less access to fresh fruit and vegetables in her impoverished urban neighborhood than she had experienced in rural DR. Perhaps the stresses of the migration and relocation led to depression, which may have put her at greater risk of obesity. Perhaps she has a more sedentary lifestyle than when she was in the DR. Perhaps there is something about her acculturation process that contributes to her obesity. These are all possible, as well as concurrent, social risk factors.

Spiritual Risk and Protection

The research on the relationship of religion, faith, and spirituality to obesity is emerging but is very limited in scope (Sloan & Bagiella, 2002). The few studies that examine this relationship can be divided into two categories. One group of researchers attempt to establish whether or not spirituality or religion is either a protective or risk factor. Another group of researchers is examining the effectiveness of various intervention programs that are emerging in religious settings with congregations that may have the highest risk for obesity, such as the African American churches. One example is an intervention called Healthy Body/Healthy Spirit in Atlanta, Georgia, that is currently under outcome evaluation. This program is based on evidence that African Americans are significantly less likely than members of other groups to engage in physical activity and to follow established food intake guidelines (Resnicow et al., 2002). A second example, the Church High Blood Pressure Program (CHBPP), based in Baltimore, is a behaviorally oriented weight control program with the goal of reducing blood pressure. It is delivered in church but does not incorporate religious practices as part of the intervention (Kumanyika & Charleston, 1992).

However, the question remains: Is spirituality/faith/religion a risk or protective factor or possibly both? A large study using national data provided little evidence that religion was either a risk or protective factor for obesity (Kim et al., 2005). Using the National Survey of Midlife Development in the United States (MIDUS) data from 3,032 adults, researchers reported that conservative Protestant men had a 1.1 + 0.45 higher BMI than those reporting no religious affiliation; no relationship between religion and BMI was found for women. However, when men's smoking was controlled for, the researchers concluded that the greater tendency to overweight in conservative Protestant men was likely due to lower smoking rates for those who were more religious (smoking is related to less body weight). Kim and Sobal (2004) also examined religion and social support in relation to fat intake and physical activity, using data from 546 adults residing in upstate New York. While they found some differences by denomination (Protestant vs. Catholic) and gender, these were not strong. Their data led to the conclusion that religion does not appear to influence the context of diet and exercise, but further study of women's health behaviors in relation to their religion and related practices is recommended.

Biopsychosocial-Spiritual Integration

Among a minority of obese individuals, obesity seems to be caused by a complex inter-action of a large number of genes. The best research indicates that most cases of obesity are the result of a complex but yet unexplained mix of biological processes, psychological processes, and social processes. Diet and activity play the major roles. And both diet and activity are biological factors that are highly influenced by a number of social factors, including family income, family relationships, community resources and community safety, family and community norms related to diet and activity, time spent watching tele-vision, and the advertising and food industries. Depression is also a risk factor, and depression has both biological and psychological components and is influenced by a number of social factors, including childhood poverty, childhood deprivation and trauma, and other interpersonal problems.

Turning to the situation of Claudia and Elias Salvatierra, these aforementioned risk and protective factors provide insight into the several reasons for Claudia's weight gain of 60 pounds to the point of obesity. While not obese as a child, she had two pregnancies, after which she did not return to the lower prepregnancy weight. Driven by poor economic and living conditions in the DR, she immigrated from her homeland to the United States, leav-ing behind a primary source of happiness, her son, and the role as his mother. Life in the United States failed to yield the level of economic security that was sought but provided considerably greater access to energy-dense foods. Claudia experienced marginal social integration and support as well as increasing marital and parental stress, possibly leading her to turn to food to satisfy these unmet social and psychological needs. Obviously, the risk and protective factors played out to her disfavor, resulting in adult obesity.

Consequences of Obesity

The rising concerns about obesity are rooted in its well-established consequences. For both children and adults, obesity is the number one risk factor for life-threatening illnesses such as type II diabetes and cardiovascular disease. The consequences of obesity in children are as severe as for adults; they include type II diabetes; sleep apnea; hypertension; and car-diovascular, musculoskeletal, and neurological complications, all of which become greater risk factors when these children become adults. Other consequences of obesity include high cholesterol, kidney and gallbladder disorders, osteoarthritis, and some forms of can-cer. These consequences also have ethnic and cultural variations. For example, minority youth (African American and Hispanic) in the United States who are obese are more likely to develop type II diabetes and cardiovascular disease compared to white youth who are obese. One group of researchers (Irei et al., 2005) reported that in Vietnamese adolescents, obesity was a risk factor for asthma, a finding that may not be specific to this population, rather just not identified in others. On the other hand, psychosocial consequences such as lowered self-esteem and poor self-concept are more prevalent for white youth, especially white females (Barker, 2004; Ebbeling et al., 2002).

To understand the physical consequences of obesity, it is important to understand the relationship of fat tissue to disease. As fat levels increase, leading to obesity, adiponectin levels fall, having an impact on insulin sensitivity; this relationship is key to understanding why diabetes is linked to obesity. Current research also is focusing on another hormone produced by fat cells, called **resistin**, which is thought to regulate insulin and energy storage. With the discovery that **macrophages,** immune system cells that protect the body by engulfing and digesting pathogens, are found in fat tissue, researchers have uncovered the link between obesity and inflammation problems that underlie certain cancers and heart disease. Other substances produced by fat tissue cause blood vessels to constrict and blood clots to form, which ultimately increases the risk of stroke and heart attack (Bray & Bouchard, 2004b).

Sexual and reproductive functioning also is impacted by obesity. Enjoyment, desire, frequency, and actual mechanics are affected. Because of the endocrine impact of adipose tissue, fertility and reproduction also are negatively impacted (Mansour, 2004). Women who are obese experience longer labor, which is a risk factor for birth outcomes (Vahratian, Zhang, Troendle, Savitz, & Siega-Riz, 2004).

Older adults who are obese face greater challenges than nonobese older adults because obesity contributes to functional impairment or disability (Jenkins, 2004). In the face of other aging problems such as arthritis and osteoporosis, obesity compounds the problem of mobility impairment, even more so than other chronic conditions (Peek & Coward, 2000).

Added to the physical challenges of obesity are psychosocial consequences such as depression, decreased self-esteem, and societal discrimination (Carpenter et al., 2000; Dixon et al., 2003; Onyike et al., 2003). As suggested earlier, obesity research indicates that the relationship between obesity and depression appears to be bidirectional, with depression serving as risk for obesity but also as a consequence of obesity (Dixon et al., 2003; Faith et al., 2002). Obese children are bullied and teased, obese adults are shunned and devalued, and both are the brunt of numerous jokes. The psychosocial consequences of obesity, such as lowered self-esteem, poor self-concept, and social isolation, can be profound, at times creating a circular causal pattern of obesity.

"Fat bias" is pervasive within U.S. society, and a large research literature indicates that this bias is shared by helping professionals whose services are needed by persons who are obese. Researchers have found that teachers and health care providers have negative views of obese persons, with a quarter of teachers saying that being obese is the worst thing that can happen to a person (Neumark-Sztainer, Story, & Harris, 1999) and a quarter of nurses saying they are "repulsed" by obese persons (Bagley, Conklin, Isherwood, Pechiulis, & Watson, 1989). At an international obesity conference in 2003, a study of 389 researchers and professionals examined their implicit attitudes towards obesity, using a word classification task. Results showed that the respondents implicitly endorsed negative stereotypes that persons who are obese are lazy, stupid, and worthless. However, some subsamples of the respondents reported lower levels of implicit antifat bias. These included persons who were male and older and persons who hold a positive emotional outlook on life, weigh more personally, have friends who are obese, and possess an understanding of the lived experience of obesity. We can well imagine that negative attitudes can lead to disparities in service delivery on the basis of weight (Puhl & Brownell, 2001; Schwartz et al., 2003). In addition, stereotyping can result in a negative impact on the self-valuation and self-esteem of persons who are obese.

Unfortunately, there is also considerable evidence of fat bias among employers. Experimental studies have found that, all other factors being equal, employers show a bias against job applicants who are obese (Pingitoire, Dugoni, Tindale, & Spring, 1994). Employers evaluated applicants they considered obese to be lacking in self-discipline and to have low supervisory potential (Rothblum, Miller, & Garbutt, 1988). Given these findings, it is not surprising that longitudinal research has found a persistent obesity wage penalty over the first two decades of the careers of both men and women (Baum & Ford, 2004).

At the same time, the macro economic consequences of obesity—the cost of obesity to society presented by negative health consequences—cannot be ignored, (Finkelstein et al., 2004; Thorpe, Florence, Howard, & Joski, 2004). Raebel et al. (2004) compared the health care costs of those who are obese (N = 539) with those who are not obese (N = 1225) and concluded that for each unit of BMI increase, health care costs increased by 2.3%, with most of this increase due to the use of prescription drugs by those who are obese. Using health care costs that rose significantly between 1987 and 2001, other researchers estimated that 12% of the health spending growth was attributed to the rise in obesity prevalence alone. Finally, based on 1998 Medical Expenditure Panel Survey data, researchers concluded that the greatest cost increases were found in white and older adults and not for blacks and persons less than 35 years of age (Wee et al., 2005). With more than two thirds of adults and as many as 17% of children and youth being overweight or obese, obesity is now considered the number one public health problem. This imperative led the nation's leading health experts to identify obesity and overweight as the second of 10 leading health indicators of the Healthy People 2010 Initiative, factors that must be addressed in order to increase the quality and years of healthy life in the United States (Anderson, 2000; Janet, 2000).

Ways of Coping

Based on the multiple and complex factors that lead to obesity, multiple interventions will be needed to respond to the underlying causes and to reflect the many variations by age, race, gender, and other circumstances. Researchers and professionals agree that there is no one solution to "globesity"; rather, a "menu" is needed so that an individualized approach can be developed to match the interplay of factors unique to each person while addressing obesity from a public health (population) perspective. Some of the current ways that persons who are obese choose to cope with the challenge are reviewed below, noting that these are rapidly changing as new data emerge to challenge their effectiveness, particularly in relation to the long-term outcomes.

Perhaps the most logical initial approach for persons who are obese is to obtain a medical evaluation to rule out possible causative illnesses, especially those that can be treated. This is recommended before attempting to manage weight with other methods. If causative illnesses are ruled out, a number of other methods of weight management are available, and others are in the experimental phase.

Self-Help Approaches

Overeaters Anonymous (OA; 2006) is a 12-step program with a spiritual basis modeled on Alcoholics Anonymous. TOPS (Taking Off Pounds Sensibly) and Weight Watchers are other organizations that offer group approaches to provide social support in the effort to lose weight (Taking Off Pounds Sensibly [TOPS], 2006; Weight Watchers, 2006). Both TOPS and Weight Watchers require membership or other fees, but OA does not. Required dues and related fees may make them inaccessible to some groups of people.

Nutrition and Diets

South Beach. Grapefruit. Atkins. Slim-Fast. Sound familiar? These diets, often referred to as "fad diets," are designed to decrease some aspect of food intake while maximizing another. They have not proven effective over time; weight may be lost initially, but it eventually is regained. And in some situations, these diets pose a threat to one's health by depleting essential nutrients and creating severe biochemical imbalances. Furthermore, the typical maximum weight lost with fad diets is only 10%, far less than desired for people who are obese and expect an outcome of normal weight for height. For those who do succeed, about half of the weight loss is regained within 1 year. In fact, 95% of people who lose weight on special diets will regain it within 5 years (Ebbeling et al., 2002). The battles continue, with some researchers and nutritionists advocating for low fat and high carbohydrates, while others promote low-glycemic index and high-protein diets (McMillan-Price & Brand-Miller, 2004). Weight Watchers (2006) is one diet plan that does not restrict foods but rather has promoted balanced eating with balanced lifestyles for the more than 40 years it has functioned. Paired with a social support approach and behavioral supports, Weight Watcher meetings, both face-to-face and Internet, are held worldwide and reflect the current state of knowledge related to weight gain and loss.

Perhaps the middle ground in the diet debate rests with the federal government, specifically the secretaries of the U.S. Department of Health and Human Services (USDHHS) and the U.S. Department of Agriculture (USDA), which every 5 years publish the *Dietary Guidelines*, an analysis of new scientific information by the Dietary Guidelines Advisory Committee (DGAC; 2006). The latest guidelines can be found at the Web site of Healthier US.Gov (www.healthierus.gov; USDHHS, 2006) and include the new food pyramid as well as information related to food preferences of different racial/ethnic groups, vegetarians, and other groups to help plan diets and develop educational programs and materials.

Exercise

The literature is replete with new programs and approaches to both prevent and treat obesity through increased exercise as a permanent lifestyle change. One study of children from Mexico City found that obesity risk decreased 10% in relation to each hour per day of physical activity, whereas risk increased 12% in relation to television viewing (Hernandez et al., 1999). Another study of the relationships between after-school activities and obesity concluded that school sports could be part of a prevention effort for adolescents (Elkins, Cohen, Koralewicz, & Taylor, 2004). Another research team focused on activity levels of preschool children and found that the amount of activity varies greatly across preschool settings, based largely on the different policies and practices of different preschools (Pate, Pfeiffer, Trost, Ziegler, & Dowda, 2004). Carrel and Bernhardt (2004) point out, however, that currently there is insufficient evidence for developing exercise guidelines to respond to child and adolescent obesity. Some guidelines are repeatedly found in the literature, but they are based on insufficient evidence in many instances (Morrow, Krzewinski-Malone, Jackson, Bungum, & FitzGerald, 2004). There are many barriers to physical activity for persons who are obese: shame fostered by negative stereotyping and discrimination; concern about one's appearance, especially in less clothing such as shorts or bathing suits (Lutter, 1993); lack of monetary resources or places to exercise; lack of time, especially in our fast-paced, competitive society; and for those who are morbidly obese, there may be physical barriers to the use of various types of equipment.

Pharmacotherapy

Drug companies are clamoring to discover substances to prevent weight gain or promote weight loss and to speed approval by the FDA by making the testing requirements less stringent, but there is strong opposition to "tinkering with nature." Furthermore, for the drugs that are on the market, the side effects can be profound (Gura, 2003). Drugs to combat obesity fall into five categories: (1) central nervous system agents, (2) leptin/insulin/central nervous system pathway agents, (3) gastrointestinal-neural pathway agents, (4) agents that may increase resting metabolic rate, and (5) other more diverse agents (Bays, 2004; Marcus, 2004). A few are overviewed in Exhibit 8.5. As you review this exhibit, please be aware that, with the exception of phentermine, these drugs are relatively new in the treatment of weight loss and the empirical evidence of both their benefits and side effects is quite preliminary. It is also possible that by the time you read this, Rimonabant and Axokine may have received FDA approval.

To date, pharmacotherapy for obesity has shown only modest weight loss for most people, far less than hoped for by those who are obese. However, a randomized trial of 224 obese adults that explored a combination of medication, diet, exercise, and group therapy with lifestyle modification counseling found that the greatest weight loss (12.1 kg vs. 6.7–7.7 kg, or 26.7 pounds vs. 14.8–17 pounds respectively at 1 year) occurred for persons who received medication along with group lifestyle modification rather than either intervention by itself (Wadden et al., 2005).

Drug	Biological Mechanism	Benefits	Side Effects
Sibutramine (Meridia) FDA-approved for long-term use	Inhibits norepinephrine and serotonin reuptake	Decreases appetite	• Slightly elevated blood pressure and heart rate • Headache • Dry mouth • Runny nose • Sore throat • Constipation • Insomnia
Orlistat (Xenical) FDA-approved for long-term use	Blocks intestinal absorption of fat	Results in 2%–3% weight loss	• Cramping • Severe diarrhea
Phentermine (Redux) FDA-approved for short-term use (3–6 weeks)	Stimulates release of catecholamines	Decreases appetite	• Insomnia • Dry mouth • Constipation • Restlessness • Euphoria • Nervousness • Increased pulse rate and blood pressure
Acomplia (Rimonabant, Zimulti) Approved in Europe but not by FDA	Blocks CB1 receptor that regulates energy balance, fat and sugar metabolism, and appetite	5%–10% weight loss for 2 years Suppresses appetite and nicotine craving	• Irritability • Anxiety • Depression • Nausea
Axokine No FDA approval	Signals hypothalamus that there is sufficient fat storage	Suppresses appetite	• Cough • Nausea

Exhibit 8.5   Examples of Pharmacotherapy for Obesity

SOURCE: Based on Bray, 2004; Gura, 2003; Mancini & Halpern, 2006; Marcus, 2004; Wadman, 2005, 2006.

On the horizon are other drugs that are not yet tested in humans. Some drug research is aimed at substances that will stimulate the brain to decrease its attraction to fatty foods. Other synthetic substances are being sought to mimic other chemical signals that influence both eating behaviors and metabolic processes. While these are only a few of the many drugs being developed, there is also skepticism about the potential of drugs as a solution to obesity because of what is known about the ways the human body is able to adapt to biochemical changes. Critics speculate, for example, that over time the use of a drug to block fat storage will be overridden by another biological mechanism to reverse the effect.

Genetic intervention has not been tried with humans, but Campion, Milagro, and Martinez (2004) provide an overview of standard methods used to manipulate genes in nutritional and obesity research. Researchers hope that these methods will help to identify new possibilities for drug and genetic interventions.

Surgical Intervention

Surgical interventions, called **bariatric surgery**, are used when a person who is obese, typically in the morbid BMI range > 40, has failed to lose weight by dieting and exercise and is of high risk for a multitude of negative health outcomes such as diabetes and cardiovascular disease. Bariatric surgery was first performed in the United States in 1953. There are several surgical techniques commonly used and others that are being developed.

Buchwald & Williams (2004) surveyed the presidents of the national societies of the 31 International Federations for the Surgery of Obesity (IFSO). Results based on the 26 that responded showed that in the year 2002/2003, 103,000 bariatric surgeries were performed in the United States and another 43,301were performed elsewhere in the world. The researchers estimated that worldwide the number of surgical interventions represents only 1% of the population that would qualify for surgery. However, between 2003 and 2006 in the United States, there has been a 150% increase in the number of surgical interventions for obesity (Strauch, Herman, Rohde, & Baum, 2006).

At least six different surgical procedures are used to treat obesity. Three procedures, gastric bypass, stomach banding, and implantable gastric stimulation (IGS), also called gastric pacing, are reviewed briefly here. The **gastric bypass** surgical technique involves the cutting and stapling of the top of the stomach to form a pouch. The remainder of the stomach is then stapled and sewn shut. Next, the small intestine is cut and the remaining section leading to the large intestine is reattached to the newly created pouch. The part of the stomach that is sewn shut is then attached to the small intestine, allowing it to drain into the digestive system even though food will bypass this section. The result is a stomach that allows only 2–4 tablespoons of food, which then bypasses the rest of the stomach as well as up to 16 inches of the small intestine to reduce the amount of nutrients that are absorbed from the food that is ingested. Weight loss after gastric bypass is approximately 33% at 2 years and 25% at 8 years. The reported complication rate is 13% and mortality is 0.2% (Everson, Kelsberg, & Nashelsky, 2003).

Another surgical procedure commonly used is **stomach banding** (gastric banding). This procedure involves the use of a band to constrict the upper part of the stomach, a procedure that is less invasive, easier to learn to do than the gastric bypass, and reversible. Recent research indicates that although gastric banding sometimes has postoperative complications such as band slippage or erosion and repeat corrective surgeries, the complication rates are low compared to bypass surgery (Parikh, Laker, Weiner, Hajiseyedjavadi, & Ren, 2006).

Implantable gastric stimulation (IGS), or gastric pacing, is a recently FDA-approved surgical procedure that is seen as a promising alternative to current forms of bariatric surgery because it is less invasive and is reversible. IGS requires an implantation of a battery-operated pacemaker-like device under the skin. Two leads from the device are placed in the stomach wall to apply periodic current to promote satiety. Data from European trials where IGS was developed indicate that 60% of people lost over 10% of their body weight within a 29-month follow-up period (Klotter, 2006). No major complications or mortalities were noted in one study of 500 Europeans who have had this minimally invasive procedure (Shikora, 2004). In another study of 103 people, 20 had a lead dislodged or broken, but this was corrected. Batteries must be replaced every 2–5 years. A similar device called Transcend awaits FDA approval in 2006.

The results of surgical intervention may not be as positive as initially expected. While most clinic sites offer, or even require, psychosocial counseling to address possible underlying emotional issues and the realities of a range of outcomes, these issues are not always sufficiently addressed, and there is wide variance in how this assessment is done (Fabricatore, Crerand, Wadden, Sarwer, & Krasucki, 2006). A recent assessment tool, the Weight and Lifestyle Inventory (WALI), has been validated for assessment (Fabricatore, Wadden, et al., 2006). There are always risks involved in any surgical procedure performed on persons who are obese because of related health issues that are intertwined with psychosocial factors. Because bariatric procedures are very invasive and require lifelong changes in behavior, emphasis on psychosocial risk factors and psychosocial consequences is rapidly increasing. Sarwer, Wadden, and Fabricatore (2005) provide a review of the literature to identify the psychosocial dimensions that are important when considering surgical treatment for obesity and propose a research agenda to advance understanding of these aspects of bariatric surgical success.

For compulsive eaters, postsurgery group therapy is recommended to prevent what has become known as grazing behavior that can lead to weight regain (Saunders, 2004a, 2004b). For the morbidly obese in particular, even successful bariatric surgery is not without further surgical consequence. After significant weight loss, skin tissue is stretched beyond its ability to recover. The excess tissue causes rashes and skin breakdown because the many folds prevent moisture from evaporating. The excess tissue on the trunk, buttocks, breasts, upper arms, and thighs also impairs walking, creates bowel and bladder problems, and impinges on sexual activity (Chandawarkar, 2006).

Although there is skepticism about most weight reduction approaches, there are examples of significant weight loss maintained over long periods of time. Research tells us that two elements are common to the many different approaches taken by individuals who have successfully dealt with obesity: limiting intake while increasing physical activity. Eating breakfast is another eating pattern found in successful weight loss efforts. Blood sugar levels that remain too low for too long put the body into survival mode, and it begins to hang on to any possible fat. Breakfast jump-starts the overnight fast, speeds metabolism, and ultimately acts like an appetite suppressant. Daily weighing to monitor eating, engaging in exercise on an ongoing basis, and journaling these behaviors are also common to successful weight loss and maintenance efforts.

Coping Strategies of Families, the Workplace, Communities, and the Federal Government

Earlier in the chapter we presented an ecological model developed to both understand and intervene with the challenge of obesity (Swinburn & Egger, 2004). The third aspect of the model is the environmental context of obesity, or as some have termed it, the "**obesogenic environment**." This model recommends a multipronged approach of behavioral, medical (medication, surgery), environmental, and psychological interventions, because no single intervention is independently effective in long-term weight loss and control.

Families, parents, and other caretakers of children play a significant role in the prevention and treatment of obesity. Repeatedly, researchers have confirmed that parental attitudes and practices related to feeding of children are significantly related to whether or not the child is at risk of obesity. For example, we know that healthy eating patterns emerge when a parent does not overemphasize or prohibit specific foods (Golan & Crow, 2004; Passehl et al., 2004).

The workplace can be a source of both prevention and remedial intervention in relation to obesity in many ways, such as providing health screens and integration of physical activity into the work environment. Yancey et al. (2004) designed a randomized posttest-only intervention trial in a USDHHS worksite in California involving 449 employees who were asked to engage in a 10-minute exercise break with moderate intensity activities during work time. More than 90% of the employees participated in the exercises. Workplaces can be designed to encourage the use of stairs instead of elevators by designing stairwells to be in closer proximity than elevators. Workplace policies and practices related to smoking, vending machines, food selections, and provision of exercise areas and equipments have demonstrated effectiveness in promoting behaviors related to weight reduction and maintenance as well as related health behaviors (O'Donnell, 2004).

Recent attention has turned to the ways that the built environment influences obesity. Reducing the distance between homes, shopping, and work has resulted in an increase in activity levels by residents (Frank, Andresen, & Schmid, 2004). Increasingly, new communities are built with sidewalks to encourage less reliance on vehicle transportation. Older communities also are being redesigned to include sidewalks, parks, and exercise equipment. Urban living centers with layouts that promote increased walking are also emerging. In these developments, pedestrians always have the right of way; driving is restricted; and restaurants, employment settings, and homes are built within walking distance of each other. For a summary of environmental factors related to obesity, see Exhibit 8.6.

A multifaceted approach to both primary and secondary prevention of obesity is supported by research as the most effective principle of intervention. Such an approach includes public education regarding nutrition and the effects of obesity. The federal government has devoted considerable resources to public education in terms of online resources, provision of research funds, and support for local programs. The NIH Obesity Research Strategic Plan is available free by going to www.obesityresearch.nih.gov/about/strategic-plan.htm. At the time of writing this chapter, the Centers for Disease Control and Prevention had provided between $300,000 and $450,000 to 23 states for capacity building

Location	Environmental Factors	Potential Impact on Energy Balance
Home	• Reduce time spent watching television and in other sedentary behaviors • Build physical activity into regular routines	• Increases daily and leisure time physical activity • Increases calories used
Schools	• Ensure that the school breakfast and lunch programs meet nutrition standards • Provide food options that are low in fat, calories, and added sugars • Provide all children, from prekindergarten through Grade 12, with quality daily physical education	• Decreases excessive calorie consumption • Increases daily physical activity
Work	• Create more opportunities for physical activity at work sites	• Increases daily physical activity; increases calories used
Community	• Promote healthier choices, including at least 5 servings of fruits and vegetables a day and reasonable portion sizes • Encourage the food industry to provide reasonable food and beverage portion sizes • Encourage food outlets to increase the availability of low-calorie, nutritious food items • Create opportunities for physical activity in communities	• Decreases excessive calorie consumption • Increases leisure time physical activity

Exhibit 8.6   Environmental Factors and Their Impact on Obesity

SOURCE: CDC, 2006b.

and between $800,000 and $1.5 million to five additional states for implementation of nutrition and physical activity programs to prevent obesity. Inclusion of information on nutritional planning in parenting classes is also recommended.

Social Justice Issues

Health disparities abound for those who are obese. People who represent minority groups in the United States, especially those of lower SES, are more likely to experience obesity and less likely to have the economic means, access to education, and the help to meet this life challenge. U.S. immigrant populations rapidly become acclimated to the U.S. diet and show rapid weight gain, as we saw in the story of Claudia Salvatierra. But immigration is not the only issue, because as previously noted, even undeveloped countries are reporting alarming increases in obesity. There is growing evidence that early malnutrition plays a role in later obesity. For poor people living in urban neighborhoods with concentrated poverty, energy-dense diets are more affordable than diets high in fresh fruits and vegetables. These urban residents also typically lack the types of physical environments that allow rigorous outdoor exercise.

Minority populations, already saddled with racism, prejudice, and discrimination, are further hampered by the continued stigma of obesity not only by society at large but also from helping professionals. Consequently, persons who are obese constitute an at-risk subgroup that is less likely to receive various types of support (social to economic) for optimal life success in personal relationships, school, the workplace, and other societal institutions in general. This may be particularly so for those persons who are obese and do not have access to the interventions supported by empirical evidence. When health care providers hold negative beliefs about obese persons, optimal services may not be provided and the negative beliefs may be internalized by obese patients.

Practice Implications

Social workers must be sensitized to the insidious, often unrecognized, beliefs and attitudes they hold about persons who are obese. This knowledge of self is foundational to any intervention. Social workers must also possess up-to-date general knowledge about causes and consequences of obesity that is supported by the most current research. Because of the epidemic proportions of obesity, it is safe to assume that social workers in any setting will work with persons who are obese. While no social worker can retain all of the information related to obesity, they can use critical thinking skills to access current information when working with clients who are obese. At the very least, social workers must understand that obesity has a wide range of multidimensional causes, frequent and far-reaching consequences, as well as promising interventions that demand a multidisciplinary approach (Eliadis, 2006). Furthermore, helping clients who are obese requires interventions that are multipronged and multidisciplinary. It is essential that social workers have a grasp of what various disciplines can contribute to understanding and intervening with obesity, such as physicians, nurses, nutritionists, dieticians, physical therapists, occupational therapists, pharmacists, community planners, and public health officials. The increasing emphasis on the psychosocial and behavioral dimensions as keys to long-term success for obesity intervention should open the door for social workers to play a greater role.

Social workers must help clients who are obese to obtain medical assistance to rule out other health issues that result in obesity, particularly those such as Cushing's syndrome that can be treated. Because morbidly obese persons are disinclined to obtain medical care, social workers must assist them in accessing services. Because prejudice and discrimination exist, social workers must play an advocacy role, especially in relation to other helping professionals who are disinclined to work with this population. Social workers can take action to educate others and to advocate for equitable access to services and humane treatment (Devlin, Yanovski, & Wilson, 2000). In addition, social workers certainly can address many of the psychosocial challenges that persons who are obese encounter, such as depression, social isolation, low self-esteem, and hopelessness, as well as access to information and even healthy foods.

Resources to assist persons challenged by obesity are increasing. Social workers can provide information and referral to clients who are seen in any setting, even if obesity is not the primary presenting problem. While social workers are encouraged to respond only to the needs and concerns that clients identify, the complex biopsychosocial-spiritual interactions related to obesity make it difficult to avoid addressing this challenge of living that is obvious when there is face-to-face contact. Social workers must acquire the skills to broach this sensitive topic and engage clients in a helping relationship to address obesity and its impacts on the various dimensions of their life.

Social workers involved with children and youth are in key positions to identify and intervene in situations of childhood and adolescent obesity (Eliadis, 2006). For example, community or neighborhood centers can develop educational and activity programs, possibly utilizing the rapidly emerging online resources or other information sources, to educate both children/youth and their parents/caregivers. Where possible, they should collaborate with other local programs in such activities. Many interactive online programs and other media are available to tailor to special populations, for example, online information can be found in both English and Spanish and in both Windows and Mac formats.

There is consensus among multiple disciplines that the obesity epidemic can be impacted only through a multidimensional and collaborative effort. Social workers must acquire the knowledge and skills of community-based, multidisciplinary, and collaborative interventions if we are to be a part of the solution. The current evidence points to the need for primary, secondary, and tertiary prevention to combat obesity. You may recall from Chapter 5 that *primary prevention* efforts are universal in scope and target the general population, attempting to prevent obesity from ever occurring. *Secondary prevention* programs target individuals identified as at heightened risk of obesity; this type of prevention work focuses on early identification in an attempt to limit the severity of obesity. Finally, *tertiary prevention* programs target individuals who are already obese. Prevention efforts must target both individuals and communities and reflect a family focus. Social workers have historically taken the requisite ecological focus on knowledge and skills for working with individuals, families, groups, communities, and organizations.

At the tertiary prevention level, a community-based social worker might help Claudia Salvatierra consider the stressors in her life and how they might be contributing to her continued weight gain. Claudia can be helped to recognize the strengths she has demonstrated in her difficult migration process and to begin to gain a greater sense of control over her life, and encouraged to consider some of the group-based self-help weight loss programs in her community. Attention should be given to raising Claudia's self-esteem and helping her feel hopeful about her ability to master situations in all spheres of her life. At the secondary prevention level, it will be important for Claudia to understand the important role she plays in the health behaviors of Sergia and Isabel and to have the necessary knowledge and skills to teach, advise, and direct their dietary and exercise habits.

Community-based social workers can also work at the secondary prevention level to confront fat bias among health and social welfare professionals in the community. At the primary prevention level, social workers can work with other community professionals to develop culturally sensitive public awareness programs about health behaviors to prevent obesity. It will be important in these efforts to recognize where community residents turn to receive health information.

Social workers are always challenged to find creative ways to apply new knowledge. Here are some examples. A recent study of the degree of physical activity among children attending preschools revealed highly variable differences by the preschool attended (Pate et al., 2004). This has implications for regulatory agencies that set standards related to minimum activity levels for children in preschools. Social workers frequently work with young parents who may not understand the critical role they play in influencing the food preferences and future lifestyles of their offspring. We can provide education about such issues as (a) the need for an emotionally positive atmosphere when eating, (b) the need to expose children to novel and low energy-dense foods such as fruits and vegetables, (c) the need to encourage but not force or restrict the benefit of certain foods as protection against obesity, and (d) the benefit of an active lifestyle (Benton, 2004). Social workers who work with families with preschool children, particularly families where other obesity risk factors exist, are in a position to help parents consider the amount of activity that is encouraged when a preschool is selected. Adequate space for active play, particularly in a geographical area where winters are harsh and serve as a barrier to outside play activity, also should be considered. School social workers can be advocates within the school environment to ensure that the school does not indirectly or unknowingly encourage obesity. For example, we can advocate for school policies related to vending machine options or recreational activities that promote healthy lifestyles. We can also develop and implement psychoeducational and/or support groups for children and youth who are obese. And last, social workers can work with policymakers to encourage a twice-monthly distribution of food stamps to help low-income caregivers avoid the monthly pattern of early food abundance followed by food insecurity.

Learning Activities

1. Ascertain the monthly allotment from public assistance, including food stamps, in your area for one person who is your age. Using the www.mypyramid.gov Web site, establish your recommended nutritional intake **(general knowledge).** Based on the recommended foods, develop a shopping list for one week. Using your local grocery store, price each item on your grocery list and compare the total cost to your weekly income. Comparison shop from the food list you prepared by visiting a grocery store in another area that is different socioeconomically from where you live **(values and ethics).** Identify and discuss any differences in food selection, quality, prices, and observations about what other shoppers are selecting. Speculate on the reasons for any differences that are noted. Finally, identify social work strategies to assist families who shop in stores in impoverished neighborhoods.

2. Similar to Activity 1 above, change the focus from you as an individual to a hypothetical mother who is obese and has three children, ages 9, 12, and 15, all of whom are overweight or obese. Establish the food intake for each person, develop your grocery list, and compare the estimated food costs to minimum-wage full-time income after taxes **(general knowledge)**. This activity can be done in a group with different students carrying out different functions and bringing the information together. Discuss the level of knowledge and skill required, and the anticipated barriers, to be successful as a mother in overseeing the household eating habits. Include in your discussion your personal beliefs about persons who are obese **(knowledge of self)**. Speculate on how various beliefs among the students could influence the helping relationship as well as the possible interventions with this family **(values and ethics)**. Interview someone you know who is challenged by obesity. What concerns does that person have about each dimension of living, that is, how has obesity impacted him or her from a biopsychosocial-spiritual perspective? What efforts has he or she made to reduce weight? What barriers have been encountered? What supports have been available? Consider what role, if any, a social worker can take in addressing these issues of social injustice **(values and ethics)**.

3. Conduct an informal survey of three or four classmates or persons with whom you work about their views about persons who are obese. What characteristics do they ascribe to others based on physical size alone? Ask them to identify behaviorally specific examples to support these attributions; also ask them to identify examples that would challenge these attributions. Then reflect on the responses you obtained in relation to your own experiences and beliefs **(knowledge of self)**. Discuss what you have found with other classmates and compare what you have found with information presented in this chapter **(general knowledge)**. Talk with your classmates about how the attributions you have heard would fit with the social work value to individualize clients and to value the dignity and worth of each person **(values and ethics)**. Speculate about how the attributions you have heard would affect the ability of a social worker who holds such attributions to engage a person who is obese in a helping relationship. What can the social worker do to become more effective with obese clients?

4. Assume that you are a social worker in a community-based agency where Sergia and Isabel Salvatierra receive after-school child care. You have noticed a considerable weight gain by their mother, Claudia, in the last 6 months, and it is time to update her file and assess her situation for the need for continued services, a task that will require you to meet with her **(knowledge of case)**. As you reflect on Claudia's circumstances, think about your personal views and expectations, if any, in relation to her weight gain over time **(knowledge of self)**. Ask yourself if your expectations or assumptions would be different were Claudia representative of a different race or ethnic group. How does social class figure in your expectations and assumptions **(knowledge of self)?** Your agency has recently begun an educational and activity program targeting residents who are obese. How would you, or would you, approach Claudia to consider joining this group **(values and ethics)?** What knowledge of self do you think you should grapple with in relation to work with Claudia? What barriers would you anticipate in her participation with the new program?

5. In this chapter we presented recent research related to the use of the prevalent definition of obesity applied to Asian populations (Chen et al., 2006; Dhiman et al, 2005; Kim et al., 2005) **(general knowledge).** Consider whether or not there is applicability to the family of Kim Tran **(knowledge of case).** What are your personal beliefs about Asian populations in relation to obesity? Were you surprised to know that this is a challenge faced not only by persons living in Asia but also by Asian Americans? Do you hold a stereotype about Asians challenged by obesity that may not be supported by the literature **(knowledge of self)?** Go online to a database such as www.pubmed.gov to search for the most recent research findings related to various Asian ethnic groups and compare what you find to what is presented in this chapter. Has the knowledge advanced? Has subsequent research supported what was presented in this chapter? Can you identify possible research questions that you think are relevant to advancing this knowledge **(general knowledge)?** Do recent findings challenge or alter how you would assess or approach the Tran family if, for example, you learned that both Kim and her two siblings had become overweight or obese?

9

HIV/AIDS

Elizabeth D. Hutchison,
Virginia Commonwealth University

Pamela J. Kovacs,
Virginia Commonwealth University

In Chapter 2, you met Estella Jackson, who has recently learned that she is infected with the HIV virus. You might be concerned about what this means for Estella's future, as well as the future of her sister, Sondra. You might also be wondering how Estella will cope with this new challenge, given her past struggles. HIV, which stands for **human immunodeficiency virus**, is a special kind of virus, called a retrovirus, that stores its genetic information in RNA rather than DNA form but has the ability to replicate by converting to DNA form. HIV attacks the immune system and is the virus that causes AIDS, which stands for **acquired immunodeficiency syndrome**. *Acquired* means that it is not hereditary but develops after birth from contact with some disease-causing agent, in this case, HIV. *Immunodeficiency* means having a faulty immune system, which makes one more vulnerable to becoming very ill or dying from a disease that others can fight off. *Syndrome* refers to a group of symptoms that collectively characterize a disease. HIV attacks the T-4 cells, one type of white blood cell that gives orders to the rest of the immune system, leaving the body susceptible to a wide range of life-threatening diseases, ones that a healthy immune system can usually defend against.

Prior to the use of **highly active antiretroviral therapy (HAART)** that became widespread in the United States in 1996, the incidence of AIDS was reported when persons' T-4 cells were below 200 and they had other physical conditions indicative of AIDS. HAART uses a combination of several antiretroviral drugs, known as **antiretroviral therapy (ART)**, which are drugs that inhibit the ability of the virus to multiply in the body. Since the more widespread use of HAART, the disease trajectory is less predictable, and trends in AIDS have become less reflective of the overall picture of HIV transmission. Therefore, currently the term *HIV/AIDS* is used to refer to persons who have been diagnosed to have the HIV infection, regardless of their AIDS status (CDC, 2003a, p. 5). In July 2006, the FDA in the United States cleared the use of a once-a-day AIDS drug, Atripla, which is predicted to make it easier for HIV-infected people to keep the virus under control (Kaufman, 2006).

HIV/AIDS is a relatively new public health problem. Its history has been conceptualized as occurring in three waves or eras (Strug, Grube, & Beckerman, 2002). The first wave dates to 1980/1981, when the disease was first identified in the United States. There was no knowledge about the cause or transmission routes, no medical intervention, and lots of death, with more than 80% of persons, primarily gay men, dead within 2 years of diagnosis. The second era, beginning around 1984, brought greater understanding, because HIV was identified as the primary factor in the development of AIDS and some hope for treatment with AZT emerged in 1986. However, despite some medical advances, most people continued to die. Demographics began to diversify as IV drug users, their sexual partners, and heterosexual women and their children, especially in communities of color, were increasingly diagnosed. One staggering fact that illustrates, unfortunately in retrospect, that HIV/AIDS was not just a gay male disease is that between 1986 and 1990, the number of HIV positive women in the United States grew by 600%, disproportionately so in the African American community (Gallegos, 1998).

In the third era, starting in 1996, the introduction of new medications, most notably the protease inhibitors (PIs) and reverse transcriptase inhibitors, radically improved the quality of life for many persons with HIV/AIDS. This altered the perception of the disease from a terminal to a chronic illness, which had implications for individuals living with the disease as well as for social workers and agencies.

A more complete history of the virus can be found in *The HIV Timeline: 1980–2001* (UCSF AIDS Health Project Training Unit, 2001). Those of us in our 50s or older remember life without HIV and each step along the way; people in their 20s do not remember life without it. In retrospect, the initial slow and ignorant response to the epidemic, perhaps driven at least partially by the stigma of being a gay disease, fueled the spread to other groups. The history of the disease sheds light on the challenges inherent in attempting to provide a comprehensive social work response to an ever-evolving epidemic. It is possible that Atripla will usher in yet another era of the life of this serious virus.

Patterns of Occurrence

At the end of 2004, an estimated 39.4 million adults and children were living with HIV/AIDS globally, 25 million in the continent of Africa. Of these, 4.9 million were new HIV infections. It is estimated that, worldwide, an average of 14,000 new infections occur per day, with 95% of new infections occurring in low- and middle-income countries (see Exhibit 9.1 for regional figures). Approximately 12,000 of the new infections are found in persons between the ages of 15 and 49; more specifically, 50% occur in persons between the ages of 15 and 24, with almost 50% of these being women. The remaining daily 2,000 new infections occur in children under 15 years of age (UNAIDS, 2005a).

Region	Adults & Children Living With HIV/AIDS	Adult Prevalence Rate (%)[a]	Adult & Child Deaths Due to AIDS (2003)
Caribbean	430,000	2.3	35,000
East Asia	900,000	0.1	44,000
Eastern Europe & Central Asia	1.3 million	0.6	49,000
Latin America	1.6 million	0.6	84,000
North Africa & Middle East	480,000	0.2	24,000
North America	1.0 million	0.6	16,000
South & Southeast Asia	850,00	0.6	460,000
Sub-Saharan Africa	25.0 million	7.5	2.2 million
Western Europe	580,000	0.3	6,000

Exhibit 9.1   Regional HIV/AIDS Estimates, End of 2003

[a] The estimated proportion of adults (15–49 years of age) living with HIV/AIDS in 2003

SOURCE: Based on HIV/AIDS Facts and Figures, WHO, 2004.

Approximately 3.1 million people throughout the world died of AIDS in 2004 (UNAIDS, 2005a), and an estimated 25 million people have died of the disease since the beginning of the epidemic (WHO, 2004). It is estimated that more than 14 million children have lost one or both parents to AIDS. World Health Organization (WHO) data (2004) indicate that AIDS kills more than 8,000 people every day, 1 person every 10 seconds. Globally, HIV accounts for the highest number of deaths by a single infectious agent.

The Centers for Disease Control and Prevention (CDC) track the HIV/AIDS epidemic in the United States. The CDC funds state and local health departments to collect and report who is being affected and how. By April 2004, all states had adopted some method for reporting new HIV diagnoses to CDC. There are limitations to these data, however, because newly diagnosed persons may have been infected recently, or they may have been infected sometime in the past; in any given year an uncounted number of infected persons have not been tested yet. Therefore, the count of new diagnoses is an imprecise way to track the epidemic. In recent years, a serologic test has been developed that can analyze blood samples to determine whether infection is recent or ongoing. Since 2000, 33 states in the United States plus Guam and the U.S. Virgin Islands have used this test for HIV surveillance. In addition, AIDS diagnoses are reported to the CDC by all states and territories (CDC, 2006a).

Overall there are an estimated 850,000 to 950,000 people living with HIV/AIDS in the United States, with approximately 40,000 new infections occurring each year, and an estimated 415,193 persons living with AIDS (CDC, 2005c, 2006a). Of those who are infected, 180,000–200,000, like Estella Jackson, do not know how they were infected, an important consideration for designing prevention strategies. Initially because HIV/AIDS appeared predominantly in the white gay communities in large metropolitan areas, specifically New York and San Francisco, the epidemic was not perceived to have broader implications. Over time, women, communities of color, and older adults reported alarming rates of increased HIV infection. In addition, new infection rates reported among men who have sex with men (MSM) are on the rise again (CDC, 2005c). The rate of HIV infection among inmates in the prison system is estimated to be 10 times the rate of the general population (Fears, 2005).

There are gender differences in the pattern of occurrence of HIV/AIDS. Men continue to account for the majority of new annual infections (70%). At the end of 2003, 73% of adults and adolescents living with HIV/AIDS in the United States were male. However, the pattern of occurrence is reversed in young people between the ages of 13 and 19; 61% of this age group living with HIV/AIDS are females and 39% are male (CDC, 2005d, 2006a). In 2004, 65% of newly diagnosed men were infected by MSM, 14% were infected by injection drug use (IDU), 5% were infected by a combination of MSM and IDU, and 16% were infected by heterosexual contact.

Although more men than women are living with HIV/AIDS, the epidemic represents a growing and persistent health threat to women, especially young women and women of color. In 1992, women accounted for an estimated 14% of people living with HIV/AIDS; this percentage had grown to 27% by the end of 2004 (CDC, 2006a). Seventy-eight percent of newly diagnosed women are infected by heterosexual contact and 20% by IDU (CDC, 2005b).

It is difficult to discuss gender variations without also considering the influence of race and ethnicity. In general, a greater number of whites live with and have died from HIV/ AIDS; however, proportionately, African Americans and Hispanics become infected and die at much greater rates. In 2004, it is estimated that 40% of all males living with AIDS in the United States were white, 38% were African American, 21% were Hispanic, 1% were Asian/Pacific Islander, and less than 1% were American Indian/Alaska Native. Among women living with AIDS, 60% were African American, 19% white, 19% Hispanic, and less than 1% were Asian/Pacific Island or American Indian/Alaska Native (CDC, 2005c). African American and Hispanic women together represent about 25% of all women in the United States but accounted for 79% of all women living with AIDS in 2004 (CDC, 2005b).

According to the 2000 Census, African Americans make up 12.3% of the U.S. population but 39% of AIDS cases diagnosed since the beginning of the epidemic. The rate is

11 times that of whites in general; broken down by gender, it is 9 times that of white men and 23 times greater than white women (CDC, 2005a). Of children born to HIV-infected mothers, 62% were African American in 2002 (CDC, 2005a). African American youth account for 56% of all HIV cases ever reported among 13- to 24-year-olds (CDC, 2005d). Although African Americans accounted for 50% of the new HIV/AIDS diagnoses in 2004, the estimated number of HIV/AIDS cases among African Americans and Hispanics decreased between 2001 and 2004. During this same time period, the estimated number of HIV/AIDS cases increased among whites, Asian/Pacific Islanders, and American Indians/Alaska Natives (CDC, 2006a).

Rates of occurrence of HIV/AIDS also vary by age group. In 2004, the estimated percentages of newly diagnosed HIV/AIDS in different age groups were as follows: less than 1% were less than 13 years old, 13% were 13–24, 26% were 25–34, 34% were 35–44, 19% were 45–54, 6% were 55–64, and 2% were 65 and older. In the same year, the estimated percentages of people living with HIV/AIDS were as follows: 1% were less than 13 years of age, 4% were 13–24, 17% were 25–34, 39% were 35–44, 29% were 45–54, 9% were 55–64, and 2% were 65 and older. From 2001 through 2004, the estimated number of HIV/AIDS cases decreased slightly for children less than 14 years of age and for the age group 30–49 years, remained the same for the age group 25–29 years, and increased in the following age groups: 15–19, 20–24, 50–54, 55–59, 60–64, and 65 and older (CDC, 2006a).

The statistics presented here focus on those living with HIV/AIDS, and greater numbers are living longer if they have access to the HAART medication. It is important, however, to remember that people continue to die of AIDS in the United States at the rate of about 16,000 per year. Through 2004, the cumulative estimated number of deaths from AIDS in the United States is 529,113 (CDC, 2006a). Thirty-nine percent of all HIV infections diagnosed in 2003 progressed to AIDS within 12 months, with persons 35 years and older, IDUs, and persons exposed by heterosexual contact more vulnerable to progress to AIDS within a 1-year period (CDC, 2006a).

Theories of Causation

It is well established that HIV/AIDS is a virus that enters the body through unprotected sex, contact with infected blood, vertical transmission from infected mother to baby, or through breast milk of an infected mother. Because the primary method of transmission is unprotected sex, theorizing about the virus has focused on sexual health behaviors. Five categories of theories (summarized in Exhibit 9.2) are discussed here: cognitive theories, gender-based theories, trauma-focused models, a multidimensional health behavior model, and a social network approach. Although these theories have been developed primarily to explain safer sex health behaviors, at least some of them may have potential to help explain behavior related to other methods of transmission as well.

Theoretical Approach	Central Ideas
Cognitive • Health Belief Model • Theory of Reasoned Action • Self-Efficacy Model	Sexual health behaviors are based on beliefs. Sexual health behaviors are based on intentions. Sexual health behaviors are based on integration of knowledge, expectancies, emotional states, social influences, and past experiences.
Gender-Based • Female Socialization and Power Disadvantage • Traditional Masculine Ideologies	Women's limited power and fear of abuse put them at risk in negotiating heterosexual relationships. Female socialization leads to conflict avoidance in sexual encounters. Traditional beliefs that men are sexually assertive and always ready for sex predispose men who hold these beliefs to risky sexual behaviors.
Trauma-Focused	Ongoing stress related to childhood adversities may lead to risky sexual behaviors. Adolescent and adult experience can trigger intrusive and aversive memories of childhood trauma. When triggered, individuals can respond with avoidance or dissociation. Avoidance and dissociation may inhibit self-protective behaviors in uncomfortable sexual situations.
Multidimensional Health Behavior Model	Vulnerability to HIV/AIDS is produced by interaction of client background variables, motivation for sexual health, knowledge about HIV/AIDS and sexual risk, emotional responses, self-esteem and attitudes, client-health professional interaction, and sexual risk behaviors.
Social Network	Interested in the whole set of persons in a particular population and the links connecting them. Interested in the role of both sexual networks and drug networks in HIV transmission.

Exhibit 9.2   Central Ideas of Theories of Sexual Health Behaviors

Cognitive Theories

A number of cognitive theories have been developed to understand risky health behaviors and to extrapolate prevention strategies from them. Three that have been applied specifically to safer sex behaviors are discussed here. One of the most widely used frameworks for HIV prevention programs is the **health belief model (HBM;** Becker, 1974; Becker & Joseph, 1988; Maiman & Becker, 1974). HBM proposes that a person will engage in health-related behaviors, such as using condoms, if he or she believes that a negative health condition (such as HIV) can be avoided, expects that taking a recommended action will avoid a negative health condition (using condoms will prevent HIV), and believes that he or she can successfully engage in the recommended health behavior (use condoms comfortably and with confidence).

The **theory of reasoned action** (Atzen & Fishbein, 1977; Hornik, 1991) assumes that humans are usually rational, use information in a systematic way to solve problems, and consider the implications of their behavior before taking action. This theory focuses on intentions rather than beliefs and attitudes. *Behavioral intention* is defined as how hard people are willing to try and how much effort they plan to exert to engage in a behavior, such as using a condom. This theory, then, is a theory of change motivation.

Although we do not know how Estella Jackson contracted HIV, given what we do know about her background, it would appear that we would need a more complex and multidimensional explanatory model than either the health belief model or the theory of reasoned action provides. Albert Bandura's **self-efficacy model of safer sex behavior**, adapted from his general theory of self-efficacy, provides a more multidimensional approach. In this model, people engage in safer sex practices because they believe they have the ability to protect themselves. Safer sex behaviors are not simply a result of knowledge or skills but of a process of integrating knowledge, expectancies, emotional states, social influences, and past experiences to develop a judgment about one's ability to master the challenges of sexual decision making and negotiating sexual relationships (Bandura, 1990).

Gender-Based Theories

Gender-based theories criticize the cognitive theories for ignoring the sociocultural context of sexuality. They call attention to the ways that gender roles and gender-based social status affect sexual risk behaviors (Amaro, 1995; Bowleg, 2004). Some theorists have focused on sexual risk behaviors of women, placing these behaviors in the contexts of unequal power and female socialization that support passivity in sexual relationships. In this perspective, women's lower social status and limited power put them at a disadvantage in negotiating heterosexual relationships. Their socialization toward connectedness leads them to avoid conflict in sexual encounters. Fear of physical and sexual abuse is also a barrier to negotiating safer sex practices. These theorists note that the major safer sex prevention method available to date is the latex male condom, and successful use of this method requires different behavior for men and women. For men, the safer sex behavior is wearing a condom. For women, the safer sex behavior is persuading the male partner to wear a condom (Amaro, 1995). Gender-based power arrangements influence the behavior of both men and women in this behavioral exchange, but women's actions are constrained by their disadvantaged power position. We might want to explore whether gender socialization and gender power arrangements played a role in Estella Jackson's pathway to HIV infection and influence her current sexual decision making.

Other theorists have focused on sexual risk behaviors of men, proposing a theory of **traditional masculinity ideologies** (Bowleg, 2004; Levant & Majors, 1997; Thompson & Pleck, 1995). This theory uses the term *masculinity ideologies* to suggest that masculinity (as well as femininity) is socially constructed by families, communities, cultures, and societies and is internalized as a set of beliefs about what is appropriate masculine behavior. Lisa Bowleg (2004) suggests that "in the domain of sexuality, traditional masculinity ideologies encourage men to be sexually assertive, be always ready to have sex, view sex primarily as pleasurable and recreational, perceive penetration as the goal of sex, control all aspects of sexual activity, and have multiple sex partners" (p. 169). Bowleg and others (see Diaz, 1998) hypothesize that embracing traditional masculinity ideologies lead men to engage in risky sexual behavior in their sexual relationships with both men and women.

Theorists also extend the sociocultural perspective beyond gender to suggest that gender ideals in relation to sexual behavior may differ by social class, race, ethnicity, sexual orientation, life stages, and historical eras (Abreu, Goodyear, Campos, & Newcomb, 2000). There is empirical support for this larger sociocultural perspective.

Trauma-Focused Models

According to trauma-focused models of health risk, ongoing stress related to childhood adversities such as physical and sexual abuse may lead to risky sexual behaviors (Tubman, Montgomery, Gil, & Wagner, 2004; Whitmire, Harlow, Quina, & Morokoff, 1999). Situations during adolescence and adulthood can trigger intrusive and aversive memories of childhood trauma and activate conditioned associations between abuse stimuli and emotional distress. When such memories are triggered, individuals may respond with maladaptive coping strategies, such as avoidance or dissociation, to keep from being overwhelmed by feelings of distress. When they are triggered by uncomfortable sexual situations, they may cope by using substances before sex and/or they may avoid negotiating self-protective behaviors.

Multidimensional Health Behavior Model

Some theorists have extended the HBM in an attempt to correct for what they see as a narrow focus on individual cognitive elements. Elizabeth Abel and Kathryn Chambers (2004) used Cox's interaction model of client health behavior (IMCHB; 1982) to propose a multidimensional health behavior model for HIV/AIDS. This model proposes that health outcomes are influenced by a complex process of interrelated variables. Vulnerability to HIV/AIDS is thought to be produced by an interaction of client background variables such as age, education, marital status, and income; motivation for sexual health; knowledge about HIV/AIDS and sexual risk; emotional responses, self-esteem, and attitudes; elements of the client-health professional interaction; and health behaviors such as sexual risk behaviors. Like Bandura's self-efficacy model, this model is multidimensional, but it has even greater capacity to incorporate more of the sociopolitical environment by introducing demographic variables such as age, education, marital status, and income. Perhaps its greatest value is recognition of the transactional nature of interactions between health care professionals and groups targeted for interventions. We don't know much about Estella Jackson's past interactions with health care professionals, but we can speculate that it was minimal, given her recent history of prostitution and heroin addiction. The IMCHB model would call attention to the interactions between Estella and the staff at the substance abuse treatment program as well as the HIV/AIDS center, suggesting that these interactions can provide either risk or protection for her future health behaviors.

Social Network Approach

The pattern of HIV infection within a population depends on complex interactions between individuals. In recent years, researchers have been concerned about the increase of HIV infections among adolescent women, particularly adolescent women of color who reside in poor urban neighborhoods (Ellen, 2003). This concern has prompted criticism of existing theories of sexual and drug risk behaviors with suggestions that they focus too exclusively on individual health behaviors and they do not adequately explain the prevalence and incidence of HIV; more specifically, they do not explain the racial/ethnic variations in the rate of HIV. A **social network approach** is offered as an alternative or complementary conceptual framework (Ellen, 2003; Jones & Handcock, 2003; Morris & Kretzschmar, 1997). This approach is based on *social network theory,* which is interested in the whole set of persons in a particular population and the links connecting them.

Epidemiologists are interested in how HIV is transmitted through sexual and drug networks and how to change the pattern of sexual and drug behavior in HIV high-risk networks. They have presented computer simulation models that demonstrate that sexual networks in which network members have *concurrent* (simultaneous, overlapping) sexual partnerships amplify the spread of HIV. Individuals have multiple partners, each partner may be connected to multiple other partners, and these others are also connected to additional partners, and so on. The structure of the network has consequences for individuals in the network and for the network as a whole. Theorists who propose a sexual network approach have recently become interested in the likelihood that high-risk sexual networks tend to exist in impoverished neighborhoods that lack social organization and cohesion (Ellen, 2003). They would suggest that the HIV/AIDS center where Estella Jackson is receiving care should be concerned about the nature of the drug and sex networks in the neighborhood where she lives. This network approach calls for a **diffusion of innovation model** of HIV prevention, in which attention is paid to how to diffuse a health behavior innovation, such as condom use or clean needle use, throughout a network (Rogers, 1983).

_____ Multidimensional Risk and Protection

Biological Risk and Protection

To examine risk and protection for HIV/AIDS, we must examine risk and protection for transmission of HIV as well as risk and protection for progression from HIV to AIDS. As demonstrated in Exhibit 9.3, researchers have looked at risk and protection in both of these ways. We look first at risk and protection for transmission and then at risk and protection for HIV progression.

	Risk for Transmission	Risk for Progression	Protection for Transmission	Protection for Progression
Biological	• Unprotected anal, oral, and vaginal sexual contact • Sharing injecting needles and other drug paraphernalia • Perinatal transmission by HIV-infected mothers • Breast-feeding by HIV-infected mothers • Few copies of CCL3L1 gene, relative to ethnic group	• Malnutrition • Few copies of CCL3L1 gene, relative to ethnic group	• Use of latex male condom during sexual contact • Oral substitution of opiods • Needle exchange programs • HIV testing for pregnant women • HAART treatment plus ZDV for pregnant women after first trimester • Elective cesarean delivery for HIV-infected women • Formula-feeding for HIV-infected women in affluent societies • More copies of CCL3L1 gene, relative to ethnic group	• Multivitamin supplements • More copies of CCL3L1 gene, relative to ethnic group
Psychological	• Lack of knowledge of HIV transmission and preventive behavior • High self-esteem in some populations • Low self-esteem in some populations • Negative beliefs about and attitudes toward condoms • Traditional masculine ideologies • Psychiatric disorders	• Psychological distress • Depressive symptoms	• Knowledge of HIV transmission and preventive behavior • High self-esteem in some populations • Motivation for sexual health • Positive beliefs about and attitudes toward condoms • Self-efficacy	

	Risk for Transmission	Risk for Progression	Protection for Transmission	Protection for Progression
Social	• Child maltreatment • Victim of physical or sexual assault • Shared needles and other drug paraphernalia in a drug network • Concurrent sexual partnerships in sex networks • Bridgers who span sexual networks • Norm of passive role for women in sexual interactions • Men who have unprotected sex with both men and women • Societal economic inequality		• Perceived supportive social network • Feeling connected to parents and community • Involvement in community-related HIV prevention activities • Norm of condom use in sexual network	
Spiritual	• Lack of meaning in life • Religious influence that discourages condom and clean needle exchange programs		• Formal role in religious activities • Personal faith or spiritual life	

Exhibit 9.3 Biological, Psychological, Social, and Spiritual Risk and Protective Factors for HIV/AIDS

There are several biological mechanisms by which HIV is transmitted. Exhibit 9.4 provides a visual image of the primary methods of transmission in the United States between 1999 and 2003 (CDC, 2004d). We discuss four primary risk factors for transmission: unprotected sex, shared drug paraphernalia, vertical transmission, and transmission through breast-feeding.

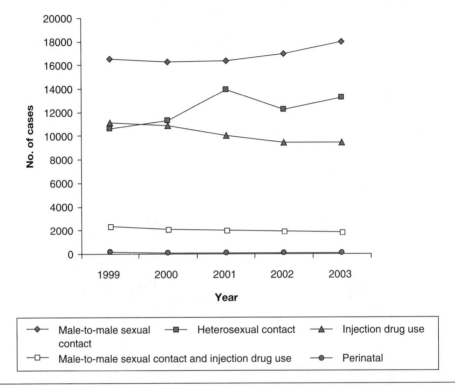

Exhibit 9.4   Estimated Numbers of AIDS Cases, by Year of Diagnosis and Transmission Category [1999–2003]

SOURCE: CDC, 2004d.

Unprotected anal, oral, and vaginal sexual contact with an HIV-infected partner is the most common method of transmission and the most commonly reported biological risk factor. Recent research has emphasized the role of unprotected heterosexual sex in the high rates of HIV among African American women in the United States (Dancy & Berbaum, 2005). Other researchers have focused on the role of **barebacking**, or the deliberate practice of unprotected anal intercourse (UAI), in the high rates of HIV among MSM (CDC, 2004c). Because of its impact on cognition and sexual decision making, alcohol and other drug use around the time of a sexual encounter has also been found to be a risk factor for engaging in unprotected sex (DiIorio, Parsons, Lehr, Adame, & Carlone, 1992; McNair, Carter, & Williams, 1998). In terms of protection, as suggested earlier, the major safer sex prevention method available to date is the latex male condom (Abel & Chambers, 2004).

Shared injecting needles and other drug paraphernalia among IDUs is another biological risk for transmission that has received considerable attention from researchers and prevention specialists. One recent report suggested that 5% to 10% of global HIV infections are the result of shared injecting needles (Gowing, Farrell, Bornemann, & Ali, 2004). The rate seems to be higher than this in the United States. According to CDC estimates, in 2003, 26% of newly diagnosed cases of HIV among men were transmitted by IDU either directly or indirectly. In the same year, IDU was the method of transmission for 27% of newly diagnosed cases among women. This figure for women does not include the numbers for HIV transmission from having sex with male IDUs, which is suspected to be a very large percentage (CDC, 2004d). We do not know how Estella Jackson contracted HIV, nor it appears does she, but we do know that she was an IDU engaged in prostitution at the time she became infected. It is quite possible that she contracted the virus either by sharing needles or from having sexual contact with an IDU.

In terms of protection, one recent review of empirical studies on HIV infection transmitted by IDUs found that oral substitution for opioid-dependent IDUs resulted in significant reductions in sharing of injecting paraphernalia (Gowing et al., 2004). One recent research team found that IDUs who participated in a needle exchange program were one third as likely to share needles and less than half as likely to lend used needles or share cookers or water (Ouellet, Huo, & Bailey, 2004).

Vertical transmission, or perinatal transmission from an HIV-infected mother to an infant, is the major risk factor for HIV/AIDS in children in the United States; it is the method of transmission for more than 90% of pediatric AIDS cases (Cotter & O'Sullivan, 2004; Nafees, 2005). It is estimated that 70% of mother-to-child transmission occurs during delivery and that the other 30% occurs in utero. Two of three in utero transmissions occur during the last 14 days before delivery (Cotter & O'Sullivan, 2004). Maternal viral load is the factor that best predicts HIV infection in newborns. The CDC found that in 29% of the vertical transmissions of HIV in 2000, the mothers were not known to be HIV infected before delivery (reported in Cotter & O'Sullivan, 2004).

Luckily, a rapidly evolving standard of care is providing protection against the risk of vertical transmission (Cotter & O'Sullivan, 2004; Public Health Service Task Force, 2004). Following this standard of care, the risk of perinatal transmission of HIV has been reduced from 25% to less than 2% for women who are aware of their HIV status early in pregnancy. Clinical trial data indicate that vertical transmission can be reduced by up to 50% even when treatment is delayed until delivery (Shaffer, Bulterys, & Simonds, 1999). The first step in effective prevention is HIV testing for the pregnant woman. The CDC recommends offering voluntary testing to all pregnant women, with a follow-up offer to those who initially refuse. Along with the Institute of Medicine (IOM), they also recommend a policy of routine rapid HIV testing of all women who present for labor and delivery using an "opt-out" approach, which means that HIV testing is included in routine panels of prenatal testing unless women specifically decline (Stoto, Almario, & McCormick, 1999). Once it is determined that the mother is HIV infected, the standard of care at the current time involves HAART for the mother, both to reduce the risk of perinatal transmission of HIV and to improve maternal health. If the mother is already on a well-tolerated HAART treatment regimen, she should continue with that regimen, with one caveat. Efavirenz should be discontinued if it is a part of the regimen because of potential teratogenic, or toxic, effect on the fetus. If the pregnant woman has not been receiving HAART, she should, in most cases, wait until the end of the first trimester to begin a regimen, to avoid any potential teratogenic effects. This is the safest course of action, given that almost all vertical transmission happens either at delivery or in the final weeks of pregnancy (Cotter & O'Sullivan, 2004).

For pregnant women, the drug zidovudine (ZDV) should be included in the HAART regimen, because it has been found to produce the greatest reduction in transmission. It is fair to say that the long-term toxicity of HAART on the fetus is still unknown, but the risks must be weighed against the transmission of a potentially fatal viral infection. There is conflicting research about whether HAART is associated with prematurity. The current standard of care also recommends elective cesarean delivery as another method to reduce the risk of perinatal transmission. And finally, the standard of care recommends 6 weeks of ZDV for the newborn as further protection (Cotter & O'Sullivan, 2004; Public Health Service Task Force, 2004).

Breast-feeding is another method of mother-to-child HIV transmission. It is estimated that more than one third of all perinatal transmission in the breast-feeding population occurs through breast milk (Nduati et al., 2000). This has led to a recommendation in the United States that HIV-infected mothers should feed their infants with baby formula rather than breast-feed them. Some public health scholars have suggested that in many parts of the world, the situation is not that straightforward, however. They suggest that mothers in some countries do not have access to clean water or the ability to boil water and prepare bottles hygienically. In these countries, formula feeding may result in severe diarrhea, even death. The risks of substitute nutrition must be weighed against the risks of HIV infection (Piwoz, Ross, & Humphrey, 2004). One research team found no difference in the 2-year mortality rates between infants of HIV-infected mothers who were breast-fed and those who were formula-fed (Mbori-Ngacha et al., 2001).

Early in the HIV/AIDS epidemic, blood transfusions were another significant method of transmission (CDC, 1982a, 1982b). Safety measures for testing donated blood have almost eliminated this as a method of transmission in the United States.

Although most of the research on risk factors for HIV has focused on methods of transmission, recent research has focused on the immune response to HIV, on the interaction of the pathogen with the individual's immune system (Whittaker, 1997). Using cross-national data, one researcher found a strong correlation between quality of nutrition and prevalence of HIV; as nutritional quality decreased, the prevalence of HIV increased (Stillwaggon, 2002). The risk of contracting HIV with each contact is far greater for malnourished persons. This finding is supported by a recent study conducted with HIV-infected women in Tanzania that found that multivitamin supplementation with vitamin B complex, vitamin C, and vitamin E significantly delayed the progression of the disease. The researchers concluded that multivitamin supplements can be a low-cost means of delaying the initiation of HAART therapy in HIV-infected women in populations with significant nutritional deficiency. It is not yet known whether multivitamins are also beneficial to HIV-infected persons with no nutritional deficiency or to persons already on a HAART regime (Fawzi et al., 2004).

Other recent research identifies a gene that can serve as either risk for or protection against becoming infected with HIV and, if infected, against developing AIDS (Gonzalez et al., 2005). The gene, called CCL3L1, controls production of an immune system-signaling chemical and may help block the HIV virus from getting into cells. People vary in the number of this gene that they have; some people have no copies of the gene at all and some people have four, five, or even more. The signaling chemical stimulates the activity of a cellular entryway known as CCR5. CCR5 is known to affect susceptibility to HIV infection and the speed with which an infected person progresses to AIDS. People who carry more copies of the gene are less likely to become infected with the virus. It is important to note, however, that it is not simply the number of extra copies of the gene that matters but whether a person has more copies than average for his or her ethnic group. HIV-negative black adults were found to have an average of four copies of CCL3L1, while HIV-negative European Americans averaged two copies each and HIV-negative Hispanic Americans had an average of three copies (Gonzalez et al., 2005).

Although there is no known cure for HIV/AIDS, a number of licensed antiretroviral drugs can slow the progression of the virus. Unfortunately, the virus can mutate to become resistant to available drugs, causing them to lose their effectiveness over time (Fawzi et al., 2004). For this reason, the current standard of care is to give a combination of drugs, including newer drugs called protease inhibitors (the method of treatment known as HAART), although this may change with the advent of once-a-day drugs. The medical staff at the HIV/AIDS clinic where Estella Jackson receives treatment are currently evaluating whether she should be started on HAART. Unfortunately, HAART makes for very expensive treatment, and the expense has led the WHO to recommend other ways of managing the opportunistic infections that are associated with HIV. Given this situation, the recent research on the benefits of multivitamins is particularly promising.

Psychological Risk and Protection

As suggested earlier, sexual contact is the most common method of HIV transmission, and the latex male condom is the accepted method of protection. Consequently, researchers who are interested in the psychological risk and protective factors related to HIV transmission have focused primarily on psychological factors that are associated with the use of condoms. These factors can serve as either risk or protection. Several psychological factors (see Exhibit 9.3) have been found to be associated with condom use in different populations: knowledge, self-esteem, intrinsic health motivation, beliefs and attitudes about condoms, self-efficacy, masculine ideology, psychological distress, and psychiatric problems. The research to date seems to indicate that different psychological factors may be related to sexual risk behaviors in different ways in different populations.

In the early days of the HIV/AIDS epidemic, knowledge of HIV/AIDS and HIV-preventive behavior was studied extensively as a risk or protective factor for HIV transmission (e.g., DiClemente, 1991; Richard & van der Plight, 1991). Knowledge dissemination was also the primary ingredient of early AIDS prevention programs (Fisher & Fisher, 1992; Oakley et al., 1995). Although knowledge may still be a concern among some populations of the world (Kelly et al., 2001; Rogers, Ying, Xin, Fung, & Kaufman, 2002), recent research in the United States suggests that in the current stage of the epidemic, knowledge plays only a small role in condom use. Meta-analysis studies of psychosocial correlates of heterosexual condom use suggest that knowledge about HIV/AIDS is a necessary but not sufficient condition for condom use (Sheeran, Abraham, & Orbell, 1999).

There are mixed findings in the research on the relationship between self-esteem and condom use. Higher self-esteem has been found to be related to condom use among black and white urban women (Abel, Hilton, & Miller, 1996), among black and white women serving in the Navy (Abel, 1998), and among black and white women in a southeastern United States family practice setting (Gardner, Frank, & Amankwaa, 1998). On the other hand, other researchers have found higher self-esteem to be related to increased sexual risk behaviors among young female Army recruits (Abel, Adams, & Stevenson, 1994) and among community college students of varying ethnic backgrounds in the western United States (Shapiro, Radecki, Charchian, & Josephson, 1999).

Having a self-directed motivation for sexual health has also been found to be associated with condom use among Hispanic women (Abel & Chambers, 2004; Abel, Tak, & Gortner, 2003). Women with a self-directed motivation for sexual health see themselves as knowledgeable about safer sex practices and believe that their views about safer sex are as important as the views of their sexual partner; they believe in themselves and their abilities to practice safer sex within the context of a relationship. Translating this motivation for sexual health into planning for condom use has been found to be one of the strongest protective factors for avoiding HIV transmission. Behaviors such as carrying condoms and having a condom available before sexual contact increase the likelihood that condoms will be used (Sheeran et al., 1999).

Condom use is also influenced by beliefs about and attitudes toward condoms. A meta-analysis of psychosocial correlates of condom use among heterosexuals found condom use to be associated with a belief that condoms can prevent HIV infection and with positive attitudes about condom use (Sheeran et al., 1999). Another research team began with the assumption that condom use is a complex interpersonal negotiation and that both sexual partners may hold a complex mix of perceptions of the advantages and disadvantages of condom use. They hypothesized that condom use is influenced by the balance between positive and negative beliefs and attitudes toward condoms (Semaan, Lauby, O'Connell, & Cohen, 2003). Their analysis of data for women from six communities with high prevalence of drug use, prostitution, poverty, sexually transmitted diseases (STDs), and high rates of infant mortality supported this hypothesis. Women who did not use condoms were more likely to see more disadvantages than advantages to condom use.

Condom use has also been found to be associated with condom use self-efficacy, or the belief in one's ability to stick to the decision to use condoms, to discuss condom use with the sexual partner, and to refuse to engage in unprotected sex. This association has been found in a number of studies (see Sheeran et al., 1999) and with a diversity of samples, including college students (Brien, Thombs, Mahoney, & Wallnau, 1994; Goldman & Harlow, 1993; O'Leary, Goodhart, Jemmott, & Boccher-Lattimore, 1992; Wulfert & Wan, 1993), urban women (Lindberg, 2000), low-income women (Dancy & Berbaum, 2005; Sikkema et al., 1995), and black and Latina heterosexual women (Bowleg, Belgrave, & Reisen, 2000).

Traditional masculine ideologies, which prescribe that men be sexually assertive, have been found to be associated with high-risk sexual behaviors such as multiple sex partners and unprotected sex. This association has been found in a sample of black, white, and Latino adolescent males (Pleck, Sonenstein, & Ku, 1993) as well as in a sample of white college men (Noar & Morokoff, 2002). Although investigations of subgroup differences in gender-based expectations about sexual behaviors are relatively new and findings not always consistent, there is evidence that factors such as age cohort, socioeconomic class, racial and ethnic identity, and geography influence gender ideologies, particularly traditional masculine ideologies (for discussion of this evidence, see Bowleg, 2004). More traditional masculine ideologies have been found among older age cohorts (Abreu et al., 2000), less affluent males (Hunter & Davis, 1992), and Latinos (Abreu et al., 2000). Some regional differences have been found for traditional masculine ideologies in the United States, and this finding warrants further empirical investigation. One study found African American men in the southern United States to have more traditional masculine ideologies than European American men in the same region, but no racial differences were found in the Northeast (Levant, Majors, & Kelly, 1998). Another study found European American men on the West Coast to have more traditional masculine ideologies than African American men in that region; Latinos in the region were found to have more traditional masculine ideologies than either European Americans or African Americans (Abreu et al., 2000). This finding of regional differences for African American males is possibly related to different structural and sociopolitical environments relative to race in different regions of the United States.

Several studies have found that *psychological distress* and *depressive symptoms* may be related to HIV disease progression (Cruess, Antoni, Kilbourn, et al., 2000; Cruess, Antoni, Schneiderman, et al., 2000; Leserman et al., 1997; Patterson et al., 1996). Reductions in psychological distress and depressed mood among HIV-infected gay men predicted a slower rate of CD4 cell decline (Ironson et al., 2002). Another study found that HIV-infected persons who received cognitive behavioral treatments for psychological distress had a drop in HIV-related symptoms as well as a decline in psychological distress (Cruess, Antoni, Kilbourn, et al., 2000; Cruess, Antoni, Schneiderman, et al., 2000).

Some researchers have also found an association between psychiatric disorders and high-risk sexual behavior. Studying a sample of youth in foster care, one research team found that youths with clinical levels of externalizing mental health problems, such as conduct disorder, were more likely than other youths to engage in high-risk sexual activity

(Auslander et al., 2002). They also found that white female youth were at greater risk of high-risk sexual behavior than other foster care youth. Another research team found an association between a lifetime history of psychiatric disorder and sexual risk behavior for a nonclinical sample of male and female young adults who had been followed longitudinally since middle school (Tubman et al., 2004).

Social Risk and Protection

As noted in Exhibit 9.3, several social factors have been found to be associated with HIV transmission. Childhood maltreatment and adult experiences with sexual and physical violence are the most frequently studied social risk factors for engaging in behavior that puts one at risk for HIV, including risky sexual behavior as well as risky drug use. Although there has been considerable research evidence for both child and adult trauma risk factors, the results are not always consistent across studies. This may be due, in large part, to the different samples studied and the different behaviors measured.

Nevertheless, there is considerable evidence that child maltreatment is a risk factor for HIV risky behaviors. One longitudinal study of a stratified random sample of youth from 10 city public health clinics found that a history of childhood physical and/or sexual abuse was associated with a variety of HIV risk behaviors during adolescence and young adulthood, including risky sexual behavior as well as risky HIV drug behaviors (Cunningham, Stiffman, Dore, & Earls, 1994). Another research team (Bensley, Van Eenwyk, & Simmons, 2000) found that early and chronic sexual abuse, without co-occurring nonsexual physical abuse, was associated with more than a sevenfold increase in risky sexual and drug behaviors. An association between childhood sexual abuse and high-risk sexual behaviors in adulthood has been found in samples of homosexual and bisexual men (Bartholow et al., 1994), college women (Johnson & Harlow, 1996), homeless female adolescents (Noell, Rohde, Seeley, & Ochs, 2001), adolescents in intensive psychiatric treatment (Brown, Lourie, Zlotnick, & Cohn, 2000), and incarcerated women (Mullings, Marquart, & Brewer, 2000). On the other hand, one research team found a stronger association between childhood physical abuse and risky sexual behavior than between childhood sexual abuse and such behavior in a sample of drug abusers who dropped out of a methadone maintenance program (Kang, Deren, & Goldstein, 2002).

There is also growing evidence that being the victim of physical or sexual assault during adulthood is a risk factor for risky sexual and drug behavior. This association has been found in samples of South African women (Kalichman & Simbayi, 2004), Latin American MSM (Nieves, Carballo, & Dolezal, 2000), low-income women (Hamburger et al., 2004; Molitor, Ruiz, Klausner, & McFarland, 2000), and sex workers (Dunkle et al., 2004; Nemoto, Operario, Takenaka, Iwamoto, & Le, 2003). Estella Jackson's intravenous drug use is a risk factor for HIV infection; the sex work that she did to support her heroin addiction put her at risk for physical or sexual assault as well as sexual transmission of HIV. In a longitudinal study with a community sample, another research team found an association between a lifetime history of physical and/or sexual abuse and risky sexual behaviors among young male and female adults (Tubman et al., 2004). Like other researchers (see Noell et al., 2001), this research team found a cumulative developmental trajectory in which early childhood sexual and physical abuse leads to later abuse, accumulating risk over time.

Social network researchers have examined both IDU networks and sexual networks for their role in the HIV/AIDS epidemic. They have found an overlap between these two types of networks. One study of IDUs in New York City found that 71% of the study respondents injected or shared syringes with others (Neaigus et al., 1994). Gender differences were found in one cross-sectional study conducted in three Los Angeles communities with known large concentrations of IDUs. In comparison to the men, the young women's personal networks were reported to have more members who use hard drugs and are current drug injectors. Women were also more likely to have overlap in their drug and sex networks, a factor that can create greater transmission risk, given that the women were also more likely than the men to report both sharing of needles and risky sexual behavior. The personal networks of both males and females were unstable, with rapid turnover of network contacts, another factor that can increase the risk of HIV transmission (Montgomery et al., 2002).

The prevention team at the HIV/AIDS center where Estella Jackson is receiving care may be interested in mapping both the drug and sex networks of which Estella is a part, in the hopes that they can intervene in these networks and prevent further spread of the infection in the neighborhood. As the treatment team works with Estella, they may want to talk with her about her current sex network and the methods she is using and can use to avoid further sexual risk behaviors.

Because the primary method of HIV transmission is through sexual contact, researchers have focused more on sexual networks than drug networks. One research team found that a 10% increase in the average number of concurrent (simultaneous) sexual partnerships increased the rate of the number of infected persons in a sexual network by about 40% (Morris & Kretzschmar, 1997). Introduction of one high-risk individual into a sexual network greatly increases the risk for the whole network. As mobility increases across the regions of the world, researchers have become interested in how mobility increases risk in sexual networks. They have been particularly interested in "bridgers," those people who span sexual networks and carry infection from network to network. Early research looked at bridgers in sexual networks of gay males (Auerbach, Darrow, Jaffe, & Curran, 1984). More recent research has focused on heterosexual men who have unprotected sex with both high- and low-risk partners (Gorbach et al., 2000; Havanon, Bennett, & Knodel, 1993) and on men who have unprotected sex with both men and women (Montgomery, Mokotoff, Gentry, & Blair, 2003). These later men, many of whom do not identify as gay, have come to be called "**men on the down low**" **(DL)**. One research team has examined the extensive use of the Internet to form sexual networks among gay men, finding that MSM who meet sexual partners over the Internet reported more sexual partners in the previous 6 months and higher rates of sexual risk behaviors than MSM who do not use the Internet to meet sexual partners (Benotsch, Kalichman, & Cage, 2002).

Social norms in the network have also been found to have an impact on risky sexual behavior of network members. One research team found that network norms that promote a passive role for women in sexual interactions increase women's risks for HIV (Dancy & Berbaum, 2005). On the other hand, another research team found that social networks may be a protective factor as well. In social networks where condom use is looked on favorably, a protective process of social modeling occurs (Wulfert & Wan, 1993).

In a cross-national analysis, Stillwaggon (2002) found that the prevalence of HIV is positively associated with the level of economic inequality in a society; higher levels of economic inequality, as measured by the Gini coefficient, are associated with higher prevalence of HIV/AIDS. This is consistent with other research that has found economic inequality to be correlated with overall morbidity and mortality (Adler, 2001).

There are preliminary findings of the important protective role of three social factors. Several researchers have found that HIV-infected adults who perceive their social support systems as helpful are less likely to engage in risky sexual behavior (Kimberly & Serovich, 1999; Peterson et al., 1992; Reilly & Woo, 2004). Perhaps this is why the social worker at the HIV/AIDS center where Estella Jackson receives care has worked with Estella to evaluate her social support system and think of ways to enhance it. Another research team found that, for female adolescents in one South African region, feeling connected to parents and community helps to decrease risky sexual behavior (Macintyre, Rutenberg, Brown, & Karim, 2004). Interestingly, they found the opposite for male adolescents; less family and community oversight was associated with less risky sexual behavior. And finally, another research team found that a sample of low-income African American women were less likely to engage in risky sexual behavior if they were involved in community-related prevention behavior such as talking to people about HIV-risk behavior and distributing condoms and HIV literature in the community (Dancy & Berbaum, 2005). These findings of the protective role of family and community connectedness, at least for women, are promising and warrant further investigation. Perhaps the prevention team at the HIV center where Estella Jackson receives care can involve her at some point in their prevention activities in the neighborhood.

Spiritual Risk and Protection

Lack of meaning in life has been found to be a risk factor for such health risk behaviors as substance abuse and suicide attempts (Coleman, Kaplan, & Downing, 1986; Harlow, Newcomb, & Bentler, 1986). One research team also found lack of meaning in life to be associated with high-risk sexual behaviors among college students (Goldman & Harlow, 1993). Consistent with this finding, spirituality and/or religion have been found to serve as a protective factor against risky sexual behavior as well as HIV progression (see Exhibit 9.3).

There are inconsistencies in the research literature, however, about the relative benefits of spirituality, defined as a personal search for meaning, versus religious practices. On the one hand, having a formal role in religious activities has been found to be associated with a reduction in risky sexual behavior in Ghana (Allain, Anokwa, Casbard, Owusu-Ofori, & Dennis-Antwi, 2004). In the United States, the greater the frequency of church attendance among HIV-infected African American women, the less likely they were to engage in high-risk health behavior and to suffer HIV progression (Morse et al., 2000). Religion has not been as important to Sondra Jackson as it was to her mother, but she has been thinking of beginning to attend church again and to ask Estella to join her. She thinks that this might help Estella find purpose and meaning in life as well as wrap her in a supportive religious community. On the other hand, some researchers have found that it is a personal faith or spiritual life, and not religious practices, that protects against HIV risk behaviors (Avants, Marcotte, Arnold, & Margolin, 2003) and against psychological distress that may contribute to HIV progression (Nelson, Rosenfeld, Breitbart, & Galietta, 2002).

These findings are difficult to interpret, because most researchers who study the role of spirituality and religion in health behaviors do not make distinctions between the spiritual aspects of religion and participation in established religious practices. It must be noted, however, that some religious groups have opposed prevention strategies that include condom use and clean needle exchanges for IDUs. Given the proven effectiveness of these prevention strategies, such religious practices can be seen as risk factors for HIV/AIDS transmission.

Biopsychosocial-Spiritual Integration

In 1994, Merrill Singer invented the term **syndemic** to describe a set of linked health problems that interact synergistically. Singer referred specifically to a substance abuse, violence, and AIDS syndemic (SAVA syndemic), because these three public health problems were seen as intertwined and mutually reinforcing, interacting synergistically to magnify the HIV/AIDS epidemic. Singer also suggested that the SAVA syndemic disproportionately afflicts people living in poverty in U.S. cities. Certainly, we can see the way that substance abuse, community violence, and HIV/AIDS are intertwined in the neighborhood where Estella Jackson lives.

More recently, one research team (Stall et al., 2003) has considered the syndemic of substance abuse, partner violence, depression, childhood sexual abuse, and HIV/AIDS among MSM. They found that there was a connection between these health problems, that each of the health problems was associated with high-risk sexual behaviors, and that a greater number of psychosocial problems was associated with higher prevalence rates for high-risk sexual behaviors and HIV infection.

The National Center for Chronic Disease Prevention and Health Promotion (2004) suggests that a syndemic orientation calls for understanding, in an integrated fashion, the common biological, psychological, social, and physical environmental risk factors for interconnected health problems. Stall et al. (2003) suggest that the role of such factors as malnutrition, stress, poverty, and racism must be considered in relation to a syndemic involving HIV/AIDS.

The discussion in this chapter indicates the integration of biological, psychological, social, and spiritual factors when HIV/AIDS is considered as a singular epidemic. HIV/AIDS is transmitted through biological processes involved in human interaction (social). Development and progression of the disease are moderated by genetics (biology), nutrition (biology), and psychological distress (psychology). Nutrition is determined largely by economics as situated in social structure (social). Psychological distress can be influenced by spiritual beliefs and practices. HIV health risk behaviors (biology) are influenced by psychological variables such as motivation, beliefs, gender ideologies, and psychological distress; by social factors such as physical and sexual abuse, the norms of the social network, and the nature of social support; and by spiritual health and religious practices. It is clear from the discussion in other chapters of this book that traumatic experiences such as physical and sexual assault (social) disrupt brain functioning (biological) and cognitive processes (psychological) and make one vulnerable to risky sexual and drug behaviors. Overall prevalence of HIV is influenced by levels of societal inequality and by the nature of social networks.

Consider the situation of Estella Jackson, who does not know how she contracted the HIV infection. We can speculate that she was having unprotected sex while she was using heroin, especially while she was prostituting to pay for the heroin. There is a good chance that she was also sharing injecting needles with other people in her drug network. As suggested earlier, from a public health perspective, it is important to learn more about Estella's drug and sexual networks. We don't know anything about Estella's genetic vulnerability to HIV, nor do we know much about her self-esteem, both of which are potential risk factors. We do know that the growing economic inequality in her urban environment is a risk factor for further spread of HIV. We can recommend that the social workers at Estella's HIV/AIDS clinic and substance abuse treatment program explore whether she has meaning and purpose in her life as she begins treatment.

Consequences of HIV/AIDS

As mentioned earlier, HIV/AIDS is a relatively new disease whose consequences have been changing over time. Early in the history of the disease, it was assumed to be a terminal disease. People sought help from AIDS service organizations (ASOs), hospitals, and hospices to ease their living and their dying. There was profound and complex bereavement in gay communities as unprecedented numbers of young people died, often cared for by partners living with the disease (Shernoff, 1990; Strug et al., 2002).

It is still the case that some die young from HIV/AIDS while others are living longer. In 2004, a UNAIDS (Joint United Nations Programme on HIV/AIDS) update delivered the sad news that the AIDS pandemic is driving the life expectancy down in 23 African countries, down below 40 years in 7 countries and as low as 33 years in some countries. HIV/AIDS is reversing the hard-fought gains in life-expectancy that had occurred in recent decades in African nations (Pavon, 2004).

AIDS deaths are presenting challenges to multigenerational families, calling for new roles across generations. It is estimated that AIDS has generated 15 million orphans worldwide (Pavon, 2004). The future of these orphans is not certain. Some are HIV infected and some are not. Some orphans in developing countries may head their own households and live largely without adult support and supervision, and many face disruptions in their education (Ainsworth, Beegle, & Koda, 2005). Many others will be cared for by grandparents and other family members who may be grieving the loss of the child's parents. This grief is often complicated by strained histories of drug use, promiscuity, and other risky behaviors. This kinship foster care often puts financial, physical, and emotional strain on grandparents who may have already suffered economic hardship in relation to their child's HIV/AIDS care and treatment, as well as the loss of potential income from the earnings of the deceased (Knodel & Wassana, 2004; Safman, 2004).

In the United States, overall, people with HIV/AIDS are living longer and have all the challenges related to living with a chronic illness—uncertainty and increased dependence on the health care system, social services, and family and other support systems. The uncertainties of chronic illness increase anxiety and depression and put stress on relationships.

In recent years, the new medications brought both hope and uncertainty and involved much decision making. Complex medication regimens have involved large numbers of pills taken at prescribed times, on empty and/or full stomach, and required access to refrigeration, as well as commitment and an organized lifestyle. Because medical information has kept changing over time, many persons living with HIV/AIDS have felt a great deal of uncertainty about adhering to treatment recommendations (Monroe, 2001). Side effects such as nausea, diarrhea, fatigue, loss of appetite, weight gain, headaches, dizziness, hair loss, and neuropathy, as well as skepticism about the medications, influence treatment adherence (Kovacs & Mutepa, 2001). As of July 2006, it is unclear how the new once-a-day drugs will change the lives of persons living with HIV/AIDS.

Managing the complexities of HIV treatment pose a serious challenge for persons coping with substance abuse, mental health problems, unemployment, and/or homelessness. It is important that Estella Jackson continue with her substance abuse treatment program to stabilize her ability to adhere to whatever treatment regimen is offered to her.

One of the triumphs to date in the fight against HIV/AIDS is the dramatic decrease in vertical transmission. Between 1992 and 1997, the rate of vertical transmission in the United States declined by 66% (Feldman, 2003). Unfortunately, vertical transmission and the care of children with HIV/AIDS remains a large problem in developing countries, as evidenced by a recent report that over half of the children admitted to South Africa's second largest hospital are admitted for HIV/AIDS-related symptoms (de Lange, Greyling, & Leslie, 2005). And in the United States, there is a significant group of children and adolescents who are growing up with HIV/AIDS. At the time they were born, there were no known effective treatments, and they were never expected to reach adolescence. However, they were able to live long enough to start the new antiretroviral medications; some were near death but improved dramatically on the new medications, reaching a point of undetectable viral loads. Unlike people who were infected as adolescents and adults, due to no behavior of their own, these youth have never known a life without HIV/AIDS. Their childhood most likely included the stressors of multiple hospitalizations, difficult medication regimens, intolerable side effects, and educational disruptions (Feldman, 2003). It is too early to predict the life course trajectories of these youth, but social workers who work with them must be sensitive to the impact of HIV/AIDS on their physical, cognitive, emotional, social, and moral development.

Now that persons are living longer and in better health with HIV/AIDS, new challenges arise for adults, in both love and work domains. The extended life course that has been afforded by the new medications presents the possibility of having children, or more children, but the decision is also often a difficult one (Kovacs & Mutepa, 2001). With increased longevity and improved health, work is becoming a valuable role for many adults who are HIV infected. Besides the important financial benefit, maintaining employment can be a real boon to emotional well-being and motivation for life (Timmons & Fesko, 2004). However, HIV/AIDS limits employment alternatives, requiring workers to avoid work situations that present environmental dangers to their compromised immune systems. They may also have to avoid jobs that require heavy labor, and employers are reluctant to hire them for positions that involve handling food. Because they must juggle work with frequent medical appointments, adults with HIV/AIDS have reported that they work part time even though they would like to work full time (Timmons & Fesko, 2004). Persons living with HIV/AIDS must also be concerned about losing government cash and medical benefits if they return to work (Brooks, Martin, Ortiz, & Veniegas, 2004).

Older adults with HIV have been referred to as "the overlooked epidemic" (Whipple & Scura, 1996, p. 23) who are "unserved, unseen, and unheard" (Emlet & Poindexter, 2004, p. 86). The number of older adults with HIV/AIDS is expected to increase as people live longer due to the new medications. Clinicians often fail to detect HIV infection in older adults because they don't consider them at risk, in part because they tend not to think of them as being sexually active or at risk from IDU. In older adults, "AIDS can be mistaken for Alzheimer's disease and other chronic illnesses" (Whipple & Scura, 1996, p. 24). Differential diagnosis is also complicated by HIV-related symptoms such as weakness, fatigue, skin rashes, swollen lymph nodes, anorexia, and weight loss that appear in many conditions that are often associated with aging.

In women, a "gynecologic condition that persists despite treatment should prompt suspicion of HIV, whatever the age of the patient." However, this is often overlooked in older women (Whipple & Scura, 1996, p. 25). Women may be at higher risk after menopause because they tend not to use condoms once pregnancy is no longer a concern. Most women are not aware that physiological changes related to normal aging, changes such as decrease in vaginal lubrication and thinning vaginal walls, as well as age-related decline in their immune function, make them more susceptible to HIV and other sexually transmitted infections than younger women.

For these and other reasons, older persons tend to be diagnosed in a late stage of infection, becoming ill with complications and dying sooner than younger counterparts. It is also unclear whether older people will benefit from the new therapies, in part because they have not been included in the clinical trials and because they tend to have other health risk factors (Ory, Zablotsky, & Crystal, 1998). Older adults with HIV/AIDS often feel isolated and lack a sufficient support network, may fear being stigmatized, and are at risk for further isolation and depression (Whipple & Scura, 1996, p. 26).

Ways of Coping

With the new and complex treatment regimens, persons living with HIV/AIDS are living longer with an illness that is both chronic and life threatening (Vosvick et al., 2002). A large research literature has investigated the strategies people use to cope with this serious illness, and a number of ways of coping have been identified, as demonstrated in Exhibit 9.5.

- Avoidant coping
  - Denial
  - Social withdrawal
  - Giving up
  - Wishful thinking
  - Disengagement
  - Passive tension-reducing behaviors
- Involved coping
  - Positive reframing
  - Acceptance
  - Seeking advice and information
  - Seeking social support
  - Health-related strategies
- Organizing at the community level

Exhibit 9.5   Ways of Coping with HIV/AIDS

Perhaps the most common line of research has focused on the psychological coping strategies used, which are typically categorized as either avoidant coping or involved coping. Avoidant coping includes denial; social withdrawal; giving up; wishful thinking; disengagement through alcohol and other drugs or through other activities to take the mind off of things; and passive tension-reducing behaviors such as emotional venting, crying, yelling, excessive eating, or sleeping (Fleishman et al., 2003; Hough, Brumitt, Templin, Saltz, & Mood, 2003; Vosvick et al., 2002; Weaver et al., 2004). Involved coping includes such strategies as positive reframing, acceptance, seeking advice and information, and seeking social support (Fleishman et al., 2003; Hough et al., 2003; Weaver et al., 2004). There is a consistent finding that avoidant coping is associated with a poorer quality of physical and emotional health for adults, but this is not the case for children who may actually benefit from avoidant coping (Hough et al., 2003; Kliewer, 1991). Adolescents with HIV/AIDS have been found to use such coping strategies as listening to music, thinking about good things, close relationships, sleeping, eating, watching television, daydreaming, and praying (Lewis & Brown, 2002).

Another commonly investigated coping strategy is religious and/or spiritual coping. There is a long line of research that indicates that people often turn to religion and spirituality to cope with life-threatening illnesses. There is much evidence that this is the case for persons with HIV/AIDS as well, including gay men (Schwartzberg, 1993), older adults (Siegel & Schrimshaw, 2002), women (Dalmida, 2006; Prado et al., 2004; Simoni, Martone, & Kerwin, 2002), and caregivers of persons with HIV/AIDS (Winston, 2003). African American and Latino HIV-infected adults have been found to use religious or spiritual advisers more often than white HIV-infected adults (Reilly & Woo, 2004). One study of older adults living with HIV/AIDS identified a variety of benefits of religious and spiritual beliefs and practices. They evoke comforting emotions, offer sense of empowerment and control, ease emotional burdens, offer social support and sense of belonging, offer support through a personal relationship with God, facilitate meaning and acceptance, and relieve uncertainty and fear of death (Siegel & Schrimshaw, 2002). A study of Thai people living with HIV/AIDS found that meditation is related to better quality of life (Molassiotis & Maneesakorn, 2004). On the other hand, one study found that religion-based harsh judgmentalism is associated with a poor quality of physical and mental health (Ironson et al., 2002).

Other researchers have found that people with HIV/AIDS often make use of social support to cope with the illness. Differences have been found, however, in the types of persons sought for support. HIV-infected gay men receive more support from friends than from family members (Hays, Magee, & Chauncey, 1994; Johnston, Stall, & Smith, 1995; Kimberly & Serovich, 1999). Women are more likely than men to receive HIV-related support from siblings, religious or spiritual leaders, mental health professionals, and community organizations (Reilly & Woo, 2004). Estella Jackson is beginning to use her sister, Sondra, as well as physical and mental health professionals, to cope with her joint challenges of substance abuse and HIV infection. Among caregivers of persons with AIDS, 86% in one study reported that they have at least one friend or relative they want to be with when they are feeling down (Turner, Pearlin, & Mullan, 1998). Female caregivers reported receiving more emotional support than male caregivers.

In terms of seeking social support, one question that HIV-infected persons must face is, "To whom do I want to disclose my HIV status?" Studies of disclosure patterns indicate that most HIV-infected people engage in selective disclosure. Disclosure may decrease isolation and loneliness, but it may also risk abandonment and job loss (Bor, 1997; Hays et al., 1993; Kovacs & Mutepa, 2001). Disclosure rates are higher to siblings than to other persons, and disclosures are higher to mothers than to fathers (Landau & York, 2004; Kadushin, 2000). HIV-infected gay men are more likely to disclose to friends and lovers than to family (Kadushin, 2000). For HIV-infected parents, whether or not to disclose HIV status to children can be an important and difficult decision. Some HIV-infected mothers openly acknowledge their HIV/AIDS status to their children; others struggle with wanting to protect their children from the embarrassment and shame they associate with their diagnosis while at the same time worrying about being dishonest if they fail to disclose (Kovacs & Mutepa, 2001).

There is more limited research on several other methods of coping with HIV/AIDS. One research team found that HIV-infected older adults use a number of health-related strategies for coping with fatigue, including dietary changes, vitamins, modification of routines, rest, exercise, acupuncture, massage, and herbal remedies (Siegel, Brown-Bradley, & Lekas, 2004). Other researchers have found that a relatively large minority of persons with HIV/AIDS use the Internet to search for health-related information and attend online support groups (Kalichman et al., 2003; Reeves, 2000). In one study, persons with HIV/AIDS described work as an important coping strategy (Timmons & Fesko, 2004).

Very little research literature could be found on how communities cope with HIV/AIDS, but one study, as well as news reports from Africa, suggests that communities are getting organized to care for orphans, present educational materials, and engage in home visitation to prevent HIV and identify people living with HIV/AIDS (Africa News Service, 2002; Kamali et al., 1996; Wax, 2005).

Social Justice Issues

As suggested earlier, the role of such factors as malnutrition, stress, poverty, racism, homophobia, and sexism must be considered in relation to a syndemic involving HIV/AIDS (Singer, 1994). The **pandemic**, the word used to refer to an epidemic that is spread over an especially wide area, in developing countries, particularly in the African region, calls for serious consideration by wealthy countries of their obligations as world citizens. The HIV pandemic is most severe in some of the poorest countries of the world, countries that have inadequate health and educational systems. Some of these countries are on the verge of being totally devastated by the pandemic. Since the beginning of the epidemic, these countries have been paying high amounts of foreign debt to Western countries, a situation that has further inhibited their ability to build an infrastructure and develop the resources to fight the epidemic. In fact, the interest on loans paid by some of these impoverished countries has exceeded the amount of aid that they have received from the lending countries to fight the epidemic (AVERT, 2005). Recently, political momentum has been growing in the developed world for offering some form of debt relief to these struggling countries, but there are disagreements about the best approach to take (Rajan, 2005).

As suggested earlier, since 1996, HARRT has been a real boon to the life chances of persons living with HIV/AIDS. But HAART is an expensive therapy. Until recently, ART was accessible only to a fortunate few, with millions of infected people around the world denied access to the new treatment technologies. In 2003, WHO and UNAIDS undertook what they called a "3 by 5" project to ensure that ART was provided to 3 million people living with HIV/AIDS in the low- and middle-income countries by the end of 2005 (UNAIDS, 2005b). Although the 3 by 5 target was not met, global access to HIV treatment more than tripled between December 2003 and December 2005. Of particular note, the number of people receiving HIV treatment in sub-Saharan Africa increased by more than eightfold in that 2-year period. These increases are promising, but it is important to note that by December 2005, only 17% of those in need of ART in sub-Saharan Africa had access to it (WHO, 2006). While most persons with HIV/AIDS in the United States have access to ART, there are countries where fewer than 10% of persons living with AIDS in June 2005 had access to ART (UNAIDS, 2005b). See Exhibit 9.6 for the percentage of HAART coverage of selected countries with the highest need in June 2005. There is a particular urgency for increased access to HIV care among children in these high-need areas, where it is projected that half of the children will die before their second birthday without treatment (UNAIDS, 2005b). The good news is that there is evidence of a growing momentum to provide universal access to HIV treatment by 2010 (WHO, 2006).

Country	Percentage Covered
Sudan	< 1%
Democratic Republic of the Congo	2–3%
United Republic of Tanzania	2–3%
Zimbabwe	3–5%
Ghana	4–5%
Lesotho	4–5%
Mozambique	5–6%
Russian Federation	4–7%
Ethiopia	5–7%
Nigeria	4–8%
India	4–9%
South Africa	10–14%
Malawi	11–14%
Kenya	12–17%
Zambia	14–18%
China	14–18%
Cameroon	11–19%

Exhibit 9.6   Estimated Percentage of ART Coverage in Selected Countries With High Unmet Need in June 2005

SOURCE: Based on UNAIDS, 2005b, Figure 1, p. 14.

The United States, through its President's Emergency Plan for AIDS Relief (PEPFAR), is the largest single donor to the worldwide effort to provide access to HIV treatment (Brown, 2006). PEPFAR has come under criticism, however, because of its emphasis on abstinence-based prevention strategies and its opposition to needle-exchange programs (Brown, 2006). There is also criticism of PEPFAR's policy of requiring U.S. health groups to denounce prostitution before they receive funds for international AIDS work. This policy, which was passed by Congress in 2003, was ruled unconstitutional by two federal judges in May 2006 (Kessler, 2006).

The research literature on risk factors for HIV/AIDS clearly demonstrates that many people, including women, children, and adolescents, are at a disadvantage to negotiate safer sex because of their low status in society (WHO, 2004). Therefore, men have a special responsibility to avoid putting others at risk, and prevention programs must recognize the vulnerable position of many women and children.

People living with HIV/AIDS have the same rights to education, employment, health care, housing, procreation, privacy, and social security as other people. And yet, the nations of the world seem to have made much more progress in improving the medications for treating HIV/AIDS than in addressing the problem of social stigma surrounding the disease and discrimination against persons with it (Parker & Aggleton, 2003; Rintamaki & Brashers, 2005). In recent years, there has been a very large international literature on discrimination against persons living with HIV/AIDS and a serious call for action to eliminate such discrimination (e.g., see Paxton et al., 2005; Uneze, 2004). There is evidence of negative attitudes toward IDUs among HIV health care providers. One study in the United States found that IDUs who were treated by physicians who held negative attitudes toward IDUs were less likely to receive HAART treatment than non-IDUs cared for by these physicians or IDUs who were cared for by physicians with less negative attitudes toward IDUs (Ding et al., 2005).

Research in the United States indicates that persons living with HIV/AIDS continue to experience some stigma in relation to HIV/AIDS, but they also report discrimination based on race and social class in their interactions with health care providers (Bird, Bogart, & Delahanty, 2004). It is not surprising that the age-adjusted rate of death due to HIV in the United States is highest among blacks and second highest among Hispanics (CDC, 2006a). Even in Canada, with its universal health care system, socioeconomic status (SES) was strongly associated with HIV/AIDS mortality (Wood et al., 2002). HIV-infected individuals of lower SES in Canada are less likely than others to receive the newer medication regimens. This suggests a need for public health efforts to consistently address the social justice issues in health disparities.

Recent research indicates that in the United States, African American suspicion of the health care system contributes to such health disparities as the ones discussed above. One study (Bogart & Thorburn, 2005) of 500 African Americans aged 15 to 44 years found that almost half of the participants believed that HIV is a humanmade virus and 44% believed that people who take the new HIV/AIDS medicines are government guinea pigs. Over half believed that a cure exists for AIDS, but it is being withheld from poor people. The authors concluded that such conspiracy theories are a barrier to HIV prevention in this population. They note that the conspiracy theories need to be understood in the context of the Tuskegee experiment conducted by the federal government from 1932 to 1972. In this experiment, black men were told that they were being treated for syphilis but actually treatment was being withheld so that scientists could study the course of the disease. Public health efforts to prevent HIV must work to obtain the trust of black communities, acknowledging the historical context of distrust (Bogart & Thorburn, 2005).

Practice Implications

There was a time when only those social workers working with gay men in ASOs and hospitals were apt to encounter HIV/AIDS. Now it is hard to imagine a setting—family, youth, mental health, substance abuse, foster care/adoption, health, or aging services—in which social workers will not work directly or indirectly with someone infected, affected, or at risk of infection, or with communities facing these issues. Indeed, HIV/AIDS has been called the "quintessential social work practice issue" (Kaplan, Tomaszewski, & Gorin, 2004, p. 158). Few health conditions call for such a broad social work response. In general, in our social work roles as clinicians, advocates, administrators, and educators, we focus on prevention, care, and services.

Prevention

Prevention remains a key focus despite promise of antiretroviral medications; prevention must be targeted to clients who are HIV negative, as well as those who are HIV positive (Mitchell & Linsk, 2004). Prevention is complex, and interventions must be multidimensional, focusing on initial behavior change as well as on sustaining or maintaining behavior change. For example, one type of program may be needed to help clients initially adopt use of condoms or clean needles, but a different intervention may be needed to help the client sustain risk-reducing behaviors. Sexual coercion and violence against women that result from gender inequality, as well as the impact of culture, are critical issues in designing prevention programs for women. These programs should emphasize empowerment and protection (Galambos, 2004). With this in mind, Estella Jackson's social worker is beginning to develop an outreach program in which HIV-positive women educate other women about ways to protect themselves against risky drug and sexual behaviors.

The public health model that considers three levels of prevention is a good fit for this complex health condition (Weitz, 2003). As you may recall from Chapter 5, *primary prevention* refers to strategies designed to keep people from becoming ill or disabled; in this case, infected with HIV. *Secondary prevention* strategies are designed to reduce the prevalence of disease through early detection and intervention; in this case, prompt testing and diagnosis to facilitate access to medication and related care and services. *Tertiary prevention* refers to strategies that minimize physical deterioration and complications among those already ill. Each of these three levels of prevention should be designed keeping in mind the developmental stage, gender, sexual orientation, social class, and culture of the target population.

Social workers at state health departments, staff at local ASOs, public health clinics, and other settings involved in designing outreach programs, billboard campaigns, literature, curricula, Web sites, and other educational materials continually assess their communities, figuring out *who* needs this information and *how* to reach them. Prevention research suggests that teens respond well to peers by age, lifestyle, and culture. Prevention strategies to protect women must include reaching their bisexual male partners who are having sex with men, many of whom are on the DL and not identifying as gay (Miller, Serner, & Wagner, 2005; Phillips, 2005). Social workers can draw on the research on sexual and drug networks to develop prevention programs to diffuse behavior innovations throughout these networks. This is a task that the staff at Estella Jackson's clinic have begun to undertake.

Care and Services

HIV is a chronic health condition that involves increased promise for longevity with proper medication adherence, but one that continues to claim the lives of thousands every day. Helping people live with this life challenge is a focus of social work practice (Linsk & Bonk, 2000; Shernoff, 1990). In addition to being knowledgeable about HIV/AIDS, practitioners need to be prepared to engage in conversations with adolescents, adults, and elders about sensitive topics such as death; sex; spirituality; childhood, domestic, and sexual violence; incarceration; and illegal behavior such as drug use and prostitution. Estella Jackson's social workers will need to be comfortable talking about most of these issues with her. The uncertainties of living with HIV/AIDS can cause psychological distress, depression, and anxiety. Social workers often function as translators (Wheeler & Shernoff, 1999) or interpreters of medical, financial, and other content, helping persons living with AIDS (PWAs) access services and navigate the health and mental health systems.

Early in the epidemic, Alperin and Richie (1989) identified the knowledge and skills social workers need to address the needs of persons with HIV/AIDS: knowledge of HIV transmission, crisis intervention skills, empathy, knowledge of AIDS programs, values clarification skills, comfort discussing sexual preferences and practices, and stress management skills. These still apply. What is known about depression, anxiety, and other adjustment reactions to chronic illness have application in work with PWAs. Guided by a comprehensive assessment with the client, whether individual, family, or community, a social work intervention would take into consideration developmental and cultural factors. The following interventions, while not intended to be exhaustive, help illustrate the importance of starting where each client is, depending upon his or her unique needs and characteristics.

Telephone support groups have been effective to decrease isolation and improve quality of life for people living with HIV/AIDS who do not have easy access to or would not feel comfortable attending face-to-face support groups, including people in small towns and rural areas (Heckman et al., 1999; Rounds, Galinsky, & Despard, 1996) and HIV-positive mothers whose children have died of AIDS (Weiner, 1999). A different approach was developed for HIV-positive adolescents in San Francisco. The Larkin Street Youth Center provides a continuum of care, including drop-in services, outreach programs, health care, and residential services (Kennedy, Spingarn, Stanton, & Rotheram-Borus, 2000). Family empowerment is important when working with families who have children living with HIV/AIDS (Kmita, Baranska, & Niemiec, 2002).

Another program illustrates the value of an interdisciplinary and culturally sensitive intervention when working with immigrant and migrant families. The culturally specific health care model, developed by Goicoechea-Balbona (1998) to increase awareness of and access to health care services, involves the use of cultural guides who are indigenous health care providers in the community. Goicoechea-Balbona notes that it is particularly important to avoid misinterpreting fear, distrust, and other personal and social factors as resistance to health care among people who fear deportation or income and job loss.

In addition to culturally specific models of care, gender-specific approaches to treatment have evolved for women whose needs were not being met. Hughes (1999) describes WHEEL (Women Helping to Empower and Enhance Lives), an HIV-prevention intervention targeting at-risk women. WHEEL involves women in designing their own interventions, most of which consist of the following components: personal and spiritual growth, networking, economic survival, advocacy, skill learning, relationships, health, self-knowledge, planning and decision making, social activities, and self-actualization. Bride and Real (2003) describe a therapeutic community modified to address the needs of homeless women who are both chemically dependent and living with HIV/AIDS. Given that women in treatment for substance abuse report more psychiatric symptoms and different patterns of substance use than men in treatment, a different approach to practice was developed that is more supportive and less confrontational than traditional programs. This program focuses on empowerment and women's strengths. This is, indeed, the approach taken by the social workers at the clinic where Estella Jackson receives treatment.

A key role for social work intervention is helping HIV-infected individuals maintain treatment adherence (Linsk & Bonk, 2000; Mitchell & Linsk, 2004). For the medications to be effective, they must be taken on precise and consistent schedules, which is challenging, given the complicated regimen of numerous pills that often cause side effects. It is difficult to live with the indefinite nature of this regimen, a daunting task for anyone but especially those living with other life challenges such as poverty, homelessness, mental illness, or substance abuse. This is a time to support, not judge, people trying to manage complex medication regimens. Case management, advocacy, supportive counseling, motivational interviewing, and other social work skills help clients maintain adherence, which is important, given that nonadherence can significantly reduce the efficacy of the medication and lead to drug resistance (Demmer, 2004). As suggested earlier, it is not yet clear what effect the once-a-day drugs will have on treatment adherence, and both PWAs and health care providers are once again charting new territory.

Learning Activities

1. **Cohort analysis.** Interview three people from three different age cohorts (e.g., someone in their 70s or 80s, someone in their 50s, and someone in their 20s or 30s) about how the HIV/AIDS epidemic has affected their lives. Ask what they know about HIV/AIDS and about the attitudes they hold toward people with HIV/AIDS. Also ask if they personally know anyone with HIV/AIDS. After you have done the interviews, reflect on how you reacted to what you heard from each interviewee. Also think about what you knew about HIV/AIDS before you read this chapter. Was there anything that you read that surprised you **(knowledge about the self)?** Write a brief paper (about four double-spaced typewritten pages) comparing and contrasting how HIV/AIDS has affected the lives of these three people. Include a brief reflection on how HIV/AIDS has affected your own life **(knowledge about the self)**.

2. **Case study exercise.** Working in small groups, reread the case of Sondra Jackson at the beginning of Chapter 2, taking particular note of Estella Jackson **(knowledge of the case)**. Also review the theoretical perspectives on HIV/AIDS and the risk and protective factors overviewed in Exhibit 9.3 **(general knowledge).** Discuss which theory or theories makes most sense for understanding Estella's infection. Make a list of the risk and protective factors that can be identified in her case scenario. Make another list of the possible risk and protection factors you would like to explore in your work with Estella **(general knowledge** and **knowledge about the case)**. Discuss potential aids for or barriers to Estella's adherence to treatment for HIV/AIDS. How would you begin to address the barriers **(values and ethics)?**

3. **Interview with social worker.** Interview a social worker who works with people living with HIV/AIDS. Some questions you might want to explore include the following: What are the biggest challenges in her or his work? What are the greatest rewards? What are the biggest challenges clients with HIV/AIDS face? What services do her or his organization provide? What are the gaps in services? What does she or he see as the trends in providing social work service to people living with HIV/AIDS? What ethical issues does she or he face working with people with HIV/AIDS **(values and ethics)?** Write a brief (about four pages) paper summarizing the main themes of the interview. Include a two-paragraph reflection on how you react to what you heard. Can you imagine yourself doing the kind of work the social worker described **(knowledge about the self)?**

4. **Community analysis and planning exercise.** Working in small groups of three or four, learn what you can about the prevalence and incidence of HIV/AIDS in your

community **(knowledge about the case).** You might want to start by talking with people at your local public health department. What groups, if any, in the community are overrepresented in the prevalence and incidence data? What social justice issues are demonstrated by the prevalence and incidence patterns **(values and ethics)?** Also investigate what agencies and organizations are involved in AIDS prevention at the primary, secondary, and tertiary levels **(general knowledge)**. Learn about the programs and activities of these agencies and organizations. Do you see issues that call for social work advocacy **(values and ethics)?**

10 Major Depression

Marcia P. Harrigan,
Virginia Commonwealth University

D avid Loefeler reports that he has been unable to hold down a steady job, primarily because he struggles with depression and anxiety issues. He also mentioned that he struggles with the side effects of the many different psychotropic medications he has tried. In contrast, the story of Kim Tran does not make specific reference to major depression, but there is reference to a pervasive "deep sadness that runs through the family," leaving the reader to be more speculative. Regardless of the work setting or service delivery system, social workers will encounter depression. Knowledge about depression is essential, because this life challenge often interferes with all dimensions of functioning. Social workers must be aware that major depression may not be the reason the client system is requesting or receiving services but may be present nevertheless. This chapter focuses on only one type of depression, termed major depressive disorder (MDD), or unipolar depression, with brief mention of other types.

Major depressive disorder (MDD) is a mood or brain disorder characterized by persistent and deep feelings of sadness or emptiness. Because all people experience moments of sadness without having MDD, there are additional criteria that must be met. The depressed mood must be present for at least 2 weeks with at least five additional symptoms from the criteria list shown in Exhibit 10.1. A diagnosis of MDD must also rule out depressed mood due to a physical illness or side effects of medications. Several subtypes of depression are described in the *DSM-IV* of the American Psychiatric Association (2000).

It is important to know that there are other types of depression that may have different causes and consequently different interventions than those recommended for MDD. **Unipolar depression** is distinguished from **bipolar depression,** which includes major depression interspersed with periods of mania, hyperactivity, or agitation. **Dysthymic disorder** is less severe than major depression and may be more chronic. A diagnosis of dysthymic disorder requires that depressed mood be present for 2 years in adults and 1 year in children or adolescents with only two, versus five, additional symptoms listed in

Exhibit 10.1. A bout of major depression may be superimposed on a chronic dysthymia, resulting in what is called **double depression**. Depression also can co-occur with certain illnesses. There is a 25% prevalence of clinical depression with such chronic illnesses as ischemic heart disease, stroke, Alzheimer's disease, arthritis, cancer, and Parkinson's disease.

- A lack of interest in most life activities that were once enjoyed
- Changes in sleep patterns (increased, decreased, or disrupted)
- Significant changes in appetite and weight (increase or loss)
- Decrease or lack of energy (fatigue)
- Feelings of guilt or worthlessness
- Physical agitation or slowed psychomotor functioning (restlessness/irritability)
- Difficulty thinking or concentrating (inability, or increased challenge, to make a decision related to matters easily addressed when not depressed)
- Thoughts of death or attempted suicide

Exhibit 10.1   Criteria List for Major Depression

SOURCES: National Institute of Mental Health (NIMH), 1999; Sadock & Sadock, 2003

Patterns of Occurrence

MDD, for most people, typically lasts from 4 to 8 months, even if untreated, and affects not only mood but also thinking and behavior. In a 1990 global study, major depression was found to be the second most common cause of disability in major market economies such as the United States (Murray & Lopez, 1996). At the first White House Conference on Mental Health in 1999, the U.S. Surgeon General declared major depression as the predominant cause of disability in all developed nations (Goldman, Rye, & Sirovatka, 1999).

It is not easy to determine the incidence and prevalence of MDD, either in the United States or globally, because different definitions are used across epidemiological studies. In addition, some studies investigate short-term prevalence, others investigate lifetime incidence, and others report both. For example, international data report a 6-month prevalence of 8.0% in Italy (Dubini, Mannheimer, & Pancheri, 2001), a 12-month prevalence of 9.3% in 15- to 75-year-olds in Finland (Lindeman et al., 2000), and a 2-week prevalence of 3%–5% in the Danish general population (Olsen, Mortensen, & Bech, 2004). In the United States, data from two large-scale studies of adults ages 18–54 provide both lifetime incidence and 1-year prevalence data for major depression: the Epidemiologic Catchment Area (ECA) study of mental health in the United States (USDHHS, 1992) and the National Comorbidity Study (NCS; Kessler & Zhao, 1999; see Exhibit 10.2). The incidence and prevalence rates vary widely between these two studies, differences that most likely are due to sampling methods, sample demographics, the year of the study, and the criteria used to define major depression. The NCS is more recent and believed to be the most representative (Kessler & Zhao, 1999; USDHHS, 1992). Indeed, the NCS was replicated between 2001 and 2003, and preliminary data analysis indicates that the past-year prevalence of major depression was 6.7%, a rate closer to the first NCS than to the ECA. In addition, recent European prevalence rates are closer to NCS estimates than to ECA estimates.

There are age, sex, racial and ethnic, and socioeconomic, as well as sexual orientation differences in the rate of MDD, both in the United States and globally.

	ECA Study[a]			NCS[b]	
	Lifetime	*Past Year*		*Lifetime*	*Past Year*
Total	4.9	2.7	Total	14.9	8.6
Male	2.6	1.4	Male	11.0	6.1
Female	7.0	4.0	Female	18.6	11.0

Exhibit 10.2   Prevalence Rates of Major Depression: A Comparison of Two National Studies

[a] *Epidemiologic Catchment Area (ECA) Study, 1980–1985* (USDHHS, 1992)

[b] *National Comorbidity Study (NCS; Kessler & Zhao, 1999)*

Age

MDD occurs at any age across the life course but typically first appears between the ages of 24 and 44, both in the United States and in European countries (see Dubini et al., 2001). Major depression in children, estimated at 2.5%, is often overlooked and may be called "**masked depression**" (Grayson, 2004a; NIMH, 2005; Sadock & Sadock, 2003). This may be a result of mistaking fluctuations in mood and other behaviors, such as clinging behaviors, as normal development, when in fact they could be symptoms of childhood depression. Children and adolescents may also experience poor academic performance as a result of depression. Masked depression for youth may include such antisocial behaviors as truancy, running away, abuse of illegal substances, and sexual promiscuity.

Overall, it is estimated that 3%–6% of teens suffer from major depression (Birmaher, Brent, & Benson, 1998; Grayson, 2004d; NIMH, 2005), although elevated depressive symptoms have been found at higher prevalence levels, 40% of girls and 30% of boys (Kubik, Lytle, Birnbaum, Murray, & Perry, 2003). Recent international prevalence and incidence studies report ranges closer to the 3%–5% estimate, a 12-month prevalence rate of 5.3% among Finnish adolescents (Haarasilta, Marttunen, Kaprio, & Aro, 2001), and a 12.2% cumulative lifetime incidence rate for a sample of German and Dutch adolescents (Oldehinkel, Wittchen, & Schuster, 1999).

Major depression is the number one mental health concern for persons age 65 and over (NIMH, 1999). It is estimated that 6 million (15%–20%) older adults in the United States experience some form of depression, but only 10% of these receive treatment. An estimated 25%–50% of older adults with dementia are reported to suffer from depression (Sadock & Sadock, 2003), and 16% of older adults in primary care settings and an even higher proportion of older adults in hospitals and nursing homes are said to exhibit depression (Reynolds & Kupfer, 1999). Major depression in older adults may be expressed less as disturbed mood and more as physical symptoms, such as lack of energy or pain, making it more complex and harder to diagnose (Small, 1998). Regardless of the high incidence of depression in older adults, it is not a part of the normal aging process and can be treated.

When major or minor depression onset occurs after 60 years of age, it is termed "late-onset depression" (USDHHS, 1999). Because symptoms are qualitatively distinct from those observed in those who are younger, the etiology may be different from major depression with earlier onset. Also, there is a lack of agreement among researchers about the character-istics of late-onset depression. These may include greater apathy, less lifetime personality dysfunction, possible cognitive deficits, structural differences in the brain, shorter periods of remission, and greater risk of recurrence when compared to onset before the age of 60 years of age (Abrams & Alexopoulos, 1994; Greenwald et al., 1997; Holroyd & Duryee, 1997; Krishnan, Hays, Tupler, George, & Blazer, 1995; Reynolds, 1994; Reynolds & Kupfer, 1999).

Gender

There are gender differences in the prevalence and incidence of major depression, but the nature of these differences change with age. For children under age 10, depression is more common in males, but by age 16, more females than males are diagnosed with major depression, a trend that persists across the rest of the life course (Grayson, 2004a; Haarasilta et al., 2001; NIMH, 2005; Oldehinkel et al., 1999; Sadock & Sadock, 2003). A number of studies have found the rate of depression in women to be twice the rate in men (Grayson, 2004c, 2004e; Oldehinkel et al., 1999), but other studies have found the gender differences to be smaller than this (Dubini et al., 2001; Haarasilta et al., 2001), and a recent prevalence study of the Danish general population found a decrease in gender differences in the past 20 years (Olsen et al., 2004). An Italian prevalence study found that major depression was 1.3 times as prevalent in females, but minor depression was 1.6 times as prevalent in males (Dubini et al., 2001).

The reasons for the gender differences in rates of depression are thought to be multi-faceted. Differences in socialization are often considered, whereby men are taught to sup-press grief as a way to appear in control and strong; they mask depression as aggression and anger, traits associated with masculinity; they are disinclined to express emotions, which is seen as a female trait; and they have greater difficulty in withstanding the stigma attached to depression. Women, on the other hand, are more inclined to express depressed mood and seek help, a trait that is considered to reflect the relational approach of females. Other gender differences for females include the following:

- Earlier life course onset and longer course
- Greater association with stressful life events such as divorce
- More sensitivity to seasonal changes
- Greater likelihood of increased sleeping and eating

- Greater association with anxiety disorders such as panic and phobias, as well as eating disorders
- Less association with substance abuse (Grayson, 2004e)

It is thought that hormonal changes may play some role in gender differences in the rate of major depression, but that explanation must be reconciled with the finding of decrease in gender differences over the past 20 years in Denmark (Olsen et al., 2004).

Race and Ethnicity

Racial and ethnic differences in the incidence and prevalence of major depression have been reported. However, these findings are often complicated by the confound of race with socioeconomic class. In a large (N = 2,046) study of adolescents ages 12–15 years, prevalence rates of major depression were as follows: Anglo-Americans (13.9%), African Americans (19.5%), Mexican Americans (25.9%), and Japanese (6.9%). However, these statistically significant differences disappeared when the father's education and family income were examined (Doi, Roberts, Takeuchi, & Suzuki, 2001). A study of 1,000 older adults with depression found that, after controlling for income, social support, and health, African Americans reported fewer symptoms of depression than did whites (Roff et al., 2005). It is also important to note that depressed African Americans and Hispanic Americans are often misdiagnosed with schizophrenia. Misdiagnosis is thought to result from different cultural norms about eye contact, different language for talking about religion, and a realistic, historically based fear of the health care delivery system that gets assessed as "paranoid ideation" (Vedantam, 2005b).

Hinton et al. (1993) examined *Diagnostic and Statistical Manual of Mental Disorders-III-R (DSM-III-R)* disorders in newly arrived Vietnamese and Chinese refugees to the United States and found that 5.5% had major depression, with higher rates occurring in the Vietnamese compared to the Chinese subsamples. This difference was explained by a greater number of traumatic events and separation from family by the Vietnamese. In a later longitudinal study, also led by Hinton (Hinton, Tiet, Tran, & Chesney, 1997), the following were significantly related to higher levels of depression: being a veteran, being older, having less English proficiency, and less attachment. These findings would suggest that the older generation of the Tran family were at particular risk for major depression.

Socioeconomic Status

Some research has indicated that rates of major depression are higher among low-income individuals, and other research has not found rates of depression to vary by socioeconomic class (Kohn, Dohrenwend, & Mirotznik, 1998). One research team conducted a systematic review of all studies published after 1979, in four languages, that examined the relationship between socioeconomic inequality and depression in persons over 16 (Lorant et al., 2003). They found that persons with lower socioeconomic status (SES) had a rate of depression 1.81 times that of persons with higher SES status and a rate of persistent depression 2.06 times as high. They also found that women are more vulnerable to major depression than men under conditions of poverty, inequality, and discrimination.

Sexual Orientation

Adolescents who are gay, lesbian, or bisexual (GLB) have a higher rate of depression than other adolescents. One longitudinal study of 1,265 New Zealand children revealed that GLB youth were 4 times as likely as other youth to experience major depression (Fergusson, Horwood, & Beautrais, 1999).

Theories of Causation

History is said to repeat itself. The history of the study of major depression reveals that in the 1800s, psychiatry focused on human physiology and what little was known about neurology, with primary attention on the brain. In part, this was a legitimate focus because of the several diseases known to affect mood and thought, such as pellagra, syphilis, and certain bacterial infections that were not easily prevented or treated at that time. However, in the 1920s, with the emergence of psychodynamic theory, the focus shifted to psychological explanations of mental illness, major depression included. Another shift occurred in the 1950s when several discoveries challenged a purely psychological explanation of all mental illnesses. These discoveries included psychotropic drugs, neurons and neurochemical transmission, and new genetic markers. Although biological theories of depression are dominant today, other theoretical perspectives are used to understand depression, including psychodynamic theory, interpersonal theory, social stress theory, and cognitive theory (see Exhibit 10.3). Although debate continues about the causative factors of depression, the current discussion is focused less on an either/or understanding and more on attempts to understand the relative importance of biological and psychological factors, both of which are recognized to be influenced by the social environment.

Biological Theories

Recent advances in understanding major depression have led to theorizing about a number of biological mechanisms and processes that are involved, including neurotransmission, genetics, hormones, problems in sleep regulation, and brain structure.

Theory of Neurotransmission

Researchers have only recently discovered the biological or chemical changes that occur in the brains of persons with major depression. This has led to a focus on **neurotransmission**, the process of transporting nerve signals from brain cell to brain cell, with

Theoretical Perspective	Central Ideas
Biological	• Problems in neurotransmission • Genetic vulnerability • Sex hormones and cortisol • Sleep disruption • Brain structure
Psychodynamic	• Problems in attachment • Internalized anger • Goal frustration
Interpersonal	• Dysfunctional relationships
Social stress	• Environmental stressors
Cognitive	• Negative views of self • Negative views of the world • Pessimistic views of the future

Exhibit 10.3   Central Ideas of Major Theoretical Perspectives on Major Depression

the suggestion that major depression is a disruption in the presence, amount, and/or processes of **neurotransmitters**, chemicals that transport signals between nerve cells or between nerve cells and muscles.

The human brain is made up of 13 billion brain cells that communicate by both electrical and chemical processes. Research related to major depression has found that there is neuron dysfunction primarily in the synapses, the spaces between the nerves where neurotransmitters carry the signal from one neuron to another (see Exhibit 10.4).

There are three groups of neurotransmitters: monoamines, neuropeptides, and amino acids. The most important neurotransmitters identified with major depression are three monoamines produced in the brain stem—serotonin, norepinephrine, and dopamine— although dozens of others have been identified. **Serotonin** is associated with arousal and the sleep/wake cycle and also mediates mood and emotion. **Norepinephrine** is typically associated with the fight/flight system of the brain that readies a person for action in the face of stress and trauma. **Dopamine** helps to regulate motor activity and the reward system. Too much dopamine can result in depression, impaired memory, and apathy. In the absence or shortage of serotonin and norepinephrine, the impulses are slowed or blocked and a person experiences the symptoms of major depression. These transmitters either are not present, or not sufficiently present, in the synapses because they are reabsorbed into the ends of the neuron, or they are out of balance with each other so as to preclude optimal transmission. Neurotransmitters also affect the receptor ends of neurons, and this process is impacted by what are called *neuromodulators,* hormones such as estrogen and testosterone, cortisol, and other steroids. These neural processes also explain how specific psychotropic medications work, which we discuss later in the section on interventions for depression (Sadock & Sadock, 2003).

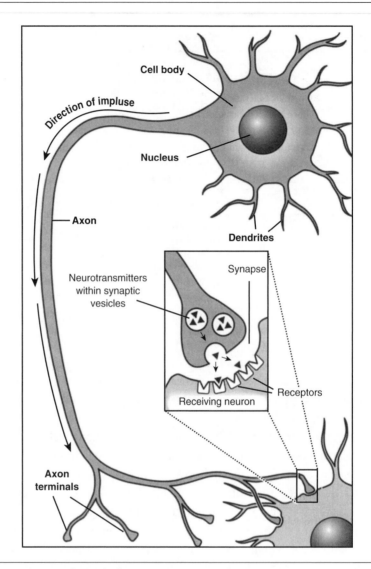

Exhibit 10.4   Features of a Typical Neuron

SOURCE: Gilson, S. (2003). The biological person. In E. Hutchison (Ed.), *Dimensions of human behavior: Person and environment* (2nd ed., pp. 107–147). Thousand Oaks, CA: Sage.

The brain does not develop or function independently of the rest of the human body or of its environment. In fact, it is widely believed that neuron development is heavily influenced by environmental factors such as nutrition and cognitive stimulation. Complex cognitive stimulation, in particular, triggers neurons to develop, function, and increase their interconnections through dentrite development. The ways that neurological brain function can be influenced are important to remember when interventions are presented later in this chapter.

New brain imaging techniques are rapidly advancing with the hope that intervention for major depression, particularly pharmacological intervention, can be specified depending on the part of the brain where dysfunction is located. Positron emission tomography (PET), single-photon emission computed tomography (SPECT), and proton spectroscopy are **neuroimaging tools** that are used to study brain function. Magnetic resonance imaging (MRI), recently paired with functional imagery (fMRI), also uses neuroimaging to show how the brain is structured and functions. Together these neuroimaging techniques provide ways to compare the differences in brain function and structure between those with and without major depression (Callicott & Weinberger, 1999). Several Web sites provide videos, brain scan images, and other neurobiological information. Check out the Laboratory of Neuro Imaging at UCLA (www.loni.ucla.edu), "The Whole Brain Atlas" from Harvard Medical School (www.med.harvard.edu/AANLIB), and the Radiological Society of North America (www.rsna.org).

Genetic Theories

Genetic research for depression initially focused on identifying *a specific* gene that either predicts or predisposes a person to major depression. Currently, the genetic link to depression is believed to be *a cluster* of genes that, together with environmental influences, predisposes a person to major depression. Even when individuals possess the same cluster of genes associated with depression, there is evidence of **variable expressivity**. For example, two persons with the same genetic background, such as found in identical twins, may differ in the presence, amount, or age of onset of depression. Environmental factors, such as precipitating life events and stress related to trauma, are known to influence gene expressivity.

Hormone Theories

Two types of hormones have been proposed as a cause of major depression. First, sex hormones have been suggested to play a role in mood regulation, based largely on the greater prevalence of major depression among women, who are known to experience greater hormonal changes (Grayson, 2004e). The hormone cortisol has also been theorized to play a role in the development of major depression. **Cortisol** is a steroid hormone that is secreted by the adrenal cortex as part of the body's response to stress. It is thought that chronic stress can disturb the daily rhythms of cortisol secretion, and such dysregulation can lead to depression (Tafet & Smolovich, 2004; Van Praag, 2005).

Theory of Sleep

Sleep disruption has been found in persons with major depression, and some researchers theorize that abnormal regulation of circadian rhythms is a causative or contributing factor. The brain patterns during sleep cycles of persons with major depression show delayed sleep onset, a shorter than typical time between falling asleep and rapid eye movement (REM) sleep, as well as abnormal delta sleep when compared to persons who do not report depression (Sadock & Sadock, 2003).

Brain Structure

Some researchers, albeit few, have found structural differences in the brain between persons with and without depression. Specifically, MRI and other imaging techniques have shown enlarged cerebral ventricles, smaller caudate nuclei, smaller frontal lobes, and abnormal hypocampal relaxation times for persons with depression compared to those without depression (Sadock & Sadock, 2003).

Psychodynamic Theories

From the psychodynamic perspective, depression is explained as a result of disruption in the mother-infant (oral stage) relationship, leading to the experience of object loss. In the face of object loss, introjection (or internationalization of authority figures) is employed as a defense mechanism to deal with the distress and conflicting feelings of love, hate, and anger that are simultaneously felt and directed inward. Sigmund Freud and Karl Abraham presented the "classical view of depression" that internalization of conflicting feelings leads to depression.

Within the psychodynamic school of thought, other theorists have proposed slightly different psychological explanations. Melanie Klein focused on internalized anger as the root cause; Edward Bibring focused on inability to meet one's goals or ideals; Heinz Kohut theorized that unmet needs of a child results in threatened self-esteem as an adult. Attachment theory, as proposed by John Bowlby, presented depression as a result of traumatic separations or disruptions in early attachment (Payne, 2005; Sadock & Sadock, 2003; Schwartz & Schwartz, 1993). From this view, when the adult experiences loss, early life trauma is relived, resulting in depression. This later conceptualization is supported by current evidence that disruptions in early attachment affect central nervous system development (Applegate & Shapiro, 2005). From a psychodynamic perspective, we might wonder about the quality of David Loefeler's early attachment relationships, given his description of his father as sometimes violent and his mother as relatively disengaged from family events.

Interpersonal Theories

Interpersonal theories of depression are an extension of psychodynamic theories; they propose that depression occurs in the context of interpersonal relationships. Interpersonal theories draw on the work of Harry Stack Sullivan (1953). The most widely known interpersonal theory is one developed at Yale University in the 1980s by a team of psychiatrists, social workers, psychologists, and nurses (Klerman Weissman, Rounsaville, & Chevron, 1984). Interpersonal theory suggests a reciprocal causal model. Depression arises from dysfunctional relationships; depression leads to relationship problems; and relationship problems lead to further depression. It suggests, in particular, that conflicted relationships, divorce, and bereavement put one at risk for depression (Hinrichsen & Clougherty, 2006). David Loefeler seems to have had a conflicted relationship with his father and more recently with his wife. It is hard to tell how much these relationship problems contributed to the substance abuse and depression and vice versa.

Social Stress Theories

Some theorists pick up where the interpersonal theories leave off, focusing on the role of environmental stressors in depression. They focus on family stress, calling particular attention to the ways that some families are situated in oppressive social structures (Hammack, Robinson, Crawford, & Li, 2004). Poverty, discrimination, and community violence are recognized as sources of chronic stress that tear at the fabric of family stability. Increasingly, social stress theorists are incorporating a biological component to explain the relationship between chronic social stress and major depression (Hammack, 2003). It is quite possible that the economic hardship and loss of the farm encountered by the Loefeler family has contributed to David's depression; certainly they were sources of great stress. And, as you may remember, financial vulnerability was an important issue in the Tran family; both of Kim's parents needed to go to work rather than complete high school when they arrived in the United States, and Kim's father had to work two low-level jobs to help support the family. In addition, the Tran family faced a whole array of stressors common to refugee families, including war, imprisonment, separation and loss, and challenges of adaptation to a new language and culture.

Cognitive Theories

Cognitive theories of depression propose that depression is related to the way people think, more specifically, to pessimistic attitudes. Aaron Beck (1967, 1976) presented the best-known cognitive theory of depression. Beck suggested that some people develop a "negative cognitive triad" that includes negative views of the self, negative views of the world, and pessimistic views of the future that make them vulnerable to depression when faced with adversity. David Loefeler's negative view of himself as a "screw-up" makes him vulnerable to the challenging situations he faces.

_____ Multidimensional Risk and Protection

Biological Risk and Protection

A number of biological risk factors for major depression have been identified, including neuron dysfunction, genetics, sex, history of depression, persistent insomnia, medication side effects, substance abuse, chronic or severe pain, and major illnesses.

Research has indicated that neuron dysfunction, primarily in the synapses in the temporal lobe, frontal lobe, and hypothalamus, contributes to depression (Sadock & Sadock, 2003). The 1999 surgeon general's report on mental health underscores the fact that mind and body are inseparable, based on evidence from new and emerging technologies that clearly show the changes in brain function when depression is present and when it is treated (USDHHS, 1999).

There is also increasing evidence of a genetic role in major depression, although specific genes have not been identified as they have for bipolar I disorder (see Craddock & Forty, 2006; Hariri et al., 2005; Hettema et al., 2006; Pezawas et al., 2005). Levinson's (2005) literature review concluded that major depression is only moderately influenced by heredity. However, evidence supporting a genetic theory of major depression is found in adoption and twin studies (Kendler, Gatz, Gardner, & Pedersen, 2006; Shih, Belmonte, & Zandi, 2004). In a recent large nationally representative twin study, Kendler et al. (2006) found a 37% **heritability** (the contribution that heredity makes to an observed behavior) of major depression, but they found a gender difference, with 42% heritability for women and 29% for men. We might want to explore the possibility that David Loefeler's mother's low profile in the family and his father's explosive outbursts are related to chronic depression, suggesting heritability.

We saw earlier that there are gender differences in the incidence and prevalence of major depression. It is not clear, however, in spite of considerable research, how much of that difference is based in biology and how much can be attributed to the social construction of gender. As noted above, there is evidence that depression is more heritable in females than in males (Kendler et al., 2006). The role of sex hormones in major depression is unclear, but existing patterns of occurrence suggest a possible role. Male mood may be influenced by hormones, but it is quite clear that women experience regular fluctuations in hormones, and frequently these are accompanied by changes in mood. Mood fluctuations occur with premenstrual syndrome (PMS), known to affect up to 75% of women. Less common is a more severe form of PMS called premenstrual dysphoric disorder (PMDD), which is reported to occur in 2%–10% of menstrual-age women. Postpartum depression and mood disturbance associated with perimenopausal and menopausal women are other points of depression associated with hormonal changes (Grayson, 2004e; Sadock & Sadock, 2003).

Unfortunately, a history of depression points to increased probability of reoccurrence, particularly if initial episodes are not treated. The NIMH estimates that up to two thirds of persons suffering with depression do not seek treatment. Childhood depression is a risk factor for major depression in adulthood, particularly if not treated. For many older adults, subclinical depression that is neither major depression nor bipolar depression is a risk factor for major depression if left untreated, as it so often is (NIMH, 1999). In fact, one may view untreated depression that is allowed to run its course as a risk factor for future depression, based on research that shows that early intervention (medication and psychotherapy such as cognitive-behavioral or interpersonal) reduces risk of subsequent depressive episodes.

Several other biological risk factors for major depression have been identified, some of them age-specific. Persistent insomnia (5%–10% occurrence rate) is a risk factor, particularly in middle-aged and older adults (Ford & Kamerow, 1989; Perlis et al., 2006). Depression can also be a result of a side effect of specific medications, such as some that are used to treat heart disease and hypertension (Alexopoulos et al., 1997; Sadock & Sadock, 2003).

Alcohol and other substance abuse, especially in adolescents and young adults, is also a known risk factor (Kubik et al., 2003). For example, weekly use of marijuana in youth doubles the risk of depression in later life (Greenblatt, 1998). Some professionals and researchers believe that substance use is an attempt to cope with depression; others maintain that substance abuse contributes to depression. Perhaps most believe that depression influences substance use and vice versa. Certainly, it would be very difficult to untangle the relationship between substance abuse and depression in David Loefeler's life. We might speculate that the combination of the two played a very large role when he quit attending school during his teen years. Given the loss of her father, and the unavailability of her mother, we might wonder whether depression preceded Estella Jackson's substance abuse problems.

Biological risk factors for older adults include the presence of other illnesses, damage to one's body image such as happens with amputation, chronic or severe pain, and use of medications to treat other illnesses (Grayson, 2004b). Vascular changes such as those caused by stroke, hypertension, coronary artery disease, and diabetes are also suspected to be risk factors for major depression (Alexopoulos et al., 1997; Steffans & Krishnan, 1998).

Biological protective factors have not been identified other than *secondary prevention,* which involves intervening with appropriate treatment at the onset of major depression, especially in children. Treating depression with psychotropic medications when it first occurs does protect from subsequent depressive episodes in terms of frequency, severity, and length (Lewinsohn, Roberts, Seeley, & Rhodes, 1994; Sadock & Sadock, 2003). In this regard, David Loefeler may reap benefit from his current treatment for depression at later stages of his life course.

Psychological Risk and Protection

Although it is not always clear in the literature which comes first, negative cognition or depression, there is some evidence to support the cognitive theory that negative cognitions put one at risk for depression under aversive circumstances and positive cognitions serve as protection. Pessimistic attitudes and low levels of self-efficacy have been found to be risk factors for depressive symptoms (Kaslow et al., 2002; Kwon & Laurenceau, 2002; Smith & Betz, 2002; Steward et al., 2004), but their role in major depression is much less clear. Likewise, self-efficacy has been found to serve as protection against depressive symptoms (Hermann & Betz, 2004). It is important to note, however, that one research team found that self-efficacy did not have the same relationship to depression in Hong Kong as it did in the United States, suggesting that culture plays an important role in the relationship between cognitions and depression (Steward et al., 2004). Psychological protection occurs when cognitive-behavioral therapy (CBT) is employed early in the course of a first depressive episode, which has been shown to have a positive biological impact on brain functioning (Goldapple, Segal, & Garson, 2004). We will want to investigate whether CBT has been a part of David Loefeler's treatment for depression.

Social Risk and Protection

Research on major depression has identified a number of social risk factors and a few social protective factors. Risk factors include traumatic stress, family dynamics, loss, parental depression, low social support, financial impoverishment, and problematic built environments. Social support is the most commonly identified social protective factor.

Many types of trauma have been identified as risk for major depression. Traumatic environmental stressors, such as major disasters like September 11, the tsunami in Southeast Asia, and Hurricane Katrina, put one at risk for depression as well as for post-traumatic stress syndrome (Kohn, Levav, Donaire, Machuca, & Tamashiro, 2005). Child sexual abuse has been found to be a particularly potent risk factor for depression (Fergusson, Horwood, & Lynskey, 1996). For example, using longitudinal data, Egeland (1997) reported that almost two thirds (64%) of children with a history of sexual abuse were diagnosed with some form of depression by the age of 17. Exposure to neighborhood violence is also a risk factor for depression (DuRant, Getts, Cadenhead, Emans, & Woods, 1995; Fitzpatrick, 1993; Latkin, & Curry, 2003; O'Donnell et al., 2002; Schwartz & Proctor, 2000; Shahinfar et al., 2000). For further discussion of community violence as risk for depression, turn to Chapter 4 and the section on consequences. One researcher (Van Praag, 2005) suggests that chronic stress and the resultant stress hormone disturbance is a causative factor in one type of depression, which the researcher labeled anxiety/aggression-driven depression. New brain imaging techniques have provided evidence that psychosocial stressors, such as severe and repeated trauma, actually result in neurobiological and physiological changes in the brain related to depression (Butler, 1996; Friedman, Charney, & Deutch, 1995; Gingsberg, Nackerud, & Larrison, 2004).

Family dynamics during childhood and adolescence can also pose a risk for depression across the life course. Chaotic or conflicted family dynamics are risk factors for major depression during childhood and adolescence. Living in a family with little cohesion or emotional expressiveness also puts children and adolescents at risk (Diamond, Reis, Diamond, Sinqueland, & Isaacs, 2002; Gilbert, 2003; Jewell & Stark, 2003; Sander & McCarty, 2005). Lack of parental support during childhood poses risks for adult depressive symptoms, as well as for other chronic health problems (Shaw, Krause, Chatters, Connell, & Ingersoll-Dayton, 2004).

Relationship loss has also been found to be a risk factor for depression. Parental loss in childhood has been found to be a more potent risk factor for major depression for males than for females (Kendler, Gardner, & Prescott, 2006). Older adults who are widowed or are suffering a recent bereavement are at increased risk for major depression (Adams, Sanders, & Auth, 2004). Widowhood is a risk factor for late onset major depression, with a 10%–20% rate of depression within the first year of bereavement (Adams et al., 2004).

Being raised by a parent with major depression is linked to depression in offspring, particularly if the mother is depressed (Pilowsky, Wickramartne, Nomura, & Weissman, 2006). From a psychodynamic perspective, this has been explained as a result of the parents' inabilities to bond and respond appropriately to children. From a social learning perspective, it is considered to be related to negative role modeling. One recent longitudinal research project found that parental depression is associated with family discord, as well as serving as risk for major depression in offspring, suggesting another possible pathway of risk (Pilowsky et al., 2006). But there may also be a biological mechanism of risk, because chronic stress in the child-rearing environment may have an impact on neurobiology (Burge & Hammen, 1991; Hammen & Rudolph, 2003).

Major depression occurs more often in persons without close interpersonal relationships, and social support is a protective factor for major depression, particularly for adolescents and for women more so than men (Dalgard et al., 2006; Heponiemi et al., 2006; Kendler, Myers, & Prescott, 2005; Leskela et al., 2006; Surkan, Peterson, Hughes, & Gottlieb, 2006). Several recent research endeavors have found that women appear to be more sensitive than men to lower social support in the face of adversity (Dalgard et al., 2006; Kendler et al., 2005), but men may be more vulnerable than women to adverse health effects related to social isolation (Kendler et al., 2005). Levels of support are not believed to explain the greater prevalence of major depression in females, however (Kendler et al., 2005). Marriage provides protection against depression for men, and divorce is a risk factor (Kendler, Gardner, & Prescott, 2006; Rohrer, Rush, & Blackburn, 2005). For children, sufficient family income as well as family support from parents, other siblings, or extended family members provide protection (DuRant et al., 1995; Thompson & Peebles-Wilkins, 1992). Peer support and acceptance by others have been identified as possible protective factors in a sample of adult Hungarians (Margitics, 2005). Finally, owning a pet may also serve as a protective factor, especially if depression is secondary to other illnesses such as HIV/AIDS (Davis, 2004).

Some researchers have found that poverty, or insufficient income, poses risk for depression (Wadsworth & Achenbach, 2005). Others note that it is the pairing of low family income with other factors, such as single parenthood, that serves as risk for childhood depression (Gilbert, 2003). Samaan's (2000) review of the literature on the influences of race, ethnicity, and poverty on the mental health of children found that children who live in impoverished families or families that have suffered economic loss report higher rates of depression, anxiety, and antisocial behavior than children without economic hardship. However, when SES is controlled for, African American, Native American, and Hispanic children have lower rates of these reported mental health problems than white children. Poverty and its associated stressors appear to be a risk factor for depression, and we might suspect that such was the case for David Loefeler. Some researchers have posited that the stress involved with financial impoverishment, both at the individual and community levels, increases the risk for major depression because of the effect of stress on neurological functioning (Manuck et al., 2005; Roy, 2004).

In recent years, more attention is being paid to the built environment and its impact on human behavior in general. With an increasing focus on cross-disciplinary research, this is an emerging academic field for a number of disciplines for which major depression is a concern. Broadly defined, the built environment is everything that is designed and constructed by humans. As such, the built environment includes residential and institutional housing, roads, parks, and even the structure of energy use. The built environment does not fit neatly into any of the four dimensions of human behavior that we have examined in this book (bio-psycho-social-spiritual), but it makes sense to place it with a discussion of social risk and protection, because both the process and products of the built environment have a social aspect (built by people who must work together to design environments that impact social interaction). Research that examines the relationship between the built environment and depression is scant, but two recent studies provide a window into an emerging line of research.

An urban study, conducted in London, used a cross-sectional survey of two electoral wards to examine the relationship between the neighborhood built environment and scores on the Center for Epidemiologic Studies Depression Scale (CES-D). Controlling for individual SES and floor of residence, they found greater odds of depression for residents living in neighborhoods with poor housing features (Weich et al., 2002). Another research team conducted a cross-sectional survey of residents living in 59 neighborhoods of New York City, examining the relationship between the urban built environment and depression. Controlling for age, race/ethnicity, sex, and individual income, the findings indicated that respondents were more likely to report both recent (last 6 months) and lifetime depression if they lived in neighborhoods identified as having poorer features of the built environment, such as dirty streets and sidewalks and buildings in dilapidated internal and external condition (Galea, Ahern, Rudenstine, Wallace, & Vlahov, 2005). This research is preliminary, and further prospective research is needed to clarify the mechanisms by which depression is related to characteristics of the physical environment.

Spiritual Risk and Protection

Religion, religiosity, and spirituality are related and complex concepts with important differences that must be considered when deciding if they provide risk or protection for MDD. In Chapter 1, we defined spirituality as a personal search for meaning, purpose, connection, and morality, and religion as a systematic set of beliefs, practices, and traditions observed within a particular social institution over time. Although research on the role of spirituality and religion in human behavior is expanding rapidly, literature to date uses different definitions or lacks definitions, making it difficult to compare findings across studies (Hackney & Sanders, 2003). Some researchers have attempted to bring greater clarity to the literature by sharpening the definitions. Kendler and colleagues (2003) studied the relationship between *religiosity* and psychiatric and substance use disorders, including MDD. They examined responses to 78 items in a sample of 2,616 male and female twins. The responses identified seven religiosity factors: general religiosity, social religiosity, involved God, forgiveness, God as judge, unvengefulness, and thankfulness. Only social religiosity and thankfulness were associated with reduced risk for major depression.

Researchers have found that spirituality, which may or may not include religious beliefs and practices, serves as both protection and risk (Koenig, 1998; Koenig, Larson, & Larson, 2001; Larson & Larson, 2003; Larson, Larson, & Koenig, 2001; Pargament, 1997; Perry, 1998). As a protective factor, both spirituality and religion can provide hope, life meaning, a source of stress relief, and a sense of control over one's circumstances (Braam, Beekman, Deeg, Smit, & Van Tilburg, 1998; Gatz, 2003; Koenig, George, & Peterson, 1998; Miller,

Warner, Wickramaratne, & Weissman, 1997). Religious beliefs also may serve as protection by limiting negative health practices such as substance abuse (Fitchett, Rybarczyk, DeMarco, & Nicholas, 1999). Perhaps the most widely accepted use of spirituality and/or religion is when a person experiences the death of a loved one (Blazer, 2001; Parappully, Rosenbaum, van den Daele, & Nzewi, 2002), a factor that has been found to be a risk for depression. However, one study that examined changes in the religious/spiritual beliefs of 103 women after widowhood indicated that an increase in religious/spiritual beliefs was associated with decreased grief but not with decreased depression (Brown, Nesse, House, & Utz, 2004).

Social support is also a benefit if religious involvement connects one to other people (Perry, 1998). In many of the studies of religion and depression, the social support that comes from religious involvement is acknowledged as an important resource to help protect against depression, its severity, or its length of occurrence (Parappully et al., 2002). Indeed, this social support function is what Kendler et al. (2003) were measuring in their variable labeled social religiosity, which they found to be one of the two aspects of religiosity associated with reduced risk for major depression. A measure of social support is frequently used in research on spirituality and religion as a protective factor, and outcome data are usually analyzed to control for its contribution to protection or risk for major depression. For example, Wink, Dillon, and Larsen (2005) examined religion as a moderator of depression for elderly persons with physical illness. Their data showed that, after controlling for social support, religiousness played a greater role than spirituality in protecting against depression. Another research team (Bosworth, Park, McQuoid, Hays, & Steffens, 2003) found that public, but not private, religious practice was associated with less depression in older adults, suggesting that the social support aspect of religious experience may play a major protective role.

Spirituality and religion may help to mediate any possible effect of racism on the development of depression (Hunter & Lewis-Coles, 2005). Although not focused on racism, a large study of 1,000 older adults stratified by rural and urban counties in Alabama, as well as by race and gender, examined depression and religiosity. After controlling for income, social support, and health, the data showed that the African Americans reported fewer symptoms of depression than did whites. Also, highly religious respondents reported fewer symptoms of depression independent of race (Roff et al., 2005).

Religion and spirituality may also serve as risk factors (Whitcomb, 2003). For example, Pearce, Little, and Perez (2003) used three standard measures of religion and spirituality with 744 adolescents. They found that religion can be protective, but when it involves a negative interpersonal religious experience, more depressive symptoms are reported. Another study of older adults differentiated between what they termed positive and negative religious beliefs (Bosworth et al., 2003). The results of this study were similar to others that examined religion/spirituality, depression, and recovery from physical disability (Fitchett et al., 1999; Koenig, Pargament, & Nielsen, 1998). For both younger adults and older adults, negative religious beliefs such as believing that one's depression is punishment by God or a form of abandonment are related to higher levels of depression and poorer recovery outcomes (Pargament, 1997).

Biopsychosocial-Spiritual Integration

As reported earlier, our understanding of the causes of major depression have varied over time, ranging from a purely biological theory to a total psychodynamic hypothesis, and now back to a primarily biological view that recognizes the influence of psychological and spiritual factors within the context of the larger social environment (Rutter, 2002). This approach was supported by a large study of 1,942 adult female twins that provided insight into the interrelatedness of risk factors. Based on interview data collected four times over a 9-year period, 18 risk factors were explored. These factors were categorized into five groups: (1) childhood (e.g., trauma, loss, genetics), (2) early adolescence (e.g., anxiety, self-esteem, conduct disorder), (3) late adolescence (e.g., substance misuse, social support), (4) adulthood (e.g., history of depression), and (5) stressful life events in the prior year. Based on structural equation modeling from these data, 52% of the variance in the likelihood of major depression episodes was explained by three broadly defined categories: internalizing symptoms, externalizing symptoms, and psychosocial adversity (Kendler, Gardner, & Prescott, 2002). As noted earlier, psychosocial adversity is now known to have an impact on several biological processes. Increasingly, the public in general is engaging in practices that represent an integrated approach to responding to depression. For example, Wright and Basco (2001) provide guidance for combining the typical CBT and drug treatment with complementary approaches, including exercise and spiritual practices for preventing and recovering from depression.

Think about the case of David Loefeler, who perceives depression as the cause of his low economic status and inability to hold a job. What are the circumstances in his life course that have presented risk of depression? Is it possible that he inherited some vulnerability to depression? What about the family conflict he experienced as a child? The harsh physical and emotional treatment he received from his father? The financial vulnerability of his family? Is it possible that his mother's low profile in the family was related to her own depression? Could his early use and misuse of alcohol and other substances have played a role? What role does his cognitive attribution of himself as a screw-up play?

Think also of Sondra and Estella Jackson. Given the many adversities in Sondra's life in recent years, what do you think has protected her from major depression? Was she lucky in her genetic inheritance? Is it a strong sense of self-efficacy? Being raised in a loving family during her early childhood? A strong social support system? A strong spiritual and religious life? How do you understand the greater vulnerability of her sister, Estella?

Speculate some about the case of Elias and Claudia, who struggled to meet their basic needs. Could Elias's abuse of alcohol have been his attempt to cope with undiagnosed depression? How might you explain the fact that Claudia did not report depression in spite of her long work hours at minimum wage coupled with social isolation and separation for many years from her son who remained in the Dominican Republic? Is it possible that Junito's current acting-out behavior is masking depression?

You may have wondered about members of Kim Tran's family as you read about the symptoms, theories of causation, and risk factors for depression. Was Kim's paternal grandmother's growing social isolation a symptom of depression? Is her father's current withdrawal from the family a marker of depression? Certainly, Kim's parents and grandparents faced many traumas, war, imprisonment, separation and loss, and traumatic resettlement. They came from a culture where group efficacy was valued and moved to the United States where individual efficacy is valued. Their Buddhist faith and traditions most likely served as a protective factor during the worst of times, but religion and spirituality are not an important part of their lives at the current time.

	Risk Factors	*Protective Factors*
Biological	• Neuron dysfunction • Genetics • Sex (female) • History of depression • Insomnia • Medication side effects • Substance abuse • Major illnesses • Chronic or severe pain • Vascular changes	• Treatment at initial depression onset, especially if occurring in childhood
Psychological	• Pessimistic attitude • Low self-efficacy	• High self-efficacy
Social	• Traumatic stress • Negative family dynamics • Loss • Parental depression • Low social support • Financial impoverishment • Problematic built environments	• Social support, especially for adolescents and women • Marriage for men
Spiritual	• Negative interpersonal religious experiences • Punitive religious beliefs	• Spirituality • Social religiosity • Thankfulness

Exhibit 10.5   Summary of Risk and Protective Factors for Major Depression

Consequences of Major Depression

The consequences of major depression include greater risk of suicide, relationship problems, school and work problems, health problems, medication side effects, as well as costs to various social institutions.

Suicide rates for persons with major depression, especially for children and adolescents, are rising. It is estimated that in the United States, annually about 500,000 teens attempt suicide and 5,000 are successful, a statistic that is considered to be an epidemic proportion, resulting in suicide being the third leading cause of death in 10- to 24-year-olds (Grayson, 2004d). The increase in suicide rates is thought to be related to increased use of alcohol and other illegal substances and to other life challenges such as community violence and early life trauma. Risk of suicide increases when a teen is withdrawing from a substance or due to the other consequences of illegal drug use (Grayson, 2004d; NIMH, 2005). An equally pressing issue is the recent concern of the FDA that the suicide and self-harm rates among adolescents may be related to the medications used to treat major depression (Elias, 2004; "FDA Seeks Warning," 2004). Gay, lesbian, bisexual, and transsexual youth are particularly at risk of suicide related to depression. A literature review by Perrin & Sack (1998) reported that up to 50% of gay youth have contemplated suicide and 25% of all gay youth are estimated to have attempted suicide. One recent study (D'Augelli et al., 2005) revealed that almost one third of the GLB respondents reported at least one suicide attempt.

A recent Finnish study (Sokero et al., 2005) of 269 adults with *DSM-IV* MDD found that 8% had attempted suicide at 18-month follow-up. The associated risk factors for suicide in this sample were a previous suicide attempt, lack of a significant other, and the length of time that the person was depressed. Men are 4 times more likely than women to commit suicide (80% of adults who commit suicide are men); women are more likely to attempt suicide but to use less lethal means (pills versus guns, for example) that do not end in death (Minino, Arias, Kochanek, Murphy, & Smith, 2002; Moscicki, 1999, 2001). Older adults have the highest suicide rate of any age group. In fact, for those ages 80–84, the suicide rate is twice that of the general population, but there are gender and racial differences in the suicide rate in old age. Older white males have the highest suicide rates of any age or racial group, with a rate 5 times the general population. For elderly women, the suicide risk is still high but lower than that for men. As with other age groups, older women *attempt* suicide more often than older men, but the rate of suicide is higher among older men. Older adults often do not actively seek treatment, and professionals do not readily diagnose major depression in older adults, especially if the depression is masked with physical complaints that do receive attention (Lebowitz et al., 1997).

As hypothesized by interpersonal theory, problems in relationships can be a risk for major depression, but problematic relationships are also often a consequence of depression. Disrupted family relationships and marital discord can result from depression, especially when depression symptoms are not well understood (Burke, 2003). Paradoxically, the social support of family serves as a protective or moderating factor for major depression but becomes threatened by major depression, compounding the likelihood of recurrent depression. One potentially serious consequence of major depression in parents is the increased likelihood of child abuse (Windham et al., 2005).

Untreated major depression affects school and work performance. The risk of school failure is high in children and adolescents with depressive disorders, particularly when these children and youth suffer relapses (Simeon, 1989; Son & Kirchner, 2000). Major depression has been found to increase the risk of unemployment and job retention problems caused by absenteeism and diminished productivity (Lerner et al., 2004; Wang et al., 2004). We might wonder if depression, as well as learning disabilities, contributed to David Loefeler's school problems in his adolescence. It seems clear that he considers his depression to interfere with his current ability to get and keep work.

Major depression may also lead to physical health problems. In older adults with major depression, there is a twofold risk of cardiac diseases, an overall increased risk of death from other illnesses, and a decreased ability to rehabilitate from a physical illness. The risk of death due to heart attack is also greater when an elderly person has major depression, as is the risk of cancer and any immune system illness such as infection (Bremmer et al., 2006; Frasure-Smith, Lesperance, & Talajic, 1995; Penninx et al., 1998). Other consequences include increased health care costs, physical disability, increased dependence on others, and poor cognitive function and decline, particularly for older adults (Oslin, Strein, Katz, Edell, & TenHave, 2000; Penninx, Leveille, Ferrucci, van Eijk, & Guralnik, 1999; Reynolds & Kupfer, 1999; Yaffe et al., 1999).

Another consequence of major depression is that psychotropic medications, like most drugs, have negative side effects. Sexual dysfunction, weight gain or loss, restlessness, sleep disturbance, and dry mouth are the most common side effects. The side effects have a differential impact on other dimensions of functioning depending on gender, age, marital status, and other characteristics. For example, a young adult male may find the inability to perform sexually more unacceptable than the actual depression. In such a situation, the drug bupropion (Wellbutrin or Zyban) may be considered because it rarely impacts sexual functioning, unlike the selective serotonin reuptake inhibitors (SSRIs) that may affect sexual function in up to 80% of cases. In another example, a young woman already concerned about her weight may be concerned about medication that further contributes to weight gain. Again, bupropion may be the drug of choice, although it is contraindicated for use with persons known to be bulimic (Sadock & Sadock, 2001, 2003).

Besides the consequences for individuals and families, major depression also has consequences for societal institutions. Between 1990 and 2000, the treatment rate for depression increased by over 50%, leading to concerns about the cost to society. Surprisingly, a study based on current epidemiologic data and population, wage, and cost information led to the conclusion that the economic burden remained relatively stable during this period (Greenberg et al., 2003). However, there are gender disparities in the economic burden of depression. Researchers examined direct costs for medical treatment, prescription drugs, and indirect costs of disability and illness-related work absence in one Fortune 100 company. They found that the company experienced $9,265 in costs for female employees compared to $8,502 for men. Women in this study had more work absentee costs but lower medical costs compared to men (Birnbaum, Leong, & Greenberg, 2003). This later finding seems to contradict the repeated finding that women are more likely than men to seek treatment. Further research is needed to clarify this situation.

Ways of Coping

People with major depression use a variety of coping strategies to manage their depression. Some of those strategies are more effective than others; some of them may even exacerbate the depression. While some persons are able to employ denial to cope with milder forms of depression, this is harder to do with major depression because of the degree of impact on functioning in all spheres. And yet, research does show that denial can lead to nonadherence to medication, which is quite common in mood disorders (Bryne, Regan, & Livingston, 2006). Men are more likely than women to use or abuse alcohol in an attempt to manage depression. Paradoxically, alcohol may be used to retreat from the psychological pain of depression when in fact it is a depressant agent (Holahan, Moos, Holahan, Cronkite, & Randall, 2003). Some persons living with major depression use religious coping.

Social stigma in regard to depression seriously and negatively impacts the ways that people cope with major depression, often making them reluctant to seek treatment (Barney, Griffiths, Jorm, & Christensen, 2006). Fortunately, with increased knowledge of the neurobiology underlying depression and recognition of depression symptoms other than depressed mood, the social stigma of depression has decreased somewhat, making it easier for persons with major depression to seek professional help. People who are depressed may encounter many barriers that limit accessibility to services or make services unavailable. These are summarized in Exhibit 10.6.

Many people with major depression, yet far too few, turn to help from professional health care providers as a coping strategy. There are a number of treatment options available to them when they do.

Medication

Let us return to the earlier discussion related to the biological causes of depression. Specifically, recall that researchers have shown that there is a difference in the presence of some neurotransmitters between those with depression and those without. This finding supports the use of a class of medications used to treat major depression, the SSRIs, sometimes referred to as the second-generation antidepressants. Examples include paroxetine HCI (Paxil), fluoxetine HCI (Prozac), and sertraline HCI (Zoloft; Sadock & Sadock, 2001).

Very simply stated, over time these medications sensitize the neuron to receiving a signal, prevent neurotransmitter absorption, or create a more effective balance of neurotransmitters. While these medications do begin to work from the start of ingestion, they require 2 to 4 or more weeks before full effectiveness is obtained and a person begins to feel relief from the depression. The time lag between starting medication and feeling relief can be discouraging to the depressed person, and many discontinue use before depression abates (Bentley & Walsh, 2006; Sadock & Sadock, 2001, 2003).

Another category of antidepressant medications is the tricyclics, which were part of the first generation of antidepressants. Examples include inipramine (Tofranil), desipramine

Client Barriers	Care Provider Barriers	Institutional/Societal Barriers
Lack of knowledge of MDD	Lack of knowledge or uncertainty of MDD and its treatment	Stigma of major depression
Belief that symptoms are normal, esp. by older adults	Lack of knowledge of community resources	Stereotyping of elderly and men
Symptoms of worthlessness and apathy	Lack of time to diagnose and/or intervene	Lack of parity with physical illness
Denial of psychological symptoms, esp. by men	Distracted by physical complaints	Housing shortages
Fear of stigma	Blinded by societal stereotypes	Managed care
Fear of cost of treatment	Reluctance to stigmatize with diagnosis	Medicare and other insurance limitations
Limited access to services	Concerns re: cost of treatment	Insufficient income supports such as Medicaid limitations
Fear of medication side effects		Complex service delivery system
Reports related physical symptoms versus mood		

Exhibit 10.6   Barriers to Diagnosis and Treatment of Major Depression

SOURCE: Expanded from information found at USDHHS, 1999.

(Norpramin), and clomipramine (Anafranil). While these drugs continue to be pre-scribed, their increased side effects in comparison to the SSRIs and SNRIs, which will be discussed below, yield them a second choice treatment option (Bentley & Walsh, 2006; Sadock & Sadock, 2001, 2003).

A third category of medications, called serotonin and norepinephrine reuptake inhibitors or SNRIs, is the most recent, or third-generation antidepressants. These drugs have multiple actions and impact more than one neurotransmitter. Examples include ven-lafaxine HCI (Effexor), mirtazapine (Remeron), and duloxetine (Cymbalta; Bentley & Walsh, 2006; Rosack, 2006a; Sadock & Sadock, 2001, 2003).

In 2004 an estimated 21 million people in the United States, Western Europe, and Japan were diagnosed with MDD but only half of these received treatment (Rosack, 2006a). For those who receive medication treatment, only an estimated one third achieve remission with the first drug that is used. Even after trying two drugs, only 50% find success. These statistics have fostered the search for new drugs called **triple reuptake inhibitors**

(TRIs), which can target serotonin, norepinephrine, and dopamine for the treatment of major depression and anxiety. Two drugs that hold promise as TRIs, DOV 216303 and NS 2359, were in the final stage of study when this chapter was written (Rosack, 2006a).

Finally, the FDA has recently approved a skin patch that delivers a monoamine oxidase inhibitor (MAOI) called selegiline to treat major depression, with the hope that this will bring depression remission to more people (Rosack, 2006a, 2006b). The breakthrough with selegiline is in the manner of administration. The MAOIs, when taken orally, require careful diet monitoring and restrictions because of negative health threats such as high blood pressure. Administration using a skin patch bypasses the digestive system, thereby reducing negative side effects and patient resistance to using a drug that impinges on other aspects of life.

While psychotropic medication is the primary intervention used to treat major depression, the selection of the best agent is sometimes thought to be more of an art than a science. Because of the side effects and social stigma attached to depression and medication use, persons with major depression may resist the use of drugs or fail to understand the need for long-term use as a preventive measure. This is important information for the social worker to convey to the person who is making a decision whether or not to take medication and then selecting the best option for medication.

We still do not understand why some individuals respond well and others seemingly not at all to the same drug(s). There is emerging evidence that may explain these drug response differences based on gender, age, and race, in addition to the class and specific drug selected. Because women have a slower gastrointestinal absorption than men, they may respond more slowly to medications. On the other hand, women may require less medication than men after adjusting for weight differences; this may be influenced by estrogen levels (Yonkers, Kando, Cole, & Blumenthal, 1992). Age also should be considered in the selection of medications. For example, not all medications have been tested with all age groups, and different age groups are known to have different responses to many medications. We know that Prozac has been approved by the FDA for use with children and teens ages 8–18, but other drugs in the SSRI class have not been tested with this age group (Bentley & Walsh, 2006; Sadock & Sadock, 2001). Older adults also may respond differently than younger adults to various medications, typically showing greater sensitivity and requiring a reduced dosage (Bentley & Walsh, 2006; Sadock & Sadock, 2001). Older adults are also more likely to be prescribed medications to treat other illnesses, and some of these may interact with antidepressants.

There is beginning to be evidence to explain other differences in medication response, depending on a person's race or ethnicity. It appears that African Americans require lower doses with smaller increases and ultimately longer start-up time to reach drug effectiveness. Asians may require a lower dose and be more prone to drug toxicity. Hispanics may have greater sensitivity to antidepressants than Caucasians (Bentley & Walsh, 2006). Unfortunately, at the moment, there are serious gaps in the scientific literature related to diversity. For example, UCLA researchers recently reviewed the best available studies of medications used to treat depression and other disorders and found little attention to ethnic and racial diversity. No American Indians were included in the 9,327 patients who participated in clinical trials. Only two Hispanic Americans were included among the 3,980 patients involved in a drug trial of antidepressant medications (Vedantam, 2005a).

Research is under way to understand the many factors that contribute to medication response. Attempts are being made to improve the classification system and diagnostic tools to more clearly discriminate between different types of depression, in the hope that this will help to clarify different medication responses. Recently a gene was discovered to play an important role in sensitivity differences to medication. Brain imaging techniques are now identifying the part of the brain that responds not only to medication but also to CBT. Isolating differences in brain processes between those with and without depression as well as those with specific types of depression may improve drug selection and reduce the time required to find the most viable intervention. These advances create hope that in the near future, persons with major depression can be tested for the presence of a gene and that medications can then be differentially prescribed to ensure a greater likelihood of a more timely alleviation of the symptoms of depression (Rosack, 2006a).

Herbal and Other Nontraditional Supplements

St. John's wort, a landscaping plant with yellow flowers, has been used extensively for many years in Europe for mild to moderate depression but with limited evidence as to its efficacy. Wong, Smith, and Boon (1998) report their analysis of the safety, side effects, drug interaction, and efficacy of a number of herbal remedies for treating a range of psychiatric problems. They reported that the published data were insufficient to make a definitive conclusion for any herbal remedies, with the exclusion of St. John's wort for mild depression and gingko for memory or dementia. In response to the increased use of herbal remedies in the United States, the National Institutes of Health (NIH) conducted a 4-year clinical trial that administered a standardized amount of St. John's wort to adults with major depression, moderate severity. The results did not find St. John's wort to be significantly more effective than a placebo (Hypericum Depression Trial Study Group, 2002). However, another study revealed a significantly greater reduction in depression ratings with St. John's wort than with placebo, especially for those with higher depression scores initially. These later researchers concluded that St. John's wort was safe and more effective than a placebo (Leerubier, Clerc, Didi, & Kieser, 2002). What is noteworthy in comparing these two studies is that the first was a U.S. sample and the second was a French sample. Neither study addressed cultural factors, but it is interesting to note that Europeans have used this herb extensively for centuries, but it is more recently used in the United States, where its efficacy is doubted.

Finally, use of herbal substances should be carefully considered in relation to other medications, particularly when there is a major health condition in addition to major depression. The best example is with persons with HIV/AIDS, a population where as many as one in three may experience major depression. St. John's wort has been shown to reduce the effects of the protease inhibitors used to control the virus, so its use is contraindicated with these life-saving medications (NIH, 2002).

Electroconvulsive Therapy

Electroconvulsive therapy (ECT) has been used since the 1930s to treat depression. However, the methods used to induce convulsions have radically changed over time, making this intervention more effective today with very few side effects, most of which are of short duration. Approximately 100,000 persons in the United States have ECT each year (Mayo Clinic Staff, 2005).

Today ECT is used to treat what is called treatment-resistant depression, typically major depression for people of all ages who cannot take medications, who do not respond to medication, or who are most at risk of suicide (Abrams, 1994; Depression Guideline Panel, 1993; Mayo Clinic Staff, 2005). An estimated 8% of psychiatrists use ECT, but use varies by when and where the physician was trained, the physician's gender, and client proximity to a mental health center. The U.S. Agency for Health Care Policy and Research (AHCPR) endorses the use of ECT and publishes guidelines that reflect evidence-based research supporting its use with persons with major depression (Hermann, Ettner, Dorwart, Langman-Dorwart, & Kleinman, 1999; Rudorfer & Lebowitz, 1999).

Psychotherapy

Recent studies have shown that certain psychotherapeutic interventions can impact brain functioning related to major depression. Specifically, two therapies have proven effective, and even more effective when used in combination with psychotropic medication: CBT and interpersonal therapy (IPT; Hinrichsen & Clougherty, 2006). These therapeutic methods are described in the later discussion of implications for practice.

Nontraditional, Complementary, and Alternative Interventions

In a nationally representative sample of 2,055 respondents in 1977/1978, 53.6% of those with severe depression reported using complementary and alternative therapies during the 12 months prior to the study (Kessler et al., 2001). These results point to the need for social workers to explore all the ways that clients have attempted to cope with major depression because of possible negative interactions with traditional interventions or potential evidence of effectiveness to support continued use.

Acupuncture is seen to have promise for relieving the symptoms of depression (Han, Li, Luo, Zhao, & Li, 2004; Manber, Allen, & Morris, 2002; Manber, Schnyer, Allen, Rush, & Blasey, 2004), but one recent meta-analysis found the evidence to be insufficient to make that claim (Smith & Hay, 2005). Phototherapy, or light therapy, may be useful as an adjunctive intervention with major depression. Although phototherapy is typically associated with treating a less severe type of depression called seasonal affective disorder that occurs when daylight is short (northern hemisphere regions or during the winter months), some people with major depression have found high-intensity light exposure to be helpful (Kripke, Tuunainen, & Endo, 2006; Lam et al., 2006; McEnany & Lee, 2005). For seasonal affective disorder, light therapy has been found to be as effective as drug therapy and to have the benefit of producing a more rapid response than medications (Lam et al., 2006). Exercise (Ernst, Olson, Pinel, Lam, & Christie, 2006; Harris, Cronkite, & Moos, 2006; Sjosten & Kivela, 2006), meditation and yoga (Pilkington, Kirkwood, Rampes, & Richardson, 2005; Sharma, Das, Mondal, Goswampi, & Gandhi, 2005; Williams, Duggan, Crane, & Fennell, 2006), massage (Field, Hernandez-Reif, Diego, Schanberg, & Kuhn, 2005), and relaxation all have been found to be helpful adjunctive interventions to medication and psychological therapeutic approaches.

Social Justice Issues

The 1999 surgeon general's report on mental health lists eight actions to meet the vision for U.S. mental health in the new millennium. One action is particularly noteworthy. It is to tailor treatment to age, gender, race, and culture. Also included in the list of populations for this action are persons with disabilities and those with varying sexual orientations. From a social justice perspective, consideration of all such characteristics or factors that shape a person's identity and image should be a screen by which to consider the remaining seven recommended actions:

- Continue to build the science base (which represents diversity by age, gender, race, culture, ability, sexual orientation, etc.)
- Overcome stigma (and how that may vary by age, gender, race, culture, ability, sexual orientation, etc.)
- Improve public awareness of effective treatment (which should vary to appeal to all persons regardless of age, gender, race, culture, ability, sexual orientation, etc.)
- Ensure the supply of mental health services and providers (to represent gender, race, ethnic, ability, and sexual orientation variations in the client population)
- Ensure delivery of state-of-the-art treatments (with treatment outcome evidence that reflects diversity)
- Facilitate entry into treatment (by actions that reflect approaches amenable to diverse populations)
- Reduce financial barriers to treatment (particularly where there are disparities that are population specific; USDHHS, 1999; comments in parenthesis are those of this author, not of USDHHS)

Children and older adults are at risk of invisibility in the mental health system. Children with major depression may not be diagnosed or referred for treatment. In fact, with the rising national debate related to overdiagnosis and inappropriate drug treatment of attention-deficit disorder and attention-deficit/hyperactivity disorder (ADD/ADHD) for children, social workers should use caution not to generalize these concerns of misdiagnosis and drug overuse in such a way that they overlook or downplay assessment and treatment of major depression in children (Bentley & Collins, 2006). Depression is also underreported in older adults, leading to a lowered quality of life that could easily be changed through earlier and better assessment and treatment. Social workers working with older adults need knowledge of the risk factors for depression in this population as well as knowledge about how depression is expressed in older adults compared to younger adult populations.

Another social justice issue related to major depression is the use of inappropriate diagnostic methods with persons from less-developed countries. This becomes particularly important with the increase in cultural and ethnic groups in the United States (Kessler, 2000). Overall, underdiagnosis of major depression in these groups is partially attributed to differences in racial or cultural background between the professional and the person with depression (Sadock & Sadock, 2003). As noted earlier, this seems to lead to overdiagnosis of psychosis and underdiagnosis of depression in African Americans and Hispanic Americans (Vedantum, 2005b) compared to Caucasians. Social workers are in key positions to provide linkage to appropriate resources and can be advocates for change in policy and programs at all levels, ranging from agency-based to national policies, to help ensure more appropriate response to the unique needs of these populations.

Gender differences in the prevalence of major depression have been explored in relation to the varying roles and statuses of males and females (Birnbaum et al., 2003). There are various explanations of why women are more likely to experience major depression than men. As indicated earlier, there is some evidence that biology may play a role. But some believe that women are socialized to be more expressive of inner feelings and willing to accept help, that is, less prone to avoid treatment because of social expectations and stigma. Women also may carry more of the emotional work of a family or household, making them more prone to ongoing stress that may impact neurotransmission over time. On the other hand, men express depression more outwardly, oftentimes involving aggression or violence. With twice as many women as men diagnosed with major depression, perhaps men are underdiagnosed and not provided with appropriate intervention. This is the major rationale behind the NIMH campaign called Real Men, Real Depression (http://menanddepression.nimh.nih.gov/infopage.asp?ID=5), which has the goal of providing more public education about men's depression and treatment.

The use or availability of some interventions also may vary by geographical area or the setting where services are delivered. For example, Hermann et al. (1999) reported that ECT is currently underutilized outside of major metropolitan areas and within public versus private hospitals. Perhaps two of the most pressing and emerging injustices is the rising cost of medications used to treat major depression and the continued tendency for insurance or governmental medical assistance programs to fail to cover the cost of care or to severely restrict the amount of care for mental illness, which results in lack of parity with physical illness. Unlike other biologically based but socially influenced illnesses, such as diabetes, where medical insurance and governmental assistance programs continue coverage indefinitely, coverage for intervention for depression may be more difficult to obtain and, when obtained, may impose time limitations that are not consistent with the course of this challenge of living. Obviously, with medical care costs rising, it is those persons with marginal incomes who are the most likely to be without any ability to access care for major depression.

Recently, many drug companies have developed indigent programs to assist those unable to afford medication. In addition, other services have developed to screen people by income level, geographical residence, and medication(s) prescribed and to link them with drug assistance programs through drug manufacturers but also through state assistance and other programs. Most of the drug manufacturers of medications used to treat major depression operate Web sites that provide assistance program information. Current research findings of drug efficacy as well as information about major depression, resources, and links to other sites are available. However, consumers must use caution and critical thinking to decide if the claims that are made, such as the effectiveness of the medications, are influenced by the manufacturer. Unfortunately, there are significant barriers to these online resources for persons unable to access a computer or with limited English language skills, although some online sites provide information in both English and Spanish.

Practice Implications

For the challenge of living, major depression, as with other challenges of living, social workers may work at the micro level of individual and family or engage in policy practice at the mezzo and macro levels. Obviously the social work role is defined not only by the challenges that a client faces but also by the agency context of services that are delivered. We discuss micro practice assessment and intervention and then turn to discussion of implications for policy practice.

Micro Practice Assessment

Armed with the knowledge that many persons with major depression may not be diagnosed and that underdiagnosis or misdiagnosis may be even greater if there is a racial or cultural difference between the social worker and the client, social workers must give greater consideration to the possibility of depression when completing a client assessment, particularly for children, older adults, adult men, and persons who represent a cultural, racial, or ethnic group different from their own. Social workers can administer various rapid assessment measures of depression but must be knowledgeable about the validity and reliability of a measure and its use with various populations (Prescott et al., 1998). Exhibit 10.7 provides examples of valid and reliable rapid measures (Bloom, Fischer, & Orme, 1999; Corcoran & Fisher, 2000; Jordan & Franklin, 2003).

Self-Rating Measures

- Beck Depression Inventory II (Beck, Steer, & Brown, 1996)
- Center for Epidemiological Studies-Depression Scale, Revised (CES-D-R; Radloff, 1977)
- Children's Depression Inventory (CDI; Kovacs, 1983)
- Geriatric Depression Scale (Yesavage et al., 1982)
- Phan Vietnamese Psychiatric Scale (Phan, Steel, & Silove, 2004)
- Zung Depression Scale (Zung, 1965)

Clinician Rating Measures

- Hamilton Rating Scale for Depression (Hamilton, 1967)
- Montgomery Asberg Depression Rating Scale (Montgomery & Asberg, 1979)

Exhibit 10.7   Selected Measures of Depression With Established Validity and Reliability

Many of these rapid assessment tools can be used with diverse populations (Beals, Manson, Keane, & Dick, 1995; Garrison, Addy, Jackson, McKeown, & Waller, 1991; Radloff & Rae, 1981; Radloff & Terri, 1986). For example, a study of elderly Asian immigrants residing in New York City was conducted to establish the reliability of the Geriatric Depression Scale (GDS) with this population. A surprising 40% of the 407 respondents were considered depressed using both long and short forms of GDS. Reliability evidence supported the use of this instrument and pointed to the need for culturally sensitive mental health assistance (Mui, Kang, Chen, & Domanski, 2004). Two screening depression tools specific to newly arrived Vietnamese refugees have been developed, the Vietnamese Depression Scale (Buchwald et al., 1995) and the Phan Vietnamese Psychiatric Scale (PVPS; Phan et al., 2004).

Although social workers in many settings may not be responsible for making mental health diagnoses, we need at least beginning knowledge to suspect, and possibly diagnose, major depression. A social worker must engage in autonomous thinking and recognize the possibility of unrecognized depression in children, youth, and older adults. School social workers must be attuned to the different symptoms of depression in children and adolescents and to the high and rising risk of suicide in these age groups. Social workers who work with an older adult population must, at times, take action to avoid the pitfalls of societal stereotypes and stigma that may hinder older adults, their families, and even helping professionals in recognizing and treating depression in this group. Kim Tran's paternal grandmother comes to mind. She was sad and withdrawn and never left the house. Could these be symptoms of depression? Certainly, she faced many traumatic events both before and during migration and had many difficult adjustments to make after arriving in the United States. To be helpful to her and her family, community mental health professionals would have a lot to consider: How is depression manifested in older adults, how is it manifested in Vietnamese culture, and what type of "help" would be acceptable to this particular older Vietnamese woman and her family?

Micro Practice Interventions

Certainly, social workers do not possess sufficient knowledge and skill, nor are we sanctioned, to independently treat major depression when psychotropic medications are indicated. However, social workers can be involved in educational roles, plan or deliver interventions, keep current on the emerging research on the effectiveness of nontraditional, complementary, and alternative interventions, and engage in referral and advocacy activities to facilitate mental health and other services for their clients with MDD.

Psychoeducation

Social workers frequently engage in the role of psychoeducator, either formally in a predesignated group or informally as part of the overall intervention plan. As the foremost provider of mental health services, social workers are well positioned to provide knowledge of major depression and the various types of interventions with known effectiveness. We can provide information to help clients and significant others such as spouses, partners, and children understand and accept intervention. We can educate significant others about the important roles they can play in providing hope and support to a depressed loved one. We can also provide information to other professionals and paraprofessionals, such as teachers and personal care staff, to help them recognize major depression and help depressed individuals get the help they need, including information about the new types and uses of medications (Bentley & Walsh, 2006). In some settings with well-established professional collaborative relationships, social workers provide suggestions of specific drugs to the person legally responsible for prescribing psychopharmacologic drugs (Bentley & Walsh, 2006).

Bentley and Walsh (2006) present a model for social workers to use not only to educate clients about the use of psychotropic medication but also to empower clients to be their own advocates with the prescribing physician. This collaborative relationship between the social worker, clients, and their families helps the client accept medication and also underscores the assertiveness skills that buttress cognitive-behavioral interventions proven to be effective in treating major depression. This collaborative approach also may prevent the client from discontinuing medication when it is not immediately effective and without consideration of alternatives. Bentley, Walsh, and Farmer (2005) provide six dimensions of quality for referring clients for psychiatric medication, as shown in Exhibit 10.8.

Psychotherapeutic Interventions

In many settings, social workers will also provide psychotherapeutic interventions, such as CBT and IPT, two intervention approaches that have been proven effective with persons with major depression.

Cognitive-Behavioral Therapy (CBT) originally developed by Aaron Beck and his colleagues, continues to show the best evidence of effectiveness for persons with major depression. This directive and structured intervention has three aims: (1) to impact the

---

- Establishing and maintaining collaborative relationships with prescribers
- Sharing up-to-date information about psychiatric medications with clients and families
- Helping clients and families understand and manage the meaning of medication
- Preparing clients and families for the actual medication evaluation and anticipating issues that might emerge
- Following up on the results of the referral
- Managing legal and ethical concerns

Exhibit 10.8   Six Dimensions of Quality for Referring Clients for Psychiatric Medication

SOURCE: Found in Bentley et al., 2005.

negative self-perception (I am a loser; I never did accomplish much; I am not a likable person); (2) to impact negative thoughts related to the environment (people are only out for what they can get); and (3) to impact the negative view of the future (life will always be depressing; I will always be ugly, a failure, no good). Negative, maladaptive actions are also challenged with CBT. The person with major depression is sequentially guided through the events that trigger a thought that leads to underlying negative thinking and ultimately is linked to specific behaviors. Specific and carefully designed instructions for change are provided, using homework assignments such as identifying and recording the type of negative thought and charting specific behaviors (Beck, 1995; Leahy, 1996, 2004).

Interpersonal Therapy (IPT) initially used for midlife-onset depression, emanates from assumptions that depression is caused by disruption in relationships or at least is exacerbated by such relational problems that may be a consequence of major depression. This brief approach focuses on the relationship between people's depression and their interpersonal relations and has shown effectiveness after 15–20 sessions. Usually the interpersonal difficulties are related to these problem areas: unresolved grief, interpersonal disputes, difficult role transitions, or interpersonal deficits (USDHHS, 1999). IPT has been shown to be as effective as the antidepressant nortriptyline in studies of older adults and more effective than a placebo (Hinrichsen & Clougherty, 2006). Combined with medication and psychoeducation groups, IPT also was found to be effective with about 80% of an older adult sample (Reynolds, 1994; Reynolds, et al., 1992).

Nontraditional, Complementary, and Alternative Interventions

Social workers, like other mental health professionals, are beginning to incorporate nontraditional approaches with known effectiveness into their practice. Meditation and relaxation exercises are used by social workers in a variety of settings (Brenner & Homonoff, 2004; McBee, Westreich, & Likourezos, 2004). To a lesser extent, social workers are also using yoga in their practice (Derezotes, 2000). Social workers may also help clients evaluate the possible benefits of using other nontraditional practitioners.

Referral and Advocacy

In settings where treatment of major depression is not available, social workers are in key positions to assist their clients in accessing appropriate resources, with particular attention to the social justice issues previously discussed.

Policy Practice

Social workers can position themselves to know not only "what is" but also to envision "what can be" in the lives of persons who are challenged by major depression at any point in the life course and in the systems that serve them (Bentley et al., 2005). The following are only a few examples of ways that social workers develop, influence, and change policy to impact persons with major depression.

As primary providers of mental health care, social workers are key informants to legislators struggling with decisions about proposed regulations that may help or hinder those persons who seek mental health assistance. To be effective policy advocates, we will need to be well grounded in social science research and understand political culture and the political process. At times, we will need to do our own empirical research to articulate the impact of existing policy. Social workers will need to work with other stakeholders to fight for mental health parity in insurance and governmental assistance programs.

Social workers also can influence the mental health system to ensure that providers of care represent the populations that are served. Bentley (2002, 2005) suggests that not only should women be represented at all levels within the mental health services systems, but women clients should have a voice in all levels of decision making for service and policy development related to major depression. Social workers can be advocates for this female voice.

Social workers who practice in school settings are in key positions to be advocates for parents and their children who may be denied access to services or presented with unnecessary barriers. For example, services for children may only be available during school hours, requiring that children miss school instruction. School policy related to absences and making up major exams, while not preventing access to services, may become a barrier as parents and children plan appointments for mental health services. Advocacy, if only for school policy exception, if not policy change, is within the purview of the school social worker.

Learning Activities

1. Select one of the assessment measures identified in this chapter and presented in Exhibit 10.7. Locate a copy of the instrument by searching by instrument name online or consulting sources such as Corcoran and Fisher (2000), Gibbs (2003), Jordan & Franklin (2003), or Shaw et al. (1997). Divide into four groups, with each group choosing one case story from Chapter 2, so that the stories of David Loefeler, Sondra Jackson, Elias and

Claudia Salvatierra, and Kim Tran are each selected by a group **(general knowledge and knowledge of case).** Within the group, review the selected case and imagine a person in that story being asked by you to complete the instrument. Consider how your selected person might respond to each of the questions **(knowledge about the case).** What recommendations, if any, would you make so that the measure is more reflective of the case situation **(knowledge about the case)?** What personal feelings or thoughts did you have **(knowledge about the self)** as you considered asking the person to complete the assessment? What ethical principles from the National Association of Social Workers (NASW) Code of Ethics would guide you in introducing the assessment **(values and ethics)** and handling the results if the instrument were to indicate that the person may have major depression?

2. Working in small groups, review the major theories of causation for major depression. Discuss what theory(ies) you would apply to understand the situation of David Loefeler **(general knowledge).** If you change one defining characteristic of David such as age or race, would you alter your theoretical explanation of his depression **(knowledge of the case and general knowledge)?** What in David's situation is not explained by the selected theory **(knowledge of the case and general knowledge)?** Is theory compatible with the core principles of the NASW Code of Ethics **(values and ethics)?** In what ways? Review the CBT and IPT practice approaches presented in the chapter **(general knowledge).** Discuss your reactions to each approach. Which approach do you believe would be the most effective with David **(general knowledge and knowledge about the case)?**

3. Using a prescription drug reference book, select a commonly used antidepressant and identify the drug manufacturing company. Ask a pharmacist to compute the cost of a month's supply of this antidepressant. Ask the pharmacist if there are any problems getting insurance coverage or governmental assistance to cover the cost of drugs **(values and ethics).** Search online for the Web site for the drug company to ascertain whether or not they sponsor an indigent drug program **(general knowledge).** Research whether Medicare or Medicaid in your state covers this medication **(general knowledge).**

4. Imagine that you are the community mental health social worker working with David Loefeler. He has just told you that he has discontinued taking his antidepressant medication because of the unpleasant side effects. Based on what you learned in this chapter **(general knowledge)** and what you know about David's situation **(knowledge about the case),** what concerns would you have about that? Take a moment to reflect on your own thoughts and feelings about psychotropic medications and how you feel about a client's rights to refuse them **(knowledge about the self).** What ethical values and principles would guide you in your approach to discussing this issue with David?

11

Afterword

Elizabeth D. Hutchison,
Virginia Commonwealth University

Themes Across the
Challenges of Living

In Chapter 1, we proposed a working model for thinking about relevant sources of knowledge to help us understand the challenges of living addressed by social workers. We suggested that this working model gives structure to the task of mining for available scientific knowledge to help us see and understand the complexity in the situations we encounter in our work. The working model is based on a set of seven questions:

1. Who is affected by the challenge of living (what is the pattern of occurrence)?

2. What are the current theories of causation, or association, related to the challenge of living?

3. What are the multidimensional (biological, psychological, social, and spiritual) developmental risk and protective factors?

4. What are the consequences of the challenge of living? Are different people affected in different ways?

5. How have people attempted to cope with the challenge of living?

6. What social justice issues are involved?

7. What do the answers to the above questions suggest about action strategies (practice implications)?

We suggested that this working model can be used to develop better understanding of any challenge of living that social workers encounter. In Chapters 3–10, we demonstrated the use of the model to build understanding of eight exemplar challenges of living: financial impoverishment, community violence, child maltreatment, traumatic stress disorders, substance abuse, obesity, HIV/AIDS, and major depression. These challenges of living were chosen because they are all commonly recognized as important public health problems and are challenges that social workers frequently confront in their various practice settings. They present across the life course, are faced by communities as well as individuals and families, and cut across age, gender, economic, racial, ethnic, sexual orientation, and other identity groups.

In this final chapter, we engage in comparison across the exemplar challenges of living to see if there are any crosscutting themes. We found some differences across the challenges of living as we expected, but we were much more struck with the commonalities than the differences. We were both impressed and saddened by the co-occurrence, bundling, and overlaps in risk factors that clearly indicate cumulative risk. We also found a tendency for the eight exemplar challenges of living to cluster and to be connected in reciprocal relationships. In addition, we identified a set of coping strategies that are used to cope with a variety of adverse situations. Social and economic inequality was a social justice theme that ran throughout the challenges of living. Although the specific social work interventions varied across the challenges of living, we recognized some common characteristics of effective practice approaches.

We turn now to comparisons across challenges of living in terms of patterns of occurrence, theoretical perspectives, multidimensional risk and protection, consequences, ways of coping, social justice issues, and practice implications. As we do so, we want to provide a word of caution. The themes addressed below may be peculiar to the particular set of challenges of living selected for this book. It is quite possible that we would have found different themes with a different set of challenges of living. Before reading the following analysis, you will want to turn back to the four life stories at the beginning of Chapter 2. You can think about how these four stories compare with the research summarized here.

Patterns of Occurrence

For each of the challenges of living discussed in this book, the task of presenting accurate incidence and prevalence data is complicated by both definitional and methodological issues. That said, the reported patterns of occurrence clearly suggest that each of the exemplar challenges of living is an important public health problem at the global, national, and local levels. Although the patterns of occurrence vary across the challenges of living, some themes emerge from considering them as a whole. As summarized in Exhibit 11.1, rates of occurrence vary by age, gender, race, ethnicity, and social class.

Age plays a role, but the vulnerable age varies across the challenges of living. Children have higher rates of financial impoverishment than other age groups, both in the United States and globally. Younger children have higher rates of child maltreatment than older children. The increasing rate of obesity among children is causing both national and international concern, but, as was the case for Claudia Salvatierra, the most pronounced

	Greater Occurrence by			
	Age	Gender	Race/Ethnicity	Social Class
Financial Impoverishment	Children	Female	African Americans, Latinos, and American Indian/Alaskan Natives	
Community Violence	Adolescents	Male	African Americans and Latinos	Impoverished Individuals
Child Maltreatment	Younger Children	Female (sexual abuse) Male (physical abuse)	African Americans and American Indians/Alaskan Natives	Impoverished Individuals
Traumatic Stress Disorders		Female (sexual abuse) Male (physical abuse)	African Americans and American Indians	
Substance Abuse		Male	American Indians/Alaskan Natives and Latinos	
Obesity	25–44	Male	Latino children and youth	Impoverished Individuals
HIV/AIDS	15–19 (worldwide) 35–44 (U.S.)	Female Teens	African Americans and Latinos	Impoverished Individuals
Major Depression	24–44	Male (under 10) Female (over 10)		

Exhibit 11.1   Crosscutting Patterns of Occurrence

period of weight gain for adults occurs between the ages of 25 and 44. Adolescence is the peak period for involvement in community violence, as both victim and perpetrator, both nationally and internationally. Isaiah Jackson was an adolescent victim of community violence, and Kim Tran has become an adolescent perpetrator. We might wonder if Junito Salvatierra is on a course that will lead him to become victim, perpetrator, or both. The majority of new cases of HIV occur in persons between the ages of 15 and 19 worldwide and between the ages of 35 and 44 in the United States. Major depression is most commonly diagnosed in the early adult years, but it is often overlooked in children and older adults, and this may skew the reported occurrence rates among these age groups. We might wonder if David Loefeler could have been diagnosed with major depression in childhood or adolescence, and we might also speculate that Kim Tran's paternal grandmother could have benefited from treatment for depression in her later years.

Gender is another important variable in the patterns of occurrence across challenges of living. But, as with age, the more vulnerable gender is not always the same from one challenge of living to another. Females have slightly higher rates of financial impoverishment than males and are twice as likely as males to be diagnosed with major depression over the lifetime. Males have higher rates of involvement in community violence and substance abuse than females. For child maltreatment and traumatic stress disorders, there are gender differences in the types of abusive situations experienced. Females are more likely to experience sexual abuse, and males are more likely to experience physical abuse. Males account for the majority of people living with HIV in the United States, except for the age group 13–19, for which the rate of infection is higher among females than among males.

There were also racial and ethnic variations in patterns of occurrence for many of the challenges of living covered in this book, but it is often difficult to untangle race and ethnicity from social class. Many of these patterns represent historical as well as current oppression and discrimination. African Americans, Latinos, and American Indians/Alaskan Natives have higher rates than other groups of financial impoverishment. African Americans and Latinos have higher rates of involvement in community violence and a higher incidence of HIV/AIDS than other groups. The rate of HIV/AIDS among African American men is 9 times that of white men; for African American women, the rate is 23 times that of white women, an astonishingly high ratio. Estella Jackson is a part of this unfortunate trend. African Americans and America Indian/Alaskan Natives have higher rates of child maltreatment and traumatic stress disorders than the general population. Although different racial and ethnic groups have different substances of choice, American Indians/Alaskan Natives and Latinos have higher rates of substance abuse than other groups. Latino children and youth have higher rates of obesity than other children and youth.

There are higher rates of community violence, child maltreatment, obesity, and HIV/AIDS among financially impoverished individuals, families, and communities. There are also regional differences in the rates of financial impoverishment, community violence, and HIV/AIDS at both the international and national levels. There are higher rates of all three of these challenges of living in regions with the highest levels of economic inequality.

Theories of Causation

Although the way that theories are classified sometimes differs across challenges of living, a very similar set of behavioral science perspectives is drawn on to explain all eight of the exemplar challenges of living. The same three historical themes can be identified in the theorizing about each challenge of living. First, multiple theoretical approaches have been presented over time, and multiple approaches still have currency. Second, there is increasing attention to biological forces in explaining the challenges of living. And third, there is a recent trend toward theoretical integration across the biopsychosocial dimensions, resulting in a current prominence of multidimensional or ecological theorizing. The theoretical perspectives used across challenges of living can be classified as biological, psychodynamic, cognitive, cultural, social process, social structure, and integrative. Each of these perspectives has received some support from empirical research. We summarize here how each is used across challenges of living, and we report how well the theory stacks up in the empirical research on risk and protection. Exhibit 11.2 provides a visual summary of how the theoretical perspectives are used across challenges of living.

Biological Theories

Theorists in the biomedical sciences have proposed a number of biological mechanisms to play a causative role in the various challenges of living. Indeed, biological approaches have been presented to explain, at least in part, each of the challenges of living discussed in this book. Genetics have been proposed to play a role in financial impoverishment, community violence, child maltreatment, substance abuse, obesity, and major depression. Technological advances in brain imaging have led to theorizing about the role of the central nervous system (CNS), including neurotransmission and brain structures, in different challenges of living. Although the structures and mechanisms are not always the same across challenges, CNS structures and processes have been proposed to play an important role in community violence, child maltreatment, traumatic stress disorders, substance abuse, obesity, HIV/AIDS, and major depression. Other biological mechanisms, such as proteins, hormones, and other chemicals, as well as sleep disruption, have been proposed to play a causal role in specific challenges of living, such as obesity and major depression. General health, a type of human capital, is proposed to play a role in financial impoverishment. There is very strong empirical evidence that a variety of biological factors play a role in each of the challenges of living discussed in this book.

Psychodynamic Theories

Although more explicitly stated in relation to some challenges of living than for others, psychodynamic approaches have been used to explain almost all of the exemplar challenges

	Theoretical Perspective			
	Biological	*Psychodynamic*	*Cognitive*	*Cultural*
Financial Impoverishment	Genetic Inferiority		Expectancy Theory	Culture of Poverty Cultural Definitions of Gender
Community Violence	Life Course Model	Vulnerable Identity Ego Deficits Threats to Self Threats to Relationships	Social Learning: Beliefs About the World	Culture of Violence Cultural Definitions of Gender
Child Maltreatment	Genetic Shaping	Parental Character Flaws	Information Processing Theory	Culture of Violence
Traumatic Stress Disorders	Interpersonal Neurobiology Dual Representation Theory	Primitive Defenses Problems in Affect Regulation Impaired Self-Esteem Ego Deficits	Cognitive-Behavioral Theory Constructivist Self-Development Theory	
Substance Abuse	Genetic Model Cognitive-Neurobehavioral Model	Personality Traits Coping Deficits	Social Learning Theory	Feminist Theory Oppression Theory Afrocentric Theory
Obesity	Genetic Explanation Nutrition/Activity Explanation Fetal Origins Hypothesis Proteins, Hormones, Chemicals	Low Self-Esteem Depression		Cultural Evolution Changing Lifestyles
HIV/AIDS	Trauma-focused: CNS	Trauma-focused: Childhood Adversities	Health Belief Model Theory of Reasoned Actions Self-Efficacy Model	Cultural Definitions of Gender Peer Subcultures
Major Depression	Genetic Vulnerability Neurotransmission Sex Hormones & Cortisol Sleep Disruption	Attachment Problems Internalized Anger Goal Frustration	Cognitive Theory	

	Theoretical Perspective		
	Social Processes	Social Structure	Integrative
Financial Impoverishment	Human Capital Theory	Social Stratification Feminization of Poverty Colonialism & Neocolonialism Environmental Geography	Ecological Theory
Community Violence	Social Interaction Social Learning Differential Association	Macro-Level Strain Lack of Collective Efficacy	Ecological Theory Life Course Theory
Child Maltreatment	Attachment Social Modeling Conditioning & Reinforcement Social Interaction	Social Isolation Blocked Opportunities Gender Inequalities	Ecological Theory
Traumatic Stress Disorders		Social Disorganization Theory	Interpersonal Neurobiological Approach
Substance Abuse	Conditioning Theories Social Affiliation Theories	Feminist Theory Oppression Theory Afrocentric Theory	Unified Theory of Behavior Conditioning Theories
Obesity	Social Modeling Conditioning and Reinforcement Associational Learning	Food Insecurity Aspects of Food Industry	Ecological Theory
HIV/AIDS	Social Network Theory		Multidimensional Health Behavior Model
Major Depression	Interpersonal Theory	Social Stress Theories	Interpersonal Theory (reciprocal causation)

Exhibit 11.2 Crosscutting Theories of Causation

of living. A number of different psychological dynamics are proposed across challenges of living, and different dynamics are focused on for different challenges. Proposed psychological dynamics include vulnerable identities, threats to self and to attachment relationships, limited ego capacities, personality traits, coping deficits, and primitive defenses. The empirical research reviewed for this book indicates that some of these psychological dynamics serve as risk factors for several challenges of living. More specifically, threats to self, threats to attachment relationships, limited ego capacities, personality factors such as poor impulse control and poor emotional regulation, and coping deficits are identified as risk factors for several challenges of living.

Cognitive Theories

Cognitive approaches are proposed in relation to seven of the eight exemplar challenges of living, all except obesity. Sometimes the focus is on knowledge, information processing, and problem solving, as is the case for child maltreatment and HIV/AIDS. More often, however, the focus is on the role that beliefs, attitudes, perceptions, attributions, expectations, intentions, and meaning play in the development of challenges of living. Low expectations about one's ability to be effective are proposed to play a role in financial impoverishment, substance abuse, and HIV/AIDS. Expectations about child behavior are proposed to play a role in child maltreatment. Beliefs about the self and about the world are proposed to play a role in community violence, traumatic stress disorders, and major depression. There is good empirical support for the cognitive theories. Low self-efficacy and negative beliefs, attitudes, and expectancies were found to be common risk factors across the challenges of living.

Cultural Theories

Culture is proposed to play a role in six out of eight challenges of living discussed in this book. A culture of poverty was once proposed as a theory of adaptation to poverty but has been revised as a theory that explains poverty. A culture of violence has been proposed to explain community violence and child maltreatment. Cultural definitions of gender roles and gender-based social status have been proposed to contribute to financial impoverishment, community violence, substance abuse, and HIV/AIDS. Peer subcultures are proposed to play a role in community violence, substance abuse, and HIV/AIDS. Cultural evolution and changing lifestyles have been proposed to play a role in obesity. For the most part, cultural theories have not been put to the same types of empirical tests as the other perspectives. However, there is empirical evidence of the role of peer subcultures in community violence and HIV/AIDS and gender role norms in child maltreatment and HIV/AIDS. There is also some evidence that some aspects of popular culture contribute to the rising rate of obesity.

Social Process Theories

Seven of the eight exemplar challenges of living are proposed to be, in part, a result of problematic social processes, or problematic interpersonal transactions. Dysfunctional role models, whether they be parental, peer, or community based, are proposed to play a causal role in community violence, child maltreatment, substance abuse, and obesity. Conditioning and reinforcement processes are proposed to play a role in community violence, child maltreatment, substance abuse, and obesity. Some note is made of the role of social construction of meaning, symbols, and rituals in community violence, child maltreatment, traumatic stress disorders, substance abuse, and major depression. Problems in attachment processes and interpersonal exchanges are proposed to contribute to community violence, child maltreatment, substance abuse, and major depression. Interactions in drug and sex networks are proposed to play a role in HIV transmission. There was clear empirical evidence that faulty attachment and interpersonal conflict play important roles in the production of almost all of the challenges of living discussed in this book. Dysfunctional role models were found to play a role in community violence and substance abuse.

Social Structural Theories

Some version of structural theory has been used to explain seven of the eight exemplar challenges of living, all except HIV/AIDS. Actions in the economic and political institutions have been explicitly proposed as causal for financial impoverishment, community violence, and obesity. Failures in the educational institution have been explicitly proposed as a causal factor for financial impoverishment. Blocked opportunities and strain that result from failures in these three social institutions have been proposed to contribute to community violence and child maltreatment. Deteriorating neighborhoods, related to problematic economic and political arrangements, have been proposed as contributing factors in community violence and traumatic stress disorders. Gender inequalities are proposed to play a role in child maltreatment, substance abuse, and HIV/AIDS. Family stress related to poverty, inequality, and racism has been proposed to play a role in child maltreatment, substance abuse, and major depression. The structure of social networks has been proposed to play a role in HIV/AIDS. The nature of the physical environment, either at the national or the neighborhood level, has been proposed to play a role in financial impoverishment, community violence, traumatic stress disorders, and obesity. There is good empirical support for the contribution of social structure to the challenges of living discussed in this book. Arrangements in the economic and political systems play a role in financial impoverishment, community violence, child maltreatment, obesity, HIV/AIDS, and major depression. Racial discrimination has been found to play a role in financial impoverishment, community violence, substance abuse, and major depression. Gender inequality has been found to play a role in financial impoverishment, child maltreatment, and HIV/AIDS.

Integrative Theories

For the past two decades, there has been a trend toward theoretical integration, an attempt to bring together theories at the individual and social levels. This approach is gaining favor across all of the exemplar challenges of living. Some integrative efforts have been more comprehensive than others, however. Ecological theories assume that no single factor can explain a given challenge of living, and ecological theories that address the interaction of biological factors, psychological factors, and multiple system levels are the most comprehensive integrative theories. Fairly comprehensive ecological theories have been proposed to explain financial impoverishment, community violence, child maltreatment, substance abuse, obesity, and HIV/AIDS. Integrative theories are well supported by the consistent findings that multiple factors across multiple dimensions serve as risk or protection for all of the challenges of living discussed in this book.

Less comprehensive integrative theories have also been developed to explain several challenges of living, and some of these theories are driving a great deal of empirical investigation. Moffitt's (1993) *life course theory* of violent behavior combines biological and social dimensions, suggesting that violent behavior occurs when biological vulnerability interacts with environmental stress. The emerging *interpersonal neurobiological approach* (Siegel, 2001; Solomon & Siegel, 2003) to understanding trauma focuses on the interdependence of the brain and interpersonal relationships, particularly attachment relationships. *Conditioning theories* of substance abuse (Childress et al., 1999; Schneider et al., 2001; Sell et al., 2000; Weiss & Porrino, 2002) integrate biological and cognitive domains. Bandura's (1990) *self-efficacy model* of safer sex behavior integrates cognitive and emotional domains with social influences.

As noted throughout the book, there is also a trend to recognize a *reciprocal* causal pattern, in which factors in different domains influence each other simultaneously. The *interpersonal theory* of depression is the best example of a theory of reciprocal causation. Interpersonal theory proposes that major depression arises from dysfunctional interpersonal relationships *and* major depression leads to dysfunctional relationships. In this view, dysfunctional relationships are both the cause and the consequence of depression. Reciprocal causation is consistent with the attention to feedback mechanisms in ecological and systems perspectives.

Multidimensional Risk and Protection _____

Across challenges of living, it is clear that researchers have paid much less attention to protective factors than to risk factors, and even less attention to how risk factors and protective factors interact and effect development across the life course. Unfortunately, that limitation in the empirical literature inhibits social work efforts to develop social work interventions that have the goal of strengthening protective factors. In the discussion that follows, you will note that identified risk factors outnumber protective factors. You will also note that more attention has been paid to social and spiritual protective factors than to biological and psychological protective factors.

In each chapter of this book, we had some difficulty untangling biological, psychological, and social factors because of their embeddedness with each other. Because of the changing nature of the behavioral sciences, we sometimes had trouble deciding in which dimension certain factors should fall. For example, intelligence, temperament, and disposition are typically studied as psychological phenomena, but there is increasing evidence of a strong biological component in each of these phenomena. In this discussion, we include these phenomena with psychological risk and protective factors. Likewise, mental illnesses have typically been thought of as psychological phenomena, but their biological base is being clarified with brain imaging studies. For the purposes of this discussion, however, we cover mental illness as a psychological factor.

Attachment is often studied as a psychological phenomenon, but it is increasingly recognized as a biopsychosocial phenomenon. We categorize attachment here as a social factor, because it develops in the context of relationships. Age is another factor that is sometimes difficult to categorize. The life course perspective recognizes biological age, psychological age, and social age as interacting forces. In this book, when we are referring primarily to the impact of biological age, we classify age as a biological factor. A similar decision rule was used in relation to psychological and social age. Another complicated variable is sex/gender. When the reference is to the role of biological sex, we include sex as a biological factor. When, however, the emphasis seems to be on socially constructed gender, we include gender as a social factor. Of course, sometimes both are involved and can be hard to untangle, in which case we included them with the dimension where the greater emphasis seems to be.

One challenge to attempts to summarize and synthesize findings about risk and protective factors across challenges of living is that researchers in different areas of inquiry sometimes use different labels, different definitions, and different measures for similar concepts. In the discussion that follows, we have chosen to err on the side of inclusion, of pooling similar concepts even when the labels, definitions, and measures had nuances of difference.

The chapters of this book illustrate that there are common risk factors that put people at risk for several different challenges of living. Common protective factors were also found. In addition to these common risk and protective factors, there are risk and protective factors that are specific to a particular challenge of living. Our social work interventions should attend to both common and specific risk and protective factors, but the following discussion focuses on common risk and protective factors. Individual chapters should be consulted for more information on specific risk and protective factors.

Biological Risk and Protection

Biological risk factors have been identified for all eight exemplar challenges of living, but there is variation in the biological factors implicated in the various challenges.

Overall, a rather large number of biological risk factors were identified, including genetic vulnerability, CNS dysfunction, biological age, use of alcohol and other substances, health problems, hormones, perinatal complications, pregnancy, nutrition, developmental delay and disability, enzymes and toxins, sexual practices, breast-feeding, insomnia, and heart rate. Here we only discuss the four factors that were found to serve as risk for half or more of the challenges of living: genetic vulnerability, CNS dysfunction, use of alcohol and other substances, and health problems (see Exhibit 11.3).

	Risk Factors			
	Genetic Vulnerability	CNS Dysfunction	Use of Alcohol and Other Substances	Health Problems
Financial Impoverishment				X
Community Violence	X	X	X	
Child Maltreatment		X	X	X
Traumatic Stress Disorders		X		
Substance Abuse	X	X	X	
Obesity	X		X	X
HIV/AIDS	X		X	
Major Depression	X	X	X	X

Exhibit 11.3   Crosscutting Biological Risk Factors

Use of alcohol and other substances was identified as posing risk for six challenges of living, but the type of substance varied by challenge of living. For child maltreatment, substance abuse, obesity, and major depression, the focus is on the use of alcohol and illegal substances, with attention to how these substances affect brain functioning. As the research reported in Chapter 7 indicates, it is hard to say which came first for David Loefeler, substance abuse or major depression, but there is much evidence that depression can be a consequence of substance abuse. Tobacco use by the mother during pregnancy is a risk factor for community violence, but smoking cessation is a risk for obesity. Use of particular prescribed medications is a risk for obesity and major depression. For HIV/AIDS, sharing of drug paraphernalia among injecting drug users presents risk. At different points in time, Estella Jackson has shared drug paraphernalia on the street, and this may well be the way HIV was transmitted to her. But Estella has also exchanged sex for drugs, and this may have been the source of transmission. As reported in Chapter 9, women often face greater HIV transmission risk than men because of the overlap in their drug and sex networks. It will be important for the social workers at Estella's substance treatment program as well as her HIV clinic to help her assess her social network for sexual risks as well as relapse risks.

Genetic vulnerability has been found to play a role in community violence, substance abuse, obesity, HIV/AIDS, and major depression. It is possible that there was genetic contribution to David Loefeler's substance abuse and depression, Claudia Salvatierra's obesity, and Elias and Junito Salvatierra's substance abuse. We don't know, but family genograms might provide some clues, although not definitive evidence, about these possibilities.

A variety of dysfunctions in CNS structures and processes are identified as risk factors for five challenges of living: community violence, child maltreatment, traumatic stress disorders, substance abuse, and major depression. Researchers studying community violence have found that perinatal complications, maternal cigarette smoking during pregnancy, and disruptions in early attachment all lead to disorganization in various brain systems and that such brain disorganization is associated with violent behavior. Premature birth and developmental delay, and related CNS function, have been found to be risk factors for child maltreatment. Right-left hemispheric disintegration and decreased gamma-aminobutyric acid (GABA) have been found to be risk factors for traumatic stress disorders. For substance abuse, affect dysregulation and increased limbic system activation have been found to be risk factors. Current research indicates that neuron dysfunction, primarily in the synapses in the temporal lobe, cerebellum, and hypothalamus, contributes to major depression.

Health problems were found to serve as risk factors for half of the challenges of living: financial impoverishment, child maltreatment, obesity, and major depression. David Loefler's mental health problems are adding to his, and his family's, vulnerability to financial impoverishment. Estella Jackson's HIV status, as well as her substance abuse problem, increases her likelihood of financial impoverishment if she cannot depend on her sister, Sondra, for financial support.

In the empirical literature on the eight exemplar challenges of living, very little attention has been paid to biological protective factors. It seems safe to say that for many factors, protection lies at the other end of a continuum from risk. This would seem to be the case for risk factors such as health, disability, heart rate, brain functioning, and nutrition. Where biological protective factors are identified empirically, they appear to be much more specific to the challenge of living; no biological protective factors are found to be crosscutting across challenges of living, with the exception of good health and good brain functioning.

Psychological Risk and Protection

A number of psychological risk factors were identified across the exemplar challenges of living. Several of them were common to several challenges of living, and others were specific to one challenge of living. Five risk factors were common to half or more of the eight challenges of living (see Exhibit 11.4). The most frequently reported psychological risk factor was mental illness, which was found to be a risk factor for seven of the eight exemplar challenges of living, including financial impoverishment, child maltreatment, traumatic stress disorders, substance abuse, obesity, HIV/AIDS, and major depression. Just as David Loefeler's substance abuse was a risk factor for major depression, likewise his anxiety and depression put him at risk for further substance abuse and financial impoverishment. In addition, untreated major depression serves as risk for subsequent episodes of major depression.

| | Risk Factors | | | | |
	Mental Illness	Low Self-Efficacy	Poor Impulse Control	Negative Beliefs	Emotion Regulation Problems
Financial Impoverishment	X	X			
Community Violence			X	X	X
Child Maltreatment	X		X		
Traumatic Stress Disorders	X	X			X
Substance Abuse	X	X	X	X	X
Obesity	X				X
HIV/AIDS	X		X	X	X
Major Depression	X	X		X	

Exhibit 11.4   Crosscutting Psychological Risk Factors

One psychological factor, problems with emotion regulation, was found to be a risk factor for five challenges of living: community violence, traumatic stress disorders, substance abuse, obesity, and HIV/AIDS. It appears that regulating his emotions is a struggle for David Loefeler, and it is quite possible that he has tried to use alcohol and other substances in an attempt to quiet strong emotional states. It is also possible that Claudia Salvatierra uses food in the same way.

Three other psychological factors were identified to present risk for half of the exemplar challenges of living. Low self-efficacy was found to be a risk factor for financial impoverishment, traumatic stress disorders, substance abuse, and major depression. Poor impulse control was found to serve as risk for community violence, child maltreatment, substance abuse, and HIV/AIDS. Negative beliefs, attitudes, and expectancies were identified as risk factors for community violence, substance abuse, HIV/AIDS, and major depression.

David Loefeler describes himself as a screw-up and appears to have negative expectancies for the future. Working with David, we would want to help him take pride in his courage and hard work to reach sobriety, to pass the high school equivalency exam, and to complete the associate's degree. We would also want to shore up Junito Salvatierra's belief in his capacity to take charge of his own life course, recognizing that he has suffered a serious setback in his sense of personal empowerment with the many losses and challenges he has faced in the past few years. We would also want to assess the beliefs and expectancies of Claudia Salvatierra and Kim Tran. Likewise, the social workers working with Estella Jackson will want to examine her expectations about her capacity for sobriety as well as her ability to practice safer sex. They may also want to work with her to improve her impulse control. Estella's sister, Sondra, seems to have made good use of impulse control, positive beliefs and expectancies, and good emotional regulation to bounce back from a number of stressful situations over time. It will be important for the child protective services social worker to acknowledge these strengths and help Sondra draw on them.

Once again, researchers have paid much more attention to psychological risk factors than to psychological protective factors in the empirical literature on the eight exemplar challenges of living. Only one psychological factor was found to serve as protection for over half of the exemplar challenges of living. High self-efficacy/locus of control was noted as a protective factor for six of the eight challenges of living: financial impoverishment, child maltreatment, traumatic stress disorders, substance abuse, HIV/AIDS, and major depression. It would appear that high self-efficacy is a potent protective factor across several challenges. It is possible that more consistent use of variables and measurements across the lines of inquiry would find that some other psychological protective factors are more common than current research indicates, but the good news is that self-efficacy is a protective factor that can respond to intervention.

Social Risk and Protection

For each exemplar challenge of living, social factors were more prominent in the empirical literature than biological, psychological, and/or spiritual factors. This was true both for risk factors and for protective factors. A number of social risk and protective factors were specific to one or two challenges of living, but eight different social risk factors and three different social protective factors were identified for half or more of the challenges of living (see Exhibits 11.5 and 11.6). The biggest story to be told centers on the leading role that relationships play in both risk and protection. Another big story is the important role of social status, poverty, and inequality in explaining a variety of challenges of living.

The most frequently noted social risk factors were child maltreatment, poverty and inequality, and problems at the community level; each of these factors was noted in six of the eight exemplar challenges of living. Child maltreatment was a risk factor for community violence, child maltreatment (parental history of maltreatment), substance abuse, obesity, HIV/AIDS, and major depression. The sporadic violence that David Loefeler suffered at his father's hands was one among other factors that put David at risk for substance abuse and major depression. Of special note in the research was the particularly strong risk that childhood sexual abuse posed for HIV/AIDS and major depression.

			Risk Factors					
	Child Maltreatment	Traumatic Stress	Attachment Problems	Low Social Support	Poverty & Inequality	Educational Problems	Community Problems	Family Conflict
Financial Impoverishment					X	X	X	X
Community Violence	X		X		X	X	X	X
Child Maltreatment	X	X	X	X	X	X	X	X
Traumatic Stress Disorders		X	X	X			X	
Substance Abuse	X	X	X	X		X	X	X
Obesity	X				X			
HIV/AIDS	X	X			X			
Major Depression	X	X	X	X	X		X	X

Exhibit 11.5 Crosscutting Social Risk Factors

	Protective Factors		
	Good Attachment Relationships	Good Social Support System	Institutional Resources
Financial Impoverishment			X
Community Violence	X		X
Child Maltreatment	X	X	X
Traumatic Stress Disorders		X	
Substance Abuse	X	X	X
Obesity	X		
HIV/AIDS	X	X	
Major Depression		X	

Exhibit 11.6   Crosscutting Social Protective Factors

Poverty and inequality was identified as a risk factor for financial impoverishment (systems of inequality), community violence, child maltreatment, obesity, HIV/AIDS, and major depression. Sometimes the risk factor was individual or family-level poverty, and other times the identified factor was community-level impoverishment. And for two challenges of living, financial impoverishment and HIV/AIDS, the risk factor was societal inequality. Of course, family and community levels of poverty are highly correlated, and for several challenges of living, both levels of impoverishment are identified as risk factors (community violence, child maltreatment, and substance abuse). The Loefeler family struggled financially and faced an economic setback. David Loefeler continues to try to make his way financially. The Salvatierra and Tran families have worked hard toward the goal of economic security. Both families had some assistance from extended family in the process, but the Tran family had a larger extended family network available for pooling resources.

Several interrelated aspects of community life were found to serve as risk for a number of challenges of living. For some challenges of living, the risk factor is neighborhood violence; this is the case for child maltreatment, traumatic stress disorders, and major depression. For three challenges of living, financial impoverishment, community violence, and child maltreatment, living in an impoverished community serves as a risk factor. Neighborhood disorganization is a risk factor for community violence, child maltreatment, and substance abuse. Given these findings, we can identify community-level risk factors for the Jackson, Salvatierra, and Tran families.

Three other social factors were identified as risk factors in five different challenges of living: traumatic stress, attachment problems, and family conflict. Traumatic stress, in general, was found to be an important risk factor for child maltreatment, traumatic stress disorders, substance abuse, HIV/AIDS, and major depression. A variety of types of trauma were identified in the literatures related to the different challenges of living, including child maltreatment, community violence, and traumatic resettlement. Loss traumas may have played a role in the lives of all four of the families presented in Chapter 2. Some of the losses may appear more serious than others, but what is important is the meaning that was made of the losses. David Loefeler faced the loss of the family farm, something for which he blames himself. Sondra and Estella Jackson faced the loss of their father when they were still in junior high school and have more recently faced the loss of their mother and Sondra's son, Isaiah. The Salvatierra family has faced the multiple losses that come with the migration experience, losses of friends and family, as well as familiar language and customs. Celia Jaes Falicov (2003) refers to this experience as "migration loss" and notes that it may be complicated, as it is for the Salvatierras, by ambiguous losses when some family members and friends stay behind and the ones who migrate may be too stressed to be present in spirit. Likewise, the Tran family legacy is full of migration loss and also includes a history of war and imprisonment.

Poor or disrupted attachments at several levels, including parent-child, peer, school, and community, were found to be a risk factor for community violence, child maltreatment, traumatic stress disorders, substance abuse, and major depression. It appears that David Loefeler was not able to build a strong attachment relationship with his parents and had some difficulties with school attachment in adolescence. Unlike her sister, Sondra, Estella Jackson also demonstrated problems in school attachment and may have been more affected for undetermined reasons by her mother's lack of emotional availability following the death of her father. Sondra Jackson seems to have developed an early healthy attachment to community, but that was disrupted as the neighborhood changed. Both the Salvatierra and the Tran families have had to cope with disruptions in attachment relationships at all levels. Kim Tran once had a strong attachment to a large extended family, but those relationships have become quite strained.

Family conflict or violence was identified as a risk factor for financial impoverishment, community violence, child maltreatment, substance abuse, and major depression. There was much conflict in David Loefeler's family of origin, as well as in his relationship with his wife. Family conflict has grown over the years in both the Salvatierra and Tran families. The conflict often spilled over into violence in the Loefeler family and has begun to do so in the Salvatierra family.

Two additional social factors were found to be risk factors for four, or half, of the exemplar challenges of living, low social support and educational problems. Given the role that attachment plays in the capacity for interpersonal relationships, it is not surprising that limited social support showed up as a risk factor for most of the same challenges of living for which attachment problems served as risk: child maltreatment, traumatic stress disorders, substance abuse, and major depression. Kim Tran felt abandoned and isolated as her family grew apart, and it appears that she has joined up with the gang, in part, to reclaim a sense of belonging to others. One important finding across three challenges of living— substance abuse, HIV/AIDS, and major depression—is that limited social support is a more serious risk factor for females than for males. For HIV/AIDS, limited social support was found to be a risk factor for females, while the opposite was the case for males for whom greater social support was found to be a risk factor. This gender difference deserves further investigation but is important to keep in mind as we plan our social work interventions.

Measured in different ways, educational problems have been found to be a risk factor for financial impoverishment, community violence, child maltreatment, and substance abuse. School problems were found to pose risk for community violence and substance abuse. Low educational achievement was noted to be a risk factor for financial impoverishment and child maltreatment. David Loefeler, Estella Jackson, and Junito Salvatierra all struggled with school and eventually dropped out of high school. David has had the encouragement to return to school, however, and has completed an associate's degree. Kim Tran's parents had limited opportunity for education in their country of origin as well as in the United States, and this places some limits on their financial opportunities.

Three social protective factors were also found to be common across several challenges of living: good attachment relationships, good social support system, and institutional resources (see Exhibit 11.6). Good attachment relationships across a number of social levels and good social support were the most commonly reported social protective factors, each noted in five different challenges of living. Good attachment relationships were noted to serve as a protective factor for community violence, child maltreatment, substance abuse, obesity, and HIV/AIDS. Good social support systems, a related variable, were identified as protection against five challenges of living: child maltreatment, traumatic stress disorders, substance abuse, HIV/AIDS, and major depression. When these related variables are combined, positive relationships are found to be a protective factor for seven of the eight exemplar challenges of living, all except financial impoverishment. We will want to be mindful of the importance of positive relationships as we work with the families and communities of David Loefeler, Sondra Jackson, Elias and Claudia Salvatierra, and Kim Tran. We could work with the Salvatierra and Tran families to help them repair estranged relationships and assist them to communicate about their migration losses and the toll they have taken on each generation. Both families may benefit from reengaging with cultural rituals that once provided coherence and connectedness to both family and community. It will be important for David Loefeler and Estella Jackson to be connected to recovery communities instead of addiction communities.

Governmental social welfare policies and other institutional resources were found to be protective factors in half of the challenges of living: financial impoverishment, community violence, child maltreatment, and substance abuse. David Loefeler has been unable to develop a sound economic base for his family, but he has benefited from state-supported mental health services and a strong state community college system. Sondra Jackson has an adequate income, but her neighborhood has become economically precarious in the past few years. The situation for her sister, Estella, would be much more insecure without the governmental and nongovernmental resources of the HIV/AIDS clinic and substance abuse treatment program. The Tran family was buffered during their resettlement period by a nongovernmental refugee resettlement program that received some governmental funds. The Salvatierra family has not had access to such institutional resources and has been more dependent on family and friends.

Spiritual Risk and Protection

Spirituality and religion have only recently been studied in a serious way for their risk and protective relationship to specific challenges of living. Consequently, researchers are just now beginning to develop instruments that are sensitive to different aspects of spiritual and religious experiences. Therefore, the reports of spiritual and religious influence on challenges of living tend to be rather global in nature. With that said, it is clear that some aspect of spiritual and religious experience serves to protect against seven of the eight exemplar challenges of living. Researchers have paid much less attention to spirituality and religion as a risk factor, but there is beginning evidence that some types of religious beliefs can serve as risk for some challenges of living. Exhibit 11.7 summarizes the crosscutting spiritual risk and protection factors. We will turn first to the discussion of spiritual risk factors and then overview the findings for religion and spirituality as a protective factor.

Some religious beliefs and styles of religious coping have been identified as a risk factor for five of the eight exemplar challenges of living. Religious beliefs that promote a high regard for child obedience and corporal punishment have been noted to be a risk factor for child maltreatment. Beliefs in a punitive deity were also found to be risk factors for substance abuse and major depression. For traumatic stress, despair is a spiritual risk factor. Religious groups that oppose such HIV transmission prevention strategies as condom use

	Challenge of Living
Risk Factor	
Religious beliefs that emphasize punishment	Child Maltreatment Substance Abuse Major Depression
Protective Factors	
Active personal involvement in spiritual search for meaning, purpose, hope	Financial Impoverishment Community Violence Traumatic Stress Disorders Substance Abuse HIV/AIDS Major Depression
Religious connectedness and supportive affiliation	Financial Impoverishment Community Violence Child Maltreatment Traumatic Stress Disorders Substance Abuse HIV/AIDS Major Depression

Exhibit 11.7   Crosscutting Spiritual Risk and Protective Factors

and clean needle exchange present a risk for HIV/AIDS. Spiritual crises and lack of meaning have been identified as risk factors for traumatic stress disorders and HIV/AIDS. However, there is also some indication that a spiritual crisis can foster greater meaning in connection, for example, enhanced spirituality can come from confronting crisis in meaning. Cross-sectional research may not always pick up this reciprocal process. One of the more promising areas of research on religion as a risk factor makes a distinction between positive religious coping, which focuses on collaborating with God and feeling spiritual support, and negative religious coping, which focuses on punishment and abandonment. Researchers who have followed this line of inquiry have found negative religious coping to be a risk factor for substance abuse and major depression. More research is needed in this area.

As mentioned earlier, spirituality and/or religion was found to be a protective factor for seven of the eight exemplar challenges of living. Researchers have just begun to tease out the elements of spirituality and religion and to understand which elements are responsible for the protective effect. Active involvement in a spiritual life can provide meaning and purpose, hope, relief, and a sense of control, particularly under adverse conditions. One research team recently attempted to tease out the elements of spiritual and religious protection in relation to major depression and found that thankfulness and the social support aspect of religious participation (social religiosity) were the only elements that provided protection against major depression (Kendler et al., 2003). It is important that researchers continue to examine the specific protective elements of spiritual and religious life.

Although she does not regularly attend church, Sondra Jackson has a strong spiritual life that is grounded in her earlier religious training. This type of spirituality seems to be an important protective factor against financial impoverishment, community violence, traumatic stress disorders, substance abuse, HIV/AIDS, and major depression. Affiliation with a religious institution can provide social connectedness and social support, and this aspect of religious affiliation has been found to be a protective factor against seven of the eight challenges of living, all except obesity. The Tran family once maintained a strong relationship with the Buddhist center in their community but has fallen away from the congregation and Buddhist practices. In a more specific way, religious institutions may provide tangible as well as intangible support, for example, food, clothing, and job leads to protect against poverty and weight control programs to protect against obesity. Indeed, the refugee resettlement program that assisted the Tran family in their resettlement was connected to the Catholic church. In addition, religious involvement has been found to inhibit negative health practices such as risky sexual and drug behaviors.

Biopsychosocial-Spiritual Integration

In Chapter 1, we indicated that we would be analyzing risk and protection for specific challenges of living by teasing out biological, psychological, social, and spiritual dimensions. We noted that this is an artificial way to examine the knowledge base given the linked and overlapping nature of these dimensions, but we hoped that by taking this analytical approach, we would be able to draw on a more multidisciplinary literature and get a fuller picture of the factors involved in risk and protection across the life course. Throughout the book, we have noted how difficult it can be to separate the factors this way, even though they are often studied in this segmented manner. It does appear, however, that being intentional in our search for risk and protective factors in all four dimensions has, indeed, led to a fuller understanding of risk and protection. Sticking to our plan has also helped to clarify some of the integrated processes and mechanisms of risk and resilience across the life course.

In the chapters of this book, a large number of risk and protective factors have been identified. Once a risk factor has been identified, we are left with the question, *How* does this factor pose risk? What is the process and what are the mechanisms by which risk occurs? As evidenced throughout this book, behavioral scientists are beginning to understand some of the integrative biopsychosocial processes of risk. We are not as far along in understanding the processes by which specific protective factors contribute to resilience, but there are beginning efforts to answer this question as well.

As we look at the most commonly identified biological, psychological, social, and spiritual risk factors summarized above, we can begin to identify some of the biopsychosocial mechanisms of risk. Genetic vulnerability can play a role in the process of risk, and the likelihood of a number of public health problems, including the ones covered in this book, increases when genetic vulnerability is combined with a harsh environment. Specific outcomes are influenced by the nature of the genetic vulnerability, the nature of the environmental stressors, and the developmental status of the person. Environmental stressors come in many varieties, many of which tend to co-occur. They can come in the form of inadequate resources for developmental tasks, whether they are inadequate physical resources such as poor nutrition or substandard housing, or they are inadequate social resources, such as parental neglect, problematic attachments, or inadequate support systems. They can also come in the form of traumatic events, family and community conflict, or family loss and disruption. Chronic and severe environmental stressors can result in further biological vulnerability, affecting a number of biological systems, including the immune system, resulting in a variety of mental and physical health problems. Mental and physical health problems become risk factors for a number of other challenges of living.

We do not have evidence of specific genetic vulnerabilities in the Loefeler, Jackson, Salvatierra, or Tran families. As suggested earlier, family genograms might begin to provide some clues about this. We do know, however, that all four of these families have faced a variety of environmental stressors.

The Loefeler family became financially destitute in spite of their very hard work. As financial pressures mounted, harsh and occasionally violent discipline turned into chronic family conflict. David's developmental trajectory was complicated by becoming a father in the midst of his adolescence, before he had developed the cognitive, emotional, and social resources needed for parenting. David believes that the financial stress increased his father's vulnerability to lung cancer, and indeed there is good evidence that severe chronic stress can impair the immune system.

Sondra and Estella Jackson were raised in a loving home with sufficient financial resources and a strong connection to a supportive community. But just as they were making the challenging transition into adolescence, they faced the death of their father and their mother's preoccupation with her own grief. Sondra and Estella were left to navigate adolescence with little guidance. Later, while Sondra was worrying about the growing disorganization in her neighborhood, Estella was putting herself into hazardous situations that, no doubt, produced much stress, maybe even traumatic stress, in her life. Sondra has faced much loss trauma in the recent past: the murder of her adolescent son followed closely by the loss of her mother and most recently the knowledge of her vulnerable infant grandson and the HIV status of Estella.

The Salvatierra family faced harsh economic realities in their native Dominican Republic and, like many other families, immigrated one at a time to the United States to try to make a better life. This meant family separations and complicated reunifications and also brought new challenges related to language and customs. They have also sometimes faced ethnic discrimination both in their native Dominican Republic and in the United States.

The Tran family still struggles with a family legacy of war, imprisonment, and forced migration. They also faced family separation and loss during the premigration and migration processes. Like the Salvatierra family, they have also had to adjust to new language and customs and suffered family conflict about different approaches to the acculturation process.

For the past 10 years, epidemiologists worldwide have studied an important potential mechanism of risk, proposing a *"developmental origins of health and disease,"* or life course, model (Gluckman & Hanson, 2004; Gluckman, Cutfield, Hofman, & Hanson, 2005). The exact mechanisms are not yet fully understood but appear to involve early nutrition and may also involve genetic vulnerability (Ijzerman, Boomsma, & Stehouwer, 2005). Originally, the hypothesis, called the "fetal hypothesis," was that fetal undernutrition was the important risk factor. After 10 years of animal experiments and human observation, the current evidence indicates that the situation is more complex than that. Current evidence indicates that if impaired fetal growth caused by maternal undernutrition, either just previous to or during pregnancy, is followed by rapid weight gain by the infant in the first few postnatal months, or perhaps even at later developmental periods, the individual is at increased risk for a number of later health problems, including obesity, cardiovascular disease, diabetes, osteoporosis, polycystic ovarian syndrome, mood disorders, and psychoses (Gluckman & Hanson, 2004; Longo et al., 2005). The theory is that the fetus adapts to a deprived environment and is ill suited for a more abundant postnatal environment. Risk is produced by the "mismatch" between the environment of the early developmental period and the later environment. This linkage between fetal and adult development is called "programming" (Gluckman, Hanson, et al., 2005; Gluckman, Cutfield, et al., 2005.).

Mismatch between the fetal environment and the later environment might help to explain why many immigrants become obese after migration to the United States. It is quite possible that this type of process plays a role in Claudia Salvatierra's obesity. Claudia's early development occurred in a climate of scarce resources, and in her adulthood she relocated to the United States, where finances were tight, but food, especially calorie-dense foods, was in greater abundance. The mismatch concept might also suggest that societies could face further health problems in the future as nutritional intake in childhood and adulthood rises rapidly in many societies. Research indicates that several intrauterine factors besides maternal nutrition may inhibit fetal growth and serve as long-term risk, factors such as infection, season of birth, and maternal smoking during pregnancy (Gluckman, Hanson, Morton, & Pinal, 2005; Moore & Davies, 2005). If we assume that a healthy citizenry increases the chances of a strong and viable society, these findings suggest that it is in the best interest of societies to attend to the health of women in the reproductive years (Eriksson, 2005).

Recent brain imaging research is beginning to clarify another very important biopsychosocial risk process (see Exhibit 11.8). Chronic stress, traumatic stress, malnutrition, and inadequate social nurturance or stimulation can impair CNS development and functioning. Different neurobiological mechanisms have been identified as risk for different challenges of living, and individual chapters of this book can be consulted for greater detail about the specific mechanisms involved with specific challenges of living. Animal studies indicate that the development of CNS regulatory systems requires attachment to dependable and nurturing caregivers. Inadequate CNS organization often leads to poor impulse control and problems with emotional regulation, common psychological risk factors for a number of challenges of living. Attachment happens in the context of social relationships. The quality of attachment has an effect on CNS functioning, which has an effect on psychological functioning and also on future interpersonal relationships. Reciprocally, the ongoing quality of interpersonal relationships will have an effect on CNS functions. To add to the complexity, biomedical researchers are noting an increasing inability to separate mind from body.

Social relationships are an important part of the chains of risk discussed above. Likewise, social relationships are an important source of protection. Strong attachments to

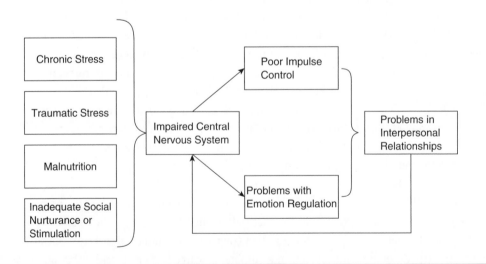

Exhibit 11.8   Possible Mechanism of Risk as Evidenced in Epidemiological Research

family, peers, school, and community, and strong social support systems, are protective in the face of adversity. This persistent finding has implications for the development of social work prevention as well as remedial interventions. There is good longitudinal evidence that supportive relationships, even in adulthood, can mediate against early deprivation and trauma (Valliant, 2002; Werner & Smith, 2001). There is also increasing evidence that spirituality and religion can serve as protection under conditions of adversity. We are just beginning to understand the mechanisms by which protection happens. We are also learning that the brain remains more plastic throughout the life course than we once thought. It will be important for social workers to keep abreast of research that examines the possibilities of using biological, psychological, social, and spiritual interventions not only for prevention but also for healing the brain and the rest of the body.

We would be remiss, however, if we did not point out that the above biopsychosocial-spiritual processes occur in specific economic and political contexts. Resource allocation is shaped by the arrangements in the economic and political institutions. Throughout the book, we have provided evidence that social policies can prevent some of the chronic environmental stressors that play such an important role in the challenges of living discussed in this book. Governmental safety nets to support vulnerable families at key life transitions have been found to reduce the ill effects of deprivation and trauma on health (Bartley, Blane, & Montgomery, 1997).

Consequences

We have reviewed the common risk and protective factors identified in the literatures on the eight exemplar challenges of living. The discussion in this book has demonstrated that just as these eight challenges of living have antecedents, they also serve as important public health problems themselves, with serious consequences for individuals, families, communities, and societies. Indeed, most of the eight challenges of living serve as risk for at least one other challenge of living and sometimes, as in the case of financial impoverishment and child maltreatment, for most of the other challenges of living. The chapters in this book demonstrate a tendency for these challenges to cluster in an unfortunate cumulative chain of risk and perhaps to interact synergistically at times to produce severe outcomes. It is also the case, as suggested throughout the book, that the relationships between conditions are often reciprocal, and it can be difficult to note what is antecedent and what is consequence. For example, poverty puts one at risk for family and community violence and a variety of mental and physical health problems. Reciprocally, violence and ill health undermine the economic well-being of families, communities, and even societies.

Looking across the challenges of living, several common consequences can be identified. There are economic costs, including health care costs, public safety costs, social welfare costs, educational costs, and costs of lost labor productivity. Each of the eight challenges of living has been found to contribute to mental and/or physical health problems. A number of them contribute to academic problems and work-related problems.

The social costs come primarily in the form of disrupted interpersonal relationships, whether it be parent-child relationships, peer relationships, school relationships, community relationships, or workplace relationships. Disrupted relationships eat at the fabric of families, communities, and societies and interfere with social cohesion at all levels. They also interfere with brain development and emotional regulation. Instability at one system level impacts functioning at other system levels.

Although there appear to be some general consequences for specific challenges of living, researchers have also found that the consequences can be influenced by a number of factors. Some factors that have been found to influence consequences include age at which the challenge is experienced, gender, whether one is victim or witness, the nature of relationships, the nature of the stressor, intensity of exposure, frequency of exposure, duration of exposure, accumulation of stressors, and coping strategies. For example, child maltreatment has a more serious impact on brain functioning if it occurs in infancy or early childhood rather than at a later age. Boys have been found to be more vulnerable to trauma and deprivation during early childhood, but girls are more vulnerable during early adolescence. Poverty during early childhood has been found to have more severe consequences than poverty during later childhood (Elder, 1974). Because of the differences in how women and men process alcohol and drugs in the body, the physical consequences of substance use are accelerated in women, through a process known as "telescoping." Males are more likely to develop externalizing symptoms and females to develop internalizing symptoms as a consequence of traumatic stress. Also, internalizing symptoms are more likely in children who witness community violence, and externalizing symptoms are more likely in children who are victimized. Greater intensity and more frequent and longer duration of exposure to environmental stressors increase the likelihood of negative consequences of child maltreatment and other traumas. It is also clear from the risk and resilience research that an accumulation of risk factors increases the likelihood of negative consequences (Werner & Smith, 2001).

Ways of Coping

As suggested above, the consequences of a particular challenge of living depend in part on the types of coping strategies used by individuals, families, and communities. Several coping strategies are employed across the various challenges of living, while others are employed to cope with specific challenges of living. Some coping strategies produce better outcomes than others, and indeed, some coping strategies may actually produce further risk.

Perhaps the most common line of research focuses on psychological coping strategies. There are several different typologies of psychological coping strategies, but one common typology is to dichotomize coping strategies as either avoidant coping or involved or action-oriented coping. *Avoidant coping* includes denial, social withdrawal, giving up, wishful thinking, disengagement through alcohol and other drugs or through other activities to take the mind off things, and passive tension reduction methods, such as emotional venting, crying, yelling, or excessive eating or sleeping. *Involved* coping strategies include positive reframing, problem solving, recognition of danger, seeking advice and information, seeking social support, and health-related strategies, including use of medical and social service professionals. This line of research consistently finds that involved coping is more effective than avoidant coping for adults but not always for children. Indeed, some types of avoidant coping, such as abuse of alcohol and other drugs, produce further risk.

It appears that David Loefeler and Estella Jackson used alcohol and other substances as avoidant coping. Claudia Salvatierra appears to be using eating in the same way. It is also possible that Junito Salvatierra and Kim Tran are using gang activity to take their minds off things at home. On the other hand, David Loefeler used involved coping when he sought social support, advice, and information from his cousin and when he sought professional assistance for his substance abuse and other mental health problems. Estella Jackson has recently begun to use professional assistance for substance abuse and HIV. Sondra Jackson appears to rely primarily on involved coping strategies such as problem solving and recognition of danger.

Another well-researched area is the role that social support networks can play in helping people cope with adversity. There is much evidence that asking for and receiving social support can be an effective coping strategy across the challenges of living. For children, the capacity to build a positive relationship with one supportive adult can be a source of resilience. Friends, family, and professionals can all be important sources of support under adverse conditions. Increasingly, people are reaching out to build support networks through use of the Internet, bringing technology and social support together, even in impoverished and remote areas.

Although it is not as well researched, political activism has been identified as an effective way to cope with community violence and may be an effective coping strategy for other challenges of living as well. There is evidence that impoverished mothers who participated in the welfare rights movement of the 1960s and 1970s drew strength and a sense of self-efficacy from their political involvement. They also seem to have benefited from the social networks that they established in their social movement activities (Piven & Cloward, 1977). It could be empowering for Sondra Jackson to become active with other community leaders to try to reverse the increasing disorganization in her neighborhood.

A number of adaptive cognitive coping strategies appear to be effectively used across the challenges of living. These include positive reappraisal, positive self-talk, appropriate externalization of blame, and problem solving.

There is much evidence that use of spiritual and religious coping can be very helpful across the board. However, recent research that dichotomizes religious/spiritual coping into positive and negative coping suggests that religious coping that focuses on a punishing God can be harmful rather than helpful under conditions of adversity. In addition, religious coping that focuses on the power of religion alone to heal might inhibit the use of beneficial health-related strategies such as use of medications and healthy lifestyle changes.

Social Justice Issues

Several highly related social justice issues were prominent across the challenges of living discussed in this book. Social inequality is the large umbrella under which the other issues fall. We are living in a time of growing economic inequality, both between regions of the world and within the United States. Some people are living in very adverse environments with multiple entangled risk factors, and other people are living in ever-increasingly enriched environments. Those at the bottom of the economic structure face a cluster of environmental risks, including overcrowding, poor nutrition, unsafe dwellings, unsafe neighborhoods, and poor school systems. They also face constant financial worries, overstimulation of the threatening kind, and understimulation of the nurturing kind. These adverse environments can contribute to biological vulnerability, including poor brain development and disorganized nervous systems, and health disparities. Problems in brain development can contribute to violence, mental health problems, relationship problems, and school and work problems. Accumulation of disadvantage can lead to impairment in every sphere of life and may compromise the nature of supportive relationships to which one has access.

Historical and current systems of racial oppression and discrimination further exacerbate the consequences of economic disadvantage. Historical systems of oppression have robbed African Americans, American Indians/Alaskan Natives, and some Latinos of opportunities to build intergenerational assets that protect against fluctuations in the economic system. Discrimination in housing, education, employment, and the criminal justice system constrain the developmental opportunities of many persons of color in the United States.

Other types of social stigma, besides racial and ethnic stigma, also can limit opportunities. Social stigma about substance abuse, obesity, HIV/AIDS, or mental health problems can place real constraints on opportunities for people living with these conditions. The adversity is compounded if people with these conditions also face racial or ethnic discrimination or discrimination based on sexual orientation. There is clear evidence that racial and ethnic bias plays a role in diagnosis of mental illness. Even though schizophrenia is known to occur in all ethnic groups at a similar rate, African Americans are 4 times as likely to be diagnosed with the disorder as whites, and Hispanics are 3 times as likely to receive this diagnosis as whites. There is evidence that this differential diagnosis across racial and ethnic groups is due in large part to such factors as different cultural norms about eye contact, differences in language used in relation to religious meaning and experiences, and real fears that are often misdiagnosed as "paranoid ideation" among racial and ethnic minority groups (Vedantam, 2005b). It is not clear if social stigma about mental health problems contributes to current policies that put stricter limits on mental health care than on physical health care, but these arrangements are harmful to people living with mental illness.

Gender inequality also plays a role in several of the challenges of living discussed in this book. Women are more likely than men to be impoverished, to be held accountable for the quality of care of children, whether or not they have the resources for that care, and to suffer from major depression. Females are more vulnerable to sexual abuse, and women are also at a disadvantage in negotiating safer sex because of their low status in society. On the other hand, males are more likely to be both victims and perpetrators of physical assault, to abuse substances, and to become infected with HIV.

Social justice issues related to both children and older adults showed up in several chapters of the book. It is imperative that societies recognize the vulnerability of children and accept responsibility for protecting them. It is in a society's best interest to do so, because the environments that children face will play a major role in their ability to contribute as adults to the stability of the society. We have read about the heavy costs to individual development and societal stability caused by early deprivation and mistreatment. Care and protection of children is also the just approach for societies to take, for the strong to protect the weak. We also saw evidence that the needs of both children and older adults can go unrecognized in the mental and physical health systems.

And finally, a focus on social justice calls attention to the need for health and social services to be offered in an ethnic-sensitive manner. Lack of sensitivity to ethnic cultures and folkways by majority service providers poses a major barrier to access to health and social services for persons of minority status. Cultural insensitivity can also result in faulty diagnosis and assessment and inappropriate intervention. In addition to developing ethnic-sensitive assessments and intervention, social work scholars should help to build a behavioral science base that represents diversity along a number of dimensions, including age, gender, race, culture, ability, social class, and sexual orientation. At the moment, there are serious gaps in the scientific literature related to diversity. For example, UCLA researchers recently reviewed the best available studies of medications used to treat depression, bipolar disorder, schizophrenia, and attention deficit disorders and found far too little attention to ethnic and racial diversity. They found that no American Indians were included in the 9,327 patients who participated in clinical trials. Only two Hispanic Americans were included among the 3,980 patients involved in a trial of antidepressant medications (Vedantam, 2005a). Indeed, it was not until 1993 that the FDA required drug trials to include participants other than white males.

Practice Implications

In Chapter 2, we identified four interrelated elements that we think are the most important ingredients in the process of turning knowledge into social work practice: knowledge about the case, knowledge about the self, values and ethics, and general knowledge from the social and behavioral sciences. In subsequent chapters, we focused on the fourth element, general knowledge from the social and behavioral sciences. In the process, we identified a number of effective social work interventions. In this final chapter, we want to emphasize again that the general knowledge about a particular challenge of living, as well as knowledge about effective interventions for preventing or ameliorating that challenge of living, must be integrated with the other three elements: knowledge about the case, knowledge about the self, and values and ethics.

Throughout the book, we have noted that effective practice begins with a comprehensive multidimensional assessment of the situation (knowledge about the case). We cannot assume that the situation we are encountering is just like, or even very similar to, the general knowledge about such situations. In fact, we want to identify what is unique to the situation. We want to know who is involved in the situation and how they are involved. We want to understand the nature of the relationships between different players. We want to understand the societal, cultural, and community contexts of the situation. We want to understand contextual constraints and contextual resources for bringing about change. We want to understand prior attempts to cope with the situation. And we also want to understand what preferences the client system has for intervention strategies.

As we build the professional relationship and work with the client system to assess the situation and to plan intervention, we will need to be aware of our own beliefs and perceptions that may lead us to overlook, discount, or misinterpret information (knowledge about the self). We want to maintain a creative stance that allows us to see possibilities. We must also recognize our own emotional states that get aroused by the situation and be able to use our emotions in ways that are helpful and avoid using them in ways that are harmful. And finally, we must reflect on our own social locations in terms of social identities such as race, ethnicity, gender, social class, sexual orientation, religion, ability/disability, family structure, and age and to imagine how those identities might facilitate or hinder our work in this particular situation.

We will also use the social work value base to guide relationship building, assessment, and intervention. We will want to be continuously reflective about how our work stacks up with the six core social work values of service, social justice, dignity and worth of the person, importance of human relationships, integrity, and competence. We will often need to use critical appraisal to resolve conflicts among competing values.

With knowledge of the self and guidance of the value base of the social work profession, social workers use general knowledge as a screen against which knowledge about the case is considered. The chapters of this book have identified a number of effective approaches to practice in relation to specific challenges of living. There are also some general themes about effective practice that cut across the literatures of the various challenges of living. When possible, social workers should make use of interventions that have been carefully evaluated. That means that we must constantly identify those interventions with the strongest empirical evidence of success. At the current time, those interventions have the following characteristics:

- Successful interventions make use of multidimensional assessment and intervention. We have provided clear evidence that challenges of living are multidetermined by risk and protective factors in multiple dimensions. Therefore, effective practice requires multidimensional assessments and multidimensional interventions. Interventions must address both individual and contextual factors and bridge biological and socioenvironmental conditions. Social workers must be able to help distressed communities as well as distressed individuals and families. They must also be capable advocates, prepared for legislative advocacy as well as case advocacy. They must be able to help individuals and families navigate a number of different systems.

- Successful interventions target empirically identified risk and protective factors. Social workers must draw on the best epidemiological research on risk and protection in relation to specific challenges of living to use or, if necessary, to develop interventions that reduce risk and enhance protection. Interventions must target both common and specific risk and protective factors, taking into consideration those factors that are most amenable to change.

- Successful interventions involve multiple parties working in a collaborative fashion. Social workers should build collaborative partnerships with individuals, families, communities, and with other professionals to pool resources and engage in focused action.

- Successful interventions are intense and long term in nature when the risk factors are tightly bundled. They tailor the intervention to the client system stage in the change process.

- Successful interventions are developmentally appropriate, targeting the risk factors that are particularly salient at different developmental periods.

- Successful interventions are culturally congruent.

We have demonstrated that each of the challenges of living addressed in this book is an important public health problem. We also think that a public health framework that identifies three levels of prevention—primary, secondary, and tertiary—is a helpful way to think about social work intervention with these challenges of living. *Primary prevention* efforts are universal in scope and are designed to keep people from developing public health problems such as child maltreatment and substance abuse. Some primary prevention programs that target the early postnatal environment have been found to be effective in reducing the occurrence of several different challenges of living. These include universal home visitation with families of newborns, parent education, and family strengthening programs that encourage healthy attachments. Public service announcements have also been effective in educating the public about methods of HIV transmission. *Secondary prevention* efforts are designed to reduce the prevalence of a public health problem through early detection and intervention. This includes such interventions as HIV testing for pregnant women, regular screening for major depression, respite care for families of children with special needs, and social development programs for children and youth who need help with emotional regulation and social skills. *Tertiary prevention* efforts attempt to minimize the severity and complications of the public health problem and where possible to facilitate recovery. This includes such interventions as helping to maintain treatment adherence, resource linking, cognitive behavioral therapy, family therapy, and experiential methods such as journal writing, art therapy, and guided imagery.

Implications for Further
Use of the Working Model

We set out to develop and demonstrate a working model for building knowledge about specific challenges of living faced by social workers. We identified questions that should guide the process of searching for and integrating the best possible scientific knowledge, and we utilized those questions to establish a knowledge base for eight challenges of living that are important public health problems in the United States and globally.

Having used the working model to examine eight challenges of living, we continue to think it has merit as a framework for giving structure to the process of transferring general knowledge about human behavior to specific practice situations. We believe that it serves well as a working model to develop understanding of any challenge of living social workers encounter. We did find, however, that financial impoverishment has not been studied often in terms of multidimensional risk and protection, and the model had to be used more flexibly with that challenge of living than with others. There may well be other challenges of living for which that would be the case. Further use of the model is needed to determine that.

As noted throughout the chapters of the book and earlier in this chapter, the division of risk and protective factors into biological, psychological, social, and spiritual dimensions is artificial, given the growing evidence that these dimensions are intricately interwoven. However, we do believe that by being very intentional in our efforts to locate research on risk and protective factors in each of these dimensions, we were led into a more multidisciplinary literature and were able to develop a fuller understanding of multidimensional risk and protection. In this regard, we note particularly the benefits of our very focused efforts to include both biological and spiritual risk and protection in our multidimensional understanding. Having said this, we want to emphasize that understanding is fragmented and incomplete until we put these dimensions together in an integrative fashion and understand their reciprocal relationships. It is the integration of risk and protective factors across dimensions that helps us understand the mechanisms and processes by which risk and protection happen.

Application of the working model to several different challenges of living gave us an opportunity to examine both common and specific risk and protective factors. Both types of information are important. We can think of *common* risk and protective factors as common pathways to a variety of problematic situations. Consequently, where they are amenable to change, they suggest the most powerful interventions, the ones that will probably have the biggest impact on individual, family, and community well-being. On the other hand, knowledge about specific risk and protective factors can be used to prevent major public health problems like HIV/AIDS, which is a totally preventable and very costly disease. There is a pressing need for more research on protective factors in adulthood that can modify the effects of early risk. There is recent evidence from longitudinal research that humans have the ability to bounce back from early deprivations and trauma, a capacity for "self-righting" over time, and the ability to develop "earned secure" attachments across the life course, but we currently know far too little about the mechanisms by which that happens (Valliant, 2002; Werner & Smith, 2001).

Froma Walsh (2003) has attempted to address the need for understanding of common protective factors. She has drawn from recent longitudinal research to describe the key processes by which families "bounce forward" from challenging situations. She proposes the following key processes in family resilience:

Belief systems: making meaning of adversity, maintaining positive outlook, and transcendence and spirituality

Organizational patterns: flexibility, connectedness, and social and economic resourcefulness

Communication/problem solving: clarity, open emotional expression, and collaborative problem solving

It is important to note that social workers typically practice within an agency context that circumscribes the social work role. This may help to contain the demanding job of understanding and intervening from the complex multidimensional approach we advocate. But it also can constrain our efforts and our effectiveness unless we retain a strong commitment to critical analysis, flexibility, and creativity.

Social workers can play a major role in preventing, ameliorating, and managing major public health problems like the ones discussed in this book. To be effective, we must draw on the best epidemiological research on risk and protection *and* the best practice effectiveness research that evaluates specific interventions with specific populations. But such knowledge alone will not guarantee success. We must also have a thorough multidimensional understanding of the specific situation we are encountering in practice, a good understanding of our own cognitive and emotional processes and how they can help and hinder our effectiveness in a specific practice situation, and a solid grounding in the values and ethics of our profession.

Glossary _____

Absolute poverty: A term used to describe poverty in economic terms. Measures of absolute poverty utilize formulas that take into account monetary assets only. It is not affected by changing norms and needs within a society. An example of this approach is Molly Orshansky's economy food plan.

Acquired immunodeficiency syndrome (AIDS): A syndrome that occurs when the HIV infection has severely damaged the immune system, making the person vulnerable to becoming very ill or dying from a wide range of diseases or infections that others can fight off.

Adipocytes: Cells within the body that store fat.

Adiponectin: A protein produced by fat cells that blocks production of blood glucose in the liver and increases muscle activity to make energy.

Adolescent-limited group of violent offenders: A large group of people who engage in aggressive and violent behavior only during adolescence.

Afrocentric perspective: A cultural perspective with principles that embrace a collectivist worldview and spiritual base. The Afrocentric perspective suggests that violation of these fundamental principles (e.g., spiritual alienation and social isolation) may help to explain a community's substance abuse behavior.

Amygdala: A brain structure that is responsible for assigning "emotional value" to an event. The amygdala is the filter that responds to threatening stimuli and puts the body on high alert if danger is assessed, charging the body with action. The amygdala, in some cases, may become overstimulated by innocuous stimuli that mimic an original traumatic event but yet which are not a current threat.

Antecedent factors: In research on risk and protection, those risk or protective factors that came before the troublesome situation.

Antiretroviral therapy (ART): Treatment with drugs that inhibit the ability of the human immunodeficiency virus (HIV) to multiply in the body.

Barebacking: The deliberate practice of unprotected anal intercourse (UAI), thought to play a role in the high rates of HIV among men who have sex with men.

Bariatric surgery: Surgery on the stomach and/or intestines to help the person with extreme obesity lose weight.

Best practices: Programs or activities considered exceptional models for others to follow. At the organizational or individual level, best practices typically have a solid body of experience or empirical support indicating that when implemented as intended, the approach reliably leads to a desired result.

Biosocial approach (community violence): A theoretical approach that suggests that violent behavior occurs when biological vulnerability interacts with social vulnerability.

Bipolar depression: A mood disorder that includes major depression interspersed with periods of mania or hyperactivity or agitation.

Body mass index (BMI): An index of a person's weight in relation to height with established cutoff points to designate normal, overweight, obese, and morbidly obese states.

Child and Family Services Reviews: Reviews of state child and family service programs to examine compliance and support overall system improvement in the areas of safety, permanency, and family and child well-being. Mandated by the 1994 Amendments to the Social Security Act (and outlined in the 2000 *Federal Register),* the process and products are administered by the Children's Bureau, which is part of the Administration for Children and Families within the U.S. Department of Health and Human Services.

Child fatality review boards: Locally administered boards that focus on systematic examination of all child deaths within a designated geographic area. They typically focus upon a systematic approach to understanding and documenting the causes and circumstances of each child death in the region. Additional goals often include enhanced cross-agency communication and development of policies and programs to improve child health and safety in order to prevent child fatalities.

Cholecystokinin: Hormone that signals that the meal is over and triggers the release of digestive enzymes from the gall bladder and pancreas.

Cognitive-behavioral therapy (CBT): A psychotherapeutic approach with known effectiveness for treating major depression; focuses on negative perceptions of the self, negative thoughts about the environment, and negative view of the future.

Cognitive damage: Significantly diminished capacity for judgment and reasoning due to impaired brain functioning. Among children, such damage detrimentally impacts the otherwise naturally expanding intellectual capacity to perceive, evaluate, understand, and communicate information.

Cognitive-neurobehavioral model of alcoholism: A model that suggests alcoholism may lead to heightened reactivity of the limbic system, which impairs the regulatory functioning of the prefrontal cortical structures that, ultimately, leads to problems in behavioral control.

Collective efficacy: The capacity of residents of a neighborhood to achieve social control over the environment and to engage in collective action for the common good; involves a working trust, a shared belief in the neighborhood's ability for action, and a shared willingness to intervene to gain social control.

Collectivist: Typically used to describe certain aspects of a culture's basic values and beliefs; refers to an emphasis on social connections, in particular the importance of prioritizing group rather than individual goals and needs and an emphasis on relationships among family and community members.

Colonialism: The practice of dominant and powerful nations to go beyond their boundaries utilizing military force to occupy and claim less dominant and powerful nations and to impose their culture, laws, and language upon the occupied nation through the use of settlers. The purpose of colonization is for the more powerful nation to gain control over the markets, resources, and labor within the colonized nation

Community violence (CV): Violence between unrelated individuals who may or may not know each other; takes place outside the home of the perpetrator.

Comorbidity: Substance use disorder that occurs simultaneously with another mental health condition (e.g., substance dependence and posttraumatic stress disorder).

Conditioning theories: Based on stimulus-response chains; suggest that drug-related behaviors are linked to specific cues that may trigger a physiological reaction that heightens craving response and ultimately drives the drug use behavior.

Coping: Efforts made by individuals, families, or other social systems to master the demands of stress, including the thoughts, feelings, and actions that constitute those efforts.

Cortisol: A steroid hormone that is secreted by the adrenal cortex as part of the body's response to stress; can become disturbed by chronic stress, possibly leading to depression.

Craving: An intense urge to drink or take drugs, often intensified in the presence of stimuli (i.e., triggers) that are associated with substance use.

Cue reactivity: Physiological and psychological reactions that are directly related to drug/alcohol cues (e.g., sights, sounds, smells, visual images related to substance use).

Cultural relativism: The position that beliefs or behaviors in a particular culture should not be judged by the standards of another culture.

Culture of honor: A concept used to explain violent behavior in some cultural groups; proposes that Scotch Irish immigrants brought a culture that prescribed violence as the appropriate reaction to disrespect and insult, the appropriate defense of manhood and reputation, to the southern region of the United States.

Culture of poverty: A term coined by Oscar Lewis to legitimize the unique culture and way of life of those who are impoverished. The term was popularized by the Moynihan report (Senator Daniel Patrick Moynihan's 1965 report on the black impoverished family). It has changed from its original meaning to one that looks at impoverished people as having cultural deficits.

Declarative memory: Memory that is accessible to verbal recall and is a cognitively conscious awareness. Declarative or "explicit" memories typically involve the hippocampus and are characterized by recalling of facts and a temporal ordering of events.

Defense mechanisms: Unconscious, automatic thought processes that enable a person to minimize perceived psychological threats or keep them out of awareness entirely.

Developmental domains: Areas of growth and development; the typical major domains examined when assessing a child's developmental progress are physical/motor, emotional/psychological, social, and cognitive.

Developmentally appropriate parenting: Parenting that reflects understanding of and responsiveness to the child's developmental stage-related needs and abilities in each developmental domain.

Differential association theory: A theory that focuses on the important role of deviant peers in modeling and reinforcing aggression and violence, particularly during adolescence.

Diffusion of innovation model: A model of HIV prevention, in which attention is paid to how to diffuse a health behavior innovation, such as condom use or clean needle use, throughout a social network.

Disease concept: The "medical model" of addiction that explains substance use disorders and drug addiction as a brain disease.

Disorders of extreme stress (DES): Disruption in affect regulation, attention, self-perception, interpersonal relationships, and meaning schemas that occur in people who have experienced chronic and intense traumatic events.

Dissociation: An unconscious psychological detachment from an event, situation, person, and so on, often operating as a primitive defensive response to a traumatic event. This symptom is often found in people who have PTSD and have undergone chronic traumatic exposure.

Dissociative disorder: A type of mental state characterized by a sudden, temporary change in the normal functions of consciousness, identity, and memory.

Distal environment: The environment beyond the family.

Dopamine: A neurotransmitter that plays a part in mood, cognition, and motor activity.

Double depression: The presence of dysthymia on which major depression is superimposed.

Dysthymic disorder: A mood disorder that is less severe than major depression and may be more chronic.

Earned Income Tax Credit (EITC): A tax program that provides the working poor with a tax credit or return at the end of the fiscal year. The credit/refund varies depending on income and family size.

Ecological model (Swinburn and Egger): The simultaneous consideration of three major influencing factors: biological (genes, hormones, age, gender, ethnicity, and drugs), behavioral (sedentary lifestyle and overconsumption of food), and environmental (physical, economic, political, and sociocultural).

Economy food plan: The least expensive way to buy an adequate amount of nutritionally sound food for a family; the basis of poverty measure used in the United States; poverty is calculated as 3 times the economy food plan.

Electroconvulsive therapy: Administration of a mild electrical current to the brain to treat a major depressive disorder that is unresponsive to other interventions.

Emotional intelligence: Ability to process information about emotions accurately and effectively and consequently to regulate emotions in an optimal manner.

Empirical research: A careful, purposeful, and systematic observation of events with the intent to note and record them in terms of attributes, to look for patterns in those events, and to make our methods and observations public.

Epidemiology: The study of the distribution of disease and health in a population; can identify causal factors of diseases, social problems, and troubling situations as well as identify the different patterns of occurrence across age, gender, socioeconomic status, cultural groups, geographic regions, and so on.

Expectancy theory: A psychological theory that proposes that individuals behave in ways because they expect their behavior will yield a certain result.

Externalizing symptoms: Responses to stressors that involve behaviors directed at the external world, such as aggression and delinquency.

Extreme poverty: A measure developed by the World Bank to count the number of poor worldwide. Extreme poverty refers to people who do not have regular access to food, shelter, clothing, health care, or education. The World Bank defines the extreme poor as having U.S. $1 per day per person or less in purchasing power. The measure for extreme poverty has been widely adopted by international agencies, including the United Nations.

Family preservation programs: Efforts to provide knowledge, resources, and other supports to help families stay intact. Government-sponsored family preservation programs are often crisis-oriented, home-based, intensive, and time-limited, with a focus on preventing imminent foster care placement or abandonment.

Family support programs: Community-based preventive services, including but not limited to child care and parenting support, designed to reduce stress and help families care for their children before crises occur.

Feminization of poverty: A term that refers to the trend starting in the 1970s of a disproportionate number of females (and their children) experiencing poverty as a result of gendered roles and discrimination within society.

Fetal origin hypothesis: The proposition that persons who experienced chronic malnutrition prior to a period of adequate nutrition are at greater risk of gaining weight as children.

Food insecurity: "The limited or uncertain ability to acquire acceptable foods in socially acceptable ways" (Townsend, Peerson, Love, Achterberg, & Murphy, 2001, p. 1739).

Gastric bypass: A surgical procedure to treat obesity that creates a pouch from the upper stomach that allows ingestion of only two to four tablespoons of food and is connected to the lower portion of the small intestine. The remaining portion of the stomach as well as up to 16 inches of the small intestine do not receive food but are reattached to the large intestine for drainage.

Ghrelin: A hunger hormone that stimulates appetite by signaling the hypothalamus in the brain that it is time to eat.

Globesity: The rising prevalence and incidence of obesity worldwide.

Habitus: Individual choices made within the confines of a societal structure defined by Pierre Bourdieu as a "set of dispositions developed through a personal history of self-reinforcing experiences of one's social location."

Health belief model (HBM): A model for understanding health-related behaviors; proposes that people will engage in health-related behaviors if they believe that a negative health condition can be avoided, expect that taking a recommended action will avoid a negative health condition, and believe that they can successfully engage in the recommended health behavior.

Heritability: Contribution that heredity makes to an observed behavior.

Highly active antiretroviral therapy (HAART): A combination of several antiretroviral drugs given together to slow the progression of the HIV infection.

Hippocampus: The brain structure that helps to contextualize memory in time and place and is involved in the conscious recall of facts and events associated with memory. The hippocampus serves to facilitate linguistic evaluation of experience. Some studies have found hippocampal impairment in people with PTSD.

Human capital theory: Individual skills, abilities, knowledge, and health that aid an individual in gaining wealth.

Human immunodeficiency virus (HIV): A special kind of virus, called a retrovirus, that stores its genetic information in RNA rather than DNA form but has the ability to replicate by converting to DNA form; the virus attacks the immune system and causes AIDS.

Hypervigilance: A state of intense preoccupation with surrounding stimuli and a heightened alertness to one's environment, such that focal attention to other aspects of one's surroundings is limited. This is a common symptom of people who have PTSD.

Implantable gastric stimulation (IGS): Also called **gastric pacing** to treat obesity, it is a minimally invasive surgical implantation of a battery-operated pacemaker-like device that stimulates the stomach to simulate fullness.

Incidence: The rate of new occurrences of a troubling situation within a given time period.

Individual or contact racism: Discrimination based on race expressed on the individual level that results in unequal treatment and social segregation.

Individualistic: Typically used to classify certain aspects of a culture's basic values and beliefs; refers to an emphasis on the importance of independence and attainment of individual goals, personal initiative, and achievement.

Information-processing theory: A sensory theory of cognition that sees information flowing from the external world through the senses to the nervous systems, where it is coded.

Institutional racism: Racism carried out and perpetuated by sociocultural institutions (e.g., schools, banks, governmental agencies) that serves to exclude people of color from equal access and opportunity, serving to maintain and or worsen their societal disadvantage.

Internalizing symptoms: Responses to stressors that involve internal symptoms such as withdrawal, somatic complaints, anxiety, or depression.

Interpersonal intelligence: Understanding other people.

Interpersonal neurobiology: An approach to understanding trauma that focuses on the relationship between brain structure development and functioning and interpersonal relationships.

Interpersonal therapy (IPT): A psychotherapeutic approach with known effectiveness for treating major depression; focuses on the relationship between depression and interpersonal relations.

Intrapersonal intelligence: Having an understanding of yourself.

Leptin: A naturally occurring protein produced by fat cells that signals the brain (hypothalamus) that there is sufficient fat in the body and therefore appetite decreases.

Life-course-persistent group of violent offenders: A small group of people who continually engage in a high level of aggressive and violent behavior across the life course and across social contexts.

Macro-level general strain theory (MST): A theory used to explain the differential levels of community violence in different neighborhoods. The major thesis is that the aggregate level of strain within a neighborhood affects the level of violence in the neighborhood.

Macrophages: Immune system cells that are found in fat tissue that provide a link between obesity and inflammation that underlie certain cancers and heart disease.

Major depressive disorder (MDD): Also termed **unipolar depression**, a mood or brain disorder characterized by persistent feelings of sadness or emptiness that must meet additional criteria established by the American Psychiatric Association.

Masked depression: Attributing the behaviors, thoughts, and mood of major depression to developmental characteristics of children and others.

Men on the down low (DL): Men who have unprotected sex with both men and women.

Metabolic syndrome: A combination of both obesity and coronary factors that place a person at higher risk of major health consequences that are life threatening.

Metacognition: Thinking about one's own thinking.

Minor physical anomalies (MPAs): Very minor structural deviations found in many areas of the body. Common examples are asymmetrical ears, curved fifth fingers, wide-set eyes, and large gap between the first and second toes. They indicate disruption in fetal development and are thought to be observable indicators of central nervous system dysfunction.

Moderate poverty: A measure developed by the World Bank to measure the number of poor worldwide. Moderate poverty refers to people who are just barely able to meet their basic needs of food, shelter, and clothing. The World Bank defines the moderately poor as having between U.S. $1 and $2 a day per person of purchasing power. The measure for moderate poverty has been widely adopted by international agencies, including the United Nations.

Neocolonialism: The practice of dominant and powerful nations to go beyond their boundaries utilizing international financial institutions such as the World Bank and the International Monetary Fund to exert influence over impoverished nations by imposing their culture, laws, and language upon the occupied nation through the use of financial incentives (loans) and disincentives. The purpose of neocolonialism is for the more powerful nation to gain control of the markets, resources, and labor within the less powerful nation.

Neuroimaging tools: Methods and techniques used to obtain images of the structure and functions of the nervous system, include magnetic resonance imaging (MRI), positron emission tomography (PET), single photon emission computed tomography (SPECT), and proton spectroscopy.

Neurotransmission: The process of transporting nerve signals from brain cell to brain cell.

Neurotransmitters: Chemicals that transport signals between nerve cells or between nerve cells and muscles.

Nondeclarative memory: Memory that is not accessible to verbal recall and is not in cognitively conscious awareness. Nondeclarative or "implicit" memories exist in sensory format, such as visual images or bodily sensations.

Norepinephrine: A neurotransmitter that is secreted by the adrenal glad that helps to regulate mood as well as impacting learning and memory.

Obesity: The point at which an adult's BMI is > 30.0, and/or WC > 40 inches for men, 35 inches for women, and/or WHR is > 1.0; and for children, weight falls in the > 97 percentile.

Obesogenic environment: Factors external to a person who is obese that create or foster obesity, such as lack of a variety of foods, prohibitive food costs, easier access to high-fat and salted foods, lack of safety to engage in outdoor activities, and other ecological contributing factors.

Orbitofrontal cortex: A brain structure that is responsible for linking the limbic system (emotional material) to the prefrontal cortex (cognitive capacities) and helps a person to self-regulate. This structure has been found to be influenced by interpersonal relationships and attachment processes.

Pandemic: An epidemic that is spread over an especially wide area.

Paradigm: A scientific discipline's general orientation or way of seeing its subject matter.

Perinatal complications: Complications of pregnancy and childbirth such as pregnancy complications, low birth weight, and delivery complications.

Posttraumatic stress disorder (PTSD): An anxiety disorder resulting from exposure to a life-threatening traumatic event characterized by reexperiencing symptomotology, intrusion of trauma-related stimuli, a numbing or restriction in affect, and hypervigilance.

Prefrontal cortex: The part of the frontal lobe of the brain responsible for motivation, attention, and sequencing of actions.

Prevalence: A rate of the number of existing cases (of a troubling situation) at a particular point in time divided by the total population studied.

Primary prevention: Efforts that are universal in scope and target the general population; applied to child abuse and neglect, such efforts can be thought of as attempting to prevent maltreatment from ever occurring.

Protective factors: Resources that decrease the probability of developing and maintaining problem conditions.

Proximal environment: The family environment.

Psychobiological attachment theory (PAT): Theory that proposes that the infant's nervous system requires attachment to a dependable and nurturing caregiver to develop normal regulatory systems and that disruptions in early attachment lead to disruptions in neurobiological regulatory systems.

Relapse prevention model: A substance abuse treatment model that helps clients to identify and successfully manage high-risk situations related to substance use, in order to prevent relapse.

Relative poverty: A term used to describe poverty in economic terms. Measures of relative poverty utilize formulas that include changing norms and needs within a society and are responsive to these changes.

Religion: A systematic set of beliefs, practices, and traditions observed within a particular social institution over time.

Residual social welfare programs: Social welfare programs that target citizens most in need of resources.

Resilience: Healthy development in the face of risk factors.

Resistin: A hormone produced by fat cells that is thought to regulate insulin and energy storage.

Restorative justice: An approach to public criminal justice policy that treats crimes as wrongs against individuals and communities, rather than against society, and emphasizes making amends to wronged parties.

Retributive justice: An approach to public criminal justice policy that focuses on paying one's "debt to society," matching the severity of the punishment to the seriousness of the offense; the type of justice on which criminal justice policy is based in the United States.

Risk factors: Events or situations that increase the probability (likelihood) of developing and maintaining problem conditions.

Safety net or **social safety net:** A set of governmental policies intended to prevent citizens from experiencing severe poverty. The social safety net often includes but is not limited to governmental health, income support, jobs, and educational programs.

Satiety: The inhibition of food consumption at the end of a meal and before the next meal.

Secondary prevention: Programs that target individuals or families identified as at heightened risk of maltreatment; this type of prevention work focuses on early identification in an attempt to limit the extent or severity of the maltreatment.

Self-efficacy: Personal beliefs in the ability to accomplish a goal; in the area of substance abuse, one's personal beliefs in being able to effectively resist using drugs.

Self-efficacy model of safer sex behavior: Model proposed by Albert Bandura; proposes that safer sex behaviors are not simply a result of knowledge or skills but of a process of integrating knowledge, expectancies, emotional states, social influences, and past experiences to develop a judgment about one's ability to master the challenges of sexual decision making and negotiating sexual relationships.

Self-regulation: The capacity to self-soothe and manage emotions under extreme stress conditions or high-risk situations.

Serotonin: A neurotransmitter that is a derivative of an amino acid that helps to regulate mood as well as motor activity, anxiety, and thought processes.

Sex trafficking: Movement of persons—typically girls and women—across borders for the purposes of sexually exploiting those persons. Diversity in form and definition exists; may include the recruitment, harboring, transportation, provision, or obtaining of a person for the purposes of any type of sexual exploitation.

Social capital: A network of relationships between people and various institutions that serves to financially advantage or disadvantage individuals.

Social exclusion: The political, economic, social, and cultural marginalization of a group of people based on a group characteristic such as class, race, or gender.

Social learning theory (community violence): A theoretical approach to community violence that suggests that some children develop a pattern of cognition that supports social aggression.

Social location: Where a person fits in a system of social identities such as race, ethnicity, gender, social class, sexual orientation/sexual preference, religion, ability/disability, and age.

Social network approach (to HIV transmission): An approach that is interested in how HIV is transmitted through sexual and drug networks and how to change the pattern of sexual and drug behavior in HIV high-risk networks.

Social welfare programs: Governmental policies and programs intended to care for citizens' needs. Policies and programs can range from health care to education. Nations structure their social welfare programs differently, based upon history, culture, and political will. Some nations favor universal social welfare programs, while others favor means-tested programs.

Socially constructed: An approach focusing upon how people socioculturally learn and label the meaning of self, others, and all phenomena; linked to the social constructionist theoretical perspective.

Somatization: Psychological material that becomes expressed as physical problems or symptomotology. This is a common symptom in people who have experienced extreme stress and/or have PTSD.

Spirituality: A personal search for meaning, purpose, connection, and morality.

Stomach banding: A surgical procedure typically done laparoscopically that places a band around the upper portion of the stomach, creating a small pouch that is then connected to the lower intestine.

Stress vulnerability model: A model that proposes that stress impacts the body's physiological response system (e.g., produces changes in stress hormones and brain structure function), which leads to drug craving. This model suggests that stress operates along a similar neural trajectory as direct exposure to the drug itself, and therefore stress in isolation from the drug can produce drug-like cravings and subsequent behavioral response to use.

Structural racism: Institutional policies that appear to be race neutral but which, in effect, work to maintain the status quo because of the inequalities created by historical institutional racism.

Substance abuse: Impairment in major life areas such as work, interpersonal relationships, educational, recreational, financial, health, and so on related to continued substance use and an inability to quit despite experiencing adverse consequences.

Substance dependence: Impairment in major life areas such as work, interpersonal relationships, educational, recreational, financial, health, and so on related to continued substance use and an inability to quit despite experiencing adverse consequences. Substance dependence is also marked by tolerance and withdrawal.

Syndemic: A set of linked health problems that interact synergistically.

Telescoping: The phenomenon that women develop more physical symptoms and problems from substance use, and in a shorter period of time, as compared to men.

Tertiary prevention: Programs that target families in which a problem like child maltreatment has already occurred or is occurring. This type of prevention generally focuses on stopping the maltreatment, facilitating recovery from its effects, and developing supports and strengths to prevent its return.

Theory: A system of concepts and hypotheses designed to explain and predict phenomena.

Theory of reasoned action: A theory of health-related behaviors that assumes that humans are usually rational, use information in a systematic way to solve problems, and consider the implications of their behavior before taking action; focuses on intentions rather than beliefs and attitudes.

Tolerance: A body's need for higher dosages of the drug to achieve the same effects, in a person who is substance dependent.

Traditional masculinity ideologies: A theory that suggests that traditional beliefs about appropriate masculine behavior can put men and their sexual partners at risk for sexually transmitted diseases such as HIV. These traditional beliefs are thought to encourage men to be sexually assertive, always ready to have sex, view sex primarily as pleasurable and recreational, perceive penetration as the goal of sex, control all aspects of sexual activity, and have multiple sex partners.

Transtheoretical model (TTM): A readiness to change model that explains movement toward behavioral change as progressing through various stages, to include precontemplation, contemplation, preparation, action, maintenance, and relapse.

Triple reuptake inhibitors (TRIs): A class of pharmacological agents currently under development that target serotonin, norepinephrine, and dopamine for the treatment of major depression.

Twelve-step program: A self-help program with wide membership that is based on sponsorship and a careful following of the guiding 12-step principles that undergird the program.

Type I trauma: Trauma that is characterized by one event.

Type II trauma: Trauma that is characterized by more than one event, such as ongoing or continuous child sexual abuse.

Unipolar depression: *See* **major depressive disorder**.

Universal social welfare programs: Social welfare programs that benefit all citizens regardless of income, age, gender, race, and so on. Examples include universal health care, universal child care, and universal free education.

Variable expressivity: Differences in the way a gene manifests itself in one person in comparison to another person who has the same gene.

Vertical transmission: Transmission of HIV from an HIV-infected mother to a fetus or infant.

Waist circumference (WC): The measure of a person's waist in either centimeters or inches.

Waist-to-hip ratio (WHR): The measure of the waist in relation to the measure of the hip circumference as a risk indicator of overweight or obesity when it is > 1.0.

Withdrawal: The body's physical reaction to stopping use of a drug when a person has become drug dependent.

References

Abadie, A. (2004). *Poverty, political freedom, and the roots of terrorism* (Working Paper No. 10859). Cambridge, MA: National Bureau of Economic Research.

Abe, J., Zane, N., & Chun, K. (1994). Differential responses to trauma: Migration-related discriminants of posttraumatic stress disorder among Southeast Asian refugees. *Journal of Community Psychology, 22,* 121–135.

Abel, E. (1998). Sexual risk behaviors in ship- and shore-based Navy women. *Military Medicine, 163,* 250–256.

Abel, E., Adams, E., & Stevenson, R. (1994). Self-esteem, problem solving, and sexual risk behavior among women with and without chlamydia. *Clinical Nursing Research, 3,* 353–370.

Abel, E., & Chambers, K. (2004). Factors that influence vulnerability to STDs and HIV/AIDS among Hispanic women. *Health Care for Women International, 25,* 761–780.

Abel, E., Hilton, P., & Miller, I. (1996). Sexual risk behavior among urban women of childbearing age: Implications for clinical practice. *Journal of the American Academy of Nurse Practitioners, 8,* 115–124.

Abel, E., Tak, S., & Gortner, E. (2003). Reliability and validity of motivation for sexual health. *Western Journal of Nursing Research, 25*(5), 548–560.

Abrams, R. (1994). The treatment that will not die: Electroconvulsive therapy. *Psychiatric Clinics of North America, 17*(3), 525–30.

Abrams, R. C., & Alexopoulos, G. S. (1994). Assessment of depression in dementia. *Alzheimer Disease and Associated Disorders, 8*(Suppl. 1), S227–S229.

Abreu, J., Goodyear, R., Campos, A., & Newcomb, M. (2000). Ethnic belonging and traditional masculinity ideology among African Americans, European Americans, and Latinos. *Psychology of Men and Masculinity, 1*(2), 75–86.

Abromovitz, M. (1996). *Regulating the lives of women: Social welfare policy from colonial times to the present.* Boston: South End Press.

Adams, K. B., Sanders, S., & Auth, E. A. (2004). Loneliness and depression in independent living retirement communities: Risk and resilience factors. *Aging and Mental Health, 8*(6), 475–485.

Aderinto, A. A. (2000). Social correlates and coping measures of street-children: A comparative study of street and non-street children in south-western Nigeria. *Child Abuse & Neglect, 24*(9), 1199–1213.

Adler, N. (2001). A consideration of multiple pathways from socioeconomic status to health. In J. Auerbach & B. Krimgold (Eds.), *Income, socioeconomic status, and health: Exploring the relationships* (pp. 56–66). Washington, DC: National Health Policy, Academy for Health Services Research and Health Policy.

Africa News Service. (2002, December 23). *Communities coping with HIV and AIDS.* Retrieved October 27, 2006, from http://archives.hst.org.za/af-aids/msg00674.html

Agathonos-Georgopoulou, H. (1992). Cross-cultural perspectives in child abuse and neglect. *Child Abuse Review, 1,* 80–88.

Agnew, R. (1992). Foundation for a general strain theory of crime and delinquency. *Criminology, 30,* 47–87.

Agnew, R. (1999). A general strain theory of community differences in crime rates. *Journal of Research in Crime and Delinquency, 36,* 123–155.

Ai, A. L., Peterson, C., & Huang, B. (2003). The effect of religious-spiritual coping on positive attitudes of adult Muslim refugees from Kosovo and Bosnia. *International Journal for the Psychology of Religion, 13,* 29–47.

Ainsworth, M., Beegle, K., & Koda, G. (2005). The impact of adult mortality and parental deaths on primary schooling in north-western Tanzania. *Journal of Development Studies, 41*(3), 412–440.

Aldwin, C. (2000). Stress, coping, and development: An integrative perspective. New York: Guilford Press.

Alexopoulos, G. S., Meyers, B. S., Young, R. C., Campbell, S., Silbersweig, D., & Charlson, M. (1997). "Vascular depression" hypothesis. *Archives of General Psychiatry, 54*(10), 915–922.

Allain, J., Anokwa, M., Casbard, A., Owusu-Ofori, S., & Dennis-Antwi, J. (2004). Sociology and behaviour of West African blood donors: The impact of religion on human immunodeficiency virus infection. *Vox Sanguinis, 87*(4), 233–240.

Alperin, D., & Richie, N. (1989). Community-based AIDS service organizations: Challenges and educational preparations. *Health & Social Work, 14*(3), 165–173.

Alter, C., & Egan, M. (1997). Logic modeling: A tool for teaching practice evaluation. *Journal of Social Work Education, 33*(1), 103–118.

Amaro, H. (1995). Love, sex, and power: Considering women's realities in HIV prevention. *American Psychologist, 50*(6), 437–447.

Amaya-Jackson, L., Reynolds, V., Murray, M. C., McCarthy, G., Nelson, A., Cherney, M. S., et al. (2003). Cognitive-behavioral treatment for pediatric posttraumatic stress disorder: Protocol and application in school and community settings. *Cognitive and Behavioral Practice, 10*(3), 204–213.

American Psychiatric Association. (2000). *Diagnostic and statistical manual of mental disorders, text revision* (4th ed.). Washington, DC: Author.

Anand, A., & Shekhar, A. (2003). Brain imaging studies in mood and anxiety disorders: Special emphasis on the amygdala. *Annals of the New York Academy of Science, 985,* 370–388.

Anderson, M., Kaufman, J., Simon, T., Barrios, L., Paulozzi, L., Ryan, G., et al. (2001). School-associated violent deaths in the United States, 1994–1999. *Journal of the American Medical Association, 286,* 2695–2702.

Anderson, R. (2000). Healthy People 2010: Steps in the right direction. *The Physician and Sports Medicine, 28*(10), 7–8.

Anderson, R. (2002). Deaths: Leading causes for 2000. *Monthly Vital Statistics Report* (Vol. 50, no. 16), 1–85. Hyattsville, MD: National Center for Health Statistics.

Anderson, T. (2004, November 24) Restorative justice places power in victims' hands. *Wisconsin Law Journal,* p. NA.

Applegate, J., & Shapiro, J. (2005). *Neurobiology for clinical social work.* New York: Norton.

Argyris, C., & Schön, D. (1974). *Theory in practice: Increasing professional effectiveness.* San Francisco: Jossey-Bass.

Aronowitz, S. (2003). Global capital and its opponents. In S. Aronowitz & H. Gautney (Eds.), *Implicating empire: Globalization & resistance in the 21st century world order* (pp. 179–195). New York: Basic Books.

Arseneault, L., Tremblay, R., Boulerice, B., Séguin, J., & Saucier, J. (2000). Minor physical anomalies and family adversity as risk factors for violent delinquency in adolescence. *American Journal of Psychiatry, 157,* 917–923.

Arterburn, D. E., Crane, P. K., & Sullivan, S. D. (2004). The coming epidemic of obesity in elderly Americans. *American Geriatric Society, 52*(11), 1907–1912.

Ashby, L. (1997). *Endangered children: Dependency, neglect, and abuse in American history.* New York: Twayne.

Aspy, C., Oman, R., Vesely, S., McLeroy, K., Rodine, S., & Marshall, L. (2004). Adolescent violence: The protective effects of youth assets. *Journal of Counseling and Development, 82*(3), 268–276.

Associated Press. (2006, March 2). *Surgeon general: Obesity epidemic will dwarf terrorism threat.* Retrieved June 14, 2006, from http://www.livescience.com/humanbiology/ap_06302_obesity.htm

Atzen, I., & Fishbein, M. (1977). Attitude-behavior relations: A theoretical analysis and review of empirical research. *Psychological Bulletin, 84,* 888–918.

Auerbach, D., Darrow, W., Jaffe, H., & Curran, J. (1984). Cluster of cases of the acquired immune deficiency syndrome: Patients linked by sexual contact. *American Journal of Medicine, 76,* 487–492.

Auerbach, J., & Krimgold, B. (2001). Improving health: It doesn't take a revolution. In J. Auerbach & B. Krimgold (Eds.), *Income, socioeconomic status, and health: Exploring the relationships* (pp. 1–11). Washington, DC: National Policy Association, Academy for Health Services Research and Health Policy.

Auslander, W., McMillen, J., Elze, D., Thompson, R., Jonson-Reid, M., & Stiffman, A. (2002). Mental health problems and sexual abuse among adolescents in foster care: Relationships to HIV risk behaviors and intentions. *AIDS and Behavior, 6*(4), 351–359.

Avants, S., Marcotte, D., Arnold, R., & Margolin, A. (2003). Spiritual beliefs, world assumptions, and HIV risk behavior among heroin and cocaine users. *Psychology of Addictive Behaviors, 17*(2), 159–162.

Avants, S., Warburton, L. A., & Margolin, A. (2000). The influence of coping and depression on abstinence from illicit drug use in methadone-maintained patients. *American Journal of Drug and Alcohol Abuse, 26*(3), 399–416.

AVERT. (2005). Funding the fight against HIV/AIDS. Retrieved on June 29, 2005, from http://www.avert.org/aidsmoney.htm

Ayala, G. X., Elder, J. P., Campbell, N. R., Slymen, D. J., Roy, N., Engelberg, M., et al. (2004). Correlates of body mass index and waist-to-hip ratio among Mexican women in the United States: Implications for intervention development. *Women's Health Issues, 14*(5), 155–164.

Bagley, C., Conklin, D., Isherwood, R., Pechiulis, D., & Watson, L. (1989). Attitudes of nurses toward obesity and obese patients. *Perception and Motor Skills, 68,* 954.

Bailey, F. (2003). Honor, class, and white southern violence: A historical perspective. In D. Hawkins (Ed.), *Violent crime: Assessing race and ethnic differences* (pp. 331–353). New York: Cambridge University Press.

Baker, R. (1992). Psychological consequences for tortured refugees seeking asylum and refugee status in Europe. In M. Basoglu (Ed.), *Torture and its consequences* (pp. 82–105). New York: Cambridge University Press.

Baker, T. B., Piper, M. E., McCarthy, D. E., Majeskie, M. R., & Fiore, M. C. (2004). Addiction motivation reformulated: An affective processing model of negative reinforcement. *Psychological Review, 111*(1), 33–51.

Bandura, A. (1977). *Social learning theory.* Englewood Cliffs, NJ: Prentice Hall.

Bandura, A. (1986). *Social foundations of thought and action: A social cognitive theory.* Englewood Cliffs, NJ: Prentice Hall.

Bandura, A. (1990). Perceived self-efficacy in the exercise of control over AIDS infection. *Evaluation and Program Planning, 13,* 9–17.

Bane, M. J., & Ellwood, D. T. (1994). *Welfare realities: From rhetoric to reform.* Cambridge, MA: Harvard University Press.

Banfield, E. C. (1990). *Unheavenly city revisited.* Long Grove, IL: Waveland Press.

Barefoot, J., Heitmann, B., Helms, M., Williams, R., Surwit, R., & Siegler, I. (1998). Symptoms of depression and changes in body weight from adolescence to mid-life. *International Journal of Obesity and Related Metabolic Disorders, 22,* 688–694.

Barker, D. J. (2004). Fetal origins of obesity. In G. A. Bray & C. Bouchard (Eds.), *Handbook of obesity: Etiology and pathophysiology* (2nd ed., pp. 109–133). New York: Marcel Dekker.

Barnett, O. W., Miller-Perrin, C. L., & Perrin, R. D. (1997). *Family violence across the lifespan: An introduction.* Thousand Oaks, CA: Sage.

Barney, L., Griffiths, K., Jorm, A., & Christensen, H. (2006). Stigma about depression and its impact on help-seeking intentions. *Australian and New Zealand Journal of Psychiatry, 40*(1), 51–54.

Bartholow, B., Doll, L., Joy, D., Douglas, J., Bolan, G., Harrison, J., et al. (1994). Emotional, behavioral, and HIV risks associated with sexual abuse among adult homosexual and bisexual men. *Child Abuse and Neglect, 18*(9), 747–761.

Bartley, M., Blane, D., & Montgomery, S. (1997). Health and the life course: Why safety nets matter. *British Medical Journal, 314*(7088), 1194–1196.

Bastian, L. A., West, N. A., Corcoran, C., & Munger, R. G. (2005). Number of children and the risk of obesity in older women. *Preventive Medicine, 40*(1), 99–104.

Basu, R., Brar, J. S., Chengappa, K. N., John, V., Parapally, H., Gersyhon, S., et al. (2004). The prevalence of the metabolic syndrome in patients with schizoaffective disorder-bipolar subtype. *Bipolar Disorders, 6*(4), 314–318.

Batavia, A. I., & Beaulaurier, R. L. (2001). The financial vulnerability of people with disabilities: Assessing poverty risks. *Journal of Sociology and Social Welfare, 28*(1), 139–162.

Baum, C., & Ford, W. (2004). The wage effects of obesity: A longitudinal study. *Health Economics, 13*(9), 885–899.

Bauman, L., Silver, E., & Stein, R. (2006). Cumulative social disadvantage and child health. *Pediatrics, 117*(4), 1321–1328.

Bays, H. E. (2004). Current and investigational antiobesity agents and obesity therapeutic treatment targets. *Obesity Research, 12*(8), 1197–1211.

Beals, J., Manson, S. M., Keane, E., & Dick, R. W. (1995). Factorial structure of the Center for Epidemiologic Studies Depression Scale among American Indian college students. *Psychological Assessment, 3,* 623–627.

Beauvais, F., & Oetting, E. R. (1999). Drug use, resilience, and the myth of the golden child. In M. D. Glantz & J. L. Johnson (Eds.), *Resilience and development* (pp. 101–107). New York: Plenum.

Beck, A. (1967). *Depression: Clinical, experimental and theoretical aspects.* Philadelphia: University of Pennsylvania Press.

Beck, A. (1976). *Cognitive therapy and emotional disorders.* New York: International Universities Press.

Beck, A. T., Steer, R. A., & Brown, G. K. (1996). *Manual for the Beck Depression Inventory* (2nd ed.). San Antonio, TX: Psychological Corporation.

Beck, J. (1995). *Cognitive therapy: Basics and beyond.* New York: Guilford Press.

Becker, G. (1994). *Human capital: A theoretical and empirical analysis, with special reference to education* (3rd ed.). Chicago: University of Chicago Press.

Becker, M. (1974). The health belief model and sick role behavior. *Health Education Monographs, 2,* 409–419.

Becker, M., & Joseph, J. (1988). AIDS and behavioral change to avoid risk: A review. *American Journal of Public Health, 78,* 384–410.

Beckett, K., & Sasson, T. (2000). *The politics of injustice: Crime and punishment in America.* Thousand Oaks, CA: Pine Forge Press.

Begun, A. (1993). Human behavior and the social environment: The vulnerability, risk, and resilience model. *Journal of Social Work Education, 29*(1), 26–35.

Behl, L. E., Crouch, J. L., May, P. F., Valente, A. L., & Conyngham, H. A. (2001). Ethnicity in child maltreatment research: A content analysis. *Child Maltreatment, 6,* 143–147.

Belgrave, F. Z., Chase-Vaughn, G., Gray, F., Addison, J. D., & Cherry, V. R. (2000). The effectiveness of a culture and gender specific intervention for increasing resiliency among African-American preadolescent females. *Journal of Black Psychology, 26,* 133–147.

Bell, D. (1953). Crime as an American way of life. *Antioch Review, 13,* 131–154.

Bell, L. (1997). Theoretical foundations for social justice education. In M. Adams, L. Bell, & P. Griffin (Eds.), *Teaching for diversity and social justice* (pp. 1–15). New York: Routledge.

Bell, P. A. (2005). Reanalysis and perspective in the heat-aggression debate. *Journal of Personality and Social Psychology, 89*(1), 71–73.

Bellamy, C. (2004). *The state of the world's children 2005.* New York: UNICEF.

Belle, D., & Doucet, J. (2003). Poverty, inequality, and discrimination as sources of depression among U.S. women. *Psychology of Women Quarterly, 27,* 101–113.

Belsky, J. (1980). Child maltreatment: An ecological integration. *American Psychologist, 35,* 320–335.

Belsky, J. (1984). The determinants of parenting: A process model. *Child Development, 55*(1), 83–96.

Bendick, M., Jr., Jackson, C., & Reinoso, V. (1994). Measuring employment discrimination through controlled experiments. *Review of Black Political Economy, 23,* 25–48.

Bennett, M. E. (2002). Interrelationship of substance abuse and mental health problems. In W. R. Miller & C. M. Weisner (Eds.), *Changing substance abuse through health and social systems* (pp. 113–141). New York: Plenum.

Bennett, M. E., McCrady, B. S., Johnson, V., & Pandina, R. J. (1999). Problem drinking from young adulthood to adulthood: Patterns, predictors and outcomes. *Journal of Studies on Alcohol, 60,* 605–614.

Benotsch, E., Kalichman, S., & Cage, M. (2002). Men who have met sex partners via the internet: Prevalence, predictors, and implications for HIV prevention. *Archives of Sexual Behavior, 31*(2), 177–183.

Bensley, L., Van Eenwyk, J., & Simmons, K. (2000). Self-reported childhood sexual and physical abuse and adult HIV-risk behaviors and heavy drinking. *American Journal of Preventive Medicine, 18*(2), 151–158.

Bentley, K. J. (Ed.). (2002). *Social work practice in mental health: Contemporary roles, tasks, and techniques.* Pacific Grove, CA: Brooks/Cole.

Bentley, K. J. (2005). Women, mental health, and the psychiatric enterprise: A review. *Health & Social Work, 30*(1), 56–63.

Bentley, K. J., & Collins, K. S. (2006). Psychopharmacological treatment for child and adolescent mental disorders. In C. Franklin, M. B. Harris, & P. Allen-Mears (Eds.), *School social work and mental health worker's training and resource manual* (pp. 15–30). New York: Oxford University Press.

Bentley, K. J., & Walsh, J. (2006). *The social worker and psychotropic medication: Toward effective collaboration with mental health clients, families, and providers* (3rd ed.). Pacific Grove, CA: Brooks/Cole.

Bentley, K. J., Walsh, J., & Farmer, R. L. (2005). Referring clients for psychiatric medication: Best practices for social workers. *Best Practices in Mental Health, 1*(1), 59–71.

Benton, D. (2004). Role of parents in the determination of the food preferences of children and the development of obesity. *International Journal of Obesity and Related Metabolic Disorders, 28*(7), 858–869.

Berlin, S., & Marsh, J. (1993). *Informing practice decisions.* New York: Macmillan.

Bernstein, J., Bernstein, E., Tassiopoulos, K., Heeran, T., Levenson, S., & Hingson, R. (2005). Brief motivational intervention at a clinic visit reduces cocaine and heroin use. *Drug and Alcohol Dependence, 77*, 49–59.

Berry-Edwards, J., & Richards, A. (2002). Relational teaching: A view of relational teaching in social work education. *Journal of Teaching in Social Work, 22*(1/2), 33–48.

Billingsley, A., & Giovannoni, J. M. (1972). *Children of the storm: Black children and American child welfare.* New York: Harcourt, Brace, Jovanovich.

Biorck, G. (1977). The essence of the clinician's art. *Acta Medica Scandinavica, 201*(3), 145–147.

Birch, L. L., & Fisher, J. O. (1998). Development of eating behaviors among children and adolescents. *Pediatrics, 101*(3), 539–549.

Birch, L. L., Johnson, S. L., & Fisher, J. A. (1995). Children's eating: The development of food acceptance patterns. *Young Children, 50,* 71–73.

Bird, S., Bogart, L., & Delahanty, D. (2004). Health-related correlates of perceived discrimination in HIV care. *AIDS Patient Care and STDs, 18*(1), 19–26.

Birmaher, B., Brent, D. A., & Benson, R. S. (1998). Summary of the practice parameters for the assessment and treatment of children and adolescents with depressive disorders. *Journal of the American Academy of Child and Adolescent Psychiatry, 37*(11), 1234–1238.

Birnbaum, H. G., Leong, S. A., & Greenberg, P. E., (2003). The economics of women and depression: An employer's perspective. *Journal of Affective Disorders, 74*(1), 15–22.

Bishaw, A., & Iceland, J. (2003, May). *Poverty: 1999* (Census Brief No. C2KBR-19). Washington, DC: U.S. Census Bureau.

Blazer, D. G. (2001). Spirituality, aging, and depression. In J. A. Thorson (Ed.), *Perspectives on spiritual well-being and aging* (pp. 161–169). Springfield, IL: Charles C. Thomas.

Bloom, M., Fischer, J., & Orme, J. (1999). *Evaluating practice: Guidelines for the accountable professional* (3rd ed.). Boston: Allyn & Bacon.

Blundell, J. E., & Stubbs, J. (2004). Diet composition and the control of food intake in humans. In G. A. Bray & C. Bouchard (Eds.), *Handbook of obesity: Etiology and pathophysiology* (2nd ed., pp. 427–460). New York: Marcel Dekker.

Boardman, J., & Robert, S. (2000). Neighborhood socioeconomic status and perceptions of self-efficacy. *Sociological Perspectives, 43*(1), 117–136.

Bogart, L., & Thorburn, S. (2005). Are HIV/AIDS conspiracy beliefs a barrier to HIV prevention among African Americans? *Journal of Acquired Immune Deficiency Syndrome, 38*(2), 213–218.

Bogen, D. L., Hanusa, B. H., & Whitaker, R. C. (2004). The effect of breast-feeding with and without formula use on the risk of obesity at 4 years of age. *Obesity Research, 12*(9), 1527–1535.

Bolen, R. M., & Lamb, L. J. (2004). Ambivalence of nonoffending guardians after child sexual abuse disclosure. *Journal of Interpersonal Violence, 19*(2), 185–211.

Bolland, J., Lian, B., & Formichella, C. (2005). The origins of hopelessness among inner-city African-American adolescents. *American Journal of Community Psychology, 36*(3/4), 293–305.

Boney-McCoy, S., & Finklehor, D. (1995). Psychosocial sequelae of violent victimization in a national youth sample. *Journal of Consulting and Clinical Psychology, 63*(5), 726–736.

Bor, R. (1997). Vancouver summaries: Disclosure. *AIDS Care, 9,* 49–52.

Boston, G. A. (2004). The hypothalamic path to obesity. *Pediatric Endocrinology Metabolism, 17*(4), 1289–1295.

Bosworth, J. B., Park, K., McQuoid, D. R., Hays, J., & Steffens, D. C. (2003). The impact of religious practice and religious coping on geriatric depression. *International Journal of Geriatric Psychiatry, 18*(10), 905–914.

Bouchard, C., Perusse, L., Rice, T., & Rao, D. C. (2004). Genetics of human obesity. In G. A. Bray & C. Bouchard (Eds.), *Handbook of obesity: Etiology and pathophysiology* (2nd ed., pp. 157–200). New York: Marcel Dekker.

Bowleg, L. (2004). Love, sex, and masculinity in sociocultural context: HIV concerns and condom use among African American men in heterosexual relationships. *Men and Masculinities, 7*(2), 166–186.

Bowleg, L., Belgrave, F., & Reisen, C. (2000). Gender roles, power strategies, and precautionary sexual self-efficacy: Implications for black and Latina women's HIV/AIDS protective behaviors. *Sex Roles: A Journal of Research, 42*(7/8), 613–635.

Braam, A., Beekman, A., Deeg, D., Smit, J. H., & Van Tilburg, W. (1998). Religiosity as a protective or prognostic factor of depression in later life: Results from a community survey in the Netherlands. *Acta Psychiatrica Scandinavica, 96,* 199–205.

Brach, J. S., VanSwearingen, J. M., FitzGerald, S. J., Storti, K. L., & Kriska, A. M. (2004). The relationship among physical activity, obesity, and physical function in community-dwelling older women. *Preventive Medicine, 39*(1), 74–80.

Bracher, M. (2000). Adolescent violence and identity vulnerability. *Journal for the Psychoanalysis of Culture & Society, 5*(2), 189–212.

Bradshaw, Y., Healey, J., & Smith, R. (2001). *Sociology for a new century.* Thousand Oaks, CA: Pine Forge Press.

Bray, G. A. (2004). Classification and evaluation of the overweight patient. In G. A. Bray & C. Bouchard (Eds.), *Handbook of obesity: Clinical applications* (2nd ed., pp. 1–32). New York: Marcel Dekker.

Bray, G. A., & Bouchard, C. (2004a). *Handbook of obesity: Clinical applications* (2nd ed.). New York: Marcel Dekker.

Bray, G. A., & Bouchard, C. (2004b). *Handbook of obesity: Etiology and pathophysiology* (2nd ed.). New York: Marcel Dekker.

Bray, J. H., Adams, G. A., Getz, J. G., & McQueen, A. (2003). Individuation, peers and adolescent alcohol use: A latent growth analysis. *Journal of Consulting and Clinical Psychology, 71,* 553–564.

Bremmer, M., Hoogendijk, W., Deeg, D., Schoevers, R., Schalk, B., & Beckman, A. (2006). Depression in older age is a risk factor for first ischemic cardiac events. *American Journal of Geriatric Psychiatry, 14*(6), 523–530.

Bremner, J. D. (2005). *Does stress damage the brain?* New York: Norton.

Bremner, J. D., Southwick, S. M., Johnson, D. R., Yehuda, R., & Charney, D. S. (1993). Childhood physical abuse and combat-related posttraumatic stress disorder in Vietnam veterans. *American Journal of Psychiatry, 150*(2), 235–239.

Brennan, P., Mednick, S., & Raine, A. (1997). Biosocial interactions and violence: A focus on perinatal factors. In A. Raine, P. Brennan, D. Farrington, & S. Mednick (Eds.), *Biosocial bases of violence* (pp. 163–174). New York: Plenum.

Brenner, M., & Homonoff, E. (2004). Zen and clinical social work: A spiritual approach to practice. *Families in Society, 85*(2), 261–269.

Breslau, N., Kessler, R. C., Chilcoat, H. D., Schultz, L. R., Davis, G. C., & Andreski, P. (1998). Trauma and posttraumatic stress disorder in the community. *Archives of General Psychiatry, 55,* 626–632.

Brewer, D. D., Catalano, R. F., Haggerty, K., Gainey, R. R., & Fleming, C. G. (1998). A meta-analysis of predictors of continued drug use during and after treatment for opiate addiction. *Addiction, 93*(1), 73–92.

Brewin, C. R. (2001). A cognitive neuroscience account of posttraumatic stress disorder and its treatment. *Behaviour Research and Therapy, 39,* 373–393.

Brewin, C. R. (2003). *Posttraumatic stress disorder.* New Haven, CT: Yale University Press.

Brewin, C. R., Andrews, B., & Valentine, J. (2000). Meta-analysis of risk factors for posttraumatic stress disorder in trauma-exposed adults. *Journal of Consulting and Clinical Psychology, 68,* 748–766.

Brewin, C. R., Dagleish, T., & Joseph, S. (1996). A dual representation theory of posttraumatic stress disorder. *Psychological Review, 103*(4), 670–686.

Bride, B., & Real, E. (2003). Project Assist: A modified therapeutic community for homeless women living with HIV/AIDS and chemical dependency. *Health & Social Work, 28*(2), 166–168.

Brien, T., Thombs, D., Mahoney, C., & Wallnau, L. (1994). Dimensions of self-efficacy among three distinct groups of condom users. *Journal of American College Health, 42,* 167–174.

Briggs, C., & Cutright, P. (1994). Structural and cultural determinants of child homicide: A cross-national analysis. *Violence and Victims, 9,* 3–16.

Brocato, J., & Wagner, E. F. (2003). Harm reduction: A social work practice model and social justice agenda. *Health & Social Work, 28*(2), 117–125.

Brockbank, A., McGill, I., & Beech, N. (2002). *Reflective learning in practice.* Burlington, VT: Gower.

Brodsky, A. E. (1999). "Making it": The components and process of resilience among urban, African-American, single mothers. *American Journal of Orthopsychiatry, 69*(2), 148–160.

Bronfenbrenner, U. (1977). Toward an experimental ecology of human development. *American Psychologist, 32,* 513– 531.

Bronfenbrenner, U. (1979). *The ecology of human development: Experiments by nature and design.* Cambridge, MA: Harvard University Press.

Brooks, R., Martin, J., Ortiz, D., & Veniegas, R. (2004). Perceived barriers to employment among persons living with HIV/AIDS. *AIDS Care, 16*(6), 756–766.

Brown, B., & Bzostek, S. (2003, August). Violence in the lives of children. *CrossCurrents.* Retrieved November 23, 2004, from http://www.childtrendsdatabank.org

Brown, D. (2006, May 31). Progress on AIDS is focus of assembly. *The Washington Post,* p. A10.

Brown, L., Lourie, K., Zlotnick, C., & Cohn, J. (2000). Impact of sexual abuse on the HIV-risk-related behavior of adolescents in intensive psychiatric treatment. *American Journal of Psychiatry, 157*(9), 1413–1415.

Brown, R. (1991). *No duty to retreat: Violence and values in American history and society.* New York: Oxford University Press.

Brown, S., Nesse, R. M., House, J. S., & Utz, R. L. (2004). Religion and emotional compensation: Results from a prospective study of widowhood. *Personality & Social Psychology Bulletin, 30*(9), 1165–1174.

Brunner, E. (1997). Stress and the biology of inequality. *British Medical Journal, 314*(7092), 1472–1476.

Bryne, N., Regan, C., & Livingston, G. (2006). Adherence to treatment in mood disorders. *Current Opinion in Psychiatry, 19*(1), 44–49.

Buchwald, D., Manson, S. M., Brenneman, D. L., Dinges, N. G., Keane, E. M., Beals, J., et al. (1995). Screening for depression among newly arrived Vietnamese refugees in primary care settings. *Western Journal of Medicine, 12*(4), 341–345.

Buchwald, H., & Williams, S. E. (2004). Bariatric surgery worldwide 2003. *Obesity Surgery, 14*(9), 1157–1164.

Bugental, D. B., & Happaney, K. (2004). Predicting infant maltreatment in low-income families: The interactive effects of maternal attributions and child status at birth. *Developmental Psychology, 40,* 234–243.

Burge, D., & Hammen, C. (1991). Maternal communication: Predictors of outcomes at follow-up in a sample of children at high and low risk for depression. *Journal of Abnormal Psychology, 100*(2), 174–180.

Burgess, A. W., Hartman, C. R., & Baker, T. (1995). Memory presentations of childhood sexual abuse. *Journal of Psychosocial Nursing, 33,* 9–16.

Burke, B. L., Arkowitz, H., & Menchola, M. (2003). The efficacy of motivational interviewing: A meta-analysis of controlled clinical trials. *Journal of Consulting and Clinical Psychology, 71,* 843–861.

Burke, L. (2003). The impact of maternal depression on familial relationships. *International Review of Psychiatry, 15*(3), 243–255.

Butler, K. (1996). The biology of fear. *Family Therapy Networker, 20,* 39–45.

Butterfield, F. (1995). *All God's children, the Bosket family and the American tradition of violence.* New York: Knopf.

Cachelin, F. M., Rebeck, R. M., Chung, G. H., & Pelayo, E. (2002). Does ethnicity influence body-size preference? A comparison of body image and body size. *Obesity Research, 10*(3), 158–166.

Cai, G., Cole, S. A., Bastarrachea-Sosa, R. A., Maccluer, J. W., Blangero, J., & Comuzzie, A. G. (2004). Quantitative trait locus determining dietary macronutrient intakes is located on human chromosome 2p22. *American Journal of Clinical Nutrition, 80*(5), 1410–1414.

Callicott, J. H., & Weinberger, D. R. (1999). Functional brain imagining: Future prospects for clinical practice. In S. Weissman & M. Sabshin (Eds.), *Psychiatry in the new millennium* (pp. 119–139). Washington, DC: American Psychiatric Press.

Cameron, A. (1996). Comparing amnesic and nonamnesic survivors of childhood sexual abuse: A longitudinal study. In K. Pezdek & W. P. Bank (Eds.), *The recovered memory/false memory debate* (pp. 41–68). New York: Academic Press.

Campbell, C., & Schwarz, D. (1996). Prevalence and impact of exposure to interpersonal violence among suburban and urban middle school students. *Pediatrics, 98*(3), 396–402.

Campion, J., Milagro, F., & Martinez, J. (2004). Genetic manipulation in nutrition, metabolism, and obesity research. *Nutrition Reviews, 62*(8), 321–330.

Carlson, V., Cicchetti, D., Barnett, D., & Braunwald, K. (1989). Disorganized/disoriented attachment relationships in maltreated infants. *Developmental Psychology, 25*(4), 525–531.

Carpenter, K. M., Hasin, D. S., Allison, D. B., & Faith, M. S. (2000). Relationships between obesity and DSM-IV major depressive disorder, suicide ideation, and suicide attempts: Results from a general population study. *American Journal of Public Health, 90*(2), 251–257.

Carrel, A. L., & Bernhardt, D. T. (2004). Exercise prescription for the prevention of obesity in adolescents. *Current Sports Medical Report, 3*(6), 330–336.

Carroll, K. M. (1996). Relapse prevention as a psychosocial treatment: A review of controlled clinical trials. *Experimental and Clinical Psychopharmacology, 4*, 46–54.

Caspi, A., McClay, J., Moffitt, T., Mill, J., Martin, J., Craig, I., et al. (2002). Role of genotype in the cycle of violence in maltreated children. *Science, 297*(5582), 851–854.

Caspi, A., Moffitt, T., Kim-Cohen, J., Morgan, J., Rutter, M., Taylor, A., et al. (2004). Maternal expressed emotion predicts children's antisocial behavior problems: Using monozygotic-twin differences to identify environmental effects on behavioral development. *Developmental Psychology, 40*(2), 149–161.

Catalano, R., & Hawkins, J. (1996). The social development model: A theory of antisocial behavior. In J. Hawkins (Ed.), *Delinquency and crime: Current theories* (pp. 149–197). New York: Cambridge University Press.

Centers for Disease Control and Prevention. (1982a, July 16). Update on acquired immune deficiency syndrome (AIDS) among patients with hemophilia A. *Morbidity and Mortality Weekly Report, 31*, 644.

Centers for Disease Control and Prevention. (1982b, December 10). Possible transfusion-associated acquired immune deficiency syndrome (AIDS): California. *Morbidity and Mortality Weekly Report, 31*, 652.

Center for Substance Abuse Treatment. (1998). *Addiction counseling competencies: The knowledge, skills, and attitudes of professional practice* (Technical Assistance Publication 21, DHHS Pub. No. SMA 98–3171). Rockville, MD: Author.

Centers for Disease Control and Prevention. (2003a). *HIV/AIDS surveillance report, 15.* Atlanta, GA: Author.

Centers for Disease Control and Prevention. (2003b). *Prevalence of overweight among children and adolescents: United States (1999–2000).* Retrieved April 20, 2005, from http://www.cdc.gov/nchs/products/pubs/pubd/hestats/overweight99.htm

Center for Science in the Public Interest. (2004). *School vending machines "dispensing junk."* Retrieved June 16, 2005, from http://www.cspinet.org/new/200405111.html

Centers for Disease Control and Prevention. (2004a). *Assault/homicide.* Retrieved December 20, 2004, from http://www.cdc.gov/nchs/fastats/homicide.htm

Centers for Disease Control and Prevention. (2004b). *Basic statistics.* Retrieved March 15, 2005, from http://www.cdc.gov/hiv/stats.htm

Centers for Disease Control and Prevention. (2004c). High-risk sexual behavior by HIV positive men who have sex with men: 16 sites, United States, 2000–2002. *Morbidity and Mortality Weekly Report, 53*(38), 891–894.

Centers for Disease Control and Prevention. (2004d). *HIV/AIDS Surveillance Report, 2003* (Vol. 15). Atlanta, GA: Author.

Centers for Disease Control and Prevention. (2004e). Youth risk behavior surveillance: United States, 2003. *Morbidity and Mortality Weekly Report, 53*(SS02), 1–96.

Centers for Disease Control and Prevention. (2005a). *HIV/AIDS among African Americans.* Retrieved January 26, 2005, from http://www.cdc.gov/hiv/pubs/facts/afam.htm

Centers for Disease Control and Prevention. (2005b). *HIV/AIDS among women.* Retrieved January 26, 2005, from http://www.cdc.gov/hiv/pubs/facts/women.htm

Centers for Disease Control and Prevention. (2005c). *HIV/AIDS update.* Retrieved February 20, 2005, from http://www.cdc.gov/hiv/stats.htm

Centers for Disease Control and Prevention. (2005d). *Young people at risk: HIV/AIDS among America's youth.* Retrieved January 26, 2005, from http://www.cdc.gov/hiv/pubs/facts/afam.htm

Centers for Disease Control and Prevention. (2006a). Cases of HIV infection and AIDS in the United States, 2004. *HIV/AIDS Surveillance Report* (Vol. 16). Atlanta, GA: Author.

Centers for Disease Control and Prevention. (2006b). Overweight and obesity: Contributing factors. Retrieved July 25, 2006, from http://www.cdc.gov/nccdphp/dnpa/obesity/contributing_factors.htm

Centers for Disease Control and Prevention. (2006c). *Youth violence: Fact sheet.* Retrieved June 4, 2006, from http://www.cdc.gov/ncipc/factsheets/yvfacts.htm

Centers for Disease Control and Prevention, National Center for Injury Prevention and Control. (2005). *Child maltreatment: Fact sheet.* Atlanta, GA: Author. Retrieved May 2, 2005, from http://www.cdc.gov/ncipc/factsheets/cmfacts.htm

Central Intelligence Agency. (2006). *The world factbook: Dominican Republic.* Retrieved June 9, 2006, from http://www.cia.gov/cia/publications/factbook/geos/dr.html

Cervantes, R. C., Salgado de Snyder, V. N., & Padilla, A. M. (1989). Posttraumatic stress in immigrants from Central America and Mexico. *Hospital & Community Psychiatry, 40,* 615–619.

Chadwick Center for Children and Families. (2004). *Closing the quality chasm in child abuse treatment: Identifying and disseminating best practices.* San Diego, CA: Author.

Chaffin, M., Wherry, J. N., & Dykman, R. (1997). School age children's coping with sexual abuse: Abuse stresses and symptoms associated with four coping strategies. *Child Abuse & Neglect, 21*(2), 227–240.

Chagnon, Y. C., Rankinen, T., Snyder, E. E., Weisnagel, S. J., Perusse, L., & Bouchard, C. (2003). The human obesity gene map: The 2002 update. *Obesity Research, 1,* 313–367.

Chambon, A. S., McGrath, S., Shapiro, B. Z., Abai, M., Dremetsikas, T., & Dudriak, S. (2001). From interpersonal links to webs of relations: Creating befriending relationships with survivors of torture and war. *Journal of Social Work Research, 2,* 157–171.

Chandawarkar, R. Y. (2006). Body contouring following massive weight loss resulting from bariatric surgery. *Advances in Psychosomatic Medicine, 2,* 61–72.

Chapel, T. (2004). Constructing and using logic models in program evaluation. In A. Roberts & K. Yeager (Eds.), *Evidence-based practice manual* (pp. 636–647). New York: Oxford University Press.

Charlesworth, L. W. (1997). *Welfare reform: A case study analysis of closed cases and initial community outcomes.* Doctoral dissertation, Virginia Commonwealth University.

Chassin, L., & Barrera, M. (1993). Substance use escalation and substance use restraint among adolescent children of alcoholics. *Psychology of Addictive Behaviors, 7,* 3–20.

Chassin, L., Pitts, S. C., DeLucia, C., & Todd, M. (1999). A longitudinal study of children of alcoholics: Predicting young adult substance use disorders, anxiety, and depression. *Journal of Abnormal Psychology, 108,* 106–119.

Chen, J. L., & Kennedy, C. (2005). Factors associated with obesity in Chinese-American children. *Pediatric Nursing, 31*(2), 110–115.

Chen, Y. M., Ho, S. C., Lam, S. S., & Chan, S. S. (2006). Validity of body mass index and waist circumference in the classification of obesity as compared to percent body fat in Chinese middle-aged women. *International Journal of Obesity, 30*(6), 918–925.

Chilcoat, H. D., & Breslau, N. (1998). Posttraumatic stress disorder and drug disorders: Testing causal pathways. *Archives of General Psychiatry, 55*(10), 913–917.

Children Data Bank. (n.d.). *Poverty rates for households with children (poverty line defined as 50 percent of the median equivalent disposable household income) of the world (countrywide).* Retrieved June 19, 2006, from http://www.childrendatabank.org/international/childpoverty/childpoverty1.html

Children's Defense Fund. (2005). *Defining poverty and why it matters to children.* Retrieved August 10, 2006, from http://www.childrensdefense.org

Children's Safety Network Economics & Data Analysis Resource Center. (2000). *State costs of violence perpetrated by youth.* Retrieved June 5, 2005, from http://www.edarc.org/pubs/tables/youth-viol.htm

Childress, A. R., Mozley, P. D., McElgin, W., Fitzgerald, J., Reivich, M., & O'Brien, C. P. (1999). Limbic activation during cue-induced cocaine craving. *American Journal of Psychiatry, 156,* 11–18.

Christiaensen, L., & Subbarao, K. (2005). Towards an understanding of household vulnerability in rural Kenya. *Journal of African Economies, 14*(4), 520–528.

Christopher, K., England, P., McLanahan, S., Ross, K., & Smeeding, T. (2000, January). *Gender inequality in poverty in affluent nations: The role of single motherhood and the state.* Retrieved July 7, 2005, from www.olin.wustl.edu/macarthur/working%20papers/wp-genderinequality.pdf

Christopher, K., England, P., Ross, K., Smeeding, T., & McLanahan, S. (2000). *Women's poverty relative to men's in affluent nations: Single motherhood and the state.* Retrieved May 20, 2005, from http://www.jcpr.org/org/research_summaries/v011_num1/html

Cicchetti, D., & Carlson, V. (Eds.). (1989). *Child maltreatment: Theory and research on the causes and consequences of child abuse and neglect.* New York: Cambridge University Press.

Cicchetti, D., & Rogosch, F. A. (1997). The role of self-organization in the promotion of resilience in maltreated children. *Development and Psychopathology, 9,* 799–817.

Cicchetti, D., Toth, S., & Lynch, M. (1995). Bowlby's dream comes full circle: The application of attachment theory to risk and psychopathology. In T. Ollendick & R. Prinz (Eds.), *Advances in clinical child psychology* (Vol. 17, pp. 1–75). New York: Plenum.

Claes, S. (2004). Corticotropin-releasing hormone (CRH) in psychiatry: From stress to psychopathology. *Annals of Medicine, 36*(1), 50–61.

Clarke, A. (1993). Social rearing effects on HPA axis activity over early development and in response to stress in young rhesus monkeys. *Developmental Psychobiology, 26,* 433–447.

Clearinghouse on International Developments in Child, Youth and Family Policies at Columbia University. (n.d.). *Family allowance.* Retrieved May 20, 2005, from http://www.childpolicyintl.org

Cloninger, C., Svrakic, D., & Svrakic, N. (1997). A multidimensional psychobiological model of violence. In A. Raine, P. Brennan, D. Farrington, & S. Mednick (Eds.), *Biosocial bases of violence* (pp. 39–54). New York: Plenum.

Cloward, R., & Ohlin, L. (1960). *Delinquency and opportunity.* New York: Free Press.

Cnaan, R. (1997). Recognizing the role of religious congregations and denominations in social service provision. In M. Reisch & E. Gambrill (Eds.), *Social work in the 21st century* (pp. 271–284). Thousand Oaks, CA: Pine Forge Press.

Cochran, S. D., Keenan, C., Schober, C., & Mays, V. M. (2000). Estimates of alcohol use and clinical treatment needs among homosexually active men and women in the U.S. population. *Journal of Consulting and Clinical Psychology, 68*(6), 1062–1071.

Cohen, S., & Wills, T. A. (1985). Stress, social support, and the buffering hypothesis. *Psychological Bulletin, 98,* 310–357.

Coleman, S., Kaplan, J., & Downing, R. (1986). Life cycle and loss: The spiritual vacuum of heroin addiction. *Family Process, 25,* 5–23.

Coles, R. (1990). *The spiritual life of children.* Boston: Houghton Mifflin.

Collins, R. L., & McNair, L. D. (2002). Minority women and alcohol use. *Alcohol Research & Health, 26*(4), 251–258.

Comas-Diaz, L., & Greene, B. (Eds.). (1995). *Women of color: Integrating ethnic and gender identities in psychotherapy.* New York: Guilford Press.

Conger, R. (2004, October 13). *Family and peer factors: Child factors.* Paper presented at the Preventing Violence State of the Science Conference, National Institutes of Health, Bethesda, MD.

Conte, H., Plutchnik, R., Picard, S., Galanter, M., & Jacoby, J. (1991). Sex differences in personality traits and coping styles of hospitalized alcoholics. *Journal of Studies on Alcohol, 52,* 26–32.

Cook, C. C. H. (2004). Addiction and spirituality. *Addiction, 99,* 539–551.

Cooper, M. (2000). The heartland's raw deal: How meatpacking is creating a new immigrant underclass. In M. Adams, W. J. Blumenfeld, R. Castaneda, H. W. Hackman, M. L. Peters, & X. Zuniga (Eds.), *Readings for diversity and social justice: An anthology on racism, anti-Semitism, sexism, heterosexism, ableism, and classism* (pp. 99–104). New York: Routledge.

Corcoran, K., & Fisher, J. (2000). *Measures for clinical practice: A sourcebook* (3rd ed.). New York: Free Press.

Corcoran, M., Danziger, S., & Tolman, R. (2004). Long term employment of African-American and white welfare recipients and the role of persistent health and mental health problems. *Women & Health, 39*(4), 21–40.

Costa, F. M., Jessor, R., & Turbin, M. S. (1999). Transition into adolescent problem drinking: The role of psychosocial risk and protective factors. *Journal of Studies on Alcohol, 60,* 480–490.

Cotter, A., & O'Sullivan, M. (2004). Update on managing HIV in pregnancy: It's imperative to identify more HIV-infected women earlier in pregnancy through HIV testing and to reduce mother-to-child transmission of the virus that causes AIDS. *Contemporary OB/GYN, 49*(11), 57–66.

Courtney, M., Needell, B., & Wulczyn, F. (2004). Unintended consequences of the push for accountability: The case of national child welfare performance standards. *Children & Youth Services Review, 26*(12), 1141–1154.

Courtney, M., & Skyles, A. (2003). Racial disproportionality in the child welfare system. *Children & Youth Services Review, 25*(5/6), 355–358.

Covington, J. (2003). The violent black male: Conceptions of race in criminological theories. In D. Hawkins (Ed.), *Violent crime: Assessing race and ethnic differences* (pp. 254–279). New York: Cambridge University Press.

Cox, C. (1982). An interaction model of client health behavior: Theoretical prescription for research. *Advances in Nursing Science, 5,* 41–56.

Craddock, N., & Forty, L. (2006). Genetics of affective (mood) disorders. *European Journal of Human Genetics, 14,* 660–668.

Crittenden, A. (2001). *The price of motherhood: Why the most important job in the world is still the least valued.* New York: Metropolitan Books.

Cross, T., & Miller, A. B. (2006). Ethnicity in child maltreatment research: A replication of Behl et al.'s content analysis. *Child Maltreatment, 11*(1), 16–26.

Cruess, D., Antoni, M., Schneiderman, N., Ironson, G., McCabe, P., Fernandez, J., et al. (2000). Cognitive-behavioral stress management increases free testosterone and decreases psychological distress in HIV-seropositive men. *Health Psychology, 19*(1), 12–20.

Cruess, S., Antoni, M., Kilbourn, K., Ironson, G., Klimas, N., Fletcher, M., et al. (2000). Optimism, distress, and immunologic status in HIV infected gay men following Hurricane Andrew. *International Journal of Behavior Medicine, 7,* 160–182.

Cunningham, R., Stiffman, A., Dore, P., & Earls, F. (1994). The association of physical and sexual abuse with HIV risk behaviors in adolescence and young adulthood: Implications for public health. *Child Abuse and Neglect, 18*(3), 233–245.

Curtis, W. J., & Nelson, C. A. (2003). Toward building a better brain: Neurobehavioral outcomes, mechanisms, and processes of environmental enrichment. In S. S. Luthar (Ed.), *Resilience and vulnerability* (pp. 463–488). Cambridge, England: Cambridge University Press.

Cusack, K., Falsetti, S., & De Arellano, M. (2002). Gender considerations in the psychometric assessment of PTSD. In R. Kimerling, P. Ouimette, & J. Wolfe (Eds.), *Gender & PTSD* (pp. 150–176). New York: Guilford Press.

Cutrona, C., Russell, D., Brown, P., Clark, L., Hessling, R., & Gardner, K. (2005). Neighborhood context, personality, and stressful life events as predictors of depression among African American women. *Journal of Abnormal Psychology, 114*(1), 3–15.

Dalgard, O., Dowrick, C., Lehtinen, V., Vazquez-Barquero, J., Casey, P., Wilkinson, G., et al. (2006). Negative life events, social support and gender difference in depression: A multinational community survey with data from the ODIN study. *Social Psychiatry and Psychiatric Epidemiology, 41*(6), 444–451.

Dalmida, S. G. (2006). Spirituality, mental health, physical health, and health-related quality of life among women with HIV/AIDS: Integrating spirituality into mental health care. *Issues in Mental Health Nursing, 27,* 185–198.

Dancy, B., & Berbaum, M. (2005). Condom use predictors for low-income African American women. *Western Journal of Nursing Research, 27*(1), 28–44.

Daro, D., & Donnelly, A. C. (2002). Child abuse prevention: Accomplishments and challenges. In J. E. B. Myers, L. Berliner, J. Briere, C. T. Hendrix, T. A. Reid, & C. A. Jenny (Eds.), *The APSAC Handbook on Child Maltreatment* (pp. 431–448). Thousand Oaks, CA: Sage.

D'Augelli, A. R., Grossman, A. H., Salter, N. P., Vasey, J. J., Starks, M. T., & Sinclair, K. O. (2005). Predicting the suicide attempts of lesbian, gay, and bisexual youth. *Suicide and Life Threatening Behavior, 35*(6), 646–660.

Davis, D. R., & DiNitto, D. M. (1996). Gender differences in social and psychological problems of substance abusers: A comparison to nonsubstance abusers. *Journal of Psychoactive Drugs, 28*(2), 135–145.

Davis, J. L. (2004). *Five ways pets can improve your health.* Retrieved May 18, 2005, from http://my.webmd.com/content/Article/81/97060.htm?printing=true2005

De Lange, N., Greyling, L., & Leslie, G. (2005). What do we know about the perception educators have of HIV/AIDS and its impact on the holistic development of adolescent learners? *International Journal of Adolescence & Youth, 12*(1/2), 29–48.

DelBello, M. P., & Strakowski, S. M. (2003). Understanding the problem of co-occurring mood and substance use disorders. In J. J. Westermeyer, R. D. Weiss, & D. M. Ziedonis (Eds.), *Integrated treatment for mood and substance use disorders* (pp. 17–41). Baltimore: Johns Hopkins University Press.

Demmer, C. (2004). Treatment adherence among clients in AIDS service organizations. *Journal of HIV/AIDS & Social Services, 2*(3), 33–47.

Dempsey, M., Overstreet, S., & Moely, B. (2000). "Approach" and "avoidance" coping and PTSD symptoms in inner-city youth. *Current Psychology, 19,* 28–45.

Depression Guideline Panel. (1993). Retrieved June 16, 2006, from http://www.allaboutdepression.com/res_08.html

Derezotes, D. (2000). Evaluation of yoga and meditation trainings with adolescent sex offenders. *Child and Adolescent Social Work Journal, 17*(2), 97–113.

Devlin, M. J., Yanovski, S. Z., & Wilson, G. T. (2000). Obesity: What mental health professionals need to know. *American Journal of Psychiatry, 157*(6), 854–866.

DeVries, M. W. (1996). Trauma in cultural perspective. In B. A. Van der Kolk, A. C. McFarlane, & L. Weisaeth (Eds.), *Traumatic stress* (pp. 398–413). New York: Guilford Press.

Deykin, E. Y., & Buka, S. L. (1997). Prevalence and risk factors for posttraumatic stress disorder among chemically dependent adolescents. *American Journal of Psychiatry, 154,* 752–757.

Dhiman, R. K., Duseja, A., & Chawla, Y. (2005). Asians need different criteria for defining overweight and obesity. *Archives of Internal Medicine, 165*(19), 2169–2175.

Diamond, G. S., Reis, B. F., Diamond, G. M., Sinqueland, L., & Isaacs, L. (2002). Attachment-based family therapy for depressed adolescents: A treatment development study. *Journal of the American Academy of Child and Adolescent Psychiatry, 41*(10), 1190–1197.

Diamond, J. (1999). *Guns, germs, and steel: The fates of human societies.* London: W. W. Norton.

Diaz, R. (1998). *Latino gay men and HIV: Culture, sexuality and risk behavior.* New York: Routledge.

DiClemente, C. C. (2003). *Addiction and change.* New York: Guilford Press.

DiClemente, R. (1991). Predictors of HIV-preventive sexual behavior in a high-risk adolescent population: The influence of perceived peer norms and sexual communication on incarcerated adolescents' consistent use of condoms. *Journal of Adolescent Health, 12,* 70–78.

Dietary Guidelines Advisory Committee. (2006). *2005 Dietary Guidelines Advisory Committee report.* Retrieved June 16, 2006, from http://www.health.gove/dietaryguidelines/dga2005/report/

Dietz, W. H. (1995). Does hunger cause obesity? *Pediatrics, 95,* 766–767.

DiIorio, C., Parsons, M., Lehr, S., Adame, D., & Carlone, J. (1992). Measurement of safe sexual behaviors among adolescents and young adults. *Nursing Research, 41,* 203–208.

DiLorenzo, P., Johnson, R., & Bussey, M. (2001). The role of spirituality in the recovery process. *Child Welfare, 80*(2), 257–273.

Dinan, B., McCall, G., & Gibson, D. (2004). Community violence and PTSD in selected South African townships. *Journal of Interpersonal Violence, 19*(6), 727–742.

Ding, L., Landon, B., Wilson, I., Wong, M., Shapiro, M., & Cleary, P. (2005). Predictors and consequences of negative physician attitudes toward HIV-infected injection drug users. *Archives of Internal Medicine, 165*(6), 618–623.

DiNitto, D. M. (2003). *Social welfare: Politics and public policy* (5th ed.). Boston: Allyn & Bacon.

Dirkzwager, A. J. E., Bramsen, I., & Van der Ploeg, H. M. (2005). Factors associated with posttraumatic stress among peacekeeping soldiers. *Anxiety, Stress, and Coping, 18,* 37–51.

Dixon, J. B., Dixon, M. E., & O'Brien, P. E. (2003). Depression in association with severe obesity. *Archives of Internal Medicine, 163*(17), 2058–2065.

Doi, Y., Roberts, R., Takeuchi, K., & Suzuki, S. (2001). Multiethnic comparison of adolescent major depression based on the DSM-IV criteria in a U.S.-Japan study. *Journal of the American Academy of Child and Adolescent Psychiatry, 40*(11), 1308–1315.

Dollar, D. (2000). *Governance and social justice in Caribbean states.* Washington, DC: Development Research Group, The World Bank.

Donnellan, B., Ge, X., & Wenk, E. (2000). Cognitive abilities in adolescent-limited and life-course-persistent criminal offenders. *Journal of Abnormal Psychology, 109*(3), 396–402.

Dougherty, M., James, W. H., Love, C. T., & Miller, W. R. (2002). Substance abuse among displaced and indigenous peoples. In W. R. Miller & C. M. Weisner (Eds.), *Changing substance abuse through health and social systems* (pp. 225–239). New York: Plenum.

Drake, B., & Zuravin, S. (1998). Bias in child maltreatment reporting: Revisiting the myth of classlessness. *American Journal of Orthopsychiatry, 68*(2), 295–304.

Driscoll, A., Sugland, B., Manlove, J., & Papillo, A. (2005). Community opportunity, perceptions of opportunity, and the odds of an adolescent birth. *Youth & Society, 37*(1), 33–61.

Dubini, A., Mannheimer, R., & Pancheri, P. (2001). Depression in the community: Results of the first Italian survey. *International Clinical Psychopharmacology, 16*(1), 49–53.

Dubowitz, H., & DePanfilis, D. (2000). *Handbook for child protection practice.* Thousand Oaks, CA: Sage.

Dubrow, N., & Garbarino, J. (1989). Living in a war zone: Mothers and young children in a public housing development. *Journal of Child Welfare, 68,* 3–20.

Dujon, D., & Withorn, A. (Eds.). (1996). *For crying out loud: Women's poverty in the United States.* Boston: South End Press.

Dulmus, C., Ely, G., & Wodarski, J. (2003). Children's psychological response to parental victimization: How do girls and boys differ? *Journal of Human Behavior in the Social Environment, 7*(3/4), 23–36.

Dunkle, K., Jewkes, R., Brown, H., Gray, G., McIntryre, J., & Harlow, S. (2004). Transactional sex among women in Soweto, South Africa: Prevalence, risk factors and association with HIV infection. *Social Science & Medicine, 59*(8), 1581–1592.

DuRant, R. H., Getts, A., Cadenhead, C., Emans, S. J., & Woods, E. R. (1995). Exposure to violence and victimization and depression, hopelessness and purpose in life among adolescents living in and around public housing. *Developmental and Behavioral Pediatrics, 16*(4), 233–237.

Dybicz, P. (2004). An inquiry into practice wisdom. *Families in Society, 85*(2), 197–203.

Ebbeling, C. S., Pawlak, D. B., & Ludwig, D. S. (2002). Childhood obesity: Public health crisis, common sense cure. *The Lancet, 360,* 473–482.

Edin, K., & Lein, L. (1997). *Making ends meet: How single mothers survive welfare and low-wage work.* New York: Russell Sage Foundation.

Edleson, J. L., Daro, D., & Pinderhughes, H. (2004). Finding a common agenda for preventing child maltreatment, youth violence, and domestic violence. *Journal of Interpersonal Violence, 19*(3), 279–281.

Edwards, V. J., Holden, G. W., & Felitti, V. J. (2003). Relationship between multiple forms of childhood maltreatment and adult mental health in community respondents: Results from the adverse childhood experiences study. *American Journal of Psychiatry, 160,* 1453–1460.

Egeland, B. (1997). Mediators of the effects of child maltreatment on developmental adaptation in adolescence. In D. Cicchetti & S. Toth (Eds.), *Rochester symposium on developmental psychopathology: Vol. 8. The effects of trauma on the developmental process* (pp. 403–434). Rochester, NY: University of Rochester Press.

Ehlers, A., Clark, D. M., Hackmann, A., McManus, F., & Fennell, M. (2005). Cognitive therapy for PTSD: Development and evaluation. *Behaviour Research and Therapy, 43,* 413–431.

Ehrenreich, B. (2001). *Nickel and dimed: On (not) getting by in America.* New York: Owl Books.

Ehrenreich, B., & Hochschild, A. R. (2002). *Global woman: Nannies, maids, and sex workers in the new economy.* New York: Metropolitan Books.

Eikelis, N., & Esler, M. (2005). The neurobiology of human obesity. *Experimental Physiology, 90*(5), 673–682.

Elder, G., Jr. (1974). *Children of the Great Depression.* Chicago: University of Chicago Press.

Eliadis, E. E. (2006). The role of social work in the childhood obesity epidemic. *Social Work, 51*(1), 86–88.

Elias, M. (2004, January 22). Antidepressants and suicide. *USA Today,* p. 7D.

Elkins, W. L., Cohen, D. A., Koralewicz, L. M., & Taylor, S. N. (2004). After school activities, overweight, and obesity among inner city youth. *Journal of Adolescence, 27*(2), 181–189.

Ellen, J. (2003). The next generation of HIV prevention for adolescent females in the United States: Linking behavioral and epidemiologic sciences to reduce incidence of HIV. *Journal of Urban Health: Bulletin of the New York Academy of Medicine, 80*(4), ii40–iii49.

Ellickson, P., Saner, H., & McGuigan, K. (1997). Profiles of violent youth: Substance use and other concurrent problems. *American Journal of Public Health, 87*(6), 985–991.

Elliott, D. (2004, October 14). *Commonalities among safe and effective interventions.* Paper presented at the Preventing Violence State of the Science Conference, National Institutes of Health, Bethesda, MD.

Emlet, C. A., & Poindexter, C. C. (2004). Unserved, unseen, and unheard: Integrating programs for HIV-infected and HIV-affected older adults. *Health & Social Work, 29*(2), 86–96.

Engstrom, D. W., & Okamura, A. (2004). A plague of our time: Torture, human rights, and social work. *Families in Society, 85*(3), 291–301.

Ericson, N. (2001). *Substance abuse: The nation's number one health problem.* Princeton, NJ: Robert Wood Johnson Foundation.

Eriksson, J. (2005). The fetal origins hypothesis—10 years on. *British Medical Journal, 330,* 1096–1097.

Ernst, C., Olson, A., Pinel, J., Lam, R., & Christie, B. (2006). Antidepressant effects of exercise: Evidence for an adult-neurogenesis hypothesis? *Journal of Psychiatry and Neuroscience, 31*(2), 84–92.

Ernst, J. S., Meyer, M., & DePanflis, D. (2004). Housing characteristics and adequacy of the physical care of children: An exploratory analysis. *Child Welfare, 83*(5), 437–452.

European Monitoring Centre for Drugs and Drug Addiction. (2003). *National prevalence estimates of problem drug use in the European Union, 1995–2000: Final Report CT.00.RTX.23.* Lisbon, Spain: Author.

Everson, G., Kelsberg, G., & Nashelsky, J. (2003). How effective is gastric bypass for weight loss? *Journal of Family Practice, 53*(11), 914–918.

Fabri, M. (2001). Reconstructing safety: Adjustments to the therapeutic frame in the treatment of survivors of political torture. *Professional Psychology: Research and Practice, 32,* 452–457.

Fabricatore, A. N., Crerand, C. E., Wadden, T. A., Sarwer, D. B., & Krasucki, J. L. (2006). How do mental health professionals evaluate candidates for bariatric surgery? Survey results. *Obesity Surgery, 16*(5), 567–573.

Fabricatore, A. N., Wadden, T. A., Sarwer, D. B., Crerand, C. E., Kuehnel, R. H., Lipschutz, P. E., et al. (2006). Self-reported eating behaviors of extremely obese persons seeking bariatric surgery: A factor analytic approach. *Obesity, 14*(2), 83S–89S.

Faith, M., Matz, P., & Jorge, M. (2002). Obesity-depression associations in the population. *Journal of Psychosomatic Research, 53*(4), 935–942.

Falicov, C. (2003). Immigrant family processes. In F. Walsh (Ed.), *Normal family processes: Growing diversity and complexity* (3rd ed., pp. 280–300). New York: Guilford Press.

Faller, K. C. (1999). *Maltreatment in early childhood: Tools for research-based intervention.* New York: Haworth Maltreatment & Trauma Press.

Fallot, R. D., & Heckman, J. P. (2005). Religious/spiritual coping among women trauma survivors with mental health and substance use disorders. *Journal of Behavioral Health Services & Research, 32*(2), 215–226.

Farrington, D. (1987). Implications of biological findings for criminological research. In S. Mednick, T. Moffitt, & A. Stack (Eds.), *The causes of crime: New biological approaches* (pp. 42–64). Cambridge, England: Cambridge University Press.

Farrington, D. (1989). Early predictors of adolescent aggression and adult violence. *Violence and Victims, 4,* 79–100.

Farrington, D. (1997). The relationship between low resting heart rate and violence. In A. Raine, P. Brennan, D. Farrington, & S. Mednick (Eds.), *Biosocial bases of violence* (pp. 89–105). New York: Plenum.

Farwell, N., & Cole, J. B. (2002). Community as a context of healing. *International Journal of Mental Health, 30*(4), 19–41.

Fass, P. S., & Mason, M. A. (Eds.). (2000). *Childhood in America.* New York: New York University Press.

Fava, M. (2000). Weight gain and antidepressants. *Journal of Clinical Psychiatry, 61*(Suppl. 11), 37–41.

Fawzi, W., Msamanga, G., Spiegelman, D., Wei, R., Kapiga, S., Villamor, E., et al. (2004). A randomized trial of multivitamin supplements and HIV disease progression and mortality. *New England Journal of Medicine, 351*(1), 23–32.

FDA seeks warning for depression drugs. (2004, March 22). *Richmond Times Dispatch,* p. A01.

Feagin, J. R. (2000). *Racist America: Roots, current realities and future reparations.* New York: Routledge.

Fears, D. (2005, February 7). U.S. HIV cases soaring among Black women. *The Washington Post,* p. A01.

Federal Interagency Forum on Child and Family Statistics. (2003). *America's children: Key national indicators of well-being 2003.* Retrieved April 20, 2005, from http://www.nichd.nih.gov/publications/pubs/childstats/report2003.pdf

Feldman, M. (2003). The challenges of working with perinatally infected adolescents: Clinical and concrete possibilities. In R. Willinger & A. Rice (Eds.), *A history of AIDS social work in hospitals: A daring response to an epidemic* (pp. 277–286). New York: Haworth Press.

Felitti, V. J., Anda, R. F., Nordenberg D., Williamson D. F., Spitz, A. M., Edwards, V., et al. (1998). Relationship of childhood abuse and household dysfunction to many of the leading causes of death in adults: The Adverse Childhood Experiences (ACE) Study. *American Journal of Preventive Medicine, 14,* 245–258.

Fergusson, D., Horwood, L., & Beautrais, A. L. (1999). Is sexual orientation related to mental health problems and suicidality in young people? *Archives of General Psychiatry, 56*(10), 876–880.

Fergusson, D., Horwood, L., & Lynskey, M. (1996). Childhood sexual abuse and psychiatric disorder in young adulthood: Psychiatric outcomes of childhood sexual abuse. *Journal of the American Academy of Child and Adolescent Psychiatry, 35,* 1365–1374.

Fergusson, D., Horwood, L., & Nagin, D. (2000). Offending trajectories in a New Zealand birth cohort. *Criminology, 38*(2), 525–551.

Fernandez, J. R., Redden, D. T., Pietrobelli, A., & Allison, D. B. (2004). Waist circumference percentiles in nationally representative samples of African-American, European-American, and Mexican-American children and adolescents. *Journal of Pediatrics, 145*(4), 439–444.

Ferraro, V. (2003). *Globalizing weakness: Is global poverty a threat to the interests of states?* Retrieved May 27, 2005, from http://www.wilsoncenter.org/index.cfm?fuseaction=news.ietm&news_id=34999

Ferris, C., & DeVries, G. (1997). Ethological models for examining the neurobiology of aggressive and affiliative behaviors. In D. Stoff, J. Breiling, & J. Maser (Eds.), *Handbook for antisocial behavior* (pp. 255–268). New York: Wiley.

Field, T., Hernandez-Reif, M., Diego, M., Schanberg, S., & Kuhn, C. (2005). Cortisol decreases and serotonin and dopamine increase following massage therapy. *International Journal of Neuroscience, 115*(10), 1397–1413.

Field, T., & Winterfeld, A. P. (2000/2003). *Tough problems, tough choices: Guidelines for needs-based service planning in child welfare.* Englewood, CO: Casey Family Programs & Annie E. Casey Foundation.

Fields, S. (2004). The fat of the land: Do agricultural subsidies foster poor health? *Environmental Health Perspective, 112*(14), A820–A823.

Finkelhor, D. (1984). *Child sexual abuse: New theory and research.* New York: Free Press.

Finkelhor, D. (1994). Current information on the scope and nature of child sexual abuse. *The Future of Children, 4*(2), 31–53.

Finkelstein, E. A., Ruhm C. J., & Kosa, K. M. (2004). Economic causes and consequences of obesity. *Annual Review of Public Health, 26*(3), 239–257.

First, J., & Cardenas, J. (1986). A minority view on testing. *Educational Measurement: Issues and Practice, 5,* 6–11.

Fishbein, D., Hyde, C., Coe, B., & Paschall, M. J. (2004). Neurocognitive and physiological prerequisites for prevention of adolescent drug abuse. *Journal of Primary Prevention, 24*(4), 471–495.

Fisher, G. M. (1997, Winter). The development and history of the U.S. poverty thresholds: A brief overview. *Newsletter of the Government Statistics Section and the Social Statistics Section of the American Statistical Association,* pp. 6–7.

Fisher, J., & Fisher, W. (1992). Changing AIDS-risk behaviour. *Psychological Bulletin, 111*(3), 455–474.

Fitchett, G., Rybarczyk, B. D., DeMarco, G. A., & Nicholas, J. J. (1999). The role of religion in medical rehabilitation outcomes: A longitudinal study. *Rehabilitation Psychology, 44*(4), 333–353.

Fitzpatrick, K. M. (1993). Exposure to violence and presence of depression among low income, African-American youth. *Journal of Consulting and Clinical Psychology, 61*(3), 528–531.

Fitzpatrick, K. M., & Boldizar, J. P. (1993). The prevalence and consequences of exposure to violence among African-American youth. *Journal of the American Academy of Child & Adolescent Psychiatry, 32*(2), 424–430.

Flegal, K. M., Troiano, R. P., Pamuk, E. R., Kuczmarski, R. J., & Campbell, S. M. (1995). The influence of smoking cessation on the prevalence of overweight in the United States. *New England Journal of Medicine, 333,* 1165–1170.

Fleishman, J., Sherbourne, C., Cleary, P., Wu, A., Crystal, S., & Hays, R. (2003). Patterns of coping among persons with HIV infection: Configurations, correlates, and change. *American Journal of Community Psychology, 32*(1/2), 187–204.

Foa, E. B., Keane, T. M., & Friedman, M. J. (Eds.). (2000). *Effective treatments for PTSD: Practice guidelines from the International Society for Traumatic Stress Studies.* New York: Guilford Press.

Foa, E. B., & Kozak, M. J. (1986). Emotional processing of fear: Exposure to corrective information. *Psychological Bulletin, 99,* 20–35.

Foa, E. B., Molnar, C., & Cashman, L. (1995). Change in rape narratives during exposure therapy for PTSD. *Journal of Traumatic Stress, 8*(4), 675–690.

Follette, V. M., Polusny, M. M., & Milbeck, K. (1994). Mental health and law enforcement professionals: Trauma history, psychological symptoms, and impact providing services to child sexual abuse survivors. *Professional Psychology: Research and Practice, 25,* 275–282.

Food and Drug Administration. (2006). *Questions and answers about trans fat nutrition labeling.* Retrieved June 16, 2006, from http://www.cfsan.fda.gov/~dms/qatrans2.html

Ford, D. E., & Kamerow, D. B. (1989). Epidemiologic study of sleep disturbance and psychiatric disorders: An opportunity for prevention. *Journal of the American Medical Association, 262*(11), 1479–1484.

Forehand, R., & Jones, D. J. (2003). Neighborhood violence and coparent conflict: Interactive influence on child psychosocial adjustment. *Journal of Abnormal Child Psychology, 31*(6), 591–604.

Fortune, A., & Reid, W. (1999). *Research in social work* (3rd ed.). New York: Columbia University Press.

Foster, J. D., Kuperminc, G. P., & Price, A. W. (2004). Gender differences in posttraumatic stress and related symptoms among inner-city minority youth exposed to community violence. *Journal of Youth and Adolescence, 33*(1), 59–69.

Fram, M. S. (2004). Research for progressive change: Bourdieu and social work. *Social Service Review, 78*(4), 553–576.

Francis, D. D., & Meaney, M. J. (2002). Maternal care and the development of stress responses. In J. T. Cacioppo, G. G. Berntson, R. Adolphs, C. S. Carter, R. J. Davidson, M. K. McClintock, et al. (Eds.), *Foundations in social neuroscience* (pp. 763–773). Cambridge: Massachusetts Institute of Technology Press.

Frank, J. W., Moore, R. S., & Ames, G. M. (2000). Historical and cultural roots of drinking problems among American Indians. *American Journal of Public Health, 90*(3), 344–351.

Frank, L., Andresen, M. A., & Schmid, T. L. (2004). Obesity relationships with community design, physical activity, and time spent in cars. *American Journal of Preventive Medicine, 27*(2), 87–96.

Franklin, C., & Jordan, C. (2003). An integrative skills assessment approach. In C. Jordan & C. Franklin (Eds.), *Clinical assessment for social workers: Quantitative and qualitative methods* (2nd ed., pp. 1–52). Chicago: Lyceum.

Fraser, M. (2004). The ecology of childhood: A multisystems perspective. In M. Fraser (Ed.), *Risk and resilience in childhood: An ecological perspective* (2nd ed., pp. 1–12). Washington, DC: National Association of Social Workers Press.

Fraser, M., & Galinsky, M. (2004). Risk and resilience in childhood: Toward an evidence-based model of practice. In M. Fraser (Ed.), *Risk and resilience in childhood: An ecological perspective* (2nd ed., pp. 385–402). Washington, DC: National Association of Social Workers Press.

Frasure-Smith, N., Lesperance, F., & Talajic, M. (1995). Depression and 18-month prognosis after myocardial infarction. *Circulation, 91,* 999–1005.

Freisthier, B., Merritt, D. H., & Lascala, E. A. (2006). Understanding the ecology of child maltreatment: A review of the literature and directions for future research. *Child Maltreatment, 11*(3), 263–280.

Friedman, M. J., Charney, D. S., & Deutch, A. Y. (1995). *Neurobiological and clinical consequences of stress: From normal adaptation to PTSD.* Philadelphia: Lippincott-Raven.

Friedman, P. (2003, April). An update on the earned income and child tax credits. *Resources for Welfare Decisions, 7*(6). Retrieved June 30, 2005, from http://www.financeproject.org /Publications/anupdateoneitcRN.htm

Fritz, C. (2005). *Executive summary: Older women and poverty: A demographic profile.* Washington, DC: Population Resource Center.

Frongillo, E. A. (2003). Understanding obesity and program participation in the context of poverty and food insecurity. *Journal of Nutrition, 133*(7), 2117–2118.

Fujiura, G. T., & Yamaki, K. (2000). Trends in demography of childhood poverty and disability. *Exceptional Children, 66,* 187–199.

Functional Family Therapy. (2003). *Functional family therapy provides positive family strengthening resources to youth at risk and in need.* Retrieved January 10, 2005, from http://www.fftinc.com/whatis.php

Galambos, C. M. (2004). The changing face of AIDS. *Health & Social Work, 29*(2), 83–85.

Galea, S., Ahern, J., Rudenstine, S., Wallace, Z., & Vlahov, D. (2005). Urban built environment and depression: A multilevel analysis. *Journal of Epidemiological Community Health, 59*(10), 822–827.

Gallegos, S. M. (1998). Providing services to HIV-positive women. In D. M. Aronstein & B. J. Thompson (Eds.), *HIV and social work: A practitioner's guide* (pp. 431–443). New York: Haworth Press.

Gambrill, E. (1990). *Critical thinking in clinical practice: Improving the accuracy of judgments and decisions about clients.* San Francisco: Jossey-Bass.

Gambrill, E. (2003a). Ethics, science, and the helping professions: A conversation with Robyn Dawes. *Journal of Social Work Education, 39*(1), 27–41.

Gambrill, E. (2003b). From the editor: Evidence-based practice: Sea change or the emperor's new clothes? *Journal of Social Work Education, 39*(1), 3–23.

Gambrill, E. (2004). Contributions of critical thinking and evidence-based practice to the fulfillment of the ethical obligations of the professionals. In H. D. Briggs & T. L. Rzepnicki (Eds.), *Using evidence in social work practice* (pp. 3–19). Chicago: Lyceum.

Gambrill, E. D. (2005). Decision making in child welfare: Errors and their context. *Children & Youth Services Review, 27*(4), 347–352.

Gans, H. J. (1995). *The war against the poor: The underclass and antipoverty policy.* New York: Basic Books.

Garbarino, J. (1999). *Lost boys: Why our sons turn violent and how we can save them.* New York: Free Press.

Garbarino, J., & Crouter, A. (1978). Defining the community context for parent-child relations: The correlates of child maltreatment. *Child Development, 49,* 604–616.

Garbarino, J., Dubrow, N., Kostelny, K., & Pardo, C. (1992). *Children in anger.* San Francisco: Jossey-Bass.

Gardner, H. (1993). *Multiple intelligences: The theory in practice.* New York: Basic Books.

Gardner, H. (1999). *Intelligence reframed: Multiple intelligences for the 21st century.* New York: Basic Books.

Gardner, L., Frank, D., & Amankwaa, L. (1998). A comparison of sexual behavior and self-esteem in young adult females with positive and negative tests for sexually transmitted diseases. *American Black Nurses Foundation Journal, 9*(4), 89–94.

Garrison, C. Z., Addy, A., Jackson, K. L., McKeown, R., & Waller, J. L. (1991). The CES-D as a screen for depression and other psychiatric disorders in adolescents. *Journal of the American Academy of Child and Adolescent Psychiatry, 30,* 636–641.

Gartner, R. (1990). The victims of homicide: A temporal and cross-national comparison. *American Sociological Review, 55,* 92–106.

Gatz, M. (2003). Aging women and depression. *Professional Psychology: Research & Practice, 34*(1), 3–9.

Gelles, R. (1997). *The book of David: How preserving families can cost children's lives.* New York: Basic Books.

George, L., Larson, D., Koenig, H., & McCullough, M. (2000). Spirituality and health: What we know, what we need to know. *Journal of Social and Clinical Psychology, 19,* 102–116.

Gershoff, E. T. (2003). *Low income and the development of America's kindergartners: Living at the edge* (Research Brief No. 4). New York: Columbia University, National Center for Children in Poverty. Retrieved June 2, 2005, from http://www.nccp.org/media/lat03d-text.pdf

Gfroerer, J., & De La Rosa, M. (1993). Protective and risk factors associated with drug use among Hispanic youth. *Journal of Addictive Diseases, 12,* 87–107.

Giaconia, R. M., Reinherz, H. Z., Silverman, A. B., Pakiz, B., Frost, A. K., & Cohen, E. (1995). Traumas and posttraumatic stress disorder in a community population of older adolescents. *Journal of the American Academy of Child Adolescent Psychiatry, 34,* 1369–1379.

Giancola, P. R., & Moss, H. B. (1998). Executive cognitive functioning in alcohol use disorders. *Recent Developments in Alcoholism, 14,* 227–251.

Gibbs, L., & Gambrill, E. (1999). *Critical thinking for social workers.* Thousand Oaks, CA: Pine Forge Press.

Gibbs, L. E. (2003). *Evidence-based practice for the helping professions: A practical guide with integrated multimedia.* Pacific Grove, CA: Brooks/Cole-Thomson Learning.

Gibson, C., & Tibbetts, S. (2000). A biosocial interaction in predicting early onset of offending. *Psychological Reports, 86,* 509–518.

Gil, A. G., Wagner, E. F., & Tubman, J. G. (2004). Associations between early-adolescent substance use and subsequent young-adult substance use disorders and psychiatric disorders among a multiethnic male sample in South Florida. *American Journal of Public Health, 94*(9), 1603–1609.

Gil, D. (1970). *Violence against children: Physical child abuse in the United States.* Cambridge, MA: Harvard University Press.

Gil, S., Caspi, Y., Ben-Ari, I. Z., Koren, D., & Klein, E. (2005). Does memory of a traumatic event increase the risk for posttraumatic stress disorder in patients with traumatic brain injury? A prospective study. *American Journal of Psychiatry, 162*(5), 963–969.

Gilbert, M. C. (2003). Childhood depression: A risk factor perspective. In M. E. Fraser (Eds.), *Risk and resilience in childhood* (2nd ed., pp. 315–346). Washington, DC: National Association of Social Workers Press.

Gilens, M. (1999). *Why Americans hate welfare.* Chicago: University of Chicago Press.

Gingsberg, L., Nackerud, L., & Larrison, C. R. (2004). *Human biology for social workers: Development, ecology, genetics, and health.* Boston: Pearson.

Ginzburg, K., Solomon, Z., Dekel, R., & Neria, Y. (2003). Battlefield functioning and chronic PTSD: Associations with perceived self efficacy and causal attribution. *Personality and Individual Differences, 34*(3), 463–476.

Glaser, D. (2002). Emotional abuse and neglect (psychological maltreatment): A conceptual framework. *Child Abuse & Neglect, 26*(6/7), 697–714.

Gluckman, P., Cutfield, W., Hofman, P., & Hanson, M. (2005). The fetal, neonatal, and infant environments: The long-term consequences for disease risk. *Early Human Development, 81*(1), 51–59.

Gluckman, P., & Hanson, M. (2004). Living with the past: Evolution, development, and patterns of disease. *Science, 305*(17), 1733–1736.

Gluckman, P., Hanson, M., Morton, S., & Pinal, C. (2005). Life-long echoes: A critical analysis of the developmental origins of adult disease model. *Biology of the Neonate, 87*(2), 127–139.

Goicoechea-Balbona, A. (1998). Children with HIV/AIDS and their families: A successful social work intervention based on the culturally specific health care model. *Health & Social Work, 23*(1), 61–70.

Golan, M., & Crow, S. (2004). Parents are key players in the prevention and treatment of weight-related problems. *Nutrition Reviews, 62*(1), 39–50.

Goldapple, K., Segal, Z., & Garson, C. (2004). Modulation of cortical-limbic pathways in major depression. *Archives of General Psychiatry, 61*(1), 34–41.

Goldman, H., Rye, P., & Sirovatka, P. (Eds.). (1999). *Mental health: A report of the surgeon general.* Retrieved June 17, 2006, from http://www.surgeongeneral.gov/library/mentalhealth/home.html

Goldman, J., & Harlow, L. (1993). Self-perception variables that mediate AIDS-preventive behavior in college students. *Health Psychology, 12*(6), 489–498.

Goldman, M. S., Brown, S. A., Christiansen, B. A., & Smith, G. T. (1991). Alcoholism and memory: Broadening the scope of alcohol expectancy research. *Psychological Bulletin, 110,* 137–146.

Goleman, D. (1995). *Emotional intelligence: Why it can matter more than IQ.* New York: Bantam.

Gonzales, E., Kulkarni, H., Bolivar, H., Mangano, A., Sanchez, R., & Catano, G. (2005). The influence of CCL3L1 gene-containing segmental duplications on HIV-1/AIDS susceptibility. *Science, 307*(5714), 1422–1424.

Goode, J., & Maskovsky, J. (2001). *The new poverty studies: The ethnography of power, politics, and impoverished people in the United States.* New York: New York University Press.

Goodhand, J. (2001, May). *Violent conflict, poverty, and chronic poverty.* (Working Paper No. 6). Manchester, England: Chronic Poverty Research Centre.

Goodman, E., & Whitaker, R. C. (2002). A prospective study of the role of depression in the development and persistence of adolescent obesity. *Pediatrics, 110*(3), 497–504.

Goodson-Lawes, J. (1994). Ethnicity and poverty as research variables: Family studies with Mexican and Vietnamese newcomers. In E. Sherman & W. Reid (Eds.), *Qualitative research in social work* (pp. 22–31). New York: Columbia University Press.

Goodwin, D. W. (1988). *Is alcoholism hereditary?* (2nd ed.). New York: Ballantine.

Gorbach, P., Sopheab, H., Phalla, T., Leng, H., Mills, S., Bennett, A., et al. (2000). Sexual bridging by Cambodian men: Potential importance for general population spread of STD and HIV epidemics. *Sexually Transmitted Diseases, 27*(6), 320–326.

Gordon-Larsen, P., Adair, L. S., & Popkin, B. M. (2003). The relationship of ethnicity, socioeconomic factors, and overweight in U.S. adolescents. *Obesity Research, 11*(1), 121–129.

Gorman, J. (2006). Gender differences in depression and response to psychotropic medication. *Gender Medicine, 3*(2), 93–109.

Gorman-Smith, D., & Tolan, P. (1998). The role of exposure to community violence and developmental problems among inner-city youth. *Development and Psychopathology, 10,* 101–166.

Gorman-Smith, D., & Tolan, P. (2003). Positive adaptation among youth exposed to community violence. In S. Luthar (Ed.), *Resilience and vulnerability: Adaptation in the context of childhood adversities* (pp. 392–413). Cambridge, England: Cambridge University Press.

Gottman, J., & Katz, L. (1989). Effects of marital discord on young children's peer interaction and health. *Developmental Psychology, 25,* 373–381.

Gottschalk, P., & Danziger, S. (1993). Family structure, family size, and family income. In S. Danziger & P. Gottschalk (Eds.), *Uneven tides* (pp. 167–193). New York: Russell Sage Foundation.

Gowing, L., Farrell, M., Bornemann, R., & Ali, R. (2004). Substitution treatment of injecting opiod users for prevention of HIV infection. *Cochrane Database of Systematic Reviews, 4.* Retrieved February 9, 2005, from http://www.cochrane.org/cochrane/revabstr/AB004145.htm

Graff, H. (1995). *Conflicting paths: Growing up in America.* Cambridge, MA: Harvard University Press.

Grayson, C. E. (2004a). *Depression in children.* Retrieved May 10, 2005, from http://my.webMD.com/content/article/45/1663_51230htm?z

Grayson, C. E. (2004b). *Depression in elderly.* Retrieved May 10, 2005, from http://my.webMD.com/content/article/45/1663_51234htm?z

Grayson, C. E. (2004c). *Depression in men.* Retrieved May 10, 2005, from http://my.webMD.com/content/article/45/1663_51232htm?z

Grayson, C. E. (2004d). *Depression in teens.* Retrieved May 10, 2005, from http://my.webMD.com/content/article/45/1663_51231htm?z

Grayson, C. E. (2004e). *Depression in women.* Retrieved May 10, 2005, from http://my.webMD.com/content/article/45/1663_51233htm?z

Greenberg, K. (1996). *Honor and slavery.* Princeton, NJ: Princeton University Press.

Greenberg, P. E., Kessler, R. C., Birnbaum, H. G., Leong, S. A., Lowe, S. W., Berlund, P. A., et al. (2003). The economic burden of depression in the United States: How did it change between 1990 and 2000? *Journal of Clinical Psychiatry, 64*(12), 1465–1475.

Greenblatt, J. (1998). *Adolescent self-reported behaviors and their association with marijuana use.* Retrieved June 16, 2006, from http://oas.samhsa.gov/NHSDA/Treatan?treana17.htm

Greenfield, S. F. (2003). The assessment of mood and substance use disorders. In J. J. Westermeyer, R. D. Weiss, & D. M. Ziedonis (Eds.), *Integrated treatment for mood and substance use disorders* (pp. 42–67). Baltimore: Johns Hopkins University Press.

Greenwald, B. S., Kramer-Ginsberg, E., Bogerts, B., Ashtari, M. N., Aupperle, P., Wu, H., et al. (1997). Qualitative magnetic resonance imaging findings in geriatric depression. Possible link between later-onset depression and Alzheimer's disease? *Psychological Medicine, 27*(2), 421–431.

Greenwood, E. (1976). Attributes of a profession. In N. Gilbert & H. Specht (Eds.), *The emergence of social welfare and social work* (pp. 302–318). Itasca, IL: Peacock. [Reprinted from *Social Work* (1957) *2*(3), 45–55]

Grinstein-Weiss, M., Zhan, M., & Sherraden, M. (2006). Saving performance in individual development accounts: Does marital status matter? *Journal of Marriage and Family, 68*(1), 192–204.

Guerra, N., Huesmann, R., & Spindler, A. (2003). Community violence exposure, social cognition, and aggression among urban elementary school children. *Child Development, 74*(5), 561–576.

Gulliford, M. C., Mahabir, D., & Rocke, B. (2003). Food insecurity, food choices, and body mass index in adults. *International Journal of Epidemiology, 32*(4), 516–517.

Gunay-Aygun, M., Cassidy, S. B., & Nicholls, R. D. (1997). Prader-Willi and other syndromes associated with obesity and mental retardation. *Behavior Genetics, 27*(4), 307–324.

Gura, T. (2003). Obesity drug pipeline not so fat. *Science, 299,* 849–852.

Gustafson, T. B., & Sarwer, D. B. (2004). Childhood sexual abuse and obesity. *Obesity Review, 5*(3), 129–135.

Gustafsson, M., Persson, L.-O., & Amilon, A. (2002). A qualitative study of coping in the early stage of acute traumatic hand injury. *Journal of Clinical Nursing, 11,* 594–602.

Guthrie, B. J., Rotheram, M. J., & Genero, N. (2001). *A guide to understanding female adolescents' substance abuse: Gender and ethnic considerations for prevention and treatment policy* (DHHS Pub. No. SMA 00-3309). Washington, DC: Substance Abuse Mental Health Services Administration.

Haarasilta, L., Marttunen, M., Kaprio, J., & Aro, H. (2001). The 12-month prevalence and characteristics of major depressive episode in a representative nationwide sample of adolescents and young adults. *Psychological Medicine, 31,* 1169–1179.

Hackney, C. H., & Sanders, G. S. (2003). Religiosity and mental health: A meta-analysis of recent studies. *Journal of the Scientific Study of Religion, 42*(1), 43–55.

Haight, W. L. (1998). "Gathering the spirit" at First Baptist church: Spirituality as a protective factor in the lives of African American children. *Social Work, 43,* 213–221.

Halfon, N., & Newacheck, P. W. (1993). Childhood asthma and poverty: Differential impacts and utilization of health services. *Pediatrics, 91*(1), 56–61.

Hall McEntee, G., Appleby, J., Dowd, J., Grant, J., Hole, S., & Silva, P. (2003). *At the heart of teaching: A guide to reflective practice.* New York: Teachers College Press.

Hamburger, M., Moore, J., Koenig, L., Vlahov, D., Schoenbaum, E., Schuman, P., et al. (2004). Persistence of inconsistent condom use: Relation to abuse history and HIV serostatus. *AIDS and Behavior, 8*(3), 333–344.

Hamilton, M. (1967). Development of a rating scale for primary depressive illness. *British Journal of Social and Clinical Psychology, 6,* 278–296.

Hammack, P. (2003). Toward a unified theory of depression among urban African American youth: Integrating socioecologic, cognitive, family stress, and biopsychosocial perspectives. *Journal of Black Psychology, 29*(2), 187–209.

Hammack, P., Robinson, W., Crawford, I., & Li, S. (2004). Poverty and depressed mood among urban African-American adolescents: A family stress perspective. *Journal of Child and Family Studies, 13*(3), 309–323.

Hammen, C., & Rudolph, K. D. (2003). Childhood mood disorders. In E. J. Mash & R. A. Barkley (Eds.), *Child psychopathology* (2nd ed., pp. 233–278). New York: Guilford Press.

Han, C., Li, X., Luo, H., Zhao, X., & Li, X. (2004). Clinical study on electro-acupuncture treatment for 30 cases of mental depression. *Journal of Traditional Chinese Medicine, 24*(3), 172–176.

Hansen, W. B., & Graham, J. W. (1991). Preventing alcohol, marijuana and cigarette use among adolescents: Peer pressure resistance training versus establishing conservative norms. *Preventive Medicine, 20,* 414–430.

Harder, J. (2005). Research implications for the prevention of child abuse and neglect. *Families in Society, 86*(4), 491–501.

Hariri, A., Drabant, E., Munoz, K., Kolachana, B., Mattay, V., Egan, M., et al. (2005). A susceptibility gene for affective disorders and the response of the human amygdala. *Archive of General Psychiatry, 62,* 146–152.

Harlow, L., Newcomb, M., & Bentler, P. (1986). Depression, self-erogation, substance use, and suicide ideation: Lack of purpose in life as a mediational factor. *Journal of Clinical Psychology, 42,* 5–21.

Harris, A., Cronkite, R., & Moos, R. (2006). Physical activity, exercise coping, and depression in a 10-year cohort study of depressed patients. *Journal of Affective Disorders, 93*(1–3), 79–85.

Harris, J. (1999). Review and methodological considerations in research on testosterone and aggression. *Aggression and Violent Behavior, 4,* 273–291.

Haugaard, J. J. (2000). The challenge of defining child sexual abuse. *American Psychologist, 55*(9), 1036–1039.

Haugaard, J. J., Reppucci, N. D., & Feerick, M. M. (1997). Children's coping with maltreatment. In S. A. Wolchick & I. N. Sandler (Eds.), *Handbook of children's coping: Linking theory and intervention* (pp. 73–100). New York: Plenum.

Havanon, N., Bennett, A., & Knodel, J. (1993). Sexual networking in provincial Thailand. *Studies in Family Planning, 24*(1), 1–17.

Hawkins, D., Laub, J., & Lauritsen, J. (1998). Race, ethnicity, and serious juvenile offending. In R. Loeber & D. Farrington (Eds.), *Serious and violent juvenile offenders: Risk factors and successful interventions* (pp. 30–46). Thousand Oaks, CA: Sage.

Hawkins, J., Catalano, R. F., & Miller, J. Y. (1992). Risk and protective factors for alcohol and other drug problems in adolescence and early adulthood: Implications for substance abuse prevention. *Psychological Bulletin, 112,* 64–105.

Hawkins, J., Herrenkohl, T., Farrington, D., Brewer, D., Catalano, R., & Harachi, T. (1998). A review of predictors of youth violence. In R. Loeber & D. Farrington (Eds.), *Serious & violent juvenile offenders: Risk factors and successful interventions* (pp. 106–146). Thousand Oaks, CA: Sage.

Haynes, K. S., & Mickelson, J. S. (2005). *Affecting change: Social workers in the political arena* (6th ed.). Boston: Allyn & Bacon.

Hays, R., Magee, R., & Chauncey, S. (1994). Identifying helpful and unhelpful behaviors in loved ones: The PWA's perspective. *AIDS Care, 6,* 379–392.

Hays, R., McKusick, I., Pollack, I., Hillard, R., Hoff, C., & Coates, T. (1993). Disclosing HIV seropositivity to significant others. *AIDS, 7,* 425–431.

Hays, S. (2003). *Flat broke with children: Women in the age of welfare reform.* New York: Oxford University Press.

Healthlink Worldwide. (2003). *Poverty and health.* Retrieved July 7, 2005, from http://www.healthlink.org.uk/PDFs/poverty-health-nl.pdf

Heckman, T., Kalichman, S., Roffman, R., Sikkema, K., Heckman, B., Somlai, A., et al. (1999). A telephone-delivered coping improvement intervention for persons living with HIV/AIDS in rural areas. *Social Work With Groups, 21*(4), 49–61.

Heflin, C., Siefert, K., & Williams, D. (2005). Food insufficiency and women's mental health: Findings from a 3-year panel of welfare recipients. *Social Science & Medicine, 61*(9), 1971–1982.

Heinrichs, M., Wagner, D., Schoch, W., Soravia, L., Hellhammer, D., & Ehlert, U. (2005). Predicting posttraumatic stress symptoms from pretraumatic risk factors: A 2-year prospective follow-up study in firefighters. *American Journal of Psychiatry, 162*(12), 2276–2286.

Henry, B., Caspi, A., Moffitt, T., & Silva, P. (1997). Temperamental and familial predictors of criminal conviction. In A. Raine, P. Brennan, D. Farrington, & S. Mednick (Eds.), *Biosocial bases of violence* (pp. 305–307). New York: Plenum.

Heponiemi, T., Elovainio, M., Kivimaki, M., Pulkki, L., Puttonen, S., & Keltikangas-Jarvinen, L. (2006). The longitudinal effects of social support and hostility on depressive tendencies. *Social Science and Medicine, 63*(5), 1374–1382.

Hermann, K., & Betz, N. (2004). Path models of the relationships of instrumentality and expressiveness to social self-efficacy, shyness, and depressive symptoms. *Sex Roles: A Journal of Research, 51*(1–2), 55–66.

Hermann, R. C., Ettner, S., Dorwart, R. A., Langman-Dorwart, N., & Kleinman, S. (1999). Diagnoses of patients treated with ECT: A comparison of evidence-based standards with reported use. *Psychiatric Services, 50,* 1059–1065.

Hernandez, B., Gortmaker, S. I., Colditz, G. A., Peterson, K. E., Laird, M. S., & Para-Cabrera, S. (1999). Association of obesity with physical activity, television programs and other forms of video viewing among children in Mexico City. *International Journal of Obesity, 23,* 845–854.

Herrenkohl, T., Hill, K., Chung, I., Guo, J., Abbott, R., & Hawkins, D. (2003). Protective factors against serious violent behavior in adolescence: A prospective study of aggressive children. *Social Work Research, 27*(3), 179–191.

Herrnstein, R., & Murray, C. (1996). *The bell curve: Intelligence and class structure in American life.* New York: Simon & Schuster.

Hesselbrock, M. N., Hesselbrock, V. M., & Epstein, E. E. (1999). Theories of etiology of alcohol and other drug use disorders. In B. S. McCrady & E. E. Epstein (Eds.), *Addictions: A comprehensive guidebook* (pp. 50–74). New York: Oxford University Press.

Hesselbrock, V. M. (1995). The genetic epidemiology of alcoholism. In H. Begleiter & B. Kissin (Eds.), *Alcohol and alcoholism: The genetics of alcoholism* (pp. 17–39). New York: Oxford University Press.

Hettema, J., An, S., Neale, M., Bkuszar, J., van den Oord, E., Kendler, K., et al. (2006). Association between glutamic acid decarboxylase genes and anxiety disorders, major depression, and neuroticism. *Molecular Psychiatry, 11*(8), 752–762.

Hill, A. (2005). Patterns of non-offending parental involvement in therapy with sexually abused children: A review of the literature. *Social Work, 5*(3), 339–358.

Hill, H., Hawkins, S., Raposa, M., & Carr, P. (1995). Relationship between multiple exposure to violence and coping strategies among African American mothers. *Violence and Victims, 10,* 55–71.

Hillson, J. M. C., & Kuiper, N. A. (1994). A stress and coping model of child maltreatment. *Clinical Psychology Review, 14*(4), 261–285.

Himes, J. H., Obarzanek, E., Baranowski, T., Wilson, D. M., Rochon, J., & McClanahan, B. S. (2004). Early sexual maturation, body composition, and obesity in African-American girls. *Obesity Research* (Suppl.), 64S–72S.

Himmelstein, D. U., Warren, E., Thorne, D., & Woolhander, S. (2005). MarketWatch: Illness and injury as contributors to bankruptcy. *Health Affairs* Web exclusive, February 2, 2005. Retrieved June 28, 2005, from http://content. healthaffairs.org/cgi/content/abstract/hlthaff. w5.63v1

Hines, A. M., Lemon, K., & Wyatt, P. (2004). Factors related to the disproportionate involvement of children of color in the child welfare system: A review and emerging themes. *Children & Youth Services Review, 26*(6), 507–527.

Hinrichsen, G. A., & Clougherty, K. F. (2006). *Interpersonal psychotherapy for depressed older adults.* Washington, DC: American Psychological Association.

Hinton, W. L., Chen, Y. C., Du, N., Tran, C. G., Lu, F. G., Miranda, J., et al. (1993). DSM-III-R disorders in Vietnamese refugees. Prevalence and correlates. *Journal of Nervous and Mental Disorders, 181*(2), 113–122.

Hinton, W. L., Tiet, Q., Tran, C. G., & Chesney, M. (1997). Predictors of depression among refugees from Vietnam: A longitudinal study of new arrivals. *Nervous and Mental Disorders, 185*(1), 39–45.

Hirschi, T. (1969). *Causes of delinquency.* Berkeley: University of California Press.

Ho, M., Rasheed, J., & Rasheed, M. (2004). *Family therapy with ethnic minorities* (2nd ed.). Thousand Oaks, CA: Sage.

Hodge, D. R. (2005a). Spiritual ecograms: A new assessment instrument for identifying clients' spiritual strengths in space and across time. *Families in Society, 86*(2), 287–296.

Hodge, D. R. (2005b). Spiritual life maps: A client-centered pictorial instrument for spiritual assessment, planning, and intervention. *Social Work, 50,* 77–88.

Hodgins, S., Kratzer, L., & McNeil, T. (2001). Obstetric complications, parenting, and risk of criminal behavior. *Archives of General Psychiatry, 58,* 746–752.

Hodgkinson, V., Weitzman, M., Kirsch, A., Noga, S., & Gorski, H. (1993). *From belief to commitment.* Washington, DC: Independent Sector.

Holahan, C., Moos, R., Holahan, C., Cronkite, R., & Randall, P. (2003). Drinking and alcohol use and abuse in unipolar depression: A 10-year model. *Journal of Abnormal Psychology, 112*(1), 159–165.

Holroyd, S., & Duryee, J. J. (1997). Differences in geriatric psychiatric outpatients with early versus late onset depression. *International Journal of Geriatric Psychiatry, 2*(11), 1100–1106.

Holzer, H. (1994). Black employment problems: New evidence, old questions. *Journal of Policy Analysis and Management, 13*(4), 699–722.

Holzer, H., & Wissoker, D. (2001, October). How can we encourage job retention and advancement for welfare recipients? (Number A-49). In series, *New federalism: Issues and options for states*. Washington, DC: Urban Institute. Retrieved June 9, 2006, from http://www.urban.org/url.cfm?ID=310360

Hornik, R. (1991). Alternative models of behavior change. In J. Wasserheit, S. Aral, K. Holmes, & P. Hitchcock (Eds.), *Research issues in human behavior and sexually transmitted diseases in the AIDS era* (pp. 201–218). Washington, DC: American Society for Microbiology.

Horowitz, K., Weine, S., & Jekel, J. (1995). PTSD symptoms in urban adolescent girls: Compounded community trauma. *Journal of the American Academy of Child and Adolescent Psychiatry, 34,* 1353–1361.

Hough, E., Brumitt, G., Templin, T., Saltz, E., & Mood, D. (2003). A model of mother-child coping and adjustment to HIV. *Social Science & Medicine, 56,* 643–655.

Hourani, L. L., & Yuan, H. (1999). The mental health status of women in the Navy and Marine Corps: Preliminary findings from the perceptions of wellness and readiness assessment. *Military Medicine, 164,* 174–181.

Hovens, J. G., Cantwell, D. P., & Kiriakos, R. (1994). Psychiatric comorbidity in hospitalized adolescent substance abusers. *Journal of the American Academy of Child and Adolescent Psychiatry, 33*(4), 476–483.

Hsieh, S. D., & Muto, T. (2006). Metabolic syndrome in Japanese men and women with special reference to the anthropometric criteria for the assessment of obesity: Proposal to use the waist-to-height ratio. *Preventive Medicine, 42*(2), 135–139.

Huesmann, L. (1997). Observational learning of violent behavior: Social and biosocial processes. In A. Raine, P. Brennan, D. Farrington, & S. Mednick (Eds.), *Biosocial bases of violence* (pp. 69–88). New York: Plenum.

Huesmann, L. (1998). The role of social information processing and cognitive schema in the acquisition and maintenance of habitual aggressive behavior. In R. Geen & E. Donnerstein (Eds.), *Human aggression: Theories, research, and implications for policy* (pp. 73–109). New York: Academic Press.

Huesmann, L., & Guerra, N. (1997). Normative beliefs about aggression and aggressive behavior. *Journal of Personality and Social Psychology, 75*(2), 408–419.

Hughes, A. C. (1999). *HIV prevention, women and the kitchen sink model*. In M. Shernoff (Ed.), *AIDS and mental health practice: Clinical and policy issues* (pp. 55–65). Binghamton, NY: Haworth Press

Hunter, A., & Davis, J. (1992). Constructing gender: An exploration of Afro-American men's conceptualization of manhood. *Gender and Society, 6*(3), 464–479.

Hunter, C., & Lewis-Coles, M. E. (2005). Coping with racism: A spirit-based psychological perspective. In J. L. Chin (Ed.), *The psychology of prejudice and discrimination: Racism in America* (Vol. 1, pp. 207–222). Westport, CT: Praeger.

Hutchison, E. (2003a). Aspects of human behavior: Person, environment, time. In E. Hutchison (Ed.), *Dimensions of human behavior: Person and environment* (2nd ed., pp. 11–43). Thousand Oaks, CA: Pine Forge Press.

Hutchison, E. (2003b). *Dimensions of human behavior: The changing life course* (2nd ed.). Thousand Oaks, CA: Pine Forge Press.

Hutchison, E. (2003c). *Dimensions of human behavior: Person and environment* (2nd ed.). Thousand Oaks, CA: Pine Forge Press.

Hutchison, E. (2003d). The physical environment. In E. Hutchison (Ed.), *Dimensions of human behavior: Person and environment* (2nd ed., pp. 285–316). Thousand Oaks, CA: Pine Forge Press.

Hutchison, E., & Charlesworth, L. (2000). Securing the welfare of children: Policies past, present, and future. *Families in Society, 81*(6), 576–585.

Hutchison, E., & Waldbillig, A. (2003). Social institutions and social structure. In E. Hutchison (Ed.), *Dimensions of human behavior: Person and environment* (2nd ed., pp. 356–403). Thousand Oaks, CA: Pine Forge Press.

Hypericum Depression Trial Study Group. (2002). Effect of Hypericum perforatum (St. John's wort) in major depressive disorder: A randomized, controlled trial. *Journal of the American Medical Association, 287*(14), 1807–1814.

Iceland, J. (2003). *Poverty in America*. Institute for Research on Poverty. Berkeley: University of California Press.

Ijzerman, R., Boomsma, D., & Stehouwer, C. (2005). Intrauterine environmental and genetic influences on the association between birthweight and cardiovascular risk factors: Studies in twins as a means of testing the fetal origins hypothesis. *Paediatric and Perinatal Epidemiology, 19*(Suppl. 1), 10–14.

Institute for Research on Poverty. (2005). *Who was poor in 2004?* Retrieved June 12, 2006, from http://www.irp.wisc.edu/faq3.htm

Irei, A. V., Takahashi, K., Le, D. S., Ha, P. T., Hung, N. T., Kunii, D., et al. (2005). Obesity is associated with increased risk of allergy in Vietnamese adolescents. *European Journal of Clinical Nutrition, 9*(4), 571–577.

Ironson, G., Solomon, G., Balbin, E., O'Cleirigh, C., George, A., Kumar, M., et al. (2002). The Ironson-Woods Spirituality-Religiousness Index is associated with long survival, health behaviors, less distress, and low cortisol in people with HIV/AIDS. *Annals of Behavioral Medicine, 24,* 34–48.

Irwin, K. (2004). The violence of adolescent life: Experiencing and managing everyday threats. *Youth & Society, 35*(4), 452–479.

Jaccard, J., Dodge, T., & Dittus, P. (2002). Parent-adolescent communication about sex and birth control: A conceptual framework. In S. Feldman & D. A. Rosenthal (Eds.), *Talking sexuality: Parent-adolescent communication.* San Francisco: Jossey-Bass.

Jago, R., Baranowski, T., Yoo, S., Culen, K. L. W., Zakeri, I., Watson, K., et al. (2004). Relationship between physical activity and diet among African-American girls. *Obesity Research, 12*(9), 55S–63S.

Janet, P. (2000). Healthy people 2010: Helping patients change. *Hippocrates, 14*(1), 25–30.

Janko, S. (1994). *Vulnerable children, vulnerable families: The social construction of child abuse.* New York: Teachers College Press.

Jenkins, E. (2002). Black women and community violence: Trauma, grief, and coping. *Women & Therapy, 25*(3/4), 29–44.

Jenkins, E., & Bell, C. (1994). Violence exposure, psychological distress, and high risk behaviors among inner-city high school students. In S. Friedman (Ed.), *Anxiety disorders in African-Americans* (pp. 76–88). New York: Springer.

Jenkins, K. R. (2004). Obesity's effects on the onset of functional impairment among older adults. *The Gerontologist, 44*(2), 206–216.

Jessor, R., Donovan, J. E., & Costa, F. M. (1991). *Beyond adolescence: Problem behavior and young adult development.* New York: Cambridge University Press.

Jewell, J., & Stark, K. (2003). Comparing the family environments of adolescents with conduct disorder or depression. *Journal of Child and Family Studies, 12,* 77–89.

Jha, R. (2006). *Vulnerability and natural disasters in Fiji, Papua New Guinea, Vanuatu and the Kyrgyz Republic* (Economics RSPAS, Departmental Working Papers). Canberra: Australian National University.

Johnson, B. D. (1980). Toward a theory of drug subcultures. In D. J. Letteri, M. Sayers, & H. W. Pearson (Eds.), *Theories on drug abuse: Selected contemporary perspectives* (NIDA Research Monograph No. 30, pp. 110–119, DHHS Publication No. ADM 80–967). Washington, DC: National Institute on Drug Abuse.

Johnston, D., Stall, R., & Smith, K. (1995). Reliance by gay men and intravenous drug users on friends and family for AIDS-related care. *AIDS Care, 7,* 307–319.

Johnson, J., Cohen, P., Smailes, E., Kasen, S., & Brook, J. (2002). Television viewing and aggressive behavior during adolescence and adulthood. *Science, 295*(5564), 2468–2471.

Johnson, K., Bryant, D. D., Collins, D. A., Noe, T. D., Strader, T. N., & Berbaum, M. (1998). Preventing and reducing alcohol and other drug use among high-risk youths by increasing family resilience. *Social Work, 43*(4), 297– 308.

Johnson, L., & Harlow, L. (1996). Childhood sexual abuse linked with adult substance use, victimization, and AIDS-risk. *AIDS Education and Prevention, 8,* 44–57.

Johnston, L. D., O'Malley, P. M., Bachman, J. G., & Schulenberg, J. E. (2004). *Monitoring the future national results on adolescent drug use: Overview of key findings, 2003* (NIH Pub. No. 04–5506). Bethesda, MD: National Institute on Drug Abuse.

Johnson, S., & Birch, L. (1994). Parents' and children's adiposity and eating style. *Pediatrics, 94,* 653–661.

Joint Center for Poverty Research. (2001). *Poverty information. Populations in poverty. How many households headed by women are in poverty.* Retrieved June 19, 2006, from http://www.jcpr.org/faq/faq_populations2.html

Jones, D. P. H. (1997). Editorial: Social support and coping strategies as mediators of the effects of child abuse and neglect. *Child Abuse & Neglect, 21*(2), 207–209.

Jones, J., & Handcock, M. (2003). An assessment of the preferential attachment as a mechanism for human sexual network formation. *Proceedings of the Royal Society of London, 270,* 1123–1128.

Jones Harden, B., & Nzinga-Johnson, S. (2000). Young, wounded, and black: The maltreatment of African American children in the early years. In R. Hampton & T. Gullotta (Eds.), *Interpersonal violence in the African American community.* Netherlands: Springer.

Jordan, C., & Franklin, C. (2003). *Clinical assessment for social workers: Quantitative and qualitative methods* (2nd ed.). Chicago: Lyceum.

Kadushin, G. (2000). Family secrets: Disclosure of HIV status among gay men with HIV/AIDS to the family of origin. *Social Work in Health Care, 30*(3), 1–17.

Kaiser, L. L., Melgar-Quinonez, H. R., Lamp, C. L., Johns, M. C., Sutherlin, J. M., & Harwood, J. O. (2002). Food security and nutritional outcomes of preschool-age Mexican-American children. *Journal of the American Dietetic Association, 102,* 924–929.

Kaiser, L. L., Townsend, M. S., Melgar-Quinonez, H. R., Fujii, M. L., & Crawford, P. B. (2004). Choice of instrument influences relations between food insecurity and obesity in Latino women. *American Journal of Clinical Nutrition, 80*(5), 1372–1378.

Kalichman, S., Benotsch, E., Weinhardt, L., Austin, J., Luke, W., & Cherry, C. (2003). Health-related internet use, coping, social support, and health indicators in people living with HIV/AIDS: Preliminary results from a community survey. *Health Psychology, 22*(1), 111–116.

Kalichman, S., & Simbayi, L. (2004). Sexual assault history and risks for sexually transmitted infections among women in an African township in Cape Town, South Africa. *AIDS Care, 16*(6), 681–690.

Kamali, A., Seeley, A., Nunn, J., Kengeya-Kayondo, J., Ruberantwari, A., & Mulder, W. (1996). The orphan problem: Experience of a sub-Saharan African rural population in the AIDS epidemic. *AIDS Care, 8*(5), 509–516.

Kambouropoulos, N., & Staiger, P. K. (2004). Reactivity to alcohol-related cues: Relationship among cue type, motivational processes, and personality. *Psychology of Addictive Behaviors, 18*(3), 275–283.

Kandel, E., & Mednick, S. (1991). Perinatal complications predict violent offending. *Criminology, 29,* 519–529.

Kandel, E., Mednick, S., Kirkegaard-Sorenson, L., Hutchings, B., Knop, J., Rosenberg, R., et al. (1988). IQ as protective factor for subjects at high-risk for antisocial behavior. *Journal of Consulting and Clinical Psychology, 56,* 224–226.

Kandel, E. R. (1998). A new intellectual framework for psychiatry. *American Journal of Psychiatry, 155,* 457–469.

Kang, S., Deren, S., & Goldstein, M. (2002). Relationships between childhood abuse and neglect experience and HIV risk behaviors among methadone treatment drop-outs. *Child Abuse & Neglect, 26,* 1275–1289.

Kaplan, H., & Sadock, B. (1998). *Synopsis of psychiatry* (8th ed.). Baltimore: Williams & Wilkins.

Kaplan, H., & Sadock, B. (2002). *Synopsis of psychiatry* (9th ed.). Baltimore: Williams & Wilkins.

Kaplan, L. E., Tomaszewski, E., & Gorin, S. (2004). Current trends and the future of HIV/AIDS services: A social work perspective. *Health & Social Work, 29* (2), 153–160.

Kaplan, M. S., Huguet, N., Newsom, J. T., & McFarland, B. H. (2004). The association between length of residence and obesity among Hispanic immigrants. *American Journal of Preventive Medicine, 27*(4), 323–326.

Karoly, L. A. (2002). Investing in the future: Reducing poverty through human capital investments. In S. H. Danzinger & R. H. Haveman (Eds.), *Understanding Poverty* (314–358). Cambridge, MA: Harvard University Press.

Karson, M. (2001). *Patterns of child abuse: How dysfunctional transactions are replicated in individuals, families, and the child welfare system.* Binghamton, NY: Halworth Maltreatment and Trauma Press.

Kaslow, N., Thompson, M., Okun, A., Price, A., Young, S., Bender, M., et al. (2002). Risk and protective factors for suicidal behavior in abused African American women. *Journal of Consulting and Clinical Psychology, 70*(2), 311–319.

Katz, L., Kling, J., & Liebman, J. (2001). Moving to opportunity in Boston: Early results of a randomized mobility experiment. *Quarterly Journal of Economics, 116*(2), 607–654.

Kaufman, M. (2006, July 13). FDA clears once-a-day AIDS drug. *The Washington Post,* p. A01.

Kellam, S., & Van Horn, Y. (1997). Life course development, community epidemiology, and prevention trials: A scientific structure for prevention research. *American Journal of Community Psychology, 25*(2), 177–188.

Kelly, J., Amirkhanian, Y., McAuliffe, T., Dyatlov, R., Granskaya, J., Borodkina, O., et al. (2001). HIV risk behavior and risk-related characteristics of young Russian men who exchange sex for money or valuables from other men. *AIDS Education and Prevention, 13*(2), 175–188.

Kendall, A., Olson, C. M., & Frongillo, E. A. (1996). Relationship of hunger and food insecurity to food availability and consumption. *Journal of the American Dietetic Association, 96,* 1019–1024.

Kendler, K. S., Gardner, C. O., & Prescott, C. A. (2002). Toward a comprehensive developmental model for major depression in women. *American Journal of Psychiatry, 159,* 1133–1145.

Kendler, K. S., Gardner, C. O., & Prescott, C. A. (2006). Toward a comprehensive developmental model for major depression in men. *American Journal of Psychiatry, 163,* 115–124.

Kendler, K. S., Gatz, M., Gardner, C. O., & Pedersen, N. L. (2006). A Swedish national twin study of lifetime major depression. *American Journal of Psychiatry, 163,* 109–114.

Kendler, K. S., Heath, A. C., Neale, M. C., Kessler, R. C., & Eaves, L. J. (1992). A population-based twin study of alcoholism in women. *Journal of the American Medical Association, 268,* 1877–1882.

Kendler, K. S., Liu, X. Q., Gardner, C. O., McCullough, M. E., Larson, D., & Prescott, C. A. (2003). Dimensions of religiosity and their relationship to lifetime psychiatric and substance use disorders. *American Journal of Psychiatry, 160*(3), 496–503.

Kendler, K. S., Myers, M. S., & Prescott, C. A. (2005). Sex differences in the relationship between social support and risk for major depression: A longitudinal study of opposite-sex twin pairs. *American Journal of Psychiatry, 162*(2), 250–256.

Kendler, K. S., Neale, M. C., Heath, A. C., Kessler, R. C., & Eaves, L. J. (1994). A twin-family study of alcoholism in women. *American Journal of Psychology, 151*(5), 707–715.

Kennedy, M., Spingarn, R., Stanton, A., & Rotheram-Borus, M. (2000). A continuum of care model for adolescents living with HIV: Larkin Street Youth Center. *Drugs & Society, 16*(1–2), 87–106.

Kesner, R., Gilbert, P., & Barua, L. (2002). The role of the hippocampus in memory for the temporal order of a sequence of odors. *Behavioral Neuroscience, 166*(2), 286–290.

Kessler, G. (2006, May 19). Prostitution clause in AIDS policy ruled illegal. *The Washington Post,* p. A16.

Kessler, R. C. (2000). Psychiatric epidemiology: Elected recent advances and future directions. *Bulletin of the World Health Organization, 78*(4), 464–474.

Kessler, R. C., Crum, R. M., Warner, L. A., Nelson, C. B., Schulenberg, J., & Anthony, J. C. (1997). Lifetime co-occurrence of DSM-III-R alcohol abuse and dependence and other psychiatric disorders in the National Comorbidity Survey. *Archives of General Psychiatry, 54,* 313–321.

Kessler, R. C., Sonnega, A., Bromet, E., Hughes, M., & Nelson, C. B. (1995). Posttraumatic stress disorder in the National Comorbidity Survey. *Archives of General Psychiatry, 52,* 1048–1060.

Kessler, R. C., Soukup, J., Davis, R. B., Foster, D. F., Wilkey, S. A., VanRompay, M. I., et al. (2001). The use of complementary and alternative therapies to treat anxiety and depression in the United States. *American Journal of Psychiatry, 158*(2), 289–294.

Kessler, R. C., & Zhao, S. (1999). Past-year use of outpatient services for psychiatric problems in the National Comorbidity Survey. *American Journal of Psychiatry, 156*(1), 115–123.

Kilpatrick, D. G., Acierno, R., Saunders, B., Resnick, H. S., Best, C. L., & Schnurr, P. P. (2000). Risk factors for adolescent substance abuse and dependence: Data from a national sample. *Journal of Consulting and Clinical Psychology, 68,* 19–30.

Kilpatrick, D. G., Edmunds, C. N., & Seymour, A. K. (1992). *Rape in America: A report to the nation.* Arlington, VA: National Victim Center and Charleston, SC: Crime Victims Research and Treatment Center.

Kim, E., Hwang, J. Y., Woo, E. K., Kim, S. S., Jo, S. A., & Jo, I. (2005). Body mass index cutoffs for underweight, overweight, and obesity in South Korean schoolgirls. *Obesity Research, 13*(9), 1510–1514.

Kim, K. H., & Sobal, J. (2004). Religion, social support, fat intake and physical activity. *Public Health Nutrition, 7*(6), 773–781.

Kim, T. (2004). *Youth gangs.* Unpublished paper. Southern California Center of Excellence on Youth Violence Prevention, University of California, Riverside.

Kimberly, J., & Serovich, J. (1999). The role of family and friend social support in reducing risk behaviors among HIV-positive gay men. *AIDS Education and Prevention, 11,* 465–475.

Kindlon, D., Tremblay, R., Mezzacappa, E., Earls, F., Laurent, D., & Schaal, B. (1995). Longitudinal patterns of heart rate and fighting behavior in 9- through 12-year-old boys. *Journal of American Academy of Child and Adolescent Psychiatry, 34,* 371–377.

King, K. M., & Chassin, L. (2004). Mediating and moderated effects of adolescent behavioral undercontrol and parenting in the prediction of drug use disorders in emerging adulthood. *Psychology of Addictive Behaviors, 18*(3), 239–249.

Kinzie, J. D. (2001). Cross-cultural treatment of PTSD. In J. P. Wilson, M. J. Friedman, & J. D. Lindy (Eds.), *Treating psychological trauma and PTSD* (pp. 255–277). New York: Guilford Press.

Kipke, M. (2004). *Preventing violence and related health-risking social behaviors in adolescents: An evidence assessment report.* Paper presented at the Preventing Violence State of the Science Conference, National Institutes of Health, Bethesda, MD.

Kirby, P., & Paradise, L. (1992). Reflective practice and effectiveness of teachers. *Psychological Reports, 70,* 1057–1058.

Kirk, S., & Reid, W. (2002). *Science and social work: A critical appraisal.* New York: Columbia University Press.

Klerman, G., Weissman, M., Rounsaville, B., & Chevron, E. (1984). *Interpersonal psychotherapy of depression.* New York: Basic Books.

Kliewer, W. (1991). Coping in middle childhood: Relations to competence, Type A behavior, monitoring, blunting, and locus of control. *Developmental Psychology, 27,* 689–697.

Kliewer, W., Lepore, S. J., Oskin, D., & Johnson, P. D. (1998). The role of social and cognitive processes in children's adjustment to community violence. *Journal of Clinical & Consulting Psychology, 66,* 199–209.

Klotter, J. (2006, February–March). Gastric pacing. *Townsend Letter for Doctors and Patients, 39,* 271–272.

Kmita, G., Baranska, M., & Niemiec, T. (2002). Psychosocial intervention in the process of empowering families with children living with HIV/AIDS: A descriptive study. *AIDS Care, 14*(2), 279–285.

Knodel, J., & Wassana, I. (2004). The economic consequences for parents of losing an adult child to AIDS: Evidence from Thailand. *Social Science & Medicine, 59*(5), 987–1001.

Koenen, K. C., Stellman, J. M., Stellman, S. D., & Sommer, J. F. (2003). Risk factors for course of posttraumatic stress disorder among Vietnam veterans: A 14-year follow-up of American Legionnaires. *Journal of Consulting and Clinical Psychology, 71*(6), 980–986.

Koenig, H. G. (1998). *Handbook of religion and mental health.* San Diego, CA: Academic Press.

Koenig, H. G., George, L. K., & Peterson, B. L. (1998). Religiosity and remission of depression in medically ill older patients. *American Journal of Psychiatry, 155,* 536–542.

Koenig, H. G., Larson, D. B., & Larson, S. S. (2001). Religion and coping with serious medical illness. *Annals of Pharmacotherapy, 35*(3), 352–359.

Koenig, H. G., McCullough, M. E., & Larson, D. B. (2001). *Handbook of religion and health.* New York: Oxford University Press.

Koenig, H. G., Pargament, K. I., & Nielsen, J. (1998). Religious coping and health status in medically ill hospitalized older adults. *Journal of Nervous and Mental Disease, 186,* 513–521.

Kohn, R., Dohrenwend, B., & Mirotznik, J. (1998). Epidemiological findings on selected psychiatric disorders in the general population. In B. Dohrenwend (Ed.), *Adversity, stress and psychopathology* (pp. 235–284). New York: Oxford University Press.

Kohn, R., Levav, I., Donaire, I., Machuca, M., & Tamashiro, R. (2005). Psychological and psychopathological reactions in Honduras following Hurricane Mitch: Implications for service planning. *Pan American Journal of Public Health, 18*(4), 287–295.

Kondrat, M. (1999). Who is the "self" in self-aware: Professional self-awareness from a critical theory perspective. *Social Service Review, 73*(4), 451–477.

Koop, C., & Lundberg, G. (1992). Violence in America: A public health emergency. *Journal of the American Medical Association, 267,* 3075–3076.

Korbin, J. E. (Ed.). (1981). *Child abuse & neglect: Cross-cultural perspectives.* Berkeley: University of California Press.

Korbin, J. E. (1997). Culture and child maltreatment. In M. E. Helfer, R. S. Kempe, & R. D. Krugman (Eds.), *The battered child* (5th ed., pp. 29–48). Chicago: University of Chicago Press.

Korbin, J. E. (2002). Culture and child maltreatment: Cultural competence and beyond. *Child Abuse & Neglect, 26,* 637–644.

Korbin, J. E., Coulton, C. J., & Lindstrom-Ufuti, H. (2000). Neighborhood views on the definition and etiology of child maltreatment. *Child Abuse & Neglect, 24*(12), 1509–1527.

Kovacs, M. (1983). *The Children's Depression Inventory: A self-rated depression scale for school-aged youngsters.* Pittsburgh, PA: University of Pittsburgh.

Kovacs, P. J., & Mutepa, R. (2001, May). *An exploratory study of women who are long-term survivors of HIV/AIDS.* Paper presented at the National Conference on Social Work and HIV/AIDS, Philadelphia, PA.

Kozol, J. (1988). *Savage inequalities: Children in America's schools.* New York: HarperPerennial.

Kozol, J. (1995). *Amazing grace: The lives of children and the conscience of a nation.* New York: HarperPerennial.

Kozol, J. (2000). *Ordinary resurrections: Children in the years of hope.* New York: Crown.

Kozol, J. (2005). *The shame of the nation: The restoration of apartheid schooling in America.* New York: Random House.

Kraemer, G. (1992). A psychobiological theory of attachment. *Behavioral and Brain Sciences, 15*(3), 493–511.

Kraemer, G. (1997). Social attachment, brain function, aggression and violence. In A. Raine, P. Brennan, D. Farrington, & S. Mednick (Eds.), *Biosocial bases of violence* (pp. 207–229). New York: Plenum.

Kraus, D., Smith, G. T., & Ratner, H. H. (1994). Modifying alcohol-related expectancies in grade-school children. *Journal of Studies on Alcohol, 55,* 535–542.

Krieger, N., Chen, J., Waterman, P., Rehkopf, D., & Subramanian, S. (2005). Painting a truer picture of U.S. socioeconomic and racial/ethnic health inequalities: The public health disparities geocoding project. *American Journal of Public Health, 95*(2), 312–323.

Kripke, D., Tuunainen, A., & Endo, T. (2006). Letter to the editor: Benefits of light treatment for depression. *American Journal of Psychiatry, 163*(1), 162b–163.

Krishnan, K. R., Hays, J. C., Tupler, L. A., George, L. K., & Blazer, D. G., (1995). Clinical and phenomenological comparisons of later-onset and early-onset depression. *American Journal of Psychiatry, 152*(5), 785–788.

Krohn, A. (2000). The anatomy of adolescent violence. *Journal for the Psychoanalysis of Culture & Society, 5*(2), 212– 216.

Krohn, M., & Thornberry, T. (2002). Common themes, future directions. In T. Thornberry & M. Krohn (Eds.), *Taking stock of delinquency: An overview of findings from contemporary longitudinal studies.* New York: Plenum.

Kroner, D., & Mills, J. (1998). The structure of antisocial attitudes among violent and sexual offenders. *International Journal of Offender Therapy & Comparative Criminology, 42*(3), 246–257.

Krug, E., Dahlberg, L., Mercy, J., Zwi, A., & Lozano, R. (2002). *World report on violence and health.* Geneva, Switzerland: World Health Organization.

Kubik, M. Y., Lytle, L. A., Birnbaum, A. S., Murray, D. M., & Perry, C. L. (2003). Prevalence and correlates of depressive symptoms in young adolescents. *American Journal of Health Behavior, 27*(5), 546–553.

Kuh, D., & Ben-Shlomo, Y. (Eds.). (1997). *A life course approach to chronic disease epidemiology.* New York: Oxford University Press.

Kumanyika, S. K., & Charleston, J. B. (1992). Lose weight and win: A church-based weight loss program for blood pressure control among black women. *Patient Education and Counseling, 19*(1), 19–32.

Kuo, F. E., & Taylor, A. F. (2004). A potential natural treatment for attention-deficit/hyperactivity disorder: Evidence from a national study. *American Journal of Public Health, 94*(9), 1580–1586.

Kuo, F. E., & Taylor, A. F. (2005). Kuo and Faber Taylor respond. *American Journal of Public Health, 95*(3), 371–372.

Kuther, T., & Wallace, S. (2003). Community violence and sociomoral development: An African American cultural perspective. *American Journal of Orthopsychiatry, 73*(2), 177–189.

Kwon, P., & Laurenceau, J. (2002). A longitudinal study of the hopelessness theory of depression: Testing the diathesis-stress model within a differential reactivity and exposure framework. *Journal of Clinical Psychology, 58*(10), 305–321.

Laester, R. (1997). The labor force participation of young black men: A qualitative examination. *Social Service Review, 71*(2), 72–88.

Lahey, B. (2004, October 13). *Child factors.* Paper presented at the Preventing Violence State of the Science Conference, National Institutes of Health, Bethesda, MD.

Lam, R., Levitt, A., Levitan, R., Enns, M., Morehouse, R., Michalak, E., et al. (2006). The CAN-SAD study: A randomized controlled trial of the effectiveness of light therapy and fluoxetine in patients with winter seasonal affective disorder. *American Journal of Psychiatry, 163*(5), 805–812.

Lancaster, C. (2003). *Should global poverty be considered a U.S. national security issue? Poverty, terrorism and national security: A commentary.* Retrieved July 7, 2005, from http://www.wilsoncenter.org/index.cfm?fuseaction=news.item&news_id=34999

Landau, G., & York, A. (2004). Keeping and disclosing a secret among people with HIV in Israel. *Health & Social Work, 29*(2), 116–126.

Langley, A., & Jones, R. (2005). Coping efforts and efficacy, acculturation, and post-traumatic symptomatology in adolescents following wildfire. *Fire Technology, 41*(2), 125–143.

Larimer, M. E., Palmer, R. S., & Marlatt, G. A. (1999). Relapse prevention: An overview of Marlatt's cognitive-behavioral model. *Alcohol Research & Health, 23*(2), 151–160.

Larson, D. B., & Larson, S. S. (2003). Spirituality's potential relevance to physical and emotional health: A brief review of quantitative research. *Journal of Psychology & Theology, 31*(1), 37–51.

Larson, D. B., Larson, S. S., & Koenig, H. K. (2001). The patient's spiritual/religious dimension: A forgotten factor in mental health. *Directions in Psychiatry, 21,* 307–334.

Latkin, C. A., & Curry, A. D. (2003). Stressful neighborhoods and depression: A prospective study of the impact of neighborhood disorder. *Journal of Health and Social Behavior, 44*(1), 34–44.

Latzman, R., & Swisher, R. (2005). The interactive relationship among adolescent violence, street violence, and depression. *Journal of Community Psychology, 33*(3), 355–371.

Law, M., & Dunn, W. (1993). Perspectives on understanding and changing the environments of children with disabilities. *Physical and Occupational Therapy in Pediatrics, 13*(3), 1–18.

Layzer, J. I., Goodson, B. D., Bernstein, L., & Price, C. (2001). *National evaluation of family support programs: Final Report Volume A: The Meta-Analysis.* Cambridge, MA: Abt Associates.

Lazarus, R. S. (1993). Coping theory and research: Past, present, and future. *Psychosomatic Medicine, 55,* 234–247.

Lazarus, R. S., & Folkman, S. (1985). *Stress, appraisal and coping.* New York: Springer.

Le, B. P. (n.d.). *Asian gangs: A bibliography.* Retrieved March 24, 2006, from http://www.communitypolicing.org/publications/iag/asian_gangs/index.htm

Leahy, R. L. (1996). *Cognitive therapy: Basic practice and applications.* New York: Guilford Press.

Leahy, R. L. (2004). *Contemporary cognitive therapy: Theory, research, and practice.* New York: Guilford Press.

Lebowitz, B. D., Pearson, J. L., Schneider, L. S., Reynolds, C. F., Alexopoulos, G. S., Bruce, M. I., et al. (1997). Diagnosis and treatment of depression in late life: Consensus statement update. *Journal of the American Medical Association, 278*(14), 1186–1190.

Leerubier, Y., Clerc, G., Didi, R., & Kieser, M. (2002). Efficacy of St. John's wort extract WS5570 in major depression: A double-blind, placebo-controlled trial. *American Journal of Psychiatry, 159,* 1361–1366.

Leigh, J., Bowen, S., & Marlatt, G. A. (2005). Spirituality, mindfulness and substance abuse. *Addictive Behaviors, 30*(7), 1335–1341.

Lengerman, P. M., & Niebrugge-Brantley, J. (2000). Contemporary feminist theory. In G. Ritzer (Ed.), *Modern sociological theory* (pp. 307–355). New York: McGraw-Hill.

Lerman, R. (2005, May). *Are low-income households accumulating assets and avoiding unhealthy debt? A review of recent evidence.* Washington, DC: Urban Institute.

Lerner, D., Adler, D., Chang, H., Lapitsky, L., Hood, M., Perissinotto, C., et al. (2004). Unemployment, job retention, and productivity loss among employees with depression. *Psychiatric Service, 55*(12), 1371–1378.

Leschied, A. W., Chiodo, D., Whitehead, P. C., Hurley, D., & Marshall, L. (2003). The empirical basis of risk assessment in child welfare: The accuracy of risk assessment and clinical judgment. *Child Welfare, 82*(5), 527–540.

Leserman, J., Pettito, J., Perkins, D., Folds, J., Golden, R., & Evans, D. (1997). Severe stress, depressive symptoms, and changes in lymphocyte subsets in human immunodeficiency virus-infected men. *Archive of General Psychiatry, 54,* 279–285.

Leskela, U., Rytsala, H., Komulainen, E., Melartin, T., Lokero, P., Lestela-Mielonen, P., et al. (2006). The influence of adversity and perceived social support on the outcome of major depressive disorder in subjects with different levels of depressive symptoms. *Psychological Medicine, 36*(6), 779–788.

Levant, R., & Majors, R. (1997). Masculinity ideology among African American and European American college women and men. *Journal of Gender, Culture, and Health, 2,* 33–43.

Levant, R., Majors, R., & Kelly, M. (1998). Masculinity ideology among young African American and European American women and men in different regions of the United States. *Cultural Diversity and Ethnic Minority Psychology, 4*(3), 227–236.

Leventhal, J. M. (2003). The field of child maltreatment enters its fifth decade. *Child Abuse & Neglect, 27,* 1–4.

Levin, E., Wilkerson, A., Jones, J., Christopher, N., & Briggs, S. (1996). Prenatal nicotine effects on memory in rats: Pharmacological and behavioral challenges. *Developmental Brain Research, 97,* 207–215.

Levinson, D. F. (2005). The genetics of depression: A review. *Biological Psychiatry, 60*(2), 84–92.

Lewinsohn, P. M., Roberts, R. E., Seeley, J. R., & Rhodes, P. (1994). Adolescent psychopathology: Psychosocial risk factors for depression. *Journal of Abnormal Psychology, 103*(2), 302–315.

Lewis, C., & Brown, S. (2002). Coping strategies of female adolescents with HIV/AIDS. *American Black Nurse's Foundation Journal, 13*(4), 72–77.

Lewis, D., Shanok, S., & Balla, D. (1979). Perinatal difficulties, head and face trauma, and child abuse in the medical histories of seriously delinquent children. *American Journal of Psychiatry, 136,* 419–423.

Lewis, O. (1968). The culture of poverty. In D. Moynihan (Ed.), *On understanding poverty.* New York: Basic Books.

Life Skills Training. (2002). *Program description.* Retrieved January 10, 2005, from http://www.lifeskillstraining.com/program.cfm

Lillie-Blanton, M., Anthony, J. C., & Schuster, C. R. (1993). Probing the meaning of racial/ethnic group comparisons in crack cocaine smoking. *Journal of the American Medical Association, 269*(8), 993–997.

Linares, L., Heeren, T., Bronfman, E., Zuckerman, B., Augustyn, M., & Tronick, E. (2001). A mediational model for the impact of exposure to community violence on early child behavior problems. *Child Development, 72,* 639–652.

Lind, C. (2004). Developing and supporting a continuum of child welfare services. *Welfare Information Network Issue Note, 8*(6). Washington, DC: Finance Project. Retrieved May 23, 2005, from http://www.financeproject.org/Publications/developingandsupportingIN.pdf

Lindberg, C. (2000). Knowledge, self-efficacy, coping, and condom use among urban women. *Journal of the Association of Nurses in AIDS Care, 11*(5), 80–90.

Lindeman, S., Hämäläinen, J., Isometsä, E., Kaprio, J., Poikolainen, K., Heikkinen, M., et al. (2000). The 12-month prevalence and risk factors for major depressive episode in Finland. *Acta Psychiatrica Scandinavica, 102*(3), 178–184.

Lindsey, D. (2004). *The welfare of children* (2nd ed.). New York: Oxford.

Lindy, J. D., & Wilson, J. P. (2001). An allostatic approach to the psychodynamic understanding of PTSD. In J. P. Wilson, M. J. Friedman, & J. D. Lindy (Eds.), *Treating psychological trauma and PTSD* (pp. 125–138). New York: Guilford Press.

Linsk, N. L., & Bonk, N. (2000). Adherence to treatment as social work challenges. In V. J. Lynch (Ed.), *HIV/AIDS at year 2000: A sourcebook for social workers* (pp. 211–227). Boston: Allyn & Bacon.

Lipset, S. (1991). American exceptionalism reaffirmed. In B. E. Shafter (Ed.), *Is America different? A new look at American exceptionalism* (pp. 1–45). Oxford, England: Clarendon Press.

Lipsey, M., & Derzon, J. (1998). Predictors of violent or serious delinquency in adolescence and young adulthood: A synthesis of longitudinal research. In R. Loeber & D. Farrington (Eds.), *Serious and violent juvenile offenders: Risk factors and successful interventions* (pp. 86–105). Thousand Oaks, CA: Sage.

Litt, M. D., Kadden, R. M., Cooney, N. L., & Kabela, E. (2003). Coping skills and treatment outcomes in cognitive-behavioral and interactional group therapy for alcoholism. *Journal of Consulting and Clinical Psychology, 71,* 118–128.

Longo, M., Jain, V., Vedernikovy, Y., Bukowski, R., Garfield, R., Hankins, G., et al. (2005). Fetal origins of adult vascular dysfunction in mice lacking endothelial nitric oxide synthase. *American Journal of Physiology. Regulatory, Integrative and Comparative Physiology, 288*(5), R1114–R1121.

Loprest, P., & Maag, E. (2001, January). *Barriers to and supports for work among adults with disabilities: Results from the NHIS-D.* Washington, DC: Urban Institute.

Lorant, V., Deliege, D., Eaton, W., Robert, A., Philippot, P., & Ansseau, M. (2003). Socioeconomic inequalities in depression: A meta-analysis. *American Journal of Epidemiology, 157,* 98–112.

Loue, S. (2003). *Diversity issues in substance abuse treatment and research.* New York: Plenum.

Loury, G. C. (2002). Politics, race, and poverty research. In S. H. Danzinger & R. H. Haveman (Eds.), *Understanding poverty* (pp. 447–453). Cambridge, MA: Harvard University Press.

Lovett, B. B. (2004). Child sexual abuse disclosure: Maternal response and other variables impacting the victim. *Child & Adolescent Social Work Journal, 21*(4), 355–371.

Luckenbill, D., & Doyle, D. (1989). Structural position and violence. *Criminology, 27,* 419–436.

Ludwig, D., & Gortmaker, S. (2004). Programming obesity in childhood. *Lancet, 364*(9430), 226–227.

Ludwig, J., Hirschfield, P., & Duncan, G. (2001). Urban poverty and juvenile crime: Evidence from a randomized mobility experiment. *Quarterly Journal of Economics, 116*(2), 665–679.

Lum, D. (2003a). *Culturally competent practice: A framework for understanding diverse groups and justice issues* (2nd ed.). Pacific Grove, CA: Brooks/Cole.

Lum, D. (2003b). *Social work practice and people of color.* Belmont, CA: Wadsworth.

Lustig, D., & Strauser, D. (2004). Editorial. Poverty and disability. *Journal of Rehabilitation, 70*(3). Retrieved May, 24, 2005, from http://www.findarticles.com/p/articles/mi_m0825/ is_3_70/ai_n6237484

Luthar, S. (2003). *Resilience and vulnerability: Adaptation in the context of childhood adversities.* Cambridge, England: Cambridge University Press.

Luthar, S., & Zelazo, L. (2003). Research on resilience: An integrative review. In S. Luthar (Ed.), *Resilience and vulnerability: Adaptation in the context of childhood adversities* (pp. 510–549). Cambridge, England: Cambridge University Press.

Lutter, J. M. (1993). Obstacles to exercise for larger women. *Obesity and Health, 8*(1), 12–13.

Luxembourg Income Study. (2000). *LIS quick reference guide.* Syracuse, NY: Maxwell School of Citizenship and Public Affairs, Syracuse University.

Luxembourg Income Study. (2004). *Relative poverty rates for the total population, children and the elderly.* Retrieved June 16, 2004, from http://www.lisproject.org/keyfigures/povertytable.htm

Lynam, D., Wikstrom, P., Caspi, A., Moffitt, T., Loeber, R., & Novak, S. (2000). The interaction between impulsivity and neighborhood context on offending: The effects of impulsivity are stronger in poorer neighborhoods. *Journal of Abnormal Psychology, 109*(4), 563–574.

Lynch, M., & Cicchetti, D. (2002). Links between community violence and the family system: Evidence from children's feelings of relatedness and perceptions of parent behavior. *Family Process, 41*(3), 519–532.

MacDonald, R., Shildrick, T., Webster, C., & Simpson, D. (2005). Growing up in poor neighbourhoods: The significance of class and place in the extended transitions of "socially excluded" young adults. *Sociology, 39*(5), 873–891.

Macintyre, K., Rutenberg, N., Brown, L., & Karim, A. (2004). Understanding perceptions of HIV risk among adolescents in KwaZulu-Natal. *AIDS and Behavior, 8*(3), 237–250.

Maguire, K., & Pastore, A. (1999). *Sourcebook of criminal justice statistics, 1998* (U.S. Department of Justice, Office of Justice Programs, Bureau of Justice Statistics, NCJ 176356). Washington, DC: U.S. Government Printing Office.

Mahoney, A., Pargament, K. I., Tarakeshwar, N., & Swank, A. B. (2001). Religion in the home in the 1980s and 1990s: A meta-analytic review and conceptual analysis of links between religion, marriage, and parenting. *Journal of Family Psychology, 15*(4), 559–596.

Maiman, L., & Becker, M. (1974). The health belief model: Origins and correlates in psychological theory. *Health Education Monographs, 2,* 336–353.

Manber, R., Allen, J., & Morris, M. (2002). Alternative treatments for depression: Empirical support and relevance to women. *Journal of Clinical Psychiatry, 63*(7), 628–640.

Manber, R., Schnyer, R., Allen, J., Rush, A., & Blasey, C. (2004). Acupuncture: A promising treatment for depression during pregnancy. *Journal of Affective Disorders, 83*(1), 89–95.

Mancini, M., & Halpern, A. (2006). Pharmacological treatment of obesity. *Arquivos Brasileiros de Endocrinologia & Metabologia, 50*(2), 377–389.

Mansour, D. (2004). Implications of the growing obesity epidemic on contraception and reproductive health. *Journal of Family Planning and Reproductive Health Care, 30*(4), 209–211.

Manuck, S., Bleil, M., Petersen, K., Flory, J., Mann, J., Ferrell, R., et al. (2005). The socio-economic status of communities predicts variation in brain serotonergic responsivity. *Psychological Medicine, 35*(4), 519–528.

March, J., Amaya-Jackson, L., Terry, R., & Costanzo, P. (1997). Posttraumatic symptomatology in children and adolescents after an industrial fire. *Journal of the American Academy of Child and Adolescent Psychiatry, 36*(8), 1080–1088.

Marcoux, A. (1997). *The feminization of poverty: Facts, hypotheses, and the art of advocacy. SD (sustainable development) dimensions.* Retrieved May 20, 2005, from http://www.fao.org/WAICENT/FAOINFO/SUSTDEV/Wpdirect/Wpan0015.htm

Marcus, C. (2004). Pharmacological treatment of childhood obesity. *Pediatric and Adolescent Medicine, 9,* 211–218

Margitics, R. (2005). Role of protective factors in the development of depression. *Psychiatry Hungary, 20*(3), 224–237.

Marlatt, G. A. (1985). Relapse prevention: Theoretical rationale and overview of the model. In G. A. Marlatt & J. R. Gordon (Eds.), *Relapse prevention* (pp. 250–280). New York: Guilford Press.

Marlatt, G. A., & Gordon, J. R. (Eds.). (1985). *Relapse prevention: Maintenance strategies in the treatment of addictive behaviors.* New York: Guilford Press.

Marlatt, G. A., Wikiewitz, K., Dillworth, T. M., Bowen, S. W., Parks, G. A, MacPherson, L. M., et al. (2004). Vipassana meditation as a treatment for alcohol and drug use disorders. In S. C. Hayes, V. M. Follette, & M. M. Linehan (Eds.), *Mindfulness and acceptance: Expanding the cognitive-behavioral tradition* (pp. 267–287). New York: Guilford Press.

Marshall, I. (2002). The criminological enterprise in Europe and the United States: A contextual exploration. In S. Cote (Ed.), *Criminological theories: Bridging the past to the future* (pp. 14–22). Thousand Oaks, CA: Sage.

Martin, S., Sigda, K., & Kupersmidt, J. (1998). Family and neighborhood violence: Predictors of depressive symptomatology among incarcerated youth. *Prison Journal, 78*(4), 423–432.

Martinez, P., & Richters, J. (1993). The NIMH Community Violence Project: II. Children's distress symptoms associated with violence exposure. In D. Reiss, J. Richters, M. Radky-Yarrow, & D. Scharff (Eds.), *Children and violence* (pp. 22–35). New York: Guilford Press.

Martyn, K., & Hutchinson, S. (2001). Low-income African American adolescents who avoid pregnancy: Tough girls who rewrite negative scripts. *Qualitative Health Research, 11*(2), 238–256.

Marx, K., & Engels, F. (1848/1982). *The communist manifesto.* New York: International Publishers.

Mason, M. (2005). Overweight people suppress their hunger hormone. *Discover, 26*(1), 38.

Masten, A., & Garmezy, N. (1985). Risk, vulnerability and protective factors in developmental psychopathology. In B. Lahey & A. Kazdin (Eds.), *Advances in clinical child psychology* (Vol. 8, pp. 1–52). New York: Plenum.

Masten, A., & Powell, J. (2003). A resilience framework for research, policy, and practice. In S. Luthar (Ed.), *Resilience and vulnerability: Adaptation in the context of childhood adversities.* Cambridge, England: Cambridge University Press.

Masten, A. S. (2004). Regulatory processes, risk, and resilience in adolescent development. *Annals of the New York Academy of Sciences, 1021*, 310–319.

Masters, R., Hone, B., & Doshi, A. (1998). Environmental pollution, neurotoxicity, and criminal violence. In J. Rose (Ed.), *Environmental toxicology: Current developments* (pp. 13–48). New York: Gordon & Breach.

Matto, H. C. (2004). Applying an ecological framework to understanding drug addiction and recovery. *Journal of Social Work Practice in the Addictions, 4*(3), 5–22.

Matto, H. C. (2005a). A bio-behavioral model of addiction treatment: Applying dual representation theory to craving management and relapse prevention. *Substance Use & Misuse, 40*(4), 529–541.

Matto, H. C. (2005b). An integrated sensory-linguistic approach for drug addiction: A synthesis of the literature and new directions for treatment research. *Stress, Trauma, and Crisis: An International Journal, 8*, 79–92.

Matto, H. C., Berry-Edwards, J., Hutchison, E., Bryant, S., & Waldbillig, A. (2006). An exploratory study of multiple intelligences and social work education. *Journal of Social Work Education, 42*(2), 405–416.

Matto, H. C., Miller, K., & Spera, C. (2005). Ecological Assessment of Substance-abuse Experiences (EASE): Findings from a new instrument development pilot study. *Addictive Behaviors, 30*(7), 1281–1289.

Mayo Clinic Staff. (2005). Electroconvulsive therapy: Dramatic relief for severe mental illness. Retrieved June 4, 2005, from http://www.mayoclinic.com/invoke.cfm?id=MH00022

Mazur, A., & Booth, A. (1999). The biosociology of testosterone in men. In D. Franks & S. Smith (Eds.), *Mind, brain, and society: Toward a neurosociology of emotion* (Vol. 5, pp. 311–338). Stamford, CT: JAI.

Mbori-Ngacha, D., Nduati, R., John, G., Reilly, M., Richardson, B., Mwatha, A., et al. (2001). Morbidity and mortality in breastfed and formula-fed infants of HIV-1-infected women: A randomized clinical trial. *Journal of the American Medical Association, 286*(19), 2413–2420.

McAvoy, M. (1999). *The profession of ignorance: With constant reference to Socrates.* Lanham, NY: University Press of America.

McBee, L., Westreich, L., & Likourezos, A. (2004). A psychoeducational relaxation group for pain and stress management in the nursing home. *Journal of Social Work in Long Term Care, 3*(1), 15–28.

McBurnett, K., Lahey, B., Rathouz, R., & Loeber, R. (2000). Low salivary cortisol and persistent aggression in boys referred for disruptive behavior. *Archives of General Psychiatry, 57*, 38–43.

McCann, I. L., & Pearlman, L. A. (1990). *Psychological trauma and the adult survivor: Theory, therapy, and transformation.* New York: Brunner/Mazel.

McCord, J., & Ensminger, M. (2003). Racial discrimination and violence: A longitudinal perspective. In D. Hawkins (Ed.), *Violent crime: Assessing race & ethnic differences* (pp. 319–330). New York: Cambridge University Press.

McEnany, G., & Lee, K. (2005). Effects of light therapy on sleep, mood, and temperature in women with nonseasonal major depression. *Issues in Mental Health Nursing, 26*(7), 781–794.

McGue, M. (1994). Genes, environment, and the etiology of alcoholism. In R. Zucker, G. Boyd, & J. Howard (Eds.), *The development of alcohol problems: Exploring the biopsychosocial matrix of risk* (NIAAA Research Monograph No. 26, pp. 1–40). Washington, DC: U.S. Government Printing Office.

McKay, J. R. (1999). Studies of factors in relapse to alcohol, drug and nicotine use: A critical review of methodologies and findings. *Journal of Studies on Alcohol, 60*, 566–576.

McMillan-Price, J., & Brand-Miller, J. (2004). Dietary approaches to overweight and obesity. *Clinical Dermatology, 22*(4), 310–314.

McNair, L., Carter, J., & Williams, M. (1998). Self-esteem, gender and alcohol use: Relationships with HIV risk perception and behaviors in college students. *Journal of Sex & Marital Therapy, 24*, 29–36.

McQueen, A., Getz, J. G., & Bray, J. H. (2003). Acculturation, substance use, and deviant behavior: Examining separation and family conflict as mediators. *Child Development, 74*(6), 1737–1754.

McWhiney, G. (1988). *Cracker culture: Celtic ways in the Old South.* Tuscaloosa: University of Alabama Press.

Mendel, R. (2000). *Less hype, more help: Reducing juvenile crime, what works—and what doesn't.* Washington, DC: American Youth Policy Forum.

Merton, R. (1938). Social structure and anomie. *American Sociological Review, 3*, 672–682.

Messner, S., & Rosenfeld, R. (1997). Political restraint of the market and levels of criminal homicide: A cross-national application of institutional-anomie theory. *Social Forces, 75*, 1393–1416.

Meyer, C. (1993). *Assessment in social work practice.* New York: Columbia University Press.

Meyers, R. J., Miller, W. R., Hill, D. E., & Tonigan, J. S. (1999). Community reinforcement and family training: Engaging unmotivated drug users in treatment. *Journal of Substance Abuse, 10,* 291–308.

Meyers, R. J., Miller, W. R., Smith, J. E., & Tonigan, J. S. (2002). A randomized trial of two methods for engaging treatment-refusing drug users through concerned significant others. *Journal of Consulting and Clinical Psychology, 70,* 1182–1185.

Mezirow, J. (1998). On critical reflection. *Adult Education Quarterly, 48,* 185–198.

Miller, B. A., & Downs, W. R. (1993). The impact of family violence on the use of alcohol by women. *Alcohol Health and Research World, 17*(2), 137–143.

Miller, J. (1996). *Search and destroy: African-American males in the criminal justice system.* New York: Cambridge University Press.

Miller, J. (2002). Social workers as diagnosticians. In K. Bentley (Ed.), *Social work practice in mental health: Contemporary roles, tasks & techniques* (pp. 43–72). Pacific Grove, CA: Brooks/Cole.

Miller, L., Warner, V., Wickramaratne, P., & Weissman, M. (1997). Religiosity & depression: Ten-year follow-up of depressed mothers and offspring. *Journal of the American Academy of Child and Adolescent Psychiatry, 36,* 1416–1425.

Miller, L., Wasserman, G., Neugebauer, R., Gorman-Smith, D., & Kamboukos, D. (1999). Witnessed community violence and antisocial behavior in high-risk, urban boys. *Journal of Clinical Child Psychology, 28*(1), 2–11.

Miller, M., Serner, M., & Wagner, M. (2005). Sexual diversity among black men who have sex with men in an inner-city community. *Journal of Urban Health: Bulletin of the New York Academy of Medicine, 82*(1), 26–34.

Miller, W. R., Meyers, R. J., & Tonigan, J. S. (1999). Engaging the unmotivated in treatment for alcohol problems: A comparison of three strategies for intervention through family members. *Journal of Consulting and Clinical Psychology, 67,* 688–697.

Miller, W. R., & Rollnick, S. (2002). *Motivational interviewing: Preparing people for change.* New York: Guilford Press.

Miller, W. R., & Weisner, C. M. (2002). *Changing substance abuse through health and social systems.* New York: Plenum.

Milner, J. S. (1993). Social information processing and physical child abuse. *Clinical Psychology Review, 13,* 275–294.

Minino, A. M., Arias, E., Kochanek, K. D., Murphy, S. L., & Smith, B. L. (2002). Deaths: Final data for 2000. *National Vital Statistics Reports, 50*(15). Hyattsville, MD: National Center for Health Statistics.

Mink, G. (1998). *Welfare's end.* Ithaca, NY: Cornell University Press.

Mirza, N. M., Kadow, K., Palmer, M., Solano, H., Rosche, C., & Yanovski, J. A. (2004). Prevalence of overweight among inner city Hispanic-American children and adolescents. *Obesity Research, 12*(8), 1298–1310.

Mish, F. (Ed.). (1998). *Merriam-Webster's collegiate dictionary* (10th ed.). Springfield, MA: Merriam-Webster.

Mishel, L., Bernstein, J., & Allegretto, S. (2005). *The state of working America.* Ithaca, NY: Cornell University Press.

Mitchell, C. G., & Linsk, N. L. (2004). A multidimensional conceptual framework for understanding HIV/AIDS as a chronic long-term illness. *Social Work, 49*(3), 469–477.

Mizuno, T., Shu, I. W., Makimura, H., & Mobbs, C. (2004). Obesity over the life course. *Science of Aging Knowledge Environment, 24,* 4.

Moffitt, T. (1990). The neuropsychology of juvenile delinquency. In M. Tonry & N. Morris (Eds.), *Crime and justice: A review of research* (Vol. 12). Chicago: University of Chicago Press.

Moffitt, T. (1993). "Life-course-persistent" and "adolescence-limited" antisocial behavior: A developmental taxonomy. *Psychological Review, 100,* 674–701.

Moffitt, T., Caspi, A., Fawcett, P., Brammer, G., Raleigh, M., Yuwiler, A., et al. (1997). Whole blood serotonin and family background related to male violence. In A. Raine, P. Brennan, D. Farrington, & S. Mednick (Eds.), *Biosocial bases of violence* (pp. 231–249). New York: Plenum.

Moffitt, T., Caspi, A., Harrington, H., & Milne, B. (2002). Males on the life-course persistent and adolescence-limited antisocial pathways: Follow-up at age 26. *Developmental Psychopathology, 14,* 179–206.

Mohr, W., Fantuzzo, J., & Abdul-Kabir, S. (2001). Safeguarding themselves and their children: Mothers share their strategies. *Journal of Family Violence, 16,* 75–92.

Mokhiber, R. (2003, May). Trafficking in children. *Multinational Monitor, 24*(5), 4.

Molassiotis, A., & Maneesakorn, S. (2004). Quality of life, coping and psychological status of Thai people living with AIDS. *Psychology, Health and Medicine, 9*(3), 350–361.

Molitor, F., Ruiz, J., Klausner, J., & McFarland, W. (2000). History of forced sex in association with drug use and sexual HIV risk behaviors, infection with STDS, and diagnostic medical care results from the Young Women Survey. *Journal of Interpersonal Violence, 15*(3), 262–278.

Monroe, A. (2001). *Psychological issues and HIV: Dealing with the uncertainty of changing treatment strategies: Community forum summary: Robert H. Remien and Michael Shernoff, Speakers.* Retrieved June 12, 2005, from http://www.thebody.com/cria/forums/psychology

Montgomery, J., Mokotoff, E., Gentry, A., & Blair, J. (2003). The extent of bisexual behaviour in HIV-infected men and implications for transmission to their female sex partners. *AIDS Care, 15*(6), 829–837.

Montgomery, S., Hyde, J., De Rosa, C., Rohrbach, L., Ennett, S., Harvey, S., et al. (2002). Gender differences in HIV risk behaviors among young injectors and their social network members. *American Journal of Drug and Alcohol Abuse, 28*(3), 453–475.

Montgomery, S. A., & Asberg, M. (1979). A new depression scale designed to be sensitive to change. *British Journal of Psychiatry, 134,* 382–389.

Moore, V., & Davies, M. (2005). Diet during pregnancy, neonatal outcomes and later health. *Reproductive Fertility Development, 17*(3), 341–348.

Morgan, C. A., Wang, S., Southwick, S. M., Rasmusson, A. M., Hazlett, G., Hauger, R. L., et al. (2000). Plasma neuropeptide-Y concentrations in humans exposed to military survival training. *Biological Psychiatry, 47,* 902–909.

Morris, M., & Kretzschmar, M. (1997). Concurrent partnerships and the spread of HIV. *AIDS, 11*(5), 641–648.

Morrow, J. R., Krzewinski-Malone, J. A., Jackson, A. W., Bungum, T. J., & FitzGerald, S. J. (2004). American adults' knowledge of exercise recommendations. *Research Quarterly Exercise Sports, 75*(3), 231–237.

Morse, E., Morse, P., Klebba, K., Stock, M., Forehand, R., & Panayotova, E. (2000). The use of religion among HIV-infected African American women. *Journal of Religion and Health, 39*(3), 261–276.

Moscicki, E. K. (1999). Epidemiology of suicide. In D. Jacobs, (Ed.), *The Harvard Medical School guide to suicide assessment and intervention* (pp. 40–71). San Francisco: Jossey-Bass.

Moscicki, E. K. (2001). Epidemiology of completed and attempted suicide: Toward a framework for prevention. *Clinical Neuroscience Research, 1,* 310–323.

Moss, H., Vanyukov, M., Yao, J., & Kiriflova, G. (1999). Salivary cortisol responses in prepubertal boys: The effects of parental substance abuse and associations with drug use behavior during adolescence. *Biological Psychiatry, 45,* 1293–1299.

Mowbray, C., Schwartz, S., & Bybee, D. (2000). Mothers with a mental illness: Stressors and resources for parenting and living. *Families in Society, 81*(2), 118–129.

Moynihan, D. P. (1965). *The negro family: The case for national action.* Washington, DC: Office of Planning and Research, U.S. Department of Labor.

Mui, A. C., Kang, S. Y., Chen, L. M., & Domanski, M. D. (2004). Reliability of the Geriatric Depression Scale for use among elderly Asian immigrants in the USA. *International Psychogeriatrics, 16*(3), 253–271.

Mullahy, J., & Wolfe, B. L. (2002). Health policies for the non-elderly poor. In S. H. Danzinger & R. H. Haveman (Eds.). *Understanding poverty* (pp. 278– 313). Cambridge, MA: Harvard University Press.

Mullings, J., Marquart, J., & Brewer, V. (2000). Assessing the relationship between child sexual abuse and marginal living conditions on HIV/AIDS-related risk behavior among women prisoners. *Child Abuse & Neglect, 24*(5), 677–688.

Multisystemic Therapy. (2004). *Treatment model.* Retrieved January 10, 2005, from http://www.mstservices.com/text/treatment.html

Murray, C., & Lopez, A. (Eds.). (1996). *The global burden of disease and injury series: A comprehensive assessment of mortality and disability from diseases, injuries, and risk factors in 1990 and projected to 2020.* Cambridge, MA: Harvard University Press.

Myers, M., & Brown, S. (1990a). Coping and appraisal in potential relapse situations among adolescent substance abusers following treatment. *Journal of Adolescent Chemical Dependency, 1,* 95–115.

Myers, M., & Brown, S. (1990b). Coping responses and relapse among adolescent substance abusers. *Journal of Substance Abuse, 2,* 177–189.

Nafees, A. (2005). The vertical transmission of human immunodeficiency virus type 1: Molecular and biological properties of the virus. *Critical Reviews in Clinical Laboratory Sciences, 42*(1), 1–34.

Najavits, L. M., Weiss, R. D., & Liese, B. S. (1996). Group cognitive-behavioral therapy for women with PTSD and substance use disorder. *Journal of Substance Abuse Treatment, 13,* 13–22.

Najavits, L. M., Weiss, R. D., Shaw, S. R., & Muenz, L. R. (1998). "Seeking Safety:" Outcome of a new cognitive-behavioral psychotherapy for women with posttraumatic stress disorder and substance dependence. *Journal of Traumatic Stress, 11*(3), 437–456.

Narayan, D. (2005). Conceptual framework and methodological challenges. In D. Narayan (Ed.), *Measuring empowerment: Cross-disciplinary perspectives* (pp. 3–38). Washington, DC: World Bank.

Nasar, S., & Mitchell, K. (1999, May 23). Booming job market draws young black men into fold. *The New York Times,* pp. A1, A21.

Nash, J., & Randolph, K. (2004). Methods in the analysis of risk and protective factors: Lessons from epidemiology. In M. Fraser (Ed.), *Risk and resilience in childhood: An ecological perspective* (2nd ed., pp. 67–87). Washington, DC: National Association of Social Workers.

National Association of Social Workers. (1999). *Code of ethics* (Rev. ed.). Washington, DC: Author.

National Center for Chronic Disease Prevention and Health Promotion. (2004). *What principles characterize a syndemic orientation?* Retrieved February 26, 2005, from http://www.cdc.gov/syndemics/overview-principles.htm

National Clearinghouse on Child Abuse & Neglect Information. (2005). *Definitions of child abuse and neglect.* Washington, DC: Author. Retrieved April 27, 2005, from http://nccanch.acf.hhs.gov/general/legal/statutes/define.cfm

National Dissemination Center for Children with Disabilities. (2002). *General information about disabilities: Disabilities that qualify infants, toddlers, children, and youth for services under IDEA.* Retrieved May 23, 2005, from http://www.nichy.org/pubs/genresc/gr3.htm

National Institutes of Health. (1998). *Clinical guidelines on the identification, evaluation, and treatment of overweight and obesity in adults* (NIH Publication No. 98–4083). Bethesda, MD: Author.

National Institutes of Health. (2002). *Depression and HIV/AIDS* (NIH Publication No. 02–5005). Bethesda, MD: Author.

National Institutes of Health. (2004, October 13–15). *Preventing violence and related health-risking social behaviors in adolescents: An NIH state-of-the-science conference.* Bethesda, MD: Author.

National Institute of Mental Health. (1999). *Depression research at the National Institute of Mental Health.* (NIH Publication No. 00–4501). Bethesda, MD: Author.

National Institute of Mental Health. (2005). *Depression in children and adolescents.* Retrieved April 16, 2005, from http://nimh.nih.gov/HealthInformation/depchildmenu.cfm

National Library of Medicine. (2005). *Health information.* Retrieved July 2, 2005, from http://www.nlm.nih.gov/

National Research Council. (1993). *Understanding child abuse and neglect.* Washington, DC: National Academy Press.

Nduati, R., John, G., Mbori-Ngacha, D., Richardson, B., Overbaugh, J., Mwatha, A., et al. (2000). Effect of breastfeeding and formula feeding on transmission of HIV-1: A randomized clinical trial. *Journal of the American Medical Association, 283*(9), 1167.

Neaigus, A., Friedman, S., Curtis, R., Des Jarlais, D., Furst, R., Jose, B., et al. (1994). The relevance of drug injectors' social and risk networks for understanding and preventing HIV infection. *Social Science and Medicine, 38*(1), 67–78.

Nelson, C., Rosenfeld, B., Breitbart, W., & Galietta, M. (2002). Spirituality, religion, and depression in the terminally ill. *Psychosomatics, 43*(3), 213–220.

Nemoto, T., Operario, D., Takenaka, M., Iwamoto, M., & Le, M. (2003). HIV risk among Asian women working at massage parlors in San Francisco. *AIDS Education and Prevention, 15*(3), 245–256.

Nestle, M., & Guttmacher, S. (1992). Hunger in the United States: Rationale, methods, and policy implications of state hunger surveys. *Journal of Nutrition Education, 24,* 18S–22S.

Neuberger, N., Fremstad, S., & Parrott, S. (2003, February 12). *$16,000 per family? Administration's claim that its budget increases welfare-to-work funding is incorrect.* Retrieved May 23, 2005, from http://www.cbpp.org/2–12–03tanf.htm

Neumark-Sztainer, D., Story, M., & Harris, T. (1999). Beliefs and attitudes about obesity among teachers and school health care providers working with adolescents. *Journal of Nutrition Education, 31,* 3–9.

Newman, K. S. (1999). *No shame in my game: The working poor in the inner city.* New York: Alfred A. Knopf.

Niaura, R. (2000). Cognitive social learning and related perspectives on drug craving. *Addiction, 95,* 155–163.

Nieves, R., Carballo, D., & Dolezal, C. (2000). Domestic abuse and HIV-risk behavior in Latin American men who have sex with men in New York City. *Journal of Gay and Lesbian Social Services, 11*(1), 77–90.

Njie, A. B. H. (2001). Poverty and ill health: The Ugandan national response. *Development, 44*(1), 93–98.

Noar, S., & Morokoff, P. (2002). The relationship between masculinity ideology, condom attitudes, and condom use stage of change: A structural equation modeling approach. *International Journal of Men's Health, 1*(1), 43–58.

Noell, J., Rohde, P., Seeley, J., & Ochs, L. (2001). Childhood sexual abuse, adolescent sexual coercion and sexually transmitted infection acquisition among homeless female adolescents. *Child Abuse & Neglect, 25,* 137–148.

Noonan, K., Reichman, N., & Corman, H. (2005). New fathers' labor supply: Does child health matter? *Social Science Quarterly, 86*(Suppl.), 1399–1417.

North American Association for the Study of Obesity. (2006). *Obesity statistics.* Retrieved June 14, 2006, from http://www.naaso.org/statistics/obesity_trends.asp

Nurius, P. (1995). Critical thinking: A meta-skill for integrating practice and information technology training. *Computers in Human Services, 12*(1/2), 109–126.

O'Donnell, D., Schwab-Stone, M., & Muyeed, A. (2002). Multidimensional resilience in urban children exposed to community violence. *Child Development, 73*(4), 1265–1282.

O'Donnell, M. P. (2004, May 24–26). Plenary: *Creating workplace environments to combat obesity.* Obesity and the Built Environment Conference, National Institute of Environmental Health Services, Washington, DC.

O'Leary, A., Goodhart, F., Jemmott, L., & Boccher-Lattimore, D. (1992). Predictors of safer sex on the college campus: A social cognitive theory analysis. *Journal of American College Health, 40,* 254–263.

O'Rand, A. (1996). The precious and the precocious: Understanding cumulative disadvantage and cumulative advantage over the life course. *The Gerontologist, 36*(2), 230–238.

Oakley, A., Fullerton, D., Holland, J., Arnold, S., France-Dawson, M., Kelley, P., et al. (1995). Sexual health education interventions for young people: A methodological review. *British Medical Journal, 310*(6973), 158–162.

Oesterle, S., Hill, K. G., Hawkins, J. D., Guo, J., Catalano, R. F., & Abbott, R. D. (2004). Adolescent heavy episodic drinking trajectories and health in young adulthood. *Journal of Studies on Alcohol, 65,* 204–212.

Oldehinkel, A., Wittchen, J., & Schuster, P. (1999). Prevalence, 20-month incidence and outcome of unipolar depressive disorders in a community sample of adolescents. *Psychological Medicine, 29,* 655–668.

Olds, D. (1997). The prenatal/early infancy project: Fifteen years later. In G. W. Albee & T. P. Gullotta (Eds.), *Primary prevention works.* Thousand Oaks, CA: Sage.

Olds, D. (2003). Reducing program attrition in home visiting: What do we need to know? *Child Abuse & Neglect, 27*(4), 359–361.

Oliver, L., & Shapiro, T. M. (2000). A sociology of wealth and racial inequality. In M. Adams, W. J. Blumenfeld, R. Castaneda, H. W. Hackman, M. L. Peters, & X. Zuniga (Eds.), *Readings for diversity and social justice: An anthology on racism, anti-Semitism, sexism, heterosexism, ableism, and classism* (pp. 402–406). New York: Routledge.

Olsen, L., Mortensen, E., & Bech, P. (2004). Prevalence of major depression and stress indicators in the Danish general population. *Acta Psychiatrica Scandinavica, 109*(2), 96–103.

Olson, C. M. (1999). Nutrition and health outcomes associated with food insecurity and hunger. *Journal of Nutrition, 129*(2S Suppl.), 521S–524S.

Olweus, D., Limber, S., & Mihalic, S. (1998). *Bullying prevention program.* Boulder: University of Colorado, Center for the Study and Prevention of Violence, Blueprints for Violence Prevention.

Onyike, C. U., Crum, R. M., Lee, H. B., Lyketsos, C. G., & Eaton, W. W. (2003). Is obesity associated with major depression? Results from the Third National Health and Nutrition Examination survey. *American Journal of Epidemiology, 158,* 1139–1147.

Ortiz, I. (n.d.). *Backgrounder: Poverty reduction. Initiative for policy dialogue.* Retrieved October 4, 2006, from http://www2.gsb.columbia.edu/ipd/j_poverty_bk.html

Ortiz, J., & Raine, A. (2004). Heart rate level and antisocial behavior in children and adolescents: A meta analysis. *Journal of American Academy of Child and Adolescent Psychiatry, 43*(2), 154–162.

Ory, M. G., Zablotsky, D. L., & Crystal, S. (1998). HIV/AIDS and aging: Identifying a prevention research and care agenda. *Research on Aging, 20*(6), 637–653.

Oslin, D. W., Strein, J., Katz, I. R., Edell, W. S., & TenHave, T. (2000). Change in disability follows inpatient treatment for late life depression. *Journal of the American Geriatrics Society, 48*(4), 357–362.

Osofsky, J. (1995). The effects of exposure to violence on young children. *American Psychologist, 50*(9), 782–788.

Osofsky, J., Wewers, S., Hann, D., & Fick, A. (1993). Chronic community violence: What is happening to our children? *Psychiatry, 56,* 36–45.

Ostman, J., Britton, M., & Jonsson, E. (Eds.). (2004). *Treating and preventing obesity: An evidence based review.* Weinheim, Germany: Wiley-VCH.

Ouellet, L., Huo, D., & Bailey, S. (2004). HIV risk practices among needle exchange users and nonusers in Chicago. *Journal of Acquired Immune Deficiency Syndromes, 37*(1), 1187–1196.

Overeaters Anonymous. (2006). 12-step recovery program from compulsive overeating. Retrieved June 16, 2006, from http://www.oa.org/index.htm

Overstreet, S. (2000). Exposure to community violence: Defining the problem and understanding the consequences. *Journal of Child and Family Studies, 9*(1), 7–25.

Ozer, E., Best, S., Lipsey, T., & Weiss, D. (2003). Predictors of posttraumatic stress disorder and symptoms in adults: A meta-analysis. *Psychological Bulletin, 129,* 52–73.

Palmer, C. J. (2003). Body mass index, self-esteem, and suicide risk in clinically depressed African American and white American females. *Journal of Black Psychology, 29*(4), 408–428.

Pangestu, M., & Sachs, J. (2004, February). *Interim report of Task Force 1 on poverty and economic development.* New York: United Nations.

Parappully, J., Rosenbaum, R., van den Daele, L., & Nzewi, E. (2002). Thriving after trauma: The experience of parents of murdered children. *Journal of Humanistic Psychology, 42*(1), 33–70.

Pargament, K. (1997). *The psychology of religion and coping: Theory, research, practice.* New York: Guilford Press.

Pargament, K. I., Smith, B. W., Koenig, H. G., & Perez, L. (1998). Patterns of positive and negative religious coping with major life stressors. *Journal for the Scientific Study of Religion, 37*(4), 710–724.

Parikh, M., Laker, S., Weiner, M., Hajiseyedjavadi, O., & Ren, C. (2006). Objective comparison of complications resulting from laparoscopic bariatric procedures. *Journal of American College of Surgeons, 202*(2), 252–261.

Parker, R., & Aggleton, P. (2003). HIV and AIDS-related stigma and discrimination: A conceptual framework and implications for action. *Social Science & Medicine, 57*(1), 13–24.

Parson, E. R. (1994). Post-traumatic ethnotherapy (P-TET): Processes in assessment and intervention in aspects of global psychic trauma. In M. B. Williams & J. F. Sommer (Eds.), *Handbook of post-traumatic therapy* (pp. 221–239). Westport, CT: Greenwood Press.

Parson, E. R. (1997). Post-traumatic child therapy (P-TCT): Assessment and treatment factors in clinic work with inner-city children exposed to catastrophic community violence. *Journal of Interpersonal Violence, 12,* 172–194.

Passehl, B., McCarroll, C., Buechner, J., Gearring, C., Smith, A. E., & Trowbridge, F. (2004). Preventing childhood obesity: Establishing healthy lifestyle habits in the preschool years. *Journal of Pediatric Health Care, 18*(6), 315–319.

Pate, R. R., Pfeiffer, K. A., Trost, S. G., Ziegler, P., & Dowda, M. (2004). Physical activity among children attending preschools. *Pediatrics, 114*(5), 1258–1263.

Patel, V., & Kleinman, A. (2003). Overt and common mental disorders in developing countries. *Bulletin of the World Health Organization, 81*(8), 609–615.

Patterson, C. M., & Newman, J. P. (1993). Reflectivity and learning from aversive events: Toward a psychological mechanism for syndromes of disinhibition. *Psychological Review, 100,* 716–736.

Patterson, T., Shaw, W., Semple, S., Cherner, M., McCutchan, J., Atkinson, J., et al. (1996). Relationship of psychosocial factors to HIV disease progression. *Annals of Behavioral Medicine, 18,* 30–39.

Pavon, B. (2004). AIDS slashes life expectancy in 23 African countries. *UN Chronicle Online Edition.* Retrieved May 29, 2005, from http://www.un.org/Pubs/chronicle/2004/issue3/0304p54.asp

Paxton, S., Gonzales, G., Uppakaew, K., Abraham, K., Okta, S., Green, C., et al. (2005). AIDS-related discrimination in Asia. *AIDS Care, 17*(4), 413–524.

Payne, M. (2005). *Modern social work theory* (3rd ed.). Chicago: Lyceum Books.

Pearce, M., Jones, S., Schwab-Stone, M., & Ruchkin, V. (2003). The protective effects of religiousness and parent involvement on the development of conduct problems among youth exposed to violence. *Child Development, 74*(6), 1682–1696.

Pearce, M. J., Little, T. D., & Perez, J. E. (2003). Religiousness and depressive symptoms among adolescents. *Journal of Clinical Child & Adolescent Psychology, 32*(2), 267–276.

Pearlman, L. A., & Saakvitne, K. W. (1995). *Trauma and the therapist: Countertransference and vicarious traumatization in psychotherapy with incest survivors.* New York: Norton.

Pecora, P., Whittaker, J., Maluccio, A., & Barth, R. P. (2000). *The child welfare challenge: Policy, practice, and research.* New York: Aldine de Gruyter.

Peek, M. K., & Coward, R. T. (2000). Antecedents of disability for older adults with multiple chronic health conditions. *Research on Aging, 22*(4), 422–444.

Penninx, B., Guralnik, J., Pahor, M., Ferrucci, L., Cerhan, J., Wallace, R., et al. (1998). Chronically depressed mood and cancer risk in older persons. *Journal of National Cancer Institute, 90*(24), 1888–1893.

Penninx, B., Leveille, S., Ferrucci, L., van Eijk, J., & Guralnik, J. (1999). Exploring the effect of depression on physical disability: Longitudinal evidence from the established populations for epidemiologic studies of the elderly. *American Journal of Public Health, 89*(9), 1346–1352.

Perlis, M., Smith, L., Lyness, J., Matteson, S., Pegeon, W., Jungquist, C., et al. (2006). Insomnia as a risk factor for onset of depression in the elderly. *Behavioral Sleep Medicine, 4*(2), 104–113.

Perlman, H. (1957). *Social casework: A problem-solving process.* Chicago: University of Chicago Press.

Perrin, E. C., & Sack, S. (1998). Health and development of gay and lesbian youths: Implications for HIV/AIDS. *AIDS Patient Care STDA, 12*(4), 303–313.

Perrin, S., Smith, P., & Yule, W. (2000). Practitioner review: The assessment and treatment of posttraumatic stress disorder in children and adolescents. *Journal of Child Psychology & Psychiatry & Allied Disciplines, 41*(3), 277–289.

Perry, B. (1997). Incubated in terror: Neurodevelopmental factors in the "cycle of violence." In J. Osofsky (Ed.), *Children in a violent society* (pp. 124–149). New York: Guilford Press.

Perry, B. G. (1998). The relationship between faith and well-being. *Journal of Religion and Health, 37*(2), 125–126.

Peterson, D. (1995). The reflective educator. *American Psychologist, 50*(12), 975–983.

Peterson, J., Coates, T., Catania, J., Middleton, L., Hilliard, B., & Hearst, N. (1992). High-risk sexual behavior and condom use among gay and bisexual African-American men. *American Journal of Public Health, 82,* 1490–1494.

Peterson, R., Krivo, L., & Harris, M. (2000). Disadvantage and neighborhood violent crime: Do local institutions matter? *Journal of Research in Crime and Delinquency, 37*(1), 31–63.

Pezawas, L., Meyer-Lindenberg, A., Drabant, E., Verchinski, B., Munoz, K., Kolachana, B., et al. (2005). 5-HTTLPR polymorphism impacts human cingulated-amygdala interactions: A genetic susceptibility mechanism for depression. *Nature Neuroscience, 6,* 828–834.

Phan, T., Steel, Z., & Silove, D. (2004). An ethnographically derived measure of anxiety, depression and somatization: The Phan Vietnamese Psychiatric Scale. *Transcultural Psychiatry, 41*(2), 200–232.

Pharr, S. (2000). Reflections on liberation. In M. Adams, W. J. Blumenfeld, R. Castaneda, H. Hackman, M. L. Peters, & X. Zuniga (Eds.), *Readings for diversity and social justice: An anthology on racism, anti-Semitism, sexism, heterosexism, ableism, and classism* (pp. 450–457). New York: Routledge.

Phillips, L. (2005). Deconstructing "down low" discourse: The politics of sexuality, gender, race, AIDS, and anxiety. *Journal of African American Studies, 9*(2), 3–16.

Pilkington, K., Kirkwood, C., Rampes, H., & Richardson, J. (2005). Yoga for depression: The research evidence. *Journal of Affective Disorders, 89*(1–3), 13–24.

Pilowsky, D., Wickramartne, P., Nomura, Y., & Weissman, M. (2006). Family discord, parental depression, and psychopathology in offspring: 20-year follow-up. *Journal of the American Academy of Child and Adolescent Psychiatry, 45*(4), 452–460.

Pincus, F. (2000). Discrimination comes in many forms: Individual, institutional, and structural. In M. Adams, W. J. Blumenfeld, R. Castaneda, H. Hackman, M. L. Peters, & X. Zuniga (Eds.), *Readings for diversity and social justice: An anthology on racism, anti-Semitism, sexism, heterosexism, ableism, and classism* (pp. 31–35). New York: Routledge.

Pine, D., Goldstein, R., Wolk, S., & Weissman, M. (2001). The association between childhood depression and adulthood body mass index. *Pediatrics, 107,* 1049–1056.

Pingitoire, R., Dugoni, R., Tindale, S., & Spring, B. (1994). Bias against overweight job applicants in a simulated employment interview. *Journal of Applied Psychology, 79,* 909–917.

Piquero, A., Gibson, C., Tibbetts, S., Turner, M., & Katz, S. (2002). Maternal cigarette smoking during pregnancy and life-course-persistent offending. *International Journal of Offender Therapy & Comparative Criminology, 46*(2), 231–247.

Piquero, A., & Tibbetts, S. (1999). The impact of pre/perinatal disturbances and disadvantaged familial environment in predicting criminal offending. *Studies on Crime and Crime Prevention, 8,* 52–70.

Piquero, A., & White, N. (2003). On the relationship between cognitive abilities and life-course-persistent offending among a sample of African Americans: A longitudinal test of Moffitt's hypothesis. *Journal of Criminal Justice, 31,* 399–409.

Piven, F., & Cloward, R. (1977). *Poor people's movements: Why they succeed, how they fail.* New York: Pantheon.

Piwoz, E., Ross, J., & Humphrey, J. (2004). Human immunodeficiency virus transmission during breastfeeding: Knowledge, gaps, and challenges for the future. *Advances in Experimental Medical Biology, 554,* 195–210.

Pleck, J., Sonenstein, F., & Ku, L. (1993). Masculinity ideology: Its impact on adolescent males' heterosexual relationships. *Journal of Social Issues, 49*(3), 11–29.

Popkin, S., Rosenbaum, J., & Meaden, P. (1993). Labor market experiences of low-income black women in middle-class suburbs: Evidence from a survey of Gautreaux program participants. *Journal of Policy Analysis and Management, 12*(3), 556–573.

Popple, P. R., & Leighninger, L. (2003). *The policy-based profession: An introduction to social welfare policy analysis for social workers* (3rd ed.). Boston: Allyn & Bacon.

Potter, L. (1999). Understanding the incidence of origins of community violence: Toward a comprehensive perspective of violence prevention. In T. Gullotta & S. McElhaney (Eds.), *Violence in homes and communities: Prevention, intervention, and treatment* (pp. 101–132). Thousand Oaks, CA: Sage.

Poulin, F., Dishion, T., & Burraston, B. (2001). 3-year iatrogenic effects associated with aggregating high-risk adolescents in cognitive-behavioral preventive interventions. *Applied Development Science, 5*(4), 214–224.

Prado, G., Feaster, D., Schwartz, S., Pratt, I., Smith, L., & Szapocznik, J. (2004). Religious involvement, coping, social support, and psychological distress in HIV-seropositive African American mothers. *AIDS and Behavior, 8*(3), 221–235.

Prescott, C. A., McArdle, J. J., Hishinuma, E. S., Johnson, R. C., Miyamoto, R. H., Andrade, N., et al. (1998). Prediction of major depression and dysthymia from CES-D scores among ethnic minority adolescents. *Journal of the American Academy of Child & Adolescent Psychiatry, 37*(5), 495–503.

Prochaska, J. O., & DiClemente, C. C. (1983). Transtheoretical therapy: Toward a more integrative model of change. *Psychotherapy: Theory, research and practice, 20,* 161–173.

Prochaska, J. O., DiClemente, C. C., & Norcross, J. (1992). In search of how people change: Applications to addictive behaviors. *American Psychologist, 47,* 1102–1114.

Public Health Service Task Force. (2004, December 17). *Recommendations for use of antiretroviral drugs in pregnant HIV-1-infected women for maternal health and interventions to reduce perinatal HIV-1 transmission in the United States.* Retrieved February 9, 2005, from http://AIDSinfo.nih.gov

Puhl, R., & Brownell, K. D. (2001). Bias, discrimination, and obesity. *Obesity Research, 9,* 788–805.

Quigley, L. A., & Marlatt, G. A. (1996). Drinking among young adults. *Alcohol Health & Research World, 20*(3), 185–191.

Radloff, L. S. (1977). The CES-D scale: A new self-report depression scale for research in the general population. *Applied Psychological Measurement, 1,* 385–401.

Radloff, L. S., & Rae, D. S. (1981). Components of the sex difference in depression. *Residential Community Mental Health, 2,* 111–137.

Radloff, L. S., & Terri, L. (1986). Use of the Center for Epidemiological Studies Depression Scale with older adults. *Clinical Gerontologist, 5,* 119–136.

Raebel, M. A., Malone, D. C., Conner, D. A., Xu, S., Porter, J. A., & Lanty, F. A. (2004). Health services use and health care costs of obese and nonobese individuals. *Archives of Internal Medicine, 164*(19), 2135–2140.

Raine, A. (1993). *The psychopathology of crime: Criminal behavior as a clinical disorder.* San Diego, CA: Academic Press.

Raine, A. (2002a). Annotation: The role of prefrontal deficits, low autonomic arousal, and early health factors in the development of antisocial and aggressive behavior. *Journal of Child Psychology and Psychiatry, 43,* 417–434.

Raine, A. (2002b). Biosocial studies of antisocial and violent behavior in children and adults: A review. *Journal of Abnormal Child Psychology, 30*(4), 311–326.

Raine, A., Brennan, P., & Farrington, D. (1997). Biosocial bases of violence: Conceptual and theoretical issues. In A. Raine, P. Brennan, D. Farrington, & S. Mednick (Eds.), *Biosocial bases of violence* (pp. 1–20). New York: Plenum.

Raine, A., Brennan, P., Farrington, D., & Mednick, S. (Eds.). (1997). *Biosocial bases of violence.* New York: Plenum.

Raine, A., Brennan, P., & Mednick, S. (1994). Birth complications combined with early maternal rejection at age 1 year predispose to violent crime at age 18 years. *Archives of General Psychiatry, 51,* 984–988.

Raine, A., Buchsbaum, M., Stanley, J., Lottenberg, S., Abel, L., & Stoddard, J. (1994). Selective reductions in prefrontal glucose metabolism in murderers assessed with positron emission tomography. *Society of Biological Psychiatry, 36,* 365–373.

Raine, A., Park, S., Lenca, T., Bihrle, S., LaCasse, L., Widom, C., et al. (2001). Reduced right hemisphere activation in severely abused violent offenders during a working memory task: An fMRI study. *Aggressive Behavior, 27,* 111–129.

Raine, A., Reynolds, C., Venables, P., & Mednick, S. (1997). Biosocial bases of aggressive behavior in childhood. In A. Raine, P. Brennan, D. Farrington, & S. Mednick (Eds.), *Biosocial bases of violence* (pp. 107–126). New York: Plenum.

Raine, A., Stoddard, J., Bihrle, S., & Buchsbaum, M. (1998). Prefrontal glucose deficits in murders lacking psychosocial deprivation. *Neuropsychiatry, Neuropsychology, and Behavioral Neurology, 11,* 1–7

Raine, A., Venables, P., & Williams, M. (1990). Relationships between central and autonomic measures of arousal at age 15 years and criminality at age 24 years. *Archives of General Psychiatry, 47,* 1003–1007.

Rajan, R. (2005). Straight talk: Debt relief and growth. *Finance and Development, 42*(2). Retrieved June 29, 2005, from http://www.imf.org/external/pubs/ft/fandd/2005/06/straight.htm

Rallings, M. (2002). The impact of offending on police officers. *Issues in Forensic Psychology, 3,* 20–40.

Rank, M. R., Yoon, H. S., & Hirschl, T. A. (2003). American poverty as a structural failing: Evidence and arguments. *Journal of Sociology and Social Welfare, 30*(4), 3–29.

Rasmussen, A., Aber, M., & Bhana, A. (2004). Adolescent coping and neighborhood violence: Perceptions, exposure, and urban youths' efforts to deal with danger. *American Journal of Community Psychology, 33*(1–2), 61–75.

Rauch, S. L., Van der Kolk, B. A., Fisler, R. E., Alpert, N. M., Orr, S. P., Savage, C. R., et al. (1996). A symptom provocation study of posttraumatic stress disorder using positron emission tomography and script-driven imagery. *Archives of General Psychiatry, 53*(5), 380–387.

Reeves, P. (2000). Coping in cyberspace: The impact of internet use on the ability of HIV-positive individuals to deal with their illness. *Journal of Health Communication, 5*(1), 47–59.

Reilly, T., & Woo, G. (2004). Social support and maintenance of safer sex practices among people living with HIV/AIDS. *Health & Social Work, 29*(2), 97–105.

Resick, P. A., & Schnicke, M. K. (1992). Cognitive processing therapy for sexual assault victims. *Journal of Consulting and Clinical Psychology, 60*(5), 748–756.

Resnicow, K., Jackson, A., Braithwaite, R., DiIorio, C., Blisset, D., Rahotep, S., et al. (2002). Healthy Body/Healthy Spirit: A church-based nutrition and physical activity intervention. *Health Education Research, 17*(5), 562–573.

Reynolds, C. F. (1994). Treatment of depression in late life. *American Journal of Medicine, 97*(6A), 395–465.

Reynolds, C. F., & Kupfer, D. J. (1999). Depression and aging: A look to the future. *Psychiatric Services, 50*(9), 1167–1172.

Reynolds, C. F., Perel, J. M., Imber, S. D., Cornes, C., Morycz, R. K., Mazumdar, S., et al. (1992). Combined pharmacotherapy and psychiatric therapy in the acute and continuation treatment of elderly patients with recurrent major depression: A preliminary report. *American Journal of Psychiatry, 149,* 1687–1692.

Rhodes, J. E., & Jason, L. A. (1990). A social stress model of substance abuse. *Journal of Consulting and Clinical Psychology, 58,* 395–401.

Rhodes, R., & Johnson, A. D. (1997). A feminist approach to treating alcohol and drug addicted African-American women. *Women and Therapy, 20,* 23–37.

Richard, R., & Van der Plight, J. (1991). Factors affecting condom use among adolescents. *Journal of Community & Applied Social Psychology, 1*(2), 105–116.

Richardson, L. P., Davis, R. D., Poulton, R., McCauley, E., Moffitt, T. E., Caspi, A., et al. (2003). A longitudinal evaluation of adolescent depression and adult obesity. *Archives of Pediatric and Adolescent Medicine, 157,* 739–745.

Richmond, M. (1917). *Social diagnosis.* New York: Russell Sage Foundation.

Rintamaki, L., & Brashers, D. (2005). Social identity and stigma management for people living with HIV. In E. Ray (Ed.), *Health communication in practice: A case study approach* (pp. 145–156). Mahway, NJ: Lawrence Erlbaum.

Roberts, A., Jackson, M. S., & Carlton-Laney, I. (2000). Revisiting the need for feminist and Afrocentric theory when treating African-American female substance abusers. *Journal of Drug Issues, 30,* 901–918.

Roberts, J., & Stalans, L. (2004). Restorative sentencing: Exploring the views of the public. *Social Justice Research, 17*(3), 315–334.

Roby, J. L. (2005). Women and children in the global sex trade: Toward more effective policy. *International Social Work, 48*(2), 136–147.

Roche, H. M. (2004). Dietary lipids and gene expression. *Biochemical Social Transactions, 32*(6), 999–1002.

Roe, C. M., & Schwartz, M. (1996). Characteristics of previously forgotten memories of sexual abuse: A descriptive study. *Journal of Psychiatry and Law, 24,* 189–206.

Roff, L. L., Klemmack, D. L., Parker, M., Koenig, H. G., Crowther, M., Baker, P. S., et al. (2005). Depression and religiosity in African American and white community-dwelling older adults. *Journal of Human Behavior in the Social Environment, 10*(1), 175–189.

Rogers, E. (1983). *Diffusion of innovations.* New York: Free Press.

Rogers, S., Ying, L., Xin, Y., Fung, K., & Kaufman, J. (2002). Reaching and identifying the STUD/HIV risk of sex workers in Beijing. *AIDS Education and Prevention, 14*(3), 217–227.

Rogers, W. A. (2003). Evidence based medicine and justice: A framework for looking at the impact of EBM upon vulnerable or disadvantaged groups. *Journal of Medical Ethics, 30,* 141–145.

Rohrer, J. E., Rush, P. J., & Blackburn, C. (2005). Lifestyle and mental health. *Preventive Medicine, 40*(4), 438–443.

Rohsenow, D., Corbett, R., & Devine, D. (1988). Molested as children: A hidden contribution to substance abuse? *Journal of Substance Abuse Treatment, 5,* 13–18.

Rohsenow, D. J., Martin, R. A., & Monti, P. M. (2005). Urge-specific and lifestyle coping strategies of cocaine abusers: Relationship to treatment outcomes. *Drug and Alcohol Dependence, 78,* 211–219.

Roisman, G. I., Padron, E., Sroufe, L. A., & Egeland, B. (2002). Earned-secure attachment status in retrospect and prospect. *Child Development, 73*(4), 1204–1219.

Rolls, D. J. (2000). The role of energy density in the overconsumption of fat. *Journal of Nutrition, 130,* 268S–271S.

Rolls, D. J., Engeli, D., & Birch, I. I. (2000). Serving portion size influences 5-year-old but not 3-year-old children's food intake. *Journal of the American Dietary Association, 100,* 232–234.

Rosack, J. (2006a). Companies desperately seek antidepressant breakthrough. *Psychiatric News, 41*(11), 22–29.

Rosack, J. (2006b). MAOI skin patch wins FDA approval for depression. *Psychiatric News, 41*(7), 31.

Rosario, M., Schrimshaw, E. W., & Hunter, J. (2004). Predictors of substance use over time among gay, lesbian, and bisexual youths: An examination of three hypotheses. *Addictive Behaviors, 29,* 1623–1631.

Rose, D. (1997). *Assessing food insecurity in the United States.* Washington, DC: USDA Economic Research Service, Food and Consumer Economics Division No. 9706.

Rose, D., Basiotis, P. P., & Klein, B. W. (1995). Improving federal efforts to assess hunger and food insecurity. *Food Review, 18,* 18–23.

Rose, S. J., & Hartmann, H. I. (2004). *Still a man's labor market: The long-term earnings gap.* Washington, DC: Institute for Women's Policy Research.

Rosenthal, B. (2000). Exposure to community violence in adolescence: Trauma symptoms. *Adolescence, 35*(138), 271–284.

Rosenthal, B., & Wilson, W. (2003). The association of ecological variables and psychological distress with exposure to community violence among adolescents. *Adolescence, 38*(151), 459–479.

Rothblum, E., Miller, C., & Garbutt, B. (1988). Stereotypes of obese female job applicants. *International Journal of Eating Disorders, 7,* 277–283.

Rotton, J., & Cohn, E. G. (2004). Outdoor temperature, climate control, and criminal assault: The spatial and temporal ecology of violence. *Environment and Behavior, 36*(2), 276–306.

Rounds, K., Galinsky, M., & Despard, M. (1996). Evaluation of telephone support groups for persons living with HIV disease. *Research on Social Work Practice, 5*(4), 442–459.

Rounds-Bryant, J. L, Kristiansen, P. L, & Hubbard, R. L. (1999). Drug abuse treatment outcome study of adolescents: A comparison of client characteristics and pretreatment behaviors in three treatment modalities. *American Journal of Drug and Alcohol Abuse, 25*(4), 573–591.

Rowe, C. L., Liddle, H. A., Greenbaum, P. E., & Henderson, C. E. (2004). Impact of psychiatric comorbidity on treatment of adolescent drug abusers. *Journal of Substance Abuse Treatment, 26,* 129–140.

Roy, J. (2004). Socioeconomic status and health: A neurobiological perspective. *Medical Hypotheses, 62*(2), 222–227.

Rudorfer, M. V., & Lebowitz, B. D. (1999). Letter to the editor: Progress in ECT research. *American Journal of Psychiatry, 156,* 975.

Runyan, D. K., & Litrownik, A. J. (2003). Introduction to special issue: LONGSCAN and family violence. *Journal of Family Violence, 18,* 1–4.

Russell Sage Foundation. (2000). *Preliminary findings from the Multi-City Study of Urban Inequality (MCSUI).* Retrieved June 9, 2006, from http://www.russellsage.org/special_interest/mcsui_points.html

Rutter, M. (2000). Resilience reconsidered: Conceptual considerations, empirical findings and policy implications. In J. P. Shonkoff & S. J. Meisels (Eds.), *Handbook of early childhood intervention* (2nd ed., pp. 651–682). New York: Cambridge University Press.

Rutter, M. (2002). The interplay of nature, nurture, and developmental influences. *Archives of General Psychiatry, 59*(11), 996–1000.

Rutter, M. (2003). Genetic influences on risk and protection: Implications for understanding resilience. In S. Luther (Ed.), *Resilience and vulnerability: Adaptation in the context of childhood adversities* (pp. 489–509). Cambridge, England: Cambridge University Press.

Ryan, J. P., Marsh, J. C., Testa, M. F., & Louderman, R. (2006). Integrating substance abuse treatment and child welfare services: Findings from the Illinois Alcohol and Other Drug Abuse Waiver Demonstration. *Social Work Research, 30*(2), 95–107.

Ryle, G. (1949). *The concept of mind.* London: Hutchinson.

Saakvitne, K. W., Gamble, S. J., Pearlman, L. A., & Tabor Lev, B. (2000). *Risking connection: A training curriculum for working with survivors of childhood abuse.* Lutherville, MD: Sidran Press.

Saal, D., Dong, Y., Bonci, A., & Malenka, R. (2003). Drugs of abuse and stress trigger a common synaptic adaptation in dopamine neurons. *Neuron, 37*(4), 577–582.

Sachs, J. D. (2005). *The end of poverty: Economic possibilities for our time.* New York: Penguin.

Sadker, M., & Sadker, D. (1994). *Failing at fairness: How America's schools cheat girls.* New York: Scribner.

Sadock, B. J., & Sadock, V. A. (2001). *Pocket handbook of psychiatric drug treatment* (3rd. ed.). Philadelphia: Lippincott, Williams & Wilkins.

Sadock, B. J., & Sadock, V. A. (2003). *Kaplan & Sadock's synopsis of psychiatry: Behavioral sciences, clinical psychiatry* (9th ed.). Philadelphia: Lippincott, Williams & Wilkins.

Safman, R. (2004). Assessing the impact of orphanhood on Thai children affected by AIDS and their caregivers. *AIDS Care, 16*(1), 11–19.

Saigh, P., Yasik, A., Sack, W., & Koplewicz, H. (1999). Child-adolescent posttraumatic stress disorder: Prevalence, risk factors, and comorbidity. In P. Saigh & J. D. Bremner (Eds.), *Posttraumatic stress disorder: A comprehensive text* (pp. 18–43). Needham Heights, MA: Allyn & Bacon.

Samaan, R. A. (2000). The influences of race, ethnicity, and poverty on the mental health of children. *Journal of Health Care for the Poor & Underserved, 11*(1), 100–110.

Samantrai, K. (2004). *Culturally competent public child welfare practice.* Pacific Grove, CA: Thomson.

Sampson, R. (2003). The neighborhood context of well-being. *Perspectives in Biology and Medicine, 46*(3), S53–S65.

Sampson, R., Morenoff, J., & Earls, F. (1999). Beyond social capital: Spatial dynamics of collective efficacy for children. *American Sociological Review, 64*, 633–660.

Sampson, R. J., Raudenbush, S. W., & Earls, F. (1997). Neighborhoods and violent crime: A multilevel study of collective efficacy. *Science, 277*, 918–924.

Sander, J. B., & McCarty, C. A. (2005). Youth depression in the family context. Familial risk factors and models of treatment. *Clinical Child and Family Psychological Review, 8*(3), 203–219.

Sanders-Phillips, K. (1997). Assaultive violence in the community: Psychological responses of adolescent victims and their parents. *Journal of Adolescent Health, 21*, 356–365.

Sandler, I. N., Wolchick, S. A., MacKinnon, D., Ayers, T. S., & Roosa, M. (1997). Developing linkages between theory and intervention in stress and coping processes. In S. A. Wolchick & I. N. Sandler (Eds.), *Handbook of children's coping: Linking theory and intervention* (pp. 3–40). New York: Plenum.

Sapolsky, R. (2005). Sick of poverty: Poor people more prone to diseases due to stress. *Scientific American, 293*(6), 92–99.

Sarwer, D. B., Wadden, T. A., & Fabricatore, A. N. (2005). Psychosocial and behavioral aspects of bariatric surgery. *Obesity Research, 13*(4), 639–648.

Satter, E. (1995). Feeding dynamics: Helping children to eat well. *Journal of Pediatric Health Care, 9,* 178–180.

Satter, E. (1996). Internal regulation and the evolution of normal growth as the basis for prevention of obesity in children. *Journal of the American Dietetic Association, 96,* 860–862.

Saunders, R. (2004a). Grazing: A high-risk behavior. *Obesity Surgery, 14*(1), 98–102.

Saunders, R. (2004b). Post-surgery group therapy for gastric bypass patients. *Obesity Surgery, 14*(8), 1128–1131.

Scarpa, A. (1997). Aggression in physically abused children: The interactive role of emotion regulation. In A. Raine, P. Brennan, D. Farrington, & S. Mednick (Eds.), *Biosocial bases of violence* (pp. 341–343). New York: Plenum.

Schiele, J. (2000). *Human services and the Afrocentric paradigm.* New York: Haworth Press.

Schiffer, F., Teicher, M. H., & Papanicolau, A. C. (1995). Evoked potential evidence for right brain activity during the recall of traumatic memories. *Journal of Neuropsychiatry & Clinical Neuroscience, 7,* 169–175.

Schiller, B. (2004). *The economics of poverty and discrimination* (9th ed.). Upper Saddle River, NJ: Prentice Hall.

Schmeelk-Cone, K. H., & Zimmerman, M. A. (2003). A longitudinal analysis of stress in African-American youth: Predictors and outcomes of stress trajectories. *Journal of Youth and Adolescence, 32*(6), 419–430.

Schmidt, C. (2003). Obesity: A weighty issue for children. *Environmental Health Perspectives, 111*(13), 700–707.

Schneider, F., Habel, U., Wagner, M., Franke, P., Salloum, J. B., Shah, N. J. S., et al. (2001). Subcortical correlates of craving in recently abstinent alcoholic patients. *American Journal of Psychiatry, 158*(7), 1075–1083.

Schneider, R. L., & Lester, L. (2001). *Social work advocacy: A new framework for action.* Belmont, CA: Brooks/Cole.

Schore, A. (1994). *Affect regulation and the origin of the self.* Hillsdale, NJ: Erlbaum.

Schuckit, M. A., & Sweeney, S. (1987). Substance use and mental health problems among sons of alcoholics and controls. *Journal of Studies on Alcohol, 48,* 528–534.

Schulenberg, J., Maggs, J. L., & Hurrelmann, K. (1997). Negotiating developmental transitions during adolescence and young adulthood: Health risks and opportunities. In J. Schulenberg, J. L. Maggs, & K. Hurrelman (Eds.), *Health risks and developmental transitions during adolescence* (pp. 1–19). New York: Cambridge University Press.

Schulenberg, J., Maggs, J. L., Steinman, K. J., & Zucker, R. A. (2001). Development matters: Taking the long view on substance abuse etiology and intervention during adolescence. In P. M. Monti, S. M. Colby, & T. A. O'Leary (Eds.), *Adolescents, alcohol, and substance abuse* (pp. 19–57). New York: Guilford Press.

Schulz, A., Israel, B., Zenk, S., Parker, E., Lictenstein, R., Shellman-Weir, S., et al. (2006). Psychosocial stress and social support as mediators of relationships between income, length of residence and depressive symptoms among African American women on Detroit's eastside. *Social Science & Medicine, 62*(2), 510–522.

Schwartz, A., & Schwartz, R. (1993). *Depression theories and treatments: Psychological, biological, and social perspectives.* New York: Columbia University Press.

Schwartz, D., & Proctor, L. (2000). Community violence exposure and children's social adjustment in the school peer group: The mediating roles of emotional regulation and social cognition. *Journal of Consulting and Clinical Psychology, 68,* 670–683.

Schwartz, M. B., Chambliss, H., Brownell, K. D., Blair, S. N., & Billington, C. (2003). Weight bias among health professionals specializing in obesity. *Obesity Research, 11,* 1033–1039.

Schwartzberg, S. (1993). Struggling for meaning: How HIV-positive gay men make sense of AIDS. *Professional Psychology: Research and Practice, 24,* 483–490.

Sciammacco, C. (1998). Feminists call for closing of wage gap: Equal pay day shows women still behind [Electronic version]. *National NOW Times.* Retrieved May 19, 2005, from http://www.now.org/nnt/05-98/wagegap.html

Sedlak, A. J., & Broadhurst, D. D. (1996). *Executive summary of the Third National Incidence Study of Child Abuse & Neglect.* Washington, DC: U.S. Department of Health and Human Services.

Seidell, J. C., & Rissanen, A. M. (2004). Prevalence of obesity in adults: The global epidemic. In G. A. Bray & C. Bouchard (Eds.), *Handbook of obesity: Etiology and pathophysiology* (2nd ed., pp. 93–107). New York: Marcel Dekker.

Seipel, M. M. O. (2003). Global poverty: No longer an untouchable problem. *International Social Work, 46*(2), 191–207.

Sell, L. A., Morris, J. S., Bearn, J., Frackowiak, R. S. J., Friston, K. J., & Dolan, R. J. (2000). Neural responses associated with cue evoked emotional states and heroin in opiate addicts. *Drug and Alcohol Dependence, 60,* 207–216.

Semaan, S., Lauby, J., O'Connell, A., & Cohen, A. (2003). Factors associated with perceptions of, and decisional balance for, condom use with main partner among women at risk for HIV infection. *Women & Health, 37*(3), 53–69.

Seymour, B., Kinn, S., & Sutherland, N. (2003). Valuing both critical and creative thinking in clinical practice: Narrowing the research-practice gap? *Journal of Advanced Nursing, 42*(3), 288–296.

Shaffer, N., Bulterys, M., & Simonds, R. (1999). Short courses of zidovudine and perinatal transmission of HIV. *New England Journal of Medicine, 340,* 1042–1043.

Shaham, Y., Erb, S., & Stewart, J. (2000). Stress-induced relapse to heroin and cocaine seeking in rats: A review. *Brain Research Reviews, 33,* 13–33.

Shahinfar, A., Fox, N., & Leavitt, L. (2000). Preschool children's exposure to violence: Relation of behavior problems to parent and child reports. *American Journal of Orthopsychiatry, 70*(1), 1115–1125.

Shapiro, J., Radecki, S., Charchian, A., & Josephson, V. (1999). Sexual behavior and AIDS-related knowledge among community college students in Orange County, California. *Journal of Community Health, 24,* 29–42.

Sharma, V., Das, S., Mondal, S., Goswampi, U., & Gandhi, A. (2005). Effect of Sahag Yoga on depressive disorders. *Indian Journal of Physiology and Pharmacology, 49*(4), 462–468.

Shaw, A., Herbert, R., Lewis, S., Mahendran, R., Platt, J., & Bhattacharyya, B. (1997). Screening for depression among acutely ill geriatric inpatients with a short geriatric depression scale. *Age and Aging, 26*(3), 217–223.

Shaw, B., Krause, N., Chatters, L. M., Connell, C. M., & Ingersoll-Dayton, B. (2004). Emotional support from parents early in life, aging, and heath. *Psychology and Aging, 19*(1), 4–12.

Shaw, C., & McKay, H. (1942). *Juvenile delinquency and urban areas.* Chicago: University of Chicago Press.

Sheeran, P., Abraham, C., & Orbell, S. (1999). Psychosocial correlates of heterosexual condom use: A meta-analysis. *Psychological Bulletin, 125*(1), 90–132.

Sheppard, D., Smith, G. T., & Rosenbaum, G. (1988). Use of the MMPI subtypes in predicting completion of a residential alcoholism treatment program. *Journal of Consulting and Clinical Psychology, 56,* 590–596.

Sher, K. J. (1991). *Children of alcoholics: A critical appraisal of theory and research.* Chicago: University of Chicago Press.

Sherman, L., Gottfredson, D., MacKenzie, D., Eck, J., Reuter, P., & Bushway, S. (1997). *Preventing crime: What works, what doesn't, what's promising. A report to the United States Congress* (NCJ 171676). Washington, DC: U.S. Department of Justice, Office of Justice Programs.

Shernoff, M. (1990). Why every social worker should be challenged by AIDS. *Social Work, 35*(1), 5–8.

Shih, R. A., Belmonte, P. L., & Zandi, P. P. (2004). A review of the evidence from family, twin and adoption studies for a genetic contribution to adult psychiatric disorders. *International Review of Psychiatry, 16*(4), 260–283.

Shikora, S. A. (2004). Implantable gastric stimulation—the surgical procedure: Combining safety with simplicity. *Obesity Surgery, 14,* S9–S13.

Shipler, D. K. (2004). *The working poor invisible in America.* New York: Alfred A. Knopf.

Shlonsky, A., & Wagner, D. (2005). The next step: Integrating actuarial risk assessment and clinical judgment into an evidence-based practice framework in CPS case management. *Children & Youth Services Review, 27*(4), 409–427.

Shoal, G., Giancola, P., & Kirillova, G. (2003). Salivary cortisol, personality, and aggressive behavior in adolescent boys: A 5-year longitudinal study. *Journal of the American Academy of Child and Adolescent Psychiatry, 42*(9), 1101–1107.

Shonkoff, J. P., & Phillips, D. A. (2000). *From neurons to neighborhoods.* Washington, DC: National Academy Press.

Shor, R. (1998). The significance of religion in advancing a culturally sensitive approach towards child maltreatment. *Families in Society, 79*(4), 400–409.

Shulman, B. (2003). *The betrayal of work: How low wage jobs fail 30 million Americans.* New York: New Press.

Siegel, D. J. (1999). *The developing mind.* New York: Guilford Press.

Siegel, D. J. (2001). Memory: An overview, with emphasis on developmental, interpersonal, and neurobiological aspects. *Journal of American Academy of Child and Adolescent Psychiatry, 40*(9), 997–1011.

Siegel, D. J. (2003). An interpersonal neurobiology of psychotherapy: The developing mind and the resolution of trauma. In M. Solomon & D. Siegel (Eds.), *Healing trauma: Attachment, mind, body, and brain* (pp. 1–56). New York: Norton.

Siegel, K., Brown-Bradley, C., & Lekas, H. (2004). Strategies for coping with fatigue among HIV-positive individuals fifty years and older. *AIDS Patient Care and STDs, 18*(5), 275–288.

Siegel, K., & Schrimshaw, E. (2002). The perceived benefits of religious and spiritual coping among older adults living with HIV/AIDS. *Journal of Scientific Study of Religion, 41*(1), 91–102.

Sikkema, K., Koob, J., Cargill, V., Kelly, J., Desiderato, L., Roffman, R., et al. (1995). Levels and predictors of HIV risk among women in low-income public housing developments. *Public Health Reports, 110,* 707–713.

Silove, D., Steel, Z., McGorry, P., & Mohan, P. (1998). Trauma exposure, post-migration stressors and symptoms of anxiety, depression and posttraumatic stress in Tamil asylum seekers: Comparison with refugees and immigrants. *Acta Psychiatrica Scandinavica, 97,* 175–181.

Simeon, J. (1989). Depressive disorders in children and adolescents. *Psychiatric Journal of the University of Ottawa, 14*(2), 356–361.

Simon, T., Mercy, J., & Craig, P. (2001). *National crime victimization survey: Injuries from violent crime, 1992–98.* (NCJ Publication No. 168633). Washington, DC: U.S. Department of Justice and U.S. Department of Health and Human Services.

Simoni, J., Martone, M., & Kerwin, J. (2002). Spirituality and psychological adaptation among women with HIV/AIDS: Implications for counseling. *Journal of Counseling Psychology, 49*(2), 139–147.

Singer, M. (1994). AIDS and the health crisis of the U.S. urban poor: The perspective of critical medical anthropology. *Social Science and Medicine, 39*(7), 931–948.

Sjosten, N., & Kivela, S. (2006). The effects of physical exercise on depressive symptoms among the aged: A systematic review. *International Journal of Geriatric Psychiatry, 21*(5), 410–418.

Skinner, C. (1995). Urban labor markets and young black men: A literature review. *Journal of Economic Issues, 29*(1), 47–65.

Skinner, D., Slattery, E., & Lachicotte, W. (2002). *Disability, health coverage, and welfare reform.* Washington, DC: Kaiser Commission on Medicaid and the Uninsured.

Sloan, R. P., & Bagiella, E., (2002). Claims about religious involvement and health outcomes. *Annals of Behavioral Medicine, 24*(1), 14–21.

Small, G. W. (1998). Treatment of geriatric depression. *Depression and Anxiety, 1*(Suppl.), 32–42.

Smeeding, T. M., Rainwater, L., & Burtless, G. (2001). U.S. poverty in a cross-national context. In S. H. Danzinger & R. H. Haveman (Eds.), *Understanding poverty.* New York: Russell Sage Foundation.

Smith, C., & Carlson, B. (1997). Stress, coping, and resilience in children and youth. *Social Service Review, 71,* 231– 256.

Smith, C., & Hay, P. (2005). Acupuncture for depression. Cochrane Database of Systematic Reviews 2004, Issue 3. Art. No.: CD004046. DOI: 10.1002/14651858.CD004046.pub2.

Smith, G. T. (1994). Psychological expectancy as mediator of vulnerability to alcoholism. *Annals of the New York Academy of Sciences, 708,* 165–171.

Smith, G. T., McCarthy, D. M., & Goldman, M. S. (1995). Self-reported drinking and alcohol-related problems among adolescents: Dimensionality and validity over 24 months. *Journal of Studies on Alcohol, 56,* 383–394.

Smith, H., & Betz, N. (2002). An examination of efficacy and esteem pathways to depression in young adulthood. *Journal of Counseling Psychology, 49*(4), 438–448.

Smith, M., & Fong, R. (2004). *The children of neglect: When no one cares.* New York: Brunner-Routledge.

Smith, P. (2002). A reflection on reflection. *Primary Voices, 10*(4), 31–34.

Sokero, T. P., Melartin, T. K., Rytsala, H. J., Leskela, U. S., Lestela-Mielonen, P. S., & Isometsa, E. T. (2005). Prospective study of risk factors for attempted suicide among patients with DSM-IV major depressive disorder. *British Journal of Psychiatry, 186*(4), 314–318.

Solomon, M. F., & Siegel, D. J. (2003). *Healing trauma: Attachment, mind, body, and brain.* New York: W. W. Norton.

Son, S., & Kirchner, J. (2000). Depression in children and adolescents. *American Family Physician, 62*(10), 2297–2308.

Song, Y. J., Hofstetter, C. R., Hovell, M. F., Paik, H. Y., Park, H. R., Lee, J., et al. (2004). Acculturation and health risk behaviors among Californians of Korean descent. *Preventive Medicine, 39*(1), 147–156.

Spencer, N. (2003). Social, economic, and political determinants of child health. *Pediatrics, 112*(3), 704–706.

Stack, C. (1974). *All our kin.* New York: Basic Books.

Stacy, A. W., Ames, S. L., Sussman, S., & Dent, C. W. (1996). Implicit cognition in adolescent drug use. *Psychology of Addictive Behaviors, 10*(3), 190–203.

Stacy, A. W., Widaman, K. F., & Marlatt, G. A. (1990). Expectancy models of alcohol use. *Journal of Personality and Social Psychology, 58*(5), 918–928.

Stall, R., Mills, T., Williamson, J., Hart, T., Greenswood, G., Paul, J., et al. (2003). Association of co-occurring psychosocial health problems and increased vulnerability to HIV/AIDS among urban men who have sex with men. *American Journal of Public Health, 93*(6), 939–942.

Stamm, B. H. (1997). Work-related secondary traumatic stress. *PTSD Research Quarterly, 8*(2), 1–8.

Steele, W., & Raider, M. (2001). *Structured sensory interventions for traumatized children, adolescents, and parents: Strategies to alleviate trauma.* New York: Edwin Mellen Press.

Steffans, D. C., & Krishnan, K. R. (1998). Structural neuro-imaging and mood disorders: Recent findings, implications for classification and future directions. *Biological Psychiatry, 4,* 705–712.

Steward, S., Kennard, B., Hughes, C., Mayes, T., Emslie, G., Lee, P., et al. (2004). A cross-cultural investigation of cognitions and depressive symptoms in adolescents. *Journal of Abnormal Psychology, 113*(2), 248–257.

Stewart, E., Simons, R., & Conger, R. (2002). Assessing neighborhood and social psychological influences on childhood violence in an African-American sample. *Criminology, 40*(4), 801–829.

Stewart, S. H., Ouimette, P., & Brown, P. J. (2002). Gender and the comorbidity of PTSD with substance use disorders. In R. Kimerling, P. Ouimette, & J. Wolfe (Eds.), *Gender and PTSD* (pp. 233–269). New York: Guilford Press.

Stillwaggon, E. (2002). HIV/AIDS in Africa: Fertile terrain. *Journal of Developmental Studies, 38*(6), 1–22.

Stoller, E., & Gibson, R. (2000). *Worlds of difference: Inequality in the aging experience* (3rd ed.). Thousand Oaks, CA: Pine Forge Press.

Stoto, M., Almario, D., & McCormick, M. (Eds.). (1999). *Reducing the odds: Preventing perinatal transmission of HIV in the United States.* Washington, DC: National Academy Press.

Strauch, B., Herman, C., Rohde, C., & Baum, T. (2006). Mid-body contouring in the post-bariatric surgery patient. *Plastic and Reconstructive Surgery, 117*(7), 2200–2211.

Straus, M. A., Hamby, S. L., & Finkelhor, D. (1998). Identification of child maltreatment with the Parent-Child Conflict Tactics Scales: Development and psychometric data for a national sample of American parents. *Child Abuse & Neglect, 22*(4), 249–270.

Straus, M. A., & Kantor, G. K. (2005). Definition and measurement of neglectful behavior: Some principles and guidelines. *Child Abuse & Neglect, 29*(1), 19–29.

Stronski, S. M., Ireland, M., Michaud, P.-A., Narring, F., & Resnick, M. D. (2000). Protective correlates of stages in adolescent substance use: A Swiss national study. *Journal of Adolescent Health, 26,* 420–427.

Strother, P. (2003). Exit from poverty: How "welfare mothers" achieve economic viability. *Journal of Human Behavior in the Social Environment, 7*(3/4), 97–119.

Strug, D. L., Grube, B. B., & Beckerman, N. L. (2002). Challenges and changing roles in HIV/AIDS social work: Implications for training and education. *Social Work in Health Care, 35*(4), 1–19.

Substance Abuse and Mental Health Services Administration. (2005). *Overview of findings from the 2004 National Survey on Drug Use and Health* (Office of Applied Studies, NSDUH Series H-27, DHHS Pub. No. SMA 05–4061). Rockville, MD: Author.

Substance Abuse and Mental Health Services Administration, Center for Substance Abuse Treatment. (1998). Addiction counseling competencies: The knowledge, skills, and attitudes of professional practice (DHHS Pub. No. SMA 98–3171). Rockville, MD: U.S. Department of Health and Human Services.

Sullivan, H. (1953). *The interpersonal theory of psychiatry.* New York: Norton.

Surkan, P., Peterson, K., Hughes, M., & Gottlieb, B. (2006). The role of social networks and support in postpartum women's depression: A multiethnic urban sample. *Maternal and Child Health Journal, 11,* 1–9.

Sutherland, E. (1942). The development of the concept of differential association. *Ohio Valley Sociologist, 15,* 3–4.

Sutherland, E. H. (1947). *Principles of criminology.* New York: Harper & Row.

Sweatt, L., Harding, C., Knight-Lynn, L., Rasheed, S., & Carter, P. (2002). Talking about the silent fear: Adolescents' experiences of violence in an urban high-rise community. *Adolescence, 37*(145), 109–120.

Swinburn, B. A., & Egger, G. J. (2004). Influence of obesity-producing environments. In G. A. Bray & C. Bouchard (Eds.), *Handbook of obesity: Clinical applications* (2nd ed., pp. 97–114). New York: Marcel Dekker.

Szalay, L. B., Strohl, J. B., & Doherty, K. T. (1999). *Psychoenvironmental forces in substance abuse prevention.* New York: Plenum.

Tafet, G., & Smolovich, J. (2004). Psychoneuroendocrinological studies on chronic stress and depression. *Annals of the New York Academy of Sciences, 1032,* 276–278.

Taking Off Pounds Sensibly. (2006). Home page. Retrieved June 16, 2006, from http://www.tops.org/

Taylor, A. F., Wiley, A., Kuo, F. E., & Sullivan, W. C. (1998). Growing up in the inner city: Green spaces as places to grow. *Environment & Behavior, 30*(1), 3–28.

Teets, J. M. (1995). Childhood sexual trauma of chemically dependent women. *Journal of Psychoactive Drugs, 27,* 231–238.

Teicher, M. (2002). Scars that will not heal: The neurobiology of child abuse. *Scientific American, 286*(3), 68–75.

Teicher, M. H., Ito, Y., Glod, D. A., Anderson, S. L., Dumont, N., & Ackerman, E. (1997). Preliminary evidence for abnormal cortical development in physically and sexually abused children using EEG coherence and MRI. *Annals of the New York Academy of Sciences, 821,* 160–173.

Ten Bensel, R. W., Rheinberger, M. M., & Radbill, S. X. (1997). Children in a world of violence: The roots of child maltreatment. In M. E. Helfer, R. S. Kempe, & R. D. Krugman (Eds.), *The battered child* (5th ed., pp. 3–28). Chicago: University of Chicago Press.

Terr, L. C. (1991). Childhood traumas: An outline and overview. *American Journal of Psychiatry, 148*(1), 10–20.

Thomas, D., Leicht, C., Hughes, C., Madigan, A., & Dowell, K. (2003). *Emerging practices in the prevention of child abuse and neglect.* Washington, DC: U.S. Department of Health and Human Services, Administration for Children and Families.

Thomlison, B. (2003). Characteristics of evidence-based child maltreatment interventions. *Child Welfare, 82,* 541–569.

Thomlison, B. (2004). Child maltreatment: A risk and protective factor perspective. In M. W. Fraser (Ed.), *Risk and resilience in childhood: An ecological perspective* (2nd ed., pp. 89–132). Washington, DC: National Association of Social Workers Press.

Thompson, D., Jago, R., Baranowski, T., Watson, K., Zakeri, I., Cullen, K. W., et al. (2004). Covariability in diet and physical activity in African-American girls. *Obesity Research, 12*(9), 46S–54S.

Thompson, E., & Pleck, J. (1995). Masculinity ideologies: A review of research instrumentation on men and masculinities. In R. Levant & W. Pollack (Eds.), *A new psychology of men* (pp. 129–162). New York: Basic Books.

Thompson, L. S., & Story, M. (2003). Perceptions of overweight and obesity in their community: Findings from focus groups with urban, African-American caretakers of preschool children. *Journal of National Black Nurses Association, 14*(1), 28–37.

Thompson, M. S., & Peebles-Wilkins, W. (1992). The impact of formal, informal and societal support activities on the psychological well-being of black adolescent mothers. *Social Work, 37*(4), 322–328.

Thorpe, K. E., Florence, C. S., Howard, D. H., & Joski, P. (2004). Trends: The impact of obesity on rising medical spending (W4–480–486). *Health Affairs,* Jul–Dec. Web Exclusive, October 20, 2004.

Tiffany, S. T. (1990). A cognitive model of drug urges and drug-use behavior: Role of automatic and nonautomatic processes. *Psychological Review, 97,* 147–168.

Timmons, J., & Fesko, S. (2004). The impact, meaning, and challenges of work: Perspectives of individuals with HIV/AIDS. *Health & Social Work, 29*(2), 137–144.

Todd, J. L., & Worell, J. (2000). Resilience in low-income, employed, African American women. *Psychology of Women Quarterly, 24,* 119–128.

Tolin, D. F., & Foa, E. B. (2002). Gender and PTSD: A cognitive model. In R. Kimerling, P. Ouimette, & J. Wolfe (Eds.), *Gender and PTSD* (pp. 76–97). New York: Guilford Press.

Tolman, R., & Wang, H. (2005). Domestic violence and women's employment: Fixed effects models of three waves of Women's Employment Study Data. *American Journal of Community Psychology, 36*(1–2), 147–158.

Townsend, M., Peerson, J., Love, B., Achterberg, C., & Murphy, S. (2001). Food insecurity is positively related to overweight in women. *Journal of Nutrition, 13,* 1738–1745.

Trattner, W. I. (1998). *From poor law to welfare state: A history of social welfare in America* (6th ed.). New York: Free Press.

Tremblay, R., Schaal, B., Boulerice, B., Arseneault, L., Soussignan, R., & Perusse, D. (1997). Male physical aggression, social dominance, and testosterone levels at puberty: A developmental perspective. In A. Raine, P. Brennan, D. Farrington, & S. Mednick (Eds.), *Biosocial bases of violence* (pp. 271–291). New York: Plenum.

Tubman, J., Montgomery, M., Gil, A., & Wagner, E. (2004). Abuse experiences in a community sample of young adults: Relations with psychiatric disorders, sexual risk behaviors, and sexually transmitted diseases. *American Journal of Community Psychology, 34*(1–2), 147–153.

Turner, H., Pearlin, L., & Mullan, J. (1998). Sources and determinants of social support for caregivers of persons with AIDS. *Journal of Health and Social Behavior, 39*(2), 137–151.

Tzeng, O. C. S., Jackson, J. W., & Karlson, H. C. (1991). *Theories of child abuse and neglect: Differential perspectives, summaries, and evaluations.* New York: Praeger.

UCSF AIDS Health Project Training Unit. (2001). *HIV timeline: 1980–2001.* San Francisco: University of California at San Francisco.

UNAIDS. (2005a). *Global summary of the HIV and AIDS epidemic in 2004.* Retrieved April 24, 2005, from http://www.unaids.org/en/resources/epidemiology

UNAIDS. (2005b). *Progress on global access to HIV Antiretroviral Therapy: An update on "3 by 5."* Geneva, Switzerland: World Health Organization.

Uneze, A. (2004, Dec. 7). PLWHAS discrimination, barrier to AIDS prevention efforts. *Africa News Service.*

UNICEF. (2003). A league table of child maltreatment deaths in rich nations. *Innocenti Report Card, 5.* Florence, Italy: Innocenti Research Centre.

UNICEF. (2005). *Child poverty in rich countries 2005: Report card no. 6.* Florence, Italy: Innocenti Research Centre.

United Nations. (1996, December 3). *Focus on poverty and disability.* Retrieved May 20, 2005, from http://www.un.org/ecosocdev/geninfo/diasbeled/disabday.htm

United Nations. (2005). *What are the Millennium Development Goals?* Retrieved October 3, 2006, from http://un.org/millenniumgoals/

United Nations Millennium Project Task Force on Poverty and Economic Development. (2004, February). *An enhanced strategy for reducing extreme poverty by the year 2015.* Retrieved October 29, 2006, from http://www.unmillenniumproject.org/documents/tfoneinterim.pdf

United Nations Office on Drugs and Crime. (2005). *World drug report, 2005.* Vienna, Austria: Author.

United Nations Office on Drugs and Crime. (2006). *Trafficking in persons: Global patterns.* Retrieved May 24, 2006, from http://www.unodc.org/pdf/traffickinginpersons_report_2006-04.pdf

United States of America. (2005). *Response to United Nations Secretary-General's Study on Violence against Children questionnaire to governments.* Washington, DC: U.S. Government Printing Office.

U.S. Bureau of Justice Statistics. (2003). *Crime characteristics: Summary findings.* Retrieved November 23, 2004, from http://www.ojp.usdoj.gov/bjs/cvit_c.htm

U.S. Bureau of Justice Statistics. (2004). *Homicide trends in the U.S.: Regional trends.* Retrieved November 23, 2004, from http://www.ojp.usdoj.gov/bjs/homicide/region.htm

U.S. Census Bureau. (2002). *The big payoff: Educational attainment and synthetic estimates of work-life earnings.* Washington, DC: U.S. Government Printing Office.

U.S. Census Bureau. (2003). *Income, poverty, and health insurance coverage in the United States.* Washington, DC: U.S. Government Printing Office.

U.S. Census Bureau. (2004). *Income stable, poverty up, numbers of Americans with and without health insurance rise.* Retrieved June 23, 2005, from http://www.census.gov/Press-Relaease/www/releases/archives/ income_wealth/ 002484.html

U.S. Census Bureau. (2005a). *People: Disability.* Retrieved June 11, 2004, from http://factfinder.census.gov/jsp/saff/SaffInfo.jsp?_pageID=tp4_disability

U.S. Census Bureau. (2005b). *Poverty thresholds 2004.* Retrieved May 13, 2004, from http://www.census.gov/hhes/poverty/threshld/thresh04.html

U.S. Commission on Civil Rights. (1982). *Toward equal educational opportunity: Affirmative admissions programs at law and medical schools.* Washington, DC: U.S. Government Printing Office.

U.S. Department of Health and Human Services. (n.d.). *The 2005 HHS poverty guidelines: One version of the [U.S.] federal poverty measure.* Retrieved May 12, 2005, from http://aspe.hhs.gov/poverty/05poverty.html

U.S. Department of Health and Human Services. (1992). *Epidemiologic Catchment Area Study, 1980–1985* (ICPSR Study No. 6153). Rockville, MD: U.S. Department of Health and Human Services, National Institute of Mental Health.

U.S. Department of Health and Human Services. (1999). *Mental health: A report of the surgeon general.* Rockville, MD: U.S. Department of Health and Human Services, Substance Abuse and Mental Health Services Administration, Center for Mental Health Services, National Institutes of Health, National Institute of Mental Health.

U.S. Department of Health and Human Services. (2001a). *Mental health: Culture, race, ethnicity: A supplement to mental health: A report of the surgeon general* (SMA 01–3613). Rockville, MD: Substance Abuse Mental Health Services Administration.

U.S. Department of Health and Human Services. (2001b). *Youth violence: A report of the surgeon general.* Washington, DC: Author.

U.S. Department of Health and Human Services. (2004). *Child neglect demonstration projects: A synthesis of lessons learned.* Washington, DC: National Clearinghouse on Child Abuse and Neglect Information.

U.S. Department of Health and Human Services. (2005). *Computations for the 2005 annual update of the HSS poverty guidelines for the 48 contiguous states and the District of Columbia.* Retrieved May 13, 2005, from http://aspe.hhs.gov/poverty/05computations.shtml

U.S. Department of Health and Human Services. (2006). *Healthier US.Gov.* Retrieved June 16, 2006, from http:www.healthierus.gov

U.S. Department of Health and Human Services, Administration for Children and Families. (n.d.). *Fourth National Incidence Study of Child Abuse and Neglect: FAQ.* Washington, DC: Author. Retrieved May 12, 2005, from http://www.nis4.org/faq.asp

U.S. Department of Health and Human Services, Administration on Children, Youth, and Families. (2003). *Child maltreatment, 2001.* Washington, D.C: U.S. Government Printing Office.

U.S. Department of Health and Human Services, Administration on Children, Youth, and Families. (2004). *Child maltreatment 2002.* Washington, DC: U.S. Government Printing Office.

U.S. Department of Health and Human Services, Administration on Children, Youth, and Families. (2005). *Child maltreatment 2003.* Washington, DC: U.S. Government Printing Office.

U.S. Department of Health and Human Services, Administration for Children and Families. (2006a). *Child welfare monitoring.* Washington, DC: Author. Retrieved May 31, 2006, from http://www.acf.hhs.gov/programs/cb/cwmonitoring/index.htm

U.S. Department of Health and Human Services, Administration for Children and Families. (2006b). *What is child abuse and neglect?* Washington, DC: Author. Retrieved June 19, 2006, from http://www.childwelfare.gov/pubs/factsheets/whatiscan.cfm

U.S. Department of Health and Human Services, National Center on Child Abuse & Neglect. (1996). *Child maltreatment 1994: Reports from the states to the National Center on Child Abuse and Neglect.* Washington, DC: U.S. Government Printing Office.

U.S. Department of Health and Human Services, National Institute on Drug Abuse. (2003). *Preventing drug use among children and adolescents* (2nd ed.) (NIH Pub. No. 04–4212A). Bethesda, MD: Author.

U.S. General Accounting Office. (2004). *Child and family services reviews: Better use of data and improved guidance could enhance HHS's oversight of state performance.* Washington, DC: Author.

Vahratian, A., Zhang, J., Troendle, J. F., Savitz, D. A., & Siega-Riz, A. M. (2004). Maternal pre-pregnancy overweight and obesity and the pattern of labor progression in term nulliparous women. *Obstetrics and Gynecology, 104*(5), 943–951.

Valliant, G. (2002). *Aging well: Surprising guideposts to a happier life from the Landmark Harvard Study of Adult Development.* Boston: Little Brown.

Van der Kolk, B. (2006). *Traumatic antecedents questionnaire.* Retrieved August 21, 2006, from http://www.trauma center.org/assessment.html

Van der Kolk, B. A., & Fisler, R. (1995). Dissociation and the fragmentary nature of traumatic memories: Overview and exploratory study. *Journal of Traumatic Stress, 8,* 505–536.

Van der Kolk, B. A., Hopper, J. W., & Osterman, J. E. (2001). Exploring the nature of traumatic memory: Combining clinical knowledge with laboratory methods. *Journal of Aggression, Maltreatment & Trauma, 4*(2), 9–31.

Van der Kolk, B. A., Roth, S., Pelcovitz, D., Sunday, S., & Spinazzola, J. (2005). Disorders of extreme stress: The empirical foundation of a complex adaptation to trauma. *Journal of Traumatic Stress, 18*(5), 389–399.

Van Praag, H. (2005). Can stress cause depression? *World Journal of Biological Psychiatry, 6*(Suppl. 2), 5–22.

Van Soest, D., & Bryant, S. (1995). Violence reconceptualized for social work: The urban dilemma. *Social Work, 40*(4), 549–557.

Van Wilsem, J. (2004). Criminal victimization in cross-national perspective: An analysis of rates of theft, violence and vandalism across 27 countries. *European Journal of Criminology, 1*(1), 89–109.

Vedantam, S. (2005a, June 26). Patients' diversity is often discounted. *The Washington Post*, pp. A1, A10–A11.

Vedantam, S. (2005b, July 28). Racial disparities found in pinpointing mental illness. *The Washington Post*, pp. A1, A16.

Vega, W. A., Aguilar-Gaxiola, S., Andrade, L., Bijl, R., Borges, G., Caraveo-Anduaga, J. J., et al. (2002). Prevalence and age of onset for drug use in seven international sites: Results from the international consortium of psychiatric epidemiology. *Drug and Alcohol Dependence, 68,* 285–297.

Vega, W. A., Aldrette, E., Kolody, B., & Aguilar-Gaxiola, S. (1998). Illicit drug use among Mexicans and Mexican Americans in California: The effects of gender and acculturation. *Addiction, 93,* 1839–1850.

Venkatesh, S. (1994). Getting ahead. Social mobility among the urban poor. *Sociological Perspectives, 37*(2), 157–182.

Videka, L. (2003). Accounting for variability in client, population, and setting characteristics: Moderators of intervention effectiveness. In A. Rosen & E. K. Proctor (Eds.), *Developing practice guidelines for social work intervention* (pp. 169–192). New York: Columbia University Press.

Vieweg, W. V., Thomas, M., Janisko, M., Booth, M., Fernandez, A., Pandurangi, A., et al. (2004). Patient and direct-care staff body mass index in a state mental hospital: Implications for management. *Acta Psychiatrica Scandinavica, 110*(1), 69–72.

Viggiani, P., Charlesworth, L., Hutchison, E., & Faria, D. (2005). Utilization of contemporary literature in human behavior and social justice coursework. *Social Work Education, 24*(1), 57–96.

Violanti, J. M., & Paton, D. (1996). *Traumatic stress in critical occupations: Recognition, consequences and treatment.* Springfield, IL: Charles C. Thomas.

Virk, S., Schwartz, T. L., Jindal, S., Nihalani, N., & Jones, N. (2004). Psychiatric medication induced obesity: An aetiologic review. *Obesity Review, 5*(3), 167–170.

Volkow, N., Tancredi, L., Grant, C. Gillespie, H., Valentine A., Mallani, N., et al. (1995). Brain glucose metabolism in violent psychiatric patients: A preliminary study. *Psychiatry Research: Neuroimaging, 61,* 243–253.

Volkow, N. D., Fowler, J. S., Wang, G. J., & Swanson, J. M. (2004). Dopamine in drug abuse and addiction: Results from imaging studies and treatment implications. *Molecular Psychiatry, 9*(6), 557–569.

Von Kries, R., Koletzko, B., Sauerwald, T., Von Mutius, E., Barnert, D., Grunert, V., et al. (1999). Breastfeeding and obesity: Cross sectional study. *British Medical Journal, 319*(7203), 147–150.

Vosvick, M., Gore-Felton, C., Koopman, C., Thoresen, C., Krumboltz, J., & Spiegel, D. (2002). Maladaptive coping strategies in relation to quality of life among HIV+ adults. *AIDS and Behavior, 6*(1), 97–106.

Wadden, T. A., Berkowitz, R. I., Womble, L. G., Sarwer, D. B., Phelan, S., Cato, R. K., et al. (2005). Randomized trial of lifestyle modification and pharmacotherapy for obesity. *New England Journal of Medicine, 353*(20), 2111–2120.

Wadman, M. (2005). Appetite downer awaits approval. *Nature, 437*(7059), 618.

Wadman, M. (2006). Rimonabant adds appetizing choice to slim obesity market. *Nature Medicine, 12*(1), 27.

Wadsworth, M. (1976). Delinquency, pulse rates, and early emotional deprivation. *British Journal of Criminology, 16,* 245–256.

Wadsworth, M., & Achenbach, T. M. (2005). Explaining the link between low socioeconomic status and psychopathology: Testing two mechanisms of the social causation hypothesis. *Journal of Consulting and Clinical Psychology, 73*(6), 1146–1153.

Waldfogel, J. (1998). Understanding the "family gap" in pay for women with children. *Journal of Economic Perspectives, 12*(1), 137–186.

Walker, N. E., Brooks, C. M., & Wrightsman, L. W. (1999). *Children's rights in the United States: In search of a national policy.* Thousand Oaks, CA: Sage.

Wallace, J., & Brody, C. M. (1994). Introduction. In C. M. Brody & J. Wallace (Eds.), *Ethical and social issues in professional education* (pp. 1–12). Albany: State University of New York Press.

Walsh, F. (2003). Family resilience: Strengths forged through adversity. In F. Walsh (Ed.), *Normal family processes: Growing diversity and complexity* (3rd ed., pp. 399–423). New York: Guilford Press.

Wang, C., & Daro, D. (1997). *Current trends in child abuse: The results of the 1996 Annual Fifty State Survey.* Chicago: National Committee to Prevent Child Abuse.

Wang, P., Beck, A., Berglund, P., McKenas, D., Pronk, N., Simon, G., et al. (2004). Effects of major depression on moment-in-time work performance. *American Journal of Psychiatry, 161*(10), 1885–1891.

Wardle, J., & Watters, R. (2004). Sociocultural influences on attitudes to weight and eating: Results of a natural experiment. *International Journal of Eating Disorders, 35*(4), 589–596.

Warner, B., & Fowler, S. (2003). Strain and violence: Testing a general strain theory model of community violence. *Journal of Criminal Justice, 31*(6), 511–521.

Wasilow-Mueller, S., & Erickson, C. K. (2001). Drug abuse and dependency: Understanding gender differences in etiology and management. *Journal of the American Pharmaceutical Association, 41,* 78–90.

Wax, E. (2005, Feb. 19). A crushing choice for Ethiopian mothers with HIV. *The Washington Post,* p. A01.

Weaver, K., Antoni, M., Lechner, S., Duran, R., Penedo, F., Fernandez, M., et al. (2004). Perceived stress mediates the effects of coping on the quality of life of HIV-positive women on high active antiretroviral therapy. *AIDS and Behavior, 8*(2), 175–183.

Webb, N. B. (2004a). A developmental-transactional framework for assessment of children and families following a mass trauma. In N. B. Webb (Ed.), *Mass trauma and violence: Helping families and children cope* (pp. 22–49). New York: Guilford Press.

Webb, N. B. (2004b). The impact of traumatic stress and loss on children and families. In N. B. Webb (Ed.), *Mass trauma and violence: Helping families and children cope* (pp. 3–22). New York: Guilford Press.

Webster-Stratton, C. (2000, June). The Incredible Years Training Series. *Juvenile Justice Bulletin.* Retrieved January 10, 2005, from http://www.ncjrs.org/html/ojjdp/2000_3_/contents.html

Wee, C. C., Phillips, R. S., Legedza, A. T., Davis R. B., Soukup, J. R., Colditz, G. A., et al. (2005). Health care expenditures associated with overweight and obesity among U.S. adults: Importance of age and race. *American Journal of Public Health, 95*(1), 159–165.

Weich, S., Blanchard, M., Prince, M., Burton, E., Erens, B., & Sproston, K. (2002). Mental health and the built environment: Cross-sectional survey of individual and contextual risk factors for depression. *British Journal of Psychiatry, 180,* 428–433.

Weight Watchers. (2006). Home page. Retrieved June 16, 2006, from http://www.weightwatchers.com

Weiner, L. (1999). Telephone support groups for HIV-positive bereaved mothers of young children. In M. Shernoff (Ed.), *AIDS and mental health practice: Clinical and policy issues* (pp. 43–53). Binghamton, NY: Haworth Press.

Weisner, C. M. (2002). What is the scope of the problem and its impact on health and social systems? In W. R. Miller & C. M. Weisner (Eds.), *Changing substance abuse through health and social systems* (pp. 3–14). New York: Plenum.

Weiss, D. S., Marmar, C. R., Metzler, T. J., & Ronfeldt, H. M. (1995). Predicting symptomatic distress in emergency services personnel. *Journal of Consulting and Clinical Psychology, 63,* 361–368.

Weiss, F., & Porrino, L. J. (2002). Behavioral neurobiology of alcohol addiction: Recent advances and challenges. *Journal of Neuroscience, 22*(9), 3332–3337.

Weitz, R. (2003). *The sociology of health, illness, and health care: A critical approach.* Belmont, CA: Wadsworth/Thompson Learning.

Wen, M., Browning, C. R., & Cagney, K. A. (2003). Poverty, affluence, and income inequality: Neighborhood economic structure and its implications for health. *Social Science & Medicine, 57,* 843–860.

Werner, E., & Smith, R. (2001). *Journeys from childhood to midlife: Risk, resilience, and recovery.* Ithaca, NY: Cornell University Press.

Westat, Chapin Hall Center for Children, & James Bell Associates. (2002). *Evaluation of family preservation and reunification programs: Final report.* Washington DC: U.S. Department of Health and Human Services.

Westermeyer, J. J. (2003). Addressing co-occurring mood and substance use disorders. In J. J. Westermeyer, R. D. Weiss, & D. M. Ziedonis (Eds.), *Integrated treatment for mood and substance use disorders* (pp. 1–16). Baltimore: Johns Hopkins University Press.

Whealin, J. M., Morgan, C. A., & Hazlett, G. (2001). The role of military studies in enhancing our understanding of PTSD. *PTSD Research Quarterly, 12*(1), 1–8.

Wheeler, D. P., & Shernoff, M. (1999). The role of mental health professionals in medical decision making regarding protease inhibitors. In M. Shernoff (Ed.), *AIDS and mental health practice: Clinical and policy issues* (pp. 3–18). Binghamton, NY: Haworth Press.

Whipple, B., & Scura, K. W. (1996). The overlooked epidemic: HIV in older adults. *American Journal of Nursing, 96*(2), 23–29.

Whitcomb, J. F. (2003). Religiosity and other selected variables as predictors of current and retrospective depression scores. *Dissertation Abstracts International Series A: The Humanities & Social Sciences, 6* (10), 3488A.

White, A. M., & Swartzwelder, H. S. (2004). Hippocampal functioning during adolescence a unique target of ethanol effects. *Annals of New York Academy of Sciences, 1021,* 206–220.

White, J., Moffitt, T., & Silva, P. (1989). A prospective replication of the protective effects of IQ in subjects at high risk for juvenile delinquency. *Journal of Consulting and Clinical Psychology, 57,* 719–724.

Whitmire, L., Harlow, L, Quina, K., & Morokoff, P. (1999). *Childhood trauma and HIV.* New York: Brunner-Routledge.

Whittaker, R. (1997). Re-assessing the virological approach to HIV pathogenesis: Can it explain AIDS as an immunological disease? *Journal of Theoretical Biology, 187*(1), 45–56.

Widom, C. (1989). Does violence beget violence? A critical examination of the literature. *Psychological Bulletin, 106,* 3–28.

Widom, C. S. (1999). Childhood victimization and the development of personality disorders: Unanswered questions remain. *Archives of General Psychiatry, 56*(7), 607–608.

Williams, D. M., & Lawler, K. A. (2003). Importance of macro social structures and personality hardiness to the stress-illness relationship in low-income women. *Journal of Human Behavior in the Social Environment, 7*(3/4), 121–140.

Williams, J., Duggan, D., Crane, C., & Fennell, M. (2006). Mindfulness-based cognitive therapy for prevention of recurrence of suicidal behavior. *Journal of Clinical Psychology, 62*(2), 201–210.

Wilson, A. E., Calhoun, K. S., & Bernat, J. A. (1999). Risk recognition and trauma-related symptoms among sexually revictimized women. *Journal of Consulting and Clinical Psychology, 67*(5), 705–710.

Wilson, J. P., Friedman, M. J., & Lindy, J. D. (2001). *Treating psychological trauma and PTSD.* New York: Guilford Press.

Wilson, J. P., & Moran, T. (1997). Psychological trauma: PTSD and spirituality. *Journal of Psychology and Theology, 26*(2), 168–178.

Wilson, W. J. (1987a). *The declining significance of race: The inner city, the underclass, and public policy.* Chicago: University of Chicago Press.

Wilson, W. J. (1987b). *The truly disadvantaged: The inner city, the underclass, and public policy.* Chicago: University of Chicago Press.

Wilson, W. J. (1996). *When work disappears: The world of the new urban poor.* New York: Random House.

Windham, A., Rosenberg, L., Fuddy, L., McFarlane, E., Sia, C., & Duggan, A. (2005). Risk of mother-reported child abuse in the first 3 years. *Child Abuse & Neglect, 29*(3), 209–213.

Windle, M., Windle, R., Scheidt, D. M., & Miller, G. B. (1995). Physical and sexual abuse and associated mental disorders among alcoholic inpatients. *American Journal of Psychiatry, 152,* 1322–1328.

Wink, P., Dillon, M., & Larsen, B. (2005). Religion as moderator of the depression-health connection: Findings from a longitudinal study. *Research on Aging, 27*(2), 197–220.

Winston, C. (2003). African American grandmothers parenting grandchildren orphaned by AIDS: Grieving and coping with loss. *Illness, Crisis, & Loss, 11*(4), 350–361.

Winters, K. C. (2001). Assessing adolescent substance use problems and other areas of functioning. In P. M. Monti, S. M. Colby, & T. A. O'Leary (Eds.), *Adolescents, alcohol, and substance abuse* (pp. 80–108). New York: Guilford Press.

Winton, M. A., & Mara, B. A. (2001). *Child abuse and neglect: Multidisciplinary approaches.* Needham Heights, MA: Allyn & Bacon.

Wisse, B. E. (2004). The inflammatory syndrome: The role of adipose tissue cytokines in metabolic disorders linked to obesity. *Journal of the American Society of Nephrology, 15*(11), 2792–2800.

Witkiewitz, K., & Marlatt, G. A. (2004). Relapse prevention for alcohol and drug problems. *American Psychologist, 59*(4), 224–235.

Wolfer, T. (2000). Coping with chronic community violence: The variety and implications of women's efforts. *Violence and Victims, 15,* 283–302.

Wolfgang, M., & Ferracuti, F. (1967). *The subculture of violence.* London: Routledge

Wong, A. H., Smith, M., & Boon, H. S. (1998). Herbal remedies in psychiatric practice. *Archives of General Psychiatry, 55*(11), 1033–1044.

Wood, E., Montaner, J., Chan, K., Tyndall, M., Schechter, M., Bangsberg, D., et al. (2002). Socioeconomic status, access to triple therapy, and survival from HIV-disease since 1996. *AIDS, 16*(5), 2065–2072.

Woodward, L., & Fergusson, D. (2000). Childhood and adolescent predictors of physical assault: A prospective longitudinal study. *Criminology, 38*(1), 233–251.

Woody, D. J. (2003). Infancy and toddlerhood. In E. D. Hutchison (Ed.), *Dimensions of human behavior: The changing life course* (pp. 113–158). Thousand Oaks, CA: Sage.

World Health Organization. (2002). *The world health report 2002.* Geneva, Switzerland: Author.

World Health Organization. (2003a). Today's challenges. In *Global health* (chap. 1). Retrieved May 19, 2005, from http://www.who.int/whr/2003/chapter1/en/print.html

World Health Organization. (2003b). *The world health report 2003: Shaping the future.* Geneva, Switzerland: Author.

World Health Organization. (2004). *HIV/AIDS facts and figures.* Retrieved January 17, 2005, from http://w3.whosea.org/en/Section10/Section18/Section348.htm

World Health Organization. (2005a). *Achievement of health-related Millennium Development Goals.* Proceedings of the Fifty-Eighth World Health Assembly. Geneva, Switzerland: Author.

World Health Organization. (2005b). *International statistical classification of diseases and related health problems* (ICD-10, 2nd ed.). Geneva, Switzerland: Author.

World Health Organization. (2006). *Global access to HIV therapy tripled in past two years, but significant challenges remain.* Retrieved June 24, 2006, from http://www.who.int/hiv/mediacentre/news57/en/index.html

Wright, B., Caspi, A., Moffitt, T., Miech, R., & Silva, P. (1999). Reconsidering the relationship between SES and delinquency: Causation but not correlation. *Criminology, 37,* 175–194.

Wright, J. H., & Basco, M. R. (2001). *Getting your life back: The complete guide to recovery from depression.* New York: Free Press.

Wright, R., Mitchell, H., Visness, C., Cohen, S., Stout, J., Evans, R., et al. (2004). Community violence and asthma morbidity: The inner-city asthma study. *American Journal of Public Health, 94*(4), 625–632.

Wulfert, E., & Wan, C. (1993). Condom use: A self-efficacy model. *Health Psychology, 12*(5), 346–353.

Yaffe, K., Blackwell, T., Gore, R., Sands, L., Reus, V., & Browner, W. S. (1999). Depressive symptoms and cognitive decline in nondemented elderly women: A prospective study. *Archives of General Psychiatry, 56*(5), 425–430.

Yancey, A. K., McCarthy, W. J., Talor, W. C., Merlo, A., Gewa, C., Weber, M. D., et al. (2004). The Los Angeles LIFT OFF: A sociocultural change intervention to integrate physical activity into the workplace. *Prevention Medicine, 38*(6), 848–856.

Yates, T. M., Egeland, B., & Sroufe, A. (2003). Rethinking resilience: A developmental process perspective. In S. S. Luthar (Ed.), *Resilience and vulnerability* (pp. 243–266). Cambridge, England: Cambridge University Press.

Yesavage, J. A., Brink, T. L., Rose, T. L., Lum, O., Huang, V., Adey, M., et al. (1982). Development and validation of a geriatric depression screening scale: A preliminary report. *Journal of Psychiatric Research, 17*(1), 37–49.

Yonkers, K. A., Kando, J. C., Cole, J. O., & Blumenthal, S. (1992). Gender differences in pharmacokinetics and pharmacodynamics of psychotropic medication. *American Journal of Psychiatry, 149,* 587–595.

Zagorsky, J. (2005). Marriage and divorce's impact on wealth. *Journal of Sociology, 41*(4), 406–424.

Zelizer, V. (1985). *Pricing the priceless child: The changing social value of children.* New York: Basic Books.

Zelli, A., Dodge, K., Laird, R., & Lochman, J. (1999). The distinction between beliefs legitimizing aggression and deviant processing of social cues. *Journal of Personality and Social Psychology, 77*(1), 150–151.

Zelli, A., Huesmann, L., & Cervone, D. (1995). Social inferences in aggressive individuals: Evidence for automatic processing in the expression of hostile biases. *Aggressive Behavior, 21,* 405–418.

Zimmerman, M. A., & Maton, K. I. (1992). Life-style and substance use among male African-American urban adolescents: A cluster analytic approach. *American Journal of Community Psychology, 20,* 121–138.

Zimring, F., & Hawkins, F. (1997). *Crime is not the problem: Lethal violence in America.* New York: Oxford University Press.

Zoellner, L. A., Fitzgibbons, L. A., & Foa, E. B. (2001). Cognitive-behavioral approaches to PTSD. In J. P. Wilson, M. J. Friedman, & J. D. Lindy (Eds.), *Treating psychological trauma and PTSD* (pp. 159–182). New York: Guilford Press.

Zucker, R. A. (1994). Pathways to alcohol problems and alcoholism: A developmental account of the evidence for multiple alcoholisms and for contextual contributions to risk. In R. A. Zucker, G. Boyd., & J. Howard (Eds.), *Research Monograph No. 26: The development of alcohol problems: Exploring the biopsychosocial matrix of risk* (NIH Pub. No. 94–3495) (pp. 255–289). Bethesda, MD: National Institute on Alcohol Abuse and Alcoholism.

Zung, W. W. (1965). A self-rating depression scale. *Archives of General Psychiatry, 12,* 63–70.

Index

About the Authors _____

Leanne W. Charlesworth, LMSW, PhD, received her MSW from the University at Albany and PhD from Virginia Commonwealth University. She is currently an Assistant Professor in the Department of Social Work at Nazareth College of Rochester, where she teaches a variety of courses, including human behavior and the social environment. She has served in child protection and other capacities within child welfare systems and has been an evaluation consultant to diverse public and private human service agencies. Her research and practice interests focus on poverty, child and family well-being, and child welfare system issues.

Marcia P. Harrigan, MSW, PhD, received her MSW and PhD in Urban Services from Virginia Commonwealth University. She is currently an Associate Professor in the School of Social Work at Virginia Commonwealth University, where she serves as Associate Dean of Academic and Student Affairs. She is a field liaison and teaches the integrative seminar for MSW/MDiv students. Her research and writing have focused on nontraditional family structures, family functioning of foster care and long-distance caregiving families, as well as human behavior within the context of family and the larger environment. She is the coauthor of *Measures of Family Functioning for Research and Practice* (1994).

Elizabeth D. Hutchison, MSW, PhD, received her MSW from the George Warren Brown School of Social Work and PhD from the University at Albany. She is currently an Associate Professor in the School of Social Work at Virginia Commonwealth University, Northern Virginia Program, where she teaches courses in human behavior and the social environment, social work and social justice, and child and family policy, along with serving as a field practicum liaison. She has been a social worker in health, mental health, and child and family welfare settings. She is the editor of the two-volume *Dimensions of Human Behavior* textbook and is committed to providing social workers with comprehensive, current, and useful frameworks for thinking about human behavior. Her other research interests focus on child and family welfare.

Pamela J. Kovacs, MSW, PhD, received her MSW from Boston College and PhD from Florida International University. She is currently an Associate Professor in the School of Social Work at Virginia Commonwealth University, where she teaches practice and research courses and serves as field liaison. Her social work practice and research experience include hospice, oncology, HIV/AIDS, and aging, with a special interest in the impact of these life experiences on families. She also is engaged in researching educational approaches for preparing social workers to work with these issues.

Holly C. Matto, MSW, PhD, received her MSW from the University of Michigan and PhD from the University of Maryland. She is currently an Assistant Professor in the School of Social Work at Virginia Commonwealth University, where she teaches courses in human behavior and the social environment and research methodology. Her social work practice experience and current research interests are in substance abuse treatment.

Pamela A. Viggiani, LMSW, PhD, received her MSW and PhD from the University at Albany. She is currently an Adjunct Professor in the Department of Social Work at Nazareth College of Rochester, where she teaches courses in social justice, social advocacy, diversity, policy, and social work methods. She has worked in schools with at-risk children and has served as the legislative liaison for the National Association of Social Workers, New York State Chapter. She also has served as an evaluator and consultant for several grants funding public child welfare professionalization. Her research focuses on poverty and pedagogy.